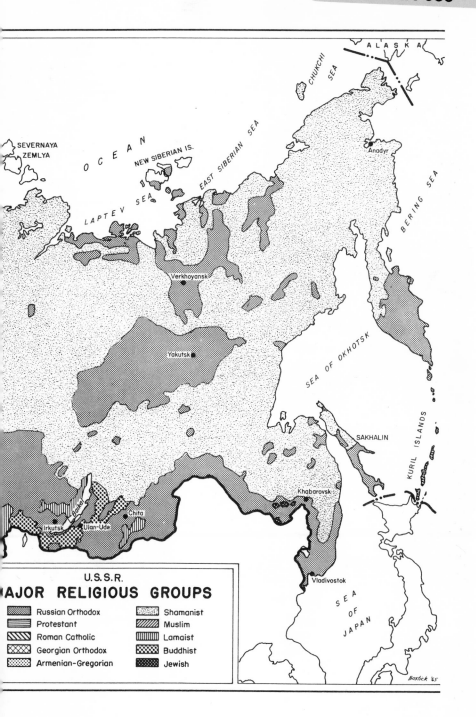

SEVERNAYA
ZEMLYA

OCEAN

NEW SIBERIAN IS.

LAPTEV SEA

EAST SIBERIAN SEA

CHUKCHI SEA

ALASKA

Anadyr

BERING SEA

Verkhoyansk

Yakutsk

SEA OF OKHOTSK

SAKHALIN

KURIL ISLANDS

Khabarovsk

Chita

Irkutsk   Ulan-Ude

Vladivostok

SEA OF JAPAN

Bostick '65

U.S.S.R.
MAJOR RELIGIOUS GROUPS

- Russian Orthodox
- Protestant
- Roman Catholic
- Georgian Orthodox
- Armenian-Gregorian

- Shamanist
- Muslim
- Lamaist
- Buddhist
- Jewish

SILENT CHURCHES

ACKNOWLEDGEMENTS

The publication of SILENT CHURCHES has been made possible through the aid of many institutions and because of the efforts of many individuals.

Recognition must be given to INSTITUTUM BALTICUM, RADIO LIBERTY RESEARCH, RADIO FREE EUROPE and their staffs for providing factual and statistical information through their research and symposia.

Too numerous to mention individually are the governmental agencies—both foreign and domestic—as well as private organizations that have supplied data supportive of my contentions.

By the same author

BALTIC YOUTH UNDER COMMUNISM

SILENT CHURCHES

PERSECUTION OF RELIGIONS

IN THE SOVIET-DOMINATED AREAS

by

PETER J. BABRIS

RESEARCH PUBLISHERS,
ARLINGTON HEIGHTS, ILLINOIS 60005

274,7
B119

79080221

First Printing, 1978

LIBRARY OF CONGRESS CATALOG CARD NUMBER: 78-052811

ISBN 0911252-02-9

DEDICATED

TO THE MARTYRS FOR FAITH

"I mean to tell everything and shall preserve silence only when it is required by decency..."

Josef Cardinal Mindszenty

CONTENTS

PREFACE

The extension of the Soviet sphere of influence since World War II has put tens of millions of believers at the mercy of a political system sworn to the liquidation of God. Armed with weapons and techniques denied to earlier foes of religion, Marxist-Leninist atheism is making the most of the situation. The long list of Catholic, Protestant, Orthodox and Jewish leaders arrested, deported or executed, the laws that have been enacted, the libelous press campaigns, are all unmistakable signs that the death sentence has already been passed upon religion. That sentence is now in the process of execution. If religion survives, this will only be because its sentence has been commuted to perpetual and degrading servitude to the godless.

The "Church of Silence" is the name given by His Holiness Pope Pius XII to the Christian communities now feeling the full weight of Communist oppression. The description is all too apt. The world knows far too little about what is happening behind the Iron Curtain. Personal contacts and the transmission of news between East and West are limited. But one can guess at the dramatic struggle now going on in the hearts and souls of millions of believers whose faith is being systematically undermined. Who will ever know the true martyrdom of those people? Who can grasp their feelings? But the word "silence" can also, unfortunately, describe the weakness of the protests that go forth from that part of the world that still enjoys freedom.

Communist attacks vary from country to country, and they are conducted quietly and systematically by means of harassment and covert persecutions.

People are said to have a right to agitate against religion, while priests and ministers do not have a civil right to defend themselves against such attacks. Communists run atheist clubs and conduct atheistic instructions in labor unions, youth organizations and schools. Meanwhile, priests and ministers who conduct religious instructions are liable to be sent to Siberia even without a judicial hearing.

Other anti-religious tactics of the Communists include the undermining of the people's faith in baptism and matrimony, and the discrediting of Christian burial by priests or ministers.

Thus, for more than half a century the Soviet Union, despite alternating periods of reckless assault and cautious retreat, has been the most prominent example of an officially inspired program of hostile confrontation with the existing religions. This state-versus-religion confrontation in the Soviet Union is aimed not merely at dis-establishment of the Church and other religious institutions, depravation of their power and influence as a social force, but it is aimed also at individuals, who must be persuaded to be intolerant toward all traditional religious beliefs and practices in order to acquire the psychological outlook of a new type of social being, the "new Soviet man." Willie Brandt, however, stated the fact that "people like me renounced long ago the outdated utopia of shaping 'a new man.'"

Concerning the Soviet dominion, objective data on religion are not easily available; any statistics presented officially conceal more than they reveal. The interested scholar must cope with a greater amount of subjective evidence than he would care to, but the absence of more reliable and objective data leaves him little choice. The claim to scholarly objectivity in many fields of western study of Soviet reality must rest heavily therefore on scrupulous observance of the norms of the "scientific method" of inquiry and weighing of evidence, whether objective or subjective. To support such evidence various books, articles, reports to scholarly conferences, seminar papers, and current news media have been dealt with.

— PJB

1

———~———

Russia's Religious Past and Present

That great prophet of the Russian revolution, Dostoyevsky, managed to forecast with striking accuracy the essential features of socialism in Russia. Generations of pre-revolutionary Russian intellectual and ideological spokesmen, bewitched by the audacity of "progressive" nineteenth-century atheistic thought, helped to disseminate among the people seditious ideas about destruction in the name of universal happiness. Dostoyevsky, on the other hand, perceived behind all this the frankly apostate nature of socialism in general, and of Russian socialism in particular. He was the first to see that socialism was taking the place not of capitalism but of Christianity, and that the key to an understanding of what was happening lay in the spiritual rather than the material-economic sphere. Dostoyevsky argued that, in place of the Christian idea of the absolute value of each human soul, socialism, under the pretense of liberating mankind, was asserting the idea of denial of the individual's independent value and proclaiming this idea as a method of achieving a social goal. This was nothing but a doctrine of unprecedented total enslavement of people, incorporating not only physical coercion to obedience but also compulsory spiritual bondage.

Recognizing the religious mentality of the Russian people, Dostoyevsky realized that, having begun a rebellion against God, the people would not stop at half-measures. Indeed, they would not stop at all until they had traveled this road to the end, and would then create their own religious cult of atheism.

This is why the age of Russian liberalism was so short-lived. This is why the Bolsheviks were ultimately bound to come to power, inspired as they were by the idea of limitless destruction and limitless violence in the name of limitless happiness for mankind in a limitless future. This is why all attempts to offer the people sensible, moderate programs for organizing society were futile, just as were appeals to return to Christ, against whom the people had risen.

Having exhausted themselves in the rampages of revolution and civil war, the people created for themselves an atheistic religion which, because of the

1

people's profoundly Christian mentality, was—as those outstanding twentieth century religious thinkers, (Berdiaev, Frank, Zen'kovski, and others) have shown—merely the negative of Christianity. Represented in this new religion were nearly all the attributes of Christianity, but of course turned inside out: a golden age—primitive Communism; the expulsion from paradise into the land of sin—the class society; the coming entry into paradise—Communism. Even the idea of original sin was included—exploitation; a chosen people—the proletariat; the four gospels—according to Marx, Engels, Lenin and Stalin; savage suppression of all kinds of heresy; and a cult of saints with adoration of relics—Lenin in his mausoleum. Thus, the people created for themselves an immortal living god on earth and worshipped it as they had previously worshipped Christ.

This is why the Soviet state—founded on monstrous violence and horrifying poverty—far from collapsing, emerged strengthened from endless crises, notwithstanding common sense and the prophecies of famous politicians in the various decades of the twentieth century. This is why the people did not rise in revolt, despite the unbearable burdens of their existence; for they were devoted to their new religion and the time for new religious rebellion had not yet come. This is why the theoretical refutation of Communist doctrine, like the refutation of Communism by life itself, led to no practical results, for Communism was a faith, and reason is powerless against faith.

In a short time Communism evolved and brought into everyday use its symbol of faith and system of rituals mandatory for all members of a society which itself carefully made sure at all levels that any manifestation of thought was brought into strict conformity with the dogmata of Communism and its scholasticism. A unique "comparative" method of cognition became an inherent feature of Soviet thinking: everything that contradicted the writings of the Communist holy father and his apostles was a lie and should be exposed, and if possible destroyed. Understandably, the people could only be liberated from such a truly diabolical obsession by an event of eschatological significance, some sort of apocalyptic sign. Just such an event was the death of the very god of the Communist religion—Stalin.

The ideological vacuum created after Stalin's death was filled by two main trends: rationalistic criticism of Marxism—revisionist and, in the final analysis, liberal-democratic; and religion—Christian.

In his efforts to shore up his Communist religion, now bereft of its god, Stalin's successor, the "great reformer," Khrushchev, desperately resisted both trends; but, as is now evident, his resistance was hopeless. Having ceased to be a religion, Communist doctrine had lost its magic power over the souls of men, and was in effect rejected not only by the intelligentsia and the people, but by the party and government apparatus as well. To save itself, the latter proceeded to throw overboard, together with many dogmas, the great reformer himself, and set about trying to hold together Soviet society by encouraging nationalism, which overflowed into outright imperialism in foreign policy and chauvinism on the domestic scene.

The last decade in Russia has revealed to the world a striking phenomenon which is perhaps without parallel and is very different from what in the West today is called the civil rights campaign. The strivings of the intelligentsia in the Soviet Union in the years since Stalin's death have been directed not outwardly, but inwardly; not to the service of the great future, but to achieving human dignity; not to the happiness of an abstract mankind of a social class, but to helping specific people; not to the liberation of the individual from any restrictions or obligations to society, but to the assertion of the absolute value of the individual and the acknowledgement of individual responsibility to one's own conscience.

The road to achievement of internal freedom proved very fruitful in asserting civil and political freedoms as well. But, however great the successes of this campaign, or, if you prefer, the human rights movement, have been, this has been, and remains, a purely intellectual movement, enjoying practically no support among other social strata. Nevertheless, it was relatively invulnerable, because, first, it did not basically go outside the law; second, it had neither an external form nor an internal party structure and therefore at any specific point in time constituted not an organization, a suitable target for destruction, but a varying number of individuals; third, it enjoyed the support of Western public opinion, which was important as long as the Soviet government was seeking to win that opinion over to its side in order to exert internal influence on the governments of Western countries.

The broad mass of ordinary Russians is traditionally indifferent to democratic transformations, to civil and political freedoms and rights, but are at the same time sensitive to truth in the Russian meaning of that word—which comprises goodness, justice, and conscience. Leaving aside the period preceding the XX CPSU Congress, one would point to the obvious fact that the dethronement of Stalin and the collapse of the Communist faith that followed it led to a revival in the religious life of the people. The swift increase in the number of believers was reflected in two ways: in a strengthening of the influence of the Orthodox Church as a reaction to the anti-Christ of Communism, and in the spread of sectarianism as a reaction to the impiety of official Orthodoxy's submissiveness to the regime.

The end of the fifties and the beginning of the sixties were marked by countermeasures on the part of the Khrushchev government: mass closures of Orthodox churches and numerous arrests of sectarians. Suffice it to say that, of a total of some five thousand political prisoners in the Mordvinian camps in 1961, at least one-fifth had been convicted for belonging to some Christian sect. At the same time, it cannot be forgotten that sectarians are often convicted under articles of the Criminal Code and sent to serve their terms in criminal camps scattered all over the country. Consequently, their total number cannot be even approximately estimated.

However, these punitive measures failed to halt the new turn toward Christianity, either toward the sects or toward the Orthodox Church. Evidence of this is provided by the continuing trials of believers and the famous campaign by Orthodox Christians to have a church opened in the Naro-Fominsk Raion of Moscow Oblast. Particularly striking was the attendance of about fifty thousand people at the burial of Patriarch Aleksei, who died at the height of the Lenin centenary celebrations. To appreciate the significance of this event, it should be remembered that an open avowal of faith in the Soviet Union is tantamount to an oath of disloyalty toward the regime; and such an act requires great courage and, naturally, no little faith.

As mentioned earlier, as long as the Soviet government regarded Western public opinion as an instrument for bringing pressure to bear on the governments of Western countries in its own foreign policy interests, the Kremlin had to allow for possible adverse reaction from this source in cases where the suppression of freedoms in the Soviet Union itself became public knowledge. A very clear example of this was the world-wide indignation at the sentences passed on the Soviet writers Sinyavski and Daniel. The gains achieved in intimidating the internal opposition were not commensurate with the loss of prestige entailed, and thereafter the Soviet government showed greater caution in dealing with writers, tolerating Solzhenitsyn and Maksimov, for example, despite their far greater sins in the eyes of the regime.

However, the latest developments in Soviet-American relations, which offer the illusory promise of resolving world problems by means of direct negotiations between Moscow and Washington, have both diminished world interest in the problem of freedoms in the Soviet Union and relieved the Soviet Union of the need to reckon with foreign public opinion. This has enabled the Soviet government to embark upon a massive campaign to suppress all forms of dissidence in the country, which it has been pursuing unimpeded now for at least a year, if one ignores the slight "deviation" on the Jewish question.

Moreover, for internal consumption, the Soviet government has managed to find a fairly successful substitute for the bankrupt religion of Communism. That is a chauvinistic form of nationalism, which has to no small degree neutralized the attractiveness of the idea of struggling for civil rights and at the same time undermined the desire to achieve justice in a Christian spirit by playing on one of the most ingrained delusions of Russian Orthodoxy—the identification of Russianness with true Christianity. Nationalism has also given the government an opportunity to do what might appear to be the impossible—surreptitiously to rehabilitate Stalin, not, it is true, as a god and the leader of world Communism, but as the great and formidable Russian czar-patriot who overcame the internal and external enemies of the fatherland. The crisis in the human rights movement was brought about not only by repressive countermeasures, but also by the fact that the movement itself was approaching a definite limit. Beyond this limit, under present conditions, it could only go if there were to be a profound reorientation of a significant majority of the thinking intelligntsia. The latter had embarked upon the path of martyrdom in the quest for truth with an astonishingly scanty—Marxist, or at least People's Will—collection of ideas and moral-ethical views. It was proving necessary to imbue the sincere striving for freedom with a life-saving idea which would lend it strength to move ahead and help it to gain the support of the broad masses.

The move which began in the sixties toward Christianity, toward the culture and the historical past of Russia, toward universal philosophy, and simply toward truth, has become characteristic of a certain section of the intelligentsia, both in its works and in its socio-political statements. What is more, Christianity has begun to penetrate the way of life of the intelligentsia—celebration of church festivals, attendance of services, and practice of ceremonies (baptism, marriage, etc.).

The search for ideas led to reinterpretation of the works and philosophy of Dostoyevsky, from whom there opened up two roads: to the Slavophilism of the last century, and to the great legacy of the *Vek-hovtsy*. The former was burdened with the temptations of official pre-revolutionary Orthodoxy, the concept of state, and the idea of Russian exclusiveness. Given the slight faith—or complete lack of it—among the modern disciples of Slavophilism, this path leads to unrestrained national-ism with a most perceptible brownish tinge. Examples of this are the offi-cial journal *Molodaya gvardiya* of the late sixties, the underground mani-festo "Word of the Nation," and the *samizdat* journal *Veche*. The second road is via the great legacy of the Russian religious thinkers like Berdiaev, Frank, Shestov, and Florenski. Their work—which incorporated all the best of Slavophilism, underwent the horrors of revolution, fascism, Com-munism, and the two world wars, and was imbued with a longing for the religious purity of the first Christians—inevitably leads to active participa-tion in socio-political life and the struggle for freedom in the name of God.

The books of the aforementioned religious thinkers are presently en-joying a wide currency among the intelligentsia. Moreover, there are known cases of "Berdiaev circles" being formed, and even of an attempt to set up an underground party based—strange as it may seem—on the ideas of Berdiaev (e.g., the Ogurtsov group in Leningrad). The influence of Christianity is becoming more and more perceptible in the works of artists, poets, and writers, quite apart from the direct appeal of Solzhenit-syn and Maksimov to Christianity. Many active participants in the struggle for human rights who are unknown in the West are inclining toward Christianity. Sure evidence of this is provided by the cross on the grave of the martyred Yuri Galanskov in the Mordvinian ASSR, the one and only cross in the camp cemetery, which was set up only as a concession forced upon the camp administration.

One would add that deeply religious circles, too, are showing interest in the human rights struggle, and attempts are already being made to stand up for the rights of the Church, using methods borrowed from the arse-nal of the champions of human rights; publicity, open letters, *samizdat*, appeals to world public opinion, and so on. In the bosom of the Church itself, more and more calls are going out to the hierarchs not to yield "to Caesar what is God's." In this connection one need only mention the names of the priests Yakunin and Eshliman, the religious writers Krasnov-Levitin and Karelin, Petrov-Agatov, Talantov, and others. Spe-cial mention should be made of Solzhenitsyn's "Lenten Letter," in which, as a simple layman, he exhorts the Patriarch to carry out the immediate duty of the Church—Christian education of society.

Thus, in the life of Russian society today, two trends can be clearly discerned: among the intelligentsia is a trend leading via awareness of rights to Christianity, and among the rest of the people a trend leading via Christianity to a realization of the need for civil rights. If both these trends develop further and at some point in time coalesce, the govern-ment will find itself in a difficult situation.

There are, it seems, no other roads to freedom in Russia, and none can be envisaged. Of course, this does not exclude popular uprisings for the most varied reasons; but even if they were to succeed, which is highly

improbably, there would be no progress toward freedom unless awareness of rights, permeated with Christian attitudes, were to become widespread among the people.

The Soviet government is well aware of this danger of Christianity
being put forward as a basis for political opposition.

Speaking over *Radio Moscow*, the executive secretary of the journal
Nauka i religiya, said:

> One of these methods of anti-Communist propaganda is the treatment of
> religious problems. It is no coincidence that religion has been chosen for this
> purpose. The face of the matter is that in our country it has remained the
> sole more or less mass ideology alien to Marxism-Leninism and the Com-
> munist outlook.

In the journal *Voprosy filosofii* in an article entitled "Militant Materialism
and Atheism," P. Filippov writes:

> Religion, having lost its former political and spiritual hegemony, presents to
> certain young people aspects which are capable of attracting by their
> unusualness, colorfulness, and aesthetic allure . . . things religious, to
> admiration for the Church, which pretends to be the age-old bearer of na-
> tional and spiritual values.

The religious-civil disturbances in Lithuania which broke out in the spring
of 1972 demonstrate what hidden possibilities a combination of religion with
the human rights struggle holds. The Lithuanian people, who had seemed
to be finally exhausted in their desperate and hopeless struggle for freedom,
suddenly took heart in a miraculous manner and demonstrated their
indestructible desire for freedom. Behind this miracle lay a policy
deliberately chosen by Lithuanian priests—in particular, Sheshkiavicius and
Zdebskis—of standing up for religious rights using the basically legal
methods of the human rights movement.

The Soviet Constitution guarantees every citizen the right to practice his
religion and states that anyone who prevents him from doing so is liable to
punishment. *Samizdat* sources, however, not only provide evidence of religious persecution but also show that Soviet laws are so framed as to enable
the authorities to imprison believers for nothing more than the normal
practice of their faith.

Most *samizdat* documents on religious matters come from Russian Orthodox and Baptist sources although some protests have been made by
Catholics, Uniates, Jews and Muslims. Religious protesters have tended to
be preoccupied with their own denominational affairs. Only a few individuals, notably the religious writers, A. E. Levitin (pseudonym Krasnov),
Rev. S. Zheludkov, the late Boris Talantov, have signed other non-religious protest documents; but it seems probably that, like national dissidents, they will become increasingly a part of the civil rights movement in
the Soviet Union.

Modification of the constitution is one of the believers' chief demands
because it prevents real freedom of worship. Since May, 1929, when the
constitution was amended to bring it into line with the still-valid law of
April, 1929, "concerning Religious Associations," "freedom of religious
propaganda" has been excluded. Believers do not have the right to teach
religion to children or to adults (other than in officially recognized

seminaries). Soviet believers have also appealed for their constitutional rights; petitioned the officially approved religious authorities to allow a democratically elected hierarchy; appealed for the registration of illegal sects (such as the dissident Baptists), for the reinstatement of dismissed churchmen and against the closure of churches.

Believers are frequently charged under Article 142 of the Russian Federation Criminal Code—"violation of the laws on separation of Church from State and school from Church"—for which the maximum punishment is three years' deprivation of freedom. They may also be charged under Article 227 for encouraging religious activities "harmful to the health of citizens" or inciting people "to refuse to participate in social activity or to fulfill their civic obligations." Since 1961 this has carried a maximum sentence of five years' deprivation of liberty or exile. Some *samizdat* documents report sentences of five years under Article 142, plus five years under Article 227; or five years under Article 142, plus five years' exile. Both sentences are illegal. The longest known sentences of believers were those of 15, 13 and 10 years' imprisonment given to leaders of the All-Russian Social-Christian Union for the Liberation of the People in Leningrad in 1967 and 1968. This group has produced a political program for democratic reform and was engaged in clandestine para-military self-education and organization work.

In prison, believers are often subjected to additional discrimination. In *My Testimony* Anatoli Marchenko gives some indication of the large numbers of religious prisoners.

> Religious prisoners are the ones who have been arrested and tried precisely because of their religion. And what variety there is! Muslims from the Caucasus and Central Asia, Orthodox Christian, Baptists, Jehovah's Witnesses, Evangelists, Sabbatarians and many others. . . . Here, in the cells I was thrown together with a large number of them. Almost every cell had its Evangelist, Sabbatarian, or Jehovah's Witness, and in some cells there were several together. The prison authorities humiliated them in every possible way. I had seen that on my very first day. Many believers had a rule that they must wear beards, yet they were all forcibly shaven while wearing handcuffs.

According to a protest letter sent to the Presidium of the Supreme Soviet in 1969 by the imprisoned writers Daniel, Ginzburg and Galanskov, believers are prohibited from receiving any religious literature and may not even have a Bible while in prison.

One result of putting so many believers in prisons and labor camps has been that they have sometimes formed religious groups there. Mikhail Sado, serving a long sentence in one of the strict regime prison camps for criticizing Khrushchev, founded the All-Russian Social-Christian Alliance, according to a *samizdat* document written and distributed by Alexander Petrov-Agatov, himself a prisoner.

Many churches have been forcibly closed and others are used for storage, workshops, etc. In his essay *Along the Oka* Solzhenitsyn said the secret of the peaceful influence of the Russian countryside was in the churches:

> But when you get into the village you find that not the living but the dead greet you from afar. The crosses have been knocked off the roof or twisted

out of place long ago. The dome has been stripped, and there are gaping holdes between its rusty ribs. . . . The murals over the altar have been washed by the rains of decades and obscene inscriptions are scrawled over them. On the porch there are barrels of lubricating oil and a tractor is turning towards them. Or else a lorry has backed in at the church doorway to pick up some sacks. In one church there is the shudder of lathes. Another is locked up and silent.

Protests by believers against such treatment are only known to have succeeded on one occasion—after a Catholic Church in Byelorussia had been turned into a grain store. According to the *Chronicle of Current Events*, local peasants said "they could not live without the church" and refused to work for several days or to send their children to school. Eventually, the chairman of the collective concerned ordered the removal of the grain. The church was repaired and the ritual plate restored.

A great deal of documentation about persecution of their members has been provided by the Evangelical Christian Baptists or *initsiativniki*, who broke away from the Baptist Church in 1965 and have never received official recognition. They have at least two regular *samizdat* publications—including a monthly, *Bratsky Listok*, an a quarterly, *Vestnik Spaseniya*.

The *initsiativniki*, who had objected to the compromises made by the leaders of the Baptist Church to placate the communist regime, are particularly active, and some 500 of them have been imprisoned since 1961. The repressive measures taken against them were described in an appeal to the party leadership by 1,453 women in March, 1969. They said their children were victimized and beaten up at school and sometimes forcibly removed from the parents by the KGB and placed in children's homes. They had addressed thousands of petitions to the authorities begging for an end to persecution but it became even harsher:

> Fines beyond our means, beatings-up, dismissal from jobs and institutes, confiscation of flats, arrests of fathers, husbands and improbable as it may seem, mothers—this is the reply we have received so far from you to all our complaints.

It is impossible to give an exhaustive treatment of the countless aspects of human suffering that occur under the reign of the godless. Even amidst the horrors of the world of concentration camps that crush behind the Iron and Bamboo curtains, those attributes of existence which are necessary for a man to be fully human, the Spirit of the Living God is drawing people unto Himself.

Victims and captives of the subhuman world marked the reign of hatred to all that is conductive to godliness subjected to ideological coercion and unrestricted tyranny, and are demonstrating that the blood of the martyrs continues to be the seed of the Church.

The behavior of the Communist authorities toward the Christians is motivated by an atheistic ideology that of necessity incorporates religious persecutions.

Faith continues in the Church of Silence despite the fact that

> this Church, savagely persecuted and tortured for its faithfulness to Christ in the midst of treason and apostasy is forced to live in modern catacombs

and despite the fact that there is

> practiced in thousands of prisons, hard-labor camps and psychiatric asylums

across the Soviet empire all methods of degradation and torture that man has known.

In order to secure its ideological dictatorship, communism crushes without mercy or shame all opposition. It seeks out dissenting world views, ferreting them out rigorously and persistently the more so as they declare themselves incompatible with it. Christianity is the natural obstacle of Communism.

In order to remain true to its nature, the Soviet regime, born anti-religious, can really never tolerate the free activity of the Christian communities, and all agreements with this regime are but a trap that results in their undoing.

Pierre de Villermarest writes that "we live in an age and in a world that considers 'freedom' to mean the right to buy on credit and protest verbally and safely. For several decades this world has acquiesced with the 'course of history.' "

Communism, states Pierre Courthial, is more than just an economic theory or a political doctrine. It is, "a universal religious system, a general view of the world, of history and of man, inspired by faith in Man as God."

Communism (systematic humanism) and Christianity (systematic theism) are rigorously antithetical. Any true Communist is systematically anti-Christian; any faithful Christian is systematically anti-Communist.

The spirit of death and inhumanity that belong to humanism can be conquered only by systematic Christianity (which is more than anti-Communism), the religion of creation and redemption by the Triune of God.

Faithful Christians, he warns, can and must oppose Communism in every sphere of human existence—conjugal, family, professional, denominational, and cultural—with a persevering quest toward transformation in the light of what God reveals, teaches, and commands in His Word.

A battle of systems is being waged, the outcome of which is life eternal and temporal for men. Faithful Christians must regain a continually renewed spirit of evangelization and dedication.

In the words of Alois Regensburger, author of *Thunder in China*,

> the Communists share with Satan the hatred of God and the desire to abolish all religion; they share with him the hatred of men, for whom they have an unprecedented lack of respect and whom they treat with savage cruelty; they share with him the uncompromising execution of their plan.

With appropriate logic the Marxist dictators call good that which serves Communism and evil that which does not. Lying, pretense, breaking promises, murder, reducing man to slavery, any spirit who rejects Communism is evil. And good must be done and evil eradicated.

One of the most complicated and disputed questions in the Soviet Union involves the number of religious believers in that country. Because no official statistics for the entire USSR are available, researchers are obliged to draw on a variety of sources to arrive at even approximate figures. For this reason, estimates vary. There are conflicting statistics, for instance, on the number of Orthodox Christians, with the lowest estimate being 30 million and the highest 115 million.

A brochure titled *Religiya y bor'be idei* was primarily designed for "propagandists of scientific atheism, for teachers and students." Its author, E. I. Lisavtsev, flatly rejects the methods used by Western researchers as well as their data on the numbers of believers in the USSR. He states:

> Usually the numbers of religious believers in the Soviet Union are greatly exaggerated. The BBC, for example, has been assuring us that the number of believers in the USSR is no less than it was just before the October Revolution. Consequently, we must have about 110 million Orthodox Christians, 17 million Old Believers and schismatics, 13.6 million Catholics, more than 10 million Moslems, 7.6 million Protestants and 1.7 million sectarians, making a grand total of about 166 million believers.

> The *New York Times* reported on April 14, 1974, that there were 30 million Orthodox, 5 million Catholics, 5 million Lutherans, and about 1 million Baptists in the USSR.

> The American journal *Pravoslyavnaya Rus'*, on September 5, 1973, claimed that there are 115 million Orthodox believers in the Soviet Union.

> The French paper *Le Figaro*, on December 24, 1974, put the number of Orthodox in the USSR at 100 million with the same number of Moslems, about 12 million Catholics and 600,000 Baptists.

Lisavtsev explains that "in citing these statistics, bourgeois propagandists pretend that the figures speak for themselves" and that "sovietologists are deliberately manipulating quantitative data regarding religious believers in the USSR in order to prove the impotence of socialism in the face of the religiousness of the masses." To substantiate his claim, Lisavtsev makes several contradictory assertions. He says, for example, that sovietologists excuse the failure to cite the sources of their data by simply stating that there is a lack of material on the state of religion in the USSR.

Further on, however, Lisavtsev acknowledges:

> Some bourgeois literature abounds with references to the titles of books, brochures, and articles published in the Soviet Union. For instance, of the 725 sources named in Robert Conquest's *The Great Terror*, 535, or three-quarters of them, were published in the Soviet Union. Nikita Struve cites a total of 705 sources in his book *Christians in the USSR*, of which 486 are Soviet. Michael Bourdeaux's *Religious Ferment in Russia* lists 297 Soviet publications.

> A recent *Reuter* report, for instance, claims: Thousands of Russians crowded into Moscow's churches to take part in Easter services. Police squads controlled crowds outside the Elokhovsky Cathedral, where Patriarch Pimen was conducting the Easter service. Crowds of believers gathered in the four churches of the Sergieva Lavra Monastery at Zagorsk.

Since mass attendance at churches in the Soviet Union is an indisputable fact, Lisavtsev tries to belittle its significance. He claims that many who attend church are not believers—an allegation that he tries to substantiate by stating that "in many Western European countries, sociological studies are conducted—some of them even by 'ecclesiastics'—to examine the extent of the populace's religiosity." The difference is that in the West, religious problems are examined mainly by church organizations, which have a vital interest in obtaining as accurate a picture as possible of religious life. In the Soviet Union, however, sociological investigations into religiosity are conducted by atheist institutions, whose aim is to combat religious activity. In addition, religious polls in the USSR are conducted on a minor scale; usually they involve only a single city or oblast. The results therefore reflect a situation specific to only one locality. Lisavtsev explains that this method was suggested by Lenin when he said: "Take your information about practical experience, even if it is only based on one district." But the level of religiosity cannot of course be identical everywhere, a fact Lisavtsev himself acknowledges.

> According to estimated date, roughly ninety per cent of the adult population in Soviet cities are nonbelievers. This percentage is somewhat lower in the villages.

> On the basis of information obtained from a study of the level of religiosity in a number of regions in the Soviet Union, it can be inferred that between twenty-five and thirty per cent of the adult population in particular regions are still to one extent or another under the influence of religion.

> A comparison of the results of sociological research carried out in our country in the 1920s with information obtained in the 1960s and 1970s shows that there has been quite a considerable evolution towards the erosion of religious feeling in the minds of believers. With every passing year the percentage of staunch believers grows smaller.

Western research on religious problems in the USSR is inaccessible to the average Soviet reader. Since this material is not available in Soviet bookstores, the reader has no opportunity to form personal opinions.

In an abstract of a brochure entitled *Obhchestvennoe mnenie i nauchnoateisticheskaya propaganda* (Public Opinion and Scientific Atheist Propaganda), P. P. Slavnyi provides some unusual information on the subject of religious believers. In his review, Slavnyi gives an account of each of the three chapters into which the brochure is divided. The first chapter is devoted to the problem of "the complete overcoming of religiosity during the period of gradual transition towards Communism." In this connection, Slavnyi presents figures that show the number of believers in the USSR. He writes:

> According to general sociological data, at the present time believers represent some twenty per cent of the adult population of the country; about ten per cent of the population is undecided, and the rest of the population consists of nonbelievers. However, the stability of religiosity bears witness to the existence of processes contributing to its regeneration, the more so since a certain number of believers are members of a generation that has been reared in the Soviet period. It is also worrying to note that many people are uninformed in matters of religion and atheism and that a part of the young people are interested in religion.

It was reported that there were an estimated 163.5 million persons eighteen years of age and over in the USSR in 1975. Hence if Slavnyi's breakdown is correct, it would mean that some 32.7 million persons are religious believers. Adding to this another 10 per cent of the adult population, or those Slavnyi describes as undecided, yields a provisional total of 49 million persons who may be religious believers. Interestingly, this figure corresponds with the estimates of Western analysis, whose research and calculations have been categorically dismissed by Soviet commentators.

In the second chapter of the brochure, continues Slavnyi, the authors consider the results of sociological investigations carried out in Leningrad and the Leningrad Oblast among various segments of the population (including school-aged children). These studies indicated that "the number of believers depends on the existence of a church in the vicinity." Among the workers who were surveyed, "only 9.1 per cent thought that religious feast-days have any everyday significance." But of all those interviewed, 41 per cent said that they observe religious feast-days "in the family or among friends," which tends to give a somewhat different picture of the number of those who may be convinced atheists.

The authors of the brochure also note with obvious concern that "in some of the answers there was an acceptance of religion's positive role in matters of morality."

> The sociological surveys also established that there are signs of the influence exerted by religious ideology of sympathy with religion, and of the remarkable prevalence of attitudes on non-interference and indifference.

The reviewer mentions that the investigations "did not establish the existence of any religious feeling in the true sense of the word" among students, but goes on to say that "some students stated that religion preaches humanism and offers a moral ideal." Furthermore, over a tenth of the students questioned (11.8 per cent) pronounced themselves "to be opposed to scientific atheist propaganda." Almost a fifth of the representatives of the intelligentsia polled (19.6 per cent) considered that "a person should be able to believe if he so desires." Such figures would seem to suggest a fair-sized spread of tolerant attitudes towards religion among these segments of society despite the anti-religious posture of the educational system.

The third chapter of the brochure is devoted to "problems of the formation of atheistic public opinion." This chapter enumerates the forms of atheism that exist in the contemporary world and underscores "the Marxist-Leninist nature of atheism in our society."

In any consideration of the information offered in the brochure it should not be forgotten that admission of religious leanings in the Soviet Union may entail unpleasant consequences and even reprisals. The higher the social position of the person questioned, the more risky it may be for him to profess that he is a believer. While it may be inferred on the basis of sociological studies that 20 per cent of the population consists of believers, what would the percentage be if there were not persons among the sample interviewed afraid to admit that they believe in God?

A. Pusin, leader of the Center for Scientific Atheism in Moscow, during a travel in which he visited Communist Parties in different Western European countries, stated that 60 per cent of the population in the Soviet Union admitted that they believed in God—about 150 million people. It is known that about 40 million of those are adherents of Islam, Jews, or Buddhists, but then there are still 110 million people left who confess that they are Christians.

Although there are over 100 million Christians in the Soviet Union, there are only 5,400 churches left. But, although, there are only 30 churches and temples left, the Center for Scientific Atheism in Moscow has 15,000 full-time employees trying to wipe out Christianity and other religions. This is mainly done through indoctrination in the kindergartens, intermediate schools, and universities. It is also accomplished through violence and torture, by locking them in prisons, labor camps, and psychiatric clinics.

The repression of the Church is well documented. Visitors see the many churches which are open in the large cities but forget that 10,000 Orthodox churches alone have been closed.

Today there are not more than 7,000 Russian Orthodox churches operating in the whole of the Soviet Union and some observers believe the figure may be as low as 4,000 churches. Before 1917 there were 55,173 Russian Orthodox Churches in Russia, not counting nearly 25,000 chapels over and above that figure. This figure has dropped to only two or three thousand by 1938, rose to 4,225 after the USSR added new western territories in 1940-41, and jumped to about 22,000 for the period from 1949 to 1959.

This is the grim side of the story, but the optimistic side is that more young people in the Soviet Union are turning to the Christian religion. This is reflected in the ages of those receiving sentences for attempted missionary work—18, 19 and many in their early 20's. The fact is best corroborated not by going to the religious but to the atheists—the Soviet press, inside Moscow and out, where young people are named, held up to ridicule, their characters blackened for religious activity.

To sense the real meaning of this "gradual resurgence" in the face of persecution, one must reflect on the position of organized religion in the Soviet Union today. It is estimated, but cannot be proven because the Kremlin will not allow statistics on it, that there are approximately 30 million members of the Russian Orthodox Church and somewhere between a million and a million and a half Protestants, largely Baptists.

In present day culture there exist important trends that are not contrary to religion but are favorable to it. It could be opportunely mentioned that a considerable percentage of believers (estimated at about 50 million) exists in the USSR in spite of more than a half century of systematic indoctriation in atheism. One could mention the explosion of religious movements among young people in America and Japan. Some famous German sociologists(Luckmann, Gehlen) and American sociologists (Berger, McLuhan) have shown that religion is not at all a secondary and contingent superstructure of society, but is, on the contrary, its carrying structure and the foundation of all culture. Even some exponents of British analytical philosophy (Austen, Ramsey, Ferre, etc.) consider a rational justification of religion possible today. But what is even more striking is that the importance of the religious dimension is admitted today even by various philosophers of Marxist extraction, such as Bloch, Garaudy, Machovec, Horkheimer. In their judgment, religion is not the opium of the people, but a positive ferment with regard to the construction of that ideal society. The arguments of the author of *Das Kapital* are still flaunted as incontrovertible.

However, historians have shown that Marx had a superficial and erroneous knowledge of Christianity, a knowledge based more on the writings of its critics than of its supporters; so that it can be affirmed that
Marx's support of atheism was due to a large extent more to prejudices
than to solid reasons.

> Not even one of the best-known Socialists of the first hour (including Marx)
> seems to have been in a living relationship with Christian piety. They are
> irritated by the irrationality of earthly situations, interested in science, con-
> centrated on the problem of earthly happiness and on the increase of the
> possibilities of reaching it for all men; the fatalism with which the people,
> under the influence of religion, submits to the pressure of circumstances,
> disgusts them. They are not interested in religious questions in the stricter
> sense, and their criticism strikes only the Church, as it unfortunately is.

Throughout the USSR there are only three Russian Orthodox
seminaries, one near Moscow, one in Leningrad and the third in Odessa.
Enrollment is about 250 students in each. If a student wishes to attend, he
must not only apply to the church but also to the state, and it is the latter
that makes the final decision on his acceptance. Thus the student who is
accepted is under state control from the outset.

There are no seminaries for any of the Protestant denominations. At
this time there are between 7 and 8 thousand legally recognized Russian
Orthodox churches in the Soviet Union and somewhere between 2,500
and 5,000 Protestant. Thus, if the individual Christian, regardless of his
faith, lives in a town or province where there is no church and he legally
seeks to form one, the state will suppress it. If he persists, he will be fined
and receive an automatic sentence of 15 days. If he attempts to organize a
worship group clandestinely, and he is caught—and many are—he goes to
prison.

There is, of course, in this modern day determination, a familiar
correlation in the suppression of the early Christians by the Romans. The
Soviets do not physically feed the offenders to the lions, but they try to
break the religious spirit in other ways. Even in those places where a
church is permitted, the individual who is a student or a professor had
better not be caught going to worship. He can be expelled from the university or lose his job as a result.

It would be incorrect to say that the Kremlin dictates the policy of the
Russian Orthodox Church. It does not have to, for church leaders are
chosen by the state through rigid appointment. Only conformists are
wanted.

As in the case of the Uniate Church and Judaism, Islam has close ties
with nationalist aspirations. *Samizdat* Islamic documents have not reached
the West, but their existence was revealed by the Soviet party organ
Pravda, when it spoke of one called *Extracts from the Decision of the Congress*.
This had been compiled by Murids in the Chechen-Ingush Republic at a
secret congress held in the Nazranov district. The document instructed
"every person of Ingush nationality to comply strictly with the 'ten
commandments' or else break 'all contacts with other people.' " Following
the Soviet custom of attacking religion by smears or exaggeration, *Pravda*
accused the Murids, who have fought for national and religious freedom

since the mid-19th century, of favoring "the kidnapping of young girls, *kalym* (bride-money) and blood feuds."

Some very limited successes from these protests have been reported. The officially recognized Baptist Church, has gained a small measure of independence in its appointment of its churchmen—for example, since 1966 its Moscow headquarters have been staffed solely by Church members. And a few churches have been saved from closure or conversion into atheist museums.

The continuing existence of the Evangelical Christian Baptists despite increasing persecution may also be regarded as a success. Indeed, the activities of believers and the circulation of *samizdat* publications have not been reduced by retaliation; rather, the religious issue has been brought before a wider audience and more Soviet citizens, especially young intellectuals, are now taking an interest in religion.

The Soviet media have drawn considerable attention to the question of religion—in particular to the Russian Orthodox and Baptist denominations—and Soviet society. A large number of articles devoted to the subject has appeared in the central Soviet press approximately within the last three months of 1971. Although there is no direct evidence available, it seems virtually certain they were published as a prelude to the conference of the heads of the state offices for religion affairs from Communist-ruled countries reported to have been held in Moscow.

A short list of titles projects the anti-religious spirit of all the published material surveyed: "The Struggle Continues Against Religious Vestiges and Renovated Dogmas," "Train Militant Atheists," "Truth Against Mysticism," "The Danger is Near," and "To Overcome Religious Superstitions."

If compared with the cruder harangues under Khrushchev, the latest pronouncements are marked by a relative sobriety of tone. There is no sign, however, that the imperative of totally eradicating religious beliefs and practices has been assigned a lesser priority. Indeed, a *Pravda* editorial considered the eclipse of religious views as "the most important condition for forming the new man."

The official Marxist-Leninist ideology is still regarded as "the only true scientific and materialist world outlook" while religion, according to the party's ideological journal,

> is outliving its era, but it is an ideological form that has vitality and tenacity and is a typical vestige of the past in the consciousness of people. It is alien to the Marxist-Leninist world conception and not infrequently acts as a brake to socio-political activity, to the growth of the culture and consciousness of that certain part of the population which is under its influence.

Moreover, although religion is allegedly destined to wither away, a passive attitude toward any form of religiosity is considered intolerable.

The major portion of commentary represents little in the way of innovation of traditional attitudes and seems more important for quantity than content. A number of articles are of particular interest, however, for their relatively strong emphasis on factors that appear to be of special concern: youth; the search for new ethical norms; a veneration of the past, especially of Russia's religious past; and the popularity of religious traditions.

A complex situation is distilled to simplistic formulas. The Church is depicted as a predator capitalizing on the naivete of the ideologically un-stable—especially young people—and using ethics as bait. Simultaneously, a complimentary—and from the Soviet view, excessive—interest by the laity in church traditions and Russia's past undermines atheist vigilance. Critical of two students who were christened in the Tikhvin chapel near Leningrad, a certain Belyayev notes that,

> the number of these ceremonies is increasing. Today they have become perhaps the fundamental sources of the church's income. And the partici-pants of such rites as christening and weddings—are naturally young people.

Nor is criticism of attachment to church ceremony limited to persons outside the party. One commentator, noting that "for some people it is now even the fashion to christen children," told of a young couple, he a biologist and party member and she a member of the Komsomol, who appear to have had no ideological qualms about christening their son. A number of other articles admit that both Komsomols and party members participate in church ceremonies, although they provide virtually no de-tails. Criticism is also levelled against the popularity of icons, crosses, and an interest in religious themes in the arts:

> It was not too long ago when an icon was to be found only among the elderly in remote little villages. But today an icon hangs on the wall of this or that contemporary apartment—it is considered to be something of an attribute of good taste. It would be at least justifiable if it were drawn by a master, but, as a rule, it is a product of mass production.

> On the beach during the summer one can see young boys and girls with crosses on their chest. Who are they? Believers? No, this is also in its own way a demonstration of devotion to that which is "truly" Russian.

> Not a few films have appeared which in full force and "tastefully" film church services and prayers and which are not always directly related to the subject of the film. And books have appeared which, under the appeal to respect antiquity opaquely suggest the necessity to respect religion. And god is portrayed as kind, and religion as a panacea.

Given the traditional reluctance of Soviet sources to offer substantive quantifiable date on this subject, the suggestion of a quantitative increase in the citations above is of significance. The absence of such data, how-ever, only raises the question as to the actual scope of this phenomenon.

Two articles touch upon a different, although related, aspect of religion and its influence. While the specific term *samizdat* is not mentioned, refer-ence to circulating manuscripts and to "illegally published literature" strongly suggests that *samizdat* method of distributing, in this case reli-gious, information. Indirectly admitting that the official atheist tack of arguing the incompatibility of science and religion is less than successful, two Moscow educators note the existence of *samizdat*-type material among young people apparently attracted by a counter-argument.

> It is extremely characteristic for defenders of religion to point to the alleged religiosity of great scientists of the past and present. This has a strong influ-ence on youth. In many of the religious compositions in manuscript form circulating among youth, there are anthologies of quotations from prom-

inent personalities concerning god and religion; moreover, atheist scientists are frequently registered in the category of believers.

Similar manuscripts are directly associated with the Baptists, in particular the *initsiativniki*. The intensity of their faith is reflected even in the short quotations that are cited in the Soviet press. One that is described is an

> anthology dedicated to the theme of suffering and compiled by a group of young Baptist-Initiativniki. It contains advice on the manner of deportment for a young man during moments of loneliness and fear, sorrow and grief, and how a person must bolster himself spiritually when depressed by a feeling of imperfection and shortcomings.

Another is entitled "Messenger of Salvation" and is described as containing a parable praising a student for not allowing his faith to waver despite the arguments of adult atheists. The parable supposedly ends with a question directed to young people:

> How do you act when you begin to be persecuted? Do you pray, as Shura prayed, or do you shamedly and cowardly repudiate your faith? Examine yourself!

Although without textual citation, a document entitled "Brotherly Advice to Young Christians" is mentioned as an example of "illegally published literature" among Baptist sectarians.

The concern reflected in the articles surveyed seems justified by other evidence available through *samizdat* and from recent arrivals in the West of the importance of religiosity as a phenomenon connected with an increasing loss of interest among the Russian population in anything connected with the CPSU. If that is what these articles were about, then the absence of any indications of a responsive initiative, seeking to steal the Church's thunder or adapt its methods to the party's needs, is significant. At times the anti-religious press has proposed such efforts, but indications are that this is not at present being considered. Coupled with an unwillingness to accept open dependence on administrative means (repression) for restricting religion's impact, it is difficult to see where the party is planning to go unless it has had to settle on a formula of "more of the same."

Probably the most outstanding advance in the life of the reformers is the establishment of the printing agency, *The Christian*. This is a rare case in which the instigators have not given their names and addresses in their statements. They say without concealment that this is because they know if they did give such details, everything would at once be requisitioned by the authorities.

Assuming that the deterioration of relations between the two Baptists groups is to a very large extent due to the incendiary actions of the state, what is the future of negotiations between the two groups? To the impartial observer there seems to be a simple solution: for the state to stop interfering in internal church affairs and to allow discussion of such issues as the current legislation on religion. However, the Soviet regime seems as little inclined to allow this in the sixth as in the previous five decades of its existence. The difference now, however, is that there are well-educated young people in several religious denominations who are prepared to press the issue. They cannot expect to find it otherwise than crucially difficult, but the indications are that they are unlikely to give in.

Lately has been seen an unusual barrage of attacks by Soviet media on the publicity which the West is giving now to the matter of religious liberty in the USSR. The increasing interest of the Western public in documented facts and precise details about the religious situation in the Soviet Union, which is being fed by a constant and rapid flow of *samizdat* publications reaching the West, clearly disturbs the Soviet authorities. Repeated attempts to undermine the credibility of material being published, however, generally fail to convince the Western reader, and must be equally unconvincing to all but a very small minority of Soviet citizens.

What has caused the intensification of Soviet reaction? First, no doubt, it is an internal matter. There is no sign that those inside the country who are taking a stand in favor of religious liberty are going to yield. They base their case solidly on their own constitutional guarantees or on the principles of the United Nations proclamations on the Rights of Man. They may not be forcing the Soviet authorities to back down, but their case is so impressive that more and more people in the Soviet Union are coming forward to endorse it; the Soviet press itself regularly testifies that young people are coming under the influence of religion. There can be no doubt that one of the chief reasons for this is the moral integrity of those who seek just opportunities for the expression of the tenets of the faith.

Secondly, the Soviet authorities do have a point when they express their anxiety about what is happening outside the country. More and more people in the West are concerned to know the facts: they will not accept the tendentious declarations of Soviet propaganda, on the one hand, nor the nakedly political statements of a few anti-Communist religious organizations on the other. The Christian—and a growing general public in the West—want the facts unadorned. It is this which so disturbs the Soviet authorities and which they find so hard to shrug off.

The main target for the recent attacks within the USSR is the Baptist Council of Prisoners' Relatives, which over the past eight years has maintained an unimpeachable record of objective and accurate reporting of instances of persecution of *initsiativniki* Baptists. Never yet, however, have the Soviet authorities been able to demonstrate that this group has forwarded a single incorrect fact or falsified document.

Konstantinov, in his article, attacks various organizations in the West which published the Moiseev story, among them the Centre for the Study of Religion and Communism in London, the German mission *Licht im Osten* and the Swedish *Slaviska Missionen*. He accuses them of misrepresentation for political reasons and winds up with a repetition of the familiar statement that "freedom of religious profession is guaranteed for all citizens of the USSR without exception."

A similar line is taken by an article in *Trud* of January 4, 1973, only this time the attack is on the broadcasters of religious programs into the USSR. The thin disguise of clericalism, it claims, fails to hide the "emigre traitors and fascists" who seek only to discredit the socialist system. Associates of Christian radio stations have been caught visiting the USSR in the guise of tourists, attempting to make contact with members of "illegal" sects and allegedly trafficking in anti-Soviet literature. In contrast to these, however, many religious visitors have reported enthusiastically on the evidence of religious freedom they have found. One Ibrahim Hussein, from Indonesia, is quoted as saying: "I saw with my own eyes that all citizens of the USSR enjoy complete freedom of conscience." The question as to what qualifications the gentleman quoted has for making such a statement is passed over in silence.

The same Hussein was cited also in a broadcast made on *Radio Moscow* by Vladimir Kuroedov, Chairman of the (State) Council for Religious Affairs in Moscow. Kuroedov used Hussein's testimony to back up a detailed description of the freedom of conscience enjoyed by Soviet citizens, in terms whose theoretical soundness is no doubt irreproachable. He continued, however: "The essence of this guarantee (of freedom of conscience) lies in the fact that the government does not interfere in the internal affairs of religious organizations. . . ."

It is only necessary to refer to Article 14 of the 1929 Law on Religious Associations to see the untruth of this statement. The article states that "the registering body (i.e., the government organ) shall have the right to exclude certain persons from membership of the executive body of the association." In other words, since the authorities have the legal right to regulate the choice of office-holders in a religious organization, how could this be described as other than interference in its internal affairs?

Further, Kuroedov spoke of the separation of schools from the church in these terms: "The education of children is the exclusive right of the family, the school, and the state—but not the church."

Kuroedov in his book *The Soviet State and the Church* has intended to demonstrate how utterly absurd are the Western press assertions about the "religious persecution" in the USSR.

> Soviet law forbids the closing down of churches, if the population supports them. Today there are over 20,000 functioning Orthodox churches, Catholic cathedrals, Lutheran churches, old-believers' temples, mosques, synagogues, Buddhist datsans, Evangelical Christian and Baptist prayer-houses, etc., in the Soviet Union. There are 20 monasteries and convents in the Soviet Union, and 18 specialized theological schools. The majority of church buildings are kept in a good state. That is another thing noticed by overseas visitors. The socialist state has placed hundreds of historical and architectural church monuments under its own protection and spends much money on their restoration by the best specialists and craftsmen.
>
> Religious associations in the USSR enjoy the right and opportunity to publish various religious literature.
>
> Discrimination against believers is a criminal offence under Soviet law. However, in accordance with these same laws, the believers and non-believers alike have, as citizens, not only rights, but also certain responsibilities, including abiding by generally accepted norms. How do the clergy and the believers regard this Soviet order? In the vast majority of cases they treat it with complete understanding and approval. Here is, for example, the statement, cited in the book, by M. Nigri, Vice-President of the General Conference of Seven-Day Adventists: The real freedom is to live in agree-

ment with the law, and not the freedom to break laws. Alas, so many people, not excluding Christians, are substituting discourses on the right to do what one likes for the correct concept of freedom. People in the socialist countries are more inclined and interested in living correctly, rather than doing un- lawful things, whereas people in the West are too free from responsibilities and are, therefore, prone to mix up the concept of freedom with that of taking liberties.

Nevertheless, the West has launched a propaganda campaign whose aim is to distort the true state of affairs. The bourgeois press is trying to portray as 'religious martyrs' church and sect extremists, sentenced in our country for unlawful activities. The book shows what some of these people are really like.

One of them is G. Vins, who was publicly tried in the Kiev Regional Court. He had spread provocative material, calling upon the believers not to abide by Soviet laws and had long carried on a campaign against our state system. N. Voloshin is another example. He organized a sect and forced people who joined it to ignore Soviet laws. He used physical violence and maimed people. Other 'religious dissidents' had also committed crimes.

Vladimir Kuroedov draws attention to the fact that the anti-Soviet activities of this handful of people are actively supported and even directed by sub- versive organs in the West.

No other social system in history is as united as socialism. In the Soviet Union atheists and believers alike are patriots of their country and they de- spise the handful of renegades.

Pope Pius XI's encyclical *Mit brennender Sorge*, on the situation of the Catholic Church under the Nazi regime, bears the date of March 14, 1937. The encyclical condemned Nazism for its "frightful horrors and anti-Christian principles." Five days after publishing *Mit brennender Sorge*, an encyclical *Divini Redemptoris* appeared condemning essential principles of Communism, with its atheism, oppression and lack of freedom.

After 40 years "the unheard-of-injustice of the economic structure of liberal capitalism created the atmosphere in which Communism could flourish. And the failure of these structures was due to an absence of justice and of love."

The fundamental principles of Communism leave no room for God, for a spiritual principle of life or for a life after death. This remains exactly the same today. The principle explains the hostility to the Church and to religion in Communist countries today. The most fundamental error of the system is to create the idol of self-redemption.

Inconsistency, contrast and contradiction have characterized state policy toward religion, both under the Czars and throughout the six decades of the Soviet period. The historian would divide church-state relations since 1917 into four major phases or periods, each lasting well over a decade and each differing radically from the preceding period.

Khrushchev, who was the initiator and chief architect of the new anti- religious strategy designed to bring about the final removal of the church and religious belief from Soviet life, calculated that the threshold of Communism could be reached in 20 years. His successors have long ago buried Khrushchev's 20-year plan both in the economical and social mobilization fields; one seldom reads these days, for example, about the "withering away of the state" or the administration of governmental affairs by voluntary social groups.

Yet one facet of Khrushchev's plan which his successors did not modify in any major respect was his multifaceted, comprehensive program to throttle and eventually to eradicate religion.

Whatever may be the hopes and plans of the Communist leaders, however, life itself has made all target dates unrealistic. For the evidence from many sides shows that religion in the Soviet Union today is more alive, more influential and—even statistically—of a greater social force than it was when the anti-religious policy of 1960 was begun.

Metropolitan Yuvenaly, head of the Foreign Relations Department of the Moscow Patriarchate, made in London in early 1975 a statement which deals with the qualitative side of religious life in the USSR. Complaining that western observers and commentators tend to speak only about "the dark side of Russian Orthodox Church life," Yuvenaly said: "I would like everyone everywhere to remember that what today exists in the Russian Orthodox Church . . . is a spiritual revival. . . ." This statement was also for foreign consumption, having been made during an interview for the BBC, but this fact in no way diminishes its importance as a frank revelation. Increasing church membership, new church buildings, a spiritual revival within the churches—what a glowing contrast to the unabated hopes and plans of the atheist leaders of the Soviet state! Religious belief in the USSR is not dead, it is not even dying, as a Communist dogma repeatedly insists it is.

There is in fact a certain degree of religious freedom but there is also a very large degree of religious persecution, much of it subtle or covert and all of it officially denied.

Khrushchev, in his "secret speech" to the 20th Party Congress in 1956, considered that Stalin left the "path of Lenin" about the time of the Kirov murder in December,1934 , by making two-fold errors: During the period of the purges he went to excess in abolishing all religious associations, halting the publication of all religious journals, arresting leading churchmen for alleged foreign espionage conspiracies, and even allowing the preparing of a "show trial" for Patriarch Sergei on similar charges, except that this failed to take place because of Stalin's hesitancy and the outbreak of the Second World War. And the war period, in Khrushchev's view, produced Stalin's second major error: He made peace with the churches, permitted the Holy Synod to be reestablished, and allowed, before his death in 1953, the reopening of between 15,000 and 17,000 Russian Orthodox churches. Stalin also was guilty of making similar concessions to the Evangelical Christian Baptists, allowing them to establish an All-Union Council in 1944 with the result that membership of the ECB churches in areas such as Rostov doubled in the period from 1947 to 1954.

Khrushchev's new anti-religious policy was calculated to avoid both these Stalinist extremes. On the one hand, the authority of the Patriarch and the Holy Synod as well as the All-Union Council of ECB were to be preserved; their regular monthly publications, the *Journal of the Moscow Patriarchate* and *Bratsky Vestnik* were to continue; in fact, the established central organs of the churches were to be infiltrated and utilized for party and state purposes rather than abolished. On the other hand, the main target was to wipe out the gains religion had made in Soviet society during World War II and the decade and a half which followed. This meant, statistically, reducing the number of operating churches in the USSR to the level of 1941—if, indeed, not to the level of 1939. But it also meant the removal of religious influence as an attractive ideological alternative to Communism. And for this purpose the policy of 1929 must have seemed to Khrushchev the ideal starting point.

The new state-church policy which was evolved within the CPSU leadership in 1959-60 had the following major features: (a) the number of operating churches was to be reduced to the lowest feasible minimum as quickly as possible and to continue, thereafter, to be reduced gradually; (b) the restrictive Law on Religious Associations of 1929 was to be enforced to the letter; (c) the existing mechanisms of state control of religious affairs, working with and through the centralized religious unions and boards would help insure the scrupulous observance of Soviet laws on religion in every local church and by every individual believer; (d) atheist propaganda machinery was to be reorganized and revitalized and atheist periodical publications were to reappear; (e) the older generation of believers was regarded as probably lost to Communism, but it would become the duty of every single party and government official, of every school teacher and of every "public" organization to see that all young people would, without exception, be imbued with a materialist ideology.

It was precisely in the years 1959-1961 that the Khrushchev regime was trying to discover the basis for creating an historic ideological revival, a "Back-to-Lenin" psychology, a return to the elan and enthusiasm of the Soviet system before Stalin. In order to achieve this goal there was a need of revision of the codes of criminal law and by drafting outlines of a historically new society—a society in which there was no room for "religious prejudice."

The church-state relations since 1960 have seen the expansion of the network of direct administrative controls over church activities at both the local and central levels of governments. The role of the local soviets in religious affairs has been enhanced and given a regularized form throughout the USSR by the simple means of *Instructions* issued to the executive committees of local soviets by the Council on Affairs of Religious Associations (CARC) under the USSR Council of Ministers. Two such *Instructions*, in 1961 and 1968, are a matter of public record. These ostensibly had only economic and organizational aims: all church buildings and inventory of religious articles were considered either as state or as cooperative property and therefore could be held by a given church congregation only with permission of the local soviet; the "registration" of a recognized church was, after 1961, put legally in the hands of the executive committees of the local soviets, although a local government still could not sanction the opening of a new church (i.e., "registration") without specific approval of the district commissioner (*upolnomochie*) of the CARC; and, finally, in order that churches could exercise the functions of a "juridical person", each church was required to establish by election a three-man executive board and a three-man auditing committee, whose members must be acceptable to the local soviet and any member of which can be removed at any time by action of the local soviet. Thus, without benefit of any new legislation, merely by means of a central *Instruction* clarifying existing legislation rather than introducing new laws, a radical reform and expansion of the state mechanisms for interference officially in church affairs was introduced in 1961 and is still in effect today.

The text of an *Instruction* issued to local soviets in 1962 became known only much later through *samizdat*. This document instructed local soviets to form under their own aegis "auxiliary commissions" to exercise control over the strict enforcement and observance of the state laws on religious associations (i.e., the law of 1929). The committees could be formed from members of the local soviet as well as from volunteer atheist activists. What were these committees supposed to do? Their tasks and duties are spelled out in Paragraph 4 of the *Instruction* and include the following:

> a) to study systematically religious conditions in the given populated area, without regard to the absence or presence of an officially operating church; to collect and analyze data on the number of believers who attend worship services; to study the names of persons who attend church and take part in religious rites such as christenings, funerals, weddings, confession and to assess the degree of influence of the religious body and its leaders which might attract young people and children to religion and to worship in church.
>
> b) to make known the names of young persons whom the servitors of a religious body have attempted to prepare for or attract into religious activities;
>
> c) . . . .;
>
> d) to study the composition of religious societies, especially members of church executive organs, and to pinpoint those who are its most active believers;
>
> e) . . . .;
>
> f) . . . .;
>
> g) to seek out persons who are not registered servitors of a church but who have appeared "illegally" in a given populated area and carry out religious rites; to report their names to the local soviet executive committee. . . .

All this anti-religious snooping activity, designed to bring down on overly-religious individuals the full weight of the criminal law was to be carried out under the authority of the local soviet. There has never been any mention of these "auxiliary commissions" in the Soviet press, so one does not know for certain how widespread or how active they may have become.

The new church-state policy which began in 1960 and continues to the present time was the enforced acquiescence of the top church officials in every legally-permitted denomination to help carry out the new anti-religious policy; this was the price they had to pay in order to preserve some part of the religious organization at all. The exact dates and means by which the appropriate officials of the Soviet government communicated this information and delivered their ultimatum to religious leaders is not known, because the churchmen who bowed to these intolerable demands and pressures have never been allowed to explain; those who refused to bow were imprisoned or removed from office. What is known is that both the Russian Orthodox Church and the All-Union Council of Evangelical Christian Baptists were compelled to adopt new church "constitutions" and to make basic changes of church rules which would insure that the diocesan or district leaders of the church would become pliable instruments of the CARC in strict enforcement of all existing laws and regulations of the Soviet state upon local churches, their priests and presbyters, as well as upon individual church members. The subtle and contemptible nature of this approach can be discerned in the fact that it passed to the top religious leaders themselves the onus of ordering new restrictions on religious freedom, and thereby made unnecessary any general public statements on religious restrictions by the Soviet organs or by the CPSU.

The Russian Orthodox Church bowed to the new demands by convening an unannounced Church Council (*sobor*) at Zagorsk on July 18, 1961 which adopted a new set of amendments on administration of the church hierarchy. This *sobor* was hardly more canonical than the 19-member Council of September, 1943 at which a kind of concordat between Stalin and the Moscow Patriarchate was ratified, a fact which many critics of the Patriarchate have pointed out. By accepting the state demands, the Moscow Patriarch, as well as all bishops and priests of the Russian Orthodox Church, were condemned to silence and deprived of any possibility to publicly protest against the wave of forced church closings which over the following three years caused thousands of operating Russian Orthodox Churches in the USSR to officially go out of existence.

During the World War II there was some relaxation in the attempts to destroy the Church, partly on account of a realization that religion was indestructible and partly because of the need for religious support in the war effort. After the clergy, with the approval of the Soviet regime, had performed immense services to the state during the war, it was to be expected that the persecution of believers would cease and that the clergy would be protected from the type of repression which they had experienced during the pre-war years. However, as soon as the war was ended, the Party press set to work with its former vigor. The popular reaction was so strong that the Party Central Committee issued on November 10, 1945, a decree condemning "errors in carrying on scientific and atheistic propaganda among the people."

Evidence of the continued attempt to destroy the Church appears in the number of clergy in Soviet concentration camps. Returnees from such camps report that of every 1,000 prisoners at least 20 are priests and of these at least one-half are Russian Orthodox. In an effort to throw on Beria and his henchmen the blame for religious persecution, the authorities released a few of the more subservient clergy, but this was again followed by a flow of priests, monks and laymen to the camps. It is remarkable that those now being persecuted are members of the generations brought up under the Soviet regime and adherents to the Moscow Patriarchate but still regarded as dangerous and requiring to be isolated. The program of genocide applied to the Russian Orthodox Church as a group still continues.

It must be said that whereas the attempted destruction of the Church was carried on under cover of the decree on the separation of Church and State, the present apparent collaboration of Church and State is based on complete absorption of the Church by the State. Even so, the members of the present hierarchy are able to some extent to bring to human souls the grace which creates a spiritual world far removed from the Communist system and from Marxist ideology.

The theoretical and practical position of the founders of Marxism-Leninism with regard to religion is well known. While the Marxists of West Europe are engaged in the difficult attempt to convince others of the possibility of changing their traditional attitude with regard to religion, remaining consistent with their ideological origins, the Communist parties in countries in the East are steadfastly "orthodox" in reaffirming Marxist-Leninist theses and acting accordingly.

Recent Czechoslovakian publications have made it possible to know clearly and without any possibility of doubt the theses regarding the problem of education sustained by the Communist party of that country and the consequent practical directives. They are texts eloquent in themselves, which it is opportune to know and meditate upon, and they do not require long comments.

The fundamental premise is that for the Czechoslovakian Communist Party the problem of compatibility between the ideology of the Socialist State and "religious ideology" is not even raised: they will remain perenially and radically incompatible. This is clearly seen from the speeches and writings of Communist representatives:

> We are convinced that the educative process must be centered on the formation of a Marxist-Leninist conception of the world which makes it possible, on the basis of scientific knowledge, to shape one's own future actively and consciously, without waiting with passive resignation for what will happen. At this point, therefore, I cannot but repeat that in this field there exists and will always exist an insuperable divergence between the ideology of the Communists, between the ideology of the Socialist State and the Religious and ecclesiastical ideology. For the whole period of the building up of Socialist society, we will struggle for man's conscience, so that he may really become the creator of his own future.

In this rigid and unchanging position, Czechoslovakian Communists know they are faithful to the doctrine of the founders of Marxism-Leninism, who always saw religion as "an upside-down consciousness of the world:"

> ... the substance and the role of religion do not change: it remains in clear antithesis with science and Marxist teaching and curbs the process of emancipation of the working masses. It remains an illusory and fantastic reflection of reality—the opium of the peoples. Therefore to wish to integrate Socialism with the values and ideals of religion is incompatible with Marxism-Leninism.

It follows from this that every moment of dialogue and collaboration with believers, as well as every concession made to "religious survivals" in Socialist society, are accompanied by careful preservation of the ideological purity of Communism from all religious contamination:

> It is possible to begin dialogue with the faithful and with theologians, to collaborate with them in the solution of some practical political questions (the struggle for world peace, the edification of the Socialist country, etc.), but it is never possible to recede from the fundamental positions of Marxist-Leninist ideology. We must not be deceived when some individual

case, when an ecclesiastical ideologist, a priest or even a Jesuit, gives a positive evaluation of the work of Karl Marx (which in most cases they would christianize very willingly) or supports the idea that Christ can be completed by Marx and thus strengthen both Christianity and Socialism. Religious ideology and the Communist one are completely different ideological systems, contrary and opposed on principle, for which reason they are ideologically incompatible.

Scientific atheism is an inseparable part of Marxist ideological education and of the formation of the personality of Socialist man. It is from this fundamental premise that we must start out if we do not wish to limit the sphere of scientific atheism or reduce it to a struggle against religion that is an end in itself. A starting point laid down in this way is important not only from the methodological standpoint, but is also a qualitatively new, scientific way to tackle the religious phenomenon.

The informative and formative function of scientific-atheistic education is ensured by various factors: family education, pre-scholastic and scholastic education at all levels, education by means of the radio, television, artistic and preferential activity (hobby), scientific and educative work itself, etc.

In the educative system outside teaching and schools, atheistic education offers not only a rich source of instructions with which the notions acquired in academic education are completed, but also space for the development of moral, aesthetic, patriotic and international sentiments. The methods of ideological education are chosen according to age, interests, preparation and maturity of the environment.

An article in *Ucitelske noviny* of June 17, 1976, entitled "Forming a Socialist conscience," reviews civic education, history, natural sciences, literature, linguistics and stylistics, giving suggestions in this connection. Then it concludes:

Consequently, the consistent accomplishment of the tasks springing from ideological education should run through, like a red thread, all school subjects and all elements of scholastic formation.

Our effort is to prepare youth for life in such a way that they will succeed in every situation in doing without religion and the lower middleclass solution. Atheism is not just an intellectual but also a sentimental attitude to reality, which sometimes arms man better than any knowledge and helps him to overcome the difficult moments of life. Unfortunately, a set of problems that have rather been forgotten in atheistic education today are those of emotional nature. The churches, on the contrary, exploit the sentiments of believers very shrewdly for the purposes of religious faith. Thanks to the activity of the Council for civil affairs, we will see in how many different ways we can enrich citizen's lives from the point of view of sentiment.

What is to be done, then, . . . to educate as quickly as possible a young generation to be convinced materialists and atheists and to have a scientific attitude to the world? In the schools today atheism can be instilled only by atheists for whom the scientific ideology is not just knowledge, but a conviction, a unique vital confession. The atheist teacher remains such consistently even in private and is not indifferent to the fact that others are of a contrary conviction.

The atheist teacher puts his whole soul into his work, he tries to influence the pupils also on the emotional plane. The personality of the teacher, his arguments, his fervor whould be such as to destroy even family influence and authority in religious questions. The whole activity of the atheist-teacher must therefore be presented as a struggle against something that is useless for man, that does not bring him anything, that is false and invented.

At this point there is not much need to stress the fact that in Czechoslovakian scholastic perspectives there cannot exist, even to the slightest extent, space for any alternative approach to teaching:

> Another matter is when the teacher manifests his own idealistic (that is, religious) convictions, with which he clearly nullifies the efforts of the school and of society to educate the individual in a Socialist way. This cannot be tolerated in any case, but it would be too little to be content merely with a 'renunciation' of the exterior manifestations of the non-scientific conception of the world, though this, too, is inevitable. We must aim at the scientific conception of the world becoming, as far as possible, the inner conviction of every teacher, of every educator, because only in this way can the individual carry out, in his daily activity, a work that is in harmony with the fundamental principles of Socialist education.

In addition to atheistic formation promoted more or less directly through the ordinary teaching of the various subjects, there is also, where possible, the direct teaching of atheism in special clubs and circles connected with scholastic activity.

> In many schools direct forms of scientific-atheistic formation have been reached. Atheistic circles and clubs are set up, which often have very interesting names, such as: "The dialectical key", "The world around us", "The world and ourselves". The attempt is being made to ensure the permanent integration of these clubs in the fabric of the school and of youth organizations. The clubs are increasing. Just in the region of West Slovakia in the academic year 1974-75, there were 155 of them in the secondary schools, with 4,130 members and in the year 1975-76 the number of these clubs had increased to 231 with 5,968 student members. In the primary schools of the region of West Slovakia 160 atheistic clubs with 1,679 pupils worked during the past scholastic year.

Nor is there lacking, of course, action to involve the families and other youth organizations in the global program of ideological and atheistic formation:

> For the next period a list of fundamental and subsidiary tasks is already planned for the Communist youth association and for the association of parents and friends of the school. It is a question of the manifestation of unity between the school and the family.

The aspects of atheistic ideological formation of youth described so far, which can be defined "positive" or regarding formation "of the Socialist new man," are inevitably accompanied also by a "negative" action of clear struggle against "religious survivals" in Socialist society. The priests, the religious family environment, the teaching of religion are the supports of these survivals and they must be opposed forcefully to neutralize their harmful influence and beat them once and for all.

> It is certain that in the minds of many pupils, who have remained for a long time under the influence of the priest and the family environment, there are convictions concerning the world, life, the universe and man influenced by religion; because the priest has a strong influence on the child especially in the period when his sentimental evolution is most unstable, that is, between the age of 6 and 9.

Our pupils often meet the concept of god, not only in fairy tales, of course.
They often hear it in the hours of religion and in families that have a religious foundation. We not only explain this concept in a Marxist way, but we
also use other forms of teaching.

First of all avoid formalisms which take so much time, but have little effect. I say so because it might be thought that, if we carry out actions of
disturbance on Sundays and feast days, if the atheist club is working well, if,
in the survey on ideological convictions, the pupils give us satisfactory
answers, if only 4 of the 680 pupils in our school (in the town of Michalovce)
attend religious instruction, everything is all right and we have done everything necessary. Even if all this represents a certain success . . . it is still only
an external indication of our activity. We are concerned, however, with the
deep, interior indication, which shows us the level of thought of the pupils.

Our meetings deal also with the organization of various activities of interest
during religious instruction. The premises are created for atheist clubs, for
revolutionary traditions, with the aims of disturbing the hours of religious
instruction.

Once more it is useful to note that the action against religious activities
is not an end in itself, but accompanies the attempt to substitute the new
traditions of Socialist society for the customs connected with faith:

The creation of new traditions has turned out very effective to counter-
balance the action of the Church. These are, in primary schools, the
pioneers' oath, the solemn presentation of identity cards, the oath of fidelity
as citizens. These ceremonies become a tradition, are held in collaboration
with the Councils for civil affairs and in the presence of parents, relatives
and a vast public which includes representatives of the party and State organs which are in the area of the school.

A systematic effort is made to reduce the participation of the pupils in
religious instruction.

One of the forms to overcome religious prejudices is the effort to reduce the
number of pupils attending the hours of catechism. Although the percentage of children attending catechism is not generally a valid proof of the
level of the teacher's educative work, scientific analysis, however, testifies to
a direct correlation between the number of years in which the children attend the religious instruction lessons and the final results that the school
reaches in the formation of the scientific ideology in them.

Action on the parents to reduce enrollments of religious instruction is
explicitly encouraged:

For educative action in the field of atheistic propaganda, some help comes
also from the support of the rural organizations of the party, the cell of the
school-family Association and from the collaboration of the party organizations in schools with the basic organization of the Czechoslovakian CP in the
factories. That it is a question of a systematic action is shown also by the fact
that the number of pupils enrolled in catechism decreases also in the course
of the year. The most effective form of immediate action is represented by
individual talks with the parents carried out by the class teachers, the headmaster of the school and, in some cases, also the members of the
school-family Association.

Unfortunately this mass action for the destruction of religious instruction
cannot fail to have results: As various surveys show, the ideas and ideological attitudes of students in all school grades have changed or are changing in

a positive sense, that is, the percentage of children whose parents ask for religious instruction is falling.

In our town (Brezno) no one has enrolled for religious instruction. Behind this fact there is the daily work of educators, talks with parents, lectures, meetings, etc.

The success of this work is testified to by the reduced percentage of pupils who have failed (as compared with last year), better attendance at school and the fact that none of the 721 pupils attends religious instruction.

Cardinal Paul Yu Pin, the Chinese Archbishop of Nanking, living in exile in Free China of Taiwan, who was condemned to death by Peking in absentia, at a press conference at St. Martin of Tours parish in Philadelphia, made the following statement:

Communism is the moral enemy of God and man. It is atheistic and intrinsically evil. Communism is the total negation of everything that the Church ever stood for: justice, human rights, freedom of religion, personal freedom and legitimate governments. It claims to promote a 'classless society' but actually functions as a dictatorship of despots who exploit the toiling masses more viciously than any other tyrannical ruling class in the history of the world.

From a platform of absolute oppression, Communism unceasingly tries to mold the thinking of its victims. Communism has been provoking and conducting wars of oppression.

In China alone Communism has slaughtered more than 60 million innocent people. Millions more may perish following Mao's death.

There have been more Christian martyrs in Communist countries than in all history before the advent of Communism.

The Church can no longer remain silent. By default we are contributing to the enslavement of millions whose future is bondage without hope.

You cannot be a Christian and a Communist. You cannot enter into detente with the Devil. A Christian cannot be an accomplice to terrorism.

We are standing at the turning point of history. The fate of mankind hangs in the balance. We must stop compromising with Communism. We must no longer indulge in the perversion of providing money and moral support for Communist ventures. We must reassert the meaning of Christianity against Communist atheism.

After 25 years of Communist oppression on mainland China the bell of freedom on April 6th, 1976, was sounded in Peking when 100,000 Chinese at the Gate of Heavenly Peace Square (Tien An Men) opposed publicly the Communist government. They were the forerunners of other millions of Chinese people all over mainland China now rebelling against the Communist regime.

In the early years of Communism, the government did everything it could—and nearly succeeded—to stamp out not only any idea of organized religion but even belief in God; it was indeed atheistic Communism. Now the government rejects the accusation that there is no freedom of religion in Russia by pointing out the number of churches open for worship.

Actually, the churches in Russia are divided into two groups: the active and the non-active churches. The non-active churches, and these are the majority, are used as museums and are controlled by the state. Many of them house government-sponsored art and historical exhibits. Admission is paid for entrance. The state assumes responsibility for their maintenance and repair. This is but a subtle form of desecration. These magnificent churches, rich in history and icons, were built only for worship, not for cultural and political shows.

Three of these historic churches are within the Kremlin walls. Thousands of tourists, Russian and foreign, pass through these churches every day, admiring the architecture and paintings, without giving one thought to prayer.

The active churches, nearly all Russian Orthodox, are open for worship on Sundays. According to the Byzantine tradition they are generally very small in comparison with our churches in the West. For this reason also their small number is without question out of all proportion with the large crowds of worshippers.

The problem of numbers is complicated by the heterogenous composition of the Orthodox Church, which nowadays also includes non-Russians. The most important non-Russian group in the Church by virtue of its size, is the Ukrainian Orthodox. To this group belong the Ukrainian Uniates who inhabited the territories that were annexed from Poland and Czechoslovakia at the end of the Second World War. The Ukrainian Uniates merged with the Russian Orthodox Church in 1946. The Georgian Orthodox Church, which was absorbed in 1917, and its independence was acknowledged by the Russian Orthodox Church in 1943. The Armenian Apostolic Church, which has historically retained certain distinctions from the other Orthodox churches, has also succeeded in maintaining its independent status in the Soviet Union, even though its activities have been restricted by the government.

In the Soviet Union, religion and nationality are closely intertwined. The state, in the interest of furthering its nationality policy, has opposed autonomous Orthodox churches of non-Russian believers. In particular, strong objections were raised to the establishment of an Autonomous Ukrainian Church. Because the Ukrainians are the closest of the non-Russian ethnic groups in culture and language to the Great Russians and also constitute the largest non-Russian nationality in the Soviet Union, the desire to integrate the Ukrainians into the Russian nation has been a lasting element of Soviet nationality policy.

Data on numbers of religious persons in the USSR ought to be handled with great care. There is hardly any official information on the subject, and estimates in Western and non-Western sources show considerable variation. To illustrate, the principal religious institution in the Soviet Union, the Russian Orthodox Church, was reported by the *New York Times* of August 30, 1967 and the *Baltimore Sun* September 29, 1968, to have between 30 million and 50 million members. More recently, Gleb Rahr, an expert on Russian Orthodoxy, stated that there are some 115 million Orthodox believers in the Soviet Union, while elsewhere it has been claimed that the Orthodox Church gives the number of its baptized members as 70 million, 35 million of whom are said to be active believers.

The next important religious group to the Russian Orthodox Church is the Catholic Church, which is reported to have over four million members. Some 80 per cent of the population of the Lithuanian SSR is Latin-rite Catholic, but the proportion of Roman Catholics in the Soviet Union as a whole is not large, particularly since the Uniate or Eastern-rite Catholic groups were forcibly merged with the Russian Orthodox Church.

The wounds inflicted by the massive assault on Catholicism thirty years ago have not yet been healed in Lithuania, while in the western Ukraine the continued persecution of the "catacomb" Uniate Church keeps the old wounds open.

The Evangelical-Lutheran Church numbers about 850,000 members, most of them living in Estonia and Latvia. There are now 92 Lutheran ministers in Latvia. Because of an influx of Volga Germans, there are three German congregations in Riga with about two hundred members each.

The membership of the All-Union Council of Evangelical Christians and Baptists is estimated to be 535,000. This figure represents "registered" Baptists, who live mostly in the Ukraine, Kazakhstan, the North Caucasus, the Novosibirsk region, Lithuania, and the Kirghiz SSR. There is, in addition, a sizeable group of "unregistered" Baptists, perhaps as many as 400,000, who represent two movements: the Pentecostalists and the *Initsiatvniki*. The history of the Soviet Pentecostalists dates back to the beginning of this century, but the *Initsiativniki* withdrew from the All-Union Council in the early 1960's in protest against government restrictions. These two groups may be considered the most active religious elements in the Soviet Union today.

The results of the last full census carried out in the Soviet Union, in 1970, show a Jewish population of somewhat more than two million. But this figure very likely understates the number of Jews in the USSR, since the census data are based on nationality and many Soviet Jews hold passports that indicate a non-Jewish nationality. It is particularly difficult to define the borders between national and religious feeling among Jews. The number of Jews in the Soviet Union who practice the Jewish religion is not known. Some 55 synagogues officially remain open, but there is no way of guessing the extent of unofficial observance. While Jews are scattered all over the territory of the Soviet Union, there are larger concentrations in Central Russia, the Ukraine, the Baltic countries, Central Asia, and Georgia. Soviet Jews as a rule live in large cities.

The total number of Soviet Muslims may be as high as 45 million. Bennigsen states:

> In the case of Islam a confusion between religion and nationality is still valid. Islam is more than a religious belief: it is a way of life, a culture, a means of national identification. Nowadays in the USSR there is even the expression 'the non-believing Muslim.'

Among many of the Muslims, the percentage of those who declare their national language to be their native tongue is increasing. This is true of the Kazakhs, Usbeks, Kirghiz, Azerbaidzhanis, and Tadzhiks.

There are some 50,000 Buddhists in eastern Siberia. Most Buddhists live in the Buryat, Tuva, and Kalmyk Autonomous Republics. Under Stalin, organized Buddhism was crushed with a severity experienced by few other religious groups in the USSR. However, a revival of Buddhism set in slowly after Stalin's death. Not only did pilgrims constantly come to the seat of the religious leader of the Buddhists, as reported by Soviet press, but also there appeared heightened interest in Buddhism among young Soviet intellectuals in Moscow and Leningrad. In December, 1972 a trial of several Buddhist scholars accused of having organised "a secret Buddhist sect" took place in Ulan-Ude, the capital of the Buryat Republic.

There are also a number of "illegal" sects in the USSR, including Jehovah's Witnesses (who are mostly to be found in Lithuania, Byelorussia, the estern part of the Ukraine, and Latvia), the True Orthodox Christians, and the Uniates.

Two observable phenomena illustrate the dimensions of the religious revival in the USSR; the systematic intensification of the campaign in the Soviet press against adherence to religious traditions, which on the evidence persist stubbornly among the Orthodox and Islam believers, and the steady increase over the past decade in the volume of *samizdat* dealing with religious developments. Among the various types of *samizdat* materials on religion, the journal *Chronicle of the Lithuanian Catholic Church*, written and published in the Lithuanian language, deserves special mention, for "the dissent it chronicles involves and is supported by almost the entire population of Lithuania."

In China the Christians are being persecuted in a dreadful way and are being forced to underground activities. The persecution of Christians rages especially cruelly in Albania. Most churches and mosques are torn down or used for other purposes. In 1972 the Catholic priest, Stephan Kurti, was shot because he baptized a child upon the mother's request in a concentration camp. In 1973 fourteen priests still lived in all of Albania; all except one found themselves in concentration camps. In the draft of a new Albanian constitution, which is to replace the one in effect since March 14, 1946, recognition of every religion is deleted.

In Communist Eastern Europe the situation is different from country to country, but everywhere the Christians, be they Orthodox, Uniate, Protestants, or Catholics, are being persecuted and repressed in a gripping ecumenicity of common suffering. The terror since the end of the "Prague Spring" in Czechoslovakia rages especially fiercely. There the pastoral effect of the church is ever increasingly being throttled by shifty administrative acts. The church also suffers from the pressure of the regime in Hungary; that is how, for example, the new generation of priests is handicapped.

Even in Poland, where the great majority of the people are true to the Catholic faith and where the priests and religious vocations are as numerous as in hardly any other country of the world, the church is severely oppressed by the Communist authorities. Recently the Primate of Poland, Cardinal Wyszynski, declared before tens of thousands of Catholics that it is unbelievable that the state is setting up "a political campaign against the Church" and is mobilizing its power in order to destroy religion. "I pray for those" he continued, "who have shown brutality and inconsideration. Father forgive them, for they know not what they do" (Lk. 23:14).

The conditions in the DDR are known. In April, 1976 the Lutheran bishop, D. Albrecht Schonherr, sadly pointed out the intention of the ruling SED party to introduce atheism for all citizens. With that, continued the bishop, "the freedom of faith and conscience would no longer be unequivocally guaranteed for those citizens, who cannot accept the Marxist-Leninist point of view." It is often suggested to Christian parents that their children should no longer go to church instruction for the sake of their future.

For sixty years the Soviet Union has been the model and harbinger of Christian persecution. Lenin, the founder of the Soviet Union, recoined the Marxist slogan about religion being "the opium of the people" into the saying "religion is unrefined spirits"—bad alcohol.

The people become extremely dull through a belief in God. Whoever believes in God, spits on himself "in the worst manner!" Lenin views all churches and religious institutions as the helpers' helpers of reaction; as instruments of slave holders, feudal lords, and capitalists, as a part of their super structure. The fight against religion is intrinsic to atheistic Marxism.

In article 124 of the Soviet constitution it says: "the freedom to practice religious rites and the freedom of anti-religious propaganda are recognized for all citizens." Soviet interpretation of this sentence means: "Outside of God's house the church is permitted nothing and inside not everything." Whereas atheist propaganda receives full support of the state and the party, the church is forbidden openly to announce its beliefs. The new religion law of June 23, 1975 no longer even tolerates "the religious influence of parents on their children." Parents, who still do this, are punished. The Church is also prohibited from performing charitable and social services. Through the new law all religious organizations and the individual believers are subjugated more severely to state control.

The church buildings and ritual objects are the property of the state. If at least twenty persons commit themselves to keeping the church in good repair, the state rents the building to this group. The pastor is its employer and receives a registration certificate, without which he is not allowed to conduct worship services.

Religious freedom appears to have fared no better since Helsinki. In Lithuania two Catholic bishops sentenced to internal exile under the Khrushchev regime have appealed for relief from the Kremlin but have as yet received no reply. One hundred Lithuanian priests sent a letter to the government protesting that the continued exiles violated the Helsinki accords. Again, there was no reply.

July 28, 1976, almost a year to the day after the treaty was signed, the Supreme Soviet of Lithuania approved new regulations that actually tightened state control over religious practices. Under the new regulations, two Lithuanian Catholics were arrested in October, and their religious literature confiscated. They were then charged with "disseminating anti-Soviet fabrications."

In August, 1976, six Baptists were sentenced to prison for operating Sunday schools—a crime in the Soviet Union. Georgi Vins, a well known Baptist leader, remains in a strict-regime labor camp despite international appeals for his release.

Fourteen years before he came to power, Russian revolutionary V. I. Lenin told a group of peasants that "everyone should have full freedom not only to adhere to the faith of his choice, but also to propagate any creed." The religious tolerance Lenin pledged in 1903 proved to be a politician's broken promise. But Christianity is far from dead in the Soviet Union, and currently it is showing remarkable vitality. Bored by lectures on atheism, younger urbanites in the U.S.S.R. are reappearing at Orthodox churches to worship. Defiant Roman Catholics and dissident Protestant evangelicals are growing bolder in asserting their religious beliefs. Baptists risk incarceration in order to turn out copies of John Bunyan's "Pilgrim's Progress" on underground presses, and even in prison, draft-resisting Jehovah's Witnesses meet clandestinely to pray and read miniature copies of *The Watchtower*.

In an unprecedented display of ecumenical solidarity, a Russian group of 28 Christian clergy and laymen in June, 1976 published an open appeal to Soviet authorities for "a rational way of coexistence between the state and Christian congregations in our country." The appeal warned that state control of the churches and systematic persecution of dissenting sects

> does great harm to the state itself. (When) tens of millions of our citizens . . . are discriminated against, artificially set apart and against the state, the life of the whole people is crippled.

Included in the appeal is a list of grievances—notably, "arbitrary closure of churches" and "interference by authorities" in the lives of clergy and congregations. The petitioners urged the state to recognize the rights of all religious societies to publish and sell their literature, to hold services outside of churches and to make religious instruction an alternative to the atheism that is taught in Soviet schools. "Religion is spreading and young people are coming to the churches no matter what obstacles are put in their way."

The major grievances of a group of Soviet Christian leaders, listed in a 15-page appeal to the Soviet government for freedom of religion, have been detailed in dispatches from Western news agencies.

The appeal, addressed in June to the Supreme Soviet, said "the difficulties of professing the Christian faith" were "particularly arduous in the USSR" and were "becoming more and more oppressive."

Among the signatories were clergy and laity of the officially recognized Russian Orthodox and Lithuanian Roman Catholic Churches, and the unrecognized, unregistered Baptists, Pentecostals, Adventists, and the fundamentalist Church of Christ. The statement charged:

> Christians are authorized only to attend worship services, but are not allowed to voice their opinions on matters of church policy.

> Anti-religious publications are printed and widely circulated with state funds, part of which comes from the pockets of believers, but believers are denied the right to explain their thinking or to respond to the accusations.

> No religious community may begin its rightful activity without prior authorization and without submitting to particularly humiliating conditions of control.

> Religious organizations do not have the right to carry out welfare activities, in spite of the fact that the state, in all good will, is not in a position to meet all concrete family needs.

> Religious organizations have no right to own property. All objects used in worship are the property of the people, and the religious community is responsible for their preservation.

Religious teaching is completely forbidden. Many parents have suffered serious consequences for having gone against this prohibition.

A Byelorussian court has imprisoned four Evangelical Baptists in a wide-ranging crackdown on small religious groups.

Of the victims in recent months have been a Buddhist scholar who had followers from the Mongolian border to the Baltic and an underground group of Jehovah's Witnesses in Lithuania, Latvia and northwestern Russia.

A court in Lithuania has sentenced four Jehovah's Witnesses to five years in labor camps and five others to lesser terms.

The Witnesses were accused of building an underground organization, printing and disseminating anti-Soviet literature and urging disobedience of Soviet laws.

Sovietskaya Litva said the Witnesses had a tightly organized, "multistage" leadership structure throughout the Soviet Union that was highly efficient in arranging secret meetings for Bible readings, smuggling pamphlets into the country and reproducing and distributing them.

Most of the signers are known religious dissenters. But the fact that organizers were able to persuade leaders of the Seventh-day Adventists, Pentecostals and other "churches in the catacombs" to join people from the Orthodox and Catholic churches was significant. Their appeal has so far attracted only silence from the government and the Orthodox Church. But for the millions of Russian Christians who proselytize clandestinely, the appeal was proof that at least some Christians from the officially approved churches are now prepared to stand up for the rights of oppressed sects. "To be a believer in Russia is to be with Christ as he is crucified."

Despite signing of the Helsinki Declaration and promising religious freedom for citizens, the Soviet Union continues to deny such freedom and discriminates against believers, according to a report published by three Western research institutes:

> In spite of all statements and false testimonies, the legislation on religion, which was carefully revised in 1975 on the eve of the Helsinki conference, serves as a convincing, objective and ready-made proof of the fact that there is in the USSR religious discrimination sanctioned by the state.

The Declaration of Human Rights states in Paragraphs 18 and 19 that it is each individual's right to believe whatever he wants, to change his beliefs, and to propagate his beliefs. However, the citizens of the Soviet Union do not have this right.

Although their constitution stipulates religious freedom, this is not the truth. The law states that atheistic propaganda is allowed everywhere, but religious propaganda is forbidden. Stalin's law of 1929 stated that religious propaganda was allowed in the churches however, too many people attended Mass so the law has now been changed. Religious worship is allowed in a church, but the interpretation of the law is that it is forbidden to worship God outside the church which, in fact, means that it is forbidden to be a Christian. If you can't worship God in the morning when you rise, and thank Him in the evening when you go to bed, then you are not allowed to be a Christian. It is not only the Christians who are persecuted, but also the Jews, the Buddhists, the Moslems, Jehovah's Witnesses and other religions.

The law concerning religious societies states in Paragraph 17, that it is forbidden to: (a) raise funds in order to provide assistance, (b) to support members with financial help, (c) to organize special children's meetings, youth meetings, women's meetings, and prayer groups, and other special gatherings, for instance, to study the Bible and other literature, to arrange needlework groups, to do physical work, study religion, or any other gathering of special groups. It is also forbidden to arrange picnics or to play with children, (d) to found a library or to lend books, (e) to help sick people, pray for the sick or set up any kind of sanatorium. This is only what Paragraph 17 states about the separation of Church and State. The law also states that nobody under the age of 18 is allowed to go to church. Parents are not allowed to teach their children religion. In the Soviet Union, children do not belong to the parents, they belong to the State because they are born as Soviet citizens. The parents, therefore, are obliged to raise their children as good Soviet citizens which, of course, is not done if they believe in God.

Because of the lack of religious freedom, many children suffer in the Soviet Union. Rev. Hans Kristian Neerskov has a document signed by 1,453 mothers living in the Soviet Union in seven different republics and in 45 different cities. This document states that children are persecuted when they believe in God. A school teacher, for instance, induced the children in class to persecute a child because he came from a Christian home and believed in God. The children went so far as to try and kill the child, but they didn't succeed. The boy who came from a religious home was moved from the school to a special school for "difficult children" because he caused problems. Nothing was done to the children who tried to kill him or to the teacher who induced them to do so.

The same document tells us how children are forced to be pioneers and wear the red scarf and to deny God at school. Additional evidence is given to support the fact that children are taken away from Christian homes and brought to atheistic orphanages because the parents taught them to believe in God.

One piece of evidence in particular is the Sloboda family living in Byelorussia in the Vitebsk district in Dubrovo village. In 1966, their eldest two girls (11 and 9 years) were taken away from school to an orphanage. In 1970, the three youngest children were picked up in their home. An ambulance came to the home and seven adults went into the house and took by force the three children. The youngest one (Pavlik, at the age of 5 years) refused to go away from his mother, so both of them were taken to the police station by ambulance where they could be separated without neighbors witnessing the scene. The children were then brought to three different orphanages and since that time the parents have not seen their children, even during the holidays when they are brought to the Black Sea where good atheistic Communists take care of children.

Hundreds and hundreds of documents signed by Christians in the Soviet Union have reached the Western world. Many Christians have signed these documents, giving names and addresses to help their suffering Christian brothers and sisters. Many of those who have signed the documents are now being persecuted, tortured, imprisoned, and many are in labor camps. Of course, they are not sentenced because they are Christians, but most of them are sentenced because they make religious propaganda or because they gather in private houses after their church has been closed down by the authorities. Officials from different organizations have estimated that five million people are detained in prisons and labor camps in the Soviet Union. Many of them are Christians who should be protected by the Declaration of Human Rights but those rights are not observed in the Soviet Union.

In the Soviet Union, 90 per cent of all churches have been closed down. This is not because there is no need for churches as every guide and official would tell you. This is because the government wants to get rid of religion.

Official policy allows freedom of religion but unofficial policy has had specific objectives to disallow it as much as the traffic will allow.

The unofficial policy is to: Control and destroy the Church.

Separate the Church from state, school and social involvement—especially by prohibiting the instruction of children and the distribution of religious information by any media.

Reduce church attendance by closing churches, by not building new churches, and by social and economic pressures so that those with families, jobs and a hopeful future "will not dare step inside a church."

Restrict the celebration of holy days and religious ceremonies.

Convert believers and non-believers to atheism through widespread propaganda efforts.

Create the ideal citizen who is a militant atheist and "a brave new builder of Communism."

2

Atheism vs. Religion

The consequences of an unlimited faith in the supremacy of the free will of man based on the assumption that God's will acts independently of this wisdom, have inevitably been tragic and catastrophic for human beings. The first consequence has been authoritarianism, totalitarism, tyranny, the rule of might—is right, on the part of those who accept voluntarianism as a philosophy of authority.

This has reached its climax in the crimes of an Adolf Hitler, who decided on the theory that his will as a ruler made his commands automatically good, to murder more than six million Jews, together with countless old people, priests and ministers, and political opponents. Hitler's crimes were matched—if not surpassed—by those of Russia's Communist rulers, who, in the name of freedom, combined with power, took the lives of at least 10 million of their own people.

More than fifty years after the Bolshevik Revolution, which was to stamp out the "evil influence of the Church of Russia for all time," a Soviet head of state pays a visit to the Pope, a commissar lauds Patriarch Aleksei, and a novel is published which includes a vivid and moving description of Christ's meeting with Pilate and the Crucifixion. Does this mean that the commissars have given way to the church after the years of mass arrest, exiled clergy and purges of believers? No. News of the rounding up of Baptists, arrests of priests, criticism of churchgoers still appears regularly in the Soviet press. but there is clear evidence that atheism and Communism have not necessarily provided the answer to man's spiritual needs in Communist society. The ambiguity of the Soviet position on the religious situation can be seen in the increasing number of religious dissidents and church-goers.

The response to the plight of Soviet Jewry is heartening. What is less heartening is the absence of visible concern for the Soviet Christians who are experiencing today an oppression unprecedented since the 1930's. Unfortunately, this has gone virtually unnoticed in this country partly because of the unbalanced report of the Appeal of Conscience Foundation and a similar shortcoming in the *America* article by Fathers Davis and Culhane. Both reports vastly exaggerate the relative differences between the status of Christians and Jews in the Soviet Union.

It would be both misleading and unfair to investigate the state of religion in the Soviet Union without some reference to the historical pattern of official policy vis-a-vis the churches. This is lacking in the *America* account, which gave the impression that the post-Stalin thaw had affected the government's dealing with the Christian churches. Hence: "The atheistic over-zealousness of some officials during previous regimes, which had been more ruthless in their fight against religion, seems to be tapering off a bit." The fact is that the "tapering off" ended long ago and the government has increased its campaign against religion since Stalin's death.

While facts and figures vary about the status of the Russian Orthodox churches, the general picture has never been much in doubt. Before the revolution there were some 50,000 Orthodox churches; by 1939 there were around 3,200. Those years also saw a legal change in the status of the churches. In 1939 the law allowing freedom of worship and freedom of religious and anti-religious propaganda was changed to exclude freedom of religious propaganda. This change was embodied in the 1936 Constitution when the churches were forbidden to provide religious education. Even today, children may not receive Bible instruction from their pastors.

When Germany attacked Russia in 1941, Stalin, needing all the national support he could muster, relaxed the restrictions on the Orthodox Church and restored the Patriarchate. This period of comparative freedom, which continued into the postwar years saw an increase in the number of churches to over 22,000 by 1958.

It is ironic that during the post-Stalin thaw a new offensive was mounted against the churches. The authorities found the resurgence in the number of churches embarrassing and beginning in 1958, atheistic propaganda intensified. Since 1961 this has been supplemented by more vigorous measures: church councils are empowered to depose parish priests, sermons are often censored, believers and priests are sometimes removed to mental hospitals and churches are again forcibly closed. This last is always undertaken in the "public interest"—i.e., a street needs widening, a park or a school must go up on a church site; a congregation cannot raise the necessary taxes and maintenance costs. The result: a drop in the number of Orthodox churches to approximately 10,000.

These reports were verified by a letter from two Russian priests to President Podgorny on December 15, 1965, charging the Council on the Affairs of the Russian Orthodox Church with having closed "no less than 10,000 churches and dozens of monasteries" as well as having inflicted a host of illegal harassments upon believers and clergy. On May 13, 1966 both men were suspended from the priesthood.

Similarly disturbing is the reduction in the number of seminaries. Fathers Davis and Culhane reported that there were only three Orthodox seminaries in the Soviet Union; they failed to ask why five other Orthodox seminaries had closed since 1958.

Things are little better with the Baptists. Although there are approximately 5,000 Baptist congregations in the Soviet Union, the *America* editors reported on their visit to only one. The authors learned from the Moscow pastor and his son that in their parish "they felt things were going along rather well." This would seem to contradict other press reports in the past years which tell of strident and vulgar attacks on Russia's Baptist communities.

G.Z. Anashkin, Chairman of the Soviet Supreme Court's collegium for criminal cases wrote that because religion will not die out by itself "there must be militant aggressive scientific-atheist propaganda exposure of the activity of the wild fanatical sects that cause physical and moral injury to people and are openly anti-social in character." The tenor of the remarks that followed clearly indicated that the Protestant sects were being especially singled out.

Soon after *Izvestia* published a 1,700-word "expose" about a young man trapped by a Baptist sect. Following his hour-long baptism in the cold waters of a canal, the young convert was taken ill and hospitalized. The Baptist preacher told him it was sinful to remain in the hospital and so he left. The preacher gave him injections of morphine three times a day which cost the young man 238 rubles. He was despondent to the point of suicide when "rescued" by the authorities.

First, the Soviet government's atheist campaign over the last few years had made the Baptist target number one. It is almost certain that when the authorities tightened up the laws on religion in March, 1966, they did so with Baptist activities specifically in mind. Secondly, the Baptists themselves have repeatedly taken grave risks to inform opinion both in their own country and abroad about the true nature of "religious freedom" in Russia.

It is a fair guess, therefore, that the Soviet government is more worried about the program of this particular group than about any other religious activity since the revolution. In 1961, a reform movement, led by a certain Alexei Prokofiev, came into being. It criticized the alleged weakness of the official church leadership (the All-Union Council of Evangelical Christians and Baptists) in the face of the new wave of persecution that struck all religions under Khrushchev. In 1965 they went into schism and called themselves the Council of Churches of the Evangelical Christians and Baptists, but they have consistently been denied any legal status by the government. It is they who have been the principal objects of the systematic reprisals. The full background to this is extremely complicated, and there is undoubtedly real Christian goodness both in the reformers and the official Church.

Three documents of appeals, written in April, June and August, 1967, by the Council of Prisoners' Relatives, a group of women who since 1964 have been seeking publicity and justice for their persecuted menfolk, and who have kept resolutely active despite the determined efforts of the Soviet secret police to extirpate them and stop their activities, have become available to public. An organization such as this group has never before been known in Soviet society.

These new letters were addressed to U Thant, with copies to the UN Commission on Human Rights and the International Commission of Jurists, as well as to the Soviet authorities. They total over 30,000 words and, although some points are repeated in more than one appeal, they give the longest and the most concrete, detailed and up-to-date account of religious persecution ever to come out of the U.S.S.R. The letter of June 5 lists under 17 separate headings the different illegal methods of pressure employed by the authorities and provides examples in every case.

Appended to these appeals (so far as one knows, there has as yet been no answer to any of them from those they were addressed to) are various other documents. The most important of these is a list, with full personal details, of 202 prisoners being held at present, almost all of whom have been arrested since the new law of March, 1966. It is now known, too, that nearly 200 others arrested in 1961-64, were released in 1965.

Many of these prisoners are now being adopted by Amnesty International, the London-based organization for freeing prisoners of conscience, but we should not delude ourselves into thinking that if they are released the problem will be at an end. This is merely the running score of an ailment that penetrates into the depths of Soviet society. Yet, as with the writers, Sinyavsky, Daniel, Delaunay, Galanskov, Ginsburg and many others, both imprisoned and awaiting trial, Soviet surgical methods have proved completely ineffective, and these young intellectuals have shown themselves increasingly in sympathy with the stand Christians have been making

The new Baptist appeals are so vivid and gripping that the logical way of presenting them is to allow them to speak for themselves, with a minimum of commentary. No summary or extracts can replace the impact of reading a whole document.

The interesting sequel to this case was contained in one of the short documents appended to the main appeals. This was a petition to the Moscow judicial authorities by the parents of 12 children whom Braun and Chernetskaya had taught. It was dated Aug. 8, 1967, and signed in the city of Frunze. As it is very short I quote it in full:

> We parents appeal to you because on March 11, 1966, the Evangelical Christian and Baptist believers Y. Chernetskaya and M.I. Braun were convicted by the People's Court of the Kirgiz S.S.R., under Article 136 of the Penal Code of the Republic. They were accused because they had been teaching religion to our children. They were sentenced to five years' imprisonment each, despite our repeated statement that we parents of the children concerned had entrusted them with this task. We petition that the cases of Chernetskaya and Braun should be re-examined and that they, who are innocent of any crime, should be liberated.

This appeal raises a key issue. The Soviet Constitution guarantees the right of parents to bring up their children in their own faith if they so desire. Yet in practice this right is absolutely denied. Not only are classes in religion savagely penalized and the production of Christian literature for children banned; parents who attempt to teach their children privately run the risk of having them forcibly removed and sent to boarding schools where they can be brainwashed with atheism. The documents contain heartrending details of this practice, too.

In the face of this incontrovertible evidence of systematic persecution and the complete powerlessness of the Soviet legal system to support those puny rights that the Christian has managed to retain on paper, the cynicism of the Soviet authorities in their self-justifying statements to the West can hardly be believed. On November 6, 1967, the special supplement of the London *Times* devoted to Russia 50 years after the Revolution contained a single anonymous article on religion. In fact, it was written by Yuri Alexandrov, a Moscow lawyer, who had been allowed to say the same thing in the same newspaper a year earlier, even though a correspondence had been published refuting many of his points. His authorship can be proved, because a longer version of the same article had appeared in *Soviet Life* two months earlier. He admits the arrests, but says they were for violating the law on the separation of church and school. He concludes:

> So far as the law is concerned, the Soviet government makes no distinction between believers and nonbelievers. Both have equal rights and both have to observe the laws that protect the guarantee of freedom of conscience for all.

There are now major indications that public opinion in the West is no longer deceived by such statements, which quite simply bear no relation whatsoever to Soviet reality. The socio-religious broadcasts to the Soviet Union, from various radio stations all over the world, are on the Western reaction to these acts of repression against Russian Christians. "Feeling is now running so high that it seems certain this will form one of the key issues that will engage the attention of responsible opinion during Human Rights Year, which has now been inaugurated."

A turning point was reached on November 15, when the London *Times* published a letter answering Alexandrov's article of a week earlier. It came from the British Council of Churches, signed by Bishop Kenneth Sansbury, the General Secretary, and Kenneth Johnstone, chairman of the Joint International Department. This seems to have been the first public condemnation of religious persecution in the Soviet Union by high-ranking British churchmen or by an official body since the 1930's. Even responsible American church bodies have not made such pronouncements in recent years. Not the least remarkable feature of the British letter was its forthright language:

> Laws designed to protect the rights of Christians are not invoked, while those curbing their activities are enforced with severity. An unregistered group such as the Reform Baptists, . . . which has rejected the official Baptist leadership for alleged weakness, has no rights whatever.

Yet so adamant has the present Soviet regime been in its systematic repression of writers, Ukrainian nationalists and any other potentially powerful minority group, that one is tempted to ask: "What's the use?" Then one remembers that two-thirds of the new group of Baptist prisoners are under 45; that university students have demonstrated in court in favor of the accused; that Pavel Overchuk, N. P. Matyukhina, Maria Braun and Yelena Chernetskaya have already imprinted their ideals on a new generation of school children as worth going to prison for. The question then becomes: "How long can the visible victory of the Holy Spirit be delayed?" The moral victory has already been won.

However, the Soviet press states that before the Revolution the Baptists had been a persecuted sect. Baptists were first given the opportunity to practice their creed freely in 1918, when a Soviet government decree separated Church from State.

Lenin pointed out that the God-seekers and God-makers were merely bringing grist to the mills of the bourgeoisie, to which the God concept was a convenient practical means for keeping the people in slavery. Thus, by polishing up the God concept, the creators of the "New Religion" at the same time gave a fresh polish to the chains into which the exploiters had put the working people.

In its atheistic propaganda of that time, the Party made the fullest possible use of the persecution of all sectarians, heretics and dissenters, and, by exposing the criminal anti-alliance of church and state, it unveiled the reactionary countenance of the clergy.

The newly established Soviet regime now started to put into practice the demands of the first program of the Communist Party regarding the possibilities for realizing freedom of conscience. The fulfillment of these demands was embodied in the famous October decrees and in the historic Leninist decree of the Council of People's Commissars of January 23, 1918, "On the Separation of the Church From the State and of the Schools From the Church."

This decree laid down the main guarantee for freedom of conscience: the church was separated from the state, thus being deprived of state support and of all privileges it had enjoyed before the revolution.

The decree not only assured the working people of the right to exercise any religious faith, but also guaranteed them the freedom of not belonging to any religious association whatsoever. The school was freed from clerical domination and guided toward the road to Soviet education.

From 1921 onwards a great effort was made to obtain from all religious groups in the USSR a committment of loyalty to the new State. In most cases this required a fair amount of coercion, and led to the actual persecution of key religious leaders who were unwilling to meet the government's demands. Emigre church sources with close contacts with the Soviet Union at the time, estimated that between 1917 and 1923 over 1,200 priests and 28 bishops of the Russian Orthodox Church met their deaths and other leaders who refused to express loyalty to the government were eventually forced more or less underground.

Before Lenin died, the basic framework of Soviet legislation on religion had been completed. Under this legislation, religious organizations ceased to exist as corporate, hierarchically ordered national bodies: the Moscow Patriarchete, its diocesan administrations and deaneries, were now reduced to an extra-legal if not illegal existence. The law now recognized only local "religious associations" — groups of at least twenty believers (the so-called *dvadtsatki* — which, after their registration by the local soviets, could lease from them houses of worship and liturgical objects.

Recently a book of secret Soviet laws on religion has been leaked to the West. Under the Soviet government's own rules, certain types of laws and decrees need not be published.

The leaked documentation shows that the Soviet ban on religious ceremonies in private homes dates back to 1962 and not to public decrees of 1975.

The lawbook is marked "for official use only," and to restrict its circulation, each of the 21,000 copies was numbered. Entitled "Legislation on Religious Cults," it was published in 1971 and was edited by V. A. Kuroedov, chairman of the Council for Religious Affairs, and A. S. Pankrotov, deputy procurator general of the USSR.

In his article, researcher Walter Sawatsky gave three reasons why he considers the lawbook valuable to Western scholars; it provides a useful collection of party and government pronouncements on religion; it gives the content of legislation on religion not available to the general public; and it enables scholars to see how Soviet policy toward religion has changed.

In some respects the 1971 lawbook is already out of date because of revisions of the basic Soviet law on cults which were approved and made public in July, 1975 — and thus were known about in the West before there was any general knowledge of the legislation being amended.

What had seemed particularly restrictive changes in the 1975 amendments are now discovered, in fact, to date back to an earlier amendment made in December, 1962, of the 1929 Law on Religious Associations.

Thus it was in 1962 that the ban on religious ceremonies in private homes was introduced, and that it became possible for a religious association to lose its registration for "violation of the law on cults' rather than for breaking the terms of the contract.

According to Sawatsky, from the fuller picture of Soviet legislation on religion that the book gives, "it is clear that the amendments of . . . 1975 are of a comparatively liberal kind."

The lawbook shows that the power of the Council for Religious Affairs has been centralized. Summing up, Sawatsky concluded:

> At present the state appears to be following a two-pronged policy towards religion. . . . On the one hand, religious associations which abide by the legislation may register and fewer obstacles are put in their way. On the other hand, those which refuse to accept the restrictive legislation are liable to be punished more severely. At all events, the state still insists on having the final word.

Now, with the demands of the first party program concerning the safeguarding of freedom of conscience having been realized, the Communist Party put the task of liberating Soviet citizens from religious prejudices in the foreground.

Of extremely great importance for the solution of the vast and complex task was the Eighth Party Congress. This congress emphasized that the adoption of the decree on the separation of Church and State and of the schools from the church, as well as the other measures destroying the alliance of state and religious associations, were regarded by the Communist Party as the beginning of its work for the atheistic education of the working people.

In the development of scientific atheistic propaganda, a decisive part was played by an article written by V. I. Lenin. "On the Importance of Militant Atheism" directed criticism against the party and state organs because of their shortcomings in the unfolding of atheistic work. A number of suggestions, all of them highly valuable, were made on the nature and proper organization of this work.

Lenin demanded that atheistic propaganda should be put on a firm scientific foundation and that one should be implacable in one's stand on idealism and clericalism.

One of the important practical measures taken in the ideological struggle against religion was the publication, started as far back as 1922, of the weekly *Bezbozhnik (The Atheist)*. Printed in mass editions, this periodical played an important part in the organization and carrying out of atheistic work among the population.

The year 1924 saw the founding of the Society of Friends of the Newspaper *Bezbozhnik*. Here was the founding stone for the League of Militant Atheists, an association which soon developed into a nationwide, atheistic mass organization.

> The Communist party and the Soviet state have scored great successes in the atheistic education of the masses. At the present stage of world history, our country is the country of mass atheism, the country where the scientific atheistic world view holds unchallenged dominance.

> The destruction of the social roots of religion is the chief task to be accomplished on the road toward its elimination. The fundamental transformation of society according to Communist principles creates such relations among people as will automatically remove the causes of the fantastic religious distortion of reality, and it will establish to the full extent the prerequisites for the complete elimination of religion.

As N. S. Khrushchev said:

> Our believers love earthly life. They do not aspire to a heavenly paradise. They want to have their paradise on earth. It is here that they want to live, to work and to enjoy the fruits of their work. And they are not doing too bad a job of it. In the 44 years which have passed since the revolution, we have achieved great successes. Now the road into the true Communist paradise has been mapped out by the new draft program of our party. We will devote all our strength to the fulfillment of this program.

On January 14, 1929, relict Krupskaya wrote:

> The need is imperative that the State resume systematic anti-religious work among children. We must make our school boys and girls not merely non-religious but actively and passionately anti-religious. . . . The home influence of religious parents must be vigorously combated. Skill and persuasion must be used. I do not approve of the over-zealous methods of some school teachers who make a practice of tearing off every cruicifix which they espy on a child's neck. Such methods are not efficacious. We must be more subtle.

The Communist newspaper, *Pravda,* in a front-page editorial, reiterated its continuing war against God. "Each Communist must become a militant atheist," said the editorial. Of course, this is in tune with Marx who sought to publish a "Journal of Atheism" and who did declare that "Religion is the opium of the people." Lenin, too, said, "Marxism cannot be conceived without atheism." He also said, "We must combat religion — this is the ABC of all materialism, and consequently Marxism."

Pravda warned fellow Communist Party members about taking part in religious ceremonies. It seems that some Communists are attending weddings and baptisms and listening to religious and national music in church services. According to *The New York Times* travelers to Armenia encounter numbers of Party members who acknowledge going to the rejuvenated Armenian Church on major holidays, for weddings, etc

The Communist newspaper editorialized,

> In modern conditions, it is very important to reveal the inter-connections between religion and nationalist superstitions. It is known that in a number of

cases, churches and sects claim to play the role of the preservers of national values. We sometimes encounter attempts to represent religious feelings as a feature of national impersonality and the nonobservance of religious holidays as a departure from the will of the forefathers.

To further the Communist Party's aim toward atheism the editorial noted that in Byelorussia, with a population of nine million, the State has opened 1,000 schools designed to teach "basic knowledge of nature and society." This is a euphemism for atheism and party indoctrination. According to the *Times* article, other party publications have been complaining about the weakness of "atheist education" and the lack of books to counter what has been called the flexibility of modern churchmen and their moral influence among young people.

The *Times* further noted that on other occasions such strongly worded editorials have foreshadowed decrees by the Central Committee which result in special campaigns directed at believers. For those living under Communism this is nothing new. The war against God and his people has been waged in Russia since the Bolshevik Revolution in 1917. Hundreds of clergy and thousands upon thousands of Christians have paid the ultimate price for their faith in Christ.

On January 17, 1973, Pope Paul told a general audience:

> A well known French review informs us recently of the ban imposed in a certain country, which even has great religious traditions, upon writing the name of God with a capital letter. We've arrived even at this today.

According to Pope Paul, the absence of God seems to characterize current history and civilization.

> Have some representatives of modern man become enemies even of the holy and ineffable name of God? This is only the extreme and outward aspect of modern atheism. But there are other aspects that merit our reflection
>
> It is said that modern man is allergic to religion. He no longer has a bent toward thinking, toward seeking, to praying to God. He is indifferent and spiritually insensitive.
>
> At bottom lies a more serious objection, which might be the dynamic force: we modern men have no need of God; religion is useless and accomplishes nothing; it even constitutes a brake, an unnecessery and paralyzing embarrassment.
>
> How many people think like that? Is it true—but we wouldn't like to think so—that youth, the new generation, is orienting itself toward this facile and victorious irreligion?

The Pope did not answer his own question. But he did observe that the absence of God from the thoughts and words of men "afflicts us deeply, and gives us the desolate impression of an anachronistic solitude."

The Catholic Bishops of East Germany write:

> Since (according to Marxists) dialectical materialism and faith in God are irreconcilable, it follows that Religion must be considered as an outdated conception, which must of course disappear. If it does not die by itself, then it must be persecuted with the instruments of propaganda and also of psychological persuasion in order to accelerate this process of extinction.

If these affirmations of the Bishops of the German Democratic Republic were contested by anyone, they could be confirmed by quoting many clear statements of Marxists in Eastern European countries on the incompatibility between any religion, Christianity in the first place, and Marxism-Leninism.

Peter Prusak, in *Nova Mysl*, a theoretical and political review of the central committee of the Czechoslovakian Communist Party, after pointing out that technico-scientific progress obliges the Church to adapt itself to changed conditions, goes on as follows:

> However, the substance and the role of religion do not change: it remains in clear antithesis with science and Marxist teaching and curbs the process of emancipation of the working masses. It remains an illusory and fantastic reflection of reality: the opium of the people. Therefore, to wish to integrate Socialism with the values and ideals of religion, is incompatible with Marxism-Leninism. This is what revisionists such as Garaudy, Fisher and the right-wing opportunist forces of the CSSR in the critical years 1968-69 tried to do and it is what international revisionism is also trying to do today.

It is significant to recall also the voice that comes from the influential leader of Romanian Communism, a country which claims a sphere of autonomy within the Socialist countries and differs, therefore, from Czechoslovakia, but which, with regard to atheistic propaganda, is perhaps even more drastic. Ceausescu says, therefore, in *Scinteia*, the organ of the Central Committee of the Romanian Communist Party on July 7, 1971:

> The atheistic campaign will be carried out and intensified, and mass actions organized to fight mysticism and backward conceptions and to educate all our youth in the spirit of our materialistic-dialectical philosophy.
>
> ... All the ideological, politico-educative, cultural and artistic activity developed in our country must be based on the Marxist-Leninistic directives of the Romanian Communist Party, and the programme worked out by the tenth Party Congress must ensure the assimilation and putting into practice of these directives by the whole people.

Questions of scientific atheism states that not only are students in second-level and higher education obliged to attend the course entitled "Foundations of scientific atheism" but also that all subjects, particularly astronomy, biology, chemistry and physics are to be taught in the spirit of Marxism-Leninism and atheism. The same tendency is found in a periodical published in Slovakia, *Slovak language and literature in schools*, an aid intended for teachers of literature, in which directives are given to explain in atheistic terms classics that refer to "idealistic" conceptions of the world, including the *Divina Commedia of Dante Alighieri!*

In the "Socialist" countries, religious freedom is in most cases limited to the exercise of worship. V. A. Kuroedov, President of the Council for the Religious Affairs of USSR, states expressly: "The Soviet State sets out from the principle that the task of the Church refers only to the course of religious worship" and excludes religious proclamation. Religious instruction in the schools is in fact forbidden in some Socialist countries (USSR, Bulgaria, etc.) and in others it is subjected to limitations (intimidations and measures of an administrative character, etc.), while the press and all the media of social communication are in the service of the dominant anti-religious ideology. In this connection the special law on the press in Romania is characteristic. In Article 8 of Chapter II, it says textually:

> The press contributes to the affirmation of the scientific, materialistic-dialectical and historical conception of the Party on life and society, and maintains a revolutionary intransigence with regard to obscurantist, backward and anti-humanitarian positions.

In a really democratic country, the press and the other media of social communication would not be the prerogative of the dominant ideology, but would leave sufficient free space for other voices. Even more, a country that claims to be democratic, in that delicate sector of education and the formation of the young, must respect the legitimate pluralism of conceptions of life and ideologies, if it does not wish to harm gravely the freedom and rights of the intermediary bodies, in the first place families, as regards the education the children should be given. So if there is only one State school (and this is not the ideal condition), it must try to keep *au-dessus de la melee* as regards ideologies and the various religious denominations, letting them organize, however, in the way they think best the moral and religious formation of the pupils. It is inadmissible that a non-Marxist, for example, should not be eligible, as happens unfortunately even in Yugoslavia, to teach philosophy, and that the teaching of sciences in the State school is carried out in terms of materialistic and atheistic indoctrination.

In the Soviet Union and other socialist countries people talk currently of separation between Church and State. If this were equivalent to the "secularity" of the State, which leaves individuals and various groups of the social body to decide freely about their religious membership and the internal life of the communities one would have no objections to make. Actually, however, conscience and religious life are subjected to undue interferences and limitations which have nothing to do with a just secularity, but rather take on the form of a confessionalism reversed, a State atheism. Everyone knows that, on a purely formal plane, a distinction is made between State and party organs, but everyone knows, too, that it is practically cancelled by the overpowering omnipresence of the Party. It cannot be said, therefore, that the State is secular and that only the Party professes atheistic materialism, without being contradicted at every step by the reality of a deep fusion between State and Party.

Marxist "orthodoxy" is, in theory and in practice, decidedly contrary to accepting the distinction between the fundamental philosophical view, materialism, dialectical and historical, with its consequent atheism, and the scientific analysis of the alienating social situations that must be eliminated.

There are in the western world Marxists who have taken up a more positive attitude towards religion, but this happens exclusively, or almost, to explain how believers can commit themselves in the Socialist revolution.

And there are Christians who become Marxists, but, losing the sense of their own identity, their faith founders and they cease to be Christians. There are, however, also Marxists who become Christians and who, accepting faith in the Risen Christ, reject atheistic materialism.

Christians and Marxists, in fact, regardless of their ideological counter-position, are or can be animated by love for man and by the desire to free him from oppression of every kind and from the alienations to which he is subjected.

Members of an old religious sect in a remote part of Siberia still forbid such things as sweets and singing and even bar their children from Communist youth organizations, a Soviet magazine has complained.

The atheist monthly *Science and Religion* was criticising small groups of "Old Believers"—a fundamentalist sect of the Russian Orthodox Church— in Tuvinskaya Province, bordering Mongolia.

The magazine said that in some schools the children of such families, when called on to sing, covered their mouths with their hands to minimize the religious offence.

Cinema-going, radios and books with illustrations were also forbidden.

If children defied their parents and joined young Communist groups, they were given special plates to eat off and made to pray in separate corners away from the family.

A typical parental warning was : "If you join the pioneers you won't get a winter coat and winter boots—and father will beat you."

It called for atheistic education in the region to be stepped up.

Children ran around with crucifixes on their chests.

Old Believers do not allow doctors to treat them, refuse injections and once, when the son of an Old Believer family was sent out to buy sweets, he replied: "Children should not eat sweets—it's sinful."

Moslem regions also continue to trouble Party authorities.

In a recent Party meeting the first secretary of the Party of Uzbekistan, Sharaf Rashidov, condemned the large number of religious leaders still at work in some towns like Samarkand.

According to the regional daily *Pravda Vostoka*, Rashidov said religious activists lived the life of parasites, indoctrinated children with their faith and distributed religious books. They perpetuated an incorrect attitude towards women as well.

Soviet authorities have for years fought the Moslem practice of barring women from social or communal life.

Over the past 60 years, people have witnessed a tremendous struggle developing between Biblical Christianity and atheistic Communism.

Unfortunately, the forces of atheistic and agnostic liberalism and socialism have, in the main, aligned themselves with the Communists. Biblical Christianity has received the ceaseless barrages from all three sectors of the left wing and particularly over the ultimate issues of the nature of man and the significance of the death, burial and resurrection of Christ.

The U.S. State Department in its *Background Notes of the U.S.S.R.* published in 1968 admits, "Atheism is a fundamental tenet of Communist ideology, and suppression of religious belief is an explicit policy of the ruling Communist Party of the Soviet Union."

American Christian College also teaches that Communism is totalitarian. Not only is the economy nationalized or socialized, but so also are men's bodies, souls and minds. It also argues that Communism is totally incompatible with Christianity and agree with Eugene Lyons in *Workers' Paradise Lost* that in practice there is literally nothing good one can say about Communism.

Not one item of Russia's progress is the direct result of Communism, for its equivalent can be found in other countries where it was attained with far less brutality, terror, persecution, famines, massacres, purges, slave labor camps and deportations. Never before have so many paid so much for so little.

The Communists' war against Christianity is nothing new. Karl Marx became an atheist at an early age and developed a biting hatred for Christianity and Biblical morality. Lenin, likewise, hated Christ, and in one passage in Robert Payne's *The Life and Death of Lenin* admits that Lenin was a confirmed atheist, dedicated to the destruction of all religious worship. He then states that Lenin "regarded Christ with undisguised hatred."

Since the modern-day Communists are designated as Marxist-Leninists, it is not surprising that they, too, have nothing but contempt for Christianity.

Present-day atheistic Communism is 100 per cent contrary to Biblical Christianity. By definition, Communism is religiously atheistic; politically totalitarian; economically socialistic; ethically amoral; and philosophically materialistic. Biblically speaking, not one of these positions is sound, and practically speaking, the complete system is a hellish nightmare. Whereas Christianity is Biblically oriented, Communism honors Marx, Engels and Lenin.

The other contrasts between the two world views are equally telling: It is the Church versus the Communist Party; Christian morality versus class morality; Trinitarianism versus dialectical materialism; consent of the governed versus dictatorship or totalitarianism; law and order concepts versus lawlessness and conspiratorial tactics; spirit and matter versus matter; freedom versus slavery; peaceful change versus anarchy; creation versus atheistic evolution; God is history versus historical materialism; private property versus socialism; sanctity of the home versus abolition of the family; compatibility of the ends and means versus the ends justify the means; values based on the existence of God versus economic values; and, finally, God versus atheism.

There is nothing in Communism compatible with Christianity and it is contended that those who do only deceive themselves. Then, too, there is nothing in socialism compatible with Christianity and I would agree with John Howard Yoder in his *The Christian Witness to the State* when he says

> that socialism as a panacea and centralized planning as the major guide of economic development are open to challenge both theologically and practically.

Although many well-meaning theological liberals cannot quite get themselves to acknowledge the truthfulness of the fall of man and the vicarious death, burial and resurrection of Christ, it seems quite evident that without the liberals' help in destroying the foundations of Biblical Christianity and building bridges to Iron Curtain countries, Communism would be hardpressed in its struggle with Christianity and the Free World.

Christianity, then, faces the necessity of saying something about Communism, for Communism is intrinsically evil and deceptively programmed to tear down the values of God and man. Staggering as it may seem, it has imprisoned nearly one billion human beings behind iron, bamboo and sugar curtains.

Dr. John W. Drakefort, in *Red Blueprint for the World*, says:

> The demonic forces that communism calls history aim at the elimination of the peculiar values of the Christian faith. Communism uses the church as a propaganda instrument to strengthen an atheistic regime, it muzzles all religious activities among children, tears down the family, degrades the individual into a servant of the state, carries on atheistic teachings in school, and anti-religious propaganda, destroys Christian ethical standards, nullifies missionary activity and has as its ultimate objective the complete elimination of all religious ideas, values and concepts. In all these issues, at the opposite pole from Christianity, communism is uniting with demonic history.

The Bible contains many references to a demonic world system sometimes called the "prince of this world," "the prince of the power of the air," "the rulers of the darkness of this world." . . . Communism comes with pragmatic evidence for the existence of such a system in its claim that in working for the destruction of the peculiar distinctive (Christian) values, it is only cooperating with the forces of history.

It is the struggle between good and evil, light and darkness, right and wrong, and has been going on since the dawn of time.

A liberal theologian once said that just at the time Liberals taught us there was no hell, psychologists showed there were psychological hells far worse than we had ever dreamed. Similarly, just as Liberal voices have abolished the Devil, debunked the idea of Satan and organized system of evil, communism has become a world force inexplicable in any terms other than demonic.

Marx's twofold purpose in life was (1) to dethrone God and (2) to destroy capitalism. Lenin's slogan, of course, was "Long Live Atheism." And, naturally, Stalin, Khrushchev, Kosygin and Brezhnev have all been atheists as have the present-day breed of new revolutionaries.

When Dr. Francis L. Patton, former president of Princeton said:

The only hope of Christianity is in the rehabilitating of the Pauline theology (for) it is back, back, back to the Incarnate Christ and the atoning blood, or it is on, on, on to atheism and despair.

He probably did not see the exact time when such a choice was literally to be made by the peoples of the world.

From the Soviet point of view, religion and atheism are described as follows:

Atheism is an integral part of communism. Scientific communism and religion are at opposite poles in their interpretation of natural and social phenomena. Every religion, whatever its philosophical, moral and ritual foundations, rests on the idea of a God upon whom the fate of the world and of man depends, a God whose will we cannot know. Communism, on the other hand, holds that nature and society develop in accordance with objective laws which are knowable.

The history of science shows us how man, step by step, has learned the secrets of nature. Physics is a case in point. From a knowledge of the simple laws of mechanics, it has progressed to an understanding of the vastly intricate laws governing the microworld (the atom) and the macroworld (the cosmos). Marxism-Leninism derives all its conclusions from exact knowledge and cannot therefore accept the idea of an all-powerful and all-knowing supernatural force.

There are, we know, instances of world-renowned scientists who discovered fundamental laws of nature and still believed in God (Isaac Newton, Ivan Pavlov and others). The lack of scientifically based theory of the origin of the Universe does lead some people to the belief in a creator. Belief in God is associated in many people's minds with the moral principles which religion preaches and which are so often violated in life. Be that as it may, the progress of science shows how far mankind has gone in cognizing the world and how unlimited the possibilities of further cognition are.

One more comment. When this problem is discussed, it is often presented as though communism originated atheism. Actually, atheism is immeasurably older than scientific communism. There were atheists among the ancient Hindus, Egyptians and Babylonians, in ancient Greece and in the Middle Ages.

The French encyclopedists—Voltaire, Holbach and Diderot—were atheists, as were many other philosophers and thinkers. There are non-Communist atheists today in all countries.

On becoming a Communist, a man accepts not only its goal but also its world outlook, the philosophical foundation from which this goal logically develops. Practically, however, this does not always follow. It varies with the traditions and the depth of religious feeling in the specific country. For example, the Rules of the Communist Party of the Soviet Union say flatly that a Communist has to fight vigorously against religious prejudice and other survivals of the past. From this you conclude that atheism is obligatory for a member of the CPSU. On the other hand, in some countries (those with deep-rooted religious traditions, usually) the Communist Party allows its members to be communicants of one religion or another.

By the way, we should bear in mind that joining the Communist Party is a voluntary matter everywhere. If a person does not feel he can join the Communist Party because of his religious views, there is no reason why he cannot support and work for whichever part of its program he does agree with without becoming a member.

What are the present and future plans of Communism toward religion?

The word "plans" presumes definite goals and times when these goals ,will be reached. If we think of the elimination of all religious beliefs, we can hardly set timetables. Only education will do that, a slow process which does not operate by timetables.

The only "plan" element is the conviction of Communists that religious beliefs will eventually "wither away" and be replaced by a scientific view of man and nature. This is where the logic of social development leads.

The Communist Party of the Soviet Union confines its activities in this area to education, explanation and persuasion. As Lenin said, religion can be fought by "purely ideological, and only ideological, weapons, by our press, by our word." What it comes down to is popularizing scientific and technical knowledge, giving people an understanding of the world around them, of the laws of development of nature and society. At one time—this applies mainly to the early Soviet period—the local authorities in some parts of the country closed down churches without the consent of the members of the parish, interfered in the affairs of church councils, and so on. The party fought that kind of anti-religious activity vigorously.

What is the true, present status of religion in the Soviet Union at all levels, particularly among upper party levels?

Churches are permitted to function, believers are not persecuted and the clergy administers all the rites called for by their religion providing they are not harmful to the health of the individual. There are no repressive measures of any kind against believers. Soviet law provides penalties for those who try to repress religious observances. The Constitution of the USSR, the fundamental law of the country, grants every person freedom of conscience and separates the church from the state and the school from the church. Prior to the 1917 Revolution the Russian Orthodox Church was the official state religion, and religious instruction was required in the schools of Russia. Moreover, only Christianity was recognized; communicants of other religions were discriminated against.

The Declaration of the Rights of the Nations of Russia, November 1917, abolished all religious privileges and restrictions. A special appeal to Toiling

Moslems of Russia and the East declared: "Henceforth your faith and your customs, your national and cultural institutions are proclaimed to be free and inviolable."

Believers in the Soviet Union are free to attend church services and observe religious holidays. Groups of believers are permitted to make pilgrimages to holy places in other countries. Seminaries educate the clergy, and religious literature is published by the church. But all children are required to go to the public schools; there are no parochial schools.

The aim of communist society is to create the most favorable conditions for the rounded development of the individual. Religious belief cannot take root in such a society. It meets no problems and answers no questions in a society in which people are the active creators of their own destinies. As they increasingly cognize nature and learn how to control it, religion gradually "withers away."

This process of spiritual emancipation from obsolete, unscientific views, religion included, is going on not only in our country but the world over. It takes different forms in different countries, depending on local conditions. But the process itself, whatever form it takes, is a reflection of today's scientific and technological revolution.

Both the decree signed by Lenin and the Soviet Constitution separate the church from the state. What does this "freedom of religious worship" mean?

The Soviet Union applies in practice the profoundly democratic idea of freedom of conscience. The essence of the official policy is briefly as follows: The church is separated from the state, the state does not interfere in the internal affairs of the church. Each Soviet citizen is free to observe any religion or none at all.

The school in the Soviet Union is separated from the church. The teaching of religious dogma in all secondary and higher schools is not permitted. Citizens can instruct and be instructed in religion privately.

Soviet law guarantees believers the right to satisfy their religious needs together in temples, churches, synagogues and mosques. The state has, without cost, transferred to religious congregations churches ritual articles, church literature and other property. Performance of religious rites and preaching are not subject to censorship if they are purely religious. The executive bodies of the religious congregations in charge of their property and finances are elected by the believers themselves from their own members.

Does not separation of church from state in effect bar believers from political activity?

Religion in the USSR is a private affair. No citizen is deprived of his civil rights on the ground of profession or nonprofession of any religious faith. All Soviet citizens, irrespective of their nationality, sex, religious beliefs and social origin, have equal rights. Believers may make their religious beliefs public or keep them secret, as they choose. There is no statement of a Soviet citizen's religious or nonreligious beliefs or affiliations in any official record. Soviet citizens, believers and nonbelievers, all work for the good of Soviet society. No citizen may, pleading religious views, avoid his civic obligations or observance of the laws.

By what practical measures, other than laws, is freedom of conscience in the USSR guaranteed?

Under Soviet law a citizen cannot be denied his rights because he is a believer. It is a crime, also, to persecute anyone for his religious beliefs. It is even illegal to insult a citizen because of his religious convictions. Under the Constitution, believers are free to observe their religious rites, to gather for services in Orthodox or Roman Catholic churches, mosques and synagogues.

Religious organizations have the right to publish religious literature, to make the articles required for their religious observances, to train clergymen and theologians, to convene congresses and conferences of religious leaders and to maintain contact with their coreligionists in foreign countries.

Soviet religious leaders took part in the conference of progressive Buddhists held in Ulan-Bator in June 1970, in the world religious conference in Japan and in the recent Fourth All-Christian Conference in Prague. In accordance with church regulations, in the past two years alone, congresses of Lutherans, Old-Believers, Moslems and Evangelical Christian Baptists have been held in the Soviet Union. A conference of Moslem leaders of the Soviet Union was convened in the Soviet Union in October 1970 around the slogan: For the Unity and Cooperation of Moslems in the Struggle for Peace.

Upon the death of Patriarch Alexei, the General Council of the Russian Orthodox Church met in June 1971 to elect Metropolitan Pimen his successor.

In March 1971 there was a conference of churchmen and representatives of the Jewish religious societies of the USSR.

The following books have been published recently to meet the needs of believers: Bibles for the Evangelical Christian Baptists and for the Orthodox Church, a Catholic prayer book, a hymnal for Evangelical Christian Baptists, a Koran for Moslems and a prayer book for the followers of Judaism. Church calendars for the Russian Orthodox Church, the Old-Believers Church, Lutherans, Seventh-Day Adventists, Jews, Moslems and Buddhists are issued annually. The religious centers of the Russian Orthodox Church, of the Armenian and Moslem religions and of the Evangelical Christian Baptists issue their monthlies in a mass edition.

Is preference given in the Soviet Union to any religion?

Soviet law prohibits categorizing citizens according to their beliefs. In czarist Russia exclusive privileges and special rights were given to the Orthodox Church. It owned millions of acres of the best land, engaged in trade and received enormous annual subsidies from the government. In 1912 alone, the Orthodox Church received 46 million gold rubles as a gift from the czarist treasury, considerably more than was allocated for public education. The Orthodox Church persecuted people of other religions and atheists. That was why the principle of equality of all religions was so welcomed by the non-Orthodox. We believe that the very existence of an official religion is discriminatory and infringes freedom of conscience.

Does the church pay taxes to the state? Does the state give any material assistance to religious congregations?

All expenses of a church are covered by the voluntary donations of its parishioners. And since living standards generally keep rising, these voluntary donations add up to quite impressive sums. The church pays no taxes to the state. The church buildings, prayer houses, religious articles and rare church books of artistic or historical value have been given to the various congregations for their use. If the church building and its rare icons, paintings or frescoes are of architectural or artistic value, they are preserved by the state. For the maintenance of church buildings and religious articles, as well as for the production of such articles, the local civil authorities supply the religious societies with the necessary building materials, wax, incense, gold and precious stones. On order from religious centers, church literature is printed at state printing houses and is distributed to believers.

By agreement with local bodies of government, any religious association or society, provided it has at least twenty members, may receive free use of the land upon which the church or other house of worship stands. Naturally the respective congregation pays for maintenance and repairs. Priests and other religious teachers are remunerated from funds made up of donations and fees for performing religious rites.

Religious associations may publish their own theological periodicals, prayer-books and other religious literature. They may also rent, erect, or purchase buildings to house chandleries and workshops making various articles for religious rites. The income and revenues of the various religious societies and churches are tax-exempt.

The following are the biggest religious denominations:

The Russian Orthodox Church. Supreme authority is exercised by the periodically convened Assembly of Sees, which elects the head of the Russian Orthodox Church, the Patriarch of Moscow and All Russia, who exercises the supreme authority in the period between Assemblies in conjunction with the Holy Synod.

The Russian Orthodox Church is divided into dioceses. Each diocese is headed by an archbishop. There are also several dioceses and other religious institutions abroad, in the USA, France, Austria, Israel, etc.

After Patriarch Alexius' death in 1970, the locum tenens for more than a year was Pimen, Metropolitan of Kruititsky and Kolomna, the senior member of the Holy Synod. On June 2, 1971, he was unanimously elected Patriarch of Moscow and All Russia by the Assembly of Sees at the Trinity Sergius Monastery in Zagorsk, near Moscow. At the same time the Assembly adopted a world-wide appeal to Christians, "to unite their efforts to prevent the threat of another world war and to strengthen friendship, understanding and co-operation among all nations."

The Georgian Orthodox Church. This is an autonomous denomination which is headed by David V, the Patriarch-Catholicos of All Georgia, who has his residence in Tbilisi, the capital of Georgia.

The Armenian Gregorian Church. Devout Armenians, whether in the USSR or abroad, belong to this Church. It is headed by Vazgen I, Supreme Patriarch-Catholicos of All Armenians, who has his residence in Echmiadzin, a monastery outside the Armenian capital of Yerevan.

The Old Believers. Or the Old Faith. First emerged in the 17th century, as the result of the Great Schism. There are congregations in central Russia, the Ukraine, Byelorussia, Moldavia and the Baltic republics.

Islam. The majority of Soviet Moslems are Sunnites. There are also Shiites.

There is no single centre. The four independent ecclesiastical centres are: the Moslem Board for Central Asia and Kazakhstan in the Uzbek capital of Tashkent, headed by Mufti Ziyauddin Babakhanov; the Moslem Board for the European part of the USSR and Siberia, in Ufa, capital of the Bashkir autonomous republic, headed by Mufti Shakir Hiyalitdinov; the Moslem Board for the North Caucasus in Buinaksk, the Daghestan autonomous republic, headed by Mufti Mohammed Hadji Kurbanov; and the Moslem Board for Transcaucasia, in the Azerbaijanian capital of Baku, headed by Sheikh-ul-Islam Suleiman-zade Ali Aga. All four boards are elected by conventions of congregational delegates, the supreme religious authorities of the Moslems.

Soviet Moslems meet at regularly convened conferences to discuss common problems and make group pilgrimages to the Holy Places.

The Roman Catholic Church. Mostly in the Western Ukraine and Western Byelorussia, the Baltic republics and some parts of the Russian Federation.

The Evangelical Lutheran Church. In Estonia, Latvia. The Estonian congregation is governed by a Consistory headed by Archbishop Tooming. The Latvian congregation is governed by the Supreme Church Assembly, headed by Archbishop Matulis.

The Evangelical Christians-Baptists. Their supreme authority is the Assembly of Evangelical Christian-Baptist Delegates, which is convened at least once every three years. It elects the USSR Council of Evangelical Christians-Baptists to exercise supreme authority in the period between Assemblies. The Chairman is Ilya Ivanov.

Judaism. There are synagogues in every city where there are Jewish congregations—in Moscow, Leningrad Kiev, Minsk, Riga, Vilnius, Kishinev, Tashkent, Tbilisi, Sverdlovsk, Lvov, Odessa, and elsewhere. The synagogues operate autonomously.

Buddhism. Practiced in the Buryat, Kalmyk and Tuva autonomous republics and some parts of the Chita and Irkutsk regions of the Russian Federation. The Central Board of Buddhists of the USSR is headed by the Chairman, the Bandido Khambo-Lama Gomboyev Zhambal-Dorzhi.

Other denominations in the USSR include the Reformed Church in the Ukraine's Transcarpathian region; the Methodists, governed by a superintendent, in Estonia; and small groups of Seventh Day Adventists, Molokani and Mennonites.

No religious instruction is given at any of the USSR general educational establishments.

The Russian Orthodox Church maintains five theological seminaries and two theological academies in Zagorsk and Leningrad. Catholics have two seminaries in Riga and Kaunas, the Armenian Church, a seminary in Echmiadzin, the Moslems, a madrasah in Bokhara and theological college in Tashkent, and the Jewish congregation has a yeshiva in Moscow. The Lutherans in Estonia and Latvia have special theological courses for training people for the priesthood.

The above-listed theological establishments may send students to the appropriate centres abroad to do graduate and post-graduate work, such as to the Al-Azhar University in Cairo, the Islamic University in El Beida in Libya, the Divinity Schools at Oxford and Cambridge, the college of the Anglican Communion at Merfield, and the University of Gottingen — mention a few.

The best known monasteries and convents in the USSR are the Trinity Sergius Monastery in Zagorsk, the Pochaev Monastery in the Western Ukraine, and the Pskov-Pechersk Monastery outside Pskov, which are maintained by the Russian Orthodox Church, and the monastery of the Armenian Church in Echmiadzin.

Soviet religious associations maintain extensive contacts with kindred organizations abroad. In addition to the various conferences and congresses that deal with purely clerical matters, clergymen attend forums to discuss safeguarding the peace.

The Russian and Georgian Orthodox Churches, the Lutherans of Estonia and Latvia, the Armenian Gregorians and the Evangelical Christians-Baptists are represented in the World Council of Churches. Soviet Christians are represented in the international federation of Christian Churches known as the Prague Christian Movement for Peace. The Evangelical Christians-Baptists are represented in the Baptist World Alliance and the European Baptist Federation. Buddhists are represented in the World Fellowship of Buddhists, and Moslems are active in the work of the Al-Azhar Academy of Islamic Research.

The Soviet government has set up a special Council for Religious Affairs for liaison between the state and the various religious denominations. It does not intervene in purely religious matters, and merely sees that pertinent Soviet legislation is observed.

The principle of the freedom of conscience, as specified in the Constitution of the the USSR, implies not only the right to espouse any religion, but also the right to voice atheistic convictions, in short, to conduct anti-religious propaganda. Scientific atheism helps the believers to rid themselves of superstitions and develop the right materialistic outlook on the world and what takes place in it. However, it should be stated that anti-religious propaganda is carried on solely by means of explanation and persuasion; it is not permissible to offend religious feelings or encroach on one's religious rights.

Soviet legislation about cults is the development of the principles of the Soviet government's decree on the separation of the church from the state and school from the church. It proceeds from the premise that religion is the private affair of the citizen of the USSR. At the same time, Soviet legislation sets limits to the activities of religious organizations. While they are free in their internal activities in the areas of doctrine, worship and traditional forms of organization, they are obliged to observe the laws of the state which determine the rights and duties of the individual and of public organizations in socialist activities. I know of no cases of people suffering for their religious convictions, but there are occasional cases of penalties being imposed for violations of financial and economic rules or of public order, and the law courts consider these cases as a matter of routine. I must say that in the Soviet Union justice is administered on a democratic basis, in public hearings, in strict accordance with legal procedure, and with the right of appeal to higher courts. This makes arbitrary judgement impossible.

Our laws strictly protect the rights of believers. Offenses against the feelings of believers or discrimination of any kind is prosecuted by law. It is only under such conditions as exist in our country that each citizen can be guaranteed the freedom of belief or disbelief, the freedom of religious worship as well as the freedom to engage in antireligious propaganda. . . .

Early this year the Presidium of the Supreme Soviet of the R.S.F.S.R. (Russian Soviet Federated Socialist Republic) adopted a resolution regarding legislation on religious cults. . . .

The resolution states that "discrimination against believers is punishable according to the criminal statutes." This refers in particular to cases in which citizens are refused employment or acceptance in educational institutions, discharged from work or expelled from educational institutions; they are deprived of relief and privileges provided by law because of their adherence to religion. No wonder, then, that believers as well as the clergy have understood and approved the new normalizing acts of the Soviet republics.

Naturally, we too have our particular laws governing religious conduct. The fundamental one is the decree of the Soviet Government on "Separation of Church from State and School from Church" issued on January 23, 1918, and signed by Lenin.

In essence religious organizations in the U.S.S.R. are required by law to limit their functions to catering to the religious needs of their members without violating general statutes and without impinging on the lives or rights of other citizens. The law forbids the use of congregations of believers as staging areas for actions aimed against the interests of Soviet society. It forbids the encouraging of believers to shirk their civic duties and to refrain from participating in governmental and socio-political life. Perverse rituals in any form, which are harmful, deceitful and tend to arouse superstitions are contrary to Soviet law.

Our legislation calls for the registration of all religious societies before they are allowed to function. This is done in the interest of believers as well as the state. By registering, the religious denomination acquires the official stamp of approval to function under the law whereby the authorities assume the protection of its members. A religious society may be refused registration only in the event that its dogmas, rituals or other activities are in conflict with the law or infringe on other citizens' well-being or rights.

It ought to be pointed out that the majority of the clergy in the U.S.S.R. are law-abiding and loyal in their attitudes toward the Soviet Government in both its domestic and foreign policies. The contribution of the Russian Orthodox Church, headed by Patriarch Aleksey, to the cause of world peace, to the prevention of a new world war, and to the strengthening of international friendship should not be left unmentioned. . . .

It is a known fact that prohibitions of any kind or administrative pressures are an ineffective way to fight religious ideology. Atheistic convictions like all other convictions and beliefs, cannot be imposed by force, legislation or any other administrative means. This fact was reiterated by the founders of Marxism-Leninism. Engels, for instance, had stressed that persecution was the most successful step in strengthening religious convictions. . . .

The ideological struggle against religion need not impinge upon the believers' rights. Religious organizations which agree to function within the framework of Soviet laws will be allowed to exist as long as believers themselves have not abandoned them.

Religious associations publish magazines, calendars, and materials used in religious services. The Old and New Testaments and the Koran are on sale in kiosks adjoining places of worship. New editions are printed as the need arises.

Concerning the authority of the Council on Religion, its chairman, Vladimir Kuroyedov, explains, "Our main concern is the strict observance of the constitutional requirement of freedom of conscience. We are responsible for the application of legislation on religion for the entire country. Though it happens very rarely, individual local officials have been known to permit an incorrect attitude toward believers. Such errors have to be corrected. Besides, problems emerge in the daily activities of religious organizations whose solution requires contact with a government body."

Though there are no statistics kept of the religious attitudes of the Soviet population, it is nevertheless obvious (and this is confirmed by sociological studies) that the proportion of believers in the country has greatly decreased in Soviet times. Many factors are responsible, including the broad dissemination of scientific views on nature and society. Of significance also is the educational work of various organizations in behalf of atheism. This activity, like freedom of religion, is sanctioned by the Soviet Constitution.

The trend away from religion is enhanced by the Soviet Union's equitable and truly socialist policy toward national minority groups. In czarist Russia, where the rights of small nationalities were trampled, the working people of the national minorities felt that their religion was to some degree an expression of national self-defense. In soviet times, with complete and real equality of large and small nations, religion no longer has this function.

Though an over-all decrease in the number of believers is observed in the country, new adherents do join one or another religious association. This is partially a result of natural migration.

The Soviet Union has over 20,000 churches, including Russian Orthodox and Catholic churches, synagogues and mosques, and about 20 monasteries and convents. The clergy is trained at specialized theological secondary schools and higher schools. Eighteen such institutions, including Russian Orthodox academies and seminaries, Catholic seminaries, a Moslem academy and a Jewish Yeshivah, are in operation today. Religious publications include the Koran, theological works, prayer books, magazines and church calendars.

Religious groups hold their congresses and conferences to consider internal church problems. Discrimination or coercion of religious believers is prohibited by Soviet law.

The first liturgical volume since the time of the 1917 Revolution was recently published in the USSR to be used at religious celebrations in the parishes. Entitled *Selected Prayers for Orthodox Liturgical Services* the book of 350 pages includes the texts used at Masses on Sunday and on the principal feast days.

The fact of religious persecution in the Soviet Union goes back to the days just following the Revolution of 1917, yet few are familiar with the facts.

In 1925 the League of Militant Atheists was formed in the Soviet Union to publish and spread anti-religious material and, like the government's economic plan, an atheistic five-year plan was launched in 1927 and again in 1932. The program aimed at the complete disappearance of God's name from the U.S.S.R. by 1937.

In the late 1930's the league was reported to have 3.5 million members, but it failed in its primary task. Religion has not been destroyed in the more than 60 years since the Russian Revolution—but not for any lack of effort on the part of the Communist regime.

Despite a 60-year campaign calling for its eradication, religion remains a force in modern Russia. A recent poll showed that 21 per cent of those questioned in a survey in Kazan (a city of 900,000 some 450 miles east of Moscow) said they were religious. More than 400 students and others at the city's university and its medical institute conducted the survey. They questioned 4,710 people. Of these, 989 said they believed in one religion or another. A surprisingly large number of the believers, 34 per cent, belonged to the working class. The report was issued by *Nauka i religiya*, the official magazine of Soviet atheism.

To appreciate the significance of such a survey, one needs only briefly to review the history of religious persecution in the Soviet Union.

Speaking on January 22, 1958, then Soviet Premier Nikita Khrushchev stated, "We are for the freedom of the religious convictions of the people and for respect for the religious views of every human being in every nation."

Those in the West who pose questions about the state of religion in the Soviet Union are referred to Article 124 of the Soviet Constitution:

> In order to insure to citizens freedom of conscience the church in the U.S.S.R. is separated from the state and the school from the church. Freedom of religious worship and freedom of (from) anti-religious propaganda is recognized for all citizens.

The clergymen were deprived of voting rights and were considered obscurants and enemies of the people, not engaged in work. By order of Lenin the All Russian Extraordinary Committee for the Suppression of Counter-revolution was established in 1918 and during the first three years of Communist rule thousands of clergy were the victims of Soviet terror.

According to official Soviet data, for example, 423 churches were closed and 322 destroyed in the first half of 1929, and 1,440 churches were closed by the year's end. Synagogues were converted into clubs. Buddhist monasteries were closed, Moslem mosques were converted into atheist museums and the printing of the Koran was prohibited.

The provision that the school shall be separated from the church denies to the church any educational functions, since these are considered to be the monopoly of the state.

Another legal document, "Decree on Religious Associations," was enacted April 8, 1929, under Stalin by the Central Executive Committee of the People's Commissars. This legislation sets forth in 19 paragraphs what religious associations must and must not do.

The right to participate in religious rites is defined by the government as worship in an approved meeting place by a registered congregation led by acceptable ministers. There is strict enforcement of the regulation against giving religious instruction to the young, including parents giving religious instruction to their own children. Public worship is forbidden, as is any attempt to preach beyond the bounds of the approved meeting place. Baptism of children is likewise forbidden, and only those religious groups which have met the approval of the government are even permitted to participate in this limited practice.

While those below the age of 21 may not be given religious instruction, they are the major target of the state's own anti-religious "propaganda " another Soviet practice contrary to Article 124.

Before the Revolution the training of Russian Orthodox clergy was ensured by 58 seminaries with 20,000 students, and by about 200 ecclesiastical schools and minor seminaries. Above the seminaries were four ecclesiastical academies. On September 6, 1918, however, all ecclesiastical establishments had to close their doors.

During World War II the Communist government sought to unify the people against the German invader, and also attempted to create the image

in the West of the Soviet Union as a democratic and freedom-loving state.
The editors of papers and magazines were instructed to stop publication of
articles attacking the church and, although the laws and regulations relating
to religion remained in force, they were not strictly applied. In 1944, in fact,
theological studies were permitted to resume on a limited basis.

With the end of the war came an increasing reign of terror. An example of
the renewed vigor with which the Soviet government attacked religion may
be seen in the case of the Ukrainian Catholic Church.

The Soviet State systematically and ruthlessly liquidated the Uniate
(Eastern-rite Catholic) Church, and the Russian Orthodox Church was its
accomplice. The dark, embroiled, and sad history of the Uniate Church in
this area goes back to the end of the 16th century, and no one would wish to
suggest that its conduct toward the Orthodox in the past was beyond reproach. But in this century it had put its affairs in order under the inspired
guidance of Metropolitan Andrei Szeptycki, a man moved by a genuine
ecumenical vision of a united Orthodox and Catholic Church. He died in
1944.

In March, 1946, the Synod of Lvov took place. The Soviet version of what
happened here states that this was a voluntary return of Eastern Christians
to their spiritual father, the Patriarch of Moscow, but it is known that all
clerics who objected were imprisoned like Archbishop Slipyj. The Archbishop had been deprived of his freedom the previous year as a preliminary measure toward eliminating opposition. Eventually the Vatican secured his release in 1963, and since he has remained in Rome.

The question Catholics have been asking for many years is: how successful
was the Moscow takeover, and have there been individuals or groups who
managed to maintain their loyalty to Rome despite the fierce penalties for
doing so?

The 20th anniversary of the Synod of Lvov was celebrated with great
pomp by the Moscow Patriarchate in 1966, and its journal printed jubilee
articles in four successive issues which set out to demonstrate that the
outcome had been an unqualified success from the Orthodox point of view.
Sporadic evidence shows, however, that this is not the whole story.

After the death of Stalin in 1953, some former Uniate priests were released from prison, and when they made their way back to their own part of
the country, rumor had it that they began organizing clandestine religious
activities.

Soviet atheists could not let the anniversary year of the Uniate Church's
demise pass without dancing on its grave. Articles appeared in *Izvestia* and
the anti-religious monthly *Nauka i religiya (Science and Religion)*, but in that
fascinating way the Soviet press has of telling a story in one place and
contradicting it in another, there were hints that continuing Uniate activity
was still very much a live issue. Indeed, one article in *Molod Ukrainy (Ukrainian Youth)* for November 12, 1965, dramatically proved that Uniates still
have an organized network in several republics. Members of a sect called the
Pokutniki (Ukrainian for "Penitents") were imprisoned at Lvov for baptizing
a 12-year-old girl, after which she allegedly caught pneumonia and died.
The article continues:

> Recently they decided to hold a council. They attracted "delegates" not only
> from the entire Ukraine, but also from Byelorussia and Moldavia. They

brought with them a brass band, they sang psalms, and the event of note was information on the "miracle of Serednaya," a recently invented legend.

What links the "Penitents" with the Uniate Church? This article does not give the answer but one that followed two months later in *Science and Religion* did. The name of the founder of the group, Fr. Ignati Soltys, and he is reported to be a former Uniate priest who "declared himself to be the representative of the Vatican, to whom the Pope himself is supposed to have handed over the task of governing the Church in the Ukraine."

Science and Religion tries to portray the group as being numerically insignificant, with not more than a hundred members in all; yet this account is directly at variance with the description of the popular demonstration in *Ukrainian Youth*. The appearance of these articles proves that the authorities must be seriously worried about the Uniate revival and that such activities are widespread. This estimate is in line with what is known about the proliferation of other underground religious groups over the last fews.

Science and Religion blames the "Penitents" for meeting illegally for worship at a spring on a hill, where the miraculous apparition of the Virgin of Serednaya is said to have taken place. It does not go on to point out that since the Synod of Lvov, it would not have been possible for a Catholic Uniate group to register and thus meet legally either in a private house or in a church. As the author of the piece, L. Smirnow, has thus proved his unreliability as a reporter in the question both of the group's legality and of its size; it is very dubious whether one may attach any credence to his account of its doctrine and activities.

Smirnow says that Fr. Soltys deluded his followers into renouncing Soviet citizenship by assuring them that the world would end, first in 1962, and then again in 1964. When a woman was dismayed at this non-event she wished to leave the sect, whereupon Fr. Soltys and his supporters reportedly dragged her possessions out of her house and burned everything she had. The stories about the apparition of the Virgin, says the author, are supported by a photograph that was crudely faked.

Whatever the Soviet press and the Russian Orthodox Church may say, it seems unlikely that one has heard the last of the Uniates in the Ukraine.

On the night of April 11, 1945, Metropolitan Josef was arrested, and with him the entire Ukrainian Catholic hierarchy. Barely two weeks after his arrest, Moscow Patriarch Alexei consecrated a Russian priest, Makarii, as Bishop of Lvov, and on April 28, 1945, a so-called Initiatory Group was organized in Lvov, whose purpose was to work to bring the Ukrainian Catholic Church into the Russian Orthodox Church.

On March 8-10, 1946, a "Council" took place and it "invalidated" the decision of the Council of Brest in 1596, and united the Ukrainian Church with the Russian Orthodox Church.

Metropolitan Josef was sentenced in 1946 and nothing was heard about him until the death of Stalin in 1953. At that time he was made the same proposition which he had refused in 1945: He must recognize the authority of the Patriarch of Moscow. He again rejected this proposal and as the result of another trial in 1958 he was sentenced to an additional seven years of compulsory labor in a concentration camp.

The Soviet government's desire to unite the Ukrainian Catholic Church with the Russian Orthodox Church illustrates an important aspect of the treatment of religion under Communism. Just as the church was needed during World War II to increase Soviet prestige in the eyes of the world and unite the people, so it is needed in peacetime to sell Soviet foreign policy and the philosophy of socialism.

Dr. Matthew Spinka, prominent church historian at the Hartford Theological Seminary, notes that the Soviet policy has

> . . . resulted in the ever increasing subjection of the church to governmental control, so that in the end but little actual difference could be discerned between the external relations *vis a vis* the church which had existed under the Czarist regime and that which existed under the Soviets. It in turn established the pattern of relations which became not only the fixed form for Russia but for all Communist-dominated countries as well.

> As such, this *modus vivendi*, whereby the church has been lulled into the belief of the possibility of a "peaceful co-existence" and a preservation of its essential rights, while in reality it has been used as a tool for eliminating all religion from society, presents perhaps the most difficult problem facing modern Christendom.

An example of the use of the Russian Orthodox Church in spreading political propaganda may be found by looking briefly at the Communist World Council of Peace which met in East Berlin on February 23, 1951. The featured speaker was Metropolitan Nikolai of Moscow, who stated:

> And so we become convinced that the spirit and substance of Fascism have not disappeared, that the delirious dreams of the fanatic Hitler have found their continuers, now trying to realize them. Their followers do not lag behind their teachers. From the first day of the lawless aggression the American neofascists began a systematic, cannibalistic destruction of the "lower" Korean race. What do we see? Cynically violated standards not only of international rights but of human morals. Executions without trial and inquisitions, secret and public. Dreadful tortures of victims, the cutting off of ears and noses, breasts, the putting out of eyes, the breaking of arms and legs. . . .

> In 1952 Metropolitan Nikolai charged that U.S. airmen in Korea were waging germ warfare: "Infected insects are being dropped from American aircraft on populated points, not only in Korea but in China. . . the Church cannot pass over in silence the suffering of the Korean people, which is perishing from the brigand-like attack and demoniac malice of these human monsters."

Testifying before the U.S. Senate Internal Security subcommittee, Petr Deriabin said, "Most of the priests in the Soviet Union, and the religious people who help the priests, they are some kind of agents of the KGB or the MGB or were at that time. It is impossible in the Soviet Union to serve God without serving the state security."

Judaism in the U.S.S.R. is subject to unique discrimination. Jewish congregations are not permitted to organize a nationwide federation or any other central organization. Judaism is permitted no publication facilities, and no Hebrew Bible has been published for Jews since 1917, nor is a Russian translation of the Jewish version of the Old Testament allowed: The study of Hebrew, even for religious purposes, has been outlawed and the production of religious objects, such as prayer shawls, is prohibited.

The number of Jews in the Soviet Union is close to three million, of whom one million have been estimated to be believers. For these there are approximately 60 synagogues and rabbis, or one synagogue and rabbi for each 16,000 believers. No new rabbis are now being trained and the average age of rabbis is over 70. Little hope remains for a continuation of Jewish religious life in the Soviet Union.

The campaign against religion has mounted in recent years. Mr. Oliver Clement, an Orthodox professor, declared that from 1959 to 1962, the number of open churches decreased from 22,000 to 11,500 and the number of priests carrying on their functions from 30,000 to 14,000. More than half of the monasteries have been closed, from 69 in 1958 to 31 in 1962. Of eight seminaries reopened in 1945, two have been closed and two have been almost stripped of their students.

News reports from the Soviet Union in the 1960's indicate that religion is in as difficult a position today as it ever was. *Pravda Ukraini* for October 3, 1966, tells the story of "Brother Prokofiev" who had already been in prison three times, but as soon as he was released, he began to organize secret Sunday schools again. The result was a fourth arrest.

Uchitelskaya gazeta on February 19, 1966. said that the "illegal" Baptist organization of Rostov has an underground printing press, and that publications are printed in which youth are called to stand up for their faith. The paper asks: "Why do teachers mix so timidly in the life of families in which children are idiotized (by religion)?"

Sovetskaya Rossia recounts how the Baptist Marinkowa has had six children taken away from her because she gave them Christian faith and forbade them to wear the Communist pioneer necktie. When she heard the sentence, she said only, "I suffer for my faith." She now has to pay the boarding school bills of her children who are now in a state institution which preaches militant atheism.

In the face of such reports it is difficult to understand why so many church leaders in the West persist in believing that somehow religious freedom has begun to exist for those who live under Communism. The protests of Jewish organizations in America and elsewhere in the West highlights the fact that this is not true.

> At a conference in Wiesbaden, Germany, Professor Will Herberg presented this assessment: Some Christian leaders have even allowed themselves to become so bemused with the idea of socialism as a kind of wave of the future and with the 'liberal' delusion that the enemy is always on the right that they cannot see the flagrantly totalitarian of the Soviet, East German, Chinese and other Communist regimes, and tend to adopt attitudes running from friendly neutralism and critical cooperation to outright support.

Religion has become the traditional enemy of all modern tyrannies. Mussolini stated that "Religion is a species of mental disease." Karl Marx called it the "opium of the people" and Hitler denounced Christianity not only because Jesus was a Jew, but because it was cowardly to speak of giving love for hate.

Though a new Soviet leadership has not brought about a fundamental change in the ideological exclusion and overt persecution of religious believers, expressions of concern over religious proclavities are increasingly common in the Soviet news media and serve to reflect the persistency and extensiveness of religious feelings in the Soviet Union.

An article entitled "Rayon Ark" describes a show trial held recently in the Vereshchaginsk rayon of the Perm oblast at which leaders of a sect of True Orthodox Christians were prosecuted. The article is notable not only because it offers a concrete example of the Soviet practice of conducting legal proceedings against religion and believers but also because it adduces many facts attesting to the extent of religious feelings among the Soviet population and to the ineffectiveness of official anti-religious propaganda. The author A. Lacis, states his intention to avoid generalizations and to confine himself to facts. These are his facts: Near the secondary school and the village of Karagay there are two "religious arks" or places for secret worship similar to the one which led to a show trial in the rayon. Since teachers constitute the main propaganda force of the regime in outlying districts, the rayon authorities dispatched a truck to the school so that its teachers could be present at the trial, but all of them declined to make the trip to the court:

> Afterwards one of them explained it this way: "I had to leave immediately to help my father mow hay." A second, a third, a fourth, and a fifth pleaded hay-mowing, domestic obligations, family responsibilities, and even health. And a sixth explained: "I am a cosmopolitan. I do not give lectures on atheism. Why should I go to the rayon center?" Six teachers, maybe sixty, and maybe even six thousand are convinced that atheism is none of their business.

Lacis adds that on the other hand "churchmen themselves can in no way be accused of underestimating mass work among the population." He cites the existence of "modern" priests in the rayons of Perm oblast who "for the sake of popularity," especially with young people, learn to play old Russian songs and dance the latest dances, record light music on tape, take a great interest in soccer, know how to drive cars quite well, and even sit down over a glass of vodka. Lacis emphasizes that his intention is not to discredit these priests. On the contrary, he denounces those anti-religious propagandists "who think that having enumerated the usual temporal faults of churchmen, they have at the same time undermined the last foundations of religion." Lacis demonstrates by example that more attention should be paid to these "modern priests," who are capable not only of "coexisting" with local educational institutions but also of successfully competing with them. For example, in one of the villages in Vereshchaginsk rayon:

> On the evening before Easter people came to the club, but the film was not shown since the projectionist was plastered to the gills. Part of the group immediately shifted from the club to the church, where there is splendor, atmosphere, in a word order.

The head of this church, Father Nestor, somewhat awkwardly but nevertheless sincerely compliments the president of the local club, remarking that the work of the club does not at all interfere with church. With respect to religious feeling among the population, Lacis draws the following general conclusion from the example of an anonymous old woman who regularly attends church apparently as part of her reaction to the callous, haughty attitude shown to her by her granddaughter: "She finds a compensation in religion for inattention, indifference, and at times even open contempt."

Lacis' facts and conclusions define and illuminate a problem that exists in a central oblast of Russia challenging description as an exceptional part of the country either in terms of ethnological conditions or history. His picture of religious life in the Perm oblast therefore demands consideration as an accurate reflection of the religious climate on a much larger scale. Of course, as formerly, the Soviet press contends that the political consciousness of Soviet citizens is steadily growing and that the number of believers extant in Soviet society is continually decreasing. If isolated occurrences occasion alarm in the press, it is argued, this is only because in a Communist society, particularly during the period of large-scale construction upon which the USSR has embarked, even random individuals must not be influenced by alien ideologies. However, an examination of Soviet press reports on so-called isolated manifestations of religious proclivities among Soviet citizens indicates that believers constitute a large percentage of the Soviet population and that this percentage shows no tendency to decline. Numerous reports appear in the Soviet press on church attendance and on observance of religious rites by Komsomol and Party members and even by shock workers of Communist labor, who have taken a special oath to live in accordance with the precepts of the "moral code for the builder of Communism." A striking example of the "split" in the spiritual life of the young Soviet citizen, as it is called by Party propaganda, is offered by Valya Shurtakova, a young specialist engaged in production work, who is known at her job in Moscow and at the institute where she studies as a shock worker and an active, effective agitator. "She is a model for others," but at the same time there is "another truth" about her. At home, forty kilometers from Moscow, Valya is an open believer and an active parishioner. Moreover, she has recently become a priest's wife. At least until she was badgered by the press, Valya apparently managed successfully to play two different, fundamentally incompatible roles:

> She became accustomed to her double life. At work she was esteemed. And here, in church, respected. . . . And she lived peacefully. In the world she is a member of a brigade of Communist labor but at home a priest's wife and an active parishioner. During the day she actively agitates for Communism; in the evening she prays earnestly and sings praise to the Lord.

Criticizing Komsomol members and leaders for their "lack of interest in atheistic work," the journal *Komsomolskaya zhizn*, in an article entitled "An Antenna Besides the Cross," cites examples of different villages in which the work of the Orthodox Church, Jehovah's Witnesses, Seventh-Day Adventists, and Free Christians has flourished simultaneously, there being "in the Free Christian sect alone eighteen persons of Komsomol age." An atheist instructor who had attended a service in an Orthodox church for the purpose of gaining some propaganda experience discovered a considerable number of young girls and boys of school age there. A curious detail was revealed about the Soviet government's policy towards the church in a conversation between priests and propagandists. A militant atheist reminded a priest that "according to regulations" he could not begin a divine service "if children are in the church." The priest's answer indicates that this "regulation" is well known to him as well as to every other Soviet clergyman. Evidently, it was issued by the Council on Church Affairs of the USSR Council of Ministers with little or no publicity since there is no mention of it in official reports of legislative acts by the Soviet government. The same issue of *Komsomolskaya zhizn* presents other interesting facts which serve to repudiate in particular the claim of Party propagandists that only children of backward, fanatical parents come under the influence of religion in the Soviet Union. Nadya Berezovskaya, a Komsomol member and a student at the Omsk Music School, is censured for her fanatical belief in God, for refusing to spend her money on movies and instead saving it in order to buy icons, crosses, and candles with which to honor saints. Her mother, an atheist, informs the district Komsomol committee of her daughter's behavior and is praised for her action in the following manner:

> An elderly woman a heroic widow, wrathfully takes icons away from her very young daughter who is a Komsomol member, a future teacher, and musician. The mother is fighting for her daughter's spiritual welfare, and when she realizes that she cannot succeed by herself, she seeks the help of a Komsomol committee.

The Komsomol organization is criticized by the editors for failing to deal with the situation effectively. Instead of remedial action involving painstaking, instructive work with Nadya, the Komsomol leaders took administrative action: they expelled her from the Komsomol organization and demanded that she also be expelled from music school. Condemning such methods of dealing with religious believers, the editors make the following general remarks:

> "Expell." "Get rid of." "Remove from sight." "Cover up the traces." As if the incident had never occurred. Such is the usual procedure of the white-washer, the bureaucrat, the lover of form. But to convince a person, to fight for him, to work with him and prevail—this, unfortunately, is dull and drawn out.

In a brochure entitled "Questions on the Formation of Scientific-Atheistic Views," published in 1964 in Moscow, data are included relating to the degree of religious activity in various cities and oblasts of the USSR. E. Lisovtsev, the author, regards as a favorable circumstance the fact, that of approximately 2,000 believers who attended Easter services at the Mironositsy Cathedral in 1963, only a third were young people, most of whom, he alleges, came out of curiosity. He also regards as a favorable indication the fact that of the Baptists, only thirty per cent were professional office, and industrial workers and that of 680 members of church administrative organs in the oblast, 225 of them were already pensioners. However, almost as an aside he notes that of these pensioners, 144 persons had been decorated at one time or another with high state awards, orders, and medals.

Frank admissions that the reason for the spread of religious beliefs in Soviet society are grounded in the social, economic, and political peculiarities of the Soviet system can increasingly be found in Soviet writings. A book entitled *Morality and Religion* maintains, as Lacis' article does, that "concrete motives for some people's conversion to religion should be sought in the practical relations between people in different spheres of life."

The same book quotes from the diary of a Komsomol member, who comments that among evangelists and Baptists one finds:

> . . . warmth, concern, attention, even. . . kissing of strangers. It is evident that young men and women attending meetings are seeking spiritual intercourse

with one another. It must be admitted that in our businesses and schools, apparnetly everywhere, there are associations and active members; yet at the same time it happens that some people are living in spiritual isolation.

A long article in *Pravda* discusses reasons for the existence of believers in Soviet society. Appropriately, the article begins by asking the question: "Where do they come from?"

> The question is not a simple one. When the believer is a person in his declining years, it may perhaps be explained. But "a slave of the Lord" at seventeen? A Baptist with a graduation certificate? How does this happen?

The newspaper attempts to disparage the spiritual world of the young believer by citing the case of Oleg Malov who belonged to a religious sect for many years but ultimately renounced his beliefs owing to prolonged, painstaking work on the part of command and political liaison personnel in his regiment. *Pravda* stresses the distinctive character of the young man's belief: "More than anything else morality enters into it. . . . Baptists do not smoke or drink, and they care for one another as brothers." No matter where Oleg's unit was transferred, he always found "brothers and sisters" around him, among the civilian population, in completely new and unfamiliar places. This admission serves to confirm the extensiveness of religious feeling and of communication among believers in the Soviet Union. The newspaper goes on to say that neglect and omissions provide fertile grounds for the cultivation of religious feeling. "Someone was treated unjustly or offended; someone had a misfortune and was not given support in time." These desperate people seek out a comforter, or else the consolers come to them. In reply to those who know Oleg and cannot understand what arguments persuaded him to falter in his belief in God, *Pravda* writes: "Only one argument, which proved to be missing on your part: more sincere, heartfelt attention for man. An irrefutable argument!"

However, this "irrefutable argument" is justifiable only if its application does not contradict general principles of Communist morality or practical measures taken by the regime. The December 15, 1964 issue of *Izvestia*, for example, brands as Pharisism and demagoguery the acts of two women believers who wrote to the editors and complained about the callousness of local authorities. A sick mother E. Strelevaya, and her daughter, Valya, who was graduating from the Roslavl Medical Academy, requested city and oblast authorities to take their family situation into account when assigning the daughter to a job and not to separate them. *Izvestia* agreed with the decision of local authorities, maintaining that in such matters the interests of the state and not those of individual citizens must prevail. Heartfelt love for one's fellow man is not expedient in this case or others which the newspaper describes, but if one bears in mind the systematic references of Soviet propaganda to the fact that socialist humanism has nothing in common with so-called abstract humanism or traditionally accepted human morality, then such contradictions between the theory and practice of Soviet atheists in their struggle against religion are not surprising.

Recently, similar contradictions as well as new aspects to religious problems are increasingly in evidence in the Soviet Union. However, it would be a mistake to see too close a connection between them and the changes that took place in the Soviet leadership in October, 1964. The new Soviet leaders are as much confirmed atheists as their predecessors were, and religion is their worst ideological enemy. Like Khrushchev, they do not personally elaborate theory and tactics for the struggle against ideologies that are alien and opposed to Communism. A sizable corps of philosophers, scientists, and propagandists whose attitude towards religion is stable exists for this purpose. Therefore, there are no grounds for expecting a relaxation in the struggle against religion as a result of a new Soviet leadership, though such a change cannot fail to have an affect on the general process of spiritual emancipation occurring throughout the Soviet Union and especially on the religious life of the Soviet people. Every change of leadership at the top serves to weaken, if only temporarily, the power structure and to stimulate potential aspirations for spiritual freedom, particularly in the Soviet Union, where the role played by public opinion is continually growing and Party leaders are increasingly compelled to take it into account.

Recent events in the world Communist movement have had a favorable affect on the position of the church and of believers in the Soviet Union: revision by the leadership of the Italian and French Communist Parties of previously inimical attitudes towards religion; exclusion from the new rules of the Communist Party of Yugoslavia of a paragraph on incompatibility of Party membership and religious affiliation: and amnesty for political prisoners in Romania, including Catholic priests. A favorable influence has also been exerted by efforts on the part of various international organizations, eminent social figures, and representatives of the sciences and arts (for example, the French writer, F. Mauriac's letters to Khrushchev and Kosygin) to promote religious freedom in the Soviet Union. In spite of an apparent lack of official reaction to such efforts, the Soviet leadership is certainly not indifferent to world public opinion, which is becoming more difficult to conceal from the Soviet people and more difficult to ignore.

Much has been written in the West about the "Patriarchal" Russian Orthodox Church in the USSR, i.e., that part of the Church which is run by the Moscow Patriarchate and officially recognized, although constantly harassed, by the Soviet government. Representatives of this Church, whose right to carry out even a highly restricted amount of religious activity has been won only at the price of a political and spiritual compromise with the authorities, are also well-known to Western churchmen from the various ecumenical congresses. At the same time, little is known in the West about the existence in the USSR of an underground, or "catacomb," Church consisting of numerous isolated religious groups and organizations all refusing to come to any sort of compromise with the atheistic Soviet regime.

The illegal "catacomb" Orthodox Church in the USSR dates from 1927 when the second post-Revolutionary schism of the Church took place as the result of a moral protest by certain members of the clergy and the laity against the acceptance by Metropolitan Sergei (Strgorodsky), Deputy Guradian of the Patriarchal See, of the conditions imposed by the Communist authorities for legally recognizing the Church's supreme administration.

Information on the catacomb Church began to leak out of the USSR in the nineteen-thirties via private correspondence and the Soviet press. Thus, in 1932 the atheistic journal *Antireligioznik* reported that in the Bashkir ASSR there were 345 "Sergian" or "legalized" parishes, 55 Revived Church parishes and 32 parishes in opposition to both groups. In his book, *A New Stage in the Fight Against Religion*, F. Poleshchuk spoke in 1933 of the appearance in Western Siberia, the Central Black-Earth Region, the Urals, and the Northern Caucasus of itinerant priests who said prayers to secret gatherings in private houses. Yaroslavsky also wrote in a brochure, *Tasks of Atheistic Propaganda*, published in 1937, that he knew of hundreds of cases of such itinerant priests' traveling around villages and workers' settlements with their "simple stock in-trade" and holding religious services. At this time, both Yaroslavsky in *Bolshevik* and S. Krushinsky in *Komsomolskaya pravda* pointed out that the "illegal" Church had become a highly intricate organization with its own conspiratorial rules and secret "dens," some in apartments, some even underground, scattered about in towns and kolkhozes. On January 11, 1938, the newspaper *Sotsialisticheskoye zemledeliye* reported that police round-ups of "tramps" had brought to light monks and persons with holy orders.

Any doubts as to the desire of many believers to break away from the Communist-controlled central administration of the Russian Orthodox Church in Moscow were finally dispelled during World War II, when Autonomous and Autocephalous Churches sprang up in the Ukraine and Byelorussia and the Baltic Exarchate and the diocese of Novocherkassk declared their independence almost as soon as the Germans occupied their territories. The priests and monks then returning from the underground to the jurisdiction of the free Churches were living witnesses to the catacomb Church's prewar existence.

A great deal of fresh information on the catacomb Church was gained when many Soviet citizens who had witnessed or directly participated in its activities fled the USSR, together with millions of their countrymen, upon the Soviet reoccupation of the German-held areas of the country. Abroad, articles and brochures began to appear containing details about the founders of the catacomb Church, such as Metropolitans Iosif (Petrovykh) and Kirill (Smirnov) and Bishops Maksim, Illarion, Viktor and Nektarii, the places of worship used by the opposition groups for their services (in Moscow these included the monastery of the Holy Cross; the Church of St. Nikolai in the Ilinka district, popularly known as the "Large Cross" Church; and the Church of the Serbian Mission (*podvorie*) in the Solyanka district); and in Leningrad the Church of the Resurrection, on the site of Czar Alexander II's assassination; the Church of St. Nikolai, at a home for aged artists; the Church of the Tikhvin Icon of the Virgin Mary; a church in Strelna and the districts where secret services were held after the centers of opposition had been smashed, e.g., the Moscow region and certain suburbs of Leningrad such as Shuvalovo, Ozerki, Kolpino, Chudovo, Gatchino, Oranienbaum, Sablino, Malaya Vishera and Okulovka. It became known that after the liquidation of the opposition clergy their initiative was taken up by Orthodox Church intellectuals (theologians, university professors, doctors, etc.), who set up secret circles and brotherhoods in an effort to spread religious enlightenment and preserve the Church's integrity in an atmosphere of militant atheism. Emigres such as Brother Zakharii and Protopresbyter Mikhail Polsky also disclosed centers of the "illegal" Church's activity in the USSR. In a report delivered at a meeting on religious philosophy in New York, B. K. Ganusovsky spoke of his meetings with Church representatives in exile in the USSR. The records of the Episcopal Synod of the Russian Church Abroad contain statements by persons imprisoned by the Soviet authorities that they had received communion bread and christening water from members of the secret clergy.

During the first few postwar years, the information on the catacomb Church supplied by the emigres was confirmed in the Soviet press. Thus, reference was made in the Moscow Patriarchate's publication *Patriarch Sergii and His Spiritual Heritage* of the purge of the Ukrainian clergy carried out by Metropolitan Ioann: (Sokolov), Exarch of the Ukraine, for the refusal of certain of its members to acknowledge the authority of the Moscow Patriarchate. The Patriarchate's mouthpiece, *Zhurnal Moskovskoi Patriarkhii*, complained of the activities of "self-styled and prohibited priests and others undermining and disorganizing ecclesiastical discipline and the principles of Orthodoxy in the dioceses" and of "anti-Patriarchal agitators" such as the Iovtsy and Solyanovtsy and recorded that bishops were being compelled to call upon the believers in their dioceses to band together and condemn those refusing to accept the authority of the "legal" Church. The journal quoted Archbishop Iosaf (Zhurmanov) of Tambov as complaining that in his diocese there were

> ... self-styled priests who are slandering the present Orthodox Church, defaming ... the Patriarch and the entire priesthood and assuming the right to perform religious ceremonies before Orthodox Christians: They are christening babies, performing funeral rites, and administering unction and even the eucharist. They consider that only they are Orthodox Christians.

The Archbishop described these priests as "enemies" of the Orthodox Church and banished them from the community of believers.

The Soviet authorities, who were assiduously cultivating the myth that complete religious freedom existed in the USSR, were embarrassed by the leakage abroad of information on the catacomb Church, particularly when this information was disseminated by the press and public emigre meetings and reference made to the Soviet sources on which it was based—as happened, for example, in the speech delivered by Bishop Nafanail (Lvov) in Brussels in 1948. Shortly afterwards, the *Zhurnal Moskovskoi Patriarkhii*, obviously acting on instructions from the Party leadership, printed an article entitled "Refute the Malicious Slander," whose author, while denying the existence of a catacomb Church in the USSR, did speak of "self-styled priests," whom he placed in the same category as the "schismatic" Russian Church abroad.

The catacomb Church inevitably attracted the attention of foreign researchers. The first to mention its existence was H. Asmussen, a representative of the German Evangelical Church. A. Gustafson's book *Die Katakombenkirche* followed in 1948. References to the Church were soon being made in both Protestant and Catholic churches. Soviet agents, however, then proceeded to take countermeasures, spreading propaganda through special channels to the effect that the catacomb Church was merely a myth created by the emigres and that all information purporting to prove its existence was "idle speculation" and "malice" on the part of anti-Soviet elements. As a result, the foreign press started to beat a retreat. In the Old Catholic journal, *Internationale Kirchliche Zeitschrift*, B. Spuler denied that there was any opposition church in the USSR. Tragically enough, this view was fostered to no little degree by many non-churchmen among the new wave of emigres. Although they had had no contact with the life of the Church while in the USSR, and thus could not have known anything about the handwritten pastoral letters of the opposition bishops or the clandestine prayer meetings held for the more trustworthy believers, these emigres stated publicly that there were no opposition church groups in the USSR and that Metropolitan Sergei's acceptance of the conditions imposed by the Soviet authorities was received unquestioningly by the rank-and-file members of the Church. The increased tolerance shown toward the Church by the Soviet authorities for purely tactical reasons between 1941 and 1957 was another reason for the doubts expressed outside the USSR as to the existence of a catacomb Church; G. G. Karpov, until 1960 Chairman of the Council for the Affairs of the Russian Orthodox Church (of the Council of Ministers of the USSR) and leading members of the Moscow Patriarchate broadcast assurances that the future of the Church in the USSR was in no danger.

Only the renewal of the antireligious campaign in 1958, which was amply reflected in the Soviet press, finally dispelled all such doubts about the "mythical" catacomb Church. Soviet antireligious specialists began to make a study of the various "sects" and religious groups, giving particular attention to those whose members observed the sacraments and other rites, worshipped icons, made the sign of the cross, wore crosses next to the skin, took vows, recognized their own secret hierarchy and worshipped saints. These groups were distinguished by their religious fanaticism and their uncompromising refusal to cooperate with the Soviet authorities and the "legal" church. The Soviet press occasionally called them "clandestine," "antisocial" and "anti-Patriarchal" and reported often on the activities of their members. It described, for example, how pilgrims swarmed down to a certain lake (Lake Svetloyar, in the Gorky Oblast, associated with the legend of Grad Kitezh), fell to the ground and began praying. They then went round the lake on their knees and dipped themselves and their children into the water "in a desire to be purified." A mother with a specialist education destroyed her diploma, which she called "a mark of Cain," and became an ascetic. Despite cold weather she went around in slippers, refused to eat meat and on Fridays partook only of bread and water in order to "sacrifice herself." A man turned the house where he lived with his wife and 25-year-old son into a chapel, in which icons hung everywhere. Prayer meetings of devout persons who had never taken part in elections or done "socially useful" work were held in the house once a week. In the town of Rubtsovsk, a community of 60 souls completely cut itself off from society and began to preach seclusion. Its members lived on "unearned" income from fruit and vegetable raising. Two sisters tramped around Abkhazian villages, refusing to work in a kolkhoz, which they branded "a work of Satan." "Illegal" prayer meetings were held in front of an improvised iconostasis erected in the vicinity of the former Kamansky Monastery by "solicitous hands." From 1942 to 1960, a girl named Anya in the Gorky Oblast lived the life of a recluse in the cellar of her father's house, which had been turned into a chapel, with icons and icon-lamps. One man renounced family life and went into the forest to live in a dug-out, which he hung with icons. Adherents of clandestine religious groups gathered at the dug-out to pray. A woman turned her back on the world and began sleeping on thorns. From 1947 onwards, Leonid, a young lad, was considered as dead. At the age of 15 he went into reclusion in a secret hide-out under a house. He was regarded by believers as holy. Maria S., in the Orel Oblast, set up an "illegal" chapel where she performed such ceremonies as baptism, funeral rites and the consecration of *kulichi* (Easter cake) and *paskha* (sweet cream cheese eaten at Easter). She also provided candles. It was also reported that persons who knew how to conduct church services and had left the legalized Church or whose church had been compulsorily closed were performing religious rites at the request of believers, who called them "unlicensed priests," adding, however, that "It's all the same now whether a priest is licensed or not."

There is little doubt that these and other fiercely religious persons mentioned in recent years by the Soviet press are the Diaspora of two groups which have come to be known in the USSR as the "True Orthodox Church" and the "True Orthodox Christians," names that were used by expeditions sent out by the Academy of Sciences of the USSR to carry out a study of sectarianism in various regions in 1960. Although members of the expeditions met representatives of the groups, their findings were inconclusive and contradictory. Some considered the "True Orthodox Christians" to be a sect which had no hierarchy of priests, while others refused to classify either group as a sect and found it difficult to distinguish between them. However, one of the expedition members L. N. Mitrokhin, did succeed in establishing the most important characteristic of both groups:

> ... these groups have no connection with traditional sectarianism; their ideology is a modification of the views of those ... who broke away from the Patriarchal Church at a time when it was entering into a loyal relationship with the Soviet authorities ... The basic dogmas of these groups are traditional Orthodox. The adherents of these groups do not recognize the existing Churches, whose clergy they declare to be the "servants of Antichrist."

The Soviet press began to call both groups 'anti-Patriarchal" and alleged that they bore a class stamp and had sprung up out of political opposition to the Soviet regime. *Voprosy filosofii* even accused them of launching a kind of ecclesiastical counter-revolution.

On the basis of what has been said about them in the Soviet press, the two movements may be outlined as follows:

The "True Orthodox Church" includes the Leontevtsy or Solyanovtsy, the Mikhailovtsy, the Podgornovtsy, the Agapitovtsy and other local groups which were formed in the territories formerly occupied by the Germans after Stalin had broken up the catacomb Church (some of whose followers joined the Imyaslavtsy). They rejected the Moscow patriachate for not fighting the "order of Satan." Since 1958, their ranks have been swelled by clergymen and laymen who had either become convinced that the Party was deceiving the Church by false promise of religious freedom, etc., or else had been deprived of their churches and their right to hold services. In the same year, adherents of the "True Orthodox Church" even began to appear in the Pochayevskaya Lavra, from where they proceeded to spread throughout the USSR.

Followers of this movement believe that the end of the world is at hand and that Antichrist is already ruling. They must avoid the "seventy-seven nets" which he has put out to ensnare humanity and are forbidden on this basis to participate in elections or "socialist" labor, to take out loans or to do military service. They live on private earnings, such as the proceeds of the produce which they grow on their small personal plots. Since they do not recognize existing Churches, their prayer meetings are held beside lakes and sacred springs. The Tatar region, "the domain of Grand Duke Mikhail," is regarded as the center of the movement, and, in 1961 at least, a certain Mikhail Yershov was its leader. In that year, followers from Siberia, Kazakhstan and other regions of the USSR congregated on the banks of the Lower Kama River to await the appearance of their Saviour, the Grand Duke, on "the last day of the world," which coincided with the opening of the World Youth Festival in Moscow.

Many supporters of the "True Orthodox Church" are young people who refuse to accept school diplomas or to belong to either the Party or the Komsomol. The Soviet authorities are currently engaged in unmasking this "anti-social" group, whose leaders and active members are frequently sentenced to long terms of imprisonment or exile. Parents who are members have their children taken away from them and put into state boarding schools to be reeducated along atheistic lines.

The "True Orthodox Church" includes the Leontevtsy or Solyanovtsy, of the "Yaroslav" branch of the Lithuanian Old Believers, or Pomortsy (under Czar Aleksii Mikhailovich, members of this branch took a vow to become hermits in order to save themselves from falling under the domination of Antichrist) are generally divided into the "True Orthodox Latter-Day Christian Believers" and the "True Orthodox Wandering Christians." The former were, until 1929, gathered together in the "Svet Mikhailovsky" (Light of Michael) agriculture artel, whose patron they considered to be the Archangel Michael, the antagonist of Antichrist. They toiled in the artel from dawn to dusk and spent their free hours praying, reading the Scriptures and singing psalms. The artel had workshops for shoemaking, tailoring and making millstones and leased out a tile factory, orchards and mills. The artel was broken up in 1930, but its remaining members formed small groups who condemned the Soviet regime as a manifestation of the rule of Antichrist. The groups were subjected to further persecution in 1937, 1940, 1946 and 1958, in which year they boycotted the elections. The "Latter-Day Believers" are required by their leaders to be spiritually vigilant and to isolate themselves completely from Soviet and other atheistic influences. They send their children to school only up to the fourth grade and do not register them in the registry offices. During the census, they described themselves as "subjects of Holy Orthodox Russia." They have secret schools for training preachers, and have been referred to as Tikhonovtsy, that is, supporters of Patriarch Tikhon. In some of their fellow-believers, they see surviving members of the Czar's family. They refuse to accept state benefits such as pensions and allowances. At the present time they are to be found in the Moscow district, the Ukraine and Central Asia. They have among their number intellectuals, specialists with a higher education and young people who have broken with the Komsomol.

The "True Orthodox Wandering Christians" consist in turn of the "illegals," that is, persons who have destroyed their personal documents (or "wiped their face clean," as they put it), do not work, live in secret dugouts and other places of refuge and in general are outside legal society, and the "benefactors," who, while living a perfectly legal existence themselves, support and care for the "illegals." From time to time the latter emerge from their seclusion and make their way along fixed routes preaching the renunciation of the "rule of Antichrist and all his works." They look upon the Communist authorities as persecutors of Christianity like Nero and Diocletian. Like the "Latter-Day Believers," they preach spiritual vigilance and the imminence of the end of the world. One of their leaders, "monk Varlaam" (Perevyshin), was recently identified by the authorities. He had allegedly built up an extensive organization with its own clandestine religious schools in Alma-Ata and Tyulkubas, drawn young people and intellectuals into his groups, held regular meetings to discuss ways and means of extending the organization's religious influence and distributed religious literature, including articles critical of materialism written by highly educated members of the organization and forming part of a collection entitled *Univers*. The "Wandering Christians" are severely persecuted for their "parasitic" and "antisocial" way of life and for their "subversive" activities. In 1964, local group leaders were sentenced to varying terms of imprisonment in an open trial in Alma-Ata. A typically colorful account of the trial was given by Alla Trubnikova. Adherents of the movement are to be found in the regions of Poltava, Saratov, Biisk and Chelyabinsk, to mention only a few.

Although these and other prohibited religious organizations do not constitute a direct political threat to the Soviet regime, since they all pursue a policy of strictly passive resistance, the regime finds their very existence intolerable, contradicting as it does the principle that the Party must exercise complete domination over Soviet intellectual life. In order to justify the expulsion of these "sectarians" to remote areas, the authorities accuse them of being political counter-revolutionaries such as "White Guardists," "kulaks" and "Hitlerites," and engaging in all possible forms of sabotage, and further maintain that they are receiving support from abroad from those anxious to "disrupt Communist construction." *Voyovnychy ateist*, for example, wrote that "the stinking corpse of the True Orthodox Church is being galvanized from abroad by the Russian Orthodox Church synod headed by Metropolitan Anastasii." In order to dissuade people from joining these "sectarian" organizations, the Party tries hard to prove that they are "anti-social." A recent article by A. Ananev entitled "The Trump Cards of Monk Griogorii" contains a whole catalogue of crimes allegedly characteristic of devout persons. It is explained that the "religious fanatics" have turned their backs on Soviet life out of hatred for a regime which has dispossessed their fathers, broken up their families and prevented them from leading a placid and well-to-do existence. According to Ananev, these persons practice various forms of religious asceticism, such as fasting, going into seclusion, taking the vow of silence and vagrancy, in order to get their own back on the authorities. They try to pass as priests out of a desire to become "large fish in small pools." Primitive and biased as the story is, it constitutes one more proof of the existence of the catacomb Church in the USSR.

Although it is, of course, impossible to come to any final judgement on the activities of these clandestine religious groups on the basis of the scattered and tendentious information given by the Soviet press, it is clear that despite the efforts of the Soviet authorities to suppress or deny the existence of the opposition to the so-called "Soviet patriotic Church" this opposition is growing. (Opposition to denominations cooperating with the atheistic authorities also exists in Poland, Hungary, Czechoslovakia, China and other Communist countries). Just as their elders rejected the October Revolution, the Soviet regime and Metropolitan Sergii's compromise with the latter, so the younger generation, despite having gone through all the stages of "Communist education," has now begun to reject the regime also in its thirst for freedom and justice and is continuing to uphold the ideals of genuine Orthodoxy.

At the same time, the various underground religious groups in the USSR have undergone a certain evolution. They no longer bear the names of their inspirers (as in the case of Iosiflyane, the Tikhonovtsy, etc.) and are headed not by bishops or intellectuals with a higher education in theology, philosophy or some other subject, but by simple people whose only qualification is their practical experience in fighting for their Church, for whose sake many have suffered imprisonment and exile. Some leaders had been active in restoring ecclesiastical life during and immediately after World War II, and had later, with the renewal of religious persecution in the USSR, become disillusioned with the Church's compromise with the regime. Unlike their predecessors in the twenties and thirties, the present leaders of the catacomb Church do not base their authority on canons, of many of which they must be ignorant. Some are inspired by the ideals of deceased bishops who have become legendary figures; others, who have adopted the Eastern attitude that Christianity is a doctrine "not of this world," are motivated by an abhorrence of opportunism; still others feel a sense of personal responsibility for the Church which leads them to oppose bitterly any kind of social order founded on atheistic principles.

Since its organization, the catacomb Church has grown numerically and territorially. According to Soviet sources, it has spread throughout the Voronezh, Saratov, Moscow and Tamboy Oblasts, the Volga region, Kazakhstan, the Caucasus and the Ukraine. In 1961, there were so many "True Orthodox Christians" in the Chernigov Oblast that plenary meetings of the local kolkhoz workers were held to discuss the matter.

Since most of their clergy have either been liquidated or forced to conceal their identity, the present catacomb Church groups give the impression of being "priestless." As has been said, in some groups the rites are performed by laymen, even by women. The recent turbulent history of the Orthodox Church has led to an agonizing reappraisal of the importance of the Apostolic Succession and qualified priests, as a result of which the general view is indeed that "it's all the same now whether a priest is licensed or not."

The groups have not clearly defined confessional structure. As far as can be gathered from fragmentary and contradictory eyewitness descriptions, their dogmas and rites are so vague and mysterious that even their adherents do not completely understand them. These dogmas and rites often combine Orthodox with Old Believers' and sectarian traditions.

If Soviet press accounts of the fanaticism, uncompromising political opposition and fervent asceticism of the catacomb Church groups and certain prohibited sects are to be believed, one is witnessing a resurgence of the *yurodstvo* (religious madness) for which Russia was once famous, especially in the sixteenth century with its injustice and terror. The philosopher Berdiaev attached great importance to *yurodstvo* and described it as a disregard for normal standards of behavior and a rejection of life itself out of protest against the "falsehoods" in the world. He claimed that the *yurodivy* appear

whenever "holiness departs from the powers that be" and that their capacity
for inspiring a people's thinking is due to their lack of a biological fear of
death. G. P. Fedotov, another expert on the Orthodox Church, characterized *yurodstvo* as "an innate reaction of sensitive souls" and wrote the
following in its defense:

> ... the injustices which exist in the world demand the correctives of the
> conscience, and the conscience passes judgement all the more freely and
> authoritatively the less it is connected with the world and the more radically it
> rejects the world. The *yurodivy* went out into the world as champion of truth
> and justice.

Yurodstvo is always eschatological. The *yurodivy* are not against the Church
as such; they do, however, dissociate themselves from the Church whenever
it alienates its followers from the basic precepts of Christ and the Apostles by
becoming "yoked together with unbelievers" (2 Cor. 6:14) out of sheer
opportunism. Both these qualities apply equally to the catacomb Church in
the USSR.

The cruel and tyrannical rulers of Russia are known to have had a mystical
terror of the *yurodivy*. It may well be that the present Soviet leaders, although
neither devout nor superstitious, are also afraid when they see that murdered or exiled believers are replaced by others just as uncompromising in
their opposition to the regime and that those returning from exile are bolder
than ever and start attracting young people by their preaching. Indeed, fear
seems to be the only explanation for the excessive attention paid by the
authorities to the catacomb Church groups and for the severity of the
reprisals taken against the latter.

Other confessions also have their secret Churches in the USSR. Ever since
the "liquidation" of the Greek Orthodox (Uniate) Church in 1945-47, this
Church has had its "wandering priests," its secret monasteries and its underground groups in the Western Ukraine. On February 27, 1964, the newspaper *Komsomolets Uzbekistana* reported that in the USSR there were illegal
groups of Baptists who had broken away from the All-Union Council of
Evangelical Christian Baptists, which, like the Moscow Patriarchate, has also
compromised itself by its services to the regime. According to another
source, these illegal groups refer to themselves as the "Free Church." There
are also "wandering mullahs" who have made themselves independent of
their spiritual administrations (*dukhovnye upravleniya*).

The catacomb Church does not only consist in specific opposition groups
of the kind it has been discussed. Religious beliefs are secretly cherished
within families and small gatherings of trusted friends centered around
priests deprived of their parishes or expelled from their monasteries. Even
Soviet children are learning to conceal their devoutness. Thus, atheist propaganda workers going round the schools in a certain district of Moscow
complained that

> ... among over one thousand children we did not succeed in finding a single
> one who wore a cross around his neck. Their crosses hang over their beds or on
> pegs inside their wardrobes ... or else are kept in small boxes ... Some
> children wear them around their necks at home after school or else put them
> on when they go to bed.

The children's discipline is so great that sometimes atheistic parents are
completely unaware that their children believe in God.

The USSR today is one vast spiritual catacomb, the heroism of whose occupants can no longer be concealed. They are awakening in others a desire to become spiritually purified, to expiate their sins, to make sacrifices and to achieve the ideals of justice and freedom. *Nauka i religiya* commented despairingly:

> . . . it is enough to tell someone that a good woman (*pravednitsa*) has appeared in a certain place for people to start filing towards the gates of her house asking for prayers and bringing gifts.

There is no doubt that the "new Soviet man" envisaged by the Party is still as remote as the stars.

There is an ever-growing body of evidence showing that the Soviet system is in a state of great ideological disarray. The "establishment" continues its proclamations to the effect that the construction of socialism has been completed and all Soviet people are united in the great effort to build Communism on that foundation. A lengthy example of such statements is the speech delivered on the 50th anniversary of the October Revolution by L. I. Brezhnev, which filled four pages of both *Pravda* and *Izvestia* of November 4, 1967. But at the same time, there are protests such as that by V. Chornovil, a Communist and at one time secretary of a unit of the Komsomol, that Soviet society lacks even the elementary forms of socialist legality, or that of the collective farm chairman Yakhimovich which speaks of the danger the Party faces of censure by the workers and peasants, with a possible rise of a new party to challenge the one now functioning in the name of Marx, Engels, and Lenin. There are even greater deviations than these, however providing such phenomena as pamphlets openly speculating about the immortality of the human soul, in terms much closer to affirmation than one might expect in an officially atheistic society.

After 60 years of the Soviet regime, and in spite of the utmost efforts of the Communist Party and the government, the open and avowed allegiance of more people is given in the Soviet Union to a religious organization than is given to any of the secular bodies which those in power so zealously attempt to foster. It is, however, true that the great majority of the religious believers of the country are to be found in those sections of the population which are either geographically or socially remote from the centers of power, among the peasantry scattered in small villages at the ends of muddy and almost impassable roads, in the lonely and disadvantaged of the cities, or among the aged survivors of an earlier era. This apartness is one of the most striking features visible as one surveys the congregation at the Cathedral of the Old Believers in Moscow, numbering perhaps 4,000, 80 per cent of whom are women, wrapped in the kerchiefs and shoddy coats of the poor, or as one notes a small group of worshippers in rubber boots and quilted jackets picking their way over the mud of a side-road toward one of the village churches which still remains open. It can be heard in the high, cracked voices of the aged in the congregational singing of the 200-odd persons gathered for Friday vespers in the great 12th century Cathedral of the Assumption in Vladimir.

Thus, the believing groups in the population are to a great degree peripheral to the major currents of Soviet life and are usually presented in the propaganda efforts of the regime as backward, even reactionary, elements who only serve as a brake on progress. And the religion to which they are so firmly attached is, in the eyes of the official spokesmen, quite truly the "opium of the people" against which, almost literally, measures should be taken as against any other addictive drug.

However, there is more in the philosophies of the great faiths which are represented in the Soviet Union than is dreamed of by the prevailing variety of Marxism, and there are questions of life and death, truth and justice for which answers cannot be found in the Party handbooks. Thus, some people among the intelligentsia look outside the dicta of the Central Committee, toward a view of life which will contain more satisfying answers and a greater portion of human truth.

It is, of course, true that this group is relatively limited, for the schism in Russia between the educated classes and religion is one which antedates the October Revolution, and the additional barriers which have been set up in the past 60 years further hinder a search for understanding. Yet one may sense in many of the works of Soviet writers something of at least an effort to reach a comprehension of the externals of religious tradition. It is easiest for the outside observer to see this relation to those writers in the Russian language who reflect the culture and traditions of the Russian Orthodox sections of the Soviet populace and the following remarks will therefore largely concern themselves with this group, but they should not be taken to mean that there are not similar phenomena to be observed among the other groups, from the Lutheran Estonians to the Moslem Uzbeks or Buddhist Buryats.

One of the ways in which the influence of the religious tradition may be noted is by an examination of what can rather awkwardly be called the neo-nationalist cultural revival which has taken place in recent years. Many of the intelligentsia have been engaged in a search for roots in a soil somewhat deeper than that of the *Pravda-Izvestia-Kommunist* line of encapsulated dogma and have in this process rediscovered something of the role of religion in at least the artistic history of the country. There has resulted a rise in interest in Russia's traditional icons, many of which have been saved from the "ashheap of history," and in the churches which, in Solzhenitsyn's words, may be seen "running up the knolls, ascending the hills, princesses in red and white, coming out to the wide rivers, with well-proportioned bell towers, tapered and carved, rising above the commonplace thatch and plank buildings, and reaching upward to the heavens." And, although one who drives from Moscow north to Yaroslavl' may see churches converted into tractor repair shops, find potatoes stored in one of the chapels of the Kremlin at Rostov-Velikii, or see that the city streetcar depot at Yaroslavl' is a sadly damaged 17th century church, they are indeed still there like princesses over the small, grey Russian log cabins of countless villages.

In the summer of 1965 *Izvestia* ran another lengthy article, this one about the reconversion to atheism of a young woman who had been a captive of the Pentecostalists and Jehovites for five years. Capitalizing upon the girl's shock when she discovered at age thirteen that she was not her parents' child, sectarians drew her into their group, baptized her and taught her that non-sectarians were her enemies. Fortunately, the young woman was rescued, is now happily married, and her section at the factory "is fighting for the title of Communist Labor Section" (*sic!*). Meanwhile the activities of the Pentecostalists and Jehovites are forbidden because of their anti-social and

anti-Soviet character. "The 'god' of this dangerous sect (Jehovah's Witnesses) is not in heaven at all but in Brooklyn (U.S.A.)," the article concluded.

Pravda got into the act by printing a letter to the editor on the illegal
activities of Baptist groups at Rostov-on-Don. The article complains that
they have been holding conclaves in houses, publicly singing religious
hymns, publicly proselytizing and mimeographing leaflets and even verses
by their sect's poets. And worst of all, an illegal children's society had been
formed to teach youth to play the sacred psalms on musical instruments. The
usual horror story is included: about a father who bound and attacked his
twenty-year-old daughter because she expressed doubts about the correct-
ness of the Baptist creed.

It is impossible to assess the accuracy of any of these stories, but the fact
that the Soviet Baptists have been the scapegoats for so much vulgar propaganda indicates that their 5,000 communities are a source of great conster-
nation to the ideologists.

The failure of the current anti-religious campaign as a whole has been
suggested by several press articles in the past year. It was reported for
example, that a new book of Biblical tales, written by a Pole, became a literary
sensation overnight. The authorities have frequently conceded that large
numbers of the people are believers and even that 30 per cent of them are
under forty years of age. While all agree that the struggle against religion
must proceed, recent failures have generated a major debate about the
effectiveness of present methods. Chairman Anashkin complains that harsh
and unjust penalties on believers often tend to make them more fanatical. In
a curious admission, another writer says that the struggle against religion
must be carried out with patience but this is how it is not being done— "that
drill sergeant's tactics result here in a score of zero."

A characteristic painting in Leningrad's famous anti-religious museum
(formerly Kazan Cathedral) shows an Orthodox priest brooding in anguish
at newspaper headlines of the latest heroics of the Soviet cosmonauts.
Perhaps it was no accident that the harsh anti-religious campaign was resumed shortly after the start of the Soviet space age. Nonetheless, several
writers have cautioned their comrades about expecting science itself to do all
the work. Many believers, they are told, pretend that they are not opposed to
science.

> "To debate with such a group of believers," one writer cautions, "requires a
> thorough knowledge of modern theology. It is even more important to know
> modern science in order to express the artificiality of fitting scientific dis-
> coveries into an analysis of the revealed texts, such as the use of geology to
> explain that six days of Biblical creation."

> One of the more interesting developments that has emerged from this
> debate is the increasing attention given to public ritual. Engels remarked that
> "Christianity never would have overcome paganism had it not replaced the
> worship of gods with the worship of saints." A case in point is the solemnity
> attached to the daily processions which arrive in Red Square to view the body of
> Lenin, part of the cult of Lenin whose picture hangs everywhere like the icons
> of old.

> More typical of the recent trend: in some regions a particular day is desig-
> nated each quarter for the formal presentation of birth certificates to new
> parents at the House of the People. The hall is richly decorated, amateur artists
> perform and speeches of congratulations are made. "This beautiful cere-

mony," so people are told, "has replaced the former church christenings.'
Greater emphasis upon ritual has also been introduced recently at weddings,
"coming of age" day (sixteenth birthday when passports are issued), and when
boys are drafted into the army. As a writer in *Komsomolskaya pravda* puts it:
"Atheism will succeed only if it arms itself still more with artistic esthetics and
psychological emotion."

That the congregations survive despite governmental pressures is, it must be
supposed, a sign of hope. Yet the most discouraging element in the picture is
neither the outward repression nor the one-sided competition with atheism;
rather, it is the inability of the Russian churches to undergo a renewal. However beautiful to the believer is the view of old women kissing frescoes and
carrying buckets of holy water, what is space age Soviet youth to think of this?
In Russia there exist secret printing presses, secret Sunday schools, so there
exists surely an underground church.

If such a powerful underground church exists about which the Soviet press
writes, and there are a hundred other articles about it, why is the underground
church not represented in the World Council of Churches? Why is the underground church never invited to send representatives here in America? Metropolitan Nikolai comes and others. They should be welcome. But why are the
heroes of the underground church never invited? And even when one member
of this church came, some of your American church leaders wish him to be
silent.

The underground church is infiltrated by the Communist secret police,
but the Communist secret police is infiltrated by religious, too.

Members of the underground church became officers of the secret police,
Members of the underground church become leaders in the official church
and tell what happens there. These are very sincere Christians.

Professor Constantinescu Iashi, the best known theological professor of
Romania, when the Communists came to power, became Communist Minister of Culture, a member of the Communist government. People opened
their eyes and asked, "But how? You have prepared for ministry thousands
of priests. How is it?" He answered, "I have been sent by the Communist
Party in the theological seminary."

Bende, the secretary of the Protestant seminary in Cluj in the capitalist
times, says that he has been sent by the Party there to prepare the students in
the radical sense.

When the Communists came to power in Romania, Orthodox priests,
Riosheanu, Patrashcoiu, and others, appeared dressed at once as colonels of
the secret police and arrested and beat their parishioners. When the
parishioners asked them, "But how is this possible? This is a nightmare. You
have been my priest; I kissed your hand; I took the sacraments from you,"
they answered: "You dupes, you idiots, the Communist Party has sent us in
the church."

These are Communists, and Communist fellow travelers who infiltrate in
churches and everywhere and destroy especially the faith of the youths.

In Romania there are three major organizations of the underground
church. There exists an Orthodox underground, *Oastea Domnului*, which
means in English *The Army of the Lord*. It is something like Salvation Army. It
is considered a forbidden secret organization.

The Communists say that it has 300,000 adult members. When they
announced a secret meeting, 6,000 farmers came to a secret meeting. One
can't arrest 6,000.

The police came, arrested just a few leaders. When the leaders were judged before court, farmers from the whole country surrounded the court. And when the prisoners were brought in, they began to cry: "We have committed the same crime. We believe like them. Arrest us, too."

"You can't arrest a whole country. With us, nobody is on the side of the Communists. Men are rather on the side of Christ."

There is a Baptist underground. They are called *The Awakened.*

There exists a Presbyterian underground. They are called *Bethanists*, something like Christian Endeavor here. They have passed and pass through prisons.

One of the leaders of the *Bethanists* has been sentenced to many years of prison for the following crime: He preached on a Sunday about a Bible verse, in St. John 21 in which Jesus says: "Throw your nets on the right side."

The next day there was a secret police officer who said: "How did you dare to say that nets should be thrown on the right side, on the side of imperialists, and not on the left side?" The pastor went to prison.

Here many Unitarian pastors are of the left wing. A Unitarian pastor was put in prison because he preached on a Christmas Eve that when Jesus was a little child, Herod wished to kill Him, but His holy mother fled with him to Egypt and there he was concealed.

The pastor was brought before the court and told: "You meant us. You wished to say that we, the Communists, like Herod, killed the Christians and that you hope in the end, Nasser will pass to your side. Therefore, you mentioned Egypt."

> Notwithstanding all this terror in the Communist camp, now being often in your cathedrals, I long for the beauties of the underground church behind the Iron Curtain.
>
> When we meet sometimes in a wood, the vault of heaven is the vault of our cathedral. We are like the Catholics. We would not worship without incense. The smell of flowers is our incense. The chirping of birds is our organ. The shabby suit on a pastor who has recently been released from prison, shines on him like the robes of a priest. And when the evening comes, then angels are our acolytes and light, as candles, the stars of the skies. The underground church is beautiful.

Popular Orthodox religion is full of sacramentals, symbols such as icons, and blessings which people need in order to come into contact with the immaterial world. There was a wonderful intermingling and familiarity between the ordinary believer and the holy in everyday life. God is to be found supremely in the liturgy. Paradoxically, people can manage without the outward forms of religion, that neither churches nor clergy are indispensible as in Western forms of Christianity. During the schism of the seventeenth century and the imposition of Peter the Great's reforms, there were considerable conflicts between the faithful and the clerical hierarchy. People became quite capable of ignoring many dictates of clerical authority, having a dislike of rigorous legalism, of precise and definite ordinances. They have retained a certain freedom, being generally more sensitive to the spirit than to the letter. Some may see the negative features of this trait rife in modern Soviet inefficiency. The moral and physical destruction of the clergy was of much less consequence to a laity well accustomed to asking little of its priests. The prohibition of dogmatic instruction has not seriously touched a religion that is more moral than intellectual, transmitted more through long standing family traditions than through catechisms. Where churches are left open and worship is allowed, with liturgy, choirs, icons and a little preaching, it has generally been enough to maintain belief.

Even the destruction of churches has not had such a desolating effect providing that there was a saint, a *staretz*, a fool for Christ, or a martyr for veneration. During the last century most people would come into touch with a living challenge at least once in their lives. Nowadays, they are probably few and far between—understandably, people keep quiet about their existence. They used to be common. There were many *stranniki*, pilgrims; and even ordinary folk would retire to a *pustyn*, a wilderness hermitage. Thousands travelled hundreds of miles to consult a *staretz* like St. Seraphim of Sarov or *staretz* Amvrosy, on whom Dostoyevsky's Fr. Zosima is based. As for the *yurodivny*, as far back as the eleventh century, the Russian had an immense respect for the genuine idiot. Even then, some men were driven so much by love of God that they acted as if out of their minds, so as to become objects of scorn and derision, an imitation of Christ in His Passion. Shimanov, in his *Notes from the Red House*, shows how even a modern educated believer can accept the loss of reason under psychiatric "treatment" as God's will.

Levitin reports that there are still 12 Bishops of the True Orthodox Church, but says that this body functions in such secrecy that the only way to find out much about it is to join it! Recently the Soviet paper, *Soviet Abhazia*, reported the sentencing of Fr. Gregory to four years in prison camp. Fr. Gennadi (as he formerly was known) was a priest of the official church who lost his registration in 1962 for having attracted young folk to his church. He created an underground parish in a city in Ukraine; took monastic vows; joined the True Orthodox Church and for ten years has been organizing many small churches in specially purchased private houses, a secret seminary and several religious communities for men and women. He now works in Abhazia, on the Black Sea coast of the Caucasus, and young men and women have travelled long distances to work in the town of Tkvartcheli and to study at the seminary in the evenings. Many have taken vows and they seem to have been able to disperse successfully when Fr. Gregory was arrested. This information suggests a fairly "orthodox" and surprisingly lively underground church.

The main concerns for religious Russian peasants are with Heaven, Hell, the Resurrection of the Dead, the world to come and the Trinity. The Orthodox have a far more vivid horror of sin than is normally believed. Their deep respect for the repentant sinner is well known through nineteenth century Russian literature. The Russian is capable of almost supernatural acts of asceticism or abnegation—a *podvig*—and this may be a result of regeneration after a fall. At the heart of Russian religion is the problem of the co-existence of evil with Divine providence, of how God's justice can be reconciled with His mercy.

Not surprisingly one feels that it is the people, by their Christian perseverance and often heroic faith, who have done far more to ensure the survival of religion, than the compromise policy of the higher ranks of official clergy. The revelations of what went on in the interwar period are not only inspiring—they are also surprising; active and open co-operation between party and believers being quite common—and even amusing. To give an example of the many anecdotes which illumine the fact; a group of peasants proclaimed themselves a brigade of godless and became "heroes of labor."

On Sundays they went off to work in a distant and difficult field where a clandestine priest quietly celebrated a rapid liturgy for them.

In the 1840's, Ivan Turgenev wrote a short story called "Bezhin Mead," a brooding tale about a hunter who gets lost on the Russian steppes and spends the night with a band of superstitious peasant boys.

Gathered around a campfire, the boys frighten each other with stories about omens, ghosts, water spirits, wood nymphs, hobgoblins, and other fantasies.

The one exception is a sturdy character named Pavlusha. He is as ignorant and superstitious as the others, but he remains undaunted by the supernatural. When he returns to the campsite after fetching water from a nearby river, he tells his freinds that he heard a voice calling, "Pavlusha, Pavlusha, come here."

The other boys shudder, invoke the name of God, cross themselves, and say it was a bad omen, the water spirit calling Pavlusha to his death.

Pavlusha shrugs it off, and, with typical Russian resignation, replies: "Don't bother about it. No one can escape his fate."

His words prove prophetic. Pavlusha dies in the end, not by drowning in the river, but by falling from a horse.

By the time the reader gets to that line, the last in the story, he is aware that Turgenev's art has woven its own kind of magic spell. The author has evoked the spirit of old Russia. It was the Russia of myths and mysticism, of folk traditions whose origins were lost in antiquity, of Russian imagination free to conjure fantastic visions and fairy tales.

That Russia is supposed to have vanished. It is supposed to have been replaced by the Soviet Union, the modern superpower. Factories now sprawl on the plans where Turgenev's huntsman roved. Hydroelectric dams have been flung across wild Siberian rivers. Rockets carry cosmonauts into orbit.

The backward peasant of Turgenev's day, chained to old traditions and believing in folk myths, has supposedly been replaced by the new Socialist man who believes in nothing more mysterious than production quotas and the progress promised in each new five-year plan.

That is the Party line, and it is something of a myth itself. If, as Pavlusha said, no one can escape his fate, then no nation can escape its past. Not completely, anyway.

Despite often ruthless attempts to wipe them out, certain folk traditions persist in the Soviet state, hanging on like the indestructible thistles that grow on the steppes. By the same token, the regime's off-again, on-again efforts to promote atheism have frequently been thwarted by the Russians' insistence on maintaining at least some of their religious customs.

Beyond that, there appears to be a recent revival of interest among Soviet citizens not only in religion, but also in rituals and legends that predate Christianity's advent in Russia in 988 A.D. Even some Communist Party members and confirmed atheists admit to being attracted to these vestiges of old Russia because they arise from the spirit of the Russian people.

It may be that that is what some modern Russians are seeking in the fables, legends, and rites of their past—a sense of mystery, of recapturing the richly mystical Russia of "Bezhin Mead."

Some hint guardedly that these old traditions, religious and otherwise, appease a hunger in the Russian soul that cannot be satisfied by the Soviet state, with its sterile worship of concrete and technology.

"We have the complicated task of developing old folk traditions and customs under new conditions," commented the weekly *Literary Gazette* recently. Some traditions that don't contradict our (Marxist) ideals have been undeservedly forgotten and attempts to revive them have been met with undergrounded censorship.

One of the traditions that has vanished is the "Night of Ivan Kuppala," a pagan holiday once observed in Russia and the Ukraine. The rite, celebrated in mid-June, honored youth and fertility, and was the background for Tchaikovsky's "The Snow Maiden."

According to legend, a man who finds the magic flower of the fern on the eve of Ivan Kuppala will be rich and happy. The holiday was celebrated by building bonfires over which young boys leaped in demonstration of strength and daring.

Girls threw garlands into the rivers. If a boy caught one before it sank, it meant good luck for the girl who threw it. If it sank, it was a portent of death.

Kolesnik, the Ukrainian teacher, said the custom fell from use after it was criticized for arousing ignorant prejudices, and, the fabric of Soviet life is the worse for it.

But other customs are still followed. In many parts of the Soviet Union there are two New Year's celebrations. As in the West, one is held on December 31 and is accompanied by the usual revelry. But something extra is added: A decorated fir tree beneath which presents are piled up.

It is the Soviet version of Christmas, which is not openly celebrated because it is religious.

The second New Year is observed on January 14, which was the beginning of the year under the old Russian calendar. Young people go out in the early morning ringing doorbells. If the door is opened, they walk inside and shower the owner of the house with grain seeds, wishing him an abundant harvest, fat cattle, and a long life.

Some who have experienced these visits get indignant, especially city dwellers who don't have any need for abundant harvests or fat cattle.

The youths, however, say that the ritual gives them satisfaction. One Ukrainian boy who said he is a confirmed atheist claimed that "God has nothing to do with it."

Easter was a major religious holiday in Czarist Russia. It still is today, and the manner in which it is celebrated provides an example of how Soviets manage to keep touch with their past without incurring the ire of their ideological watchdogs.

Both western and eastern churches were celebrating Easter at the same time in 1977. Normally their differing calendars put Easter on separate Sundays.

In Leningrad, an estimated 5,000 Russian Orthodox Christians jammed St. Nicholas Cathedral and another 5,000 stood outside for a midnight Easter service. Those able to work their way past the doors guarded by militia and auxillary policemen had stood in line since midafternoon.

They remained on their feet inside the gilded-columned structure because Russian Orthodox churches do not have pews.

Before 1917, Russians observed Easter by inviting guests over to the house for tea and an Easter cake called *kulich*. Today, they observe it by inviting guests over for tea and an Easter cake called "plum cake." Plum cake is the modern alias for *kulich*, a word with religious connotations.

The extent to which the Easter feast is celebrated here is backed up by statistics from the Moscow bakers' trading organizations. In the first, third, and fourth quarters of each year, the city's bread shops order no ingredients for plum cake. In the second quarter, when Easter falls, they order 600 tons of ingredients.

Seth Mydans, in his article, "Soviet Union Saves Its Religious Past," describes the religious restoration as follows:

> In tiny whitewashed rooms once used by monks, Soviet artisans painstakingly apply gold leaf to ornate crosses, hammer out intricate brasswork, retouch ancient icons.
>
> The religious restoration is being done with the blessing of the anti-religious Soviet government, which has undertaken a new program to refurbish some examples of the nation's church architecture.
>
> Few of the restored churches are used for worship. Of the 657 churches that existed in Moscow on the eve of the 1917 Revolution, only 100 to 150 stand today, according to Soviet officials.
>
> Of these, only 46 still hold services, the Moscow Russian Orthodox patriarchy says.
>
> Others have found new incarnations as clubs, factories, offices, aquariums and anti-religious museums.
>
> For half a century, the graceful delicately domed churches have been left for the most part to decay or have been torn down.
>
> But in the last decade, the Soviet Union has appeared to feel less threatened by the nation's past and more protective of its monuments.
>
> A law now under consideration would set up protected areas around designated historical monuments, including many churches.
>
> A number of newly restored churches now stand among Moscow's rising glass-fronted hotels and office building, and some of the most impressive of them are within the walls of the Kremlin itself.
>
> "We see these as architectural monuments, not monuments to religion," said Alexander Khalaturin, director of the Soviet Department of Fine Arts and Restoration.
>
> He quoted a proclamation issued in 1917 by the revolutionary victors, urging their comrades not to tear down the churches and destroy religious art.
>
> "This is an art that talented people could create even under the yoke of despotism, which testifies to the beauty and strength of man's soul," the proclamation read.
>
> But such sentiments were largely ignored for decades, as some of the gems of church architecture were leveled during the Stalin and Khrushchev eras.
>
> Stalin considered tearing down St Basil's Cathedral in Red Square, the baroque 16th-century cluster of onion-shaped cupolas that is Moscow's most familiar symbol. The church was to be sacrificed to ease the traffic flow through the big cobbled square.
>
> St. Basil's was saved by strenuous protests, including a suicide threat by an architect.
>
> Not so fortunate was the 19th-century Church of Christ the Savior, on the banks of the Moscow River near the Kremlin, which was described years ago as the most richly decorated church in the city.
>
> It was dynamited in the early 1930's to make room for one of the gingerbread skyscrapers that Stalin was fond of, but the subsoil was found to be too soft, and a municipal swimming pool now stands in its place.

Today, the working churches are largely responsible for their own restoration, and some of them in Moscow and other affluent areas have maintained themselves in sumptuous splendor through private donations. They are crammed with priceless icons in worked gold and silver frames.

Others struggle against poverty, declining congregations and official neglect.

The Novospassky Monastery, where the artisans work in their small, sunlit rooms, is the central workshop for state-supported restorations around the Soviet Union.

The monastery is·itself under repair, and its once quiet grounds overlooking the Moscow River are clattering with the sounds of buzz saws and cement mixers.

Crumbling walls are being shored up, cupolas rebuilt with the aid of ancient blueprints, and one 15th-century wooden tower has been completely reconstructed.

The director of the workshops, Alexander Chekmaryev, said that the monastery would eventually become a museum of church restoration.

Its workshops include a small apothecary shop where pigments are reproduced from herbs, berries, bark and roots, following the recipes of ancient books.

Churches are only part of the work of the Soviet restorers, who also work on the old palaces, Soviet memorials such as Lenin's birthplace and the Kremlin itself.

When young "hooligans" were arrested in Tblisi, Georgia, for desecrating frescoes in a church, a studied campaign to preserve and restore ancient church architecture is going on all over the Soviet Union despite some dialectical criticism. In the following article, aimed at youthful readers of *Molodaya gvardiya*, is explained and defended this new official stand:

I have had the good fortune of having been a member of of the organizing committee of the Society for the Protection of Historical and Cultural Monuments, and thanks to this, I am very familiar with the enormous scale of the destruction to which our ancient architectural monuments have been subjected until very recently. Only three or four years ago there were voices calling for the destruction or transformation of all church architecture. This attitude was reflected even in the meetings of the Society itself.   ·

Let us face it: the destruction of church architecture is tantamount to the destruction of our entire architectural heritage, which would only lead to the lowering of the country's dignity.

Let us at last stop being vulgar sociologists and look at history through the eyes of a Marxist dialectician. Did Scientific atheism appear long ago, and with it secular culture and art? I shall remind you that both Greek sculpture and the paintings of the Renaissance were essentially based on subjects, ideas and images of religious origin.

Can we really forget the past and should we really be ashamed that history was history and not a lecture on an antireligious theme?

In the days of the ancient states, or in prefeudal times, and throughout the era of feudalism practically no other ideology but the religious one existed. Through the ages the struggle between progressive and reactionary trends was waged within the framework of one and the same religious concept.

For at least the last five or six thousand years the greatest efforts and the best talents of the world's people were directed toward the creation of temple architecture, religious paintings and church music.

Fortresses were also built, but purely engineering problems predominated there; palaces were built, but the dictates of class set the limits here. To compensate for this, in buildings of a religious nature the architect could express in exalted and pure form the idea of the unity of the people as a whole and could reflect its spirit and character.

Centuries pass. Dwelling do not survive their owners by much; new generations rebuild homes, adapting them to the needs of the changing way of life. Fortresses fall to ruins. Sometimes whole cities disappear, but the ancient city cathedral remains. As a result, nine tenths of the architectural treasures of every nation consist of religious buildings, which at one time absorbed the best artistic traditions of all national architectures; porches were influenced by chapels, fortresses by monasteries, and palace architecture by the entrance chambers of monasteries.

Just think of the pagodas of Japan and China, the temples of India, the mosques of the Moslem countries, the temples and pyramids of Egypt, the Greek Parthenon and the medieval cathedrals of Europe. Imagine Paris without the cathedral of Notre Dame, Prague without the cathedral of St. Vitus. Suppose it had been decided to remove the temples from the Acropolis in Athens, to destroy the Parthenon and the Erechtheum, for the sake of combatting church ideology! It is unimaginable!

Our ancient church architecture is certainly not inferior to the architectural monuments of other nations. If anything, in its diversity, originality and vividly expressed freedom of expression it offers many superior examples. Without any exaggeration, the talents of our ancient architects can be called unprecedented. Almost every one of the independent cities of Ancient Rus' had its own school of architecture. Pskov had its belfires and original octagonal roofs. The temples of Rostov, Yaroslavl and Vologda had their unique style. Then there are the incomparable structures of white stone in Vladimir, particularly the the incomparable Pokrov Cathedral on the Nerli, whose beauty takes one's breath away and delights one's heart. Then there are the many-tiered kokoshniks in Moscow architecture; the fantastic splendor of St. Basil's; the carved ornateness of Russian baroque; the wonderful chapels of the North, and the crowning glory of the tent-shaped temples, streaming upward, the faceted pillars — timber or stone — of the Russian folk tale.

Let us not forget that the architect in Ancient Rus', with rare exceptions, came from the people. The ingenious and proud muzhiks used to build joyously and majestically at the same time. They adorned the land in their own way and to suit their own, the popular, taste. The struggle of the popular master craftsman with official church ideology at times reached great intensity. History shows that neither secular nor spiritual powers necessarily dominated or influenced their building. For instance, let us recall how many ancient buildings were mutilated at the royal will of Nikolai I, or how primitive "renovations" spoiled a heritage of world significance.

The meaning of ancient architecture was understood with extraordinary accuracy by popular Russian painters. Surikov put insurgent archers against the background of the towers of St. Basil's, using them and the cathedral as a contrast to the overpowering oppression of the monarchy.

Savrasov put a church with a tentlike bell tower in his best landscape—"The Rooks Came Flying"—which became the banner of "democratic" art. White, gleaming churches on the vast expanse of the plains became an integral part of Levitan's landscapes.

The significance of church architecture is that it in fact expresses our national character, and that is why it is unthinkable to save only individual "historical

monuments." That is why the country cannot be "'stripped bar!" Architecture
is at work constantly; one must grow up surrounded by architectural monuments, for only then do they become instilled in the national character of a
person.

The palaces of Leningrad do not instill royalist convictions in people, yet their
austere beauty has a definite influence on the character of the Leningrad
resident. The wonderful churches of Ancient Rus' do not instill in a modern
person inclinations toward obscurantism and religious fanaticism (they did not
instill such characteristics in the past either, as a rule), but they do instill the
national spirit impressed in them by our forebears, the sense of the homeland
and a love for one's own soil.

I am not speaking now about a beauty that is purely architectural or abstract,
but about the amazing mastery of "loftiness" achieved by our ancient architects.
The modern architect seems unable to handle space going upward. He can
invent nothing except a box set on end. Against the background of this boxlike
barrenness, the complicated, light, flowing forms of temples, belfires, bell
towers and porches topped by a circling chorus of onion-shaped domes above
them, from the mighty pillar of Ivan the Great to the swift lightness of the
church in the village of Kolomensl seem the creation of strangers from some
other, infinitely higher civilization.

Yes, of course it is hard at times to dismiss the idea of the church as a house of
prayer. It required almost a thousand years for European mankind to realize
the aesthetic beauties of the Greek temples. Right up to the Renaissance, the
temples of antiquity were storehouses of hewn stone, nothing more.

But our citizens are now capable of understanding the beauty of churches aside
from their religious purpose. Once, I had a conversation with a Moscow taxi
driver. When he learned about the formation of the Society for the Preservation of Historical Monuments, he was delighted.

"You know," he said, "I love to hunt. My friends and I go to the Oka River area.
There is one spot which is so beautiful . . . pine forests, and bluffs and, in the
distance, the church. You know, I can't imagine that district without it, without
that church! You can't separate it from nature. But when my friends and I went
up close to it, we saw that it was falling apart, and surrounded by junk; some
kind of rusty machines had been dumped there. It should be fixed. After all, it
decorates the whole region!"

There is not a breath of any "religion" in the minds of these people. Yet, love
for the homeland and respect for ancient architecture are inseparable to
them.

Our nation's history lives in the monuments of ancient architecture. History
should live everywhere—in Red Square and on the banks of the Oka—for with
a light of its own that comes from antiquity it warms the path to the future of
each new generation and of every human being.

That is why it is necessary to learn to protect our ancient churches, properly
and solicitously, and to use them creatively. The more successfully we go in this
direction, the sooner the legacy of the church will be reinterpreted and become
a part of our heritage and also part of the heritage of the church itself.

Incidentally, the stream of tourists heading for Suzdal (old monasteries and
churches) and Rostov Veliki (fine twelfth-century cathedral) increases every
month and already numbers hundreds of thousands of people annually. Obviously all these people, young people for the most part, cannot be accused of
being out of step with our era. The respect for one's ancestors, which Pushkin
wrote about as an indispensable feature of a cultured nation, is becoming a

part of the consciousness of a full-fledged personality, of the individual in a Communist society. I hope that in the end this respect will become the rule for our architects also.

One of the results of this interest has been the frequent appearance of protests against the razing or mutilation of buildings which, though they may be churches, are also works of art. If one could cite but a single writer who reflects this point of view it would be the essayist and poet Vladimir Soloukhin whose touching accounts of his native region of Vladimir province show his appreciation at least of the esthetics of the combination of church and village, but whose "Letters from the Russian Museum," which appeared in 1966 in the monthly organ of the Komsomol, *Molodaya gvardiya*, reach more deeply toward things of the spirit. There is a note which can only be called spiritual as he writes,

> In man, in addition to the necessity for eating, drinking, sleeping, and continuing the species, from the very beginning there have existed two great necessities. The first of them is communion with the soul of another person. And the second, a communion with the sky (*nebo* —which also means heaven). This latter need arises, "Evidently from the fact that man as a form of temporary existence is a part, be it a millionth, be it momentary, be it insignificant, but still a part of that very endlessness and boundlessness" which is represented by the sky.

Soloukhin goes on to remark that "Russia, not long ago, before the cataclysm, was multifaceted and varied." There was, it is true, Russia of the bureaucrats, such as Anna Karenina's husband or the Mayor in Gogol's *Inspector General*. Moreover, one finds the warriors, the revolutionaries, the explorers, the scientists.

> But Russia was also a praying country. The hermitages in Kerzhen, in the forests beyond the Volga, the Old Believers, the self-immolators, the female fanatics who in early life went into convents, the pilgrims, male and female, wandering from the Solovki Islands to Kiev, and from Kiev to the Solovki Islands. And it was this pious, praying Russia which the artist Nesterov put down on his canvases.

One of the inheritors of this effort to depict the old "pious, praying Russia" of whom Soloukhin speaks, was also the artist Pavel D Korin who, stemming from the icon-painting village of Palekh, spent years in the 1930's working on an enourmous painting, titled *Ukhodiashchaya Rus'*, (The Russia which is passing away), as a sort of great group portrait of the servitors of the church and their followers, painted perhaps in a style of academic realism which is not in the Western mode, but done with great fidelity to at least the outer truth of the situation. Korin, however, was more than the mere recorder of events for, as a recent catalog of his collection shows, he assembled a major group of Old Russian icons, and evidently did much to help bring a revival of pride in and understanding of this part of Russia's past.

And in commenting on a number of the paintings of mid-19th century Russian artists who sought to depict events in the life of Christ in the terms of the then-fashionable, almost photographic realism, Solouchin writes, with reference to Christ and the woman taken in adultery:

> So according to the old laws, this young woman should be killed by stoning. Christ was a revisionist. He came in order to revise the ancient laws. He was against cruelty. He considered that evil gave birth to and multiplied evil. And

that the path of mankind in this direction would lead only to a dead end. . . .
And thus He believed that it was possible to save mankind in only on way: by
limitless, boundless, all-encompassing love.

And in reference to another painting, Soloukhin states, that, though
nailed to the cross, Christ was "a symbol of love, forgiveness, and self-
sacrifice."

These are indeed strange words to be found in the Soviet press of the
mid-1960's, and particularly in a magazine which is an organ of the Central
Committee of the Komsomol. Yet, something at least of the spirit of search
for the Russian national past, including some recognition of the historical
role of religion, may be observed in other pages of this periodical, with its
frequent articles under the general headings of "preserve our relics!" These
tell of activity to save old buildings, chiefly churches, in danger of gradual
decay or of the sudden onslaughts of city-planners eager to substitute
housing developments of box-like monotony and dubious taste for old but
good buildings. These articles, and others of like nature which appeared in a
variety of publications, seem to have played their role in the formation in
1966 of the All-Russian Society for the preservation of Monuments of
History and Culture and of similar bodies in other republics in the USSR.
And one may see the physical results of this movement in little tablets such as
that attached to the Church of Elijah the Prophet in Yaroslavl', restored as a
museum, noting that restoration was carried out with the cooperation of the
Yaroslavl' branch of the society.

This movement has been significantly accompanied by a relatively large
number of publications on neonationalist themes, publications which treat
seriously, and one might say even with love, the whole religious-esthetic side
of Russian culture. One need only refer to Olga Chaikovskaia's recent
account of Old Russian religious art in her *Protiv neba na zemle* (From earth
against heaven), principally intended for adolescent readers but still a profoundly serious book, to see how the author is searching for a historical and
esthetic understanding of the role of religion in terms which do not easily
combine with the standard cliches of Marxism.

However, it may be said that esthetic and historical comprehension of a
movement do not necessarily mean sharing the values of that movement,
and so it is possible for a present-day citizen of the Soviet Union to appreciate
the glories of the churches at Kizhi with their multitude of cupolas or of
Andrei Rublev's majestic miniature *Spas v silakh* (The Savior in a mandala),
without necessarily being affected by the philosophy which lies behind these
works of art. Still perhaps one may see a deeper influence when one turns
from the things of wood and stone and paint to the world of words, to take
note of the many reflections in current Russian literature of the Christian
and Orthodox tradition, thought or bits of wording from Russia's religious
heritage. Indeed, some are venturing now, in a manner parallel to those who
protested against the violation of legal procedures in the prosecution of
Sinyavski, Daniel, Bukovski, Galanskov, and others, to claim the protection
of the Soviet Constitution and of its article 124 which, after decreeing the
separation of the church and state provides that "Freedom of religious
worship and freedom of anti-religious propaganda is recognized for all
citizens."

These protestors say that, in view of the close controls kept over religious
functions by the official supervisory body, the Council on Religious Affairs

attached to the USSR Council of Ministers, and in view of the extremely detailed laws and regulations which govern the formation of parishes and maintenance of places of worship, even this minimal freedom of religious worship is impaired. Some indeed go so far as to proclaim that many religious leaders including important clergymen of the Russian Orthodox Church , have failed in their duty to protest against the infringement of the rights of worshippers and have thereby permitted the Council of Religious Affairs to interfere illegally in the internal life of the church.

The most extensive exposition of this view is to be found in a lengthy and outspoken letter, addressed to Patriarch Aleksei, and supplemented by an appeal to N. V. Podgorny, Chairman of the Presidium of the Supreme Soviet of the USSR, which was sent in December of 1965 by two priests, Nikolai Eshliman and Gleb Yakunin of the Moscow Diocese. These documents recount, in a wealth of detail, the way in which the highly circumscribed liberty of religious worship in the Soviet State is even more limited by all sorts of what the authors term illegal and unpublished rulings by the Council, the effects of which are furthered, they say, by "a whole group of bishops and clergymen . . . who under the cover of piety knowingly and actively distort the spirit of Russian Orthodoxy." Something of the trials to which the church has been subjected lately may be gathered from reading this remarkable letter, while many further instances of single cases of persecution, throwing light on the general observations of Frs. Eshliman and Yakunin, are to be found in the work by Nikita Struve.

The Moscow priests' letter cites Article 124 of the USSR constitution which "grants all citizens of the Soviet Union freedom to practice religious cults" and a 1918 decree on the separation of church and state as the ground for their protest. They accuse the Soviet Council on the Affairs of the Russian Orthodox Church of radically changing its function "from that of an official arbitration organ to that of an unofficial and illegal control organ over the Moscow Patriarchate." The young priests charge that the council "by infraction of the laws on separation of church and state have placed themselves in the position of unlimited dictators of the Russian Church, systematically abusing the principle of freedom of conscience and hindering the free conduct of religious worship." This action, they contest, leads "to warranted dissatisfaction of the believing citizens of the U.S.S.R. and discredits in the eyes of the broad public the rightful foundations of socialist society, thereby causing great harm to our Fatherland."

This unusual letter, which on the basis of good evidence the National Council of Churches believes to be authentic, accuses the Soviet council of interfering with the nomination of clergy, closing "at least 10,000 churches and dozens of monasteries," violating civil rights of Christians by forcing them to register sacraments such as baptism with state authorities, hindering freedom of worship by requiring special permits for religious services outside churches, violating the Soviet constitutional principle of freedom of conscience by barring children from church life, interfering in the financial affairs of the church, limiting participation in parish life and administration to 20 persons per parish and obstructing the practice of religion by limiting the number of priests on church staffs. These unequivocal, specific accusations against an arm of the Soviet government compose a document of extraordinary historical importance. The letter tells nothing one did not suspect about government interference with religion, but it tells much that one did not know about the vitality of the Russian church. If the Council on the Affairs of the Russian Orthodox Church is as powerful and dictatorial as the young priests imply, their careers, even their lives, may be in jeopardy. On the other hand, their appeal, addressed as much to the conscience of mankind as to the Soviet president, may obtain as they hope "effective measures for the earliest possible uprooting of illegality and the re-establishment of the legal rights of the millions of believing citizens of the Soviet Union."

However, these two priests, Frs. Eshliman and Yakunin, were punished, although not by the secular authorities. Aleksey, Patriarch of Moscow and All Russia, in a letter of July, 1966, to the bishops of the Russian church, condemned the two for endeavoring "to spread distrust in our Supreme Church Authority among the clergy and laity of our Church, and thereby to bring temptation into the quiet stream of Church life." And, almost as if intent upon proving the allegations raised by Eshliman and Yakunin as to overzealous cooperation between the hierarchy and the state, this letter goes on to speak of

> an endeavor to cast slander on State organs. The endeavors of individual persons to step forth in the role of unappointed judges of higher Church Authority, and their desire to cast slander on State organs, do not serve the interests of the Church, and have the effect of destroying the well-intended relationships between State organs and our Church.

It is noteworthy that the "State organs" of so powerful a state would need the protection provided by the words of the 90-year-old Patriarch, or by his action to suspend the priests from performance of their sacramental functions as a result of criticism of the State.

Alarmed at the seeming failure to wean more "believers" away from the faith, the official magazine of the Communist Party points out that atheism has to strive to do everything possible to satisfy the ethical and aesthetic needs of man if it is to succeed in combating the church.

> An interesting conversation was held between a member of a committee sent to investigate the causes of religious beliefs in the Province of Orel, and the local believers, He was told by one of the religious-minded women that she finds herself in communion with God, that she talks with Christ, and associates with Him, and her happiness stems from this. "Non-believers," she said, "could never attain such bliss..."

> The clergy makes every effort to impress on the believers a conviction about the actual existence of God in various forms, so that a real, daily contact can be established with Him. The priests are supposed to be the only healers of spiritual ailments. Only they are capable of solving grave personal problems; they are the guardians of human happiness. Owing to such emotional, psychological influence, a certain number of people find peace in religious prayers, or in other experiences of a religious and ethical nature.

> The most important task of scientific atheism is to unmask the fraud of theologians who maintain that all psychological activity, all inner personal experiences represent the "estrangement" of the human soul, which can find a solution only in religion. The falsity of the notion that it is possible to "save" man by the mere strength of a genuine religious love is proved by the fact that the theologians themselves say that love of God belongs to a higher category than love of man. Consequently, religious love is transcendent and devoid of all real content, and it cannot possibly be a stimulus toward any positive social action.

In the work of re-educating the believers, one frequently encounters statements like the old woman's in Orel, when all logical arguments fail to disprove their delusions. And here we must find a specific, authoritative approach to the spiritual world of the people, showing them step by step how all the most difficult problems can be solved without the help of religion.

It is necessary to explain in scientific manner the ethical and aesthetic needs of man. But this alone is not enough. It is the duty of public opinion, of all local organizations, to do everything possible to satisfy those needs. Society must see to it that circumstances favorable to the revival of religious attitudes are eradicated. Indifference of social organizations and of the "collectives" to the human conditions, to man's difficulties, his confusion, his misfortunes — all this makes it possible for the religious activists to win people into their fold.

A relevant example is the life history of a religious woman who was actually related to a member of the above-mentioned expedition to Orel. "Up till 1956 I was not a believer, although my parents were Baptists," she recalled. "Then I went to Orel, where I worked in a knitting factory. It took me a long time to learn how to work the machine. My co-workers laughed at me, they called me stupid. A few days later a middle-aged woman approached me, said that she would always help me. She didn't mention God, and I was naturally very grateful to her. One day she asked me: "What do you do with your free time? Come to our parish." I went and liked it: the singing, the sermon, everything. After a while I felt a need to pray. . . ."

Similar instances testify time and again to the serious losses — speaking in social and ideological terms — occurring through lack of attention in the "collectives" and in social organizations to people's needs and their individual experiences.

Aware of the fact that a lifetime is a relatively short fragment of time, man finds himself strongly influenced by emotions and moods. He experiences all the adversities of earthly existence, reflects upon his fate and upon the problem of happiness. An atheist cannot shun these problems in his investigations; neither can he avoid giving a positive answer to the question: wherein lies man's happiness? It is particularly important to prove that real happiness is closely related to the complete development of man's physical and spiritual powers, and that it depends on man's participation in the life of his community. A religious ideal demands that a man remain locked within himself and direct all his strivings toward the salvation of his soul in the afterlife. Atheism, on the contrary, aspires to develop the whole personality of man, and to direct his consciousness toward the present, toward the joy of life.

Therefore, the object and the approaches of scientific atheism are twofold: on the one hand atheism must criticize religious consciousness with all its complex elements; on the other hand, atheism must be positive and constructive. As we demonstrate the effects of the religious approach to life, we must be able to explain to a believer in clear and precise terms what he could replace those concepts with if he became an atheist.

A conception of the world based on Marxism and Leninism gives us a possibility of solving in a scientific manner the problem of personality; it demonstrates to man the true, nonillusory value of his existence and stimulate him to creative activity. It is the duty of all those in charge of atheistic propaganda, all members of our intelligentsia, the whole society, to use this possibility to the full.

Since the Communist system sees in man only a degree of development of society, it is merely a rigid consequence if society is conceived as a collectivity to which individuals are ordained and subordinated as a part of the whole. While in the social doctrine of the Church society is conceived as bound in solidarity to the person and finds its task in making man's development possible, according to the Communist conception it is the social collectivity that determines all the manifestations of man's life.

It is impossible to understand Soviet policy toward religion unless one realizes the difference between its exported, propagandist position and its actual policy toward religious groups. An excellent example of this double standard was *Tass* coverage of the Nixons' attendance at the Baptist Church in Moscow — for the free press in the Western world.

Another illustration of this point concerns the Bible. The propagandist position holds that it is not an outlawed book and is available anywhere. The actual position is that a Bible can usually be bought only through the black market and costs from two weeks' to a month's wages.

Bibles are confiscated immediately when Christians are imprisoned, and one of the prime requests which prisoners make to seemingly deaf authorities is to have them returned.

There are only three Iron Curtain countries where Bible societies have been able to operate since Communist rule: Yugoslavia, East Germany and Poland. In Russia and the other satellites a church of 300 people is fortunate to have one Bible to share, usually belonging to its pastor.

Brother Andrew, author of *God's Smuggler*, heads a huge network of Bible distributors for believers behind the Iron Curtain because of the scarcity of Scriptures there.

Taking a brief backward look at history since the Bolshevik Revolution, one finds that conditions were not too hard for believers at first. In 1918 the Council of People's Commissars guaranteed separation of church and state. However, in 1929 the Law on Religious Associations was passed, stating that every religious community must be registered, supplying lists of members to local authorities so that the latter might remove any they object to who have been elected into positions of leadership.

The government became even more repressive in 1961 with Article 142 of the Criminal Code, forbidding the "organization and systematic teaching of religion to minors." Now Russian parents are denied their fundamental human right to rear their children in their own moral and spiritual standards.

In 1960 the United Nations adopted a Convention on Education which states that "parents . . . must have the opportunity of guaranteeing the religious and moral upbringing of their children according to their own beliefs." Incredibly, the USSR adopted this U.N. convention in 1962, just a year after they had expressly forbidden it by law in their own nation.

The Teachers' Gazette, published in Moscow, states unequivocally:

> Communist ideology is irreconcilable with that of religion . . . (it is the duty of every Soviet teacher) to do everything possible to make atheistic education a constitutional part of a Communist education, to root out with finality superstitions and prejudices among children, and to bring up every school child as a militant atheist.

John Milc Lochman, Czech author of *The Church in a Marxist Society*, answers the question of why the church is so vital under persecution.

> The one ground for becoming a Christian in that situation is the ground of faith. You have nothing to gain by being a Christian. Rather, you may lose. Thus the shadow of hypocrisy grows less. And here is the chance for a new credibility.

A careful survey of the major religious groups operating within the USSR appears to back up Lochman's claim.

The free world rubbed its eyes in disbelief at headlines of the Soviet refusal to let novelist Alexander Solzhenitsyn leave Russia to claim his Nobel Prize for Literature. Most people thought the author's persecution came solely because of his stand for freedom; few realized he is also an outstanding Christian layman.

A member of the Russian Orthodox Church, Solzhenitsyn charged Patriarch Pimen with Communist collaboration in his famous "Lenten Letter" of 1972. He never received an answer from the Patriarch, but he did get a moving and revealing reply from an Orthodox priest who is himself deprived of the Soviet "registration" which would enable him to function clerically or receive an income.

Sergey Zheludkov, author of *Why I Too Am a Christian* and a prominent writer for the underground press, challenged Solzhenitsyn that he was expecting too much of the "registered" church under Communism.

> The whole truth is that the legal church organization cannot be an oasis of freedom in our strictly uniformly organized society, governed from one Center. . .
>
> To work at the religious education of children — and of adults too — this is not permitted us . . . One thing only is permitted us — to celebrate divine services in the churches, and this too with the implicit understanding that it is only for the passing generation. . . .
>
> I am sorry that you did not mention at least the churchmen Boris Talantov who died in prison and Anatoly Levitin who is suffering in prison. . . ."

Thus Zheludkov affirms that even in the most privileged or at least tolerated church in Russia there is also an underground movement.

The Communist Party organ, *Pravda*, has called for renewed efforts to stamp out religious beliefs in the Soviet Union and said some party members are taking part in religious ceremonies.

The lead editorial in the paper said: "Every Communist should be a fighting atheist."

The editorial called religion "one of the strongest leftovers of the past."

Traditional Soviet anti-religious attitudes toward religion appear to have remained unchanged. Anti-religious propagandists still preach that belief in God perverts and cripples the human psyche.

But official policy can face two ways at the same time. Sometimes the emphasis is on tolerance, sometimes on elimination.

Russia's constitution guarantees freedom of belief, but there is little doubt the state ultimately hopes to root out and crush religion entirely.

In 1961, the Communist Party set a target date of 1980 — the 1,000th year of Russian christendom — as the year by which religion would be eliminated. Presumed unrealistic in recent years, this date no longer is mentioned. Religion in the Soviet Union claims too many adherents to be easily outlawed.

Far from dead in the world's leading atheist state, the Orthodox Church in the Soviet Union is believed to be upheld by at least 30 million believers, many of them military men committed by the Party to discourage religion among their troops.

A clue that the days of harrassing churchgoers is over, at least for a while, came recently when *Moskovskaya pravda*, the newspaper published by the Moscow Communist Party, appealed to its readers to treat believers as "comrades" instead of enemies.

Another newspaper, *Komsomolskaya pravda*, warned that "insults, violence and the forcible closing of churches, not only fail to reduce the number of believers, but actually tend to increase the number of believers, make clandestine religious groups more widespread, and antagonize believers against the state."

Anti-religious propaganda is still published by the ton in the government-controlled Soviet press. But the struggle against religion takes the form of efforts to convince believers of the scientific truth said to be embodied in atheism, rather than taunting worshippers and closing churches.

Marxist philosophy has it that as man's intellectual and scientific awareness grows, his need for faith in a "God in the unfathomable" should fade away.

Soviet policy is that religion may not challenge any state doctrine or practice, and that it may not be propagated.

Believers, therefore, can go to church as long as they confine their practice to the church and do not try to bring the church into areas of Soviet life that the Kremlin believes belong to the state.

The appearance of some unusual documents and letters in Moscow has unveiled dissatisfaction among Russian Orthodox Church believers, some of whom claim that the Soviet state is still closing churches.

The first document, which came to light early in January, 1974, was a complaint to Kremlin and church leaders that authorities in the Ukrainian town of Zhitomir had closed a local church.

About 30 members of the congregation of Zhitomir's Church of the Epiphany, apparently mainly old folk, said modern youth had cinemas, theaters, and dances where they could enjoy themselves and spend their free evenings, "but we old people have only one place of recreation, our Epiphany. . . ."

Next, a series of letters which became available at the end of January protested about alleged harassment of the Pochayev Monastery in the western Ukraine and complained of attempts to exert a psychological influence on its work.

Observers in Moscow could recall seeing few such documents before, although there have often been rumors of dissatisfaction among believers, especially in the provinces.

Moscow is reasonably well supplied with working churches— there are said to be 45 open Russian Orthodox churches— but many small towns and villages lost their places of worship either in the early years of Communist power or in the last years of the rule of Premier Nikita S. Khrushchev, who was toppled in 1964.

The old churches were often destined to become warehouses, clubs, or sometimes libraries.

However, there has been little evidence of churches being closed in recent years.

But the letter from Zhitomir said the Church of the Epiphany, a wooden structure next to a school, had not only been closed but was scheduled for demolition.

Officials told representatives of the congregation that a church could not stand next to a school, although the two buildings had stood together for 32 years.

Freedom of religion is guaranteed under the Soviet Constitution, but state atheism places tight controls on religious life, such as restricting worship to registered communities, while anti-religious propaganda tries to convince the population of the scientific truth embodied in atheism.

"The church does not actively fight against the atheistic Soviet government," declared Metropolitan Yuvenaly, chairman of the department of external church affairs of the Moscow Patriarchate.

> What would happen if the church in Russia, with its million of believers, would come out against the government? With the Apostle Paul, we act on the belief there is no power that does not come from God. . . .

> Like the church here, the church in Russia has some problems. We have lived under less than optimum conditions for 60 years.

> We have no church schools, no means of publicizing our services. Nevertheless, the churches have not begun to empty. We don't keep statistics, but other indicators lead us to believe there are 40 to 50 million Orthodox believers in our country.

> The majority of those attending worship services are women over 40, but the number of participating youth is growing. The youth in the cities are more involved in the church than village youth. And the young people who are attending church tend to come from the ranks of the better educated.

> Some youth have become interested in religion after reading the atheistic journal, *Science and Religion*. Atheistic propaganda seems to make people think about the religious side of the question.

> Russia is truly a country dedicated to bringing into existence a nation that will be anti-religious, where any mention of God will bring nothing but ridicule.

> In Leningrad one will find the "Museum of the History of Religion and Atheism." The museum is housed, irreverently, in the Kazan Cathedral, which was one of Leningrad's leading churches from 1801 until 1932, when the museum was founded.

> Now 40 years old, the museum is still packing them in — crowds of school children, peasants down from the collective farm, sailors strolling hand-in-hand with their girls.

> What they see is an institution, according to the Leningrad release, devoted to the idea, enshrined in the Soviet constitution, that if churches have the right to preach, the government has the right to preach against them.

> On the ground floor, beneath mosaics and frescoes of the cathedral, are hundreds of photographs and displays ridiculing religion. The glories of space travel and the failure of Soviet cosmonauts to find God in the orbit are chronicled.

> So is the support of some German churchmen for Hitler and the reactionary role of the Russian Orthodox Church in the pre-revolutionary days of Czarist Russia. Even unbiased historians have little good to say about the Russian church in those days, and it has provided rich grist for the museum.

> There are robes, crowns, icons, goblets and mitres, caked in gold and covered in jewels — all taken from church treasuries.

> The museum often manages to have it both ways. Ministers are shown as both foolish and cruel. Exhibits laugh at poor church attendance by Western youth, and lampoon the use of jazz in Western churches to recover these youth.

Old people — the bastion of religion in Russia today — are urged to forsake the church. Young people are shown pictures of lavish weddings in the many non-sectarian "palaces of marriages" or "baptisms" in "palaces of happiness," where children receive tiny Lenin medals.

While the church is condemned when its minister blesses U.S. troops in Vietnam, Charles Manson is glorified in a new exhibit on the revival of Satanism in the West. Another display shows pictures of members of a much oppressed group of dissident Soviet Baptists who, according to the captions, repented and are "now propagandists for atheism."

The Kazan Cathedral, like most of the 462 churches which graced Leningrad in 1917, is not a "working church" today. Some, particularly the most beautiful, have been restored by the Soviet regime and turned into museums. Others have been torn down.

Only 17 working churches remain. They include 12 Russian Orthodox Churches, one church of the Orthodox "Old Believers," a Roman Catholic church, a Baptist Church, a Jewish synagogue and for the city's Moslem minority — a mosque.

Despite brutal oppression, Christianity has survived in the Soviet Union. At the same time, it has been exposed to a more subtle form of opposition.

Stalin and his successors decided to take control of the faithful by appointing specially trained and conditioned agents to key positions in the church — especially the Russian Orthodox Church, but also in others.

These appointments were made in an indirect way, by allowing only those churches that suited the Communist government to function. Communist agents entered seminaries, were ordained as ministers, and started to preach blind obedience to the "ruling powers."

The existence of open churches allows the Communists to claim they respect freedom of opinion. In this way they brainwash people in the West and entice tourists. . . . By developing relations between the churches in the Soviet Union and those abroad, the government creates another way of sending agents into the West.

Lately, people trying to carry on antistate activities have put on new masks. They are now described as "fighters for freedom of religion." Actually, nothing threatens the freedom of conscience and religion guaranteed by the Soviet Constitution. Prestigious representatives of all the religions practiced in the country have made statements to that effect time and time again.

Interviewed by journalists in December 1975, Pimen, Patriarch of Moscow and All Russia, said: "I must state with full authority that there has not been a single case in the Soviet Union when a person was brought to trial or imprisoned for his religious beliefs. More than that, there are no penalties for religious beliefs under Soviet law. It is the private business of each Soviet citizen to practice religion or not."

Socialism solved the problem of freedom of conscience for the first time in history. In the Russian Empire the Russian Orthodox Church enjoyed all the privileges, but in the Soviet Union today all religious denominations are equal: Russian Orthodox, Catholic, Islam, Buddhist, Georgian Orthodox, Armenian Gregorian, Jewish, Evangelical Lutheran, Evangelical Christian Baptist and any other.

It stands to reason that groups whose activity under the guise of religious ritual, actually harms the health of citizens or urges them to shirk their civic duties are forbidden in the USSR.

The Russian Orthodox Church has found new favor by developing "Communist Christianity."

This accepts the Communist social system as just and good and supports Kremlin policies. It plays down the philosophic conflict between the Christian faith and the atheistic materialism officially espoused by the government.

Notable evidence of a changed attitude toward the Church appears in the magazine *Nauka i religiya*, the leading Soviet publication on religious matters. The magazine used to assail religion and proclaim the need for its disappearance from Soviet life.

The previous issue of the magazine, taking a similarly favorable attitude, wrote admiringly of church members as good Soviet citizens. It referred to polls taken recently which were said to have confirmed this.

The new attitude in *Nauka i religiya* reflected an apparent Kremlin attempt toward further reconciliation with religion. The post-Khrushchev leadership seems ready to live with the Orthodox church as part of the national heritage. It has made a general attempt to end divisive quarrels and rally all groups in the country.

Nauka i religiya dealt only with the Russian Orthodox Church, which still claims 50 million members despite early Communist persecution.

The magazine praised the church for giving up its old alliance with capitalism and its concentration on the inner state of man and the after life in favor of more emphasis on social justice and general human welfare on earth.

The gist of the social interpretation of Russian Orthodoxy lies in the concept of Communist Christianity. Communist Christianity appeals to believers to get involved in the struggle for socialism and Socialist conceptions.

Nauka i religiya quoted from *Zhurnal Moskovskoi Patriarkhi* to show how the church press treated the new outlook.

"The establishment of Christ's kingdom on earth is more and more associated with the Communist reconstruction of the world."

Nauka i religiya commented approvingly: "Leaders of the modern Orthodox Church proclaim that the atheistic Soviet authority carries out the will of God by establishing a new life in a just society," for instance:

There are two million weddings a year in the Soviet Union, and there is an infinite variety of wedding customs, for there are more than a hundred nationalities. But all have one thing in common — the new socialist content of the ceremony. Old humiliating customs which underlined woman's unequal position in society, the domination of man, customs like bride-money in the Caucasus and Central Asia have long been left behind. Young couples who get married these days have no class or religious barriers, and nationality too is unimportant — one marriage in four is mixed.

Weddings often go beyond the family circle, celebrated by the collectives where bride and groom study or work. There is a new tradition, especially in factories and on large building sites — the Komsomol wedding where all the workmates celebrate the wedding, and often management and the trade union give the young couple the key to their new flat.

Wedding ceremonies are memorable — festive music, good wishes from the deputy to the local Soviet who registers the marriage, the exchange of rings, congratulations, champagne, a ride through the town in flower-decked cars, and then a party in a restaurant or at home.

Country weddings are somewhat different, though the legal part of it is much the same — the marriage is recorded in the register, and the newlyweds are issued a marriage certificate.

Old folk customs have mostly been dropped in towns but they live on in village weddings. There you can still hear the special songs and see the customs that have come down to us from older times, the match-maker and the best man; the bride is "ransomed" and "sent off," the newlyweds are given bread and salt and grain, the symbol of good living. These customs have lost their original meaning but they still give pleasure.

Each nation has its own customs, but everywhere one thing is the same — the equality of the newlyweds and their equality in the family and society.

In Moscow the ornate, red-carpeted palaces have come under sharp new criticism for failing to provide more dignified and gentle settings for marriages.

At the same time, authorities across ther Soviet Union are trying to encourage simpler wedding celebrations. Lavishness, which sometimes runs into days of feasting in the Caucasus and Central Asia, is a sign of increasing affluence, a status symbol, and in part a reaction against the sutere official ceremony.

In Moscow Wedding Palaces, couples are processed at the rate of one every 10 minutes or so. After waiting in line with other wedding parties, they are called into a large room where a statue of Lenin looks down upon them. A woman official briefly lectures them on the seriousness of the marriage contract.

The couple then signs a document. A recording of Mendelssohn's Wedding March is played. The official declares the couple man and wife — and they are back on the street as other couples push past them on the way in. The fee: $2.05.

"This is not good enough," writes the head of the registrar's office of the Moscow city executive committee, S. Kulayeva, in the weekly writers' journal, *Literary Gazette*.

The ceremonies too often resemble a "conveyor belt." Officials are too often "in a hurry." More wedding palaces are needed in Moscow.

Three additional palaces are being built, according to S. Kulayeva, but a fourth, though planned, has not even been begun. Construction officials said "right to our faces" that such sites had low priority.

The registrar chief was commenting on a letter in which Masha K. and her husband Sascha said how disappointed they were to find a long queue outside their palace and haste inside.

"Our joy was simply stolen," the couple said. Of the long line outside they added, "If it had not been for the tulips, one could have thought something in short supply was on sale."

What is to be done? Several remedies have been tried, the registrar chief says.

A "theater specialist" conducted seminars for a year to teach officials to act as though each ceremony "is exclusively for this couple and happens only once in a lifetime."

In 1975, a competition was held for the best wedding ceremony, judged on decoration of the palace, clothes worn by the officials, musical background, and how the prescribed text was read.

Reception halls for parties after the ceremony have been abolished. But the resulting space is not used for weddings. It is used to register new-born babies and for other municipal functions.

The registrar chief frowns on two other traditional parts of a Soviet wedding. She would replace the Mendelssohn with "works by Soviet composers." And she dismisses as "outdated" the bright paper streamers that flutter from the hoods of the taxis or private cars that transport the wedding party, and the dolls in white dresses and the teddy bears usually affixed to the radiator grills.

On church weddings the *Moscow News* comments as follows:

> ... Most young Soviet people do not believe in God. But this doesn't mean they aren't allowed to go to church. Here religion is a personal affair. Soviet citizens can be married in a religious ceremony, but it becomes legal only when it is registered at state organs. A marriage sanctioned by religion does not allow man-wife family rights and responsibilities established by Soviet law.

For instance, "wedding palaces" in the cities of Perm Province performed 10,500 secular weddings in 1972, complete with bouquets, wedding gowns, and processions of beribboned automobiles, sometimes festooned with teddy bears and Kewpie dolls.

But this was only one-third the total number of marriages in the province. Two-thirds of the couples had to content themselves with the barren "desk, inkwell, and pen" of the registry office.

"Wedding palaces," first introduced in 1959, are lacking in most small villages. Even in the cities, couples sometimes must wait their turn as long as six months to celebrate a marriage at a "palace." And, according to the newspaper *Soviet Russia,* the scene is lamentable when five couples at a time line up with all their witnesses and friends in crowded waiting rooms before the ceremony.

Soviet Russia joined its sister-paper *Soviet Culture* in urging poets, composers, folklore specialists, and dress designers to create new and uplifting secular rites not only for weddings, but also to celebrate births and comings of age.

It said a "ministry of ceremonies" was not needed, but some kind of public council ought to be formed to devise appropriate ceremonies for the Russian public, largest region in the Soviet Union. Model ceremonies should be tried out and popularized via television, film, and recordings.

The Ukraine Republic already has embarked on such a program. In 1969 the Ukraine's Supreme Soviet established a commission to introduce new civil ceremonies. The commission has adopted new model plans for secular weddings, and other occasions. It has published a handbook of varied ceremonies which includes scripts and music.

Theater, motion picture, and television studios have combined forces to stage the new secular ceremonies for public viewing.

Architects are designing "happiness rooms" in rural government buildings for civil weddings and birth festivals.

In addition to weddings and child-naming, the new Ukraine ceremonials include memorial services on Victory Day, marking the end of World War II in Europe. On this day young Ukrainians plant trees in memory of those who sacrificed themselves for the country, and meet with war veterans and their families.

Ukrainian farms have also devised ceremonial harvest festivals and spring festivals. As farm bands sound a march, young people enter to receive a symbolic clump of earth from the hands of a veteran farmer.

A tree-planting ceremony or youth carnival concludes the festivities.

But when it comes to competing with the church in weddings and christenings, the press complains that the state has to try harder. The newspaper

Soviet Culture has chided architects for unimaginative wedding palaces that look like stores.

Through the ages the greatest artists consecrated their work to the church. It protested that Soviet architects, musicians, and poets have not yet measured up to the challenge.

Pravda of the Ukraine reported surveys showing that as many as half the newborn babes in the Ukraine are christened, even though religious belief is confined to between 12 and 30 per cent of the population.

If the function of a funeral is to consign souls to heaven, then atheists should have little interest in their final sendoff.

It is just the opposite.

The avowedly non-believing Communists of Russia have woven elaborate new trappings around the age-old ceremonies of death. Everything from the paperwork to the tombstone is bigger, fancier, and costlier nowadays. It is a poor and friendless atheist whose funeral does not rival that of a pre-revolutionary prince of Russian orthodoxy.

In fact, many of Communism's funeral rituals have been adapted, lock, stock, and coffin, from the ancient rites of the Russian church.

Death ceremonies for a non-believer last 40 days, as of old, and relatives often seek advice from pious old women on the proper way to conduct the funeral.

The funeral of a Moscow Communist usually begins with a formal lying-in-state in some public building where his body is displayed with elaborate somberness, in keeping with old custom.

All mirrors in the room are covered with black shrouds, and black and red bunting is draped throughout the room — black for tradition, red for Communism. The deceased, carefully combed and dressed, lies in a wooden coffin that is also covered with red and black cloth, and the bier is surrounded by piles of flowers and wreaths.

An orchestra may play, or recorded music may be piped in through speakers. The music almost invariably is the final movement from Tchaikovsky's 6th Symphony or the Tchaikovsky Funeral march.

In this atmosphere mourners walk past the coffin, some pausing to look, to weep, or to place a wreath. Later, the mourners gather in the hall to hear eulogies delivered in somber tones by friends and relatives. There is no priest, but the eulogists are expected to be gifted speakers able to produce ornate and poetical turns of phrase to embellish the virtues of the deceased.

The trip to the cemetery or crematorium is a bouncing, speedy affair in an ordinary passenger bus. The coffin, still open, is pushed through the back door while the mourners crowd around it in the seats.

Although most Communists choose to be cremated, the Russian Orthodox Church disapproves of the practice so many families cautiously choose burial. Just in case.

If burial is chosen, the coffin is placed by a freshly dug grave for the final eulogies. Then grieving relatives, following religious custom, kiss the feet and forehead of the corpse.

The lid is hammered down, and workmen using a pair of stout ropes lower the coffin into the grave and shovel earth upon it.

That, however, is not the end. Far from it. After the funeral, it is customary to go home for a meal of *kut'ya*, or rice pudding, pancakes, caviar, sour cream, and copious amounts of vodka drunk as toasts to the deceased. A place is set for him, with food and a glass of vodka, and it remains there untouched for the 40-day mourning period.

The feast, called *pominki,* is repeated on the ninth day after the funeral, again according to old religious custom, and a final *pominki* is held on the 40th day. Only then is the vodka and food — by now dried up — removed from the deceased's place.

There is still more to go. Families usually commission a tombstone to be built, and it is placed and dedicated in a ceremony held on the first anniversary of the death. The monuments can be incredibly elaborate, and sometimes they are grimly amusing.

In one Moscow cemetery the grave of a tank commander is topped by a large olive-drab scale model of a T-54 tank, its cannon pointing to the sky. Nearby lies a heart surgeon, remembered by a pair of granite hands grasping a heart made of translucent red glass.

The tombstone dedication usually ends the atheist's death rite. But in one famous case, the funeral has been going on for more than 50 years.

Vladimir I. Lenin, the founder of the Soviet Union, lies in perpetual state in Red Square. Every day, thousands of persons file past his body in its glass-cased bier in what must rank as the most remarkable funerary remembrance since the pyramids.

It is the only kind of immortality an atheist can have.

3

Russian Orthodox Church

At its accession to power, the Communist Party faced a formidable competitor in the church. The Russian Orthodox Church was a massive institution in 1917, exercising incalculable influence in nearly every area of society. It possessed a formidable corps of trained, experienced administrators and an apparatus of local churches which penetrated to the smallest hamlet of Russian society. The Party devoted itself to the task of destroying the influence of this vast institution, and within the brief span of sixty years the Russian Orthodox Church has been transformed into a relatively weak organization on the fringes of society, enjoying the support of only a minority of the population and at present, playing no discernable role in the decision-making processes of Soviet society. This was a truly remarkable transformation accomplished in an extremely brief period of time.

The Party, however, did supply pressure against the church, pressure which forced it into a different pattern. Through such means as large-scale arrests of clerics and believers, forcible closure of a great majority of the churches, and a seemingly limitless range of pressures, the Party stripped from the church all but its most intensely tenacious features. Out of the collapse of the old bureaucratic church a new approach to the Russian Orthodox religion emerged, one which had not been foreseen by the Bolsheviks.

The church, by concentrating on its liturgy, offers to the Soviet populace not only a cultural atmosphere which is mightily attractive, but in addition, offers that "softness of indulgence of human pity" which is so desperately lacking in much of Soviet society.

Together with this emphasis on the liturgy, the Church has undertaken a concerted attempt to increase the impact of its services through use of sermons. Sermons have become a widespread fixture in the Russian Orthodox service and great care is devoted to training clerics in using sermons to maximum effectiveness. Such sermons seem designed to attract the non-religious person, as well as to have maximum effectiveness among the believers. The result is that even if a non-believer visits the church out of casual curiosity, the church can hope to have considerable impact upon him through the medium of the liturgy and the sermon.

Baptism would seem to be one of the most pervasive of the Russian Orthodox ceremonies. When possible, Baptism is administered very soon after birth. In other cases, Baptism is administered much later and sometimes it is administered by laymen. There has even been some recent evidence of Baptism being applied by proxy. It would probably not be enough to consider this emphasis on the sacrament of Baptism to be a mere continuation of an orthodox practice; instead, it would almost seem as though during recent years there has been a revival of the sacrament.

Following World War II there was a considerable increase in the popularity of religious weddings, often at the request of parents. In fact, during the post-war period "it had become fashionable to be married in church."

The state was much concerned about this continuing practice of religious marriage, and late in the fifties resumed its earlier attempt to glamorize civil ceremonies. While on occasion these attempts enjoyed some success, in most cases the state ceremonies were woefully inadequate when compared with church weddings.

A similar index of the church's ability to influence society is found in religious holidays and festivals. Great effort in recent years has been expanded by the state on combatting these religious festivals. To date, however, there is little evidence that the state has enjoyed great success in most of its attempts in this regard.

The primary emphasis of the church during the Soviet period has been an identification with the people. According to one Russian bishop, "A Latin proverb says 'Vox populi — vox Dei.' The Russian Orthodox Church, adhering to this truth, was always one in spirit with the people."

Religious people have been observed praying and making the sign of the cross in public restaurants. A state farm was accused of supplying vehicles to transport believers to a church, while another changed its "free day" in order to please the believers.

From the identification of the church with the Russian people it is only a short step to identification of Russian Orthodoxy with the nation as a whole. The organic connection of the Orthodox Church with Russia's history, of course, goes far to make this identification of church and nation inevitable, and the state, in seeking to elicit an appreciation of Russia's national heritage, oftenhas unintentionally lent support to the church's attempts to identify with that history. The result is that identification of church and nation is still exceedingly strong in Russia, because of several major arguments: (1) Christianity is a major factor is social progress; (2) Socialism "is indebted" to Christianity for its best ideas and motivations; (3) the church is an essential "aid" in establishing communistic social relations; (4) labor is "pleasing to God;" (5) Christianity supports the peace movement; and (6) Christianity educated the people in intellectual, moral and spiritual capacities.

These views are reflected in society. Thus a letter to a newspaper claims that religion affirms beauty and harmony, while another equates religion with morality and fullness of life. In another instance, young believers caused considerable discomfort to members of a Young Communist group by the assertion that Christianity is not a passive approach to life, as examination of its saints and martyrs will demonstrate. To the suggestion that many of these stories may be myths, these young people could claim that nevertheless they exerted a powerful influence on society, just as fictional literary heroes do.

Perhaps the most meaningful attraction of Christianity is the answer it gives to those concerned with the meaning of life. It is the church which can provide an answer to the question of what there is to live for when youth is gone. Far from atypical is the case of Moscow university student who became an ardent believer after taking this question to a priest.

Late in 1965 the now famous Eshliman-Yakunin letters were composed. These were letters of protest signed by two Moscow priests, one addressed to Patriarch Aleksei protesting the failure of church authorities to resist encroachments by the Communists, and the other addressed to Podgorny, protesting the Soviet government's failure to abide by its own laws in its religious policy. These letters reached the West in the Spring of 1966, and almost concurrently with their publication in translation in the West, the Pariarchate placed the two priests under interdiction. The priests wrote a protest against this interdiction, claiming that it was contrary to Canon Law and church custom, and appealed that a Council be convened to judge their case. This appeal was followed by an Encyclical by Patriarch Aleksei denying their request and instructing all bishops to take stern measures against such protests within their dioceses.

The fact that such an encyclical was sent to all the bishops in the USSR, and that it was brought to the West not through underground channels (as had been the case heretofore) but by an official of the church, would suggest that the protest is very serious indeed. Such drastic measures would scarcely have been employed if the protests merely represented the dissatisfaction of two individual priests in Moscow. Such measures would be explicable only if the letters represent what amounts to a nation-wide movement of dissatisfaction with the current situation within the church. The existence and strength of a similar protest movement among the Russian Baptists, and these recent events within the Orthodox church make it probable that the Baptist experience may be paradigmatic.

It is not unlikely that this nascent protest movement will be of crucial importance for the continued activity of the Orthodox Church in the USSR. There is great danger that if the church has not yet attained sufficient flexibility to contain the movement, the net result may be a schism of great proportions.

Should the protest develop into a schismatic movement, not only would the result be a considerable weakening of the church as many of its most concerned members no longer would participate in its life, it would seem most unlikely that the dissidents themselves would be able to realize their full potential for exercising an influence on society. The discouraging history of earlier schismatic Orthodox movements such as the True Orthodox Church and the True Orthodox Christians demonstrates not only how small the impact of a movement is which, by withdrawing from the church in favor of a completely clandestine religious life, has severed all bonds with society, but also how successful the persistent application of police power can be in disrupting such movements entirely. Such an extreme form of protest is an ever-present temptation to a dissident movement, and there are disturbing indications that the current protest may succumb to the temptation.

Thus there is a real danger that the current Orthodox protest, if it develops into an illegal, schismatic movement, will scarcely be able to exercise more than a peripheral influence on society. If, however, the protest remains within the legalized church, it could be of profound significance.

The letter to Podgorny was careful to remain within the bounds of legitimate criticism. Beginning its address "as citizens of the Soviet Union," the letter is a carefully and thoughtfully worked out analysis which at no point questions the legitimacy of Soviet laws on religion nor attacks the basic design of socialism in the country, and it concludes,

On the basis of the above, we earnestly request you to take effective measures for the earliest possible uprooting of illegality and the reestablishment of the legal rights of the millions of believing citizens of the Soviet Union.

Provided the movement can continue to maintain a position of loyalty to the laws and statures of society in its demands, avoiding that extreme rejection of the Soviet state as "antichrist", which so often accompanies an underground Christian movement, there is no reason why the discussions could not remain within the body of the legal Russian Orthodox Church constituting a vigorous and dedicated minority devoted to the renewal of the vitality of the church.

By remaining within the church, the dissidents would then be able to stimulate widespread discussion within the Orthodox community. Unlike the Baptist dissident movement, whose protests to date seem to have been confined to an emotional, almost visceral reaction to an unbearable situation, the Orthodox, both historically and at present, have a demonstrated ability to go on from the immediate problem to a thoughtful, philosophical analysis of the deeper issues involved. The current protests raise far-reaching questions about the nature of faith in a secular world, the kind of freedom to which the church can aspire in a technological, socialistic society, and, indeed, the relation of religion to the ultimate issues of life.

As is apparent from the discussions of the ferment within the intelligentsia, it is precisely such questions which exercise the educated, articulate youth of the country today. Provided that the current protests can continue to remain within the Orthodox Church so that they may stimulate such deeper analysis of the problems involved, there is every likelihood that such thinking would strike a responsive note within the intelligentsia, and a broad alliance between them and the Orthodox might rapidly develop.

The church asserted some independence and even predominance over weak Czars during the seventeenth century, but Peter the Great brought it under the control of a department of state, a position of dependence from which it never escaped.

Moscow's inheritance of the Byzantine tradition in its widest form has largely determined the Russian political consciousness up to our time. It is not only that the church did not and could not restrain the excesses of the Czars; it did not generally feel any obligation to do so. Thus, there never arose the notion that the political conscience of the citizen should, under law, put a limit on that of the autocrat. Those who for conscientious reasons objected to either Church or State government had no separate organization from which to promote reform. They were compelled to retreat into sectarianism — a sort of internal emigration involving the rejection of all established authority rather than any attempt to reform it.

This question of keeping the church in being and what price should be paid to keep it in being arises just as acutely in Soviet Russia. The Concordat which Stalin reached with the Russian Orthodox Church in 1943 was, at any rate symbolically, an event of greater importance than that of Napoleon or

Mussolini or Hitler. For he alone of these dictators was openly and avowedly a militant atheist, dedicated to the destruction of religion in his country. His training in an Orthodox seminary in Tiflis had made him, like so many other seminarists from the French Revolution onwards, a fanatical enemy of the Church. His accession to the supreme power in 1928 heralded an intensification of the Communist anti-religious drive which coincided with the great collectivization, religion being seen as the ideological superstructure of the peasantry. Religious persecution reached new heights at this time, and the anti-religious organization, the League of the Militant Godless, attained its peak membership of over five million. But when the census of 1937 was taken it was reliably reported that some 50 million people registered themselves as believers. As a result the census figures were not published; the census officials were arrested; both the Church and the League of the Militant Godless suffered mass arrests and deportations during the great purges. Anti-religious propaganda was again intensified, particularly in the newly occupied territories from the Baltic to the Black Sea, right up to the time of the German invasion.

Then when it became necessary to mobilize all patriotic forces for the Great Fatherland War, the League of the Militant Godless was disbanded, its journal was suppressed, and the support of the Orthodox Church with its mass following and great national tradition was enlisted for the war effort. The Concordat of 1943 was the reward for the Church's patriotic efforts. The Church was recognized as the principal religious body of the USSR and allowed to elect its own Patriarch, to have its own ecclesiastical government, the Holy Synod, to publish its own journal, to have a legal right to its own property, and to take over the schismatic church hitherto favored by the Communists.

Stalin and his successors have been able to gain certain advantages from their limited toleration of the Church; but, by any standards, the faithful have got the better of the bargain. For the existence of some form of organized religion has been one of the main obstacles to that complete tyranny over the minds of men which Stalin sought by every means to establish. Their freedom may seem small enough by the standards of the non-Communist world. They can celebrate their liturgy; that is all. The missionary, teaching and social activities, which are the normal rights of religious bodies elsewhere, are forbidden. Under Khrushchev, who seems to have had strong personal feelings on the subject, hundreds of churches were closed down; monks, pilgrims and church congregations were subjected to arbitrary police interference and hooliganism. Under Khrushchev's successors there was less arbitrary persecution, but the regulations against any religious activity apart from the church services were tightened up. There are, however, limits to government pressure. Already in 1966 two priests wrote to both Church and government authorities, complaining of the subservience of the hierarchy to atheist pressure and their betrayal of the faith. It is a feeling that is fairly widespread among believers, and if, as a result of persecution, it were to grow, there would probably be a schism and a formidable increase in underground religious opposition. Already the Baptists have split into official and unofficial bodies, the latter accusing the former of selling out to the Communist authorities. Hundreds of the schismatic Baptists have been arrested. The regime has reason to fear a growth of such activity since Russia is traditionally the land of fanatical sects; and even totalitarian police measures have not been able to suppress them. The area on the Ukrainian-Moldavian border, for example has ever since the war been particularly fruitful of millennial sects which regard Communism as anti-Christ. Recently, according to the local press, one of these sectaries issued a warning that the end of the world was a at hand and that only those who retired with him into the caves would be saved. No less than 5,000 people followed him and stayed in the caves for some weeks until removed by the police. A regime which cannot prevent such an extraordinary demonstration as that cannot afford to drive more reasonable believers into a mood of desperate defiance.

In the spring of 1944 Stalin made a queer attempt at reconciliation with the Pope, an attempt with which a truly farcical episode was connected. On April 28, 1944 he received in the Kremlin a strange visitor, an American Roman Catholic priest of Polish descent, the Reverend S. Orlemanski from Springfield,Massachusetts. The priest, a simple devout soul, unaware of the pitfalls of high politics, had left his quiet parish and come to Moscow with a sense of a mission to perform. He was out to make a personal contribution to two "historic" reconciliations, one between the Kremlin and the Vatican, the other between Russia and Poland. For a few days the good man was in the limelight. To everybody's amazement, Stalin not only received him, but was twice closeted with him for long hours. Orlemanski, whom no authority in his Church had empowered to parley on its behalf and who had even left his parish without his bishop's permission, obtained from Stalin a solemn written declaration, signed in Stalin's own hand, in which he, the master of the Kremlin, offered collaboration to the master of the Vatican. What use should be made of the offer he left to Orlemanski's discretion; and Orlemanski, with the momentous document in hand, returned to his parish. There his bishop pounced upon him, charging him with a breach of ecclesiastical discipline and threatening excommunication. The hapless priest suffered a nervous breakdown and removed himself to a cloister to do penance for his vagaries. Thus, the great attempt at reconciliation between the Kremlin and the Vatican came to an end. The incident was, nevertheless, characteristic of the opportunistically rightist coloring of Stalin's policy in those days.

In recent years he had been very gratified at being mentioned in the church's prayers as the "Leader Elect of God", and this was why he had maintained the cathedral and monastery at Zagorsk from Kremlin funds. . . .

He had also ordained that Soviet people, like all Christian folk, should have their day of rest on Sunday and not on any odd day of the week; he had even re-introduced the sanctity of legal marriage, as under the Tsar, although in his time he had suffered under this. Who cared what Engels had to say on this subject?

It was true that moral standards had declined, particularly among the younger generation, and that people were losing their sense of values.

In the old days people had leaned on the Church and the priests for moral guidance. And even nowadays, what Polish peasant woman would take any serious step in life without consulting her priest?

It could be that the country now needed firm moral foundations, even more urgently that the Volga-Don Canal or the great new dam on the Angara River.

Some Marxists, reflecting on historical experience and on the behavior of Christians, have questioned the summary criticism of religion, which had been for a long time an accepted and authoritative doctrine in their official manuals. On the other hand, the Church of silence does not belong only to the past, and the violations of religious freedom, as well as vexations and abuses, have not ceased.

Although the Soviet press seldom writes about the closing of churches, they continue to be closed down, and apparently the process has slowed down. The reticence of the Soviet press to mention such events may be due in part to the unfavorable publicity and possible protest in the West.

The journal *Nauka i religiya* describes for its readers, most of whom are atheists and propagandists, under just what circumstances churches may be closed down.

The journal *Nauka i religiya* describes for its readers, most of whom are atheists and propagandists, under just what circumstances churches may be closed down.

> First of all, this may be done when there are not enough believers who wish to support and sustain their church; in other words, when the religious society has dissolved and the authorities have taken away its registration. The religious group may be relieved of its registration, or the house of worship may be closed for other reasons; for instance: for violations of Soviet laws concerning sects, failure to observe contract terms under which the church building was leased to the believers and for refusal to adhere to the legal orders of state organs. Secondly, the congregation's building may be closed if it is to be torn down to allow for the reconstruction of dwellings or if it is a dilapidated building. Thirdly, if the necessity arises for converting the house of worship to state or public use.

The journal concedes that the believers have the right to receive compensation for the closed church in the form of another building or location.

> These premises may be presented to them by private individuals or by executive committees of rayons and city soviets. In individual cases the construction of a new house of worship through the efforts and means of the believers will be allowed at the request of the religious society and with the permission of the appropriate Council for Russian Orthodox Church Affairs of the USSR Council of Ministers or of the Council for the Affairs of Religious Cults of the USSR Council of Ministers.

Local authorities do not have the power officially to close churches. Only the Council of Ministers of the appropriate autonomous republic and kray, oblast and city (Moscow and Leningrad) *ispolkoms* "by agreement with the corresponding Council for Russian Orthodox Church Affairs or Council for the Affairs of Religious Cults" have this right.

Local authorities, then, may only "initiate a petition" for the consideration of the above-mentioned organs.

1. Institute figure for church closures 1960-1962, based on Soviet press survey, about 2,000. Other reports (tourist conversations with clerics, etc.) go as high as 5,000. Latter figure used in emigre press. *Reuters* reports that in 1961, 1,500 churches were closed.

2. Churches functioning in 1961 listed as 20,000 by Moscow Patriarchate. *Nauka i religiya* reports 77,727 Orthodox religious establishments of all descriptions in 1916, "Somewhat more than 4,000" in 1941; 15,000 in 1941-48, and "from this time scarcely any churches were opened." *Nauka i religiya*

says, "In recent times now a few churches and prayer houses have been closed." Institute estimates that no more than 10,000 churches are open today in USSR.

3. XXII CPUSSR Congress stresses ". . . the necessity of re-education of those who find themselves in the captivity of anti-scientific religious ideology. . . ." ". . . the religious point of view must receive in our socialist conditions the most decisive rebuff. Attacks against it cannot be weakened." Trend: 1,500 churches closed in 1961.

4. Churches closed in certain areas include:

> *Grodenskaya Oblast:* 40 closed since 1948.
> *Brestskaya Oblast:* 108 closed in 1960-61.
> *Odesskaya Oblast:* 68 church communities and 75 churches closed in 1961.
> *Dnepropetrovskaya Oblast:* Of 180 parishes existing in 1958, 40 existed in 1962.
> *Volynskaya Oblast:* 180 churches closed "in the last few years."
> *Cherkaskaya Oblast:* 40 different religious groups and parishes closed in 1959 and beginning of 1960.

Moldavian SSR:

> *Kotovsky Rayon:* 15 churches closed.
> *Lipkansky Rayon:* 18 churches closed.

Protests by believers against such treatment are only known to have succeeded on one occasion — after a Catholic Church in Byelorussia had been turned into a grainstore. According to the *Chronicle of Current Events,* local peasants said "they could not live without the church" and refused to work for several days or to send their children to school. Eventually the chairman of the collective concerned ordered the removal of the grain. The church was repaired and the ritual date restored.

Before World War I the Russian Orthodox Church had in Russia, not including the Warsaw eparchy, 98,363,974 adherents, 72 eparchies, 77,767 churches, and 1,025 monasteries. There were 50,105 parish priests, not including army and navy chaplains, missionaries, law professors, and unregistered priests, and 94,629 monks. Church institutions included 61 religious seminaries and academies, 185 religious training schools, 37,528 parochial secondary schools, 2,171 primary schools, and 403 monastery hospitals and almshouses.

At the very beginning of the Bolshevik revolution, a campaign was inaugurated against religion, particularly aimed at destroying the Russian Orthodox Church as "the last remnant of the political organization of the vanquished classes."

During the years of collectivization and the Yezhov Purge the Soviet regime did its utmost to complete the liquidation of the "harbingers of bourgeois ideology" and "counter-revolutionaries in the country." The extent of the persecution became known to some extent following the purge, although complete lists of the martyred clergy will become known only when the Soviet archives are available, and probably not completely even then. Of 260 bishops in the Tikhon Church and 27 Revived Church bishops, by the end of 1939 only four remained and, according to propaganda reports published by the Soviet Information Bureau in London, in place of the 77,767 Orthodox churches in 1914, the total in the USSR in 1948 was only 4,225. The number of clergy had undoubtedly fallen off in proportion.

During and after the First World War, the Orthodox community in the USSR was given back several churches that had previously been seized from it. The struggle against religion in the Soviet Union has, generally speaking, not ceased for the past 60 years. Nevertheless it is possible to identify particular moments in Soviet history when the Church has succeeded somewhat in strengthening its position. After the so-called reunification of the western oblasts with the USSR (Bukovina, Galicia, Western Byelorussia, Moldavia, Zakarpat'e), several thousand churches and a number of monasteries came under the jurisdiction of the Moscow Patriarchate. Some of them had already been Orthodox before; others, like the Greek-Catholic (Uniate) monasteries and churches, were united with the Russian Orthodox Church "at the request of the people."

In the beginning, all the Orthodox churches and monasteries situated in predominantly Greek-Catholic oblasts had almost complete freedom of action. But this was a customary political gesture of the regime, directed, on the one hand, at demonstrating to new citizens of the USSR that they "enjoy complete freedom of religion" and, on the other, at furthering the "reunification" of the Greek-Catholic and Orthodox Churches with the help of the Orthodox clergy.

In the end, this policy did not succeed, and a new faith was forcibly imposed upon the Uniates. After the Orthodox Church had strengthened its position in the Ukraine, Moldavia, and Byelorussia, the authorities once again intensified their struggle against the Church. This struggle was carried out not only in the western but also in the central oblasts of the USSR. (It may be assumed that the 21st Congress of the CPSU in 1959 sanctioned this fresh attack on the Church).

From data published in the Soviet press in the period from 1959 to 1961, it emerges that 684 churches were closed in eight dioceses. The Synod of the Orthodox Church Outside Russia reported that 1,500 churches in the USSR were closed in 1961 alone. But if one takes into account the fact that at this time there were not eight but eighty-three dioceses in the USSR, then it is quite possible that many more churches suffered.

According to the *New York Times,* when the Moscow Patriarchate requested that the Russian Orthodox Church in the USSR be admitted to the World Council of Churches, the following facts were quoted in the application:

Number of Russian Orthodox dioceses	73
Number of Russian Orthodox priests	30,000
Number of Russian Orthodox parishes	20,000
Number of Russian Orthodox monasteries	40

Information on the state of the Orthodox Church in the USSR published in the encycolopedia *Der Grosse Herder* gives quite a different picture:

Number of Russian Orthodox dioceses	83
Number of Russian Orthodox priests	40,000
Number of Russian Orthodox parishes	22,000
Number of Russian Orthodox monasteries	90

The discrepancy may be explained by the fact that the encyclopedia's information was gathered in 1958 — i.e., on the very eve of the great offensive against the Church.

In January 1976, the newspaper *Izvestia* published an interview with the president of the Council for Religious Affairs under the USSR Council of

Ministers, Vladimir Alekseevich Kuroedov. Repeating that citizens of the
Soviet Union enjoy freedom of religion, as guaranteed under the basic law
by the Constitution of the USSR, Kuroedov stated among other things:

> More than 20,000 Orthodox churches, Roman Catholic churches, synagogues,
> Lutheran churches, churches of the Old Believers, mosques, Buddhist tem-
> ples, prayer houses of the Evangelical Baptists, Seventh Day Adventists, etc.,
> and about twenty monasteries and convents are active in the USSR.

Thus it may be concluded that while in 1961 there were 20,000 purely
Orthodox churches in the USSR (according to the figures of the Patriarchate
cited by the *New York Times*), the same number of churches in 1976 is said to
include Roman Catholic churches, Synagogues, Baptist prayer houses, mosques, and so on, as well as Orthodox churches. How many Orthodox
churches then still remain in the USSR? Kuroedov is silent on this point. One
thing is clear: in recent years they have become considerably fewer in
number.

In reference to monasticism in the Soviet Union Michael Bourdeaux
writes:

> Before the revolution of 1917, there was perhaps no country in Europe where
> monasticism was still as popular and revered as it was in Russia. Every year
> thousands of people took to the roads on pilgrimages to the various ancient
> monastic centers — the Cave Monastery in Kiev, the Trinity-St. Sergius Monas-
> tery at Zagorsk, and the northern island monastery of Solovki, all of which had
> hundreds of monks. In 1917, there were 1,025 Orthodox monasteries and
> convents on the territory of the Russian Empire. By 1920, when the Soviet
> government had been in power for three years, and was already zealously
> carrying out a policy of official atheism, the number of monasteries and
> convents had been reduced to 352. During the next forty years, 283 monastic
> communities were dissolved, mostly by forcible means; the monastery build-
> ings were turned into museums or concert halls, or were simply left as ruins,
> and the monks and nuns were driven away or imprisoned. The monastery
> island of Solovki was turned into a detailed account of this process in the second
> volume of *Gulag Archipelago*. Almost all the monasteries were closed by 1939,
> but some were later reopened.

> In 1958, after Stalin had been dead for five years, there were still 69 Orthodox
> monasteries and convents in the Soviet Union according to official figures.
> This was a small number for a country of 250 million people. Yugoslavia, by
> contrast, has 68 monasteries and 84 convents; Rumania has 95 monastic
> communities; and both these are much smaller countries. However, after the
> anti-religious campaign of the 1960s, the number of monasteries was again
> drastically reduced, as were the numbers of churches and theological colleges.

> Today there are six to ten Christian monasteries, two Buddhist monasteries,
> and ten to fifteen convents left in the Soviet Union. The Christian monasteries
> are all Orthodox; there are no official Catholic monasteries or convents in the
> U.S.S.R., although there are over four million Catholics. However, it is thought
> that there may be secret monastic communities — both Orthodox and
> Catholic. The numbers of these are unknown, but they are mentioned in the
> *Chronicles of the Lithuanian Catholic Church* where secret 'nuns' are said to have
> been dismissed from their jobs.

> The government campaign in the 1960s against the monasteries was one of the
> most brutal and vicious chapters in the entire anti-religious "struggle" of those
> years. Monks and nuns were subjected, in the Soviet press, to open libel of the
> most shameless kind. It was asserted that "in St. Cyprian's Monastery ten
> monks were suffering from veneral diseases" that "in pools near convents, in

wells and toilets, the bodies of new-born babies have been found, begotten by the 'holy fathers' on the 'brides of Christ;' "and that in the Tsyganesti monastery (Moldavia) one of the monks had raped another monk's daughter. "Open money-grabbing and theft, parasitism and vagrancy, synical egotism and unconcealed debauchery: these are what characterize the life of the 'holy monks,' who preach love for one's neighbor, cleanliness, and sinlessness."

Most of the closures of monasteries in recent years have been carried out with brute force, in the face of fierce opposition from believers. One of the worst deliberate affronts to the feelings of religious believers was the closure of the Kiev Cave Monastery, which was visited by 100,000 pilgrims yearly. Its monks (about 100) were evicted forcibly in 1960, and it was made into a museum. Another ancient monastery closed at this time was Optina Pustyn, Dostoevsky's model for the monastery in *The Brothers Karamazoo*, which has now been made into a training school for mechanics.

The closure of convents, especially, was described by the Soviet press as the "liberation" of its inmates, who had been "forced" to pray, read religious books, and confess their sins. Now they, too, can read Soviet books, join the Komsomol, and work on collective farms. One hundred and two former nuns from the Rechulsk Convent are now working on the Frunze collective farm, 35 nuns from the Varzareshtsk Convent also work on a collective farm, and the 104 former nuns of Tabor Monastery have been put to work in a carpet-making factory. The former abbess, Mother Tavifa, is said to have run away with "the convent funds."

As the Soviet law on religion contains no specific clauses referring to monasticism, no legal subterfuge is necessary to disband them: monasteries are thus completely at the mercy of the Soviet government. Those that remain are kept in existence only by the devotion of the Orthodox faithful and the support of public opinion abroad.

This was demonstrated in the case of the Pochaev Monastery of the Assumption, which almost met the same fate as the Kiev Cave Monastery. In 1959, several of the monastery buildings were taken over by the authorities and turned into clubs and clinics. A hostel for pilgrims was closed. Then, in the early 1960s, many of the 142 monks, including the abbot, were arrested on various charges and imprisoned in other provinces; and after they had served their terms of imprisonment they were refused residence permits in the Pochaev area. Other monks were committed to mental hospitals. By 1962, only 36 monks remained, although these continued to hold services for the thousands of pilgrims who continued to visit the monastery. Between 1962 and 1966, the local KGB carried out a campaign of terror and assault against the remaining monks and those who had returned and were living 'illegally' in the district.

A particular target for such assaults was the pilgrims and especially the so-called *chernichki* — women who were not officially nuns, but led a monastic form of life in the outside world. Such unofficial nuns were often to be found among the pilgrims and were singled out by the KGB for brutal treatment; many were beaten and raped.

However, the Pochaev Monastery achieved a great deal of publicity abroad; a long document written by the Spiritual Council of Pochaev Monastery was published by the *samizdat* journal *Phoenix 66*, edited by Yurii Galanskov. This document described the events at the monastery, and was widely published in the West. It was perhaps due to this publicity that the Soviet authorities decided to keep the monastery open. Accounts of church feast days there, attended by many clergymen and worshippers, were ostentatiously published in the *Journal of the Moscow Patriarchate*. However, many of the monks who were deported to other provinces have not been allowed to return. In August 1967, for example, two monks wrote to the Patriarch of Constantinople, asking him to accept them in a monastery on Mount Athos, as they were not being allowed to return to Pochaev nor to enter any other monastery.

The showplace of Russian monasticism is, of course, the Trinity-St. Sergius Monastery at Zagorsk. This is the center of Orthodox Church life and is a tourist attraction; it includes the largest of three Orthodox seminaries in the USSR. There is a constant stream of novices from the seminary, and it is from these that the future Orthodox hierarchy will come, as all Orthodox bishops must be monks. (Married clergymen remain as parish priests.) There are about 90 monks here at present, half of them ordained priests. Monastic life here is, in a sense, privileged: apart from the limitation placed by the authorities on the number of novices, there is little interference here with the daily rituals of monasticism — indeed, services and prayers are almost all performed in public, with huge crowds of believers in attendance.

The Uspensky Monastery, in Odessa, is the official summer residence of the Patriarch, and as such is also somewhat select and privileged; it is more secluded from the outside world than other monasteries, but has very strong links with the Odessa Seminary.

The Pskov Cave Monastery, which now has about 60 monks, is one of Russia's largest monasteries. About 30,000 pilgrims visit the Pskov Monastery on church feast days. It is 500 years old; there are cave-churches and catacombs beneath the buildings where many of the monks are buried. It is famous for preserving the structure and discipline of prerevolutionary monasteries. After the war, the abbot was tried for collaborating with the Germans, and recent official propaganda has accused all the monks of being traitors to the Soviet regime. Anatolii Levitin has written an article on the Pskov Monastery in which he gives biographical details of the monks. The late abbot, Archimandrite Alipi, was a laborer on building sites, and a soldier during the war, before becoming a monk. He believes in hard work for everyone and has no interest in intellectual argument. He is a real Russian and very close to the people. It would be impossible to imagine anyone with a greater understanding of their life. The other monks include a former railwayman, a collective farm worker, a shoemaker, and a goods manager; all these are former soldiers. "They have not come here to rest," says Levitin, "but to live in a manner pleasing to God."

The Zhirovitsy Uspensky Monastery, in the district of Minsk, has been subjected to many attacks by the authorities, but it is apparently still functioning. Archbishop Ermogen of Kaluga was confined there after his enforced retirement and is still there, as far as is known. The monastery buildings are also being used by nuns, who were transferred there after the closure of the Grodno and Polotsk Convents. This is against strict monastic rules, but the authorities refuse to give the nuns a separate building. The local regional executive committee, led by the chairman, S. T. Kobyak, has been trying to confiscate monastery bells, buildings, and kitchen gardens. Local parishioners and pilgrims appealed to them to leave the monastery alone, but they replied: "We're Communists — we'll do whatever we like."

Another Russian Orthodox monastery at which the monks are obliged to share space with a community of nuns is the Holy Ghost Monastery in Vilnius, Lithuania. The existence of two Orthodox monastic communities in an almost completely Catholic country, incidentally, is somewhat ironic, since no Catholic monasteries are allowed there.

The Zhirovitsy community of nuns is the only female monastic community on Russian soil (Belorussia). The other Orthodox convents are all in non-Russian areas of the Soviet Union. There is one convent in each of the Baltic countries, Latvia, Lithuania, and Estonia; there is one in Moldavia; and there are six in the Ukraine.

The Uspensky Convent in Estonia is at Pyukhtitsa, which means "Holy Mountain" in Estonian; the Mother of God was said to have appeared there to some Estonian shepherds. There are 150 nuns, including lay sisters. They live in cells and work on the neighboring state farm. There are a number of churches and chapels in the convent grounds. The Mother Superior is Abbess Varvara Trofimova, who entered the convent in 1952.

The Trinity-St. Sergius Convent in Riga, Latvia, also contains a number of churches and chapels. The abbess is Mother Zinaida Baranova. This convent contains a skete, or "pustyn," the so-called Wilderness of the Transfiguration. (A "pustyn" is an isolated cloister within a monastic community, and it has a small number of inmates and practices a stricter, more ascetic way of life than the monastic community as a whole).

The largest of the convents in the Ukraine, and indeed, in the USSR as a whole, is the Pokrovsky Convent in Kiev, which has 200-250 nuns. Hundreds of women wanting to enter the nunnery as novices were on the convent's waiting list at one time, but since 1960 the authorities have allowed hardly any novices to be accepted, and have reduced the number of nuns in the convent by transferring some of them to Orthodox convents in Israel. The Mother Superior is Mother Elikonida. The convent is famous for its icon-painting workshop. There is also a second, smaller convent in Kiev — the Florovsky Convent, which contains the ancient Ascension Cathedral. The abbess is Reverend Mother Agnesa.

The Rozhdestvensky Convent in Odessa diocese, near the village of Aleksandrovka, was founded in 1924 as a monastery, and was reorganized as a convent in 1934. It is remarkable for being the only officially functioning convent founded since the Soviet regime was established. The present Mother Superior, the Abbess Alevtina, was one of the first novices. The church was renovated in 1969, and was visited by the Patriarch in 1971. There are over 40 nuns; they work in a nearby collective farm as well as participate in convent services. There is purposely no electric light in the churches, so that prayers may be held by candlelight. The nuns are of five different nationalities — Russian, Ukrainian, Moldavian, Gagauz, and Bulgarian — and services are held in Church Slavonic, Moldavian, and Gagauz. The number of nationalities is probably due to the fact that some of the nuns have been transferred from convents closed in Moldavia. The only monastic community left in Moldavia is the Zhabsky Convent on the right bank of the River Dniester, of which very little except the name of the convent is known. The same is true of the Pokrovsky Convent at Krasnogorsk in the Cherkassy district; all that is known is that the abbess there is Reverend Mother Ilariya.

The Convent of St. Nicholas in Mukachevo, in the Carpathian foothills, was renovated in 1970. The abbess is Reverend Mother Afanasiya. There are 120 nuns. The former abbess, Reverend Mother Paraskeva, died in 1967 and is still famous for the testament she left behind her, which was read at her funeral service: "I can no longer speak to you with my lips and voice, as before, because I no longer have breath or voice. But I speak to you with this poor letter. The temple of my body has been destroyed and given to the earth according to the word of the Lord: 'Dust thou art and to dust thou shalt return.' But I look for the resurrection of the dead and I hope to inherit the age to come. My hope and salvation is Jesus Christ, my Lord and God. I have gone away from you on a long road, and I am walking along a road unknown to me. . . . But the time of Christ's second coming is approaching. . . . May God grant that we shall meet then."

The Trinity Convent in Korets, in the Volyn district, has two choirs which are renowned for their singing. The abbess is Reverend Mother Natalya. The nuns divide their activities between church work (making liturgical vestments) and working on the land on a neighboring collective farm.

Other monastic communities in the USSR are in Georgia and Armenia. There are four Armenian Gregorian monasteries at Gegard, Gayane, Hripsime, and Echmiadzia. The Georgian Orthodox Church has no monasteries, but it does have four convents. One of these, at Mtskheta, has only eleven nuns and no novices. There is also a seminary at Mtskheta.

The two Buddhist monasteries in the Soviet Union are the Ivolginsky Monastery, with thirty monks, near Ulan Ude, and the Aginsky Monastery, with twenty monks, near Chita. Neither community is allowed to accept novices, but Soviet Buddhists have reportedly been applying as novices to the Mongolian Buddhist monastery at Ulan Bator.

These monastic communities, which still survive despite the persecutions and vilifications directed against them by an atheist state, are still in danger. Monasticism is not countenanced as an institution by the Soviet authorities, and those wishing to become monks or nuns attract the full wrath of the state. Anatolii Levitin admits that a great many Soviet people find the idea of monasticism abhorrent: "I wrote the word 'monasticism' and shuddered involuntarily, thinking what an anachronism it sounds in the ears of the man in the street — 'Monasticism? That's something horrible. When did it arise and when did it die out?' Any average person today would ask this question."

In such circumstances, when the wish to become a monk brings such unpleasantness and persecution in its wake, why should any Soviet citizen still want to join a monastic community? In "Monasticism and the Modern World," Anatolii Levitin recalls that it was always difficult for those who entered monasteries to leave the world. St. Alexii, the man of God, left his family and young wife to enter a monastery, despite his father's entreaties and those of his family. Levitin compares this fervor to that of the nineteenth-century revolutionaries who sacrificed their family life for their ideals. The monk is called to be a light to the world by his exemplary life; this is the social role of monasticism. "Restraint and purity demonstrate to the profligate that debauchery is not a norm, but an abnormality, renunciation and voluntary poverty teach scorn of riches; self-denial is the best weapon against egotism. Thus monasticism is a healthy weapon against selfishness, banality, and uncleanliness. Naturally, however, the role of monasticism is not exhausted by this. For monasticism is a holy mystery." By "a holy mystery" Levitin means a miracle, which demands active participation on the part of man through faith; by this miracle human nature becomes superhuman and angelic. This is why monks are called "soldiers of Christ." "We firmly believe," says Levitin, "in the coming of a new wave of monasticism in the Russian Church. The future of Russia is with the ardent and zealous young people of our country who, despite opposition, are every day attaining to the faith. New monks will come from among them — zealous warriors for Christ's cause. They will transform the Church of Christ and the land of Russia."

The question is how many Orthodox monasteries have been closed over the last 30 years and how many monasteries are still active in the USSR. Official spokesmen for the Soviet authorities and for the Moscow Patriarchate have frequently stated that nobody in the USSR has closed churches and monasteries and that they continue to carry out their functions. In June 1965, for instance, Archbishop Aleksei (now Metropolitan Aleksei Rediger of Tallin and Estonia) gave an interview to a *Tass* correspondent about the press conference of Archbishop Antonii Bartashevich of Geneva (Orthodox Church Outside Russia) on the subject of the persecution of believers in the USSR, including the treatment of the Pochaev and other monasteries. Aleksei said that:

> It is not the first time that Archbishop Antonii has tried to mislead public opinion. However, whatever he may say, Pochaev monastery, one of the ancient Russian Orthodox monasteries, like our other monasteries, continues to live in complete concord with its rules and traditions.

Today, as at that time, these people continue to affirm that monasteries have not been closed and that nobody is persecuting their inmates.

According to the encyclopedia *Der Grosse Herder* in 1958, ninety monasteries were functioning in the USSR; but in 1961 there were 40. Now, however — in 1976 — Kuroedov cites the estimate: "about 20." What colloquial has happened to the other 70 that were mentioned just 18 years ago? They could not have simply disappeared. After all, the official organ of the Orthodox Church, *The Journal of the Moscow Patriarchate*, has so far not made any mention of the fact that certain monasteries have ceased to function.

On the basis of reports published in *The Journal of the Moscow Patriarchate*, commencing in 1948, it has been possible to compile a list of monasteries that were still functioning in the USSR after the Second World War and that were in the main closed between 1959 and 1961. This information is set forth below, preceded by a list of monasteries known to be functioning currently in the USSR.

Altogether there are 17 monasteries and convents left at present in the USSR. Of these nine are in the Ukraine, two in RSFSR, two in Latvia, and one each in Byelorussia, Lithuania, Moldavia, and Estonia.

1. The Monastery of the Holy Spirit, Vilnius.
2. The Zhabsky Convent of the Ascension (Diocese of Kishenev in Moldavia).
3. The Monastery of the Assumption, Zhirovitsy (Diocese of Minsk).
4. The Florovsky Convent of Ascension, Kiev.
5. The Pokrovsky Convent, Kiev.
6. The Trinity Convent, Korets (Volynsko-Rovensky Diocese).
7. The Convent of St. Nikolai, Mukachevo (Zakarpatsky Diocese).
8. The Pskov Monastery of the Caves.
9. The Monastery of the Assumption, Odessa.
10. The Rozhdestvensky Convent (Diocese of Odessa).
11. The Pochaev Monastery of the Assumption.
12. The Convent of the Assumption, Puhtitsa (Diocese in Estonia).
13. The Trinity-St. Sergius Convent, Riga.
14. The Pustyn Wilderness of the Transfiguration (under Convent of Riga).
15. The Trinity Monastery of St. Sergius, Zagorsk (Diocese of Moscow).
16. The Chumalevsky Convent of the Ascension (Zakarpatsky Diocese).
17. The Pokrovsky Convent, Kransnogorsk (Diocese of Cherkassy).

Up to 1959, there were fifteen monasteries in Moldavia, of which only one, the Zhabsky Convent of the Ascension, is still functioning. It has been possible to determine the names of nine of the monasteries that have been closed.

1. The Varzareshtsky Convent.
2. The Girzhavsky Monastery.
3. The Gerbovetsky Monastery of the Assumption.
4. The St. Cyprian Monastery (closed in 1961).
5. The Kitskansky or Novo-Nyametsky Monastery (70 km. from Kishinev).
6. The Rechulsky Convent.
7. The Tsyganeshtsky Monastery (closed in 1961).
8. The Khirovsky Convent.
9. The Frumoasky Monastery.

Up to 1959, there were 20 monasteries in Zakarpate (Mukachevo-Uzhgorodsky Diocese). Of these only two are still functioning, the Mukachevsky and Chumalevsky Monasteries. It has been possible to determine the names of six of the monasteries that have been closed.

1. The Bedevlyansky Monastery.
2. The Domboksky Convent.
3. The St. Dmitry, Monastery, Dubovsky.
4. The St. Nikolai Monastery, Izsky.
5. The Lipshansky Convent.
6. The Monastery of the Transfiguration, Tereblya.

Monasteries closed in various dioceses in the USSR.

1. Convent of St. Vasily, Ovruch (Zhitomir Diocese).
2. The Kiev Monastery of the Caves.
3. Ioanno-Bogoslovsky Monastery, Kreshchatinsk (Chernovitsky Diocese, closed in 1959).
4. The Monastery Kozatskie Mogily (Volynsky Diocese, closed in 1959).
5. The Mikhailovsky Monastery, Kiev.
6. The Vvedensky Convent (Diocese of Odessa).
7. The Vydubetsky Monastery (Diocese of Kiev).
8. The Vvedensky Monastery (Diocese of Chernovits).
9. The Trinity Convent (Chernigovsky and Nezhinsky Diocese).
10. The St. Mikhail Convent, Aleksandrovka (Diocese of Odessa).
11. The Monastery of the Ascension (Irkutsky and Chitinsky Diocese).
12. The Pavlo-Obnorsky Monastery (Vologodsky Diocese).
13. The Zosimovsky Pustyn (Formerly part of the Trinity Monastery of St. Sergius at Zagorsk).
14. The Glinsky Pustyn (Diocese of Kursk, closed in 1961).
15. The Kresto-Vozdvizhensky Convent, Poltava (closed in 1961).
16. The Lebedinsky Convent (diocese of Cherkassy).
17. The Brailovsky Convent (Diocese of Vinnitsa).
18. The Vilensky Novosvetsky Convent (closed in 1960).
19. The convent in the Town of Bar. (Dioceses of Vinnitsa).
20. The Kremenetsky Convent.
21. The Bogoyavlensky Monastery, Zhitomir.
22. The Rozhdestvo-Bogoroditsky Convent, Gorodishchensk (Diocese of Khmel'nitsk, closed in 1959).
23. The Blagoveshchensky Convent, Ufa.
24. The Hermitage of the Pochaev Monastery of the Assumption (destroyed in 1959).
25. The Dermansky Monastery (Diocese of Kremenets).

26. The Bogoyavlensky Monastery, Kremenets.
27. The Tikhvinsky Convent, Dnepropetrovsk (closed in 1959).
28. The Baltsky Monastery (Diocese of Odessa).
29. The St. Nikolai Convent, Lebedinsk (Diocese of Kiev, closed in 1961).
30. The Kozelshchansky Convent (Diocese of Poltava).
31. The Satanovsky Convent (Diocese of Kamenets-Podolsk).
32. The Grodnensky Convent (Diocese of Byelorussia).

Thus, it is possible to determine that 67 monasteries have been closed in the USSR in only the last thirty years and that for the time being, seventeen continue to function. But since neither the Soviet authorities nor the Moscow Patriarchate has furnished exact figures about the monasteries, the number of monasteries that have been closed may very well be in the neighborhood of a hundred.

It is clear from obituaries published in *The Journal of the Moscow Patriarchate* that in the period from 1959 to 1962 almost all the senior clergy of the monasteries that had been closed were no longer active. How then could it have happened that just in this very short space of time (1959-1962) both the senior clergy and ordinary monks, contrary to all monastic rules, should find themselves outside their monasteries in their old age?

Despite the fact that the closure of monasteries is passed over in silence, from meagre hints that crop up from time to time in *The Journal of the Moscow Patriarchate*, it is possible to make a rough estimate of the numbert the monasteries that have been closed in the Soviet Union. Until the monasteries have been returned to the Church, there can be no question whether freedom of religion does or does not exist in the USSR, and all the strenuous assertions by Metropolitan Nikodim (Rotov), Kuroedov, and others to the effect that it does will remain just that — assertions.

Between 1958 and 1965 about 10,000 churches were illegally closed. Such measures have not entirely ceased; parishioners are petitioning for the re-opening of Vladimir Cathedral, a recent casualty. Government activity has been turned more against the spread of religion among the young, and to the suppression of Christians involved in civil rights protest. Estimates of churches still open vary from 7,500 to a staggering low of 1,000 based on a recent *samizdat* document pointing out that only 198 churches serve the main 67 urban areas with a population of 50 million.

Incidentally, the atheists were to be on the watch for itinerant "unregistered" ministers or priests who apparently circulated to fulfill the basic religious needs of deprived worshippers, at great personal risk. The oblast representatives are to conclude a contract with the parish council of 20. It read in part:

> It should be kept in mind that at present the "Twenty" do not inspire special confidence. . . . You should recommend that they create a new "Twenty" composed of educated persons, capable of managing the community who would honorably fulfil your recommendations. . . . There should never be more than 20 persons in the "Twenty." The "Twenty" are then to elect the smaller parish executive body. It is desirable that you take part in the selection of members and select those persons who adhere to our line. I suggest that you do not employ employees of the church in the "Twenty;" priests, choir directors, janitors, etc.

The Russian Orthodox Church's experience under Communism is illustrated by the following statistics culled from official sources:

	1914	1939	1947-1957	1962	1966	1973
Dioceses	73	?	73	73	73	73
Bishops in diocesan service	163	about 4	74	63	63	64
Parish clergy	51,105	some 100s	about 20,000	14,000	10,000	?
Churches	54,174	some 100s	about 18,000	11,500	7,500	7,500
Monasteries and Convents	1,025	Nil	67	32	16	12-20
Monks and Nuns	94,629	?	about 10,000	5,000	?	?
Church Academies	4	Nil	2	2	2	2
Theological Seminaries	57	Nil	8	5	3	3
Pre-Theological Schools	185					
Parochial Schools	37,528					
Hospitals	291		Forbidden by law			
Homes for Aged	1,113					
Parish Libraries	34,497					

In a relatively short time a great number of monasteries were arbitrarily closed down. By 1920, of the 1,025 monasteries in 1914, 673 had been dissolved. Vast numbers of monks and nuns, who found themselves precipitately cast out of the cenobitic life to which they had pledged themselves, were forced to depart into the surrounding world to make their way as best as they could." The black (monastic) clergy were scattered over the face of the Russian land like cockroaches swept out from under the stove by the hand of a tidy housewife."

Some of the monasteries hastily utilized the expedient of forming themselves into "working collectives" or artels, consonant with the Soviet theory of optimum agricultural organization. This practice of forming co-operative communities, overt or covert would also play a role in the subsequent development of underground Orthodoxy.

In spite of the hostility of Marxism toward religion and the campaign against it in the USSR, the Communist auhorities there have shown on three occasions, in 1922, 1926, and 1943, that they wished to set up a legalized Supreme Administration of the Russian Orthodox Church. In 1922, they actively supported and granted numerous priviteges to the schismatic "Supreme Church Administration." Such support was aimed at (1) ensuring the selection of clergymen willing to support all official measures and capable of directing believers along lines favorable to the authorities; (2) providing the government with a pretext for taking steps against recalcitrant clergymen who refused to support the new Administration; and (3) demonstrating the "unity" of the church and government and the ostensible freedom of the church in the USSR, a step intended to neutralize the unfavorable impression created abroad by the measures against religion in the Soviet Union.

When the government realized that both the attempt to renew the church and the new clergymen were being ignored by the people at large, its representatives began to urge the church leaders to accept the conditions worked out by the authorities: (1) the publication of a declaration; (2) the removal from the administration of clergymen of no use to the authorities; (3) the condemnation of foreign Orthodox church administrations unwilling to accept the church authorities in the USSR; (4) cooperation with the authorities in the interests of the latter. The successors of Patriarch Tikhon, who were in exile at the time, rejected the conditions. They then advanced their own counter-suggestions: (1) the memorandum of the Solovetsky bishops and (2) "draft conditions for the legalization of the church administration" on June 10, 1926, submitted by Metropolitan Sergei. Both notes proposed the legalization of the church administration on the basis of the separation of church and state — complete and mutual non-interference in political and church matters. While admitting the existence of "insurmountable difficulties" between the church and Communists, the notes guaranteed the political loyalty of the clergy inside the country, while refusing to take steps against Orthodox clergy abroad. Neither proposal satisfied the Communists. Finally worn out by arrest from December 27, 1926 to March 20, 1927, Metropolitan Sergei accepted the Communists' conditions. The new administration of the Orthodox Church, later known as the Moscow Patriarchate, came into existence, thus becoming a tool in the hands of the Party and government. The speed with which all formalities were carried out reveals how interested the Soviet authorities were in setting up the new organ as fast as possible. The latter has since carried out various measures of great political importance for world Communism and the USSR. They included (1) selecting the clergy; (2) establishing complete control over all Orthodox believers in the USSR; (3) assuring the outside world that the Communist regime was granting freedom of religion and that the Russian Orthodox Church was flourishing in the USSR; (4) carrying out patriotic activities during World War II; (5) demonstrating that the Orthodox Church was flourishing in the postwar period; (6) participating in political campaigns; and (7) opening branches in the non-Communist world.

At that time those Orthodox groups anxious to maintain their religious freedom and unwilling to submit to an atheistic government ranged themselves about the various church figures. The Patriarchate was anxious to obtain control over all believers. Such a task was by no means easy and the Patriarchate had to resort to violence. The various groups were branded as "anti-Patriarchate groups" and "illegal societies" and dealt with by the organs of terror. Various groups then went underground and resistance has continued down to the present. The press attacks such groups as anti-Soviet and reports that they have been dispersed.

The comparative freedom of religion permitted during the war was maintained, the population was permitted to erect chapels in some of the major cities, and the government set about restoring the Troitse-Sergei Monastery and Moscow Cathedral and opened theological colleges. The Moscos Patriarchate thus had a very impressive facade for the benefit of visitors from abroad. Foreign church delegations, public, political and cultural figures, journalists and young persons are the constant guests of the Patriarchate. Even heads of state and ministers visiting the USSR for talks with the Soviet government find themselves invited to attend receptions held by the Patriarchate. Reports in the Soviet press show that visitors are invariably taken round the same buildings. These are the 10 most outstanding churches in Moscow; 2-3 in Leningrad and Kiev respectively; the monuments in the village of Kolomenskoe; the 4 residences of the Moscow Patriarch; the TroitsepSergiev Monastery; the Kiev Pokrovsky Nunnery; some churches of the Kiev-Pechersk Monastery; and the Moscow and Leningrad theological colleges.

It takes dedication to train for the clergy in a land of official atheism, but the Russian Orthodox Church seminaries have a steady flow of applicants, according to Archbishop Vladimir of Dmitriyev, head of the seminary and church academy at Zagorsk:

> Many come to religion even through pondering antireligious literature. When we ask applicants how they reached their faith, some say they started on the path by reading the atheist magazine *Natural Science and Religion*.

Four times as many apply for admission as the seminary can accept. The church sets admission quotas in accordance with estimates of the number of priests that will be needed.

In addition to 200 enrolled full-time in the four-year seminary and 100 in the four-year academy, which trains higher clergy, there are 765 in correspondence courses. Correspondence students come to Zagorsk three or four times a year for periods of lectures and examinations.

A Leningrad seminary and academy have similar enrollments. Odessa has a seminary with about 150 students. "They have to be dedicated men," the archbishop said.

Beside theological subjects and singing, the seminary and academy curriculum includes Latin, Greek, Hebrew, Church Slavonic, Russian, and English, French or German. Secular subjects are logic and psychology and courses in the Soviet Constitution and history.

Seminaries were reopened during World War II, when church support for the government's war effort led to reconciliation with the state. To meet the need for priests, seven seminaries were formed, but four were closed after the initial training needs were met.

Archbishop Vladimir could give no figures for the total number of parishes in the country. Asked whether all parishes had priests, he replied: "It depends on the parish."

Graduating class of 1974 at Zagorsk consisted of 89 from the seminary — most of whom will become priests — and 77 from the academy, including full-time and correspondence groups.

According to the Moscow Patriarchate statistics in the year of 1975 there were in the Soviet Union 65 metropolitans, archbishops and bishops. Besides these clergymen, there were 12 Moscow Patriarchate bishops in foreign countries. From the released information can be seen that there are still 6 monasteries in the Soviet Union.

Moscow Patriarchate office released figures concerning the priesthood of the Russian Orthodox Church were as follows: In the three theological seminaries at Zagorsk (300); Leningrad (300) and Odessa (150) were approximately 750 theological students. About the same number of theological students were enrolled in the extension courses.

The greatest dupes, the most outspoken defenders of atheistic Communism, are not residents behind the Iron Curtain.

They are citizens of countries to the west of that invisible but impassable barrier to freedom and religion and the saddest fact of all is that many of them join forces with the very foe they are pledged to fight.

They are churchmen, clergymen who are dedicated to combat the duplicity of the devil, yet ally themselves with his devotees in the unending war to stamp out religion throughout the world.

In their readiness to be "liberal," they lean backwards to admit more than is due to the devil and find themselves, if they face the facts squarely, in the horrified position of doing his work.

A classic case of how the Soviet Union achieves this coup is revealed when one studies the dossier of no less prominent an ecclesiastical personage than Metropolitan John Nikodim, whose official titles include that of Patriarchal Exarch of North and South America.

Dossier is usually associated with a criminal record and it makes sense when studying his career of deceit.

Since he succeeded Comrade Nikolai Dorofeyavich Yarushevich, Metropolitan of Moscow, as the foreign secretary of the Russian Orthodox Church, it might be well to glance first at Nikolai's career to understand why Nikodim was chosen as a logical man to don his mantle.

The narrative of fraud and villainy that runs through Nikolai's life is presented by Edgar C. Bundy. One can only refer to the highlights of how as a young man he became a monk in the old Russian Orthodox Church in 1914, graduated from a theological seminary a year later, and suddenly, following Lenin's takeover of the government and the bloody execution of top religious leaders such as the Metropolitan of St. Petersburg, the Metropolitan of Kiev, and the chief representative of the Roman Catholic Church in Russia, became head of the Peter and Paul Cathedral in Peterhof in 1918, then in 1919 was named Archimandrite and head of the Nevsky Monastery in Petrograd, and in 1922 Bishop of Peterhof and Petrograd diocese.

Patriarch Tikhon, supreme head of the Orthodox Church, died in 1925, after three years of imprisonment. The legitimate succession was wiped out with the arrest or exile of ten out of eleven ecclesiastics. From 1922 to March 25, 1926, His Lordship was located in Semipalatinsk (Southern Siberia) and then in Karkaralinsk. Here Bishop Aleksei lived in private quarters, celebrated services of worship, worked, took walks, conducted correspondence, surrounded by people holding him in great esteem. At the Feast of the Annunciation, 1926, Bishop Aleksei returned to Leningrad leaving a legacy of uncertainty regarding his real attitude toward the Soviet regime, and a short list of bishops who might serve as patriarchal *locum tenens*, depending on their receiving government permission to occupy the office. During these months also, a group of bishops in northern exile who were seeking consensus on a *modus vivendi* for relations between Church and state, drew up a statement which is known as the Solovetsk Document. None of the first few bishops listed by Patriarch Tikhon received permission to come to Moscow, but in early 1926 Metropolitan Sergei of Nizhnii-Novgorod was accorded recognition by the state, and on June 10 he issued his famous declaration of loyalty to the Soviet regime, apparently drawing upon the Solovetsk Document as motivation. Was the declaration a statement of his personal views or the consensus of bishops so far as it could be ascertained? The relationship of the newly elevated Metropolitan Aleksei to it appears in the following statement by Professor I. N. Shabatin: "There are grounds for stating that Metropolitan Aleksei was no less than the chief co-author of this most important document."

Whether he was "co-author" or not, Metropolitan Aleksei from that day onward adhered to the policy of complete loyalty to the Soviet regime. Some churchmen, both at home and abroad, have severely criticized him and even refused to acknowledge his position in the Church because of his loyalty, asserting that the anti-religious principles, policies, and practices of the Soviets completely preclude the possibility of loyalty on the part of an Orthodox Church bishop. Was Aleksei moved by St. Peter's injunction to the early Church on its relation to the then persecuting state? Perhaps this was a factor. More likely, however, both he and Metropolitan Sergei were led by rational and pragmatic considerations. The decree of January 23, 1918 and the earliest redactions of the constitution separated Church and state while permitting divine worship. The law prohibiting specific religious activities had not yet been published, for it appeared only in 1929. At the time of the declaration they could have felt that the essence of church life — the celebration of the sacraments and the preaching of the Word of God — was being preserved even under Soviet restrictions. Moreover, a publicly recognized hierarchy was essential both on canonical grounds and, tactically, in order to counter the claims of the upstart 'Renovation' bishops.

Whatever their motives, Metropolitans Sergei and Aleksei throughout their lives remained loyal to the Soviet government. Unquestionably they thereby lost a measure of credibility and even of moral authority in the minds and hearts of many faithful Christians. It may be noted, however, that all Christians in the Soviet Union were themselves facing the same issue, and they are the millions constituting the flock in a spirit of *sobornost*. They have shared with their bishops the risks of being charged with hypocrisy, levelled at them by critics, whether atheists or believers. They took this risk in order that the sacramental life of the Church might be continued in churches open to the public.

The years of violent collectivization, of the persecution of religion during the militant atheist campaign, of terror, imprisonment and injustice in the 1930s — all must have sorely tried the conscience of Metropolitan Aleksei. In his address to the faithful at his enthronement as Metropolitan of Leningrad in October 1933, one finds these words:

> I accept the obligation in full awareness of its difficulties and of the responsibility which I carry before God and Holy Church, because the pastor must give an account to God for every Christian soul entrusted to him. And the work of the pastor in the Church of Christ is not that of worldly dominance or assertion of power, but a work of serving and presenting himself as a sacrifice after the manner of Christ, who came not to be served but to serve, according to his words, "The good shepherd gives his life for his sheep" (Jn 10:11).

During this decade vast numbers of parish churches were closed, bishops, priests, and active laity were sent off to die in labor camps and, even though Stalin stated in presenting the 1936 constitution, "Not all the clergy are against us," suffering continued. When the Nazi forces invaded Russia in June, 1941, Sergei and Aleksei were the only surviving metropolitans in office, along with half a dozen other bishops, in the whole of Russia.

It is not known if Metropolitan Aleksei had any part in the appeal for patriotism issued by the patriarchal *locum tenens* at the outbreak of war, but the former's actions reveal patriotism and even readiness to lay down his life for his people. He refused to leave his post. He lived throughout the 900 days of the Leningrad blockade in a tiny apartment in the Nikol'skii Cathedral. Although neither Marshal Zhukov in his *Memoirs* nor Harrison Salisbury in his classic *Nine Hundred Days* so much as mention Metropolitan Aleksei, the citizens and the Soviet state did recognize his faithfulness, and twice he was awarded medals of high distinction.

As a churchman, however, his great reward was that of being able to join with Sergei, the patriarchal *locum tenens*, and with Metropolitan Nikolai Krutitskii in presenting personally to Stalin the two great desires of the Church — to elect a patriarch and to restore institutions for the theological training of priests. Both requests were immediately granted. The few bishops who could be brought together naturally placed Sergei officially on the patriarchal throne, which he had occupied *de facto* for seventeen years. This was in September, 1943. Eight months later the long-suffering Patriarch died, and again the Church sent its representatives to elect a new head. There was only one candidate, Aleksei of Leningrad, who was unanimously elected by the 41 bishops and 126 clergy and laymen gathered in solemn *sobor*. He was to rule the Church for twenty-five years of the most intensive activity known in Russian Church history.

One can mention only a few items: resumption of the *Journal of the Moscow Patriarchate* and publication of a few books, opening of ten theological seminaries and two academies (eventually reduced to three seminaries and two academies); inter-Orthodox visitations throughout the ancient Patriarchates and the Balkans; exchanges of visits with Anglican, Lutheran, Old Catholic, Oriental Orthodox, and finally Roman Catholic delegations; at first rejection of ecumenism (1948), then formal entry into the World Council of Churches (1961). The whole world knows of the extraordinary multiplication and extension of the interests of the Russian Church — except in its own domestic life. The magnificence of hospitality in the Soviet

Union and the impressiveness of Russian participation in world affairs tended to overshadow the darker aspects of life, not easily discernible to outsiders. Not all Christians were gratified at the "return" to Orthodox jurisdiction of some three million Uniates by a stroke of the pen in 1946. The attempt to assume leadership of all Orthodoxy by calling a pan-Orthodox conference (1948) proved abortive when the representatives of the Ecumenical Patriarch attended the religious and social functions but refused to participate in formal ecclesiological deliberations and decisions. The opening of many parish churches and release of some imprisoned bishops and clergy was followed, in the 1960's, by a new wave of anti-religious repression, closing churches and monasteries, reducing by half or even two-thirds the number which had been active in the 1950's.

Among other things the truth appears from the history of the Orthodox Church in the Soviet Union. It is the history of a Church which was successively struck, deceived, incarcerated, ridiculed and made serviceable to Communism. After multitudes of its faithful priests and bishops had sealed their loyalty to Christ with their blood, one weakling was found prepared to make concessions. He was the firstling of the prelates who have become the servants of the Communists. He honored Stalin as a wise leader whom God Himself had placed at the head of the Russian people. He organized collections to provide aeroplanes and tanks for the Red Army. He was silent about the persecution. While Communistic wolves were mangling his own sheep, he assisted them by the extermination of the Ukrainian Uniate Church. And while the Slavic peoples of Eastern Europe were sighing under Soviet terror he wrote a pastoral letter:

> The Vatican is the centre of fascism and of the international conspiracy against the Slavic peoples. It is one of the instigators of two imperialistic wards and is now playing an active part in unchaining a new war against world democracy.

Latter utterances cause to suspect that Patriarch Alexei, who, moreover, was specifically condemned by Pope Pius XII, did not write this libellous accusation through wickedness but through weakness. Yet great caution should be exercised in all dealings with him and with his collaborators. These henchmen of Communism have made the Russian Church far more subservient to the State than it ever was in the time of the Czars. It is a mistake to consider them as the undisputed leaders of Orthodoxy. The true Orthodox Church which has remained true to Christ does not acknowledge him. It declines any compromise with atheism. It is being violated in the penal institutions of Siberia. Its priests are imprisoned, degraded to the rank of unskilled laborers or live like vagrants for God. Instead of Communistic medals, they wear the calumny and shame of the Man of Sorrows. It has withdrawn into holy illegality. Although in the last few years thousands of churches and almost all the priests seminaries of the Soviet Union have been closed, it still survives in a holy and spiritual way in the catacombs. It has more right to ones interest and sympathy than the prelates who have sold themselves to Moscow and consider themselves as the official mouthpieces of Orthodoxy.

It was a conference "of all religions in the USSR" gathered at the Holy Trinity Monastery of Saint Sergius in Zagorsk near Moscow. To this meeting had been invited not only the "religious" leaders of the Soviet Union, but "personalities from the Christian churches and religious organizations" from 44 countries.

At this ostensibly religious meeting, the discussion was about (a) European security, (b) the military and political situation in the Near East, (c) the fight against "colonialism" and "neo-colonialism," (d) racism and apartheid, and (e) "Christian" opposition to the war in Viet Nam.

Each invitee was especially screened. The meeting procedures were safely in the hands of Archbishop Nikodim who, in 1963 at the age of 33, had been appointed head of the Russian Orthodox Church by the Communist authorities. In order to make the whole event "official," a message was received from Kosygin, to which meeting delegates responded by expressing approval of the "beneficial efforts of the Soviet government for peace and liberty in the world and for friendship among the nations."

Nikodim, not to be outdone, went on record by calling the Bolshevik Revolution, "A cleansing thunderstorm of divine jurisdiction," and he regarded "the armaments of NATO," "conservatism" and "the principles of private property" as the chief evil in the world and a source of innumerable suffering.

The Archbishop pointed out to the delegates, however, that the acceptable preconditions for religious activity in the Soviet Union had been laid down with certainty:

> The loyalty of the religious communities toward Soviet society is the indispensible precondition for its activity in the Soviet Union. A religious organization which takes on an attitude of opposition toward the Soviet state, inevitably loses the confidence and the support of the faithful and ceases to exist.

Nikodim assured delegates that

> the participants had entire liberty to make use of all possibilities to get to know the religious life in our country. . . . Every guest from a foreign country, visiting our country, can see for himself, that in thousands of churches, prayer-houses, convents and theological colleges in our country, cult and teaching takes place freely.

Is it the truth then, that "cult and teaching takes place freely?" Is it not, rather, that there are many groups of religious believers who are increasing their expressions of discontent in the USSR today, not only with the Orthodox church, but among Protestant groups such as Baptists and Adventists?

Take the *initiativniki* within the Baptists, for example. A truer description of their fate can be found in a letter which was signed by eleven Christians and submitted to Kosygin and a number of Soviet newspapers:

> We relatives of evangelical Christian and Baptist prisoners, persecuted for their faith and for preaching of Christ, hereby inform you of the cruelties which the local authorities in the city of Omsk imposed on one of our numbers, Alexandra Timofeevna Kozarezova, the believing wife of a prisoner. She has eight children, from one to eight years of age. The husband, who is a prisoner for the sake of the Word of God is sentenced according to paragraph 142:2, to the loss of liberty for three years. For two years he has been kept from the light of day. . . . We who are still free, are fined. They break up our prayer circles in the homes. We are dismissed from our work and expelled from our schools. They have searched our homes during which literature of a spiritual nature is

seized. In some cases we are deprived of our real property and our cattle. Wives and children in large families are left without support.

A letter dated August, 1968, sent by three persons from different Russian cities to U Thant, makes reference to the U.N. Declaration of Human Rights.

The International Year of Human Rights is characterized by new, strengthened persecutions. They break up our peaceful worship services. Believers who participate are fined and condemned to 15 days without food. Children are taken from believers that they may be raised without religion, and during raids they have seized our spiritual literature. We cannot fully describe our suffering.

In their letter they ask U Thant whether human rights are also rights for them because,

during the trial of April 15th through the 17th of this year, T. K. Fejdak and V.A. Viltjinski, believing brethern from Brest, were told by the prosecutor that the Declaration of Human Rights was introduced into the U.N. by the Soviet Union government, but was for colonialist and capitalist nations only.

The anti-religious acts by the Soviet Communist authorities continue, and increase in intensity, as a form of neo-Stalinism spreads of nation.

Archbishop Basil Velychovski of the Ukrainian Uniate Church, for example, was sentenced to three years in jail merely for giving communion to some ailing persons. In 1946, when his church was forcibly integrated into the Orthodox Church, he was sentenced to death. This was later commuted to ten years of hard labor.

Three young British tourists were arrested by the Soviet secret police for distributing, in a downtown square in Moscow, a few pamphlets demanding freedom for Soviet religious and political prisoners. The pamphlet read, "Freedom for Galanskov, (one of the Baptist *initiativniki* who later died in prison)."

During the Easter service in the Kiev Cathedral, bands of the Communist youth, Komosomol, sneaked into church and, at a given signal, began to beat old persons and children. The young thugs tore worshippers' clothes, shouted insults at them, and dragged them out of the church.

In the Ukraine, priests are forced to assemble in their own catacomb-retreats. Wandering from place to place, they secretly gather the faithful together in peasants' huts in order to hold services, baptize, preach, and exhort the faithful.

When the Communists came to power half a century ago in Russia, there were 77,765 Russian Orthodox Churches in that country. There were 1,025 monasteries and 250,000 clergymen. These have been whittled down, not from the lack of faith among the Russian people, but through systematic government anti-religious propaganda and repression.

Today it is impossible in some places to find 20 laymen, which would constitute the necessary *dwadtsatki*, to obtain permission from the State to open and operate a church. From 1957 to 1962 the number of Orthodox churches has declined from 20,000 to 11,500; the number of monasteries from 67 to 32; seminaries from eight to five, and lay-priests from 30,000 to 14,000.

Anti-religious acts have not been directed solely against Christians. Moslems and Jews have also been affected. The number of Moslem religious teachers — Mullahim, for example — have been reduced from 28,000 to 400. Their mosques have been reduced from 26,000 before the Revolution to 1,312 today.

Yet strangely enough, the constitution of the Soviet Union guarantees that,

> the churches have been separated from the State, and the schools from the churches. The liberty of practice of religious cults and the liberty of anti-religious propaganda is conceded.

Lest some Russians believe that this, in fact, assures liberty of worship, a clarification was made in 1932.

> If the capitalist separation of Church and State leads to the free and highest development of religion, the Soviet separation of Church and State leads to the free and final death of religion.

But the time has not yet come when "all forms of religion will lie on the refuse dump of history." Today in the Soviet Union there are countless thousands who living under the legacy of Communist tyranny, might take solace from the words of Stalin's daughter. Svetlana Stalina Alliluyeva declared, as she stepped on American soil as a refugee, "I found it was impossible to exist without God. . . . Since that moment the main dogmas of Communism have lost their significance for me."

In fact, after setting forth what are the errors of Bolshevik and atheistic Communism and having denounced its "violent and deceptive" methods of action, the document *Divini Redemptoris* lays down the main lines of the Christian conception of *Civitas humana,* human society, based on reason and on Revelation. They are: God the supreme reality, man a spiritual person; the nature and rights of marriage and the family purposes of society subordinate to man himself (it is the occasion for a new criticism of "individualistic liberalism"); the principles of the economic and social order. Has sufficient stress been laid on the insistent reminder of the doctrine of the State subjected to the rules of morality?

> The deprivation of man's rights and his enslavement, the denial of the first and transcedent origin of the State and of State power, the horrible abuse of public authority in the service of collectivistic terrorism, are the very opposite of what corresponds to natural ethics and to the will of the Creator.

In the seventeenth century the Patriarch and Holy Synod of the Russian Orthodox Church in Moscow instituted a series of changes in the official text of the liturgy and in the ritual. While generally accepted in the Church, a significant number of the faithful, under able leadership, rejected these changes. Known as the "Old Believers," they were much persecuted by the official church and state. In the nineteenth century some of them reached an agreement with the Russian Orthodox Church. Under the Soviets, the Old Believers have suffered from anti-religious efforts the same as all churches. It is interesting that agreement has now been reached between another segment of the Old Believers and the Russian Orthodox Church.

On July 20, 1970, on the even of the feast of the icon of the Mother of God of Kazan, there took place an event of which the significance for Orthodoxy it would be difficult to overestimate. For, on that day, in Leningrad, in the residence of the Metropolitan of Leningrad, there occurred the first official meeting known to history between representatives of the Russian Orthodox Church and those of the Maritime Old Believers' Church.

Proceeding in an atmosphere of heartfelt brotherhood, the meeting opened with prayer before the icon of the Mother of God of Tikhvin.

In the conversation which ensued, Metropolitan Nikodim explained to the Old Believers' party the present attitude of the Russian Orthodox Church towards the Old Believers, emphasizing that the church entertains no doubts about the fitness and meaning of their rituals for salvation. This declaration of an eminent prelate of the Russian Orthodox Church was received with great satisfaction by the Old Believers. Metropolitan Nikodim stressed also that there were no dogmatic divergencies between the Russian Orthodox Church and the Old Believers "We differ only in ritual" said Metropolitan Nikodim. "The Holy Orthodox Faith has been preserved intact by both you and us."

During further conversation a succession of questions about the reciprocal relations of the Russian Orthodox Church and the Maritime Church of the Old Believers was discussed. The most important were the matter about the oaths of the Council of Moscow of 1666-1667; of the co-operation of the two churches in creating Christian peace, and the possibility of the Old Believers' holding their services in the ancient Russian shrines maintained by the Russian Orthodox Church. The two sides spoke in favor of continuing contacts between representatives of the two churches.

Destruction of Ukrainian Religious Life

The rise of the Ukrainian Autocephalic Orthodox Church was the result of a movement for religious emancipation in the Ukrainian territories which belonged to the Russian Empire, a movement which assumed large dimensions after the Revolution of 1917.

In the middle of November 1917, on the initiative of the third Kiev Eparchial Council, a Ukrainian Army congress, and other organizations, an organizing committee was created to convene an All-Ukrainian Synod, for the purpose of reorganizing the Ukrainian Church. The committee consisted of priests and laymen, with Archbishop Aleksei (Dorodnitsyn) of Vladimir as honorary chairman. On November 23, 1917, the committee renamed itself the Provisional All-Ukrainian Orthodox Church Council. It included representatives of the Ukrainian eparchies, the council of bishops, the religious academies and seminaries, the monasteries, the religious brotherhoods, and the peasants', soldiers', and workers' organizations.

The All-Ukrainian Church Council began its work on January 22, 1918, while military operations were in progress between the Bolshevik and Ukrainian forces. On February 1, 1918, meetings of the synod were adjourned. They were resumed on June 20, 1918, but were again interrupted by political developments at the beginning of 1919.

Despite these unfavorable events, the whole process of national religious revival continued. In 1918 preparatory measures had been taken in the synod for the introduction of the living Ukrainian language into Church services. In the summer of 1919, in various unoccupied parts of the Ukraine, the larger part of which was already in the hands of the Soviet regime, congregations were established on the initiative of the clergy and the faithful, where religious services were held in the Ukrainian language. The All-Ukrainian Orthodox Religious Council was re-established to guide the national religious movement. The next step in the organization of the Ukrainian Autocephalic Orthodox Church was the convention of an All-Ukrainian Council which assembled in the historic Cathedral of St. Sophia in Kiev in October, 1921.

The years 1921-27 were a period of development for the Ukrainian

Autocephalic Orthodox Church. It was also the period of the NEP, with its slackening of terrorism and lessening of political activity on the part of the Communist dictatorship both economically and culturally. By the end of 1926, the Ukrainian Autocephalic Orthodox Church had no less than 2,800 parishes or, according to some reports, as many as 3,500, and about 2,000 clergymen. During these years it was one of the best organized and most cohesive non-Communist centers in the Ukraine, in the fields of both religion and national culture. The significance attributed by the Communist regime to the Church is attested by a contemporary Soviet historian, who declared:

> The most important legal centers for the dissemination of bourgeois ideology in the Ukraine during the NEP period were the independent Autocephalic Church, the branches of the cooperatives and the *Proletkult* (Society for Proletarian Culture).

A secret circular distributed by one of the district sections of the GPU in October, 1924 states:

> The GPU has called to the attention of the district sections the continuously growing influence among the Ukrainian population of the so-called Ukrainian Autocephalic Church headed by the Kiev Metropolitan Vassily Lipkovsky. . . . It has long been known that Lipkovsky and his associates are secret propagandists of Ukrainian separatism and are not so much striving to free from subordination to the Moscow Patriarchate several Church parishes in the Ukraine as they are under this screen preaching various ideas of Ukrainian nationalism harmful to the Soviet regime.

Accordingly, the circular continued, the GPU of the Ukrainian SSR regarded "the activity of this Church as of particularly dangerous significance for the Soviet regime" and issued specific instructions "to throw light on a broad scale, by political surveys, on all sides of the life and activity of this Church, devoting special attention to the sermons delivered by the priests in the churches."

The Church suffered the first heavy blows in 1927, coinciding with the slowing down of the NEP and of the conciliatory tactics connected with it. The Church leaders were accused of counter-revolutionary activity and the head of the Church, Metropolitan Lipkovsky, was forbidden to take part in religious work. In order to preserve the Church from premature destruction, the second synod, which was held in October, 1928, was compelled to remove him. However, this was only the beginning of the persecution, which in 1929 assumed mass dimensions. Five bishops and more than 700 priests were arrested between July, 1929 and March, 1930.

A deadly blow was struck against the Ukrainian Autocephalic Orthodox Church at the beginning of 1930 in connection with the trial of the Union for the Liberation of the Ukraine (SVU).

At the trial, the prosecution attempted to prove that the Church was also a tool of the capitalists and bourgeois and that it sought to restore capitalism in the Ukraine. Contemporary Soviet sources claimed that the counter-revolutionary role played by the members of the Ukrainian Autocephalic Church was completely exposed by the trial. The trial was intended not only to condemn individual representatives of the Autocephalic Church, but also the Church as a whole, which the court treated as an organized anti-Soviet force.

Preferring to use methods involving hidden pressure, the regime attempted to make its measures for the liquidation of the Church appear to be legal and to give them the appearance of voluntary acts on the part of the Church itself. On January 28, 1930, at the demand of the GPU, an "emergency council" was summoned consisting of a few bishops and 40 priests. The council, which only lasted a few hours, was compelled to adopt a resolution, the text of which had been previously drawn up by a representative of the GPU; this resolution provided for dissolution of the Church as a united religious organization. However, this compulsory self-liquidation did not save the clergy and faithful from further repressive action. In May of the same year, Metropolitan N. Boretsky, who had been elected by the synod in 1927 after the compulsory removal of Metropolitan Lipkovsky, was arrested and imprisoned in solitary confinement at Yaroslavl'. He died in prison in 1933. By the end of 1930, 14 bishops and more than 800 priests had been arrested.

In 1935 the bishops still remaining at liberty were arrested. Only Archbishop Ivan Teodorovich, who in 1924 had crossed the ocean to become head of the Ukrainian Orthodox Church in the United States and the Ukrainian Greek Orthodox Church in Canada, escaped this fate.

By the end of June, 1925, there was not a single remaining parish of the Ukrainian Autocephalic Orthodox Church.

The temporary removal of the Ukraine from the authority of the Soviet dictatorship in 1941-43, during the German occupation, resulted in a revival and a great upsurge of religious life, and especially in a revival of the Ukrainian Autocephalic Orthodox Church. This process took place with the active assistance and under the guidance of Ukrainian Orthodox Church centers in the parts of Volynia which until 1939 had formed a portion of Poland. The first Soviet occupation of this territory in 1939-41 had not succeeded in completing a campaign aimed at liquidating organized religious activity there.

The temporary withdrawal of the Soviet regime from the Ukraine caused a wave of religious activity not only in the western part of the Ukraine, which had been recently joined to the USSR, but also in the main areas of the Ukraine. Despite the hostile and prejudiced attitude of the German authorities and the unfavorable conditions caused by the occupation, the religious revival continued. Between 20 and 30 per cent of the old parishes were restored in the oblasts which had belonged to the USSR before 1939. About 580 parishes were organized in the Kiev Eparchy and about 100 each in Poltava and Zhitomir after the departure of the Soviet authorities. The revival of the parishes was made difficult by the shortage of clergy as a result of oppression by the Soviet regime.

The return of the Soviet regime virtually destroyed the Church organization of the Ukrainian Autocephalic Orthodox Church, and the remaining clergy and congregations had no opportunity to restore it under the new conditions. The new metropolitan, Ioann, coming from Moscow, proposed that they "recognize the Patriarchal jurisdiction as the only possible opportunity for further existence." The existence of the Ukrainian Autocephalic Orthodox Church in the Ukraine was thus cut short for the second time. Thenceforth it lived on only for the numerous Ukrainian Orthodox emigres outside the USSR and the satellite countries.   a

The Soviet regime, in its direct persecution of the Ukrainian Autocephalic Orthodox Church and in its creation of conditions making its existence impossible, has committed an act of genocide clearly within the United Nation's definition of "actions committed with the intention of partly or wholly destroying a national, ethnic, racial or religious group as such."

The exiled Ukrainians on several continents and both hemispheres, have for years been compiling data, case histories, irrefutable documentation and indictments against Soviet-Communist criminals, which is far more horrifying than the mine-run of reports on Nazi crimes. Moreover, the very magnitude of these Soviet crimes exceeds the statistics of those committed by the Nazis.

The theme of the Ukrainian expose is that Russian Communism is militant atheism. Communism and Christianity cannot exist together. They are like fire and water. The Ukrainians, once a free nation, have for centuries been militantly Christian, which, of course, makes them anathema to Moscow. Also marked for extinction by the Kremlin caliphs are the Estonians, Latvians and Lithuanians, all Catholic or Protestant. The basis of their persecution is the irreconcilable disparity between Communism and Christianity. The fight is atheism against all Christian civilization.

Prior to the Revolution there were 10,835 Orthodox parishes in Ukraine, organized in nine dioceses. The metropoly of Kiev possessed a higher Theological College, 10 lower theological seminaries and 35 schools. There were 188 students in higher Theological College and 3,724 pupils in the lower ones. There were, moreover, 10,000 parish schools. As a result of the anti-religious drive by the Bolsheviks, all these schools were abolished and the number of parishes declined considerably.

At the height of its growth, in 1926, the Ukrainian Autocephalous Church was divided into 20 church districts with 17 active bishops. By 1927 there were in existence, according to the most cautious estimates, about 1,100 parishes of the Church. Altogether during the 1920's there were 34 bishops of the Church. The rate of decline of the church life, compared with the pre-revolutionary period, is illustrated by the fact that while in 1914 there were 10,793 church cantors in Ukraine, by 1927 their number decreased to 4,574, i.e., by 6,219 or by more than 57 per cent.

Since the middle of the 1920's the Ukrainian Autocephalous Orthodox Church experienced increasing interference on the part of Soviet authorities, in particular the GPU secret police, which manipulated even the elections of metropolitans and bishops of the Church. Thus under the pressure from the GPU, the great Metropolitan of the Church, Archbishop Vasyl Lypkivskyi, was forced to stand down and leave active participation in Church affairs, in order not to exacerbate the relations between the Church and the Soviet regime.

The situation eased up a little towards the end of 1930 and the Ukrainian Autocephalous Orthodox Church was able to hold another extraordinary council which restored the hierarchy of the Church to some extent and created 7 dioceses. The Metropolitan see was transferred to Kharkiv which was then the capital of the Soviet Ukraine. However, there was constant surveillance and interference on the part of the Communist authorities. Incessant persecutions and arrests, intimidation and terrorisation of the bishops, priests and faithful resulted in a rapid decline of the Church as an organised body. While prior to its liquidation the Church had 22 districts with over 1,000 parishes, by the end of 1930 the number of parishes dwindled to about 300, and by 1933 to not more than 200. By 1936, it seems, this

Church disappeared completely when the last known parish went down under the assault of the atheistic regime.

Following the liquidation of the Autocephalous Church, the two other forms of the Orthodox Church in Ukraine, the so-called Patriarchal and the "Synodal" churches, were likewise almost completely wiped out by 1936-37. It appears that the last active bishop of the Orthodox Church under the jurisdiction of the Patriarch of Moscow, was arrested in Poltava in 1938 together with four priests of his Church and two priests of the Ukrainian Autocephalous Orthodox Church.

An eye-witness of the martyrdom of the Ukrainian Orthodox Church writes about its destruction by the atheistic Communist Russian regime as follows:

> ... The years 1934-36 saw the final destruction of the visible signs of religious life in Ukraine. Churches were destroyed on a mass scale then. The last mock trials of clergy and faithful, were staged by the government. Over 30 bishops, over 2,000 priests and a great number of faithful from among the flock of the Ukrainian Autocephalous Orthodox Church were annihilated. Only a few priests returned to Ukraine before the Second World War. But during the war they again organised and brought back to life the Ukrainian Autocephalous Orthodox Church.The Ukrainian Autocephalous Orthodox Church had 34 bishops and over 3,000 priests and deacons. From this number, during World War II, only two bishops, with impaired health, returned to Ukraine from exile; one of them died in 1943. The Kiev All-Ukraine Church Council registered, at the end of 1941, only 270 priests who returned to Ukraine from exile.

The Ukrainian Autocephalous Orthodox Church, which declared its independence from Moscow, became an object of hatred of the Communist Russian authorities and the Russian Orthodox leadership. Therefore the entire hierarchy and a number of the clergy of the Ukrainian Autocephalous Orthodox Church left Ukraine before the advancing Soviet armies, fearing savage reprisals on the part of the Russians. A large part of the hierarchy and clergy of the "Autonomous" Church in Ukraine also went into exile. The Soviet authorities immediately liquidated the Ukrainian Autocephalous Orthodox Church upon their return to Ukraine and the remaining clergy and faithful had to submit to the jurisdiction of the Patriarch of Moscow and his Exarch in Ukraine.

Moreover, in 1946, the Ukrainian Catholic Church of the Eastern rite which existed in the Galician part of Western Ukraine, with its 3,000 parishes and about 5,000,000 faithful, was forced under terror to submit to the Patriarch of Moscow and renounce the allegience to Rome. Its entire hierarchy and most of the priests were arrested and deported to slave labor camps before the break with Rome was announced.

In view of the fact that religious life revived to a greater extent in the areas that experienced German occupation, the proportion of Ukrainian Orthodox parishes in the Russian Orthodox Church remains very high. By the middle of the 1950's, for instance, it was reported that there were functioning in Ukraine 8,500 Orthodox parishes (out of the total of 20,000 in the USSR) with 6,800 priests, nearly 40 monasteries (out of the total number of 67 in the USSR) and three theological seminaries (out of eight in the USSR).

This relative toleration of the church life ended in November, 1958 when, on Khrushchev's insistence, the plenary meeting of the Central Committee of the CPSU decided on a sharp change of course in relation to religion and church and on the strengthening of atheistic propaganda. In the next few years, as a result of a vicious propaganda campaign and increasing pressure by means of various levers which a totalitarian state power has at its disposal, many churches were closed down and the number of parishes fell down catastrophically. By 1963 their number fell by about 50 per cent. Even in 1961 the number of Orthodox parishes in the whole USSR was given as 11,000. In Ukraine the resistance to the campaign of the closing of churches was greater than in Russia herself, as is witnessed by the fact that the decline in the number of churches was somewhat less. It is estimated that there are at present about 5,000 Orthodox parishes in Ukraine. This is a very small number indeed if one takes into account the fact that about a half of them are former Ukrainian Catholic ("Uniate") parishes in Western Ukraine and a quarter, perhaps are situated in Volynia and Bukovina (West Ukraine). Thus, at most just over 1,000 (or one quarter) are situated in the Central and Eastern provinces of Ukraine with three quarters of the population of Ukraine. It should also be remembered that Ukraine, with its population of over 40,000,000 people of Orthodox background, has 1,200 towns and urban settlements and 32,000 villages, most of which had one or more Orthodox churches before 1917. The Orthodox Church in Ukraine is divided now into 19 dioceses many of which remain, however, unoccupied owing to the fact that bishops of the old generation are dying out rapidly and there are few replacements. The same goes for the clergy. The present head of the Orthodox Church in Ukraine and Exarch of the Patriarch of Moscow is Archbishop Filaret Dmitrovsky, appointed by the Synod of Moscow Patriarchy in 1966. He is a Russian monk who, on his appointment was only 37 years old. He had already held important administrative and diplomatic posts in the Russian Church prior to his most recent appointment.

Thus there exists now in Ukraine only a fraction of the number of parishes that existed there before the Bolshevik invasion. The number of monasteries has fallen down almost to nil, so that at present only three remain open, and even these are threatened with closure. During the 60 years of existence of the Soviet regime not even one new church has been built. Many of the churches of exceptional historical and cultural value have been pulled down or fell into a deplorable state of disrepair. The process has not been halted and many churches continue to be destroyed.

The Kiev Theological Seminary was closed when its building was confiscated in 1960. The Lutsk Seminary stands before closure because of the shortage of students due to the difficulties which the regime places before the prospective priests.

One bishops was declared an unwanted person in Ukraine and another was deprived of the right to preach and the right to say Mass. In 1961, Archbishop Andriy Suchenko was sentenced to 8 years of imprisonment on trumped up charges of tax evasion and keeping minors from work.

A new anti-religious legislation was introduced in Ukraine in 1961. Article 227 of the new Criminal Code states, among other things, that

> the leaders or directors of a group the activity of which, under the pretext of a lecture, includes religious teaching or the practice of religious rites, thus endangering the health of the citizens who are members of the group . . . or which is connected with the demand for abstention from any form of social activity as well as the acceptance of minors in such a group . . . shall receive sentences of up to five years imprisonment. . . .

This article of the Code does not remain an empty threat but is applied in practice as occasional newspaper reports confirm.

In Kiev, the capital of Ukraine, with its population of 1,500,000, there are only seven Orthodox churches open today, while before the Soviet occupation there were 106 for a much smaller population of 250,000. In Kharkov, the second-largest Ukrainian city, with a population of 1,200,000, there are only four churches open, and similar situation prevails throughout Ukraine.

An official communique by *Tass* Soviet press agency announced that as of January 1, 1948 the Ukrainian Catholic Church ceased to exist and had no longer any legal rights. This was long after the Church had in fact been violently destroyed. However, even though the Ukrainian Catholic Church does not officially exist in Ukraine, it exists in the hearts of a large number of the faithful and clergy. It has been driven underground and, from time to time, newspaper reports speak about clandestine activities of the remnants of the Ukrainian Catholic Church which has been driven into the catacombs by persecution. According to some reports, the faithful meet in private homes to hear Mass celebrated by underground priests.

The real feelings of the population with regard to the "unification" with Moscow Patriarchy could be seen from the following report. In August, 1947, the Orthodox Church attempted to proclaim "unification" of the faithful from Carpatho-Ukraine with the Moscow Patriarchy. For this purpose five Orthodox bishops arrived from other parts of the USSR and took part in the church service at the Mukachiv monastery confiscated from the Catholic Church in the presence of about four to five thousand people. At the same time at the parish Church in Mukachiv the Greek-Catholic church service was attended by about 70-80,000 pilgrims.

For a period of time there still existed many parishes which refused to accept Orthodoxy, but gradually their number declined and finally the Church disappeared altogether. Only a minority of the priests submitted to the Orthodox Church; those of the others who were not arrested entered civilian life and became ordinary workers, shop attendants or book-keepers. Some of the younger unmarried priests continued to carry on their priestly duties illegally.

In 1944-45 when the Soviet Russian troops occupied West Ukraine, there were three Ukrainian Catholic dioceses of Lvov, Peremyshl and Stanyslaviv, and two circuits of the Apolstolic Visitor in Volynia and an Apostolic Administrator in the Lemko region. (Parts of the Peremyshl diocese and the Lemko area were ceded to Poland by the USSR in 1945). Together with Mukachiv diocese embracing Carpatho-Ukraine, which was incorporated into the Ukrainian SSR in 1945, and the Priashiv diocese which remained in Czecho-Slovakia, this compact Ukrainian territory contained approximately 5,000,000 Ukrainian Catholics. The Church hierarchy consisted of 1 Archbishop-Metropolitan and 10 Bishops and was divided into 5 dioceses and 2 circuits of Apolstolic Administration. There were 3,040 parishes with 4,440 churches and chapels, as well as 127 monasteries and convents. There were 2,950 diocesan priests, 520 priests in orders, 1,090 nuns. There were also 540 seminarians in 1 theological academy and 5 ecclesiastical seminaries. In addition, the Ukrainian Catholic Church possessed a great number of cultural centers, primary and secondary schools, publishing houses, libraries, welfare and aid associations, orphanages, student and youth leagues, and societies.

All these were ruthlessly destroyed in 1945-50 by the Communist Russian government and its satellite regimes in Poland and Czechoslovakia, although in the latter two countries there has been a restricted revival in the last few years. In Ukraine itself the Ukrainian Catholic Church of the Eastern rite has been placed outside the law and exists only as an underground Church.

The decree issued by the Russian Soviet government on January 23, 1918, fundamentally "regulated" the affairs of the Church inasmuch as it deprived the latter of its public legal character and status. From now onwards, communities of the Church were only to be allowed to continue to exist as private societies. This decree was extended to apply to Ukraine, too, by the Communists in 1919. The Church was also deprived of its right of ownership of property. Only if they paid rent for the future "state property" were church communities to be allowed by the administration to use church buildings for the purpose of worship. In addition, the Church was likewise strictly forbidden to engage in any form of charitable activity.

In spite of constant persecution of the Church, of the bishops, priests and the faithful, most of the people of Central and East Ukraine unwaveringly retained their Christian faith and did their utmost to preserve the organised forms of Church life, at least within the very limited rights which the Soviet decree at that time conceded to church communities as private societies. In 1921 the Greek Orthodox Ukrainians detached themselves from the supremacy of the Moscow Patriarchate which had been forced on them, and established the revived Ukrainian Autocephalous Orthodox Church, which under the spiritual leadership of its Metropolitan, Basil (Vasyl) Lypkovsky, included the whole of Central and East Ukraine and in 1927 numbered about 3,000 parishes, more than 3,000 priests and 34 bishops.

That this was possible under the Communist regime is explained by the fact that though the Soviet state power, in keeping with the Communist ideology of a militant atheism, fought the Church again and again all the time, and continues to fight it even today, this fight, however, assumes various forms according to time and circumstances.

In their fight against the Church, the Communists resorted to various methods in turn, ranging from comparative tolerance — whenever the situation demanded that the people should for the time being be pacified — to ruthless terrorism. During the transition period up to 1926 the Communist state power endeavored to destroy the organisation of the Church from within, by making use of the so-called "Living Church," founded in 1923, which in a similar way to the "New Economic Policy," was to become the instrument of the Communists for the purpose of consolidating their regime. The Communists also took part in the founding of the so-called "Active Church" so that, with the help of the latter's functionaries, they might be able to compromise religion and the Church in the eyes of the population. Thus, one of these functionaries, for instance, who posed as an orthodox priest, at the end of divine service — obviously at the instructions of the Communist elements — publicly declared in the church that he had so far been telling the people "lies" and would now, therefore, relinquish his office as a priest. In order to make this atheistic demonstration more striking, he tore off his priest's vestments and threw his priest's cross on the floor and trampled on it. Some time later, he was appointed leader of a "circle of atheists" and devoted himself to a lively anti-religious activity.

The Communist authorities exerted considerable pressure in order to make the population take part in the anti-religious campaign which they themselves organised, and readily resorted to threats and punitive measures against all those who openly refused to take part in this campaign. The Communists arranged public anti-religious rallies, usually at Christmas and Easter, which were for the most part attended by members of the "Union of Atheists," Komsomols and by countless semi-criminal elements of the rabble. They donned priests' vestments and, holding a crucifix in their hand, held wild masquerades in the streets and ridiculed God, religious faith, the Church and the priesthood. They tried to provoke the faithful who had assembled in the churches for divine service, by screaming, shouting and whistling; sometimes they even forced their way into churches where they then started maltreating and beating the priests and the members of the congregation and demolishing pictures of saints and sacred vessels. All this was done either at public instigation or with the tacit permission of the Communist authorities.

These sacreligious demonstrations were a prelude to a large-scale campaign which was intended to destroy completely religious and Church life in Central and East Ukraine. According to an official decree issued by the Soviet government on April 8, 1929, the Church ceased to exist legally as a hierarchic organisation. From now onwards, the Communist administration systematically began to close the churches and to use church buildings for other purposes or else to demolish them. Such measures were carried out in accordance with the government and Party directives.

In 1936, the last parish, which had previously declared its adherence to the Ukrainian Autocephalous Orthodox Church, was officially dissolved, and thus the last vestige of the existence of this Church as an organised community on Soviet Ukrainian soil was now obliterated. Those priests and monks who had still engaged in their profession were now obliged to do so illegally. They went from place to place, preaching the Divine Word to the population and hiding from the police. Those who were caught were shot, as for instance, the monk Pylyp (Philip) in 1937 and the abbot Arsenius, some time before 1941. The police system of informers made it practically impossible for the priests to continue their religious activity even in secret. In Kyivalvae, where prior to the Bolshevist occupation there had been 140 churches, only two churches were later allowed to remain open, and that was chiefly in order to be able to demonstrate Soviet "tolerance" to foreigners. In many other towns not a single church was allowed to remain open. Moreover, both in Kiev and elsewhere, countless churches were demolished, which, as monuments of the Ukrainian architecture of the 12th to 17th century, were of great artistic and historic value; in Poltava fourteen churches were demolished. In Odessa nineteen churches were demolished on one single occasion in 1937.

The Communist administration imposed such exorbitant taxes on the priests and the parishes that, as a rule, they were not in a position to pay them; and this fact, of course, provided the authorities with the desired "legal" reason for dissolving the church parishes. As a result of these exorbitant taxes, a number of parishes in Poltava collapsed in 1931. And most of the communities of the Ukrainian Autocephalous Orthodox Church were liquidated by this "cold" method.

As a result of the Communist persecution of religion and the Church in West Ukraine and Carpatho-Ukraine, the life of the Catholic Church there was completely disorganised. This is obvious from the following comparison of the status of the Ukrainian Catholic Church there in 1939 and its status at present:

Status in 1939		Status at Present
Dioceses	5	All liquidated.
Circuits of Apostolic Admin-istrators or Visitators	2	All liquidated.
Bishops	10	All deprived of their rank and office and arrested or deported (1 murdered, 7 died in prison).
Secular priests	2,950	About 50 per cent imprisoned (or
Priests in orders	520	murdered), about 20 per cent fled
Nuns	1,090	or hid, about 30 per cent forced to give us their religious faith.
Parishes	3,040	The majority handed over to the
Churches and chapels	4,440	Russian Orthodox Church; church
Monasteries	195	buildings party used for profane purposes.
Ukrainian Catholic primary schools	9,900	
Ukr.-Cath. secondary schools	380	All communised or closed down.
Ukr.-Cath. colleges	56	
Ukr.-Cath. publishers	35	
Ukr.-Cath. journals	38	All liquidated or confiscated.
Other Ukrainian Catholic institutions	41	

Although the official Constitution of the Soviet Union ensures freedom of religion to all Soviet citizens (Article 123), the Soviet state power has actually deprived the population of West Ukraine and Carpatho-Ukraine of the right to follow their religious faith within the Ukrainian Catholic Church, and the latter has been liquidated by terrorist measures. In addition, a considerable part of the population, starting with the primary schools, has been forced to take part in the anti-religious atheist movement.

The Bolshevik liquidation of the Greek Catholic Church in 1945-46 was not only a part of the general campaign of militant Communism against religion but also a part of the struggle of the Communist dictatorship against the national aspirations and national culture of the Ukrainian people.

In order to understand the real reason for this act on the part of the Soviet regime, it is necessary to recall the part played by the Greek Catholic Church in the life of the Ukrainian population of Eastern Galicia. The Greek Catholic, or Uniate Church had been founded in 1595-96 when a portion of the Ukrainian Orthodox clergy and lay leaders, at a synod held in Brest, decided to reunite with the Roman Catholic Church. It received official confirmation eventually only for the Western Ukrainian lands which went to the Austro-Hungarian monarchy as a result of the partitions of Poland. There it assumed a sharply nationalist character, becoming for persons of Ukrainian nationality a bulwark against Polonization. The upsurge of nationalism in Ukrainian Galicia in the nineteenth century received its main impetus from members of the Greek Catholic clergy, the Ukrainians of Galicia having for three and a half centuries gathered closely about what they had come to regard as their national Church.

The Greek Catholic Church accepted all the dogmas of the Roman Catholic Church but retained its former Byzantine Slavonic ritual, the two aspects of the Holy Eucharist, a separate Church organization and hierarchy, and several other less important special characteristics. In 1932 there were 5,162,385 Ukrainian Greek Catholics, of whom 3,602,270 were living in the Galician bishopric, 640,015 in the Carpathian Ukraine, and the remainder in the United States, Canada, Argentina, Brazil, and other countries.

The liquidation of the Greek Catholic Church was carried out by the Bolsheviks after their second occupation of the Western Ukraine. There had been an earlier occupation, in 1939-41, but at that time their treatment of the Greek Catholic Church had not differed substantially from the pattern established by the Soviet regime toward all religious cults in the Soviet Union. During this first occupation religious seminaries and monasteries had been closed and some of the priests arrested and deported. However, repressive action had not been taken against the highest religious hierarchy, headed by Metropolitan Count A. Sheptitsky.

By the time of the second occupation of the Western Ukraine by the Bolsheviks, the general policy of the Soviet regime toward religion and the Church had undergone a considerable change. The change of policy toward the Orthodox Church in the USSR during the war was reflected in relations between the Soviet regime and the Greek Catholic Church. Although religious propaganda was forbidden as before, priests were not forbidden to teach religion except in schools, and a number of categories of clergy were relieved of their obligation to perform military service. The monasteries, which had been handed back to the Church by the Germans, remained for some time in the possession of their congregations. When Metropolitan Count Sheptitsky, who had been extremely influential among the Ukrainian people, died on November 1, 1944, his funeral was attended by Khrushchev himself, at that time First Secretary of the Ukrainian Communist Party.

By the spring of 1945, the situation had radically altered. The liquidation of the Greek Catholic Church as such now began. It has been described in some detail in a "White Book" compiled by Ukrainian Catholic priests living in Rome.

The campaign of persecution of the Greek Catholic hierarchy was opened with an article by a certain Vladimir Rozovich, which first appeared in the newspaper *Vilna Ukraina (Free Ukraine)* on April 6, 1945, and was then reprinted and distributed among the population in leaflet form. The article contained a slanderous attack on the dead Metropolitan Sheptitsky. The appearance of the pamphlet was followed immediately by the arrest of all bishops living in the territory of Galicia.

After the upper hierarchy of the Greek Catholic Church had been removed by arrest and deportation, the Bolsheviks began to implement their plan for the entire liquidation of the Greek Catholic Church. Several weeks after the arrest of the Ukrainian episcopate, an ostensibly spontaneous movement to merge the Greek Catholic Church with the Orthodox Church was staged. The Bolsheviks placed the well-known religious leader and editor of the church magazine, Father G. Kostelnik, at the head of the movement. However, despite the campaign of the Communist authorities against the Greek Catholic Church and the arrest of the whole group of higher clergy, 300 Greek Catholic priests signed a protest in which they demanded the application of the Stalin Constitution to the religious life of the Western Ukraine. All were arrested and deported.

In March, 1946, Kostelnik and his supporters summoned a "synod," "which proclaimed the liquidation of the Church Union with Rome and "re-union" with the Moscow Orthodox Church. Only 204 priests attended the "synod" out of a total of 2,950.

After 350 years, the union with Rome was "officially abolished." But what is the actual situation? Is the Church of the Catacombs — or as Pope Pius XII referred to is, the "silent church," still alive in the westertn Ukraine? According to *samizdat* material that has reached the West, as well as to reports in the Soviet press, one can assume that the Ukrainian Catholic Church has gone underground but has in no way ceased to exist and that despite arrests and persecution, it continues to be active on a large scale.

In 1959 the ex-abbot of Ternopol, Vasilii Velichkovsky, was secretly nominated a bishop of the Ukrainian Catholic Church, and in 1963 one of the bishops secretly annointed him. As a legitimate bishop of the Ukrainian Catholic Church, he began extensive underground activities in the western Ukraine: he ordained new Uniate priests, prepared novices for monastic life and the priesthood, and celebrated Mass.

During the 1960's three clandestine Uniate convents were discovered in Lvov alone: the Convent of the Order of the Servants of the Blessed Virgin Mary, in which there were ten nuns, led by Mother Superior Valeria (Maria Stepanovna Dubik); the monastic order of St. Vincent; and the convent of the Vasilian Sisters. The nuns of these convents all worked as nurses but in fact continued to live a monastic life. Mass was said for them in tiny chapels by Catholic priests who had already spent time in Soviet prison camps for refusing to accept the dissolution of the union with Rome.

In 1965 Father I. M. Krivoi, who had been "converted" to Orthodoxy at the time of the reunification, was tried in Lvov. He was accused of distributing Uniate religious literature. Six others were tried with him at the same time; two of the young men, who had printed a thousand religious calendars for him in 1964, received light sentences.

In December, 1969, these same printers, M. Seneshin and G. Ya. Gavrilyak — again at the request of Father Krivoi — printed a thousand copies of the Uniate prayerbook, *Molitvennik dlya ukrainskogo naroda*, which was based on an original edition published in Toronto in 1954. In 1970 the two men printed another thousand copies; and at the end of 1972, they ran off another 1,500 copies. The fact that so many prayerbooks were printed can be taken as a good indication that there are still a fair number of Greek-Catholics in the western Ukraine.

According to information that has reached the Western press, the possibility that an illegal Catholic Church exists in the western Ukraine has been discussed at a Politburo meeting of the Ukrainian Communist Party Central

Committee. This activity has possibly been the cause of the increased persecution of practicing Uniates. For example, in the village of Mezhile in Sokalsky raion, the kolkhoz administration has stored grain on several occasions in the local church, but believers continued to gather there for prayers. When the authorities locked and bolted the doors, the believers gathered in the churchyard on feast days, set up an altar, and prayed. There they were attacked, beaten, and dispersed. An orthodox priest was sent to the area, but the people refused to accept him. In the village of Nesterovo, the residents refused to attend the Orthodox Church and have instead organized prayer meetings in private houses, for which they have been accused of arranging illegal gatherings. In all these villages, the authorities reportedly search for Uniate priests who are performing their religious functions in secret. If found, they are generally tried and sentenced to prison camps.

An oblique reference to the activity of the Ukrainian Catholic Church was made in a speech delivered by Metropolitan Filaret in Lvov on the thirtieth anniversary of the convocation of the Council on Reunification. In his speech, the metropolitan stated that "Orthodoxy is firmly implanted in the consciousness and the life of the clergy and laity of our western patriarchies. But this does not mean that bishops and priests have nothing left to do." It was revealed for the first time that Uniate priests and their relatives had had difficulty in accepting Orthodoxy. In his speech, Metropolitan Nikolai stated:

> Undoubtedly, it was not easy for the older generation of priests to persuade themselves and their relatives to cross the ecclesiastical and historical barrier. Now they are growing old and going to rest.

> Notwithstanding the various statements about the "dead and forgotten" Uniate Church that the Soviet Press has disseminated with the Soviet Union and abroad, one fact remains clear: the Ukrainian Catholic Church, despite large-scale persecution, despite the fact that it is outlawed, still survives in the western Ukraine — a Church of the Catacombs, perhaps, but still in existence.

> Metropolitan Nikolai has predicted that new clergymen dedicated to the Orthodox Church will replace older priests who have died. However, only the future will determine whether or not the metropolitan's prophecy becomes a fact.

The Byzantine-rite of the Catholic Church is represented in the Soviet Union by the now "illegal" Ukrainian Greek Catholic Church dating, in Galicia, from the Union of Brest in 1596 and, in Transcarpathia, since the Union of Uzhhorod in 1646. The flock of this largest "prohibited" religious group in the USSR still predominates in the oblasts of Lvov, Ternopil and Ivano-Frankivsk, and has a sizeable following in the Transcarpathian oblast. As a result of migration from Galicia, there is a growing Ukrainian Catholic diaspora both in the Central and Eastern Ukraine, while further east, there are still numerous Uniates in the areas of resettlement and exile in Northern Kazakhstan and Western Siberia.

The forcible nature of "reunion" of the Uniates with the Russian Orthodox Church some thirty years ago — a clearly illegal act whether in terms of the published Soviet legislation on religion or from the stand-point of both Catholic and Orthodox canons — left a legacy of illegitimacy with the Orthodox Church in the "reunited" dioceses, while conferring upon the Greek Catholic Church an aura of martyrdom for the faith and the Ukrai·

nian national cause. As a result, ¯a peculiar religious situation prevails in
Galicia. Apart from those priests and laymen who have accepted official
Orthodoxy and aspire to infuse it with Ukrainian national traditions and
values, there are at least three more categories of faithful in the Western
Ukraine.

The first group embraces those who continue to consider themselves
Greek Catholics but, in order to openly practiced their religion, formally
belong to the Orthodox Church.

> They practice there, their religion in accordance with the old rituals and
> customs and . . . have for their priests former Uniates who were officially
> converted to Orthodoxy. . . . To this group, the Orthodox Church in the
> formerly Uniate regions is like a "branch of the Catholic Church, forcefully
> separate from the Vatican and subjected to the regime."

Very likely the majority of the "reunited" clergy in the formerly Uniate
oblasts fall into this "crypto-Uniate" category, as well as most of the overt
believers. They sympathize with the "Catacomb" Uniate Church, maintain
links with the "illegal" clergy and often help them in difficulties. In 1973, for
example, three such Orthodox priests were tried together with three laymen
for their part in secretly reproducing during 1969-73 over 2,000 Uniate
prayerbooks and a number of psalm and service books, using state printing
facilities in Lvov. Should the Greek Catholic Church be legalized again they
would rejoin it, but under the circumstances they find it more practicable to
work within the framework of the official Church to keep up the faith
among the people and to counter the powerful anti-religious pressures. But
as the former Uniate clergy are dying out, some of the parishes are now
taken over by the new generation of clergy, already trained in the Orthodox
seminaries, who may not necessarily identify themselves with the Uniate
traditions and loyalties. With the shortage of new clergy, however, more and
more churches are left without a priest and are in danger of closing. One
recent account from the Western Ukraine describes the plight of believers in
such localities:

> In my village there is no priest, but people come to church every Sunday and,
> together with the psalmsinger (diak) they sing Matins and the Mass . . . while a
> chalice and lighted candles are placed on the altar.

The second group consists of the "recalcitrant" clergy and believers who
reject the Russian Orthodox Church either as "schismatic" and "Muscovite"
or as "corrupted" by its subservience to the atheistic regime. Some Uniate
laymen, particularly from among the intelligentsia, attend the few Roman
Catholic churches still open in the Western Ukraine But the majority of
them depend on the "Catacomb Church" for occasional religious services
and rites, sacraments, religious instruction, etc.

The underground Uniate Church is said to embrace at least 300-350
priests, headed by three or more secret bishops; they recognize the authority
of the Church's primate Josyf Slipyj who, after nearly eighteen years imprisonment, was released by the regime and allowed to leave for Rome. One of
the "catacomb" bishops — Vasyl Velychkovskyi — was arrested in 1969
together with two other Uniate clergymen and sentenced to three years'
imprisonment. In Lvov, alone, according to Levitin-Krasnov's recent account, there are some 80 Uniate priests. Almost invariably these clergymen
hold full-time secular jobs or have now retired from such jobs; many have

behind them a decade or more of imprisonment or exile for their refusal to "convert" to Orthodoxy. Their identities seem in most cases known to the Soviet police who frequently submit them to searches, interrogations, and fines but stop short of arresting them unless they extend their activities beyond a narrow circle of friends in private homes. The thinning ranks of the aging "recalcitrant" clergy are being replenished by an unknown number of younger priests already trained and ordained in the underground Church. They are more activist and militant than the older clergy. Outside the Western Ukraine there may be as many as thirty Ukrainian Catholic priests in Lithuania, some of them serving their Ukrainian flock from afar.

The third, smallest but most radical category of the Uniates, centers around a "neo-Uniate" movement popularly known as *Pokutniki* ("Penitents") dating since the 1950's which apparently has broken away from the "Catacomb" Church. This group, which has been subjected to ruthless repressive measures by the administration and the police, combines eschatology with radical nationalist views and urges a total repudiation of the Soviet regime. According to recent Soviet attacks on *Pokutniki*, their movement

> spreads among the population a slogan of the God-choseness of the Ukrainian people, prohibits the believers to participate in elections, in social-political life, calls upon them to reject service in the Soviet Army, the work in Soviet enterprises, education of children in schools, and medical assistance.

> On the one hand, the "neo-Uniates" proclaim themselves a purely religious movement, a "truly apostolic faith" (and) on the other hand, they speculate on the national sentiments by declaring that "the Lord elevates" now the Ukraine which allegedly has "for long centuries been under oppression, in abject slavery and captivity." Thus, they are trying to inflame hatred towards the Russian people, which allegedly has brought atheism to the Ukraine.

Since 1968 the Uniate activities in the Western Ukraine have markedly intensified, possibly in connection with the legalization of the Uniate Church in the neighboring Czechoslovakia and in line with the general upsurge of dissent in the Ukraine. There have been more and more cases of the priests and believers challenging the validity of the Church's prohibition, taking possession of the churches closed or abandoned by the Orthodox Church, and in particular sending petitions and delegations to Moscow and Kiev demanding legalization of the Uniate Church.

In 1974 one such delegation accompanied by a Ukrainian priest from Lithuania, Volodymyr Prokopiv, travelled from the Lvov oblast to Moscow to hand in a similar petition signed by 12,000 believers. Soviet response to such petitions was to sharpen repressive measures against the activist Uniate clergy, monastics and laymen and to intensify their propaganda campaign against this "bourgeois nationalist Church" which "was forever rejected by the Ukrainian people." Soviet publications have been voicing alarm about the upsurge of the Uniate activities, involving "illegal agitation for the revival of the Uniate Church" and distribution of "pamphlets, calendars and prayerbooks of anti-Soviet and anti-Communist content." Speaking at a special conference on Catholicism in the USSR that was held in Lithuania in December, 1969, a professional *antireligioznik* from the Ukrainian SSR charged that

> ... the Uniates are persistently spreading the idea that the Greek Catholic
> Church is allegedly the Ukrainian national church, the bearer of the material
> and spiritual culture of the Ukrainian people; playing on the national senti-
> ments of some berlievers, they stress the claim that the religious Poles have
> their (own) Church, but not the Ukrainians who thus do not enjoy the right of
> the freedom of conscience.

> Nurturing hopes for the restoration of the Uniate Church, its apologists are
> working on the clergy who reunited with Orthodoxy, trying to persuade them
> to repudiate the "Muscovites" and to openly or secretly carry a Uniate, pro-
> Vatican line. I some regions of the Ukraine, illegal schools were organized to
> train new Uniate priests. In a series of localities, the Uniates have wilfully
> opened the previously closed churches and were conducting religious services
> (without a license) . . .

The cause of the persecuted Uniates was taken up by Ukrainian dissent
movement. Its mouthpiece, the *Ukrainian Herald*, carried during 1970-72
accounts of the harassment, searches, arrests and trials of the Uniates and
has editorially condemned the "wanton liquidation of the Greek Catholic
Church."

During the recent years, the dissident Lithuanian Catholic clergy has also
offered its support to the demands for the lifting of the illegal ban on the
Uniate Church. In September, 1974, from a leading Russian Orthodox
dissenter, Anatolii Levitin-Krasnov, came an eloquent appeal to Sakharov's
Human Rights Committee in Moscow calling upon it to raise its voice in
defense of the Uniates and other persecuted religious groups.

> The Union in the Western Ukraine is a massive popular movement. Its perse-
> cution means not only religious oppression, but also restriction of the national
> rights of West Ukrainians.

Within the Soviet Union are Christians who are locked in prisons, concentration camps, or "special psychiatric asylums" for declaring the Word of
God.

Andre Martin, author of *Buried Alive in the Soviet Hospital-Prisons*, states
that

> some physicians in the service of the secret police do not conceal the object of
> treatment they inflict upon their patients. The goal is simple: reduce all
> "opponents" to ideological and political conformity. "You are hospitalized for
> your political ideas" they admit to those who protest . . . "When you are cured
> of your political ideas you will be set free."

In a petition to the U.S. Secretary General in 1970, the Evangelical
Christian-Baptists requested that ECB prisoners be set free, that children
taken away from parents because of religious training be given back to their
parents, and that confiscated homes be returned.

In another document, mothers protest the confiscation of their children,
pointing out that the children who have been isolated and imprisoned
because of their religious education are free from delinquency and vice, and
that the methods used by the Communist governments "were used by
Pharaoh, murder of children in ancient Egypt; by Herod; and by Nero,
renowned for centuries for his blood thirstiness."

The Free World, and Free World churches, have given little support to the
Church of the Catacombs. The members of the underground church,
Grossu states, know the meaning of "Be faithful unto death. . . . "

Anatolii Levitin-Krasnov, a Russian Orthodox layman who was allowed to leave the Soviet Union, describes the persecution of members of the Truly Orthodox Church and several outlawed churches — the *initsiativniki*, unofficial Baptists, the Reformist Seventh-Day Adventists, the Pentecostalists and Jehovah's Witnesses as follows:

> The most awful thing is the persecution of the . . . Uniates (Ukrainian Catholics) and members of the Truly Orthodox Church, which has become the norm of life, does not evoke the slightest indignation. This unheard of savagery is blatantly committed, yet calls forth no protest.

> Tracing the history of the Ukrainian Catholic Church from the time of its unification with Rome in 1596, restrictions and persecutions have followed the "Uniates" throughout their history, under the Russian Czars and under the communist government.

> In 1946 upon the final reunification of the Western Ukraine and Western Byelorussia with the USSR the Stalin regime undertook the persecution of the Uniates and arrested the head of Ukrainian Catholic Church, Metropolitan Joseph Slipyi of Lvov and six other bishops.

> Resolution of reunification of Ukrainian Catholics with Russian Orthodoxy was formulated and forced upon the Uniates. Priests who refused to comply were arrested, and those clergy who outwardly resisted the resolution were charged with treason and sentenced to 25 years in prison.

> No judicial inquiry was conducted. All repressions were carried out through a special committee of the KGB, Soviet secret police.

> If we take into account that together with the clergy, students in the Uniate seminaries, parishioners, and the most active lay people were punished, then it is not surprising that the number of victims soon reached . . . 300,000 people.

> Despite a series of persecutions over the years and the imprisonment and death of most Uniate bishops, the campaign to destroy the Uniates failed.

> Today 80 Uniate priests function almost openly in Lvov alone. They perform in their homes the Divine Service (liturgy) and, upon request, religious rites (of various kinds). Three Uniate bishops function in the underground. As soon as one dies or is arrested, another is immediately consecrated.

> Communist authorities are obliged to tolerate this situation since they seem to feel that they cannot risk again a policy of mass repressions and the arrest of individuals, fines and short term imprisonment.

> The tragic impact of the situation on thousands of human souls beaten and broken by the violation of their conscience is further aggravating tensions between Ukrainian and Russian peoples.

> It behooves the U.N. Commission to come to the defense of the persecuted Uniates. This is a matter of elementary humanity.

Christians in Ukraine and the Soviet Union generally are the 20th century counterparts of the early "catacomb-martyr Christians" according to reliable and well-documented information received in this country, only the lions of the past have been replaced by mutant Soviet bears.

It has been revealed that the Soviet government, in its efforts to exterminate Christians, has for years and now continues to employ tactics of torture, dismissal from employment, exile, commitment of sane people to mental institutions, forced removal of children from their parental homes and parents, imprisonment, sentences to forced labor in concentration camps, the commission of cold-blooded murder and atrocities and crimes against humanity which are unparalleled in the annals of the history of manking.

Specifically on May 2, 1973, 1,500 Ukrainian Protestant (Baptist) young people gathered in a forest near Kharkov, Ukraine, for an Easter worship service after the government had denied them the use of a church or hall. As the service began, Soviet militia forces and civilian authorities charged into the congregation, brutally assaulted, molested, and arrested many who were present.

Ukrainian Christians and Christians living in other member States of the Soviet Union are not seeking the right to emigrate from their countries primarily. Moreover, they are not engaging in activities prohibited by Soviet law, nor are they defying the Soviet government. They also are not attempting to coerce others to accept their faith. The Christians being viciously persecuted by the Soviet power structure are merely seeking the right to worship in accordance with the dictates of their conscience, a right supposedly guaranteed every Soviet citizen by Section 9 of the "Decree Regarding Separation of Church and State and by the International Convention against Discrimination in Child-rearing" which became law in the Soviet Union on November 1, 1962.

Both the United States and the Soviet Union are signatories of the U.N. Charter and as such are also bound by the U.N. Declaration of Human Rights. The Soviet Government is in clear violation of the Declaration. Moreover, the methods being employed by the Soviet government are crimes against humanity and, as was done in the case of Nazi Germany, must be condemned and resisted by civilized humanity.

> Recently the Ternopil members of the Komsomol planted a bomb in a church. The bomb exploded but no great damage was caused. In Lvov a church was converted into a restaurant. The church is situated in Zyblikevich Street now Ivan Franko Street. The Ecclesiastical Seminary was destroyed during the war. Its clock tower is still standing. The church on Rus Street has now been under repair for a long time.
>
> The Stavropihia is also closed. The Armenian church is being repaired. St. George's Church is open. The majority of those who attend mass are from the east. There is no lack of agents. In Cracow Street the church is finely decorated with embroidery; the Galicians mostly go there. All the Polish Roman Catholic churches are closed except the cathedral on Halych Street. On Horodetsky Street at the Leo Sapiha corner someone who wanted to take down the cross from the church spire fell to his death. At present this church is in neglect. On Yaniv and Horodetsky Street the Polish Roman Catholic church has been converted into a furniture warehouse.

During 1976 Easter celebrations, the scolding of the faithful and the priests of the underground Ukrainian Catholic Church was increased to prevent the conducting of religious services on Eastern Sunday. This new policy arose at the end of the 25th Congress of the Communist Party of the Soviet Union in February, 1976. Police cordons, set up on the roads to the villages in the Sambir and Horodetsk regions, checked cars, buses and motorcycles, searching for priests whose photographs were in their possession.

In the village of Pidhaichyky-Sambir region, the KGB beat up a Ukrainian

Catholic so badly that he lost his hearing.

The Orthodox Church is also being persecuted. For example, in the Lvov oblast near Mykolaiv, the secretary of the Party group, the headmaster of the school and the head of the *kolhosp* called out an Orthodox priest late one evening, stabbed him in the back three times and hung him from a ladder by a bandage near his home, where the doors had been closed in advance.

In the village of Stavchany-Pustomytsk region and in many other villages, before the blessing of the *paskha*, the organized theft of holy articles in the churches took place, vestments and other embroidered materials were destroyed or damaged, and no one has tried to find the culprits.

In the Ukraine, possibly as many as one-half of the 132 Roman Catholic churches officially reported in 1961 have since been closed. Apart from the Hungarian clergy in Transcarpathia, a number of priests (nearly all Poles) are ministering to the overwhelmingly Polish flock; among them are at least a dozen graduates of the Riga seminary. The majority of the operating Roman Catholic churches are now apparently located in the old Polish communities east of the 1939 Soviet-Polish border, particularly in the oblasts of Vinnytsia and Khmelnytskyi. To the south-east, there is a Roman Catholic church in Odessa with a Lithuanian priest serving the city's multi-national congregation, as well as some distant priestless churches. The activism and popularity of some of the clergy led the Ukrainian-language atheist monthly, *Liudyna i svit*, to attack a number of Roman Catholic priests for the alleged violations of Soviet legislation on "cults," including "illegal" gatherings of the clergy, "reactionary" sermons, religious "propaganda" and, in particular, the work with youth. One of the priests attacked, Fr. Bernard Michiewicz of Stryi, Galicia, was tried in summer, 1974 by the Lvov court on such charges as systematic religious instruction of children, "performing actions directed at arousing superstition and religious fanaticism," and spreading "slanderous fabrications about the Soviet system."

On official occasion of the Ukrainian-rite bishops' presence in Rome, together with some 400 Ukrainian-rite laymen, headed by Joseph Cardinal Slipyj, exiled major archbishop of Lvov in the Soviet Union, Pope Paul VI said:

> Day after day we have participated in the anxieties and problems (of Ukrainian-rite Catholics) in the sincere desire of working them out in the manner best permitted.
>
> We have a continuing interest both for Ukrainians living abroad — the generous witnesses to the name Christian in both the new and the old world — and for your fellow countrymen who have remained in the Ukraine, to whom our fatherly, vigilant and shared concern goes out, well knowing how faithful they remain to the same cause for which St. Josephat gave up his life.

Cardinal Slipyj told Pope Paul that the Ukrainian-rite bishops present were

> happy to have the occasion to be able to show personally to Your Holiness, vicar of Jesus Christ on earth and successor of St. Peter, our sentiments of filial love, faithfulness and loyalty, along with the assurance of the unfailing loyalty to the Holy See of our particular Ukrainian Church, which . . . has suffered hard and terrible persecution for its indissoluble relationship to the Holy See.

During the day of October 3, 1974, Ukrainian-rite Joseph Cardinal Slipyj denounced religious persecution in totalitarian nations and most particularly persecution of the Ukrainian-rite Catholic Church in the Soviet Union.

The white-bearded Ukrainian-rite prelate said he thought it necessary to call the attention of the Synod of Bishops to the obstacles hostile governments create for evangelization and even for the practice of religion.

> Religion is not only subject to persecution but is in danger of extinction in many countries including the USSR, of which the Ukraine is a part.
>
> We should have before us especially the situation in the Ukraine and of the Ukrainians.

He said that while the religious picture in Poland seems to be improving, in Russia it is worsening.

Pointing to the persecution of intellectuals in Russia and their confinement in hospitals when they are judged at odds with the state, Cardinal Slipyj concluded:

> It is our duty and that of the universal Church to condemn every injustice which violates freedom of faith, of conscience, of reason and of opinion, and to demand the liberation of those who are held in public custody and those detained in psychiatric institutions, as they are called. . . . This must be done especially for those men who defend divine and human values.

Increased activity of the Uniates, who acknowledge the supremacy of the Pope, has been matched by increased persecution. According to *Chronicle,* priests have been detained and beaten up by the police. On October 18, 1968, the homes of ten were searched and religious objects confiscated.

Further information has come from a *samizdat* essay of January, 1970 *Chronicle of Resistance,* by Valentin Moroz, a Ukrainian historian. He condemned the appropriation of religious works of art from a Uniate church in the Kiev area, which belonged to a strongly nationalistic minority, the Hutsuls. Arguing that religion and national culture had become inseparable in Eastern Europe, he said:

> One must inevitably conclude that a fight against the Church is a fight against the culture. The anti-religious struggle is in fact, a *Kulturkampf*. It is more convenient to destroy the foundations of a nation as a whole under the guise of a struggle against religion. . . .

In a pastoral letter distributed in London, 84-year-old Joseph Cardinal Slipyj has called on all Ukrainians — Catholic, Orthodox and Protestant — to unite "in one particular Ukrainian Church under the leadership of the Patriarch."

However, twenty-two delegates to the general chapter of the Ukrainian-rite Basilian order have elected a new superior general who is expected to take a hardline position against Joseph Cardinal Slipyj's fight to establish a Ukrainian-rite patriarchate.

The election was seen as a severe blow to attempts by Cardinal Slipyj to establish a patriarchate with himself as its head.

Pope Paul VI has firmly squelched any hope that a Ukrainian Catholic patriarchate will be established during his pointificate.

Besides opposing Cardinal Slipyj's disobedience to Pope Paul VI, the new superior is expected to clean up abuses in the order itself and enforce stricter discipline.

The Vatican has issued a statement in London reaffirming the Roman Catholic Church's jurisdiction over Ukrainian-rite Catholics through the Apolstolic Exarch, Bishop Augustine Hornyak, and denying the authority of Joseph Cardinal Slipyj, acting in the disputed capacity of Patriarch of the Ukrainian Catholic Church.

The statement, released through the Apolstolic Delegate, Archbishop Bruno Heim, stressed that priests conducting their ministries without Bishop Hornyak's permission are automatically suspended. Several priests have been sent to Britain by Cardinal Slipyj who is claiming patriarchal authority over the Ukrainian church worldwide.

The Vatican action, which seeks to quell a raging dispute in this country as well as in other areas of the world over Cardinal Slipyj's position in the Church, expressly forbids any Ukrainian priests sent by the Rome-based Cardinal to act in a priestly capacity without local permission.

The statement said Bishop Hornyak was the only lawful authority in the Ukrainian Church in Great Britain "to the exclusion of all other Ukrainian Catholics." It said any priest carrying out a ministry requiring permission from Church authority, such as hearing confessions or conducting marriages, incurs the penalty of suspension unless he is authorized by true bishop.

The dispute has led to the closing of one Ukrainian church, the Church of the Sacred Heart.

On December 13, 1976, Pope Paul VI, at the audience of Cardinal Slipyj and some Ukrainian bishops, said:

> Allow us also to recall before you, with all the respect due to persons, the widespread uneasiness of certain Ukrainian communities and their pastors. We are referring to the expectation of a patriarchal title, which, in the present circumstances the See of Rome does not see the possibility of granting.

Pope Paul asked the bishops — who had petitioned the Pope to establish the patriarchate and permit ordination of married men — to rally around his decision regarding the controversial patriarchate.

Apart from the traditional Orthodox and Catholic Churches there exist in Ukraine a number of Protestant churches or sects. Some of them are registered with the appropriate government organs, but others have been refused registration and are working illegally, and therefore suffer from a particularly vicious persecution.

The most widespread Protestant church in Ukraine is the Union of Evangelical Christian Baptists (UECB) who form territorial communities. In 1960 the total number of Baptists in the USSR was given as about 540,000, more than half of whom lived in Ukraine. There were 170 communities in Kiev region, 56 in Kharkov, 73 in Donetsk, and 72 in Chernihiv regions.

The Union of the Seventh Day Adventists is officially recognised by the Soviet authorities and has its centre in Moscow. This sect has 300 communities of which 115 are in Ukraine. Out of their total number of 26,000 in the USSR,

9,000 are in Ukraine with bigger communities in the Donetsk and Crimea regions.

The Pentecostals are banned in the Soviet Union for their alleged "anti-social and anti-Soviet" attitude. But groups of them exist as can be judged from newspaper reports attacking them or describing their "misdeeds." Pentecostal communities exist illegally in Odessa, Volynia and Rivne regions of Ukraine.

The sect of *Jehovah's Witnesses* is banned in Ukraine and its members are severely persecuted. The Soviet press frequently relates hair-rising stories about the alleged "crimes" of members of this sect and their clandestine activities. For some time Jehovah's witnesses published their journal, *Watchtower*, illegally in Ukrainian language. Their groups are active in Donetsk, Mykolaiv and West Ukrainian regions.

According to the census of January 15, 1959 there were 840,000 Jews in Ukraine, living predominantly in the big cities.

The Judaic religion is officially recognised in the USSR, and as such, according to an authoritative statement, it enjoys "possibilites for free existence (synagogues, schools, religious literature). It has no single centre in the USSR, but synagogues have links with one another . . ."

A number of Jews from the Soviet Union managed to emigrate to Israel in the years 1946-48 and 1956-57, and in order to stop large-scale emigration; the Soviet authorities started an intensive campaign to discredit Israel, depicting life of emigres there in the darkest colors.

Jewish religious life in Ukraine has been reduced to the barest minimum. There are no Jewish schools or publications in Ukraine, most synagogues have been closed or ruined, and the process continues. Russification and abandonment of religion is rapidly progressing among the younger Jewish generation.

Before World War II the small Moslem population of the Ukrainian territory consisted largely of the Crimean Tatars. Of the 205,000 Tatars living in Ukraine in 1926, 175,000 were inhabitants of the Crimea. After their mass expulsion from the Crimea by the Russian government to Central Asia and Siberia in the wake of the war, as reprisal for alleged collaboration with the Germans, their number fell sharply. The census of 1959 shows only 62,000 Tatars in the Ukrainian SSR, some of whom are probably Volga Tatars, newcomers working in the Donbas mines and the industrial towns of East Ukraine. And although the Crimean Tatars were officially rehabilitated in September, 1967, very few of them have been given the opportunity to return to their homeland.

The sufferings that the Ukrainian Autocephalous Orthodox Church, the Ukrainian Catholic Church of the Eastern-rite and other denominations have undergone at the hands of the Communist Russian occupation regime in the last 60 years is a great tragedy which most people in the free world still fail to realise. The martyrdom of the Ukrainian Churches ought to be widely known so as to warn those who are inclined to give too readily the benefit of doubt to the Communist Russian regime. It should also encourage people in the free world to stand up in defence of the persecuted behind the Iron Curtain, in particular in defence of the rights of the Ukrainian nation to religious, national and political liberty.

5

Suffering Byelorussian Church

After the liquidation of NEP, the Moscow goverment started and intensified the Russification of the Byelorussian people and their country. To bring the Byelorussian literary language closer to Russian, on August 26, 1933, changes and simplifications in Byelorussian grammar and orthography were introduced.

The Moscow government removed from circulation and destroyed all ethnographic and patriotic Byelorussian books and periodic publications. For this purpose in 1935 a secret catalogue was printed (the "Joint Control List of Publications of the Byelorussian State Publishing House") for the use of Communist Party members in an edition of 500 copies. According to this publication, in 1935 alone, 1,778 of the listed books and magazines were destroyed, amounting to 12 million copies. Instead, Byelorussia was flooded with Russian publications of classical literature and Communist propaganda.

On March 13, 1938, by a governmental decree, the study of the Russian language was made obligatory in Byelorussian schools, and other national republics of the USSR. Immediately a final Russification of schools was pursued. Russian was the compulsory language of instruction in all higher schools and in nearly all secondary and grammar schools.

The Russian language was introduced in the cultural life administrative offices, commerce, communications, armed forces, etc.

The Moscow government commenced to liquidate the cultural achievements of the Byelorussian people of the past. Many architectural and religious monuments — cathedrals, churches and monasteries — were ruined completely. Even after the Second World War at Freedom Square in Minsk, the Roman Catholic cathedral and a medieval firehouse tower of typical Byelorussian architecture were destroyed. Byelorussian buildings were erected in the uniform present Russian style.

The names of towns, streets, institutions, schools, etc. are dedicated to Russians or international Communists. The University of Minsk is dedicated to the Russian Communist, Lenin; the military school in Minsk is dedicated to the Russian Czarist General Suvorov, the prospect in Minsk is dedicated to the Russian poet, Pushkin. In Byelorussian towns and cities many monuments were rebuilt and dedicated to Russian personalities.

It is hard to assume that the genocidal policies of the present Soviet Russian government will be able to eradicate the Byelorussian people with their desire for national independence. The historical past convincingly shows that at a suitable opportunity, Byelorussians will again take up the military fight for their liberation.

During 60 years of occupation, the Moscow government has annihilated over 6 million of the Byelorussian population.

Besides the physical extermination of people, the Soviet Russian government commenced to liquidate the national spirit, ethnic distinctions, and cultural achievements of the Byelorussian people, with the aim to create one indivisible Soviet Russian nation.

The religious life was struck by Bolsheviks first of all. The Assembly of the clergy and laymen of July 23, 1923, in Minsk, proclaimed the foundation of the Autocephalous Byelorussian Orthodox Church to secure independence from Moscow. However, the elected Head of this Church, Metropolitan Melkhisedek, was called to Moscow, imprisoned and died under mysterious circumstances. Bishop Ioan of Mazyr died in a concentration camp; Bishop Filaret of Babruisk and Bishop Nikolai of Slutsk died in prison. Subsequently, all 2,000 clergymen were shot or deported to concentratrion camps; 2,500 churches and 23 monasteries were ruined or closed. By 1937 the Orthodox Church in the BSSR was destroyed completely. The religious life of all other denominations and church organizations met a similar fate.

At the time of the Second World War, the All-Byelorussian Orthodox Assembly took place in Minsk on August 30, 1942. This Assembly composed of bishops, priests, and laymen restored the Autocephalous Byelorussian Orthodox Church and requested the Patriarch of Constantinople to grant the required *Thomos*. The believers in Eastern Byelorussia began to repair and restore the churches and resume services and religious life. However, after the occupation of Byelorussia in 1944, the Soviet Russian government liquidated this Church. The Byelorussian bishops were forced to leave the country, many priests were shot or deported to concentration camps, and many parishes were closed. Still-existing churches in Byelorussia were subordinated to the Patriarch of Moscow and Russified.

Little is known about the situation of the Catholic Church in Byelorussia and the Ukraine. Catholics — predominantly Poles — constitute a significant minority in Western Byelorussia, especially in the Grodno oblast where, according to Soviet estimates, there were at least 176,000 Catholics in the early 1960's. The 1959 total of 154 churches in Byelorussia has been reduced by at least one-third during Krushchev's anti-religious campaign and presently stands somewhere between 65 and 100 churches, some two-thirds of them located in the Grodno oblast, where Poles constituted over 30 per cent of population in 1959.

Some 40 priests are reportedly active in Byelorussia, most of whom are Poles. According to a recent Polish visitor to the republic, the local Roman Catholic clergy are working in most difficult conditions; they try to serve also the growing number of priestless parishes, but must each time seek official permission to do so. Though the believers in such parishes continue to assemble for prayer services, sooner or later their churches are being closed due to the lack of pastors. Soviet writers have noted the intense religiosity of the Catholics in the Republic, but their numbers are declining due to both the anti-religious pressures and assimilation. Some years ago, the Vatican-Soviet negotiations have reportedly come close to an agreement to have a Roman Catholic bishop appointed for Byelorussia, but opposition both from the local Polish clergy and from the Church in Poland to a Byelorussian candidate for such post has allegedly frustrated this initiative.

The attempt of the Byelorussian Greek Orthodox population to attain cultural and political independence found expression in the creation of an autocephalic Byelorussian Orthodox Church as the center of their religious life. The Church was first declared to be autocephalic in the thirteenth century and it existed as such intermittently until the seventeenth century. In later centuries the Byelorussian people lost their opportunity for independent national development and with it their autocephalic Church.

In 1918, by popular will, Byelorussia declared its independence, but suppression of independence by the Communists removed the possibility of a restoration of the Byelorussian Autocephalic Church. However, when the Soviet regime began to persecute the Russian Orthodox Church on the excuse that it was a bulwark of the former autocracy and of counter-revolution of all kinds, the Byelorussian Church took advantage of the general relaxation during the period of the New Economic Policy to assemble the national leaders in a Church synod. The synod now re-created the Byelorussian Autocephalic Orthodox Church on the basis of historic precedent and in accordance with instructions from Patriarch Tikhon and, after his arrest, his successor Metropolitan Agafangel, who had authorized local religious authorities to act independently if necessary. By restoring the Autocephalic Church, the Byelorussian Orthodox Church sought to bring about a local national spiritual revival and to protect itself from from pressure by the Revived Church and destruction by the regime.

The first blow was the indictment of the Metropolitan and the clergy of the cathedrals for concealing religious treasures earmarked for Volga famine relief, despite the fact that all these had been removed in accordance with inventories.

The second blow was the inundation of Minsk in 1924 with the clergy of the sovietophile Revived Church. The Metropolitan was summoned to Moscow, and Soviet agents and GPU guards installed Revived Church bishops in the cathedral. The people resisted resolutely. The railway workers of Minsk opposed the new clergy with special energy. Many were arrested, show trials were held, the prisoners were beaten in the GPU cells and deported.

The third blow was the arrest of the Metropolitan and his deportation to Krasnoyarsk in 1926; he was also reduced in rank.This was one of the first services performed on behalf of the Soviet regime by Metropolitan Sergei, who enjoyed Soviet confidence, before his outright declaration of loyalty in 1927.

World War II released Byelorussia from the Soviet regime, and at the very beginning, while the ruins were still smoking, the restoration of religious life began.

The rebuilding of churches which had not been completely destroyed in the cities, towns, and raions was undertaken. On September 9, 1941, a Byelorussian Church Council was called together by Metropolitan Dionisy of Warsaw. In 1941 and 1942 three bishops were appointed for the

Byelorussian bishoprics. Between August 30 and September 2, 1942, a
synod of the Byelorussian Orthodox Church held in Minsk reestablished the
Byelorussian Autocephalic Church, with Metropolitan Panteleimon as its
head. The restoratrion of religious life took place under difficult conditions
of war, partisan fighting, a shortage of building materials and with complex
relations existing between the occupation forces and the enemies of the
Byelorussian national movement. Soviet agents attempted to sue provocation to prevent this development. Many of the leaders in religious and public
life perished at the hands of Soviet partisans, or as a result of false denuncia-
tions made to the German punitive agencies.

The close of the war turned back the wheel of history. Again Soviet forces
invaded Byelorussia and again the national aspirations were suppressed. By
refusing to recognize Byelorussian autocephaly, the Moscow Patriarchate
again performed a service for the Soviet regime. The clergy and the people,
who resisted the merger with the Patriarchal Church, were cruelly mistreated by the Soviet authorities. Again there were mass deportations,
executions, and arrests.

The NKVD, in seeking out and liquidating the participants in the All-
Byelorussian Synod and the supporters of the Byelorussian Autocephalic
Church, regarded them as enemies of the Soviet system. L. Tsanava, chief of
the NKVD in the Byelorussian Soviet Socialist Republic in 1951, declared:

> The majority of the Byelorussian nationalists . . . when unearthed and seized,
> suffered well-merited punishment. . . . The majority have already gone to
> their graves, and those who have escaped will not avoid the punishment which
> they deserve.

In the Byelorussian town, Nova Ruda, the occupation government decided to close the church and to make it into a granary. Pleas of the faithful to
leave them the house of prayer were disregarded. When on July 26, 1970 the
men left for work, the militia surrounded the church and loaded all church
furniture on a truck. Since nobody paid attention to their pleas, the women
lay down across the road to prevent the plunder of the church. The true
driver refused to move although he received strict orders not to pay attention to the women wallowing in mud. A militiaman took the place of the
driver and the truck left, but first the women were forcefully removed from
the road. The church was then converted into a grain elevator.

In the summer of 1957 there were no Byelorussian parishes in the territory of Byelorussia. Of the former eparchies only Minsk and Bobruisk
remain as bishoprics. In the religious seminary, teaching is done in the
Russian language.

The hierarchy of the Byelorussian Autocephalic Orthodox Church has
been driven into exile. Parishes of the Byelorussian Autocephalic Orthodox
Church, which continue to develop its religious life in accordance with the
national aspirations of the people, now exist only in countries of the free
world — the United States, Great Britain, Australia, Canada, Germany and
Belgium.

Persecution of Religion in the Balticum

Communism now controls a third of the world's surface. Over 250 million of their captives are Christians. Bishops, priests and members of religious orders numbering over 15,000 are known to have been murdered. Another three million Christian laymen have been murdered and twelve million imprisoned or banished to Siberia where they await a lingering death.

The Vatican's 1970 yearbook estimates that there are 659 million Roman Catholics in the world.

The Vatican counts as Catholics all persons who have been baptized in the church, without reference to whether they practice their religion.

A preface says the figures cannot be considered fully accurate because of the difficulty of obtaining information about the so-called "Churches of silence" in such places as China, North Korea and the Soviet Union.

Figures published recently by the Vatican's Central Statistics Office, for January 1, 1975, give the number of Catholics in the world as 705,028,000, or 18.2 per cent of the world population of 3,873,733,000. Including Protestants and Orthodox, the number of Christians comes up to 31 per cent of the world population.

It is difficult to find accurate statistics for the different religions of the world, but the following figures may be taken as an approximation:

Catholics	705,028,000
Protestants	350,000,000
Orthodox	150,000,000
Muslims	550,000,000
Hindus	510,000,000
Confucianists	310,000,000
Budhists	280,000,000
Shintoists	75,000,000
Taoists	50,000,000
Jews	16,000,000
Others	877,705,000

When the Soviet regime came to power in 1917, the Catholic Church in Russia had: 1 Archdiocese, 4 Dioceses and the Apostolic Administration for the Armenians at Tiflis and the Apostolic Vicariate for Siberia at Vladivostock, with a total of about 2,587,000 Catholics, 980 churches, 681 parishes, three seminaries, one Ecclesiastic Academy at Petersburg, 36 institutions and religious houses and some hundreds of asylums, schools and other charitable Catholic works.

When, in 1939, the territories of Eastern Poland, East from the so-called Curzon-Riebentrop-Molotov line were annexed nine other archdioceses and Catholic dioceses fell under the Soviet-Russian domination, with a total of approximately 8,437,000 faithful, 4,843 parishes, 7,409 churches, 5,344 priests, nine major seminaries with about 800 seminarists, 888 religious houses, with about 3,000 religious men and women, 16,960 schools and, approximately, 300 orphanages, hospitals and charitable Catholic institutions.

In 1941, after the annexation of Lithuania, Estonia and Latvia, nine further Archdioceses and Catholic dioceses fell under Soviet Russia's domination. This meant a total of about 3,525,000 faithful, 1,393 churches, 1,086 parishes, 1,711 priests, six major seminaries with about 1,200 students, 103 religious houses with 827 religious men and women, 780 Catholic schools (Wilna) and a Theological Faculty annexed to the Kaunas University.

In 1945, finally following the annexation of the territories, some more 542,967 Catholics, belonging to the Mucacevo diocese with about 540 churches, 330 parishes, 487 priests and some ten religious houses, twenty schools and other charitable Catholic institutions came under the Soviet regime.

Therefore, during the period from 1917 to 1945, the following had become part of the Soviet Union:

15,091,000	Catholic faithful
8,454	priests of the secular clergy
1,170	religious men and women
45	Archbishops and bishops
3,500	nuns
10,321	churches and chapels
6,930	parishes
24	Archdioceses and dioceses
1,034	institutions, religious houses, and Catholic seminaries
20,316	schools, asylums and education institutes
1,520	hospitals, orphanages and charitable institutions
70	typographies and Catholic libraries
110	magazines and Catholic publications.

Priests and Religions:

From the 8,554 priests of the secular clergy and the 1,170 of the regular clergy, which made a total of 9,624 members of the Catholic Clergy in Russia, the following were lost:

A) *Russia* (territories before 1939)

a) Murdered priests 120
b) Died in prison 150
c) Disappeared 200
d) Deported or interned 200
e) Expelled or exiled 130
f) Dispersed or hidden   100

                                              Total   900

B) *Russia (former Polish territories)*

a) Murdered priests 70

b) Died in prison 150
c) Disappeared 1,500
d) Deported or interned 1,000
e) Living in exile 600
f) In hiding 800
g) In schism...1,111
h) Progresists 200

                                                    Total   5,431

C) *Baltic States*

a) Murdered priests..150
b) Died in prison or disappeared.................................500
c) Deported or interned 300
d) Escaped to foreign countries 200
e) Hiding in their own countries 300

                                                    Total   1,450

D) *Sub-Carpathia*

a) Murdered priests..12
b) Died or disappeared...100
c) Deported or sentenced 200
d) In schism 36
e) Hiding in their own countries 50

                                                    Total   398

A) *Human losses*

The total losses of Catholic priests and religious who were lost to Catholic Church in Russia and within the annexed territories amount to a total of 8,049.

This figure can be subdivided as follows:

a) Murdered or executed 352
b) Died or disappeared 2,600
c) Deported or interned 1,700
d) Escaped abroad 930
e) In hiding within their own countries 1,250
f) Adherants 1,147

Only some 1,575 priests are supposed to be still free in Russia, besides the 1,147 who had adhered either to the Orthodox Russian Church or to the movement of the Priests Peace Partisans.

These are distributed in the various territories as indicated hereunder:

a) Russia   (Territories before 1939)
            12 Catholic priests (there used to be 912 before)

b) Russia   (former Polish territories)
            965 Catholic priests (formerly 6,267)

c) Baltic States   1,088 priests and religious (formerly 2,538)

d) Sub-Carpathia
            56 Catholic priests (formerly 474)

B) *Material losses*

	1939	1953
1) Archdioceses and dioceses	24	2 (Kaunas and Panavezys in Lithuania)

all the others were liquidated, deprived of their titulars; those of oriental rite were turned over to Orthodox Churches.

	1939	1953
2) Parishes	6,930	1,200 (1 at Moscow, 10 at Tiraspol, 800 in Lithuania and Latvia, 300 in the Ukraine, 30 in Sub-Carpathia etc.
3) Churches and chapels	10,321	1,500 all the others were closed; requisitioned and adhibited for profane purposes.
4) Seminaries	18	All closed.
5) Religious Houses	1,019	All closed.
6) Schools, asylums, etc.	20,316	All requisitioned and nationalized
7) Hospitals, orphanages, etc.	1,520	All requisitioned
8) Typographies and libraries	70	All requisitioned and nationalized
9) Magazines and publications	110	All suppressed
10) Catholic Associations, organizations and institutions (of both rites)	3,000	All suppressed
11) Land property, buildings, etc.		All forfeited
12) Libraries, works of art, etc.		All forfeited, dispersed or re-sold.

A) Personal Losses
a) Archbishops and Bishops:

Only *two* of the 45 Archbishops and Bishops who fell under the Soviet Regime from 1917 to 1945 remained until their deaths within the Soviet territory:

1) Mons. Antonio Springovics, Archbishop of Riga (Latvia)
2) Mons. Casimiro Paltarokas, Bishop of Panevezys (Lithuania).

The following is account for the rest of those 43 Archbishops and bishops:

a) 1 murdered.
b) 6 died in jail.
c) 12 arrested, deported or expelled and died in exile.
d) 5 condemned to forced labor and still in state arrest.
e) 19 expelled from their Sees and at present living or dead in exile.

Among the members of the Catholic hierarchy in Russia, who disappeared and whose whereabouts were unknown, the following must be remembered:

1) Mons. Augustin Baumtrog, Apostolic Administrator of the Volga district; arrested in August 1950 and disappeared.

2) Mons. John Roth, Apostolic Administrator of the Caucasus, arrested in August 1930 and disappeared.

3) Mons. Stephan Demurov, Vicar *ad interim* of the Tiflis Administration and of Georgia, about whom nothing has been known for a long time.

4) Leonid Feodorof, Exarch of the Russian Catholics of Byzantine Rite, who was twice arrested in 1923 and 1930, deported to Archangelsk and died at Vjatna in March 1935.

More than 1,500,000 Polish, Lithuanian, Latvian, and German adherents to the Roman Catholic religion of the Latin-rite lived in the territory of czarist Russia. As a rule their religious needs were administered to by the Polish clergy. The parishes of the German Catholics where from 1802 until 1820 the clergy were Germans, and later on either Germans or Poles depending on the political changes in the country, constituted the chief exception.

In all there were 1,200 Roman Catholic churches in the territory of czarist Russia.

After the October Revolution, when the Orthodox Church was already being cruelly persecuted, no such drastic measures were at first taken against the Roman Catholic Church.

Another wave of persecution of the Roman Catholics resulted from the publication abroad of a letter from Pope Pius XI, dated February 2, 1930 to Cardinal Pompeli, in which the Pope sharply condemned "the very grave crimes of the Soviet atheists...," the persecution of the Orthodox and Roman Catholic Churches and the poisoning of the minds of young people with atheism. In the course of this wave of persecution, the attempt was made to root out every vestige of Roman Catholicism. in Byelorussia charges of being in contact with the Poles in the 1920's, during the Polish occupation, were brought and correspondence with foreign relatives was pointed to as a form of espionage in favor of the Vatican. Individuals were accused of resisting collectivization. During this period 221 Roman Catholic parishes and 412 priests were eliminated in Byelorussia alone. Catholic cathedrals were closed one after another. The year 1939 brought further victims. The Roman Catholic Church in the territories newly occupied by the Communist regime suffered the same type of oppression. Priests and believers filled the prisone and many were deported to concentration camps in the harsh North and in Siberia. In western Byelorussia, which has been occupied by the Bolsheviks, the highly developed Roman Catholic organization was steadily eliminated: the bishoprics were left vacant, the two religious seminaries which still existed in 1939 were closed, monasteries and convents were liquidated. The cruelty of the measures taken against the Roman Catholic clergy by the Bolsheviks is reflected in Soviet Byelorussian literature of the time.

The Roman Catholic churches of the Volga Germans suffered much the same fate as those already described. During the first years of the Soviet regime, the situation among the Volga Germans was as follows:

> The faithful could use their own churches only on payment of very high rent. All sacraments were heavily taxed. Priests were imprisoned for conducting services in secret, and frequently they ended by dying of starvation. Many were shot. With the passage of time the majority of the cathedrals were either closed or converted into Komsomol clubs. Letters from the laity all agree, "Our main wish is to escape from this hell."

At the beginning of World War II, the Volga Germans were deported to Siberia where they were forced to perform excessively hard labor. There could be no question of any religious life in the Siberian concentration camps. And even outside the camps, the Roman Catholic Volga Germans, according to reports of foreign tourists, have not been permitted to open Roman Catholic churches.

Lithuania, Latvia, and Estonia, where a large percentage of the population was Roman Catholic, endured the same destruction of their religious life. The Roman Catholics of these countries, both at home and through their governments-in-exile, repeatedly appealed to the Vatican, to the United Nations Organization, and to the conscience of the world to beg for action to stem the draining away of the life-blood of the Roman Catholic Church in these countries. There is a wealth of documentary evidence concerning the persecution of the Roman Catholic Church and the horrors which its clergy and believers are even now enduring.

The Georgian Catholic Church suffered the same degree of persecution. Ever since 1924 the Catholics of Georgia, of whom 8,000 adhered to the Armenian-rite and 32,000 to the Latin-rite, have been cruelly oppressed. A number of accounts of this period have been published. By 1930 not a single Catholic church and not a single Catholic priest remained in Georgia. Some priests were brutally tortured in the streets of cities and villages, others were exiled, others forcibly converted to Orthodoxy.

The Armenian Catholic Church, both in the Caucasus and in Lvov, where an Armenian Catholic eparchy had existed since 1632, was deprived of its clergy, who were executed or deported.

The Catholic Church of the Eastern-rite, which comprised both Russians and Byelorussians, was also destroyed by the Bolsheviks, although its members were not numerous. The parishes of Leningrad, Moscow, Nizhnyaya Bogdanovka in Kharkov Province, Albertino and many others, with a small number of monks, priests, and intellectuals who were followers of Vladimir Soloviev, were totally destroyed or liquidated during the period of the general offensive against the Catholic Church. The first victim was the Exarch of the Russian Catholic Church in Russia, Father Leonid Feodorov, who was sentenced, according to the charge of the prosecutor, Krylenko, at his trial on March 21, 1922, not only "for what he had done, but also for what he might do." He was first deported to Solovki, and later to a settlement, where he died. After his removal, the remainder of the clergy were completely eliminated. Laymen who adhered to the movement were accused of "espionage in favor of the Vatican" and "contact with foreign intelligence services" and were deported without the right to carry on correspondence.

At the time of this writing there is not a single parish, church, monastery or priest of the Eastern-rite in the USSR. Believers, if they have survived, conceal their convictions, since, unlike the pioneers of the Russian-Catholic movement prior to 1905, they have no opportunity to emigrate.

The bitter attack on the Catholic Church, including the forcible conversion of the Ukrainian Catholics of the Eastern-rite in the Western Ukraine, to the Orthodox faith, is evidenced that, quite apart from the motives behind the Communist struggle against religion, Catholicism, with its independent, supra-national directing center outside the USSR and its rejection of cooperation between the Church and an atheist regime, is regarded by the Communist leaders as a particularly serious threat.

The only bishoprics at the time of this writing are in the Lithuanian and Latvian SSRs. Moscow and Leningrad have only one Roman Catholic Church each, the former embassy church of St. Louis in Moscow and the Church of Notre Dame de France in Leningrad. Their priests are subordinated to the Bishop of Latvia and their activity is strictly limited to conducting church services.

In early 1941, the annexed territories contained some six million Roman Catholics served by 12 dioceses with over 1,740 churches and more than 2,300 priests. In addition, there were approximately three and a half to four million Ukrainian Greek Catholics (Uniates) with three dioceses, some 2,000 churches and over 2,100 clergy. The destruction of institutional Roman Catholicism in the pre-1939 USSR made it impossible for the Kremlin to employ the same methods as in the case of the Orthodox Church to "sovietize" the Catholic Church in the annexed terrtories and impose reliable political controls over its hierarchy and internal ecclesiastical activities. With the reconquest of the Catholic "borderlands" by the end of the war, the Soviet authorities launched a frontal attack upon Roman Catholicism in the Baltic republics—especially Lithuania, and the Uniate Church in the Western Ukraine. This campaign—which has largely spared the Polish and Hungarian Roman Catholics in the new Soviet territories—was evidently motivated above all by the regime's desire to destroy the links between the "national" Church and the anti-Russian nationalism of Lithuanians and Ukrainians and to deprive the latter of the Church's institutional framework. Though in Lithuania the Soviet police attempted to terrorize bishops and clergy into breaking away from Rome and imprisoned or deported all but one Lithuanian bishop and nearly one-third of the clergy, the regime stopped short of totally suppressing the Church in this northernmost outpost of Roman Catholicism. In the Western Ukraine, however, Stalin not only suppressed the Uniate (Greek Catholic) Church, arrested its entire episcopate and many hundreds of priests and monastics, but also—in the tradition of Nicholas I—forced the Uniates into "reunion" with the state-controlled Russian Orthodox Church. The wounds inflicted by this massive assault on Catholicism thirty years ago have not yet been healed in Lithuania, while in the Western Ukraine the continued persecution of the "catacomb" Uniate Church keeps the old wounds open, despite the decade-old "dialogue" between Moscow and the Vatican.

Atheism has been a constant factor affecting the Soviet treatment of all religious groups, though the intensity of attack upon any single denomination has been varying, depending on the regime's policy priorities, its perceptions of domestic stability and external security, and the anticipated reaction from believers at home and abroad.

Soviet policy towards the Catholic Church has been the traditional Russian hostility to Catholicism as a "foreign", "un-Russian" faith, historically associated with the Teutons, Lithuanians, and—in particular—Poles, and as an aggressive, hierarchically structured international Church directed from the Vatican—that "centre of the world reaction" which has always allied itself with the "enemies of Russia." Among the cohorts of the Catholic "international," monastic orders have been perceived as the most fanatical, dedicated, and cunning "shock troops" of the Vatican. An even greater hostility has been reserved for the Eastern (Uniate) branch of the Catholic Church, seen as the Vatican's "bridgehead" for the spiritual conquest of Russia, and condemned as an "illegitimate" child of the union of Polish overlords and traitorous Orthodox bishops, nurtured through the centuries of Polish and Austrian rule to separate Ukrainians and Byelorussians from their "elder brother"—the Russian people.

Also, the Catholic Church has been the traditional association of Roman Catholicism with Lithuanian and Polish nationalisms and of the Uniate

Church with Ukrainian nationalism, as well as the Church's historical importance as an integrative, and nation-maintaining force, especially when the peoples in question found themselves wholly or in part under the Russian rule.

The doctrinal, canonic and organizational features of the Catholic Church, including its dependence on the Vatican, as well as the Church's intimate links with the non-Russian national cultures and aspirations, made it more difficult for the Catholic Church than for other denominations to accept a pro-regime "patriotic" political platform. However, these features helped the Church to minimize the impact of "sovietization" on its internal life, to frustrate some of the regime's controls and to retain the confidence of the believers.

The Roman Catholics in today's USSR are largely concentrated in the Baltic republics of Lithuania and Latvia (especially in Latgalia), the western oblasts of the Byelorussian and Ukrainian SSRs. Their total number is estimated at over three million. A large Roman Catholic diaspora extends as far east as Kirghizia and Siberia. In terms of their ethnic composition, Latin Catholics include Lithuanians (some 1.9 million or two-thirds of the Republic's population), Latvians (the majority of Latvia's 265,000 Catholics who constituted 11.2 per cent of the population in the early 1970s), Poles (probably the majority of 340 thousand Poles residing in the Western oblasts of Byelorussia and at least one-third of the 295,107 Poles in the Ukraine), Byelorussians (several hundred thousand), Germans (mostly in their areas of deportation in Siberia and Kazakhstan), Hungarians (some 80,000 Roman Catholics) concentrated in the Transcarpathian oblast of the Ukraine, approximately 2,500 Estonians, and insignificant numbers of Ukrainians and other nationalities. In addition, several thousand Catholics (of both Uniate Armenian and Latin-rites) are known to reside in Georgia and Armenia.

While the Soviet authorities have favored centralization of the Orthodox Church and some other religious organizations in the USSR, presumably to facilitate governmental controls, the Roman Catholics (and some other denominations) have not been allowed to establish "Unionwide," central ecclesiastical structure. Only in Lithuania and Latvia are Roman Catholics organized in dioceses with their own hierarchy and with minimal facilities for the training of the clergy; Hungarian Catholics in Transcarpathia have been allowed to maintain a Vicariate General in Uzhhorod which in the late 1960's embraced 26 churches and 22 priests. Outside the Baltic Republics and Transcarpathia, individual Roman Catholic parishes have either been formally subordinated to the Archdiocese of Riga (the two operating Estonian parishes and the Leningrad parish) or the Archiocese of Vilnius (the Moscow and, possibly, Odessa parishes); it seems that the parishes (in the Ukraine and probably Byelorussia) have depended for new priests mostly on Riga, though the Polish Catholic Church has continued to treat Roman Catholics in the Ukraine and Byelorussia as its unofficial sphere of influence, maintaining informal links with the local clergy despite the Soviet Position that this represents an illegal interference with the affairs of Soviet believers. Some Latvian and Lithuanian priests are known to have been serving distant (mostly "unregistered") Roman Catholic congregations in the Asiatic part of the USSR.

According to official Soviet sources, there were in 1960-61, 1,235 Roman Catholic churches and chapels in the USSR with some 1,270 clergy. By 1966, the total of "working" churches declined to about 1,000.

In the Catholic areas of the Baltic States the Roman Catholic Church has suffered from a wide range of discriminatory acts. Religious pilgrimages, a vigorous tradition in East European Catholic life, have been restricted. In Lithuania, a country predominantly Roman Catholic, churches remain closed or in disrepair. Only 600 remain out of 1,202 formerly existing. Others have been converted into warehouses, clubhouses, museums, or simply kept closed. In Vilnius, only 4 of 33 churches are now open. At the moment there are only some 500 priests in Lithuania, most of them advanced in age. The death rate of these priests has been placed at 50 a year and the number is progressively increasing. Enrollment in the remaining seminary for the training of future priests is limited to 60 students. By thus restricting enrollments of students, according to one source, "the regime aims at destroying the Roman Catholic Church." The spiritual activity of Lithuanian priests are further curtailed by trials and imprisonment. Acoording to a report in 1963, five priests had been tried and imprisoned on charges of "bourgeois nationalism."

Perpetuation of the Catholic faith among those Balts, Germans, Poles, Byelorussians, and Ukrainians, transported to the virgin lands of Kazakhstan, is made extraordinarily difficult. Analysis of a body of material by one researcher indicated that no reference was made to a Catholic Church or priest functioning in the area and few references to Catholics at all. Some Catholics lived in Dzhambul, but the Catholic community in Czelinograd, the Soviets claimed, had disintegrated within the last two or three years as a result of atheistic work.

Lutheran believers, the predominant faith among Latvians and Estonians, have suffered similar acts of discrimination. The "violently antireligious policy" of the Soviet regime in Estonia was said to have eased slightly in the mid-1950's, but recently some reports indicate a quickening of the pace of persecution and discrimination. Efforts to discover and apply Communist substitutes for church rites and holidays have been enthusiastically recounted in the Soviet press. Wedding and christening ceremonies were said to be almost as attractive as those of the church. Easter has been replaced by a festival of spring, and Christmes merged with the New Year holiday.

According to *Moscow News:*

> There are Catholic communities in 10 of the 15 Republics, making up the Soviet Union. The majority of them live in Lithuania, Latvia, Western Ukraine and Western Byelorussia. A special article in the USSR Constitution and in the Constitutions of the Union Republics guarantees freedom of conscience for Catholics and other believers in all the Republics. According to information from churches in Lithuania and Latvia, the number of Catholic parishes and churches has not become smaller there under Soviet power. The church, however, lacks the data to ascertain the precise number of believers. The state is completely separated from the church; it does not interfere in church affairs, nor does it keep count of believers.
>
> Clergymen receive their stipend from church incomes, and their living standards are quite high on the whole. Therefore, they have no need to work anywhere except in the church. The state does not impose a demand on them that they work because, as we have already said, it does not interfere in church affairs.

Throughout the Soviet occupation of the Baltic States of Estonia, Latvia, and Lithuania in the years 1940-1944, about six million Christians, (and among these three million Catholics with eight blooming dioceses) were subjugated by the Moscow Soviet regime, and even more, they were suppressed mercilessly, fought, and persecuted for more than thirty years. As after Stalin's death, and Khrushchev's taking of power, one asked, if the change in the leadership had any meaning for the condition of the Church. Did it become easier for the Church, or did the struggle become sharper for it? The answer was given by the general secretary L. Brezhnev on March 29, 1966, at the twenty-third Congress of the CP of the Soviet Union,

> No power in the world can undermine or weaken our unshakable faithfulness to Marxism-Leninism. The goal of the ideological work of the Party is the formation of the scientific conception of the world, the development of the Communist morale in all strata of society.

Generally it is known that there exists a religious hostility in Marxism-Leninsim. According to their teachings, religion is a "social product" and always is combined with "a certain form of society," that religion can be the cause of social inconveniences namely because it allegedly sanctifies the interests and the mercenary attitude of the mighty and rich, the clergymen and bigshots, impresses submission upon the subjugated and exploited, and promises them everlasting bliss in the life to come. Religion also results in social inconveniences for the frustrated masses of the poor, unhappy, exploited and enslaved; looking for their consolation in the life to come promises an illusioned, deceitful, everlasting bliss. Therefore, religion for Marxism is a dangerous mystification of the exploit system—an "opium for the people." Even more objectionable, Lenin writes,

> Every god is desecration of the dead, even if it is the purest, most ideal . . . God, that makes no difference. . . . Every religious idea, every idea of every god is the most dangerous atrociousness, the most repugnant epidemic. Religion is a kind of spiritual surrogate in which the slaves of capital lose sight of their human countenance and their demand for a halfway humanly worthwhile life.

> According to Marx, the preservation of religion as the illusionary fortune of the people is at the loss of their real happiness.
> Lenin demands more radically,

> We must fight religion. That is the ABC of the whole materialism and consequently of Marxism.

The motive demand of Marxism-Leninism, in view of the destruction of religion, has more value than ever today, even after Khrushchev's depriving of power. At the Twenty-second Party Congress, a party program was adopted forming new orders for the destruction of religion. These orders were stated under the headings "Conquest of the remainder of capitalism in the awareness and conduct of human beings" and "The Party regards the fight against visions of civil ideology and morale . . . against superstition and prejudice as the component of communist education." Under the appeal for the ordinance of the Party program, Ilitschev, secretary of the Central Committee of the CPSU, explained in his speech of December 1963, before the Ideological Committee of CC of the CPSU:

> True to the instructions of Lenin, our Party has always actively risen against the religious ideology.

In the Party program, accepted at the Twenty-second Congress of the CPSU, the Party has set the task to definitely free the awareness of the Soviet human beings from the remainder of the old concepts of society, therefore, also to free it of religious prejudices.

Ilitschev demanded further:

This problem must be solved by all means that our Party and all social organizations have. No back doors to the heart of the people may remain open for clergymen and sectarians.

The following, from the Party organ *Pravda*, has given the signal for a new intensified attack against the "remainder" of religion because religion is the strongest ideological opponent of Communism. G. Anashkin, the president of the penal department of the Superior Court of the USSR, emphasized in the magazine, *Sovetskoye gosudarstvo i pravo*, an organ of the academy of the sciences of the USSR, with which courts and public prosecutions comply as much as police and other administrations conform unconditionally that "the education of the communist morale is impossible without the fight against the religious ideology." Up to date therefore,

religion is the ideological main enemy of communism, above all, Catholicism should be destroyed first of all. That is our duty, to fight Catholicism, to show forth its ideologically harmful nature, to attack it through application of the various methods and means in all its appearances, but equally through individual influence on the believers.

With notable fury, Lenin attacked the established belief at his time by warnings:

Millions of sins, acts of force, vulgarities, and epidemics of physical form are recognized by the masses more easily and therefore are much less dangerous than the cunning, spiritually clothed in magnificently "ideal" garments, idea of one God.

Clearly and categorically, the Soviets rejected through their spokesman, Ilitschev, any renewal of religion and Church and their adaptation to our time. With reference to V. I. Lenin, Ilitschev explained in his speech at the end of the year 1963:

Theologians have proven early their flexibility, their ability for adaptation to the given formalities.

Lenin designated such an ideological transformation of religious societies as a way of "house cleanings" and remarked that established religions were more dangerous.

In the Moscow paper of the Communist youth, *Komsomolskaya pravda*, which appeared during the closing period of the Council, it was emphasized:

The church stirs, the church renews itself, but still it wants to remain a church that is a combination of institutions, offices, rites which support themselves on "supernatural life," "supernatural powers," "happiness in paradise," and "misfortune in hell?"

The Soviets reject even the most eager and compliant adaptation of religion to Communism and the Soviet regime. In the year 1961 it was emphasized explicitly in the Moscow pseudo-scientific, anti-religious magazine, *Nauka i religiya*,

The incompatibility which exists between religion and us cannot be bridged through the attempt of the clergymen to adapt religion to the formalities of today, to renew and readopt a few ideas of the "Holy Scripture" to create a sign of good will and kinship between religious teachings and principles of the communist teachings. The incompatible cannot be made compatible.

Even more clearly and categorically, Ilitschev rejected every attempt at adaptation of religion and Church to Communism:

The church shows an especially great adaptability in the political area. Officially, the Church stands loyal to the Soviet power, and a few of its representatives have even come forward with proofs for the common goals of religion and Soviet state power. So said a clergyman from the area Lugansk in a sermon, "Christ teaches us to arrange life on earth in a way that there are neither poor nor rich, that all human beings be bound together in brotherly love, and have their livelihood. The program of the COSU corresponds fully and entirely to the spirit of this teaching." Even more penetrating, a representative of the cathedral of Vilnius taught his believers: "Those that claim that religion and communism are uncombinable are mistaken. They must fulfill the moral code of the builder of communism zealously—its foundation is taken from the Holy Scripture." As we see, some servants of the Church are not averted from supporting the morale code of the builder of communism with words, so that they make the conclusion plausible to all believers, so that there are no serious differences or even contradictions between the communist morale and religious rejection. It is known that Lenin had in his time decidely and categorically refused all attempts to unite scientific socialism and religion. Communism and religion have nothing in common. Any type of embellishment of religion cannot change its character in any way. Engels replied, "Even if a few parts in the Bible could be united in the spirit of Communism, the whole spirit of its teachings is hostile towards Communism through and through."

The adopted Party statutes of the Twenty-second Party Congress in October 1961, in chapter one, paragraph two, demanded:

The party member must . . . fight energetically against all forms of the bourgeoise ideology, against all religious beliefs, and the leftover residue of the past.

Ilitschev declared in his speech,

The most important task of the Party organ is to organize atheistic work, and to mobilize all ideological powers against religious imaginations and superstitions. Consequently, each Party member must be an atheist and above all, a "militant atheist."

Pravda reported that in February 1964, a resolution "About the measures for the aggravation of the anti-religious education of the people," was adopted by the CC of the CPSU:

With the present stand of the superstructure of the communist society, it is the Party's opinion that a final victory over the religious faith can only be reached through a worked out and integrated system of communist upbringing, through which all layers of the population can be reached, and which can prevent the spreading of religious ideas, especially among children and adolescents.

The resolution ordered to establish an "Institute of Scientific Atheism," for the guidance and coordination of atheistic work, to strengthen the supervision of the members of the Communist Party, in its fulfillment of the Party ordinances relating to the fight against religion, and to entrust certain Party committees with leadership for the anti-religion work. As a result of this resolution, the Party had founded in Moscow the "Institute of Scientific Atheism" in June, 1964, which was subjected to the Central Committee of the CCPSU.

The Twenty-third Congress of the CPSU in Moscow, from March 29 to April 4, 1966 did by no means change the Party regulations governing the fight against religion. On the contrary, the Congress demanded:

    a) The untrue and neglectful Party members "who violate the Party program or the Party statues" must be excluded from the Party and;

    b) The Congress obligates the Party organizations to turn their special attention to the communistic upbringing of the Komsomols and the whole Soviet youth.

With reference to the resolutions of the Twenty-third Party Congress and the Party statutes, the Soviet Latvian Party magazine, *Komunists*, reprimanded the Party members about their duty to carry on their fight against religion energetically, and the Party members should also be prepared for the fight against religion in special Party schools and courses. The same Party magazine reported that of the 72,000 Party members who studied in Latvia in the school year 1965/1966, 53,000 in other words 75 per cent, were enrolled in Marxist philosophy courses.

Like the Party members, the members of the Party organization of Komsomol, the young Communists, must be atheists and carry on merciless fight against religion. The resolutions of the Fourteenth Congress of the Soviet Union's Komsomol of 1962, read:

> It is necessary to familiarize the youth with scientific atheism and to equip them with the spiritual dexterity which is necessary for work among the youth, which have been caught in the 'loops' of religion. Children and adolescents must be protected from the trecherous nets of the servants of the church. The Congress underlines that sharpness must characterize the fight against the ideology and morals of the bourgeoise and against the remnants of the past as a whole. Not to defend oneself, but to attack on the ideological front—that's what the Party demands of us.

In Latvia, L. Bartkevics, the first secretary of CC of Soviet Latvian Komsomol, pressed for the same action in his speech before the Sixteenth Congress of the Soviet Latvian Komsomol of February 10, 1966.

The Fifteenth Congress of the Komsomol of the Soviet Union, held from May 17 - 21, 1966, in Moscow, decided with reference to the resolutions of the Twenty-third Congress of the CPSU:

> The committees of the Komsomol must watch the work of the individual influence of the youths, who have been under the influence of religion and sects daily, and make sure that the unmaskings of the religious dogmas are deeply scientific and aggressive.

In the whole Soviet Union, there were approximately 23,000,000 Komsomol members or Young Communists in the year 1966, or approximately one Young Communist to ten inhabitants. In the same year, 108,000 Komsomol members were in Estonia, 190,000 were in Latvia and 250,000 were counted in Lithuania. In all the Baltic States, there was approximately one Young Communist to twelve inhabitants.

As an elite army against religion and Church, militant atheists, qualified propagandists of atheism, are employed. "That is a noble and honorable call," *Nauka i religiya* praises the militant atheists, "To be an atheist is to help mankind find a way to spiritual freedom."

Ilitschev emphasized in his speech that, "The most important problem is the training of anti--religious cadres." The director of the University for Marxism-Leninism of the Riga Committee of the Latvian Communist Party, also emphasized the pressing need to educate good propagandists of "scientific atheism." The militant atheists are educated and trained for their job in special high schools, colleges, seminars, and courses for atheism. In addition, there are clubs of the militant atheists, where work programs are planned, conferences, contests, and assemblies in colleges and grade schools are arranged.

In the Latvian newspaper, *Komunists* of April 1964, A. Serdants, the Chairman of the Chief Council of Atheism, demanded that the propagandists of atheism conduct their monthly seminars, so that they could replenish their knowledge in atheism, and endow their work assignments. He reported further that Consultation Centers for religious and atheistic questions will be provided in many places. Experienced lecturers on atheism will give the propagandists the necessary consultation, and will also answer questions of the believers. In the school year 1962/1963 within the framework of Party schooling in the Soviet Union alone, 3,787 atheist clubs provided atheistic lessons to 75,000 persons, and 7,109 atheist seminars for 14,400 persons. At the same time, the following devoted themselves to various schools of atheism, and to studying atheism in general:

RSFSR—had 90,000 participants.
Ukraine had 79,000 participants.
Byelorussia had 12,000 participants.
In Estonia there were 1,278,000 inhabitants in 1964;
1 school of atheism by the Central Committee of the Communist Party of Estonia; 2 faculties of atheism by the CC of the CP of Estonia;
2 schools of atheism in the University; 17 atheist clubs, 46 seminars for atheism and 7 adult education classes and schools for atheism.

In every local committee of the Communist Party, a "Commission for ideological work" consists of 12 members; this commission had a special section for atheistic propaganda. This section must have an authorized agent in all plants and institutions; likewise, it must have lecturers who may eventually recite atheistic lectures in state universities. According to statements of the year 1964, on the average, 250 listeners took part in the lectures in the school for atheism at the State University in Tartu. These listeners were educated to become lecturers, agitators, and propagandists for atheism.

In 1964, in Latvia there were altogether 70 schools and affiliated institutions of adult education classes for atheism, with some 4,000 students. In 1965, on the faculty for atheism in the adult education classes of the District Rezekne alone, 70 militant atheists studied. In 1966, there were 300 students of atheism, in the District of Cesis. In March, 1966, 700 people took part in a three-day seminar for atheism in Riga "to raise the qualifications of the atheist lecturers."

In Lithuania, the college of Marxism-Leninism of Vilnius had educated, up to 1965, over 5,000 Communist leaders, and in the same year over 1,000 students studied there. In 1965, 90 militant atheists studied in the Regional Seminar of Atheism in Vilkaviskis. In 1964, 25,000 militant propagandists were under the Chief Counsel of Atheism in Lithuania.

One can, on the average, count one atheist propagandist among every 200 to 300 inhabitants. The work of the atheistic propagandist—the fight against religion and church—is directed through the so-called Chief Counsel of Atheism. Its task is "to force it into the heart and mind of everyone."

Religious classes in all schools of the Soviet Union are forbidden by law. Article 122 in the Soviet Penal Code states: "The instruction of religion in schools and institutions of learning is forbidden and also violators of this can be imprisoned up to one year."

Whatever befalls atheism, the school is the main arena for the imbuing of the atheist point of view. In the Twenty-second Party Congress, the Party has made Communist education its main task. The Moscow atheist newspaper, *Science and Religion,* demanded a strong atheistic education in an article entitled "The school cannot be neutral."

> Can the Soviet school, that is called upon to give the public the light of scientific knowledge, be indifferent and tolerant to the religious condemnation of the students? Without a materialistic, and therefore an atheistic point of view, the training of the younger generation in a communistic spirit is impossible. To imbue the youth with an inquenchable counter-will against the remnants of the past, is the main point for all the decisions and regulations of the party and government.

At the close of the Central Committee of the Communist Party of the Soviet Union in February, 1964, *Pravda* published courses for the study of the basics of scientific atheism, which must be carried through in various higher educational institutions, special seminars for atheist lectures, and anti-religious instructions in public schools must be strengthened.

> Through atheistic training, our schools must teach the children to wage an implacable, idealogical war against religion. We need an active militant atheism that will call the people to fight against all beliefs and superstitions.

The Soviet Lithuanian newspaper of the Komsomol, *Komjaunimo Tiesa,* wrote in 1964:

> The atheists in the school fight on the side of the teacher with all their might for a new man emancipated from the mildew of religion, for a strong materialistic philosophy of life.

Nauka i religiya demanded: "The teacher must be a fighter, an example in the fight against religion." The same demand was in the speech of Ilitschev. Moscow *Komsomolskaya pravda* reported, that Naschmudinsov, the principal of the school of Rudaka was fired because he didn't fulfill the atheistic propagaanda of the school with enough energy. In Estonia the official organ of the News Agency, *Noukogude Kool,* emphasized that atheistic training can be successful only with the complete conviction and activity of a teacher. All subjects should be in the service of the broadening of atheism. Ilitschev said, too, that:

> The cornerstones of a scientific, atheistic philosophy of life for all, are laid in the schools, and every subject must serve that end, every single hour.

In the Moscow monthly journal, *Kommunist,* it was stated, "The teachings of all subjects in school must be saturated with militant atheism."

The most potent method of training for atheism is the boarding school. Schools of this type were originally founded to protect the children from the religious influence of the family and to give the Party a constant direct control over the students. Besides that, the "anti-religious propaganda for the children" must begin in the pre-school years rather early.

> We must rain the militant atheists from the first childhood years and the first
> school days, because it is easier to overcome religious notions in the early years
> than later on.

In Estonia, *Noukogude Kool* said in 1966, that the base for an atheistic
philosophy is laid on the first day of school, and must be reinforced from day
to day. In all of the Soviet Union, there were over two million boarding
students in 1962/1963. According to reports from L. I. Brezhnew in the
Twenty-third Congress of the Communist Party of the Soviet Union, in the
year 1965/66, the public schools had forty-eight million students. In Latvia,
in 1965 there were thirty-four boarding schools with 10,834 students. There
were 552,000 students in the school year 1965/66, from them 190,000 were
Young Communists, 132,000 Pioneers—members of the pre-organization
of the Komsomol.

> Lithuania had in 1956/57—3 boarding schools with 745 students. 1964/65—47
> boarding schools with 15,700 students.

In the school year 1964/65 in Lithuania were 4,033 public schools with
458,100 students, and 590 evening and extension schools with 58,200 students.

In the Soviet Union and its occupied countries even the parents are forced
to raise their children godlessly. The Soviet press goes so far as to threaten to
take away the rights of the parents.

> In the event that the belief of the parents can not be changed, it would be better
> to take the children away into a boarding school and rise them there.

Nauka i religiya states that according to Article 227 of the Penal Code, a
father is subject to punishment if he calls upon his son not to join the
Komsomol, becuase this organization has taken up the fight against religion.
In Lithuania, the newspaper *Tiesa* complained in 1964 against a certain
Gutautas because he opposed his daughter Jadze's membership in the Komsomol of the high school of Skuodas. The newspaper wrote that Gutautas
"has raised his hand against the Soviet morals" and that the society and the
school were also guilty in the Gutautas case.

In 1960, a college was opened in Vilnius in which the parents were to learn
how to raise their children in the Communist spirit. The studies of that
school lasted two years. Since then, all the schools hold regular atheistic
conferences for parents.

Not only the Party and the school, but also the Soviet intelligentsia,
functionaries, doctors, academicians, and scientists must openly step forward as fighters against church and religion. There is no legal regulation,
but the regulations of the Party have in every Communist state a unity of
laws.

In the speech of Ilitschev is stated,

> The religious hysterics use such intellectuals (the believers) as examples, in
> order to make the honest people dumb—see, an educated man, but he believes
> in God. Our society must unmask such proponents of religion and fight against
> the appearance of contradiction and deceit. No Soviet intellectual can pull out
> of the fight between science and religion, between scientific idealogy and
> informable, untruthful idealogy. The entire Soviet intelligentsia: teachers,
> scientists, high school teachers, doctors, agronomists, and engineers—all who

are capable, must pass scientific knowledge to the masses and go along with the atheistic propoganda and training.

The organization *Znaniye,* which is spread throughout the Soviet Union, plays a big role in anti-religious propaganda and "in the critical fight against religious prejudice." It included in 1963 over one million intellectuals, educated people, teachers, college teachers, engineers, technicians, agronomists, doctors, writers, journalists, elite workers of industry and real estate. They are a mighty army in the fight against religion.

Tarybinis Mokytojas reported that at the beginning of 1966 there was a meeting in Siauliai of school and kolkhoz leaders, Lithuanian secretaries, representatives of the Women Council, and other organizations. The meeting discussed the means and methods of cooperation between the public and teachers how to disseminate atheistic materialism among the youth, and to convert Lithuanian believers to atheism. The doctors were especially urged to push the fight against religion. The *Komunistas* demanded in 1964, that the 5,700 doctors and the 17,000 hospital orderlies strengthen the anti-religious propaganda. It was even demanded from the doctors that they interfere with patients who wear religious symbols. In 1964 the Minister of Education, through a special decree, instituted the subject "Basics of Scientific Atheism" in all medical institutions on a compulsory basis.

In Latvia an advisory council was founded by the Ministry of Health, which had to prepare plans for atheistic training, and has the job of watching over all medical institutions. K. Arons, the chairman of this council, demanded in his article, "The Doctor Against the Darkness of Religion," that the doctors "fight against religious superstitions and promote the scientific philosophy of life."

In Estonia, Anatoli Mitt, dean of the physics-math department at the University of Tartu, has studied the entire Bible in order to combat it more effectively, and so that he could make the University of Tartu the center for atheistic propaganda.

Lenin compared the Labor Unions with the school of Communism, and explained that the main task of the unions is to train the masses in a communistic spirit, and to stand by the Party in the fight against religion. Since the opening of the Central Soviety Council of Unions on September 12, 1962, on "The division of union organizations of scientific atheistic propaganda for the service of the betterment of production," the importance of the anti-religious effect of the unions has strongly increased.

Grishin, the general secretary of unions, in his program speech on the Thirteenth Congress of Unions, explained,

> The annihilation of religious superstitions is an essential part of the fight against the remnants of the past, and for the training of the people in the spirit of a scientific, materialistic philosophy of life. This fight demands patience and individual work with every single believer.

Chairman Dobrowolsky at the Ninth Congress of Soviet Lithuanian Unions in Vilnius, demanded on September 15/16, 1965:

> We must give special consideration to the effect of unions in the field of atheistic training. In factories the atheistic counsels are impressive, and the atheistic propaganda for the formation of an atheistic philosophy of life in the people is carried on. In the future, we must strengthen this work.

In 1964 *Pravda* demanded, that all plants celebrate a day of atheism. In

Latvia in the year 1965 were 2,247,000 inhabitants of which the unions had 980,000 members.

The Soviet Army is not only godless, but it also fights against religion. A. A. Epishev, Chief of the political guidance of the army and navy in 1964 explained, that it is very important to orient the political training of the soldiers in such a way that

> he who comes to the troops with a belief in God will be freed from it, and the non believer will be strengthened in his materialistic outlook and atheistic conviction.

Further, in that presentation it was said,

> The training of the soldiers and sailors, whose conscience is darkened with religious dust material, is considered an important part in the ideological work in the armed forces. Commanders, politruks, and party organizers of the army, have the duty to see that every youth returns home as an atheist of conviction after his military duty.

Nauka i religiya demanded in 1963 that,

> all party schools and other institutions for political education must work for the atheistic training of Soviet people; all clubs and seminars must expose religion and all foreign idealogies and also religion must consequently be irreconcilably fought.

In the Soviet Union 68,000,000 people became members in the school system of political education in the school year 1964/1965, of which only 75 per cent became members.

According to N. Johanson, the secretary of CC of the CP of Tallinn, in Estonia, by the end of 1964 in Tallinn alone, there were 826 atheist seminars, 732 political clubs, 704 schools "of communistic work." Of the 320,000 inhabitants of Tallinn, 74,000 supposedly participated in this study.

In Latvia, the first secretary of the CC of the CP, A. Pelse, reported at the Twentieth Congress of the Latvian Communist Party on March 22, 1966:

> According to the instructions of the CC of the CPSU, the scientific philosophy, political economy, scientific communism, and the history of the Soviet Union Communist Party will become major subjects in the Party education system starting with the school year 1965/1966. In the party education system of Latvia, there are over 9,300 experienced propagandists.

In Lithuania, according to the *Sovetskaya Litva* of September 25, 1966, 800 people have completed their studies in the higher party school of Vilnius, and over 1,600 persons have deepened their knowledge in Marxism-Leninism.

Single believers are individually persuaded. A fight "about the people" is being waged. Every atheistic propagandist, every agitator is given a specific family or person whom he should "work over" so that he becomes a non-believer. "The best success in the fight against the 'opium of religion' can be achieved through the individual influence of solitary believers." In November, 1963, *Nauka i religiya* reminded of the conclusions of the Plenum of the CC of CPSU, and emphasized,

> In connection with the individual believer, that is the main task of the con-clusion of the June Plenum of the CC of CPSU. The inhabitants of our land as a whole have for a long time already freed themselves from superstition and religious belief. Therefore, the method of individual influence has won first priority in atheistic propaganda.

The same thing was said in Ilitschev's programmatic speech:

> The atheistic work is only then effective when the individual characteristics of the believers are eliminated. The work with the individual believer is the basis for success. The tasks and work of propaganda should be done in private apartments and community centers, in reading rooms, in factories, everywhere, where the propagandists meet the workers, it is their duty to attack religious idealogy, bring forth the harm of religion, and promote the scientific atheistic outlook. This duty holds especially in the individual visits to a believer. The choice of propagandists that are geared to individual work with believers is an important task of the Party organization. One must choose for this task a well prepared person who looks good, has authority, and induces confidence. It is especially important to watch the families that have small or growing children. The propagandist must make it clear that the strongly enforced laws of the Soviet Union forbid the clergy or fanatical sect leaders to hold the believers from a social life, and that these laws are for the benefit of the worker, of which the believer is one.

The Soviet state and the Soviet government can never undertake anything against the Party program. Consequently, it is indeed the Soviet state which persecutes religion and churches with their laws and regulations, with police, law courts, prisons, concentration camps, forced labor, etc.

The entire Soviet press is engaged in a struggle against religion and Church. In the Soviet Union, *Nauka i religiya,* in the years 1961/1962 alone, printed 607 anti-religious books and pamphlets with a total edition of eleven million copies.

In Estonia, in 1963, there were printed eight anti-religious books with a total of 2,000 pages. In the catalogue of books, the Scientific Library of Estonia contained an index of twenty-eight pages concerning atheistic and anti-religious books. Besides that, an anti-religious paper, *Atheist,* is published regularly.

In Lithuania from 1945 to 1965 were circulated 2,500,000 copies of anti-religious publications, that is almost one copy to each inhabitant including infants and old people. In Lithuania, such publications are mainly oriented against the Catholic Church. In the year 1964, two thousand books were published with a total circulation of fourteen million. In Lithuania, during the time of the Soviet rule in the years 1940-1941 and 1945-1964, five hundred titles on Marxism were printed, the total circulation of these books being withheld; also there were published 33,000 books and pamphlets with a total circulation of 209 million, of that 40 per cent with political contents, i.e., seventy copies for every inhabitant. Every day there were printed an average of 340,440 copies. Presently, there are published more than 150 periodicals and on the average, every Soviet-Lithuanian citizen receives more than one magazine or paper. The other Baltic States, Estonia and Latvia, show a similar picture. In Lithuania there have appeared the anti-religious magazine, *Mokslas ir Gyvenimas* since 1957, and since 1964, the other anti-religious magazine *Ateistas.*

Without regard to countless special anti-religious publications, there are the official Party and government journals and newspapers. On a regular basis, anti-religious articles and caricatures in which religion, worship, sacraments, clergy, the Vatican, etc. are attacked and ridiculed.

In the Moscow party magazine, *Kommunist,* it was emphasized in the year 1963 that the meaning of art for the communistic upbringing cannot be emphasized enough. In the past years, Soviet art has given special attention to the fight for freedom of man from the religious narcosis.

In the beginning of 1964, there were seventy anti-religious films available. The official film committee to the Cabinet Council of the Soviet Union decided in the same year to increase the production of anti-religious films. The yearly production plan of anti-religious films stands three to four feature films with anti-religious content among those one or two for children, four to five cartoons with anti-religious characters, ten to fifteen popular scientific films and twelve to fifteen anti-religious documentary films.

Besides the news media, there exist many atheistic anti-religious exhibitions in the Baltic countries. In a picture published in *Cina*, a student from the Forty-ninth elementary school in Riga can be seen at an anti-religious exhibition, which he was required to visit at the Vigil of Christmas. On December 31, 1965, in the Baltic countries anti-religious touring exhibitions were created, which travel from city to city in railway cars. These exhibitions show pictures and other materials of anti-religious character, anti-religious lectures are held and films are shown.

In Vilnius, the now profaned church—which was built during the Seventeenth Century in the name of holy Kasimir, the patron saint of Lithuania, which stands for a National Lithuania—this holy monument was converted into a central museum and, in order to increase the mockery, the former faithless priest, S. Markonis, was appointed director of the museum. In this museum are shown about five hundred objects and one hundred of the "authentic documents" in relation to so-called "reactionary activities" of the Roman Catholic clergymen in Lithuania. There are held regularly anti-religious reports and lectures, organized discussion evenings and anti-religious documentary films shown.

The clergymen, in press, radio, television, films, and lectures, are brought into discredit as useless wrong-doers, avaricious thieves, cheaters, obscurantists, traitors, murderers, Nazi agents and spies for capitalist countries. The evidence for this is supposedly taken from government archives, diocese offices, from secret records, "voluntary" testimonies, diaries, and other documents, which in reality never existed.

Clergymen and believers are completely helpless in the Party. The Soviet state doesn't defend them against charges and defamation. Section 143 of the Soviet Penal Law asserts: "Interference in religious ceremonies, as long as they don't disturb the all around peace and don't impose into the rights of a citizen, can be punished with forced labor up to six months and public rebuke." But according to section 227 of the same Soviet Penal Law, every religious or cult ceremony can be interpreted as intrusion into personal or citizen rights, while in section 143 is talked about interference with cults only, but not at all of the insult and defamation which clergymen and believers are exposed to; the Soviet state doesn't see such insult and defamation as an offence. Consequently, there is no Soviet court or any recourse to protect clergymen or believers from defamatory attacks from the atheists. The clergymen are completely exposed to the discretion and the mood of the local Party committees and officials when the *modus vivendi* is impossible; when worsening of relations occurs, it is wise for the clergymen to transfer into another vicarage. If a clergyman is reported to an official he also is sentenced because the Soviet state goes on the presumption that the Soviet official or authorities are not at all unjust and can proceed against the people's enemy. A clergyman, on his occupation, is classified as politically unreliable and very easily can be accused because of an offence against the penal law; thus, he is always in the position to be dismissed from office or liable to the threat of arrest. The paper *Cina,* of January 29, 1964, accused, for example, a certain Stanislavs Zomgale of laziness because he "avoided every occupation which was useful to society." He was punished with deportation and five years of forced labor.

By this law, not only the ministerial work of clergymen is reduced, but he is even prohibited to make visits and give help or comfort, when a dying person wants to see him. Then a priest must hand in a written application to the local police official, and the official makes his decision on this.

The printing or copying of religious books and writings is forbidden as well as is their import from foreign countries; this is classified as forbidden religious propaganda. The clergymen can study for their theological development and stimulation only old, outdated theological books, which still are present in the Baltic countries after thirty years of Soviet occupation and persecution. The sermons of clergymen are watched very carefully. In no instance may they rebuke or even mention anti-religious propaganda and the materialistic world outlook.

The Soviet state forces the clergymen, especially those who have higher positions to political actions, and namely to the taking part of the Communistic Peace Movement, which serves the goals of the Communistic World Revolution. What the Communist Peace Movement means in reality, Lenin explains in his "Farewell letter to the Swiss Workers."

> We are not pacifists. We are opponents of the imperialistic wars, which are held for the splitting of the prey by the capitalists; but we have always explained that it would be nonsense if the revolutionary prolitarist would refuse the revolutionary wars, which could prove necessary in the interest of socialism. To tie the enemy's hands, who is better equipped than we today, if and when we will fight with him, is foolishness and not a revolutionary deed. To take up the fight, when it is notoriously favorable for the enemy and not for us, is a crime, and politicians of the revolutionary class, who don't talk about, understand, to make agreements and compromises in order to evade a notoriously unfavorable contest are not worth a penny.

The material conditions of clergymen can be described as follows: All parsonages and church buildings are disowned as state property. The clergymen were dislodged. In some places they were allowed to rent a room in the earlier parsonage. In most localities, however, they had to look for some other places to shelter themselves. If the congregation wanted to keep its buildings, it had to pay a rent to the state equal to that of a "luxury apartment."

The Nationalization Law says, though, that the churches, on the basis of special decrees of the state organs, are given to the belivers for free use. In reality, the believers are exposed to a very sensitive economic pressure. For the use of a church, which isn't profaned yet, the believers have to pay a very high rent to the state, which isn't calculated by square meters, but by cubic meters. The average yearly rent amounts from 1,000 rubels to 4,000 rubels. For the Middle Age St. Olais Church in Tallinn, with its 138 meter high Gothic steeple, the congregation of the Baptists have to pay 6,000 rubels yearly to the state.

In order to attain a corresponding picture to reality, it does not suffice to employ examples on the basis of the official foreign money courses. One has also to consider wages and prices. In Latvia, the monthly wage of a simple worker sways between 45 and 70 rubels; the monthly wage of a qualified worker amounts to 120 rubels. A collective peasant received, according to official statements of the year 1962, 1,45 rubels and .87 kg. grain.

The enormous church rents and other funds must be raised by the plain workers, and collective peasants, the lowest and poorest class of the Soviet society. Ilitschev stated himself, that after analysis of statistics, "The part of the believers were people of not so qualifying work: homeworkers, watchmen, waitresses, housewifes" and that "they were uneducated people for the greater majority." Any raise of donations of the believers for the church is in accordance with Article 124 of the Soviet Penal Law. Moreover, a pastor is not allowed to look up believers himself or through others in order to collect money. The church is only allowed to take voluntary and spontaneous donations and collections.

The clergymen today in the Baltic States are exclusively dependent on voluntary contributions, collections, and gifts of the believers. The income of the clergyman is regarded as a private income, and accordingly is taxed with the highest tax rate of 81 per cent. The taxpayers, who are not disfited by the state or state governmental authorities or firms, but who have a private income, and whose tax is calculated from their private income belong to three groups: 1) Craftsmen, who don't work in state firms, pay 10 per cent more income tax than those in the state firms. 2) Doctors, surgeons, lawyers, and professors pay 60 per cent of their private income as taxable income. 3) Craftsmen, who are self-employed, gardeners, and clergymen pay 81 per cent of their income as income tax.

In order to avoid the suspicion that the incomes are not specified truthfully, all donations, those for masses and clerical acts, are usually thrown into a closed box by the believers in church. The key to this box is with the congregation's elder. At certain times, this offering box is opened in the presence of the minister and the congregation's committee, the money is counted, the tax rate subtracted, and rest given to the minister. The clergyman can, by no means, accept a donation which doesn't come in a closed collection box, which therefore, was not declared to the revenue office. He must live on his small income. As soon as he permits himself more, and perhaps wears more expensive clothes, even if they were given to him as presents, one would immediately suspect him of having forged his income declaration, for one knows exactly that his income, after tax deduction, does not suffice for as the raising of his living standards.

In spite of all caution of foresight in the area of tax matters, the clergy are often accused of supposedly forging declarations, and are even convicted. The exploitation of the believers by the Soviets exceeds any imaginable extent in Latvia. Some places, the income and income taxes of the clergymen are appropriated according to what would probably come in on donations from the believers.

In order to understand the materialistic condition of the clergymen, one has always to consider the poverty of the believers, who help to support the clergymen from the most modest incomes. A Soviet Latvian newspaper admits the large generosity of the population: "Most people can only afford meat on New Year's, the First of May, and during the October festivities."

All who are active in the church-life such as sextons, organists, and others are excluded from social security and pensions. This pertains to the clergymen all the more. The clergymen can be pensioned at the age of 65, if the church is capable of paying a pension from the donations of the believers.

In the Baltic states, since the Soviet occupation, pastors are subjugated to the Soviet government authorities for church affairs, who watch over and steer the whole activities of the church and the clergymen. This state office stands immediately under the first substituting government chief. The travel abroad and the participation on church days is only possible under control and in accordance with the instructions of this authority. This office is in reality, however, only a tool of the representative of the religion committee at the minister council of the USSR. The delegates of the church for lectures, the participants of church meetings, and persons who make visits abroad are not appointed by the church itself, but by the state office, which gives the concerned its instructions. The delegates must come to Moscow before the departure, as for example, the delegates of the conference "All Christian Peace Conferences" in Prague 1962, the Evangelical Lutheran archbishop of Riga, Gustav Turss, and others.

A few representatives of the Roman Catholic Church of Lithuania and Latvia were permitted to travel in order to participate at the council meetings in Rome. But no one Roman Catholic bishop of the Soveit Baltic States, since the occupation by the Soviets, has been permitted a so-called *ad limina* trip to Rome while he is obliged every five years in accordance with the Church regulations, to give the Holy Father a report about the religious life and the ministerial work in his diocese.

Only the government-authorized official has the right of nomination, transfer and advise for clergymen on the participation in any meeting, on services in any other congregation, or on the admittance and dismissal of theological students, on their admittance to the ordination, on nominations and dismissal of theology professors. He grants work books and residence permissions, or refuses or withdraws them.

There are four categories of clergymen:

1) Clergymen who are entitled to be active as ministers or vicars;

2) Clergymen who have the right only to celebrate the Holy Mass in a certain church; they are called "Altorists."

3) Clergymen who are entitled to receive a pension from the diocese curia; they are called "Pensionists."

4) Clergymen whose workbook is withheld and who are not allowed to practice any ministerial or priestly activity; they are called "Office Removed" or "Suspended."

What concerns the congregation management in accordance with the Soviet Religious Law of 1929 is that the congregation is not led and managed by a minister, but by three laymen: the congregation's elder, his helper, and the treasurer. In Lithuania, the government authorized or cult commissar, Justas Rugienis, had published his explanation in the Soviet Lithuanian paper, *Valstieciu Laikrakstis,* how this law must be followed:

> The religious fellowship can vote for a revision on commission, which exercises the control over the inventory and the incoming contributions. The religious committee is elected in a meeting of believers, out of those being present, through open voting, thus a committee of three persons is chosen. Neither the

clergymen, nor the religious central management, have the right to remove from office one or any of the members of the committee of revision commission. They also have no right to give the executive organ or revision commission of believers any kind of regulations of obliging character. The function of the clergymen is solely limited to the exercise of religious functions.

According to the law of 1929, the executive organ is subject to the Soviet congregation and is entitled to remove anyone from office who does not please them. The congregation committee, therefore, is no longer an executive organ of the church but an instrument of the Soviets.

A general spiritual resurgence now sweeping the little Baltic state is "almost like a miracle." More than at any previous time, young people are searching for spiritual freedom. Having long been surfeited with lies, they are now looking for truth.

Students respond critically to professors, and anti-Soviet literature is distributed. Young people openly wear buttons (some handmade) that proclaim "I Love Jesus" or "Jesus Loves Me."

Baptist churches are now crowded and young people are well represented. Throughout Latvia the number of Baptist church members had dropped to about half the pre-war total, but that erosion has now been checked. Roman Catholicism too is attracting open identification among many Latvians. Other denominations are experiencing some new interest also but not as much as the Baptists and Catholics.

While there is a steadily increasing amount of religious expression in the Soviet Union, it is not without its hazards.

Communist authorities are now keenly sensitive to news in the Western media about dissidents within their borders. World attention is focused on their compliance with provisions of the Helsinki accords on European security and cooperation.

"This may be the beginning of the end," Bruvers declared. He does not see how the Soviets can stop what appears to him to be a rolling tide of freedom. People all over Eastern Europe are pressing for Western recognition of their plight in light of the Helsinki guarantees. Western delegates to the Belgrade conference, including the Vatican, made a strong defense of human rights as the 35 nation meeting completed its first week.

The 420 delegates to the meeting, which began October 4, 1977, and was scheduled to run three months, represented 33 Eastern and Western European nations, plus the United States and Canada, that signed the accords at the end of the Conference on European Security and Cooperation at Helsinki, Finland, in 1975.

Among the signers of the Helsinki agreements was the Vatican which promoted the human rights section guaranteeing, among other things, religious liberty for believers of all faiths.

Vatican Radio cited the issue in an editorial as the Belgrade conference opened.

> Certainly it was not realistic, although it was a great hope, to think that certain situations would change suddenly in light of the accords.

> Much still remains to be done, but more than ever the hopes remain alive that what has not been done in these two years can be done today and in the near future in an even more complete way.

The same cautious approach was taken by the Vatican delegate to the Belgrade conference, Msgr. Achille Silvestrini. He pleaded for greater respect of religious liberty in Communist nations, especially regarding still-respressed Eastern-rites, but also cited positive gains such as the easing of travel restrictions against Church personnel.

The Helsinki agreement was important primarly for the impulse it gave to a progressive movement—even though toilsome and too slow here and there—toward the irreversible development of ever-broader freedoms.

Although Msgr. Silvestrini did not single out specific countries in his remarks, it was clear that he was referring to the Soviet Union and Eastern European nations as the chief offenders of religious liberty.

The major action arm of the U.S. Catholic bishops has urged the chief of the American delegation to the Belgrade conference to "insist strongly" on a comprehensive review of participating states' records, especially those in Eastern Europe, on religious freedom and human rights.

> There is abundant evidence that these commitments are not being observed in the USSR and the Communist states of Eastern Europe and that indeed, systematic programs of interference with religious life, religious observances and the religious instruction of children continue in effect and are ever being intensified.

At the Belgrade Conference to review the Helsinki accord, U.S. delegate Arthur Goldberg issued a sweeping indictment of the failure "by some nations of the East" to live up to the human rights provisions of the agreement. Without naming the countries, he condemned their practices of imprisoning or exiling persons "for making their thoughts known."

The section of the Final Act of the Helsinki accords committs participating states to "respect human rights and fundamental freedoms" and "to recognize and respect the freedom of the individual to profess and practice . . . religion or belief acting in accordance with dictates of his own conscience."

Lithuania

The Soviet constitutional and legal guarantees of freedom of religion and conscience are deceptive because the Penal Code and various governmental decrees and instructions concerning the implementation of the laws on religion are designed to permit the regime a virtually unlimited harassment of the faithful in the performance of their religious duties and, in fact, subject the religious communities to a complete control by the state. At the same time the state, through the constitutional right of anti-religious propaganda, violates the freedom of conscience by subjecting the school children and the society at large to an intense atheistic indoctrination, including informally applied sanctions to those who want to profess a faith. The examination of the Soviet legal materials on religion alone attests the suppression of the churches and the faithful in the Soviet state.

Soviet laws and regulations of religion are essentially derived from the decree "Concerning the Separation of Church and State and the School and Church," enacted on January 23, 1918. This decree, prepared by Lenin, separated the church from the state, confiscates all church property, prohibits religious observances in public offices, separates the church from the school, prohibits religious instructions in schools, but at the same time guarantees the freedom of conscience and practice of religion as long as it does not interfere with "public order." For instance, Lenin's policy is reflected in Article 96 of the Constitution of the Lithuanian SSR (which is identical to Article 124 of the Constitution of the USSR and is implemented in a series of articles of the Lithuanian SSR Penal Code and government decrees and instructions.

Article 143 of the Penal Code of the Lithuanian SSR provides that the violation of the constitutional separation of church and state and the school and church is punishable by imprisonment of up to one year, or by corrective labor for the same period, or by a fine of up to 100 rubles. Repeated violations are subject of up to three years in prison. On May 12, 1966, the Presidium of the Supreme Soviet of the Lithuanian SSR adopted an instruction on the application of Article 143 of the Penal Code. According to this instruction, the following acts constitute a violation of this article:

187

Compulsory collection and tithes for the benefit of religious organizations or ministers of cults; the preparation for purposes of mass dissemination or mass dissemination of handbills, letters, leaflets, and other documents making appeals for the nonobservance of the legislation on religious cults; the commission of fraudulent actions for the purposes of inciting religious superstition among the masses of the population; the organization and holding of minors in violation of established legislative rules; the refusal to employ a order; the organization and regular holding of classes for teaching religion to minors in violation of established legislative rules; the refusal to employ a citizen or to admit to an educational institution, the release from employment or the expulsion from an educational institution, the revocation of legally established advantages and privileges of citizens, also other essential limitations of the rights of citizens because of their religious views.

Another decree of the Presidium of the Lithuanian SSR Supreme Soviet on the implementation of Article 143 of the Penal Code provides administrative penalities of up to 50 rubles, imposed by administrative commissions of the executive committees of rayon and city soviets, for commission of the following acts:

The failure to register the associations with governmental organs by the leaders of religious associations; the violation of legally established rules in organizing and holding of religious meetings, processions, and other rites of cults; the organizing and holding of special meetings, and also of labor, literary, and other circles and groups, having no relation to the performance of the cult, for children and adolescents by the servants of the cult or members of religious associations.

Among other things, such provisions limit the religious communities in the propagation of their faith through organized religious instruction of children. The state goes even further in intervening with this basic right by attempting to impose limitations on the parents themselves. The 1968 legislation on the family seeks "to eliminate finally from the family relations harmful vestiges and customs of the past." The Soviet authorities hope that the isolation of children from religious influences eventually will eliminate what is usually referred to as "religious superstitions." The same legal provisions enable the authorities to impose severe limitations on religious communities and the clergy in the performance of their rites (such as processions). It is also noteworthy that not a single case is known of a conviction of anyone for interfering with religious practice.

Article 144 of the Lithuanian SSR Penal Code provides penalties of up to five years in prison, or exile for the same period with or without the confiscation of property for "the organizing of a group, whose activity, carried on under the guise of propagation of the faith or the performance or religious rites is connected with a perpetration of harm to the health of the citizens or with other violations of citizens' rights." This rule limits not just specific rites of a number of religious denominations (the Christian Scientists, for example), but it may be broadly construed and applied to prohibit such religious rites as the administration of Extreme Unction in the Catholic faith on the grounds that such rites are "injurious to the health" of a critically ill patient. In general, "harm" to the personality of an individual is nowhere specifically legally defined and the provision can and is arbitarily applied to various religious practices and the propagation of the faith.

Article 145 of the Penal Code superficially is for the protection of the believers. It provides punishment of up to one year in prison, or corrective labor for the same period, or a fine of up to 100 rubles for "the obstruction to perform religious rites, insofar as they do not violate public order or infringe on the rights of citizens." In fact, the qualifier of the first sentence alone permits a wide discretion for the regime to intervene and to harass the performance of religious rites by the clergy and the faithful. This article also has not been applied.

The constitutional separation of church and state does not mean the mutual non-interference in the affairs of the parties, but rather the complete subjection of the church to the state. According to Soviet law, the church is a private organization, does not possess a legal personality, and as an organization is completely dependent upon state authorities. Organizationally and economically the state is in a position to impose control virtually over all aspects of church life. Nowhere is this so clearly defined as in the instructions on application of laws on religion, promulgated in 1969 by the Representative for the Lithuanian SSR of the Council for Religious Affairs of the Council of Ministers of the USSR. The instruction provides for a maximum isolation of the clergy from the laity and for a maximum intervention of the state in the internal affairs of religious communities. The following are among the more significant provisions of this instruction:

5. In the agreement (between the members of the religious community and the local authorities) it is provided that the persons, who undertook to use the house of prayer and other property, have the duty:

to permit   freely at all times, except during religious rites, the representatives of rayon (city) executive committees to periodically inspect and to survey the property, given to the religious community.

8, The religious community in a meeting of its members by an open vote elects an executive organ of the members for the conduct of the affairs of the religious community, to perform the function of utilizing the property and funds of the cult.

9. An audit commission of not more than three members may be elected to audit the use of the property of the cult and of the voluntary monetary contributions of the believers.

The local executive committees have the right not to permit certain persons to become members of the executive organ or the audit commission. The servants of the cult and religious centers do not have this right.

11. The religious communities and servants of the cult may not undertake any activity, except the performance of religious rites among the faithful. They do not have the right:

a) to open mutual assistance funds and engage in welfare activity,

b) to organize sanatorias or treatment,

c) to hold excursions, children's and sport parks, to open libraries,

d) to hold any kind of a meeting, circle, etc., which is not related to religious rites.

12. Without the permission of the rayon (city) executive committee, the religious community and the servants of the cult may not:

a) hold plenary meetings of the faithful to consider questions pertaining to the conduct of affairs of the the religious community and the use of cult property,

b) hold religious processions, hold religious rites and ceremonies in the open air, also within the apartments of the believers. Special permits or notifications of religious processions which are an integral part of the services and are performed around the house of prayer are not necessary when such procession does not interfere with normal street traffic. It is permissible to perform religious rites in the apartments and homes of the believers without a permit or notification to governmental organs at the request of the dying or critically ill.

13. The religious centers, the religious communities, and the servants of the cult are prohibited:

a) to hold special prayer rites for children, adolescents, and women, also to organize circles, groups or meetings for religious instruction,

b) to hold meetings of believers in "holy places," to take deceitful actions, whose aim is to inculcate religious superstitions among the inhabitants (the proclamation of all kinds of miracles: the cure of the ill, prophesies, etc.), and to have some kind of advantage from this,

c) to organize compulsory collections and taxation of believers for the benefit of the religious community or for some other purpose,

d) to apply to the believers measures of coercion or penalities.

15. The religious centers, the curia of dioceses, the religious educational institutions, the convents, the religious communities, and other religious associations are required to permit the officials of state organs to inspect periodically the property, to audit the financial books and other documents, in order to determine whether the property in their care is properly used and to obtain information which is necessary for the taxation of the servants of the cult and other persons.

In independent Lithuania, freedom of religion was granted by the Constitution. Churches and equivalent religious organizations recognized by the state enjoyed the rights of legal entities.

In 1940, when Lithuania was occupied by and incorporated into the Soviet Union, it had approximately 3 million inhabitants. The population was divided into the following religious groups: Roman Catholics, 80.5 per cent; Protestants, 9.5 per cent; Jews, 7.3 per cent; Orthodox, 2.5 per cent; and others .2 per cent. Roman Catholics constituted 94.4 per cent of the Lithuanian ethnic group.

After the reunification of the Vilnius region in 1939, the Catholic Church in Lithuania was composed of 2 archbishoprics,, 4 bishoprics, 69 deaneries, and 681 parishes. In 1940, there were 4 archbishops, 9 bishops, 1,487 priests, 152 monk-priests, 571 monks, 963 nuns, 1,202 churches and chapels, and 2,776,000 members.

There are no available statistical data for other religious denominations in 1940. The following statistics are from 1930 and cover only Lithuanian territory outside the Vilnius region.

The Jews had 300 synagogues, 160 rabbis, and 3 rabbinical schools; the Orthodox, 24 parishes and 27 priests; the Lutherans, 95 parishes and 80 ministers; the Old Believers, 51 parishes and 51 priests; the Reformed Protestants, 13 parishes and 13 priests.

From the historical point of view, in the present survey the situation of church and religion in occupied Lithuania is divided into two periods: Lithuania under the first Soviet occupation (1940-41), and Lithuania under the second Soviet occupation (1944-   ).

Immediately after the occupation of Lithuania by the Soviet Union on June 15, 1940, the Concordat was denounced and a series of strong measures were taken for the elimination of religious influence upon public life.

The Soviet laws and regulations of 1918, 1929, and 1931 were not published in the official gazette of the Lithuanian SSR; however, they were gradually applied in Lithuania, presumably on the basis of the provisions of article 19 of the Soviet Union Constitution which prescribes that "the laws of the USSR have the same force within the territory of every union republic."

The measures taken by the Soviet authorities in Lithuania were described by an eyewitness, Bishop V. Brizgys, before the Congressional Committee on Communist Aggression and Forced Incorporation of the Baltic States into the USSR as follows:

> The Russian Army occupied Lithuania on June 15, 1940. Ten days later, June 15, the Concordat was abrogated. The Papal Nuncio received an order to leave the country by August 25. Chaplains from army hospitals, schools, and prisons were dismissed on July 2.
>
> During the next 2 weeks all private hospitals, schools, kindergartens, all charity institutions, orphanages, old people's homes were expropriated. All the property of these institutions was confiscated.
>
> . . . All leading personnel or organizations were arrested the night of July 12, 1940. Beginning that night, one by one disappeared the more or less active members of Catholic and patriotic societies. Some were shot in torture chambers, while others were sent to concentration camps in Russia.
>
> All Catholic newspapers and magazines were suppressed during the first weeks of occupation. Efforts to save at least one catechism or prayerbook were futile. Without any compensation all printing establishments were taken over. . . .
>
> All priests' seminaries were seized during the first days of the occupation. After very long and difficult efforts one seminary was allowed for the five dioceses in Kaunas, which after 4 months, however, exactly January 13, 1941, was closed. The students and professors were expelled within 12 hours.
>
> All monasteries were also closed during the first months of the Communist regime. All property and deposits in banks were also seized.
>
> With few exceptions, the rectories and the churches were taken over for various fictional purposes of the Communist party. I say fictional purposes, because the Communist Party had members in only a small number of towns.
>
> All bishops and chancery office staffs were banned from their residences. Among the last to be expelled from their residences were the archbishop of Kaunas and his auxiliary bishop. This was December 8, 1940. . . .
>
> After 4 months, in October 1940, the Communist government began a very strong movement against the observance of Christian holidays—Sundays, Christmas, Easter, and so on. . . . I personally know many cases where school children, workers, and officials were summoned, intimidated, arrested for assisting at Sunday Mass.

The following three documents, seized by the Lithuanian partisans at the beginning of the war between Nazi Germany and the Soviet Union in 1941, constitute the best illustration of the Soviet attitude toward the church and religion in Lithuania.

On October 2, 1940, Gladkov, Acting People's Commissar of the Interior of the Soviet Socialist Republic of Lithuania, issued an order to all commanders of the county branches of the GPU to place all clergymen, monks, and nuns under formal surveillance, recruit agents to obtain information on their activities, and deliver to him a memorandum concerning the action taken against the clergy by October 15, 1940.

Another order was issued on January 21, 1941, by Guzevich, the People's

Commissar for the Interior of the Lithuanian SSR, asking that a list of all Roman Catholics, Orthodox, and Protestant organizations be prepared; a list of pastors, parish priests, and leaders of sects, and a detailed report on their activities.

Finally, on April 25, 1941, priests were asked to sign a form agreeing that they would not give any religious education to children.

During the first occupation, in all of Lithuania outside the Vilnius diocese, 28 Catholic priests were arrested, 12 were deported and 15 murdered by the retreating Red Army.

The efforts completely to destroy the Church were interrupted by the outbreak of the German-Russian war in June, 1941.

This decade must be considered the most horrifying in the entire 1,000 year history of Lithuania. Had the same policies continued in effect for a longer time, not only would religion have been wiped out but the nation itself would have been annihilated. During this time about 300,000 Lithuanians were either killed or exiled to Russia. Those who remained in Lithuania lived in constant, daily terror. Anyone whom the Communists considered influential was deported or slain. Some families were deported together; others were not. Fathers were sent to one concentration camp, mothers to another, and the children were separated from both their parents. Years later, after Stalin's death, some of the children returned to Lithuania while their parents still remained in Siberia.

In Lithuania, the Roman Catholic Church had in the year 1940, about 2,290,000 believers, six dioceses, fourteen bishops, 1,439 priests; in the year 1966, after the death of the bishop Petras Mazelis on May 21, 1966, there remained only one bishop, Juozapas Labukas-Matulaitis, apostolic administrator of Kaunas and Vilkaviskis, and 850 priests. Now five bishops' seats were unoccupied; two bishops for a longer time are still under house arrest, namely Julijonas Steponavicius, former apostolic administrator of Vilnius and Panevezys, and Vincentas Sladkevicius, apostolic administrator of Kaisiadorys. The Evangelical-Lutheran Church had 93 ministers in the year of 1945; in 1962, there were only twelve ministers left. The age groups of the Catholic clergymen in the Baltic countries show the following picture: up to forty years—30 per cent; from 40-60 years—46 per cent, and from 60-70 years and over—24 per cent.

During 1945 and 1946 nearly every priest in Lithuania was required to present himself for interrogation at one of the 480 "centers of terror" set up throughout the land. At these centers the Soviets demanded that each priest sign a "loyalty" oath—a promise to spy on his own people and to make reports to the police. He was also required to help organize "The Living Church," which was to be independent of Rome and loyal to the occupational government of Soviet Russia. As a result of these terror tactics, the Bishop of Telsiai, Vincentas Borisevicius, was shot to death, and 100 priests were imprisoned and another 180 were deported, practically all of them to concentration camps in Siberia. In this latter group were three bishops; namely, the Bishop of Kaisiadorys, Teofilius Matulionis; the auxiliary Bishop of Telsiai, Pranciskus Ramanauskas; and the Archbishop of Vilnius, Mecislovas Reinys.

The occupational government of Soviet Russian sought to control the Catholic Church by forbidding the appointment of new bishops to the dioceses that had lost their bishops by death or deportation. To take charge of religious affairs in Lithuania, the government appointed a "delegate"— an ordinary Lithuanian Communist who had served in the NKVD (the secret police) for several years. He appointed others as assistants in the local districts. To this "delegate" full administrative powers, properly belonging to the bishops alone, were granted. Yet, neither he nor his aides received any real jurisdiction since they merely carried out the orders and directives coming from Moscow.

Under the new administration only one seminary remained open for the entire country. Though candidates for the priesthood were not lacking, Moscow allowed only 25 to attend the seminary at one time.

Before the young men could enter the seminary, they had to obtain the approval of the "delegate" for religious affairs. Even then, the seminarians faced frequent questioning and the possibility of dismissal if the "delegate" decided that they were unsuitable. The fact that four seminary rectors were arrested between 1944 and 1954 illustrates the political stringency with which the seminary was controlled. What harmful effect this control and the limitation in numbers has had on the Church can be judged from the fact that in 1967 only 9 priests were ordained while 24 died.

After Stalin's death the reign of terror diminished. Some of those who had been imprisoned or deported to Siberia returned—130 priests and 35,000 lay people. A considerable number of them were invalids.

Though about 130,000 perished in concentration camps, some 145,000 Lithuanians are still alive in Siberia.

The basic principle of Communist tactics, already stressed by Lenin himself, is adaptability. Accordingly, the Communist tactics and strategy toward church and religion vary from time to time. Such fluctuations became very evident in Lithuania during the second Soviet occupation which started in 1944.

In the Soviet Union the control of church activities is vested in two councils attached to the Council of Ministers of the Soviet Union: one for the Orthodox Church (since 1942) and the other for other religions (since 1943).

Besides the "delegate" for religious affairs, there is in Lithuania a government-financed Supreme Council for Atheism. Its purpose is to recruit anti-religious agents, determine policies, select tactics, and finance anti-religious activities.

In Lithuania, the control functions are performed by the director of religious affairs and may be summarized as follows:

> The administration of the church is really in the hands of the cult commissar. Without his permission, no priest can perform his duties or assume any sort of post. Some priests are forbidden to perform their priestly duties. The cult commissar also controls the assignment of priests to parishes. He himself attempts to place selected priests in vacant positions. He seeks to place the control of the dioceses in the hands of reliable priests, who are faithful to the state.

The most characteristic feature of this period is the strong action of Lithuanian partisans against the Communist administration in Lithuania and subsequent mass arrests and deportations. In order to break down the partisan movement, the leading Catholic authorities, and especially the bishops, were urged to condemn it:

> The Communists tried to use bishops as political tools for their purposes.

When the NKVD was unable to suppress the numerous partisan bands in 1946, the Commissar of the Interior requested the bishops to renounce the resistance movement and urge the partisans to surrender. When the bishops refused to do this, the NKVD began to threaten and then to act. The first victim was Bishop V. Borisevicius of the Telsiai diocese, who was arrested in 1946 and sentenced to death in a closed trial on January 3, 1947. At the end of 1946, his assistant, Bishop P. Ramanauskas, was arrested and deported to Siberia. In the same year, both Bishop T. Matulionis of the Kaisiadoriai diocese and the Archbishop of Vilnius, M. Reinys, were exiled to hard labor camps in Siberia. Archbishop Reinys died in the Vladimir prison on November 8, 1953. By 1947, only one bishop remained in Lithuania, Bishop Paltarokas of Peneveziai.

The most complete statistical data of the losses of the Catholic Church during this first period of intense struggle were provided by V. Vaitiekunas. He compiled it on the basis of the *Tass* report of 1947, information provided by the Lithuanian underground movement and the alleged statement of Bishop Paltarokas published by the pro-Communist American Lithuanian daily *Laisve* (*Liberty*), on January 13, 1954. The table compiled by V. Vaitiekunas reads:

	1939	1947 (Tass)	1948 (Lithuanian underground)	1954 (Soviet information)
Archbishops and bishops	14	2	1	1
Clergy	1,646	1,332	400	741
Religious	1,586	0	0	0
Churches	1,202	711	600	688
Parishioners	2,776,422	?	?	?

By about 1947, all monasteries were closed and most of the monks and nuns had been deported. In the period 1946-49, 180 priests were deported and sentenced to hard labor.

The Lutheran Church and the Reformed Church were almost completely destroyed and only a few pastors remained, the majority having fled to the West, the others having been deported.

The comparison of the Lithuanian Church in the years of 1940 and 1967 is as follows:

	1940	1967
Catholic Dioceses	6	6
Prelature Nullius	1	1
Archbishops and Bishops in Metropolitan Archdiocese of Kaunas	2	2
Archdiocese of Vilnius	2	0
Diocese of Vilkaviskis	2	0
Diocese of Penevezis	1	0
Diocese of Telsiai	2	1
Diocese of Kaisiadorys	1	0
(Emeritus Archbishop Karevicius was alive in 1940 and has died since)		
Deaneries	62	54
Priests	1,450	844
Priests refugees from Lithuania	257	610
Parishes and Mission churches	717	610
Other Churches and Chapels	330	5
Seminaries for Priests	4	1

Diocesan Seminarians	425	29
Seminarians of Religious Communities	141	0
Catholic Theological-Philosophical Faculty	1	0
Protestant Theological Faculty	1	0
Jewish Rabbinical Academy	1	0
Jewish Rabbinical Schools	2	0
Monasteries	37	0
Convents	85	0
Centers of Catholic Organizations	18	0
Membership in Catholic Organizations	800,000	0
Catholic Academy of Science	1	0
Catholic Secondary Schools and Lyceumns	18	0
Catholic Elementary Schools	18	0
Catholic Kindergartens	35	0
Catholic Institution for Deaf and Dumb	1	0
Catholic Orphanages	10	0
Catholic Homes for Children	10	0
Catholic Homes for Aged	25	0
Catholic Hospitals	2	0
Correctional Institution for Youth	1	0
Catholic Museum of Art	1	0
Catholic Libraries	6	0
Catholic Parish Libraries and Others	823	0
Catholic Archives	643	0
Catholic Periodicals and Daily Papers	32	0
Circulation of above	7,500,000	0
Catholic Publishing Houses	7	0

Perhaps as many as two thirds of the Lithuanians have retained links with the Church. The latter's basic organizational structure has largely remained intact. More serious was the situation with the clergy: where there were once ten bishops, only two active bishops remained by 1968 with approximately 800 active priests (a reduction by about 40 per cent since 1940), not counting some 176 retired or "unregistered" clergy.

Though over three hundred priests have been ordained since 1945, only a handful had left the Church by 1967. A few clergymen were reportedly recruited as police informers and some have become apologists for the regime's policies. But the majority, while overtly professing their loyalty to the Soviet state, have been conscientiously carrying, under difficult conditions, a heavy burden of pastoral work, abstaining from any political involvement for or against the regime. By the end of the 1960's there has also emerged an increasingly vocal group of activist clergy and young lay intellectuals who were prepared to risk their personal careers in order to break the seal of silence imposed upon the Church by more than two decades of intimidation.

Following Stalin's death, the Lithuanian Church experienced several years of a "thaw". Some 130 priests—less than half of the numbers exiled after the war—were then allowed to return home, together with two surviving bishops. Meanwhile, in 1955, the government consented to the consecration of two new bishops—Julijonas Stepanovicius and Petras Mazelis—and permitted a few "loyal" priests to pursue their advanced studies in Rome. A Catholic prayerbook was published in a small edition at that time.

By 1958, the regime resumed the harassment of the Church. Bishop Vincentas Sladkevicius, evidently ordained without the government's consent, was barred from his see and confined to a remote village; in 1961, the same fate befell Bishop Steponavicius. The enrollment in the Kaunas seminary was further reduced to 25 students. Some churches, especially in urban centres, were closed and a major church in Klaipeda—one of the two built by believers in Lithuania since 1945—was confiscated and turned into a concert hall. Chapels and crosses in the principal pilgrimage centers were destroyed by the authorities. While a massive anti-religious propaganda drive was launched in the Republic, new restrictions were imposed upon the performance of certain religious rites, and more severe sanctions were applied against the clergy for religious instruction of children and for allowing active participation of the youth in religious ceremonies.

In the wake of Khrushchev's fall came some abatement in anti-religious pressures. The authoirties permitted the ordination of two new bishops—Juozas Matulaitis-Labukas, in 1965, and Juozapas Pletkus, in 1968. The enrollment in the Kaunas seminary was raised to 30 students. The Church was able to publish, in miniscule edition, a volume containing decisions of the Second Vatican Council. Nevertheless, the antiligious propaganda—though less abusive than during the early sixties'—has not lost much of its intensity, with the authorities resorting to administrative and judicial weapons to minimize the clergy's influence upon children.

Despite nearly 30 years of legal and administrative restrictions and a steady barrage of atheist propaganda, the Roman Catholic Church in Lithuania has remained, by the end of the 1970's, still a potent force in Lithuanian society.

After Stalin's death, and especially after Khrushchev's declaration of November 10, 1954, when the central committee demanded the cessation of anti-religious actions and insults to individual religious feelings, the climate of the war against religion changed. In Lithuania this statement of Khrushchev's was interpreted by the Communist Party organ as follows:

> In the republic there are collective farmworkers and laborers who, although actively participating in collective farm production and factory work and conscientiously carrying out their political duties, are still under the influence of religious belief. The party teaches us to adopt an attitude of sympathy and understanding in dealing with these believers. It would be stupid and harmful to consider these or other Soviet citizens as politically questionable merely because of their religious beliefs. Religious superstition in man is only a remnant of the past. Therefore, we must regard the fight against religious superstition as an ideological war of the scientific-materialistic philosophies against unscientific religious philosophies.

At that time some people ventured even to engage in open discussions. For instance, on December 11, 1955, Drotvinas wrote:

> To the educated, religion is not a hindrance. Today religion has been modernized to such an extent and has made nso many compromises that it cannot act as a retarding force in the development of science, technology, and art. Technological and scientific progress can be observed in countries where religion is a state institution and where scientists are religious.
>
> On the contrary, the art of the 20th century has suffered a setback in comparison with earlier ages, even though it is definietly more atheistic today. Religion does not interfere with the initiative of the workers because it does not advocate that they do their job badly or refuse to do it at all. . . . Among the atheists today there are many deviates and therefore it cannot be asserted which is definitely better—the man who goes to church, or the man who goes to a restaurant. This

question is too broad and too deep for a quick and easy solution. . . . We must consider an educated man who goes to church. The religious fanatic is as ridiculous as the anti-religious fanatic. One believes in superstitions, the other attacks them. It is not clear what and why the former believes, nor why the latter attacks him and is so deeply worried, since God does not exist.

During this period of the thaw, the attacks against religion and priests diminished and some priests were permitted to return from exile:

During the period of relaxation (1953 to September 17, 1955) an amnesty was declared (except for a few categories of crime), after which a certain percentage of the deported were allowed to return to their homes. About 35,000 people (of the 275,000 deported) returned to Lithuania. Others did not have the right to return, but had to settle somewhere in Russia (usually in the Asian part of the country). At that time about 130 priests returned to Lithuania. A small part of these returned of their own free will to their former places of exile to serve the needs of the faithful. Two bishops, Matulionis and Ramanauskas, also were allowed to return to Lithuania, but were not permitted to resume their duties. They were told where to live and could not communicate with their priests or the faithful.

It must be stressed that those who returned were not rehabilitated, but remained "criminals" and their crime was constantly remembered in the press.

During the period of relaxation, on September 11, 1955, two bishops (Julijonas Steponavicius and Petras Mazelis) were consecrated and assigned by the Holy See to the Vilnius, Panevezys, and Telsiai dioceses.

Some churches were repaired during this liberal period and permission was given to build two new churches in Klaipeda and Svencioneliai.

In 1956 a series of articles appeared in the Lithuanian Communist press, especially in an organ of the Communist Party called *Tiesa,* which were directed against religious practice, emphasizing that it is an obstacle to the construction of Communism, the good performance of civic functions, the education of youth, etc.

In general, teachers, professors, and scholars were urged to devote more time and energy to atheistic philosophy. Atheistic indoctrination became one of the most important tasks of the schools:

The formation of a materialistic attitude (Weltanschauung) in the students and scientific atheistic education is the paramount responsibility of every teacher. Teachers of biology, physics, chemistry, history, and literature can play an exceptionally important role. By revealing from its very foundations the materialistic interpretation of the order in the universe and in human society, they can at the same time show, with vivid and pointed examples, how the slaves of religion try to falsify scientific truths and to fool the gullible public. . . . Religion must be exposed to show how the servants of the church have fooled the laboring classes with superstitions, keeping them literally in the dark, how they have preached respect and reverence for the exploiters of the working class.

In 1949 the Lithuanian Society for the Dissemination of Political and Scientific Information was established. During the thaw period its' activity was limited. However, since 1956, when general propaganda against church and religion was reactivated, this society also showed more activity. In 1957, it started publication of a journal called *Mokslas ir Gyvenimas* (Science and Life) which was entirely devoted to atheistic propaganda. It also organized lectures which increased in number from year to year, reaching 100,000 in 1962.

The press, radio, museums, and exhibitions are constantly used for atheistic propaganda. In 1960 there were 779 groups of intellectuals formed for this purpose.

When the Soviets occupied Lithuania the second time, only ten Protestant ministers were left in the entire country. Since these few could not possibly provide adequate service to the Protestant community, the faithful were forced to rely on their own selected lay preachers to lead them in worship with hymns, prayer, and the Word of God. An especially strong manifestation of this form of religious service was prevalent among the Protestants in the Klaipeda area. During the Soviet occupation, some of these lay preachers assumed full pastoral duties. In Klaipeda, where no church was available to the Lutherans, the service was conducted by preacher Blasner in private homes. Since the Communist authorities forbid these new clergymen from performing religious rites, Protestant worship goes on in secret, and the lay preachers spend their days performing full-time duties on collective farms or other Soviet-controlled enterprise.

During the Stalin era, Protestant clergymen in Lithuania were permitted to teach catechism to the children and to prepare them for Confirmation. Since then, however, these privileges have been abrogated, and any attempt "to spread superstition and inflict harm on the child's conscience," as in the case of Catholics, is punishable by law.

The Protestant clergyman, too, is subject to moral terrorism. He is driven to making public confessions and renunciations of his faith. One recent victim of such terror was the 80-year-old minister of the Reformed Church, Adomas Sernas, whose article renouncing his faith and clerical duties was printed in *Tiesa* on August 16, 1964, a few months before he died.

Another organization for atheistic education is the pioneer organization for grammar school children. It publishes two periodicals: *Lietuvos Pionierius* (The *Lithuania Pioneer*) and *Zvaigzdute* (The *Little Star*).

In order to undermine the authority of priests and break the unity between them and the faithful, attacks in the press and the radio were intensified and priests were accused of all possible crimes: collaboration with Lithuanian partisans and Germans, participation in the annihilation of innocent people under the German occupation, the undermining of Communist construction, etc. On Feburary 1, 1961, *Valstieciu Laikrastis* wrote:

> The pastor of Nedzinge, Necinskas, under the cover of night, performed the marriage ceremony for the leader of bandits of Dzukija, Ramanauskas; Jankauskas, pastor of Varsedziai, organized the distribution of anti-Soviet leaflets. . . . Bishop Borisevicius helped the nationalistic gangs to re-establish their broken radio communications. . . . P. Gustaitis, a priest of Viesvenia, transmitted radiograms of parachutists. . . . Rudzionis, pastor of Geguzine, organized gangs of bandits. . . . J. Lelesius, pastor of Lenkeliskia parish, was a leader of a bandit gang of the "Tauras District" during 1946-47.

Thus, the so-called unmasking of priests became the subject of all atheistic gatherings. In 1961, *Sovetskaya Litva*, a Communist newspaper in Russian, published a long series of articles against priests, such as "Exhorters in Soutanes", "Criminals in the Name of God", "The Black Crows", "Cross and Pistol". The following cases may be mentioned among the trials:

In the autumn of 1959, the Reverend Gilis was sentenced to 9 months' hard labor for giving 30 children lessons in the catechism twice a week.

On March. 15, 1963, *Svyturys*, a Soviet magazine, reported that Rev. Antanas Seskevicius would be tried for the distribution of crucifixes, medallions, and holy images. He was sentenced to 7 years of confinement for sending crucifixes to Siberia.

On January 6, 1962, *Tiesa* reported that the people's court of Varena had sentenced the pastor of Dubiciai, Rev. Alfredas Kanisauskas, to 6 months of corrective labor and a fine of 300 rubles for laying out cemeteries and "cutting down trees which, in falling, crushed tombstones and knocked down crosses."

In April 1961, the pastor of a newly built church in Klaipeda, Rev. L. Pavilonis, and his assistant, Rev. Burneikis, were arrested and tried for the alleged illegal purchase of construction materials for the building of a church. In January, 1962, both priests were sentenced, the former to 8 years and the latter to 4 years of confinement. The managers of the enterprises which sold the construction materials were also sentenced; namely B. Algys, J. Mikalauskas, Ant. Paskevicius, J. Krivickas, and Aga Klovaite. The church was converted into a dancehall.

In 1964, the Reverend Jankus was accused of killing 1,200 people. The Reverend Jankus, who lives in Brooklyn, was tried in absentia and was sentenced, according to *Tass* information, to 15 years of imprisonment. Interviewed by a *New York Times* correspondent the priest said: "The trial is a show trial and part of an antireligious campaign which, for some reason, the regime has stepped up lately."

Moscow's animosity toward Rome is centuries old. Moscow's attitude toward Roman Catholicism has been summarized as follows:

> The Roman Catholic Church was a major obstacle to the spreading of the world revolution; it was the ally of capitalism, reaction and fascism; it was a driving force behind the war of intervention of the capitalist world aiming at overthrowing the young Soviet regime, and it never ceased to be a major element in the anti-Soviet front.

Therefore, the first attacks against the Roman Catholic hierarchy were made in order to break the unity of the church. According to A. Michel the results were to be achieved: (1) Above all by breaking the unity with Rome, by preventing contact of the hierarchy and the faithful with this center of the Catholic Church. At the same time by skillful propaganda must be undermined the respect and affection of the clergy and faithful toward the Holy Father; (2) By breaking up the unity of the bishops among themselves; (3) By breaking up the unity between bishops and priests; (4) By breaking up the unity of the priests among themselves; and (5) By breaking up the unity of the clergy and the faithful.

During the first occupation, 1940-41, Soviet authorities had tried to break the relations with Rome by denouncing the Concordat and expelling the Papal Nuncio. These efforts were renewed in 1944 by advancing the idea of a "national church."

> The church hierarchy was ordered to sever all its relations with the Vatican; when it refused, the occupiers endeavored to organize the younger priests. Their efforts brought no significant results—neither promises nor threats availed. The Lithuanian bishops were repeatedly summoned to various government offices and informed that the Party would tolerate only a national church, not an international one. Smirnow, the chief of the MGB, was given the task of organizing such a church, while Snieckus, the first secretary of the Communist Party in Lithuania, and B. Pusinas, the director of religious affairs, applied additional pressure.

However, these efforts did not produce any results because there were no priests to support such an idea.

On Feburary 19, 1946, V. Borisevicius, Bishop of Telsiai, was arrested and on January 3, 1949, was sentenced to death. Also in 1946, the Auxiliary Bishop of Telsiai, P. Ramanauskas, was arrested and deported. Ten years later he was permitted to return but was not allowed to perform his duties. Bishop Matulionis suffered a similar fate. In 1956 he returned but without permission to perform his functions.

In 1947 Archbishop Reinys was arrested and deported. He died on November 3, 1953, in the prison at Vladimir. Bishop A. Karosas died, thus depleting the hierarchy further. Archbishop Skvireckas and Bishops V. Brizgys and V. Padolskis were deported by the Germans and did not return to Lithurania. Thus, after the arrest of Archbishop Reinys only one bishop, K. Paltarokas, remained acting in Lithuania. This situation continued until 1955 when, in accord with the Holy See, he consecrated two new bishops, P. Mazelis and J. Steponavicius. A third bishop, V. Sladkevicius, was consecrated in 1957. Bishop Paltarokas died on January 3, 1958, and Bishop Ramanauskas on October 17, 1959.

Actually, only three bishops remained in Lithuania and only one was permitted to perform his functions; namely, Bishop Mazelis. Two others, Julionas Steponavicious and Vicentas Sladkevicius were deported to other dioceses.

As was mentioned above, during the first occupation, the priests were urged to sign a form stating that they would not give religious education "to school children of preparatory school age, either in churches or in the homes of the children, or in my own apartment or elsewhere." This attitude still persists and has made religious education practically impossible. Religious education can be given only during a general celebration of Masses and sermons. Any attempt to organize such education is punishable, and not only the priests or laymen who organize such education are punished, but the parents as well. Children at schools are interrogated as to whether they are being given religious education by their parents, although this is not prohibited. Priests are not allowed to organize special religious services and sermons for children even in the churches.

The ranks of the clergy were depleted by deportations, arrests, and natural death. The situation of the seminaries was summarized as follows:

> The seminaries at Kaunas, Telsiai, Vilnius, and Vilkaviskis had been reopened during the German occupation; in the fall of 1944 those at Vilnius and Vilkaviskis were again closed and the Telsiai seminary was closed the following year. Some 300 students attended the sole remaining seminary, at Kaunas; the party decided this was too many, and in 1945 it restricted the number to 190 and in 1946 to 150. Later restrictions reduced the number to 75 and then to 69, and last year the seminary was permitted only 60 students.

> The seminary functions under extremely difficult conditions. There is a great shortage of suitable literature for the professors and textbooks for the students. Also, the department of religions frequently interferes in its internal affairs. It has tried on several occasions to initiate lectures on Marxism and Communist theory. In 1946 the police demanded that all the seminarians sign a statement promising to inform on the activities of the seminary, but in spite of great pressure not one seminarian signed. In retaliation the NKGB arrested and deported Monsignor Rauda, the rector of the seminary. His successor, Reverend Kuzmickis, met the same fate. In all, four rectors of the

seminary have been deported since 1944; one vice rector and two prefects were also arrested. In the spring of 1959 still another rector, Rev. K. Zitkus, was dismissed from his position along with three professors. They were replaced by younger priests without academic degrees, graduates of the seminary during the occupation.

Information concerning the taxes imposed upon churches and priests is very scarce.

From the very beginning, priests were charged a very high rent. For from 1 to 9 square yards of living space they had to pay 3 rubles, while employees with the highest incomes were charged only 0.8 ruble; for over 9 square yards the rent was 6 rubles for each additional square yard (decision of the Council of Ministers of the Lithuanian S.S.R. of July 18, 1952, and December 22, 1952).

Bochenski reported that a pastor in Lithuania must pay 100,000 rubles and an assistant priest 80,000 rubles in taxes. A. Namsons observed the following:

> Recently priests and churches were subjected to new taxes. Each priest for (the privilege of) performing his duties must pay 300 rubles (new ones). Also churches are subject to taxes. So, for instance, the Church of the Holy Ghost must pay 3,000 rubles per year, and the Church of St. Apostles Peter and Paul, 2,200 rubles.

> The civil authorities have forbidden 23 capable priests to exercise their priesthood, and of 80 considered "retired," some were forcibly retired—not by their bishops but by the civil government.

> This year only eight men were ordained to the priesthood (in Lithuania) and 15 priests passed away. The number of priests is diminishing, not because of the lack of vocations but because the Russian government is limiting the number of admissions to the only functioning seminary in Kaunas.

> Up to the year 1969 only five new candidates were permitted annually. Last year and this year 10 were allowed to enter.

> More than 100 Lithuanian churches either have been destroyed or converted to profane use by the Red government. The cathedral of Vilnius now is an art gallery and St. Casimir Church in Vilnius is being used as an atheistic museum.

The announcement that the Church was preparing for an Ecumenical Council caught Moscow's attention. Soviet Russia immediately began to take steps which were intended to demonstrate to the world "the good will" of the Soviets, even though some observers considered them insignificant.One of these tactics was the "tour" of Italy by Khrushchev's son-in-law, Aleksey Adzhubey, and his request for an audience with Pope John XXIII.

Before leaving for the first session of the Council, a number of bishops in the Russian satellite countries received surprising news. Each of these bishops was informed that "he alone in the whole world was being entrusted with an extraordinary mission" to ascertain whether or not the Vatican was prepared to communicate with Moscow, because the entire Communist world was prepared to change its attitude toward the Catholic Church and toward religion in general. Every one of those bishops was convinced of the genuineness of his mission, until he arrived at Rome. There, in Rome, the bishops learned from one another that more than one "exclusive   emissary" existed. At first, too, some of these bishops actually did attempt to persuade the delegates to the Council not to mention the religious persecutions taking place in Communist countries because, during the preceding months, there had been good signs indicating that the Soviets were possibly undergoing a change of heart.

Worth noting here is that not a single bishop from Lithuania, Romania, or Bulgaria was permitted to attend the Council, and that only a part of the Polish hierarchy and just a few bishops from Czechoslovakia and Hungary were allowed to leave their countries.

While the Soviets were demonstrating "good will" to the outside world, at the very same time, in Lithuania and elsewhere, centers of the Communist Party were busy discussing and evaluating plans for a more successful war against religion. Some of the measures taken were the following:

> In 1964, orders came from Moscow that the campaign against religion was to be so intensified that the Catholic Church in Lithuania would be completely wiped out by 1980.

> *Valstieciu Laikrastis,* in the October 24, 1965 issue, announced that a school for atheistic propagandists was replacing what had been the seminary at Vilkaviskis.

> On October 29, 1965, the same newspaper stated that the historical Church of Saint Casimir in Vilnius had been converted into an anti-religious museum.

> In 1966, Moscow sent to Lithuania a special emissary, Pomerancev, to ascertain the progress of the anti-religious war.

When the President of Russia, Podgorny, was preparing to visit Pope Paul VI at the beginning of 1967, the newspaper *Novosti (News)* wrote that the Catholic Church in Lithuania no longer had any difficulties because the problem of vacant dioceses had been satisfactorily resolved. That statement was a downright lie designed to deceive the uninformed readers outside of Lithuania.

The actual situation was quite different. At that time, not a single one of the six dioceses in Lithuania had a bishop who could rule his diocese according to the normal provisions of Canon Law. Four of the dioceses, Vilnius, Panevezis, Kaisiadorys, and Telsiai, had no bishop at all. (Bishop Mazelis of Telsiai died in 1966; Bishop Steponavicius of Vilnius and Panevezis, and Bishop Sladkevicius of Kaisiadorys were exiled outside their own territories). The remaining two dioceses, Kaunas and Vilkaviskis, were in the charge of an Apostolic Administrator, Bishop Matulaitis-Labukas, an infirm, old man. The situation in Lithuania is the same today except that, according to the latest information available, Juozapas Pletkus, has been named Bishop of Telsiai (February, 1968).

Presumably, the entire world understood that Podgorny made the trip to Rome merely to appease persecuted Catholics in Soviet Russia and in countries occupied by her so that there would be more favorable atmosphere prevailing while Russia celebrated the 50th anniversary of the Communist Revolution. The Communist press in Lithuania scarcely mentioned Podgorny's trip to Rome, and, even before the Russian president left for Rome, the Communist ideologist, Niunka, wrote in the periodical, *Mokslas ir Gyvenimas,* that in the war against religion any techniques, even dialogue with Catholics, are good.

The information in the following pages testifies to the spirit of the people, and is not intended to minimize the havoc resulting from the Soviet Russian occupation of Lithuania.

From 1940 to 1968 not a single Lithuanian bishop succumbed under Communist pressure.

Young men continue to study for the priesthood despite the annoying, governmental meddling in seminary affairs described earlier.

Of the 440 priests ordained in Lithuania between 1940 and 1968, only 17 abandoned their priesthood.

About 170 priests and 4 bishops died as martyrs for the faith.

Sad to say, two priests, ordained before 1940, became active anti-religious propagandists. One of them, Ragauskas, died October 11, 1967, and the other, Markonis, is the director of the anti-religious museum set up in the Church of Saint Casimir in Vilnius.

The spirit of the laity is best described by examples taken from recent Communist sources.

The Secretary of the Communist Party of Lithuania, Antanas Snieckus, observed that "religious superstitions" are deeply rooted among the common people.

The emissary, who had been sent from Moscow to Lithuania in 1963 to ascertain religious conditions, reported that in Western Ukraine, White Russia, Moldavia, and in the Baltic Republics (Estonia, Latvia, and Lithuania), the majority of the people were believers and that religious sentiment was alive among the people in their daily lives. Important events, such as the birth of a child, a marriage, a death, were bound up with religious ceremonies. He also observed the strange phenomenon that, even though churches and religious societies were decreasing, the number of religious customs and practices was still very great. The emissary also noted that, as religious influence was waning, drunkenness, sexual immorality, and a general disregard for everything were on the increase.

Recently, a broadcast over Soviet Radio claimed that about 830 Catholic priests are active in pastoral work in Lithuania. This was a broadcast aimed at Canada, answering a question from a Canadian listener.

But, in another broadcast for "home consumption" only, members of the Communist Party were urged to "combat religion" in accord with the principles enunciated by Lenin. Therefore, this must be done, the broadcast added, because "a certain number of Soviet people are still under the influence of religion" and it is the Party's duty to combat religion and propagate atheism.

There is no indication that persecution of religion in Lithuania is abating; it is more likely to go the other way, unless the force of world opinion has an effect on the rulers of Russia.

The Lithuanians are predominantly of the Catholic faith, constituting majority of the population. Although in Lithuania other religious communities still remain—there are consistories of the Evangelical Lutheran Church and the Evangelical Calvinist Church, a bishopric of the Russian Orthodox Church, and a number of other small groups of believers—the main thrust of anti-religious policies has been against the Catholic Church. The attack against the Catholic Church has been associated with the general Soviet policy of eradicating the sense of nationhood because in many respects the Catholic Church has been involved in Lithuania's struggle for freedom and independence.

It is not necessary to enumerate all the ways in which the freedom of religion and conscience is denied to the Lithuanian people. The described legal framework and especially its arbitrary application are essentially anti-religious. The intensity of attack on religion is indicated by the policies of the regime toward the clergy of the Catholic Church. In 1940, 1,450 priests served the Lithuanian Catholics. In 1960, their number declined to 929, in

1964 to 869, in 1967 to 852, and in 1972 to about 800. Between 15 and 20 priests die annually (16 in 1972). They are not effectively replaced because the only existing Interdiocesan Seminary in Kaunas is permitted to enroll less than 40 candidates for priesthood (there were 44 seminarians in 1972), of whom only 5-8 are ordained annually. (Only six clerics were ordained in 1972). The fact is that the rate of deaths is accelerating as the pre-soviet priests reach the 60's and 70's. Without substantial increases in ordination, the Catholic Church in Lithuania is facing an inevitable death with in a generation. The state determines the number of seminarians and approves the applications of candidates for priesthood. Since 1945 the number of seminarians allowed has been progressively decreased and there is no indication that this policy will appreciably change in the coming years.

The situation is worse when one considers the fact that regularly about 100 priests are forbidden to perform their pastoral duties through arbitrary administrative orders (the denial of permit to work, for example). Under the Soviet regime about 90 churches (out of the 717 in 1940) and 300 chapels (out of about 320 in 1940) have been closed. Despite the decline in the number of churches, many parishes are without pastors or have to be taken care of by old and infirm priests or by priests from other parishes on part-time basis. At the present time in Lithuania there are six bishops (12 in 1940), two of whom—Bishop J. Stepanovicius and Bishop V. Slatkevicius— have been exiled to the provinces and are forbidden to perform their pastoral duties. As a consequence, three of the six dioceses (Vilnius, Panevezys, and Kaisiadorys) are headed by administrators, contrary to church regulations.

A stirring appeal was smuggled out from the depths of the Communist-dominated world which may serve in part to bring a realization of the co-religionists' situation. This message found its way from Lithuania. It was confided, in duplicate copies, to several groups who were going to attempt to cross over into the free world. Only one copy ever reached its destination. Addressed to the Pope, under date of September 20, 1948, it read in part:

> Where are the civilized peoples of the world? Where have the millions of Christians disappeared to? Are there no longer any fighters for the truth, no great men? Do they not know that their Christian brothers and sisters are being exterminated? Have the Christians of the world gone to sleep in the vain illusion that the hordes from the East, after they have exterminated us, will stop and go back?

The writers of the message addressed themselves directly to the Pope. "Holy Father," they cried,

> ... we have hope of being heard. We have suffered sorely for our holy faith and for our loyalty to the Apostolic See. We therefore hope for Your Holiness' help. We are already in the death agony, but in dying we should wish to hear Your Holiness' consoling words and the assurance of the Catholic world that our children shall no longer suffer in spiritual slavery. We are convinced that your potent word will arouse from lethargy the leaders of the freedom-loving peoples.

This pathetic appeal concluded: "Holy Father, give your blessing to us who die for the freedom of the faith and of our people. Praised be Jesus Christ, the Lord of the living and the dead."

It is impossible to determine precisely how successful the Soviet regime has been in eradicating religious beliefs in the population. No doubt, the massive anti-religious propaganda, the isolation of youth from the church, and the ongoing physical destruction of the church must be having some impact. The freedom of conscience is basically compromised by the power and intervention of the state. Yet, despite the intense attack on religion, there are indications that the masses are adhering to religious beliefs with great tenacity. The petition of 17,054 Lithuanian Catholics to the authorities is suggestive of the continuing viability of religion among the people.

In the last few years, perceiving the threat to the survival of the church and their faith, the believers began to resist vigorously the abuse of Soviet laws by challenging their application in courts and through petitions and appeals to the appropriate state authorities. Numerous documents of such actions, as well as cases of religious persecution and harassment, have reached the West. The latest is the new underground periodical *Lietuvos Kataliku Baznycios Kronika* (*Chronicle of the Lithuanian Catholic Church*), the first two issues have reached the West in 1972.

On March 19, 1972, appeared the first issue of the clandestine *Chronicle of the Catholic Church in Lithuania.* Modelled, obviously, on the older *samizdat* newsletters—the *Chronicle of Current Events* and the *Ukrainian Herald,* soon to be suppressed in the KGB dragnet of dissidents—the Lithuanian *Chronicle* signalled a new stage in the consolidation of the Catholic dissent movement. The emergence of a more regular communication medium was an important step towards the integration of the clerical and lay dissidents in a "quasi-organization"—a loose network of the editors, informants, producers and distributors of the *Chronicle.*

In the subsequent issues of the *Chronicle,* its editors enlarged on the reasons for its appearance: it was to bring out facts about "the situation of the Catholic Church, the nation's present, the arbitrary actions, repressions and other discriminatory means of the government organs . . ." The newsletter "will stop appearing only when the Government will grant to the Church and the believers at least as much freedom as is guaranteed by the Constitution of the USSR."

Significantly, the *Chronicle* was conceived by its editors as a vehicle for articulating authentic interests of "the persecuted Church" not only to the Soviet authorities, but also to the Holy See; which, the journal noted, "while defending victims of discrimination all over the world, barely recalls the 'Church of Silence and Suffering', does not bring up and does not condemn covert and overt persecution of the faithful in the Soviet Union." Such actions of the Vatican, noted the *Chronicle,* as the conferring of ecclesiastical distinctions on "certain priests 'loyal' to the Soviet system," the nomination as bishops of "the hand-picked candidates of the government," and the Vatican's "dialogue with the Soviet government," have created among the Lithuanian Catholics, the feeling that "the Vatican is being deceived," or that they have been "betrayed" and abandoned by the Roman Curia.

> At such a difficult time, the only recourse left to Catholics in Lithuania is to trust in Divine Providence and to seek ways by which the true message might reach the Vatican and the rest of the world, that the most deadly thing for the Catholic Church in Lithuania is not persecution, but the noose being tied by some of our own people.

The Church in Lithuania will not be destroyed by repressions, declared the *Chronicle,* but it "will lose the people if it loses credibility by boot-licking the Soviet regime. This is what happened to the Orthodox Church in

Russia."

In the tradition of the Moscow *Chronicle,* the Lithuanian dissident newsletter insisted on accurate, verified information:

> The *Chronicle of the Catholic Church in Lithuania* has no use for inconcrete information and inaccurate facts . . . must be thoroughly checked, clear and accurate. Numbers, dates, last names, names of places and other data must be especially intelligible, correctly recorded and authenticated.

The informants were requested to "specify which names are to be withheld."

The readers of the *Chronicle of the Lithuanian Catholic Church* were asked to "protect the Chronicle of the L.C.C. from the KGB organs" and to pass it from "hand to hand."

The first issues of the *Chronicle,* (which has been appearing since March, 1972 on a roughly quarterly basis), have been largely devoted to the documentation of the Soviet violations of religious freedom, including complaints and declarations of the clergy and laymen; reports of arrests, interrogations and trials of the alleged violators of the "laws on cults;" administrative harassment of the clergy and believers, especially for their work with minors; anti-religious indoctrination in schools and discrimination against religious pupils and students; protests of religious parents, etc. Since its December, 1972 issue, the publication has begun to carry lengthy unsigned articles outlining the objectives and attitudes of the movement, evaluating Soviet church policy and anti-religious activities, polemicizing with the atheist writers, and criticizing the "appeasement" of the Communist regime by the official Lithuanian Church leaders and the Vatican. These evidently editorial articles speaking for the "Representatives of Lithuanian Catholics," offer an important insight into the ideological orientation and political strategy of the Lithuanian dissidents.

With the May, 1973 issue, the *Chronicle* began to dedicate more and more space to other, not strictly religious manifestations of dissent, to Soviet persecution of Lithuanian intellectuals and students suspected of "bourgeois nationalism," violations of civil rights, denationalization policies in education and culture, and occasionally, to other religious groups, most notably the Ukrainian Catholics. Along with an increasing politicization of the publication and its more open identification with Lithuanian nationalism, the *Chronicle's* style has lost some of its early naive, provincial flavor and has become more sophisticated and precise, with occasional touches of irony and sarcasm.

From a careful reading of the Lithuanian *samizdat,* it appears that the core of the Catholic dissent movement has consisted of a tightly-knit group of provincial priests, including a few survivors of Stalin's concentration camps, some younger clergy educated and ordained since World War II, and indivual clerics who, for political reasons, have been barred by the authorities from legally performing their pastoral duties. Their loyalties have not been with the officially sanctioned bishops and diocesan administrators.

In March of 1977, five years have gone since the publication of the first copy of the Lithuanian self-edited periodical, *The Chronicle of the Lithuanian Catholic Church.* This underground publication has now in the five years of its existence become a document of supreme impartiality in respect of contemporary life and gives expression to that spirit of independence and character-building of a nation which was about to be devoured by the ferocious jaws of a totalitarian regime. The *Chronicle* came into existence as a successor of the *Chronicle of Current Events* and after the alarm-tolls for truth had been ringing from the books of A. Solzhenitsyn. Together with these it gives expression to the revival of faith in the final triumph of truth and justice. *The Chronicle of the Lithuanian Catholic Church* is published in spite of the efforts on the part of the authorities, which are dominated by collaborationists, to discredit it from within. In the *Chronicle,* the bare facts registered in a dispassionate manner are the most hope-inspiring source of information about the methods by which the fight against the Catholic Church is being conducted, how the freedom of conscience and conviction is growing stronger, how the basic human rights are being crushed, how censorship is harassing the press which has been turned into a State monopoly, and, as a consequence of all this, it shows how in fact the genocide of the Lithuanian nation is carried out.

The fifteenth issue of the *Chronicle of the Lithuanian Catholic Church* contains the following circular:

> The Soviet authorities intend by means of the criminal code and the Committee of Public Safety to destroy not only the *Chronicle of the Lithuanian Catholic Church,* but also the Lithuanian Catholic Church itself. We, the Lithuanian Catholics, however, are fully resolved to fight with the Divine help for our rights. We still cherish the hope that the Soviet authorities will understand that they are making a great mistake in supporting atheists who are in a minority, while arousing against themselves the Catholic masses. The Catholics of Lithuania beseech our brothers who have emigrated, and all friends of Lithuania all over the world to inform a wide general public as well as governments about the repression of human rights in Lithuania.

The *Chronicle* publishes letters from its readers. One of the letters contains the following account:

> Recently we learned through the *Chronicle of the Lithuanian Catholic Church* about the arrest of the Doctor of biology Sergei Kovalyov. We, the Lithuanian Catholics, pray to God that He will endow this scientist with all spiritual and physical strength. What the world needs most urgently today is love. Jesus Christ said: "There is no greater love than in giving one's life for one's friends." We are confident that the sacrifice of Sergei Kovalyov and others will not be in vain . . .

The *Chronicle of the Lithuanian Catholic Church* constantly publishes lists of the victims of persecution, of persons interrogated by the KGB, not only for their religious conviction. The Catholic Church has, by means of its underground periodical, become the only reliable source of information available. It is therefore only natural that the KGB is trying with such desperate hate to destroy the *Chronicle of the Lithuanian Catholic Church* and stamp it out to the roots. The waves of arrests, the almost epidemic actions with the aim of breaking up this form of resistance from within by means of collaborationists and informers, and the draconic punishments for distributing the periodical, all these measures are put into effect. But so far, fortunately, without any noticeable results. It may be hard to understand the reasons for this success, but the obvious reasons are above all truthfullness and faith.

The *Chronicle* collects testimonies from the most remote corners of Lithuania and informs its readers about unjust perpetrations committed by certain authorities, defining the limits of the authorities' rights in a spirit of legality and acting in this respect strictly in accordance with the rights guaranteed by Soviet legislation and the Soviet Constitution.

The *Chronicle* has bravely acted in defense of the Roman Catholic priests A. Seskevicius, Y. Zdebskis, and P. Bubnys, who were sentenced to various terms of imprisonment for having provided religious education for children and for their catechization. But in the eyes of the general public it was not the servants of religion, as the authorities wished, but rather the brutal Persecutors of the Church who were guilty, since these priests had been constrained to commit these "perpetrations" owing to the laws of their consciences and the entreaties of parents.

In Lithuania, priests are forbidden to exercise their most urgent duties, which are the instruction of children, their catechization, to attend to the sick and the dying, and to administer funerals. These duties are severely prohibited for them, and, in fact, freedom of conscience which is guaranteed by the Constitution, compels them to carry out these duties as underground activities.

Thus, the Lithuanian Roman Catholic Church, the traidtional bulwark of national identity, is reduced to the same state as the first Christians who had to assemble in the Catacombs. The persecutors do not realize that in this country faith is irradicable, and persecution will only strengthen it.

In Lithuania it is not possible to enter a clerical seminary without the approbation and consent of the Communist Party and the KGB.

It is prohibited to publish, print or distribute books, booklets or newspapers dealing with religious matters. The few official publications with a ridiculously small circulation can in no way satisfy the needs of the belivers. A large part of the prints of the Holy Scriptures and of the Prayerbook is sent to the West for propaganda purposes. Some believers, trying to make amends for this shortage by taking matters into their own hands, were severely punished. On September 3, 1974 sentence was passed in case No. 345 on persons who had prepared and distributed Prayerbooks and religious literature.

To repair Roman Catholic churches or to build new ones is not permitted. Many of those built long ago are closed, or are used as storage halls, museums of atheism or as "places of culture."

Monuments and national relics of a religious character are being systematically destroyed in Lithuania, even those of an artistic value. In the past the country contained an immense number of cared crosses decorated with sculpture of a unique character. Out of the Lithuanian national popular sculpture there grew a distinct school of professional plastic art. But the organized campaigns of the Komsomol have wiped away from the face of the earth this glory of many generations. A few specimens are locked up in quite inaccessible museums or have been handed over to the unbelievers for ridicule.

The story of the Hill of Crosses at Saulai is remarkable. After the insurrection against the Czarist regime from 1861 to 1864, the Russians in this place drove the insurgents into a chapel and buried them alive by covering the chapel with earth. To this Hill the people have since then for a century been carrying beautiful crosses, indicating in this way one bloodstained path in their country's history.

In the summer of 1961 Soviet soldiers who recently had arrived destroyed a few thousand crosses during one night. The orders for this destruction were given by the representative of the Minister of the Supreme Soviet, comrade Dirzhinskaite-Plyushchenko. But after every destruction new crosses were erected in the place of those destroyed, and every year the Hill is laid waste again. During this year the people have brought new crosses to the Hill three times to replace those that had been destroyed.

The following is only a small selection of available documents from this and other underground sources, directly testifying about the serious violations of religious freedom and conscience, guaranteed by Soviet laws and international agreements accepted by the Soviet Union.

Fuller facts on this have become apparent very recently, as the Lithuanian Catholics have followed the Baptists and Russian Orthodox in making available a now considerable amount of documentation of their situation and problems. In the beginning there was a trickle of letters and petitions signed by small and larger groups of both clergy and laity. Shorty before the riots in spring of 1972, there was the widely publicized "Memorandum" of the Lithuanian Catholics, signed by 17,054 persons.

The leaders of the movement were probably able to rely on strong support from the "illegal fringe" of the Church—underground monastic communities (especially nuns working in a variety of secular jobs), unofficial candidates for priesthood, and lay producers of "illegal" religious literature and articles of worship. From the very beginning, it seems, the movement has also attracted some lay Catholics—urban intellectuals, students and workers—the so-called "clerical elements" who have shown "lively interest in the church life and its future." While the underground convents and individual monastics have been carrying much of the burden of the religious education of children and the work with youth,

> it is no secret that almost all prayerbooks, catechitical books and other religious literature were published in exceptionally difficult and dangerous conditions precisely by those clerical elements.

Judging by the numbers of priests who signed protest petitions during the years 1968-72, almost one half of the Lithuanian clergy at one time or another has expressed its solidarity with the objectives of the dissent movement, and in two dioceses—Panevezys and Vilkaviskis—the majority of the local priests joined in the movement's epistolary campaign.

Compared to the Baptist and Orthodox dissent currents, the Catholic protest movement has been able to draw upon a much larger social base. In numerical terms, most of its support has come evidently from outside the major metropolitan centres, from the provincial town and village parishes which are or have been served by the dissident priests, with church attendants and, particularly, women playing the most active part in the "grassroots" protest activities. In a number of cases, the parish executive committees have been working closely with the activist pastors. Undoubtedly, too, the dissidents could draw strength from the eschatological undercurrents among the believers which manifested themselves in certain pilgrimages, penitent movements such as the "carrying of crosses," chain "letters from heaven" and similar activities.

Like the Catacomb Uniate Church in the Western Ukraine, the Lithuanian Catholic dissidents have appealed also the national sentiments of the flock, to the widely shared belief in the interdependence and inseparability of the traditional faith and nationality. But in contrast to the Uniates whose parishes and churches have been forcibly incorporated into the Russian Orthodox Church, the Lithuanian Catholic dissenters have had the immense advantages of working within a relatively autonomous ecclesiastical organization, little infiltrated by the police; of legally operating chrurches with their physical facilities, financial base, institutional lines of communication; of open contacts with other priests and believers; and of opportunities, however limited, for socialization of the believers in the religious and national subcultures.

Eventually, as the episcopate was compelled by the authorities to condemn the protest activities and as the police intensified their reprisals against the suspected dissident leaders, their base of support among the clergy was bound to contract somewhat, though simultaneously the movement's reputation must have been attracting larger numbers of lay supporters.

"Representatives of Lithuanian Catholics"—as the movement's leaders have come to call themselves—have neither formulated nor attempted to develop a systematic political ideology. One can assume that they have included individuals of differing ideological inclinations, as well as people concerned only about certain specific, practical goals. Nevertheless, scattered throughout the Lithuanian Catholic *samizdat*—and particularly evident in some petitions and defense statements of such prominent dissidents as the priests Seskevicius and Zdebskis, as well as in the *Chronicle's* editorials—are values, behavioral norms, implied models of alternative social order, of the "proper" kind of church-state relations, of the "natural" and "just" rights of the Lithuanian nation. Some of the ideas dispersed throughout the Lithuanian dissident literature are unmistakenly products in the pre-Soviet political culture of the socialization and traditionalist Catholic education: like most of the Roman Catholic Church in other Communist states, Lithuanian dissidents have considered "modernization" and "liberation" of the Church, and, especially its "dialogue" with the Communists as either a dangerous luxury, a definite mistake, or something close to capitulation—in their own conditions of a total seige of the Church by the much more powerful atheist state.

The uncompromising "one must hearken to God rather than to man" has been perhaps the dominant note in the dissident literature. The Church cannot be destroyed from without, even if it should be deprived of legal conditions of existence: it can only be destroyed from within, through the compromise of its leaders and pastors with atheism, through abdicating some of its intrinsic spiritual duties, in particular that of teaching the young and old. One must, therefore, fight, whatever the risks, for the rights of the Church. Initially, the dissidents were restricting their demands to the actual realization of the rights specifically provided for believers in the Soviet constitution and international conventions; later the *Chronicle* has carried appeals demanding the extension to believers of the general democratic rights under Article 125 of the Constitution, including access to all mass communication media, the publication of religious books and newspapers, and the establishment of religious organizations.

The dissidents' notion of "proper" church-state relations has largely centered around the unfulfilled Bolshevik promise of a "complete" separation of church from state, i.e., the classical liberal formula which presupposes the state's indifference to various religious creeds and its impartiality in the treatment of believers and non-believers; and which also demands that religious organizations be left free to manage their own internal affairs without the state's interference. On the other hand, the dissidents have stressed on many occasions the historical and cultural inter-dependence, indeed a symbiotic relationship between Roman Catholicism and Lithuanian nationality, as well as the ultimate dependence of private and public morality on absolutist, religious ethical norms.

The nationalist orientation has in time become more pronounced in the Lithuanian Catholic protest movement, as can be seen in the more recent issues of the *Chronicle* referring to the "occupiers of Lithuania," approving of the patriotic manifestations among the youth, including the marking of Lithuania's Independence Day, and condemning the official profanation of the national monuments, neglect or distortion of the Lithuanian past, discrimination against the Lithuanian culture, and, in general, denationalization policies of the regime. One is left with little doubt that the emancipation of Lithuania from Soviet Russian control—at least to the extent enjoyed by the neighboring Poland—has been viewed by the Lithuanian Catholic dissenters as the political guarantee of the nation's survival.

At a time when Vatican diplomacy continues to push for detente with the Soviet Union, additional arrests and house searches for religious literature are being reported in Lithuania.

The account comes in the eighth issue of the underground periodical *Chronicle of the Lithuanian Catholic Church*. Now that the Russian and Ukrainian underground chronicles have been successfully terminated, the KGB or Soviet secret police seems to be zeroing in on the religious Lithuanian underground periodical.

> Ten bags of religious literature, three typewriters and several issues of the chronicle were seized at the home of the pastor of the town of Smilgiai. The search was conducted by 15 KGB officials. The altar where the Holy Sacrament is kept was combed; everything down to the toilet paper was checked.

Several priests were arrested and nearly 30 civilians were "crudely" interrogated. Students who stood up for their beliefs were dismissed from school.

This new wave of religious repression is not limited to Lithuania. "Members of the Byelorussian Catholic hierarchy also were reprimanded." Byelorussia with a population of about 10 million has many Roman Catholics.

Lutherans in the Western republics of Estonia and Latvia were molested, the report continued, and underground presses which turned out prayer books were confiscated.

In addition, Party spokesmen once again are attacking "malicious anti-Soviet clerical elements," a phrase which has not been used for some time.

But while all this goes on, the Vatican continues to work for detente. Lately, Pope Paul VI received for the fourth time Soviet Foreign Minister Andrei A. Gromyko in a private audience.

The talks dealt with "the situation of the Roman Catholic Church on the territory of the U.S.S.R." among other items.

The Vatican hoped that its condoning of the progress of East-West detente, the improvement of the Vatican's relations with Poland, and the shelving of the Hungarian Primate Cardinal Mindszenty would please Moscow.

Earlier Vatican concessions in the Ukraine hint that it will follow a similar course of noninterference in Latvia. Rome temporarily deprived the Ukrainian Uniate Cardinal Slipyj of a Vatican passport after he served for years in a Soviet concentration camp.

The Vatican needs Soviet aid to bring about a definite agreement between church and state in Poland, possibly even a concordat, and secure conditions for the Roman clergy in Hungary, Czechoslovakia, and East Germany.

In February, 1971, Pope Paul sent Archbishop Casaroli, the Vatican's unofficial foreign minister, to Moscow. In May, Cardinal Willebrands attended the inthronization of Patriarch Pimen in a gesture of ecumenical goodwill.

In August, the general of the Jesuits, the Very Rev. Pedro Arrupe, spent several days in Moscow and Leningrad "in order to bring a Christian greeting to our brothers in Christ." He, too, had talks with high Soviet officials.

The Vatican's hopes for better times for Roman Catholics in Russia have been disappointed so far.

There has been no visible response to the visit that three high Vatican officials paid to the militantly anti-religious Soviet government in the hope of easing the lot of the Kremlin's Roman Catholic subjects.

Believers are discriminated against in everyday life, fired from their jobs, and given work unsuited for them.

The clergy is severely restricted. Of the four seminaries which existed in 1940, only one remains, and only 10 students are admitted every year. Priests are forbidden to take part in retreats. Neither the catechism nor the missal can be published.

Yet religious faith has not weakened. On March 26, 1971, the head of the Lithuanian Party's office of agitation and propaganda admitted in *Sovietskaya Litva* that in 1968 more than half of all infants were baptized and nearly a third of the deceased buried religiously. Actually, the percentages are larger.

In September, more than a fifth of the inhabitants of the medium-sized town of Prienai sent a letter of protest to foreign newsmen in Moscow. Since the letter was signed only by adults, one must assume that more than half of the people of the town took part in this action.

Such organized activity would have been unthinkable under Stalin and probably also under former Premier Nikita S. Khrushchev. But while police repression has eased, believers continue to be harassed.

Yet only in Poland did the condition of the Roman Catholic Church noticeably improve. In the Soviet Union the situation of the believers seems to have changed very little.

As far as the believers are concerned, the Vatican's overtures to the Communists have been fruitless. No wonder that the Pope's Easter message once again referred to the "church of silence" which "languishes in many vast regions . . . here a legitimate and by no means subversive existence is denied believers."

Pope Paul VI imparted the traditional Easter blessing to the city of Rome and to the world April 2, after making an impassioned appeal for Christian unity and addressing a special greeting to the "Church of Silence"—the faithful denied the free exercise of their religion.

More than 100,000 in St. Peter's Square heard the Pope speak traditional Easter greetings in Russian, Ukrainian, Slovak, Czech, Chinese, Vietnamese and Japanese to emphasize his message of peace.

He said he wanted his words to penetrate "where there is still the conflict of war, hatred, bloodshed, destruction and ever more numerous and mur-

derous weapons."

He said men have demonstrated their capacity for great technological progress, but he asked: "Will they not have the wisdom and strength to defend and restore peace?"

The Pope called for a new commitment to the effort to heal the divisions among Christians, and said he wanted to express this desire with "great clarity."

"Peace be with you, brothers still so distant and yet in affection so close. May the risen Christ help us to restore the unity between us."

The message contained a special word to victims of oppression of religion:

> Will our greetings of peace reach our Churches of Silence on this feast of the risen Christ?
>
> In many vast regions of the earth there still exist, or rather there still languish, those humble, undaunted communities of individual faithful who are denied a legitimate and by no means subversive existence in the free establishment and expression of their religious life.
>
> Let these individual souls know, let these restricted and oppressed Church know—if ever the echo of our words this Easter reaches them—that they are not forgotten.
>
> They are assured of our solidarity in faith and love, together with our prayers and the hope we share in the risen Christ—Christ will never die again.

His reference to "Churches of Silence" revived a phrase often used by Pope Pius XII to refer to Catholics behind the Iron and Bamboo Curtains.

A Vatican source was quoted as saying this portion of the Pope's Easter message had been redrafted in strong language after reports that 17,054 Lithuanian Catholics signed petitions protesting suppression of the Church in that Communist-ruled country.

"Christ is your friend and He suffers with you. Isn't this enough to make you happy and feel better?"

A body which calls itself "Representatives of Lithuanian Catholics" has begun to accuse the Presidium of the Lithuanian Soviet Republic on "terrorization" and "harassment" of people who collect signatures for protests against attempts "to impose by force an alien ideology."

Signatures themselves are no longer published, but according to the Lithuanian *Chronicle*, one statement requesting the cessation of discrimination against religious students had the backing of 14,604 signatures; another statement decrying the shortage of religious publications was signed by 16,800 Lithuanians.

The seventh issue of the Chronicle conveys a surprising spirit of defiance on the part of students, parents and priests.

Bishop Julijonas Steponavicius, banished to the town of Zagare in 1961, was accused of editing the *Chronicle* and sending it to Poland, from where it was allegedly relayed to the West. The accusation was made at a Party "seminar" in Vilnius, on February 3-6, 1976. It was mentioned in the seminar that some of the issues of the *Chronicle* were not "reactionary." A report on the situation of the Kaunas Theological Seminary disclosed that, owing to the rapid decline of the number of priests, one priest will soon have to service two parishes. The activity of clandestine nuns in hospitals was also mentioned.

Devotion to the church by believers and a hardy band of priests is so strong that Lithuanian Catholic Nationalists represent what is probably the biggest underground movement challenging the authority of the ruling Communist Party and Soviet government.

A year after secret police agents (KGB) scoured apartments in Moscow, Leningrad, Kiev and other major cities attempting to stamp out the production and distribution of an underground civil rights newspaper, *The Chronicle of Current Events,* a parallel campaign was being conducted in Lithuania.

The target was *The Chronicle of the Lithuanian Catholic Church,* which is still functioning.

In addition to keeping track of arrests, searches, and unfair treatment of believers, Lithuanian Catholics have also produced the biggest and most frequently signed petitions and street protests in modern Soviet history.

The Lithuanians are a bigger group with a higher birthrate than their neighbors and between 1959 and the present were able to increase their ethnic composition to more than 80 per cent of the population while the other Baltic states were diminishing. Like their neighbors, the Lithuanians have maintained their own language.

The other major factor in the Lithuanians' inherent strength to resist ethnic and cultural subjugation is their church.

While Lithuanians are the largest single group in Vilnius (43 per cent), the Catholic population is larger because of the minority of Catholic Poles—18 per cent in the city. Twenty per cent of the population is Russian and the remainder divided among other nationalities, including Byelorussians, Jews and Ukrainians.

In their frequent petitions to both local Lithuanian Communist authorities and Moscow, the religious groups ask for the same sort of official toleration of their practices that the Polish Communist regime extends to its believers.

Unable—in contrast to the Orthodox and several other religious groups—to publish their own periodical, and severely restricted in producing the necessary liturgical and other religious books, the Lithuanian Catholics have had to depend for such literature on underground publication facilities operated by dedicated laymen. Unlike the Russian Orthodox, the Catholic Church has not been allowed since the 1940's to maintain its monastic institutions, but small clandestine convents continue to exist in Lithuania, with the "illegal" nuns carrying much of the burden of the religious education of children and youth. As elsewhere in the Soviet Union and the Communist Bloc, the socialization of youth has remained the chief area of confrontation between the Church and the atheist regime. While forcing anti-religious indoctrination upon school children, the Lithuanian authorities have been particularly severe in finding and imprisoning priests and nuns accused of religious instruction of minors.

The first manifestations of organized Catholic dissent in Lithuania date from 1968. Proclaimed by the United Nations as the Year of Human Rights, 1968 was something of a turning point for the human rights movement in the USSR; it opened with the Trial of the Four in Moscow which triggered the greatest wave of petitions ever to emerge from the Soviet intellectual community in defense of the rule of law and against the portends of re-Stalinization. This year witnessed the rise and suppression of the "socialism with a human face" experiment in Czechoslovakia and the parallel surges of hope and despair within the incipient "democratic movement"; it saw the marked politicization and radicalization of dissent epitomized by the appearance of the *Chronicle of Current Events* and the symbolic demonstration in Red Square against the invasion of Czechoslovakia; it was during 1968 that yesterday's "Jews of silence" joined the Crimean Tatars and other dissident currents in speaking out in word and deed in defence of their national rights; and it was the year characterized by significant escalation in the severity of the regime's reprisals against its critics.

In Lithuania, 63 priests of the Telsiai diocese protested to Premier Kosygin on January 8, 1968, against the arbitrary government restrictions on the training of the clergy. On August 7 of the same year, Rev. V. Sliavas of the Adakava parish addressed a similar petition to Premier Kosygin, "on behalf of all clergymen and believers." These were the first protests in the series of collective and individual petitions which marked the crystallization of a dissent movement within the Lithuanian Church, its rise undoubtedly stimulated by other manifestations of protest in the USSR. It was from the "older" dissent currents that the Lithuanian movement adopted the epistolany weapon of protest: to seek the redress of grievances by publicizing at home and abroad, in the form of open letters to the authorities, the regime's violations of its own laws and of constitutional and international guarantees of religious freedom. Underlying this quite legal tactic was the expectation that such publicity would, on the one hand, help to mobilize domestic and foreign support for the Catholic demands and, on the other hand, sufficiently embarass the Soviet authorities to bring about at least partial restoration of the Church's legitimate rights. Essential to the success of such an epistolary campaign was some kind of clandestine organization to gather and verify the facts, to document the claims, and to collect signatures under petition; such organization was also necessary for the purpose of circulating the Lithuanian protests via *samizdat* and through foreign publicity media, which in turn may have called for links with the dissident circles in Moscow and some access to the capital's foreign colony.

Undoubtedly, such an extensive involvement of the Lithuanian clergy and believers could only be explained by their acute anxiety about the prospects of the Church's institutional and spiritual survival in a hostile political environment and the progressively contracting scope of the open practice and propagation of the faith; no doubt, also, their protests were motivated—like those of the Baptist and Orthodox dissenters before them—by the realization that the established channels for the articulation of the Church's interests—via the official church leaders and the government's Council for Religious Affairs—could not anymore be relied upon either due to a combination of arbitrariness and bias on the part of the atheist CRA officials or the timidity of the episcopate.

The grievances of the clergy and believers centered around several critical issues affecting the fate of the Lithuanian Catholic Church. The first and foremost target of the clergy's protests was the existing systems of pervasive, restrictive and discriminatory regulations impeding the normal functioning of the Church even within the narrow framework provided by the Soviet Constitution and the legislation on religious cults. In particular, the protesters complained about the continuing arbitrary banishment of Bishops Steponavicius and Sladkevicius at the time when some dioceses remained for years without episcopal leadership; about restrictions on the exercise of some canonic functions by bishops, including the conferring of the sacrament of Confirmation; about the deliberately low *numerus clausus* imposed by the authorities on the sole Kaunas seminary with only 5-6 new priests allowed to be consecrated annually at the time when 12 to 22 priests die each year; about the illegal interference of the CRA officials with the work of the Seminary, as well as the official measures to prevent potential students from entering it or to recruit informers among the seminarians. The protest documents criticized numerous administrative obstacles—some of which arbitrarily "reinterpreted" the published legislation on religion, while others clearly violated this legislation—obstacles designed to further restrict the activities of the clergy to the performance of religious rites within the assigned houses of worship and to prevent them from assisting each other at the time of special local celebrations or at the traditional pilgrimage sites. Other complaints were directed against the virtual prohibition of the construction of new churches and the difficulties encountered in repairing the older shrines, as well as against discriminatory taxation and utility rates levied on churches by the authorities. Some petitions demanded the return of churches confiscated during the previous two decades. The ridiculously low printings of the few religious books allowed to be published by the authorities, the shortage of prayerbooks, and the absence of certain kinds of religious literature and of the Catholic press were also listed among the grievances of the Church.

The second category of complaints related to the arbitrary rulings by the authorities which placed the traditional examination of the children's religious knowledge by priests prior to their First Communion under the Criminal Code prohibition of any systematic religious instruction of minors; and which extended the prohibition of the individual membership of minors in religious associations to their active participation in religious processions, church choirs and orchestras and to assisting the priest at the Mass. This was a common theme of the believers' petitions which protested against the harsh court sentences and administrative penalities imposed upon the clergy and layment for these alleged violations of the "laws on cults." Closely associated with these grievances were the parents' protests against the compulsory antireligious indoctrination of their children in schools; the use of harassment, ridicule and discrimination directed against religious pupils; intimidating interrogations and questionnaires employed in schools to reveal the parents' and clergy's involvement in the religious upbringing of children; and the abuse of teachers' and administrative authority to bar pupils from attending religious services with their parents and, in general, to undermine the parents' influence over their own children.

Like the Baptist and Orthodox dissidents before them, the Lithuanian protest movement supported its demands with references to Lenin's programmatic writings and appeals to the Soviet Constitution and legislation on religion, the Universal Declaration of Human Rights, the International Convention against Discrimination in Education, and the UN Covenants on Human Rights. Significantly, several protest documents contrasted the plight of the Lithuanian Catholics with the much more tolerant treatment of the Roman Catholic Church in Poland and other "people's democracies." Progressively, the scope of Lithuanian protests extended to include other violations of "socialist legality" in the Republic; to express concern about the official treatment of the national heritage, history, culture, and language both in Lithuania and with regard to the Lithuanian diaspora elsewhere in the USSR; to plead for the restoration of the Ukrainian Greek Catholic (Uniate) Church; and to voice growing dissatisfaction of at least some clergy and faithful with what they regarded as appeasement of Moscow by the Vatican at the expense of the Lithuanian Catholic Church.

> At the time when first clergy declarations concerning restrictions on religion in Lithuania were addressed to the Soviet Government, the priests and faithful in all the dioceses approved the thought (that) one ought to fight for the faith. Many regretted that they had waited much too long and had not done anything in this direction.

The clergy's declarations soon brought their authors and supporters into an escalating series of direct confrontations with the Soviet authorities who were determined to break the protest movement at its inception by singling out and punishing the suspected leaders of this movement. As a rule, the priests' petitions remained unanswered by the authorities to which they were addressed (despite their legal duty to do so within a month); the latter usually passed them on to the republican representative of the Council for Religious Affairs (the very official whose abuses of authority have motivated many of the clergy's complaints)—a practice which seemed to be designed to impress the clergy with the utter futility of their protests. The common response of the CRA representative was to summon the petition writers, to reprimand then threaten them, and often have them transfered to other parishes.

Before long, the police and the courts were employed to isolate the most vocal spokesmen of the movement. The pretext seized upon by the authorities was the alleged "violation of the laws on cults," specifically, "the organization and systematic conduct of religious instruction of minors" prohibited under Article 143 of the Lithuanian Criminal Code. This prohibition was conveniently extended by an unpublished government instruction, to cover also the examination of the children's religious knowledge by the priests, prior to the First Communion, whenver more than one child was examined at a time of when other children were present at such an examination—the *caveats* which many Lithuanian priests found physically impossible to observe.

In July, 1970, the police arrested a Jesuit priest, Antanas Seskevicius, of Dubingiai parish, charging him with the illegal religious instruction of minors. Fr. Seskevicius had been previously exiled from Lithuania for some twenty years, fourteen of which he had spent in Siberian concentration camps. Accused of violating Article 143, he eloquently defended his actions in the Moletai court in September, as legitimate under the Constitution and international human rights conventions and attacked the arbitrary secret instructions which have been used by the CRA officials to bar the youth from the Church. Seskevicius' sentence to one year in prison evoked a series of protests signed by a total of 283 priests from four dioceses. In summer, 1971, two more priest activists were arrested on the same charges—Juozas Zdebskis of Prienai and Prosperas Bubnys of Girkalnis—and were sentenced, in separate trials in November, to a one year term each.

The case of Fr. Zdebskis was of major significance in the final crystallization of the Catholic dissent movement in Lithuania. Considered by the KGB as a principal leader of the movement, Zdebskis was reportedly brutally beaten during the pre-trial investigation. In violation of the established procedures, his trial was transferred to Kaunas and was actually held *in camera*. At the trial, Zdebskis accused the authorities of systematic discrimination against believers, persecution of the Church, and its internal subversion through some submissive ecclesiastical leaders. During the Zdebskis trial came the first major physical confrontation between some 500-600 Catholics who were barred from the court proceedings, and the police, who used force to disperse the crowd; some twenty people, including two priests, were arrested in the ensuing disorders.

The arrest and trial of Fr. Zdebskis marked the beginning of an increasing involvement of laymen in the Catholic protest movement. Within three days of the priest's arrest, a petition demanding his release was signed by 350 of his parishioners and personally delivered to the Procurator-General's Office in Moscow; representatives of believers also made personal representations to the Republican Procurator and the CRA representative, Rugienis. In September, 1971, 2,000 Prienai believers (some 25 per cent of all the parishioners) addressed to the Party and government leaders in Moscow a petition demanding the release of Fr. Zdebskis and the lifting of discriminatory restrictions on religion. They were soon joined by 1,190 members of the Santaika parish. Similar letter of protest was sent to the government in December by 1,344 believers calling for the release of Fr. Bubnys.

In December, 1971 and January, 1972, 17,054 signatures were collected throughout Lithuania under a "Memorandum of the Roman Catholics of Lithuania" addressed to Brezhnev; along with the imprisonment of Zdebskis and Bubnys, this document enumerated the main grievances of the believers.

> We therefore ask the Soviet Government to grant us the freedom of conscience, which has been guaranteed by the Constitution of the USSR but which has not been put into practice heretofore. What we want is not pretty words in the press and on the radio but serious governmental efforts that would help us, Catholics, to feel as citizens of the Soviet Union with equal rights.

An addendum to the Memorandum signed "Representatives of Lithuanian Catholics," noted that only "an insignificant portion of religious believers in Lithuania," were able to sign the memorandum "since the organs of the Militia and the KGB have used all kinds of means to interrupt the collection of signatures," including arrests of those collecting them.

This massive protest document was sent the following month to the Secretary General of the United Nations for transmission to Brezhnev. In their appeal to Kurt Waldheim, "Representatives of Lithuania's Catholics" justified this course by the fact that none of the earlier protests had elicited any official reply but only "increased repressions;" they also pointed to the fact "that religious believers in (Lithuania) cannot enjoy the right set out in Article 18 of the Universal Declaration of Human Rights.

Although the Soviet constitution guarantees freedom of religion, the Lithuanian Catholics and other religious groups have complained of official interference in church life. The dissidents told Waldheim that three previous petitions with a total of 5,000 signatures were sent last fall to Communist Party Secretary Leonid I. Brezhnev, but the police prevented the mass collection of signatures.

"Such action by the authorities prompted the conviction that the present memorandum, signed by 17,054 believers, will not attain its aim if it is sent by the same means as previous collective declarations," the letter said.

In their petition, the Lithuanians complained that Soviet officials limit the number of new priests to be trained and control the assignment of priests to parishes. They said no more than 10 youths a year can enter the seminary.

There are so few priests in Lithuania, the letter charged, that one must often serve two or three parishes and that "even invalid and aged priests must work."

The Lithuanian authorities do not enforce a law which would punish those who persecute church-goers, the petition claimed.

In addition, Catholics have not been allowed to rebuild churches destroyed during World War II and have difficulty in getting permission to hold services in private homes.

The letter repeated charges made last November that two parish priests were sent to labor camps for providing religious instruction to youngsters. Two bishops were also exiled without trial, the letter asserted.

More signatures would have been included in the peition if the Soviet police had not reacted so strongly against the dissidents, the letter said. The list of names, however, is one of the largest groups of dissidents to identify themselves publicly in recent years.

The letter suggested the presence of continued nationalist feelings in Lithuania more than 30 years since Stalin ended its brief period of independence between the two world wars.

In addition to repressing religion, the "forcible atheistic upbringing" of Soviet society has also caused increases in juvile crime, alcoholism, divorces, abortions and suicides.

An accompanying letter explains to Waldheim the unusual method was being followed because of the Soviet government's negative response to earlier protests about treatment of Catholics and Church officials in Lithuania, home of most of the estimated 3 million Roman Catholics in the USSR.

Petitions protesting the imprisonment of Father Juozas Zdebskis—signed by 2,000 of his parishioners—were sent to Moscow. The only official answer, the latest petitions say, was more repression; the same fate was accorded two other petitions.

The petition—all 123 copies of it—complain: "Freedom of conscience is still absent for the believers among our people, and the Church is still subjected to persecution."

Specific cases cited included the one-year sentences meted out to Fathers Zdebskis and P. Bubnys—for preparing children for first Communion— and the exile of Bishops Julionas Stepanavicius and Vincentas Sladkevicius— "although they committed no crime."

Complaints also cited a severe shortage of priests complicated by an unreasonable restriction of admissions to the seminary at Kaunas, a shortage of churches becuase Catholics are not allowed to rebuild those destroyed during World War II, and failure to enforce a law that makes persecution of churchgoers a crime.

The repression, the petitions said, violate the Soviet and Lithuanian constitutions and the U.N. Declaration of Human Rights. The complaints were similar in many respects to those of Soviet Jews—another minority of about 3 million whose treatment has brought increasing criticism on the Soviet government.

However, a Soviet church official has insisted there is no foundation for complaints that Catholics in Soviet Lithuania suffer religious persecution.

Msgr. Ceslovas Krivaitis was interviewed by the official *Tass* news agency after Western newsmen wrote about a bitter petition from 17,054 Lithuanian Catholics.

The interview did not mention the protest directly, although it obviously was meant as rebuttal. The interview argued issues raised by the 17,054 in their petition to Communist Party leader Leonid Brezhnev.

However, the official account is highly selective and does not deny the truth of the petition.

Krivaitis was identified as director of the archbishopric of Vilnius, capital of Lithuania. The former bishop there, Julionas Steponavicius, was sent into exile.

He said that no one prevents believers in Lithuania from giving children religious education "in the family." This pointedly ignored the fact that two Lithuanian priests were sent to jail for preparing children for their First Communion.

Krivaitis also said that Lithuania has 815 Catholic priests, most of whom studied theology after World War II.

The 17,054 maintained in their petition that many ill and aged priests have been pressed into service because of a severe shortage of clergymen.

Moreover, Western religious experts say the number of priests in Lithuania now is about half the total there in 1940, when the USSR annexed the country. Krivaitis' figure confirms the reduction.

"In Krivaitis' opinion the annual number of graduates of the seminary meets the demand of the Catholic church in Lithuania," *Tass* said.

This clearly was meant to counter the complaint in the petition that Communist authorities, who control the sole remaining seminary in Lithuania, have permitted no more than 10 students to enter each year.

Krivaitis also said that Lithuanian Catholics have been able to buy a variety of religious texts from a state printshop in Vilnius. Western analysts have suggested that the number of copies printed is totally inadequate for the demand—but Krivaitis does not give figures.

It is highly unusual for the Soviet government to emphasize the point that Soviet Catholics, so small a minority of religious practitioners that they amount almost to a splinter group, live without restrictions. Religious practice customarily is portrayed here as an aberration among old people. While freedom of religion is guaranteed by the Soviet constitution, churchgoers usually are depicted as slightly cockeyed.

Krivaitis' comments supported this theme. "Young people visit the church much less often than the elderly," he said.

However, exiled Bishop Vicent Brizgys, has suggested the priest quoted by the Soviet news agency, *Tass,* on the status of the Church in Lithuania is the "tool" of Moscow.

Bishop Brizgys does not question the "priestly integrity" of the *Tass* source—Msgr. Ceslovas Krivaitis, vicar capitular of the Archdiocese of Vilnius, Lithuania—but he recalled the same man had enjoyed special treatment from Moscow in the past:

I do not question the priestly integrity of Msgr. Krivaitis, yet I remember, that during four years of the Second Vatican Council not one bishop from Lithuania was permitted to attend the Council by Moscow.

Msgr. Joseph Stankevicius, who was invited by Pope John XXIII under the title of expert, after the second session was impeded by Moscow from attending the third and fourth session. . . .

Msgr. Krivaitis remained in Rome during all four sessions, not on an invitation of the Vatican or his own wishes, but sent and paid by Moscow. Obviously now *Tass* found that the best person to be used to deny the persecution of religion in Lithuania was the same Msgr. Ceslovas Krivaitis. . . .

He was just the tool to pronounce what was wanted by *Tass*.

Bishop Brizgys, who was removed from his diocese in 1944 by the Gestapo during the Nazi occupation of Lithuania and then was refused permission to return to it by the Soviet Union after World War II, called attention to his own recent report on the condition of the Lithuanian Church.

The report was made during a demonstration at the Civic Center in Chicago April 2, 1972, at which Chicago's Lithuanian community proclaimed its support for Catholics in their homeland who risked their safety to sign the anti-Soviet petitions.

This is the Bishop's report based on "official Russian sources:"

The population of Lithuania today is about 3,043,00—imported Russians included. With the minimum natural growth of 1% it should be about 4,300,00.

Religion: 9% officially have declared themselves without religion (almost all imported from Russia).

Communist party members are 77,500. (From those more than 50% are imported from Russia. From about 35,000 Lithuanian Communists less than 5,000 are considered sincere Communists.)

Of the 9% believers, those under 16 years of age are forbidden to be taught and to practice the religion publicly.

The military, students, employees of any age are persecuted for practicing their religion.

There were about 1,600 priests in 1940; today there are 804.

There were about 450 seminarians in 1940; today there are 30 and are allowed to be admitted those only, who are approved by the atheistic government. (Above mentioned statistics consider the part of Vilnius archdiocese, today in the limits of Lithuania.)

Private schools, organizations and religious publications are forbidden.

The few religious books that were printed, by the government, were for propaganda purposes abroad. For example, a ritual was printed, of which 500 copies were sent to Rome with the intention of being sold to Lithuanian churches in the U.S.A. and elsewhere at $5 per copy, but were not available for the churches and priests in Lithuania until a protest was voiced over the *Voice of America* and *Vatican Radio*.

All hospitals, homes for the aged and orphanages are nationalized. Spiritual assistance, even when requested by the patients, is almost impossible.

All diocesan and parochial archives are confiscated.

Four bishops and about 170 priests have died as martyrs. Some were executed by firing squads, while others died in prisons and concentration camps.

Over 100 churches have been closed or destroyed. Many of them are converted to profane use. Recently four churches were burned down by the Communists and the faithful are not permitted to rebuild them.

At present two bishops are under arrest. According to last news, arrests now are on a large scale. I could not guess how many priests are under arrest today.

About 138,000 men and women, mostly young, are now in Siberia or in other Russian territories under various pretexts, without possibility of returning to Lithuania.

Even before *samizdat* and foreign communication media gave publicity to this latest initiative of the Lithuanian dissidents, the Soviet police—already busy with the round-up of the dissident Ukrainian, Russian and Jewish intellectuals—intervened to stop further collection of signatures under the December protest petition in Lithuania and launched searches and interrogations to uncover "anti-Soviet priests" suspected of having organized this action. In April, the authorities compelled the administrator of the Vilnius Archdiocese, Msgr. Krivaitis, to offer an interview for foreign consumption in which he declared that there is "freedom of religion in Lithuania." On April 11, the functioning Lithuanian bishops and administrators of dioceses were summoned to Kaunas by the CRA representatives from Vilnius and Moscow, and told a sign a "pastoral letter" to be read in all churches on April 30. The "letter" condemned the "irresponsible individuals" who "gather signatures" under pretext of "fraud," and warned the flock that

the signing of irresponsible documents affects relations between the church and the state and gives rise to misunderstandings. These kinds of things can bring no good to the Church . . .

Despite the pressure exerted on the clergy by their canonical superiors and the civil authorities, "very few priests" have reportedly read the bishops' condemnation on the appointed date. A clandestine appeal circulated among the clergy in April exposed the "pastoral letter" as a "slanderous" and "compromising" declaration which was "forced" upon the episcopate against their will. The sequence of events in Lithuania culminated, on May 14, in the self-immolation of Romas Kalantas in protest against the suppression of freedom in the country. Though not directly motivated by religious oppression, Kalanta's tragic end triggered on the day of his funeral a mass demonstration demanding national and religious freedom and ended in clashes between the demonstrators and the militia and security troops.

The campaign for religious freedom also promotes Lithuanian nationalism and attacks the effects of official atheism on the republic's culture.

As with the other Baltic states, thousands of Lithuanians were exiled to Siberia and Central Asia after the Stalinist takeover in 1940. One million Lithuanians disappeared between 1940 and 1959. And from 1944 to 1953, when there was strong opposition to the return of Soviet power, an estimated 300,000 were killed or exiled. Only 35,000 returned from exile after Stalin's death.

There are Lithuanian nationalists in eastern exile and labor camps now, too. A *Chronicle* earlier in 1973 reported that a group of students and young professionals had been accused by the KGB of contacting deportees and prisoners and also with meeting with nationalist groups in Georgia and Armenia, two other republics where anti-Soviet and anti-Russian feelings run high.

The deepening anxiety of the Lithuanian clergy and believers about the prospects of the Church's institutional and spiritual survival in a hostile political environment, has generated a massive movement of religious protest. Between 1968 and mid-1972, some seventeen collective and individual petitions and protests have been addressed to the Soviet state and Party authorities by the Lithuanian clergy. Despite the vulnerability of the "registered" clergy to governmental reprisals, the support given by the Lithuanian clergy to this epistolary campaign was unequalled by any other religious group in the USSR: in five dioceses, nearly 47 per cent of all the priests have signed at least one of the protest documents, and in the dioceses of Penevezys and Vilkaviskis the share of protesters reached 83 and almost 56 per cent respectively. Since mid-1971, the clergy's petitions were overshadowed by a succession of protest documents signed by large numbers of believers, ranging from several hundred to more than 17,000 (petition to Brezhnev of December 1971-January 1972). Fuilled by the governmental reprisals, including arrests and trials of some leading dissident clergymen, the protests escalated into physical confrontations between believers and the authorities, confrontations which have acquired increasingly nationalistic overtones and which culminated in Romas Kalanta's self-immolation and subsequent riots in May, 1972. Earlier that year appeared the first issue of the clandestine *Chronicle of the Catholic Church in Lithuania,* supplying the dissent movement with a more regular vehicle for articulating—over the heads of submissive ecclesiastical leaders—the authentic interests of "the persecuted Church" both to the Soviet authorities and to the Holy See. Many issues of the *Chronicle Chronicle* have appeared so far, offering a unique insight into the plight of Catholicism in Lithuania.

The grievances of the Lithuanian clergy and believers have centered primarily around the existing system of pervasive, restrictive and discriminatory regulations impeding the normal functioning of the Church, a system administered by the republican plenipotentiary of the Council for Religious Affairs whose activities often violated the Soviet Constitution and the published legislation on "cults." In particular, Lithuanian protestors complained about the continued arbitrary banishment of Bishops Steponavicious and Sladkevicius; about restrictions on the exercise of some canonic functions by bishops, including the conferring of the sacrament of Confirmation; about the low enrollment quota imposed upon the Kaunas seminary and the illegal interference of the authorities with the seminary's program, instructors and students; about restrictions on the publication of the necessary religious books; about the arbitrary rulings making near impossible for the priests to examine children's religious knowldge prior to their First Communion; about the restrictions in children's participation in religious rites; about the compulsory anti-religious indoctrination in schools and the harassment of religious pupils and parents by teachers and school authorities; and, in particular, about the harsh prison sentences and fines imposed upon the clergy accused of religious instruction of minors. Progressively, the scope of Lithuanian Catholic protest widened to express anxiety about the official treatment of the Lithuanian national-cultural heritage both in Lithuania and with regard to the Lithuanian diaspora outside the Rebpulic; to plead for the restoration of the Ukrainian Greek Catholic (Uniate) Church; and to voice growing concern about the direction and consequences of the Vatican-Moscow "dialogue."

Most of these grievances have remained unresolved. To be sure, the regime has offered some concessions to the Church, presumably to strengthen the hand of the "loyalists" among the bishops and clergy. In December, 1969, the authorities consented to the consecration of two new bishops (Povilonis and Kriksciunas) and are reportedly willing to replenish the aging Lithuanian episcopate with one or more "loyal" hierarchs from among the collaborationist clergy. The 1966 quota of 30 students of the inter-diocesan theological seminary was significantly raised: by the end of 1973 there were 48 seminarians at Kaunas. But at the same time, the regime employed its coercive resources to isolate the leaders of the Lithuanian dissent, to intimidate and silence their followers, and, in particular to suppress the Lithuanian *Chronicle* and other clandestine religious-nationalist publication efforts.

To tighten their grip on the Lithuanian Church, the authorities have now undertaken to transfer completely the parish administration from the clergy to the local laymen's parish committees, —a measure which was forced upon the Russian Orthodox Church yet in 1961. During 1974, under the pretext of reviewing "registrations" of the parish congregations and of the clergy and the renewal of all "leases" on church buildings and their contents, the government proceeded to narrow further the scope of the Church's activities. According to the eleventh issue of the *Chronicle,* the local government authorities were instructed to scrutinize membership of the parish "twenties", their executive and auditing committees, and to purge these bodies of "reactionary" elements. In November, 1974, the republican plenipotentiary of the Council for Religious Affairs, K. Tumenas, announced the establishment of "permanent commissions for the control of compliance with the laws on cults" designed to strengthen the governmental controls over local parishes. In an attempt to sever the links between the Lithuanian dissenters and the Moscow dissidents who have done much to publicize Lithuanian grievances within and outside the USSR the KGB searched the homes of several leading Moscow dissidents and arrested in December, 1974 one of the principal collaborators of Andrei Sakharov, a biologist, Sergei Kovalev, suspected of serving as in important link between the Lithuanian dissenters and Moscow's diplomatic and foreign correspondents' community.

During the recent years, the dissident Lithuanian Catholic clergy has also offered its support to the demands for the lifting of the illegal ban on the Uniate Church. In September, 1974, from a leading Russian Orthodox dissenter, Anatolii Levitin-Krasnov, came an eloquent appeal to Sakharov's Human Rights Committee in Moscow calling upon it to raise its voice in defence of the Uniates and other persecuted religious groups. "The Union in the Western Ukraine," wrote Levitin-Krasnov, "is a massive popular movement. Its persecution means not only religious oppression, but also restriction of the national rights of West Ukrainians."

Perhaps the closest bonds of sympathy and solidarity united the dissident Lithuanian clergy with the "illegal" Ukrainian Catholic priests with whom they came to share years of imprisonment and exile during the wave of anti-Catholic persecution in the later 1940's and the early 1950's. At the time of the suppression of the Ukrainian Greek Catholic Church, a few Uniate priests found shelter with the Lithuanian clergy; it was rumored that for a while an underground Ukrainian Uniate bishop has had his

"base" in Lithuania. Some other Uniate clergymen, when they were re-
lased from exile along with deported Lithuanian priests, chose to accom-
pany the latter to Lithuania where they offered their pastoral services to
Lithuanian believers as "illegal," "worker-priests." Among them were
those who continued to serve their Ukrainian flock from afar, such as
priest, Volodymyr Prokopiv, of Vilnius, whose arrest in late 1973 was
reported by the *Chronicle,* after he personally accompanied to Moscow
representatives of the 12,000 Ukrainian believers who signed a petition
asking for the restoration of the Uniate Church.

Earlier, in December, 1971, a petition of 47 Vilnius diocese clergy
requested Soviet leaders, among other things, to permit "all priests living
in our country (including the Ukrainians) freely and publicly do their work
as priests." Months later, when one of the organizers of this petition, priest
B. Laurinavicius, was summoned by the CRA representative, J. Rugienis,
and accused of "insolence and anti-Soviet activity," he responded with a
lengthy written explanation of the priests' action. He justified reference to
the Uniate clergy in the following words:

> Our colleagues, the Ukrainian priests . . . are dear to us . . . We requested that
> the Ukrainian priests be allowed to go back to work, because the faithful of the
> Ukraine give us no peace, asking us to work among them. We asked that their
> priests be put back to work, since they have never been sentenced by the court.

Among the issues that united the Lithuanian dissidents and the banned
Ukrainian Uniates has been their opposition to the Vatican's *Ostpolitik,*
its "dialogue" with the Kremlin. Commenting on Gromyko's visit with the
Pope, a recent issue of the *Chronicle* obserbved that

> Dialogue, it seems, is useful to (the communist regime) only in order to (have)
> the Vatican maintain silence about the persecution of Catholics in the Soviet
> Union . . .

In trying to cope with the growing unrest among the Lithuanian clergy
and faithful, the Soviet authorities typically combined "carrot and stick"
measures to isolate the "hard core" dissidents from their following and to
strengthen the hand of the "loyal" church leaders. Together with direct
repressions—administrative fines, police interrogations and threats, and
eventually arrests and trials of the suspected animators of the protest
movement—the government applied against them indirect sanctions,
through their canonical superiors, who were compelled to restrict the
activities to order transfers of the "troublesome" priests; those clerics who
refused to submit to such orders as uncanonical were threatened or actually punished with suspension; on occasions, the authorities stepped in to
help enforce these ecclesiastical sanctions. While such use of the episcopate by the government—including the issuance of the April, 1972 "pastoral letter" slandering the organizers of protest petitions—did help to
"pacify" those strata of the clergy who offered a passive or lukewarm
support to the dissenters, it only deepened the alienation of the dissident
priests from their submissive ordinaries and contributed to the further
radicalization of the dissent movement.

Some concessions were offered to the Church. In December, 1969, two
new bishops were consecrated with prior governmental approval: the once
persecuted Klaipeda pastor, Liudas Povilonis, and the former Chanceloor
of the Kaunas Archdiocese, youthful Romualdo Kriksciunas. In the wake

of the "protest explosion" during the winter and spring of 1972, came a short-lived relaxation of anti-religious pressures and even some self-criticism in the Soviet press. In August the Vilnius daily *Sovetskaya Litva* warned that

> irreparable damage could be inflicted by administrative attacks (on the Church), by any insult to the sentiments of believers. Wrong methods of combatting religion not only fail to undermine the basis for its dissemination, but, on the contrary, they lead to the intensification of religious fanaticism, hidden forms of service and rites, cause discontent and distrust among the believers and aggravate them.

Two Lithuanian Catholic bishops who attended the August, 1976 International Eucharistic Congress in Philadelphia were subjected to "indignities" by Soviet customs agents upon their return and all religious articles carried by the prelates were confiscated, according to a report smuggled out of the Soviet territory.

The Chronicle of the Catholic Church in Lithuania said the prelates— Bishop Liudas Povilonis, Apostolic Administrator of Kaunas-Vilkaviskas, and Bishop Romualdas Kriksciunas, Apostolic Administrator of Panevezys—were "thoroughly searched:" Female customs agents derisively draped rosaries about their own necks, thereby deeply offending the high-ranking Church leaders.

Following Soviet occupation the Lithuanians of all Baltic nations offered the most stubborn resistance to the occupiers. The Lithuanian anti-Soviet partisan struggle under the name of "movement of Struggle for Freedom of Lithuania" (LLKS), commonly also known as "The Forest Brothers," continued well into the 1950's. Simas Kudirka, the Soviet-Lithuanian merchant-marine sailor who had jumped ship and tried unsuccessfully to obtain political asylum aboard a US Coast Guard vessel on November 23, 1970, stated the following at his trial in Vilnius, which took place on May 17-20, 1971. As his statement was not disputed by the court officials its factual side should not be doubted:

> I remember that when I studied in Vilnius, instead of the two prisons which were there under the Germans, there were seven under Soviet rule, and there were about 20,000 prisoners. They were overfilled until 1955. Already in 1950, waves of Lithuanians with their young went to the concentration camps. . . . The death of Stalin saved my people from physical extermination. However, the essence of the policy remained the same.

> Now we are destined to die a much slower death—assimilation. . . . For ten years our "forest brothers" fought, believing that in the West our struggle was known and supported, even if only morally. . . . Even the state security officials admit that 50,000 Lithuanian partisans died.

> The Atlantic Charter, which promised the enslaved peoples freedom, was an empty promise costing my people 50,000 dead and 400,000 deported, of whom 150,000 found their graves in the earth of Siberia.

A very heavy price indeed for a nation of three million. But Kudirka maintains that even at this exorbitant price in human lives the spirit of the nation has not been quelled: " . . . a new generation has grown up which intends to go the road of their fathers." Then he stated that he was a Roman Catholic. In conclusion Kudirka expressed the wish that his homeland become independent and then explained to the Chairman of the court what he meant by that:

> An independent Lithuania . . . has a sovereign government and is not occupied by any army. The government has . . . a free democratic system of elections.

This uncommonly erudite common sailor, who quoted Herzen, Lenin, and Marx "to explain the difference between socialist theory and practice in Lithuania," seems to have expressed the heart of the matter in Lithuania: the inseparable duality of the Lithuanian social movement—struggle for national freedom and religious freedom, for the Roman Catholic Church and the nation. Judging from the fragmentary information from unofficial sources on the latest disturbances in Kaunas, and taking into consideration what preceeded them in Lithuania, it seems to be safe to conclude that the same themes of religious and national freedom, the latter being understood in terms of basic human rights, lay at the bottom of these disturbances.

On the strength of information from Russian dissident sources in Moscow, western agencies reported that the riots in Kaunas were set off by the funeral of a 20-year-old, Roman Kalanta, who had poured gasoline over himself in a public garden in Kaunas on May 14, 1972 and set himself afire. The riots began on May 18 and were quelled only the next day by units of army troops brought into the town for that purpose. At least one policeman was killed and several hundred rioters were arrested. There were many wounded. The magnitude of the riots can be estimated from the fact that the Soviet media found it impossible to conceal the fact and the Lithuanian press, both in Lithuanian and in Russian, reported the fact of the immolation of Kalanta, adding that a *post-mortem* psychiatric commission has concluded that Kalanta was mentally disturbed. A similar statement was made at an international press conference in Moscow, where it was denied that any political motive lay at the bottom of the act and alleged that a small group of hooligans tried to use this pretext to disturb peace in Kaunas. Those who acted in a particularly negative way were detained by the organs of protection of social order. Those detained were mostly hooligans, criminal elements who had been tried earlier for thefts and debauches. There were no political motives or political aspects in the affair.

This version will hardly convince anyone. Why did it take the army and the police two days to quell but a "small group of hooligans." Why should hooligans and criminals take an act of self-immolation as a pretext for rioting? And if it was a case of hooligans and criminals, why the first source of information on the riots were the dissident circles in Moscow? The facts and precedents give an entirely different picture; some of these were already discussed above, but there are others as well.

Kalanta's case of self-immolation has not been an isolated case. According to the *Chronicle of Current Events,* this form of political protest has been appealed to in the Soviet Union several times before in the recent years.

On December 5, 1968 a Ukrainian teacher, Vasiliy Makukha, burned himself to death in the main street of Kiev with the cry, "Long live Free Ukraine!" On February 10, 1969, another Ukrainian, Nikolay Berislavsky, tried to burn himself in front of the Kiev University, but was prevented from doing so by KGB officers. He was then detained and accused of the "state crime" of anti-Soviet agitation (Article 62 of the Ukrainian Code, corresponding to Article 70 of the RSFSR Criminal Code). On January 22, 1970, a Russian worker, Gennadiy Trifonov, tried to burn himself in Leningrad in front of the Lenin Monument at the ex-Smolny Institute, which had been Lenin's headquarters at the time of the 1917 Revolution. He was protesting against the hard material conditions of life in the Soviet Union. The fire was put out and the doctors managed to save his life. On April 13, 1969, a brilliant student of mathematics, Ilya Rips, tried to burn himself in front of the Liberty Statue in Riga. He unfurled a slogan reading, "Freedom to Czechoslovakia." Rips' life was saved. He was first placed into a psychiatric prison, but later was released and allowed to leave for Israel. His mental health has been confirmed by all who knew him and by his present behavior in Israel. In all other known cases of self-immolation, no psychiatric charges are known to have been preferred against those whose life had been saved.

As to the charge that the Kaunas riots were the work of hooligans and criminals, besides the above arguments against them, Kaunas remembers the precedent of 1956 when, at the time of the Hungarian Revolution, the city was practically in revolt, demanding freedom for Lithuania. The revolt had to be crushed on November 1-2, 1956 by massive troop reinforcements.

The immediate pretext for the recent disturbances seem to have been the wave of protests against religious persecutions in Lithuania. Only a few weeks before the disturbances, the West was in receipt of a petition to Brezhnev signed by 17,054 Lithuanian Roman Catholic believers. The petition, written in January of 1972, enumerates facts of persecution, including the deportation of Bishops Steponavicius and Sladkiavicius, imprisonment of the priests Zdebskis and Bubnys for teaching the catechism to children preparing for First Communion, the closing or destruction of Roman Catholic churches in various Lithuanian townships or villages. Despite the unusually great number of signatories, the memorandum notes that

> only an insignificant number of Lithuanian believers signed the memorandum, inasmuch as the militia organs and the KGB took various measures to stop the collection of signatures ... Several persons collecting signatures were arrested ... Lists of signatures found on them were confiscated.

And the document had warned that if the Soviet authorities' attitude to the needs of believers continued to be the same, they would be forced to appeal to the Pope, to the UN Secretary General, etc., which they did the following February.

The *Chronicle of Current Events* is full of reports on the persecution of Christians throughout the Soviet Union, and a very high proportion of these reports are on Lithuania, where it is not only a question of one-sided persecution but also of considerable resistance and attempts on the part of the believers and clerics to continue some form of regular religious activities, such as elementary religious instruction to children of willing parents, attempts to rebuild or even to build churches, protests against the cutting down of the numbers of seminarians at the only remaining Roman Catholic Seminary, that of Kaunas, from 150 to 30.

It seems that the struggle is desperate and hopeless as long as this little nation of 3 million remains in its national isolation from the rest of the Soviet Union. It is probable that it was this very realization of hopelessness of struggle for national and religious freedom that brought a relative quiet to the country in the years 1956 to about 1970. There was the inevitable final bloody suppression of the "Forest Brothers" in the early '50's (the outburst in Kaunas in the fall of 1956 seems to have been but a reaction to the Hungarian Revolution and the general restlessness of the youth throughout the Soviet Union following the 20th Congress) followed by a sense of hopelessness and foresakedness. It is highly probable that the new wave of activity in Lithuania has been inspired by the existence of the Democratic Movement in Russia. That there is a regular chain of information between the Lithuanian Roman Catholic circles and the Moscow Democratic Movement can be concluded from: a. the amount of information on Lithuania that has been appearing regularly in the *Chronicle* from No. 17 of 31 December, 1970, to the last issue available; by the fact that the first information that the West received about the riots in Kaunas came from the Moscow dissident circles, i.e., the Democratic Movement. The information was direct and immediate: the first reports came from Moscow to the West already two days after the quelling of the riots. Furthermore, in the course of searches and arrests carried out in the USSR in January, 1971, following the unofficially reported Central Committee secret decision of December, 1971 to put an end to the *Chronicle*, the *Ukrainian Vestnik*, the Russian *Veche*, and *samizdat* in general, among those arrested was Vatslav Sevruk, a researcher in sociology at the Institute of History of the Academy of Sciences of the Lithuanian Republic. Sevruk is of Slavic background and has been contributing to *samizdat* in Russian. The search of his apartment and his arrest were in connection with so-called "Case No. 24." Over 100 people were called in for questioning in Vilnius in connection with the Sevruk case. All these facts point to a close relationship between the Democratic Movement and the Lithuanian human rights activists.

Events in Lithuania during 1972 drew world attention to this small republic, where a very particular blend of nationalism and religious feeling finally erupted onto the streets in demonstrations and violence. Three young men who died by self-immolation were making their protest not only against the lack of freedom for Lithuania as a national entity, but also against the non-freedom of what is still virtually the Lithuanian national religion: the Roman Catholic Church. It is also worth noting that the young sailor, Simas Kudirka, who in November, 1970 attempted unsuccessfully to defect to the United States, at his trial in May, 1971 (when he was sentenced to ten years of corrective labor) declared: "If I am condemned to death I want to be assisted by a Catholic priest."

The Catholic Church in Lithuania continues to claim the undoubted allegiance of the large majority of the population—despite a statistic in the official 1971 Vatican handbook which gave the number as a mere 420,000. This new official statistic is evoking world-wide query and protest; there can be no doubt that it falls far short of the true figure, which is likely to be something between two and three million.

The position of the Lithuanian Catholic Church is a tricky one from Moscow's point of view. Lithuania is of course a relatively recent addition to the Soviet family, and as such, like the Western Ukraine with its similarly rich religious heritage, it continues to display a degree of spiritual vitality that offers a marked and embarrassing contrast to other regions of the USSR where religion has been more effectively controlled. Khrushchev's anti-religious campaign of 1959-64, for example, closed about half of the existing Orthodox churches, but did not affect Lithuania to any comparable degree.

The Church is also compromised in Moscow's eyes by its involvement in the Lithuanian partisan struggle after Soviet annexation, but at the same time, its popular strength presents a formidable challenge to central control. The situation might even be compared to that in Poland, where the unique strength of the Catholic Church has effectively resisted almost all frontal attacks by the Party and has brought about an uneasy but workable compromise. Clearly the Soviet situation is different, and it remains to be seen how long Catholic organization in Lithuania will be permitted to survive in its present form. Already it has, of course, suffered considerable losses and repression, and a large degree of control is certainly exercised over the activities of its hierarchy.

An issue of the Russian language newspaper, *Sovetskaya Litva* (*Soviet Lithuania*), featured a review of a book, *Catholicism and the Nation.*

The reviewer of *Catholicism and the Nation* claimed that the book, written by Jakov Minkiavicius, a philosopher who teaches at the Lithuanian Academy of Sciences, shows that Catholics in Lithuania are using their Church "to sponsor anti-Russian feelings."

According to the reviewer, the book provides evidence of the effect of "nationalism" on religion, and charges the Church has exploited nationalist feelings "in its own interest."

Lithuania is the only state in the Soviet Union which has a majority of Catholics in its population—well over 2 million.

According to some specialist on the position of Catholics in Lithuania, Soviet authorities have been concerned with displays of religious fervor there because of the strong ties between the people and the Church.

Special efforts have been taken by government authorities to keep religious teaching out of the educative process. Education of children has been devised to hold the Church's influence to a minimum.

The reviewer said the Minkiavicius book also criticized the Christian conception of the Jewish people serves as a kind of foundation for the Semitism.

He quoted the book as saying people cannot fail to see "Catholicism's conception of the Jewish people serves as a kind of foundation for the Jews' exclusiveness in the family of nations—a conception that finds an echo in contemporary Judaism and in Zionism, and affords a basis for anti-Semitism."

Seventy-nine chapters of the Lithuanian-American Community of the U.S.A. were urged by their national president to follow the lead of the call for mourning, prayer and fasting to draw attention to religious suppression in Lithuania.

In a statement released here, Vytautas Volertas described a formal denunciation by the U.S. hierarchy of Soviet oppression in Lithuania as "a dramatic breakthrough" in influencing public opinion. He urged the nation's 2 million Lithuanian-Americans to support it.

Volertas referred to a statement by John Cardinal Krol of Philadelphia, president of the National Conference of Catholic Bishops, and Auxiliary Bishop John Dougherty of Newark, chairman of the Committee for International Affairs, U.S. Catholic Conference.

In their statement, Cardinal Krol and Bishop Dougherty described conditions in Lithuania under Soviet rule as "sadly scarred by oppression of religion, denial of freedom of conscience and of human rights."

This was the "first formal pronouncement" by the U.S. hierarchy critical of Soviet rule in Lithuania, and "constitutes a viable first for the Catholic Church" which dramatizes the plight of 3 million Lithuanians.

Hopefully this statement will give "added weight" in drawing public sympathy to the oppression which has existed since the Soviet Union annexed Lithuania in 1940.

Urging the U.S. Lithuanian population "to peaceably participate" in the bishops' call for a period of mourning, prayer and fasting, Volertas disclosed bulletins have been issued to all 79 chapters of the Lithuanian national organization.

In his lecture at the Politechnic Institute, K. Tumenas, Soviet official for religious affairs in Lithuania, stated that half the population of Lithuania practice their religion, about 45 per cent of the children are being baptized, about 25 per cent of the marriages are performed in churches, and about 51 per cent of the funerals are according to ecclesiastical rites.

Accounting these statistics, the Soviet official admitted that their atheistic propaganda carried on for more than 30 years was not so successful. In reality, the percentage of practicing Catholics is even larger.

In Soviet-occupied Lithuania there are 33 schools which prepare lectors for atheistic propaganda. In 1972 they had 750 students. All expenses are paid by the state. The Church is separated from the state, but atheistic movements are not; they are part of the government activities.

In spite of religious persecution the people of Lithuania are fervent in religious practices. This is indicated by the number of Confirmations: in Tytuvenai, 2,456; in Prienai, 2,702; in Silale, 5,100.

However, the Catholic underground newspaper, *Chronicle of the Catholic Church in Lithuania,* reported that the "Soviet state office" for church affairs has prohibited priests from engaging in any religious activities or ceremonies during harvest time.

The journal said Communist authorities ruled that harvest work had a top priority and religious activities should be reduced to a minimum. All church festivals were banned during the harvest period.

Every Sunday thousands of people of all ages crowd into the eleven Roman Catholic churches of Vilnius, capital of the Soviet Republic of Lithuania. Each church holds four or five Sunday services.

Two-thirds of the population of Lithuania are Roman Catholics. But the church has become much more than a place of worship. It is a rallying symbol of anti-Russian Lithuanian nationalism.

The underground *Chronicle of the Lithuanian Catholic Church* alleges persecution of Roman Catholics. Lithuanian government officials deny such charges.

There are 600 to 700 active churches in Lithuania, most of them

Roman Catholic. The most recent New Testament printing (an edition of 12,000) was in 1972. Prayer books (60,000) were last printed in 1968. Not every Lithuanian believer has a Bible and prayer book of his own.

Mr. Dilys said that the Kaunas seminary, the second Roman Catholic seminary in the Soviet Union, has about 50 students. It graduates five or ten a year. He said there are "more or less" enough priests for all the churches.

His own church gave first communion to about 300 young people every Sunday last summer. It conducts about 100 weddings, 300 christenings, and 50 funerals a year. All of these, including funerals, are taxed by the state, which categorizes them as handiwork by private craftsmen. Mr. Dilys preferred not to say how much the tax is.

In Lithuania at present there cannot be any Catholic hospital. All Catholic schools are nationalized. In the capital, 23 churches have been desecrated:

> The cathedral is transformed into an art gallery and concert hall.
>
> The Augustinian church has been turned into a storehouse of electric appliances.
>
> St. Bartholomew's Church has been converted into an art studio and in 1975 a huge sculpture of Lenin was created in it.
>
> The church of the Basilian Fathers has been made into a laboratory to test the resistance of various metals.
>
> The Church of the Bernardin Fathers now houses an art workshop.
>
> St. Ignace's Church is a storehouse of a film studio and in one chapel of that church is a restaurant.
>
> The Sacred Heart Church has been turned into a club for construction workers. St. Jacob's and St. Phillip's Church is a storehouse of opera and ballet decorations.
>
> St. John's Church is being transformed into museum and meeting hall. St. George's Church is converted into a book storehouse. St. Catherine's Church is a storehouse of groceries. St. Casimir's Church is now a museum of atheism. Holy Cross Church was destined to be a concert hall.
>
> Charity Chapel became a storeroom for books. Assumption Church has been turned into an archive. St. Michael's Church will house a permanent exposition of architecture. Missionary Church is assigned for keeping medical supplies.
>
> St. Stephen's Church is a storehouse of construction material. Holy Trinity Church became a work house for the Museum of History and Ethnography. Trinitarian Church is a depository for armed forces. The church of Trinapolis is a hospital storehouse.
>
> All Saints Church houses a permanent exposition of folk art. Visitation Church is being used as a jail for teenagers.
>
> One Evangelical church in Vilnius is converted into a film theater, another turned into a sport hall. Such is the situation of the 23 Catholic and two Evangelical churches in Vilnius.
>
> In another city, Kaunas, 14 Catholic churches and two Evangelical churches have been confiscated for profane use. However, all Russian Orthodox churches are open.
>
> In occupied Lithuania there is extremely great discrimination against pat-

riots and believers. Children of parents who were in exile in Siberia in many instances cannot get good marks of behavior in schools and that is a hindrance to continue their studies.

One art enterprise by the name *Daile* a few years ago made medals which included an old Lithuanian wayside cross constructed in the form of a pillar. People purchased these medals and wore them. Red authorities issued an order to collect all these medals from the stores and destroy them.

The underground paper, *The Chronicle of the Catholic Church in Lithuania,* announces that in the first decade of Soviet domination in Lithuania (up to 1959), 50 churches and semi-public chapels were closed, the use of cemetery chapels was prohibited, three crosses which were on the hill dominating Vilnius, were dynamited, wayside crosses in the city plazas and streets were destroyed. On the eve of the 25th anniversary of Soviet rule in Lithuania 35 chapels—Stations of the Cross at Vilnius Calvary—were dynamited.

In the closed churches many artistic statues, pictures, stained glass windows, organs, memorial plates, liturgical vestments and many other religious articles are destroyed. Even the remains of historical persons in the cellars of the churches and chapels were desecrated.

The underground paper warns the readers in free lands that Red authorities of occupied Lithuania in 1975 printed a book, *The Catholic Church in Lithuania,* in English, German and Italian, which contains pure Soviet propaganda based on some still open churches and distorted information.

Recently the Lithuanian Priests League of the U.S. published statistical data about the Church in Lithuania. It stated that 74 churches of Lithuania do not have priests. Young boys are prevented by all means from entering the seminaries, and because of this the number of priests in the last decade diminished by 97.

More than 60,000 Lithuanians have protested anti-religious measures of the Soviet Communist regime.

Citizens of the predominantly Lithuanian Soviet Republic, in protest letters to Communist officials, complained of violations of their religious rights by local authorities.

In one letter to a Communist official, some 14,000 Catholics protested atheist school education and discrimination against Catholic students. The letter said Catholic students were forced to write atheist and anti-church essays and draw anti-church cartoons.

"This violates the freedom of opinion guaranteed in the Constitution," the letter said.

Lithuanians, urban and rural, young and old, believers and non-believers alike risking imprisonment, economic security and educational opportunities, have lent their support to the *Chronicle's* publication and dissemination. Despite the best efforts of the KGB, resulting in numerous persons being arrested and imprisoned, publication of the *Chronicle* continues. Nonetheless, the American media, for all intents and purposes, have ignored the *Chronicle* and, with the exception of articles printed in local Catholic newspapers, the Catholic media have not done much better. This silence is in marked contrast to the media's extensive coverage of the mistreatment of Soviet Jews.

The Kremlin's reaction to rising discontent among Lithuanian Catholics is also instructive: Soviet authorities displayed concern about Catholic protest early in the 1970's after several petitions circulated by the Catholic militants attracted mass support. Catholic protest, along with that of dissident intellectuals and Russian Jews demanding the right of emigration, was interfering with Brezhnev's efforts to secure political and economic concessions from the West. In an attempt to discredit the militant Lithuanian Catholics, moderate prelates speaking favorably about the Kremlin's attitude toward the church gave interviews to reporters from Western Communist newspapers, such as *L'Humanite, La Unita* and *Paese Tera.*

Before the occupation, there were four seminaries for priests with an enrollment of 425 students; in 1975 there remained but one seminary with merely 29 students. Before the occupation, the Lithuanian Catholic Church could point to its 37 monasteries, 85 convents, 823 libraries and to its 32 periodicals boasting a circulation of over 7,500,000. All this has changed: Catholic organizations (whose membership totaled 800,000) are disbanded; Lutherans and other Christian denominations as well as Jews suffer the same oppression in Lithuania.

It is impossible to predict the ultimate outcome of the struggle of the Lithuanian Catholic Church to survive. It is certain that the struggle will be extremely difficult and costly and that the Soviet regime is not likely to give up its proclaimed goal of eradicating religion from the life of the people.

Latvia

According to the census of 1935, which was the last taken in independent Latvia, the population was then just slightly under two million people. With regard to religious affiliation, 56 per cent of the people were Lutheran, 24.5 per cent Roman Catholic, and 9 per cent Eastern Orthodox. The remainder included various smaller groups, from Baptists to atheists. There were 297 Lutheran Churches, served by 288 ordained pastors; 165 Catholic Churches, served by 177 priests; and 154 Greek Orthodox Churches, served by 128 priests.

The Latvian Orthodox Church had 174,389 Orthodox believers in 1935, and 107,195 Presbyterians. Altogether, there were 281,584 believers of Byzantine-rite; of this number 210,633 were Russians, 57,600 Latvians and others. There were three Orthodox bishops, 125 priests, 153 parishes, and 165 churches. The Latvian Orthodox Church was under the jurisdiction of the patriarch of Constantinopol. During the first Soviet occupation, it was placed under the jurisdiction of the Moscow patriarch. Consequently, since the second Soviet occupation in 1944, it is considered as a part of Moscow's Patriarchate, and its church life is subdued by appropriate conditions. Noticeable are the long vacancy of the hierarchal seat for the Latvian Orthodox Archdiocese in Riga. Since August 3, 1963, the former auxiliary bishop, Nikon Fomitsche, has officiated in Riga as superior of the Latvian Orthodox Church.

Today religious life in Latvia is gravely imperilled by an atheist communist regime. Article 124 of the Soviet Constitution says:

> In order to insure citizens freedom of conscience, the church in the USSR is separated from the State, and the school from the church. Freedom of religious devotion and freedom of anti-religious propaganda is recognized for all citizens.

The dubious wording of this article quite obviously denotes restrictions on religion. Although the churches, formally at least, are separated from the State, their activities are held under rigid State control. This control is vested in the Council for Religious Affairs, which is an affiliate of the USSR

Government. Through its commissioners, the Council makes it certain that the religious organizations strictly observe the decrees which regulate Church life in the USSR. The Commissioner, who by designation of the Party is in charge of all church activities in Latvia, is a Russianized Latvian by the name of Proletary Liepa.

All political power in the Soviet Union is vested with the Communist Party which is ideologically atheist. As Riga Radio declared recently:

> Religious belief is incompatible with Marxism-Leninism. Propagation of scientific atheism is one of the most important forms of communist ideological activities. Religion is an obstacle to the objective development of socialism. It diverts believers from maintaining useful social relationships.

In Soviet society, atheism is a means of stifling religion in all its forms of expression. Militant atheism enjoys the full support of the Party and government. This support consists of promoting anti-religious organizations (including atheist youth clubs) and anti-religious lectures, museums, movies, and literature. At the same time, religious organizations and their members are being harassed, directly or indirectly, in various ways. By excessive taxation, making it impossible for the congregation to maintain their churches; by making it hard for the clergy to earn a decent living; by prohibiting religious instruction to the young; and by reducing the publication of religious literature to a trickle, the Communist Party hopes to eventually extinguish religious life.

One of the most crucial devices of the Bolshevik regime to crush the worship of God in Latvia is the expropriation of churches and their transformation into museums, concert halls, warehouses, clubs or offices. The most prominent historic churches of Riga are no longer used for religious purposes. The Lutheran St. Mary's Cathedral was converted into a concert hall; the Russian Orthodox Cathedral is today a planetarium; and the ancient St. Peter's Church is to be converted into a museum of architecture. Today there are only about a hundred Lutheran churches available for worship, as compared to nearly three hundred in 1935. It is extremely difficult to obtain building materials to keep the remaining chruches in repair, even for congregations which manage to collect the necessary funds.

Nevertheless, despite great difficulties, there are still active in Latvia today six religious denominations: Lutherans, Roman Catholics, Eastern Orthodox, Baptist, Pentecostal, and Judaism. The largest religious group is still the Lutheran Church, though it has shrunk by half since Latvia lost its independence to Soviet Russia. The Latvian Lutheran Synod adopted in 1948, under governmental pressure, a new constitution, and elected the Rev. G. Turs to head the Church as Archbishop. In 1968, Turs resigned under circumstances which were brought about by a crisis in the administration of the Church. In 1969, the Rev. J. Matulis, having obtained the blessing of the Communist authorities, was elected the new head and was formally inaugurated the same year as Archbishop by the Swedish Bishop Dannell at a ceremonial service in St. John's Lutheran Cathedral in Riga. Matulis, who obviously enjoys the confidence of the regime, has been permitted to participate in several international church conferences abroad. He was induced to file a protest with the World Council of Churches against the admission of the Latvian Lutheran

Church in exile into the membership of the Council. He has signed various Soviet propaganda declarations "for international peace," or whatever, short of publicly admitting that God is dead. On the other hand, he has instilled a new vigor in the Church. He has initiated a pension fund for the clergy, and theological courses for a few young aspirants to the pastorate. At present, though, the Lutheran clergy in Latvia is still entirely composed of pastors who had received their theological education in independent Latvia.

Daniel Flaherty, editor of *America,* describes religious life in Latvia as follows:

> So much was happening the weekend of April 7 that I might have overlooked Pope Paul's message on April 8 to Bishop Julian Vaivods, Apostolic Administrator of the Archdiocese of Riga—the capital of Latvia—on the occasion of the bishop's 50th anniversary of ordination to the priesthood. But the Pope's letter of congratulations struck a peculiarly responsive chord in my memory.

> "We are not unaware," Paul wrote, "of the state of the Church in Latvia, but we hope it will develop for the better, trusting . . . in the worthy and unshakable steadfastness of which the faithful have given and are still giving proof in the midst of such distress—and above all in the prudence and zeal of their bishop, whose strength, like a noble oak tree, stretches its roots deeper and deeper, awaiting the day it can thrive again under a milder sun."

> I recalled it was just a year ago that I had been in Riga for a few brief days. I had gone with a group called the Appeal of Conscience Foundation—an ecumenical group of Protestants, Jews and Catholics—to inquire at first hand about the situation of religion today behind the Iron Curtain.

> Unfortunately, Bishop Vaivods was not in Riga while we were there. We did visit with the Orthodox Metropolitan of that city, with members of the Jewish community (like so many cities in the Soviet Union, the congregation in Riga has no Rabbi) and with the Lutheran Archbishop. But I wish now, more than ever, we had had a chance to meet with the man Pope Paul compares to a "noble oak tree."

> I remember Riga as a turreted town on the Baltic, its old section still much as it was at the height of the Hanseatic League. On our first night there, we wandered the cobblestone streets of the old town under a full moon, looking for the synagogue and a Catholic church for morning services. Ancient churches stood out black against the moonlit sky on nearly every corner of the old city—but most of them are museums or "civic centers" now.

> In the morning, with a bright, pale spring sun tempering the winds from the sea, I finally found one small Catholic church. It was the week after Easter, and the Feast of the Annunciation (postponed because it had fallen in Holy Week). A procession filled the main aisle of the little church—young girls in white and boys in blue. The church was crowded right to the doors with people of all ages, even though it was a week day and a working-day.

> It was of that moment in Riga, a year ago, that Pope Paul's letter poignantly reminded me.

The activities of the Christian congregations are subject to stringent government-imposed restrictions. Conditions for the survival of religious life are more favorable in the cities than in the country. Rural churches are dependent upon the benevolence of the local kolkhozes for such vital matters as transportation, provision of building materials for repair of the premises, and moral support of the clergy. Services are generally poorly attended, except on religious holidays. In the country some pastors attend to several congregations. Some churches maintain choirs, and church buildings are being taken care of as conditions permit. There have occurred, however, numerous cases of atheist vandals breaking windows and smashing the interiors, including organs. To repair an organ is practially impossible under prevailing conditions.

The churches are obliged to observe Communist holidays and to participate in "peace" propaganda. Religious literature is scarce and hard to obtain. The only regular Lutheran publication is a church calendar, which appears in limited copies. Some years ago, the regime permitted the publication of the New Testament and hymnal, also though in limited numbers. Churchmen who are being trusted to take part in international "peace" conferences are expected to sign Communist-inspired resolutions and to denounce American or Israeli aggression, etc. On the other hand, Western church delegations are welcome to visit Latvia and to participate in services held in some select Lutheran churches in Riga. The great majority of the Latvian clergy, however, has no opportunity to maintain contact with foreign churches, or to travel abroad.

Though the future of the Church is insecure, religious life in Latvia has not yet been destroyed. The number of believers who support church activities is still considerable. There are young students attending theological courses in preparation for the Lutheran ministry. Also the fact that the Communist regime is constantly combating "remains of religious superstition" is evidence that the church is still an entity to be reckoned with.

The Roman Catholic Church is presently headed by Bishop J. Vaivods. The Cathedral and headquarters of the diocese are located in Riga, even though the majority of the Latvian Catholics live in Latgale, the easternmost province of Latvia. The diocese maintains a seminary which is training a dozen or so seminarians for the priesthood. Relations with Rome are strictly limited, though Bishop Vaivods was allowed to attend the Second Vatican Council. The influence of the Catholic Church among its parishioners is still very strong. The press of the Komsomol never tires of reproaching some of its members for attending Mass and participating in church rites.

Three million Roman Catholics isolated in the Soviet Union gained their first voice in the Vatican with the unpublicized arrival of two bishops and three priests from Lithuania and Latvia, the Soviet-conquered Baltic republics.

The Vatican, like the United States, has never recognized Russia's ownership of Lithuania and Latvia.

The new link between the cut-off Catholics and Rome, fragile and only two weeks in duration, was achieved as a result of Pope Paul's face-to-face request to Soviet President Nikolai Podgorny during his 1962 audience.

The Bishops were Joseph Labukas-Matulaitis of Kaunas, capital of Lithuania, multilingual scholar and author of a Latin-Lithuanian dictionary, and Julian Vaivods of Riga, Latvia.

Both in their 70's, they were improvised bishops, named to fill vacancies caused by imprisonment, exile, detention and death.

They were the last free survivors of an episcopal system that required seven bishops for Lithuania and three for Latvia.

Both bishops were summoned to Moscow before coming to Rome and briefed on the conditions of their Roman stay. They were given "Cinderella visas" that elapsed March 15, 1962.

In 1973, according to the Vatican's *Annuario,* the Archdiocese of Riga and diocese of Liepaja encompassed 178 parishes with 265,000 Catholics having 4,541 baptism, served by 133 diocesan and 13 religious priests, 2 priests ordained during that year, with 18 seminarians studying in the Riga seminary; compared with its 1940 strength (216 churches and chapels, 166 parishes, 190 clergymen and 31 theological students)—the Church in Latvia suffered since then fewer losses in the number of parishes and clergy than probably any other denomination in the USSR. The Latvian Catholics have been lacking religious books; only once, in 1967, were they allowed to publish a small missal and a prayer book.

In 1975 and 1976 were published marriage, baptismal and last-rites rituals: *Ordo celebrandi matrimonium; Ordo baptismi parvulorum,* and *Ordo unctionis infirmorum eorumque pastoralis curae.* Besides that, Pope Paul VI has donated to the Latvian Church numerous volumes of new missals and Readings from the Holy Scriptures in Latin, and a certain number of breviaries for the Latvian priests.

The Latvian Catholic Church is still headed by the old apostolic Administrator of Riga and Liepaja, Julian Vaivods, assisted by, in November, 1972 consecrated Bishop Valerian Zondaks, former rector of the Riga Seminary. The senior living Latvian bishop, Kazimirs Dulbinskis, has been banished since the 1960's to a remote village and is prohibited from serving Mass in public, after he had returned from his long imprisonment in the Komi ASSR and exile in Byelorussia.

Soon after the establishment of the Soviet regime in Latvia all three denominational theological faculties—the Lutheran, the Roman Catholic, and the Greek Orthodox—of the State University of Latvia at Riga were closed by a special decree. It was not until 1956 that the supervisory agency for religious affairs attached to the Ministry of the Interior of the Latvian S.S.R. authorized the Supreme Church Board of the Lutheran Church of Soviet Latvia to open theological courses for the training of Lutheran clergymen. In 1960 twenty persons, including one woman, attended these courses, the age of the oldest being 72 years. However, according to information received from Latvia in February, 1962, the Soviet Latvian government has ordered the cessation of the above mentioned theological courses attached to the Supreme Church Board of the Evangelical Lutheran Church at Riga.

The Seminar for Catholic Priests at Riga is also subject to restrictions in a manner detrimental to its activities and making questionable its future. The Soviet Latvian government initially limited the maximum number of Catholic candidates for the priesthood to 60. However, in 1961, this number dwindled to 13.

While hundreds of universities, gymnasiums, schools, and clubs are available for the education of militant atheists, the theology studies have been brought to extinction. From five Roman Catholic seminaries in the Baltic States, today there are only two provisional seminaries left, one in

Kaunas and the other in Riga. The seminary of Vilkaviskis was changed to an atheist seminary, which in 1965 had ninety participants. Besides that, in 1963, the *numerus clausus* was introduced for theological seminary, and theology studies. Whereupon, for each diocese, only one priest can be ordained. Therefore, for the eight Roman Catholic dioceses of the Baltic, not more than eight priests can be ordained yearly; eight priests yearly for three million Catholics. In 1965, in Latvia's two Roman Catholic dioceses, only six new priests were allowed to be ordained.

Admission into a seminary is becoming more and more difficult. In practice, the State decides who can enter a seminary or an Evangelical-Lutheran course. The authorities can grant or refuse the residence permit in the place of study. The Soviet regime also is capable of infiltrating among these candidates agents or other unsuitable persons. Applicants for theology study must be prepared to be made fools of in the press. In Sveksna, even the director of a lycee was released because two of his graduates entered the theology seminary.

The economy of the clergymen seminaries is in a deplorable position. The Roman Catholic seminary of Riga is located in the parsonage of the St. Francis Church. The students of the Roman Catholic seminary from Kaunas live in narrow, small rooms, which are scattered over the entire city. The teaching hours are held in the Holy Trinity Church from Kaunas, but this was closed in the year 1965 in order to change it to a club and dance hall. The lack of textbooks is unimaginable. One has to be satisfied with the theological books on hand, all of them from pre-war years or of typewritten copies.

According to an interview in the *Moscow News,* Bishop Valerians Zondaks, the Dean of Riga's Roman Catholic seminary, gave the following account of religious life in the Soviet Latvia:

> There is absolute freedom of conscience in Latvia and all over the Soviet Union. The Constitution of the Latvian Soviet Socialist Republic guarantees it. Every citizen is free to attend religious services. His rights are protected by Soviet law.

> The number of parishes has not diminished in Latvia, nor has the number of dioceses. There is the Riga Archdiocese and the Liepaja Diocese, established about 50 years ago. They have their own administrations. The Government of the Latvian Republic puts no impediments in their way nor does it interfere in their religious activities.

> The dioceses have the right to convene conferences of clergy to discuss religious matters, to publish religious books and tracts, and so on. Decrees of the Second Vatican Council, prayer books for believers and for priests were published in Latvia in the last five years, and we have received many new books for clergymen from the Vatican.

> There are fewer priests today because some of them left Latvia during the war. But there are quite enough of them in each parish to satisfy their people's spiritual needs.

> The war brought much suffering and destruction to Latvia. It left many towns and villages in ruins, and many churches were destroyed. After the war the Soviet state made a titanic effort to restore the war-ravaged economy. We are grateful to the Government which, in that trying period, gave us the materials needed to restore and repair our churches.

> At present all the churches are in an excellent state of repair and lovingly

decorated by parishioners. It is noteworthy that some of them are, as outstanding works of architecture, protected by the state.

There is a seminary in Riga which runs a five-year course. Tuition is free, and the students are provided for by the believers. The number of the seminary's students has almost doubled in recent years.

The syllabus is coordinated with the Vatican Sacred Congregation for Catholic Education and is virtually in line with Roman Catholic universities.

The Catholic Church of Latvia keeps in touch with the Vatican, with Catholic churches and Catholic organizations abroad. We took an active part in the work of the Second Vatican Council, we have and are attending the Synod of Bishops called by Pope Paul VI, work on Vatican commissions on canonic law, take part in the European Catholic Conference, make pilgrimages and visit Catholic churches in other countries. The Soviet authorities do not interfere. Besides, Latvian Catholics keep in touch with their co-religionists abroad and invite them to the Soviet Union.

The Soviet State supports the believers, religious organizations and clergymen's work for peace, detente and better international relations. Quite recently the Soviet Peace Committee awarded the Medal of the World Peace Council, instituted in connection with the 25th anniversary of the world peace movement, to a group of religious leaders, including Bishop Julians Vaivods of the Riga Archdiocese, for their active work for peace.

However, the Latvian minister Janis Smits gave this picture of Soviet surveilance of religious activities in the state:

The Soviet Government actively scrutinizes church-goers, seeks collaborators among church leaders and those of weaker faith, and makes masked efforts to promote its own confidants into positions for which they are often not qualified.

It is considered a crime for a pastor to preach in any parish other than the one to which he is assigned, to ask parishioners to pray (in church) for those imprisoned in the Soviet Union, or to encourage youth under 18 to take an active role in church work—such as religious education or singing in a choir.

There is a great shortage of Bibles and other religious literature, with some churches possessing only a single copy for their entire congregations. Bibles printed legally in the U.S.S.R. for sale to parishes—a process supervised by Soviet officials—are extremely scarce, and usually end up being sent to the West for propaganda purposes. This is also the case with the new Orthodox Russian Bible translation.

Formal theological training is generally inaccessible to Latvians, except for Moscow-area courses open to a few government-selected candidates, and some low-level correspondence courses.

Some pastors are granted privileges to travel within and without the U.S.S.R., but the recipients are usually collaborators with the Communist Party. Some are thought to be party members.

While Latvians have open telephone contact with Western Europe—even those under religious persecution—their conversations are carefully monitored by authorities.

Broadcasts of *Voice of America, Radio Liberty* and *Radio Free Europe* are providing virtually the best source of world news for Latvians. And Bible readings by these stations make possible an exposure to the Scriptures which is largely unattainable otherwise for many who do not own Bibles.

However, the policy of detente has taken a noticeable toll on the effectiveness of such broadcasts. It has brought with it a clear decrease in broadcasts about controversial, substantive world issues, and a vast increase in more trivial programming, with the result that many Latvians have lost interest in the programs.

A visitor to the Soviet Latvia writes in a letter her observations as follows:

> Every morning and evening I went to a Catholic church, and nobody bothered me. Churches in Riga are crowded with believers on Sundays and holidays. The believers are praying and singing even more heartedly and devotedly than at the time of free Latvia. . . . Almost all church-goers receive Holy Communion. On weekdays, of course, the morning Masses are attended by more or less of a hundred people. In some of Riga's churches there are evening Holy Hours which last for three hours. There is never a lack of worshippers. Children are permitted, after a short preparation, to receive the First Holy Communion. Memorial services are held in cemeteries regularly every year. Young people and adults are solemnly baptized, married solemnly without any pomp or circumstance.

> Churches are very poor because each parish has to pay a big sum of money to the State every year. The priests also have to pay their taxes every month because they are not working for the government.

> The rates of electricity for a church is three times higher than for the rest of the people. The Church is separated from the State, however, the government controls the Church and checks every movement of the Church. In order to help the Church to pay taxes some believers are working overtime. Some older mothers revealed to me, that they fast at least two days a week so that on Sundays they could offer a ruble to the Church.

> As you see, I experienced a great joy and depressing agony at the same time in my Fatherland. . . .

Recently, 5,043 Roman Catholics from Daugavpils, Latvia, signed an undated petition in the Russian language addressed to the government of the Soviet Union. The signers fear that the local authorities still intend to tear down their church which has "beautified the city" for decades. Initially, when the first threats to demolish the church were made, a letter of protest was posted to the appropriate authorities in Riga, who answered that the Catholic church "would not be destroyed at the present time." This reply was hardly reassuring, because the local Lutheran church, which had served both the Lutheran and the Baptist congregations of Daugavpils, was confiscated—as the petitioners point out, after the ratification of the Final Act of the Conference on Security and Cooperation in Europe on August 1, 1975. The Protestant worshippers were assigned a meeting place in a private home near a cemetery at the edge of town. Bearing these events in mind, the Catholics of Daugavpils are asking the Soviet government "to put an end to the persecution of believers in our city and to safeguard the rights of the faithful to worship in their own particular churches and not in dwellings on the outskirts of town."

This brief letter of petition is not remarkable for the information that it provides on the plight of Christians in the Soviet Union, for its contents merely add more detail to what is already known. The number of signatures on it is small in comparison with the 17,000 names that appeared on the Lithuanian appeal addressed to the UN General Assembly in 1972.

However, the letter of the Daugavpils Catholics gains in significance when it is considered in terms of the milieu from which it originated.

Daugavpils is the second largest city in Latvia, and one of the oldest as well: on July 5, 1975, Daugavpils celebrated its 700th anniversary. It is the cultural and industrial center of Latgale, a province that traditionally has had the greatest concentration of Roman Catholics in Latvia. In the late 1930's, there were more than 35,600 Roman Catholics in the Daugavpils deanery, of whom more than 16,000 resided in the city. The Catholics composed nearly 25 per cent of Latvia's population, and, after the Lutherans, who comprised more than 55 per cent of the population, formed the second largest religious denomination in the country. In Daugavpils the greatest portion (nearly 36 per cent) of the inhabitants were Roman Catholics; Jews and Lutherans made up some 25 per cent and 16 per cent of the city's population respectively. By nationality, the breakdown of the city's population was 36 per cent Latvians, 25 per cent Jews, 20 per cent Russians, and 18 per cent Poles.

In the post war years the population of Daugavpils has changed considerably: the number of inhabitants has increased to 112,000 (in the late 1930's the population was 45,610), and people of 30 nationalities now live and work in the city. Latvians, are in the minority, forming only 15 per cent of the population. Figures on the present religious composition of Daugavpils are not available, but it may safely be assumed that the percentage of Christians has decreased markedly owning among other factors to changes in the national composition of the city in the post war period.

Little is known about the true conditions of the Roman Catholic Church in Latvia. According to Soviet sources, in the years immediately following World War II the Latvian Catholic Church was decidedly anti-Communist, but lately has become loyal to the Soviet regime. This assessment would appear to be not entirely unfounded, because there are reports that some Catholic clergymen in Latvia have served as mouthpieces for pro-Soviet propaganda. Also, no evidence of recent conflict between Latvian Catholics and the Soviet regime has reached the West. One explanation for this situation is the desire for survival. Some Western observers feel that the Latvian Roman Catholics have sought to maintain their identity and preserve their churches through the exercise of astute diplomacy and quiet perserverance.

If such a policy has been followed, then this petition marks a turning point: like the Roman Catholics of Lithuania, the Latvian Roman Catholics are openly protesting the injustices and harassment suffered by believers. It could also be that the authorities are placing more restrictions on believers in Daugavpils and that the previously successful means of avoiding persecution are no longer efficacious. In any case, the letter of the Daugavpils Catholics is the first document of this kind to have arrived in the West from a large group of Roman Catholics in Soviet Latvia.

For over 15 years, the Reform Baptists in the USSR have promoted a remarkable publishing enterprise, producing and circulating Christian literature under the noses of the KGB. From the outset the state outlawed the whole movement for religious liberty and for the establishment of a Protestant Church independent of government control. Over 600 of its leading figures have served periods in prison, some sentenced to as long as ten years. The state has suppressed the key leadership (Georgi Vins is currently serving a ten-year sentence in Yakutsk, Siberia; Gennadi

Kryuchkov is in hiding), yet the ideals which they represented while at liberty live on.

The persecution of Christians in Communist-ruled nations has continued unabated throughout the years. Recently Soviet secret police used radioactivie tracers to locate an underground printing press being used by an underground Baptist group to print Christian literature, including New Testaments. With the aid of helicopters, the whole district of Cesis outside Riga was carefully searched for several days in October, 1974, until one day, sensitive detection instruments responded over a farm in Ligukalns.

About 200 police were ordered to the spot. In a secret section of the basement, seven young Baptists were found on October 24, 1974, in the process of printing 30,000 New Testaments as a gift to the churches for Christmas.

The Baptists were arrested and 15,000 New Testaments and 20,000 pounds of paper were confiscated.

Most of this literature is hectographed or typed, but a few years ago the Reform Baptists established an offset press. Despite the discovery of one arm of the publishing operation in Latvia and the imprisonment of several people connected with it, the enterprise continued.

Now the press has begun to print a journal, *Vestnik istiny* (Herald of Truth). Beautifully produced in three colors, it marks an important new stage in the continued determination of the Reform Baptists to provide theological literature for their followers. It aims, too, to give the church member something which he can put into the hand of the person who is curious about the faith, but not yet committed to it, though strengthening the committment of the converted will be the primary purpose.

Western authors, as well as Soviet ones, are represented in the first issue: an article by Billy Graham, reprinted from *Christianity Today*; and the story of Nicky Cruz, author of *Run, Baby, Run*. There is also a most moving story of a Soviet atheist who burned a Bible,. but one page, not completely consumed by the flames, fluttered out of the stove and the one preserved sentence on it, "Heaven and earth will pass away, but my words will not pass away" brought the man to Christ. The journal also prints a moving letter to Gennadi Kryuchkov from Georgi Vins, written in Spring, 1975 in a transit prison en route to Siberia.

Only the first issue of 1976 has reached the West to date, and the *Hearld of Truth* is projected as a quarterly publication, so it is not yet known whether the new journal has survived the further determined efforts of the KGB to stamp out unauthorized Baptist publishing activities. A publication with the title *These Ruins Accuse* gives a pictorial survey of the destruction of churches and of their use for other purposes—as kolkhoz storehouses, sports halls, concert halls, museums, etc.

Its preface states among other things:

> In 1939 there were 297 Lutheran churches in Latvia. In 1974 there were only approximately 90 places of worship left for us by their congregations. About 40 churches were destroyed in the war, and no one cared to rebuild them. In the last few years many churches have been converted into cultural and social centres. Thus, historic churches such as the 12th century Dome in Riga, Valmiera's 13th century St. Simeon's, the church in Kuldiga and other churches have been transformed into concert halls. The Russian Orthodox

Cathedral's cross in Riga was broken off and a museum of astronomy was installed. The stately Church of St. Peter in Riga is being rebuilt as a museum . . .

The Independent Latvian Lutheran Church had in:

	Congregation members	Congregations	Pastors
1935	1,200,000	280	270
1944	1,100,000	280	260

Soviet Latvian Lutheran Church

1948	1,000,000	280	70
1962	500,000	250	110

Church buildings:

1939   300
1945 (war demolished, 42 churches; heavily damaged during the war 90 churches)   168
1963 (5 war-damaged churches repaired; 22 newly built churches; 65 Lutheran churches have not been handed back to the congregations for use)   110

The number of churches still left to the congregations constantly diminishes because the remaining church members are unable to pay the exorbitant state imposed tax on the use of the building.

The tragedy of the Church and people in Latvia is described as follows:

These ruins accuse those who, having thrown aside God's Laws and Christ's Gospel, relentlessly seek to destroy the Christian Church . . .

These ruins accuse those who look indifferently at the sufferings and persecution of their brothers and sisters in faith . . .

These ruins accuse those who know, but supress the truth . . .

These ruins accuse the leaders of the Churches who lack the courage to call the Soviet Union by name when they speak of freedom of religion and human rights . . .

Estonia

The church in Estonia is not about to die out—despite atheist propaganda—but has a vital existence and is able to withstand pressure, even economically. Services have a lively attendance.

In Tallin, for example, there are at the moment eight Lutheran communities. The two largest communities in the time of national independence, the Johannis Church (37,000 congregation members) and the Karls Church (40,000 members) have today 3,500 and 4,000 members each. The communities are enrolled as communities of belief; they have to pay the state rent for the use of the churches. The annual rent of a large-size church in Tallin amounts to 3,500 rubles. The state receives altogether 100,000 rubles annually from the 125 churches in the Russian-occupied Estonia. The community itself must pay for the renovation and current upkeep of the church.

From the income of the community (from voluntary contributions) 15 per cent goes for general expenses of church life, including the running of the Theological Institute, which has now 25 students, who are preparing, along with other work, to become pastors.

There is no religious literature, and it is forbidden to import it from abroad. The customs officials checked with a special care to see that a Swedish guest did not bring any with him. The hymn books are falling to bits. Hymns for the services are duplicated or written by hand.

According to law, the Evangelical Lutheran Church and Estonian Apostolic Orthodox Church enjoyed the rights of institutions constituted under public law, and the heads of these churches were members of the Second Chamber of the Legislature by virtue of this office.

The Lutheran Church, as well as the Estonian Apostolic Orthodox Church and other churches, became "people's churches" in independent Estonia not only in name but in essence. According to statistics, 80 per cent of the population belonged to the Evangelical Lutheran Church, 19 per cent (including districts on the Russian border) belonged to the Apostolic Orthodox Church, 1.5 per cent to churches of other Protestant denominations (Baptist, Adventist, Methodist, etc.). The Roman Catholic Church accounted for 0.3 per cent of the population.

The Estonian Apostolic Orthodox Church was established as an autocephalous church in 1923 and was recognized by the Ecumenical Patriarch in Constantinople. The word "apostolic" was inserted to make clear the definition between the Estonian and the Russian Orthodox Church. The church was headed by the Metropolitan of Tallinn and All-Estonia, and a Synod, elected by the church assembly. In order to westernize the church many liturgical reforms were introduced, the ceremonies reduced to a minimum and greater importance was attached to sermons than the Orthodox normally do.

The Theological Department at the Tartu University continued its twofold work: the preparation of ministers and pastors not only for the Evangelical Lutheran Church but also for other churches and denominations, and scholarly research and publication work.

Closer relations were established between the Estonian Evangelical Lutheran Church and the churches of Finland and the Scandinavian countries, as well as with the Church of England.

Estonia has been under Communist rule three times: for a short time from the end of 1917 through the beginning of 1918; in 1940 and 1941; and since the autumn of 1944 up to the present. All these periods left their traces in the history of the Estonian church.

The recent Communist period began in August-September of 1944 when the Soviet Union newly occupied the country and has lasted ever since.

Shortly before the reoccupation of the country about 80,000 Estonians escaped to Germany and Sweden, among them 68 pastors of the Evangelical Lutheran Church with Archbishop Johan Kopp and Bishop Johannes O. Lauri, as well as numerous priests of the Estonian Orthodox Church with the Metropolitan Alexander, and preachers of other denominations.

Precise information on the situation of churches is not available for the time being. According to some scattered and incomplete information, 10 churches were destroyed and 42 damaged during the military operations in 1941, and 20 more churches were destroyed in the operations of 1944. Out of 250 clergymen of the Evangelical Lutheran Church only about 80 were available in Estonia at the end of the war. According to some information there are now 170 church buildings used for divine services with 122 pastors. The situation of other churches is no better.

The autocephaly of the Estonian Apostolic Church was brought to an end, the chair of the Metropolitan was liquidated, the Synod dissolved, liturgical reforms introduced at the time of Estonian independence were discontinued, and the church was subordinated to the Russian Patriarchate. All this was carried out in a way which is reminiscent of the procedure of annexation of Estonia by the U.S.S.R. in 1940, when the Supreme Soviet of the U.S.S.R. declared that Estonia was admitted to the Soviet Union by "the will of the people."

The emissary of the Patriarch of Moscow, Archbishop Grigorii, arrived in Tallinn on March 5, 1945, summoned the members of the Synod of "the schismatic Estonian Church" who were available in Tallinn on that day (3 priests and 2 laymen), and, to "accelerate the matter," demanded of them the signing "on behalf of all members of the Estonian Orthodox Church" of letter of repentance with the request for readmission to the Russian Church. The letter was read in a church, and the Estonian autocephalous church was thus ended and the Estonian Diocese under the jurisdiction of the Russian

Patriarchate was born. Archbishop Bogoiavlenskii was appointed Bishop of Tallinn and Estonia in 1947. On September 3, 1961, he was replaced by Aleksei Redinger as Bishop Aleksei.

Some beautiful churches in the cities have been converted into museums. A cafe has been opened in the tower of St. Nicholas Church in Tallinn. St. Michael's Church in Tallinn has been turned into a sports hall.

In Estonia the Roman Catholic Church had in the year 1940 about 3,000 believers, one bishop, and 15 priests. Since 1945, there have been no more bishops, and only two priests, who have recently come from Latvia. The Evangelical-Lutheran church in 1961 had about 350,000 believers, one bishop and 114 ministers that is 500,000 less than in 1931 (864,994).

The Archbishop Jaan Kiivit and 114 ministers were appointed by the Soviet Government. At their disposal were 165 church buildings. The Estonian Orthodox Church in 1934 had a total of 212, 764 believers (19 per cent of the total population) among them 118,000 were Estonians, and 92,000 were Russians, and they were under the jurisdiction of the patriarch of Constantinopole. There existed two dioceses, one Estonian with its seat in Tallinn, and the other Russian with its seat in Narva, with parishes numbering 160 (in the year 1939). There were three bishops, 138 priests, and 23 deacons. During the first Soviet occupation of Estonia (1940-1941), the two Orthodox dioceses of Estonia were united into one diocese, and of course, placed under the Orthodox diocese of Estonia and the Eparch Sergei of Moscow. After the relief of the Soviet occupation by German forces (1941-1944), the Orthodox Estonians regarded the subjugation under the patriarch of Moscow as transitory. After the second Soviet occupation of Estonia at the end of 1944, the "Estonian Schism" March 6, 1945 was made invalid with a repentence service. Since then, the position of the Orthodox church of Estonia hardly distinguishes itself from the remaining provinces of the Moscow Patriarchate. From 1944-65, five times the Soviet Orthodox dioceses of Estonia have changed their hierarchy of whom only one was a native Estonian. Since September 3, 1961, Archbishop Aleksei Redinger has been superior of the Orthodox Churcn of Estonia. He has directed the foreign offices of the Moscow Patriarchate since about 1964, because he has knowledge of many West-European languages. At the meeting of the Holy Council, which took place December 22, 1964, under the direction of the Moscow patriarch, the archbishop Aleksei Redinger was elected a member of the Holy Council and manager of the patriarchate.

7

Armenian Gregorian Church

Throughout the many centuries of its history, the Armenian Church has repeatedly been persecuted by invaders. But rarely at any time in its history has the Church been so oppressed as under the Soviet regime.

The Communist rule was established in Armenia on December 2, 1920, during the period of War Communism, and continued until February 18, 1921, when it was swept away by a national uprising. In this brief interval, the authorities were unable to launch an effective campaign against the Church. But after the suppression of the uprising on April 2, 1921, the persecution of the Church and religion gradually assumed a more organized form.

In 1922 a decree of the Soviet government of Armenia not only separated the Church from the State, but also abolished the hierarchy of the Armenian Church and destroyed its universality and unity. The same decree gave the faithful the right to organize local religious communities of not less than 20 persons which were however not allowed to have organic contact with each other.

The decree confiscated the most valuable property of the Armenian Church, including the well-equipped printing press at the monastery of Echmiadzin and the ancient Armenian manuscripts with their remarkable miniatures. Only recently have the Soviet authorities published reproductions of these miniatures which had been carefully collected over the centuries by the Armenian monasteries.

The year 1938 was the culminating point of the persecution of the Church and clergy. The Soviet government did not allow the election of a new Catholicos and until 1949, the Deputy Catholicos, Archbishop Georg Chorekchian, occupied the throne.

During World War II a new religious policy on the part of the Communists was reflected in the Armenian Church. Instead of completely destroying the Church, the authorities decided to utilize it for their own ends and for this purpose to permit certain concessions. Georg VI was given an audience by Stalin as a reward for his appeal to the people to defend the "Soviet Motherland," and Stalin even promised him that the territories which had been lost to Turkey would be restored to Soviet Armenia.

At the end of the war the harsh persecution of believers ceased, and a period marked by so-called scientific atheist propaganda began. The Catholicos was permitted to open a religious seminary in Echmiadzin, and was allowed greater freedom of intercourse with the Armenian eparchies abroad. In exchange, he was compelled to take part in the "peace" campaign and to appear at various political congresses organized by the Soviet regime. It has been impossible to restore the church buildings which have been destroyed. Of those closed during the persecution of the Church, most have remained closed and continue to serve as grain storehouses or clubs. In a meeting in Moscow between the present Catholicos, Vazgen I, and Bulganin, the latter promised that 10 or 15 churches would be returned to the faithful. This promise was reported officially and was carried out. The political use made of religion by the Communists in the postwar period does not come within the scope of this study, but it should be noted that the return to the Church of a number of places of worship which had previously been closed is undoubtedly of purely political significance, intended to facilitate the subversive work of Soviet propagandists among Armenians abroad. Since there were 1,250 church buildings in Armenia before the Sovietization of the country, it goes without saying that the return of 10 to 15 is of not real significance

Bardizian, the author of a book entitled, *The Crisis of the Armenian Church and Those Responsible For It,* has summed up the situation as follows:

> The Soviet regime has stolen all the property and all the lands, all the sources of income given to the Church by the Armenian people over the centuries. Nearly all the monasteries and their lands, such as those of Sevan, Gandzasar, Tatev, Akhnat, Sakain, Tsitakavar, etc., have been expropriated.
>
> Most of the valuable manuscripts, the Church property, and all the wealth of the Echmiadzin Matenadaran Museum have either been stolen directly by confiscation or taken by misappropriation by puppet priests.
>
> Many of the clergy have been arrested and exiled. Neither the unity, nor the universality, nor the hierarchy nor the head of the Armenian Apostolic Church are now recognized by the Soviet authorities.
>
> An antireligious propaganda campaign is being waged with state funds. The legal and administrative structure of the Armenian Church has been destroyed, plunging it into chaos.

The fact remains that in its attacks on the Armenian Gregorian Church as an expression of Armenian national life, the Soviet authorities have engaged in a form of national genocide.

The Armenian Apostolic Church occupies a unique position in Soviet religious life. After the war it helped the government drive to persuade Armenians to come back to the Soviet Union (10,000 did) and won some concessions in return. It receives substantial financial help from Armenian communities abroad.

It had 1,446 parishes before Soviet rule came to Armenia: in 1962 it claimed 200. Only six monasteries survive with 25-30 monks. The church is said to have about three million members, with over half the population going to church, and it appears that nearly three-quarters of Armenian babies are baptized.

Vazgen I, Supreme Catholicos of all the Armenians, has affirmed that there is a widespread revival of religious life in Armenia, which is one of the constituent republics of the USSR:

> Soviet Armenia is the home of one of the world's most ancient Churches— the Armenian Apostolic Church. Nowdays the Armenian community is widely dispensed, with large numbers in the Middle East and America.
>
> In recent years there had been a four-fold increase in the number of baptisms being performed, with many Communists bringing their own children to be baptized. Probably the absolute figure was about seventy per cent, while, in the villages, it was not far short of one hundred per cent. Only in the Communist Party and in inttellectual circles were there a significant number of families who did not have their children baptized.
>
> Soviet law imposed restrictions on the education of children in the Christian faith, but young people were nevertheless being reached through their presence at religious meetings.
>
> The giving of the people to the Church has increased eleven-fold in the past twenty years. Although it was still possible for Armenians outside the Soviet Union to contribute to special projects such as the building of new churches, it was no longer necessary for them to subsidise the basic budget.
>
> The Armenian Church has a vigorous publishing programme, with 5,000 of each issue of the monthly journal *Echmiadzin* being printed. Additionally, this year, 20,000 copies of the Church calendar have been printed, as well as a further 10,000 wall calendars.

For reasons known, on the 20th anniversary of the election of Catholicos Vazgen I as supreme head of the three million Soviet Armenian Christians, leaders of major denominations were invited.

In response to the invitation of His Holiness Vazgen I, Supreme Catholicos-Patriarch of all Armenians, the Holy Father sent a special delegation to take part in the solemn celebrations which took place at Echmiadzin, Armenia, USSR, from September 25 to 27. The celebrations consisted in the ceremony of the blessing of the Sacred Chrism and the XX anniversary of the election of the Catholicos.

The ceremony of the blessing of the Sacred Chrism is of particular importance in the Armenian Orthodox Church. It is reserved to the Catholicos himself and it takes place only once every seven years. The Chrism is used for the administration of the sacraments of orders, baptism and confirmation and in other solemn blessings. The blessing and distribution of the Chrism is a sign of communion between the Catholicos and the other bishops of his church. Armenian Orthodox Bishops from all over the world were present, together with delegates from other Christian churches, at the ceremony in Echmiadzin.

Today the Soviet Russian government is busy sowing discord in the Armenian diaspora by exploiting the Church, the spiritual head of which, the Catholicos, resides at Echmiadzin, near Erivan. Soviet propaganda is very intensive, particularly in the Near East, where hundreds of thousands of Armenians recognize as their spiritual leader the Catholicos of the Great House of Cilicia, who resides in Lebanon. However, the intrigues of the Soviet agents have not yielded fruit, as the overwhelming majority of the Armenians living outside the Soviet Union are firmly attached to the ideal of independence. They are politically organized in the name of independence, and live in flourishing communities where the national language and culture are kept alive.

Speaking of the Christian faith, an Armenian official said:

> Our church is something special for us. There is nothing inconsistent in being a Communist and having my children christened. We suffered more because of our church, being a Christian people on the edge of the Moslem world. But we survived as a nation because it preserved our language and culture, as well as itself, through the invasions and dispersals.

8

Georgian Autocephalic Orthodox Church

The Georgian Church is one of the oldest Christian denominations. A mass christening of the Georgians, followed by the proclamation of Christianity as the state religion, took place between 325 A.D. and 337 A.D.

By the end of the fourth century, all the necessary religious books, chiefly translations from the Greek, were available in Georgia. Original literature dealing with history, including the story of the Christian martyrs and saints, appeared. The hierarchy of the Georgian Church was also established. Whereas at first the Georgian Church had been served mainly by Greek clergy, by the middle of the fifth century these had been replaced by Georgians. The head of the church was the Catholicos, the Patriarch of All Georgia. Later on, his authority was extended to Armenians and Syrians who had broken away from the Nestorians and Monophysites.

In 1783, the Russian Empress Catherine II and the Georgian Czar Irakly II signed a treaty in accordance with which Georgia accepted the protection of Russia, also a Greek Orthodox country. The treaty provided for the right of Georgia to free development of its Autocephalic Church. In 1801, Georgia was annexed by Russia and in 1811 the Catholicos of All Georgia, Anton II, was replaced and was deported to Russia by order of the commander of the Russian troops in the Causasus. The Holy Synod of the Russian Orthodox Church then abolished Georgian autocephaly and established a Russian exarchy in Georgia. This status existed for 106 years.

The February Revolution of 1917 brought about fundamental changes. A synod of the Georgian Church, held in the Cathedral of Mtskhet on March 12, 1917, restored Georgian autocephaly, which was abolished by the Holy Synod of the Russian Orthodox Church and established a Russian exarchy in Georgia. In September of the same year, a Catholicos was elected at a special synod. There was now every reason to believe that there would be broad opportunities for the independent development of the Georgian Church. But the seizure of Georgia by Soviet troops in 1921 marked the beginning of a period of persecution of the Georgian Autocephalic Church.

Following the publication of a decree separating Church and State, the Communist authorities seized the Church treasures, including valuable carpets, ancient icons, and old ornaments. Library books were removed from Georgia as "people's property." The Church lands were seized and the church buildings closed. The League of Militant Atheists was organized in one of the confiscated churches in Tiflis (renamed Tbilisi in 1937).

A wave of cruel persecution of the Church throughout Georgia followed the passage of this law. The persecution was promoted by the Communist Party, as was freely admitted by Lominadze, secretary of the Central Committee, in his report to the Third Congress of the Georgian Communist Party, held in Tiflis in 1923:

> In a number of districts the local Party organizations have set themselves the task of swiftly and fully uprooting all religious rites and cults. Because the peasantry have not received this measure with great eagerness, we have had to resort to administrative measures. The local militia have begun to close the churches. Competition between districts has commenced, and as a result up to 1,500 churches have been closed in a few months in Western Georgia alone. The practice of religious rites has been forbidden.

Of 2,455 religious buildings in pre-revolutionary Georgia, 2,355 churches, 27 monasteries, and 7 convents had been closed by 1923. Of these, the oldest and finest architecturally were the Mtskhet, built in the fifth century, the Novo-Afon and the Pischchund. The cathedral in Kutaisi was destroyed and a memorial to Lenin erected on its site. In Poti, the local church was converted into a theater; in Batum, the large church became a library for the Red Army; in Tiflis, St. George's Church was converted into a public bath; and the famous old church of Anchis-Khati became a museum. The ancient monastery Mchadis-Dzhvari became a kokkhoz storehouse. Many churches were demolished and the stones were used to build offices for the village soviets.

The barbarous treatment of the Church and the clergy by the Communist authorities aroused universal indignation. Disorders and active resistance broke out. The people were particularly indignant regarding the confiscation of the Church treasures, in the course of which sacred vessels were desecrated and stolen by the local Communists.

The extent of the loss suffered by the Georgian Church can be judged from the short but eloquent account given to a foreign correspondent by the late Catholicos Kallistrat. When he was visited in 1951 by Mr. Harrison Salisbury of the *New York Times,* who inquired about the status of the Georgian Orthodox Church, the Catholicos replied, "I shall give you some statistics from which you can draw your own conclusions. Out of 2,455 churches in Georgia there are now only 100 functioning, and the same number of priests are now practicing."

The Russian Orthodox Church, through the Moscow Patriarchiate, has recognized the autocephaly of the Georgian Orthodox Church. However, there remain only three out of the 15 former eparchies in Georgia and, as noted, there are no more than 100 churches in the whole republic. A theological seminary has been opened, but the number of students is restricted: in 1956, only seven priests were granted permission to study. There are not enough priests to satisfy the religious needs of the people. On the occasion of religious holidays, the people assemble around the ruins of the old churches to perform their religious rites. The fact that young people and even members of the Komsomol take part in such holidays has been repeatedly reported with indignation by the local press.

The assurance given by the Communists concerning their favorable attitude toward the Church are mere propaganda. The emphatic assurance given by the Moscow Patriarchate, undoubtedly on instructions from the Party, to the effect that "all religious organizations are equal in the eyes of the State" and that "the State insures the right of self-government for all religious organizations" does not accord with reality. The Church is being stamped with the imprint of the Communist regime, which compels it to further the regime's political objectives in order to mislead the free world.

It is not known what proportion of the 4 million population of the Soviet Georgia go to church. The only seminary was reported in the late 1960's to have 10 students (before the Revolution there were 400 seminarians) and educational standards are said to be low.

9

Status of Religion in Eastern Europe

Everywhere in the Red East, intellectuals and artists are fascinated by the ideal of freedom. An irrepressible spiritual revolt against Communism has broken loose. The possibility is becoming clear that God needs no war at all to destroy this system in apocalyptical manner. He is probably better served when this shame collapses from within; when nature resumes its rights; when the builders of the real empire themselves realize how their paradise has become a hell in which they are being tormented by fear, despair, distrust, terror and hate, so that they themselves destroy the work of their own hands. This process has already begun. The revolution of the young Communists, who have unmasked Communism as deceit, is on its way.

As God has no right to speak under the atheistic regime and has therefore disappeared from the consciousness of many, this revolution is being inspired less by religious than by humanistic ideas. Yet in large strata of society a spontaneous trust in the Catholic Church is still living, the latter having taken the most courageous stand against oppression. An eleventh hour co-operation with Communism would kill this trust.

The future of the Church is not safe with collaborators. The feeble shepherds and peace priests who have taken service , for whatever reason, with the oppressor, are harvesting hatred and contempt. The trust of the oppressed is with the intransigent figures, who have fearlessly denounced the sin of Communism, though in all love for the sinner, and have consistently refused to betray the poor for the sake of temporary gain. "Forgive your enemies; do good to those who hate you," was Christ's admonition to Father Werenfried van Straaten of the Flemish Norbertine Fathers, founder of the Iron Curtain Church Relief, or as he called it. A "School of Love." He traveled afar preaching and praying, as large numbers of followers sprang up in Holland, which had suffered so much from Hitler's invasion. The fields of Flanders, as has been recorded in song and story, ran red with blood as the Nazi forces swept the countryside during World War II. The Germans were thoroughly hated for their atrocities.

Then as the war ended, the Allies pushed them back into the Fatherland. But that nation, too, had suffered. Aachen, Hamburg, Bremen, Cologne, and Frankfurt were bombed corpses. To these grey skeletons of cities, filled with sickness and starvation came more than a million refugees from the Soviet zone. Some were urged to go elsewhere, many died, while hundreds who were ordered back to the Soviet committed suicide, rather than return. There were no available houses, no work, no money — just agonizing despair. Immorality, drunkenness, dope peddling developed — the chaos of hell.

Then Switzerland succumbed to his message of love, followed by France and Austria. As things settled down, Father van Straaten began an appeal among the Germans who still had their homes and were gradually recovering economically. They, too, responded generously for their less fortunate refugee brethren.

The next move was to equip 3,000 "rucksack" (knapsack) priests who were traveling all over the devastated areas offering Mass wherever they could since most of the churches were in rubble. All the stolen and destroyed chalices, ciboria and every bit of equipment for Mass had to be replaced, yet the appeals of the Bacon Priest produced a sufficient supply.

Next he organized "Building Companions" and "Christian Masons." Assisted by dedicated Belgians and Germans of exemplary character and unusual skill, great housing projects were built and chapels erected. Some 1,100 Flemish and Walloon youthful volunteers from Belgium traveled to Germany paying their own way to help in the great undertaking — a real act of forgiveness.

In 1957 the energetic priest was in the Holy Land. He found that in 12 years the Arabic-speaking Catholics had been reduced to 18,000 from 35,000 during the previous nine years. But his ever-ready group, through a mass collection of rags, bottles, metal and wastepaper, raised millions of dollars for the struggling Catholic Church in Israel.

At about the same time, under an assumed name, the apostle of charity slipped into five Iron Curtain countries, so-called People's Republics, and interviewed four Catholic bishops, the fear on their part of betrayal having been removed by trustworthy recommendations.

In the following passages Father van Straaten describes the real situation and need for the churches behind the Iron Curtain:

> It would be impossible to make concrete plans and relief programmes for the future of Eastern Europe if we had no connections with the responsible leaders of the persecuted Church. Iron Curtain Relief must not become the hobby of romantic dreamers. Our relief behind the Iron Curtain and our preparations for the day of the open doors must be guided by the most expert judges of the situation: the bishops and crypto-bishops of the East. And since only few of them are allowed to come to the West we are obliged to go to the East. So now and again one of us has to risk his liberty and his life to go and discuss the situation in the satellite states.
>
> It is very seldom that we can publish anything of these journeys as we may not bring our proteges into danger. On the other hand we feel compelled to give evidence as to everything that we have seen and heard in Eastern Europe. Especially since the ordinary tourist is not able to find out the real extent of religious persecution and is inclined to be under the impression that the Communist system has modified its anti-religious attitude. In this way the increasing travelling facilities in Eastern Europe act as a soporific, a method used deliberately by the Communists to put the Western peoples off their guard and lower their defenses against this great danger.

I myself made an excursion through five people's republics during which I visited many bishops and ecclesiastical authorities. I did not travel under my own name, and even the bishops I met did not know who I was. In every country I was accompanied by a confidential agent who opened doors and hearts for me for a confidential talk. Without the guarantee of such an agent not a single bishop can take the risk of giving to an unknown foreigner his heartfelt opinion.

After due consideration I think it possible to publish my interview with four bishops, while, of course, suppressing names of persons, places and countries and with a few modifications. In this account I shall also give some particulars which were told me during earlier meetings in Eastern Europe.

Before going into details I would like to pass on the general impression I received of Iron Curtain Church Relief, on the eastern side of the Iron Curtain. I was able to ascertain that our relief action, representing a value of millions of dollars, is useful and necessary and mostly attains the aim in view. The helping hand of our benefactors is present everywhere in Eastern Europe where the need is greatest. I myself have ridden on some of the motor vehicles given in hundreds by those who have heard my sermons, and which have become an indispensable support for numerous bishops and priests. I have visited churches that have been resurrected from their ruins by the generosity of the friends of Iron Curtain Church Relief. I have witnessed the joy of a large family when one of our gift parcels arrived by post. I have shaken hands with seminarists who were enabled to follow their vocation by an allowance from Iron Curtain Church Relief. But I was especially able to ascertain, in dozens of personal talks, how incalculably great is the moral support and the consolation that these persecuted fellow-Christians gain from our work.

It is the imperishable merit of our countless benefactors in the whole of Europe that Iron Curtain Church Relief is again and again able to strike a breach in the Iron Curtain to break the spiritual blockade of the silent Church. God alone knows the number of those who hereby were given the strength to remain faithful in this heavy affliction and to fight to the bitter and glorious end!

I met the first bishop while visiting a cathedral. He looked like a peasant in his grandfather's wedding garments. His suit was worn out, too narrow in some places and too wide in the others. There were patches on his trousers. My companion said that this was the bishop but he wore neither ring nor pectoral. His diocese, marked by death, contains many depopulated villages with burnt-out houses and half demolished churches. The people of these villages were murdered by the Communists or emigrated to the cities. The parishes where there are still people are served by itinerant priests.

The bishop invited me for a trip on the back of his heavy motorcycle to visit some churches in course of construction. A quarter of an hour later we were on our way. He had changed his clothes. He now wore a pair of yellow-brown courduroy trousers with wide black soldier's boots, a pullover, a Roman collar and a dark grey raincoat. No purple.

We drove along unbelievably bad roads and visited the first church. There were four walls without roof. It was charred black and the altar stood under a wooden lean-to. The Blessed Sacrament and a couple of praying women were in a little shed at the bottom of the tower. Between these walls Holy Mass is celebrated in the open air on Sundays. It is still a church and there is a by-law that says that a church may not be torn down as long as it is still in use. So a priest comes here every Sunday to celebrate his third Mass. He is struggling to keep this ruin standing and has been trying for five years to get permission to roof it in. He has not yet been successful but the paper war is continuing with tough persistence. He may succeed one day.

The Bishop then took me to another village. Here a church was being reconstructed. He climbed up the scaffolding and inspected the roof. He showed me
with great pride the piles of cement bags, the old bricks, the wool and the great
rolls of rusted armour for concrete that he collected in sheds and in the attics of
priests' ruined houses for the building.

He lives in the future and the present at the same time. He calls his young
priests by their Christian names. They live in dire poverty. He discusses with
them the technical and spiritual difficulties of their office as church-builders
and pastors. For years he has gone on foot, by bicycle or by motor-cycle from
priest to priest to assist them, console, finance and encourage them. A battle
has to be fought for every building licence, taking from two to six years or even
longer. If the building licence is granted there is no building material. If the
building material has been obtained there is a struggle against the claws of the
tax-collectors threatening to confiscate everything to pay arrears in taxes.
Then the building is begun, with feverish haste, often in the night by the parish
priest himself with his flock.

It is a spiritual guerilla warfare with small defeats and small victories, the only
fight—an underground fight—that is possible here. God's partisans with this
young partisan bishop as their head are no longer afraid. None of them has
joined the association of priests of peace, the priest-syndicate that provides
salary, pension and other material advantages. They have no income except
what Providence puts into their hands from day to day. They are no richer or
safer than the poor oppressed people in whose midst they were born. Many of
them have suffered imprisonment, forced labour and torture for the Kingdom
of God. Twenty priests of this diocese were murdered after the war, stabbed,
shot, burnt or hanged. Their blood was the seed for new vocations. These
young men have now become the best co-workers of this bishop.

I was on my way with him until late at night. We viewed by candlelight another
church that was roofed in and knelt before the poor tabernacle where Jesus
lives amidst His persecuted brethren. The young priest told us that the Communists were so angry at the restoration of the church that they had even
confiscated his bed and two chairs in payment of his arrears of taxes. With a
smile he showed us the straw mattress on the ground on which he sleeps.

At home with the bishop—he had only one room—we talked for a long time.
He rejects all compromise with the government because he knows that every
favour has to be paid for by a conciliatory silence with regard to some measures.
"We may not be dogs that do not bark," he said. His bright blue eyes shone in
the lamplight when I left him at dead of night.

The second bishop is dying on his feet. The patches on his worn-out cassock are
covered by the shining black overall he had wrapped himself in. His transparent face and thin hands bear the scars of the tortures he has been through. He
has long ago left his bishop's palace and found accommodation on the second
floor of his dilapidated seminary. It is one of the few seminaries in the country
that has not yet been closed. It is full to overflowing with hundreds of seminarians both boys and men from the surrounding dioceses that have lost their
seminaries. The professors look like labouring men—they still have the hard
hands and weather-beaten faces that they had in the forced labour camps from
which they were dismissed. The Rector was in prison. The vice-Rector had
been killed some years ago. The bishop is one of the uncompromising people
who would not make peace with the Communist authorities. No one in his
diocese has joined the organization of the priests of peace. Therefore his clergy
are the poorest I have met, without revenues, without fixed income and
continually exposed to Communist vexations.

There are also parts where the bishops connive at their priests joining the priests' trade union and where the severe ecclesiastical sanctions with which those who joined were punished, are not applied. There are even countries where a number of excellent priests joined were punished, are not applied. There are even countries where a number of excellent priests joined these organizations on the secret instructions of their bishops to avert worse disasters, or where entire provinces of religious orders were inscribed by their Provincials in the association of state priests.

This disastrous confusion is the fruit of Communist tactics to divide the sheep from their shepherds and to prevent contacts between the bishops themselves and with Rome. But this bishop in overalls had remained firm in his resistance, as I had already been told in many places. Yet he did not look like a fighter. He was small and old. The years of conflict with the powers-that-be and all the trouble brought upon his priests by his unyielding attitude had destroyed his health and wrecked his nerves. His hands trembled as he took me in silence to the library. There we could talk undisturbed; he was afraid there might be a microphone in his own room. The library betrayed the utter poverty of this seminary. It consisted of nothing else but a dusty collection of old fashioned priests' books of the 19th century. Only three shelves with books by Noldin, Tanquerey and a few other authors are usable. There were twenty to thirty copies of each of these works: one manual for the use of four seminarians. None of them possessed a compendium of dogmatics or moral law of his own. After their ordination they go to the appointed parishes without books. Each young priest is given at least three parishes.

Many churches and priests' houses in this diocese have been destroyed. There was method in this destruction. Flourishing Catholic provinces were in this manner demoralized and partly depopulated by mass murders. A foreign population now lives in these villages, non-Catholics that owe their new way of life to Comunism. In this way the power of the Church was broken.

In the half-light of the library the bishop unfolded a map; with short explanations he pointed out the most threatened areas. His thin hands glided over the map, sometimes with a gesture of loving protection and at other times with a violent movement as if warding off dangers. At one or two places of strategic importance he tapped nervously on the map, decisively and emphatically. This small bishop with an unbroke spirit in a decayed body was God's strategist in the spiritual guerilla war behind the iron curtain. He asked help to reconstruct three centrally situated priests' houses whence three motorized curates (even the motorcycles came from Iron Curtain Church Relief) could serve the whole country-side. He is modest in his desires. Perhaps every year a roof could be built on one parsonage—the walls were still standing—and for the present one small room made habitable. He did not require much but without our help nothing at all could be done. The people were dying without priests. With tears in his eyes he assured us that he would gladly forego all other help if we could only help him with this plan.

I promised him money and building materials for all three houses at once, although I did not yet know where I should get it, unless my readers would help me keep my promise.

This grey-haired old man is at the head of a diocese of martyrs. He showed me the death notices of his murdered priests, young men in the prime of their lives. He told me how bravely his priests spoke up before the court that condemned them. His soft voice trembled as he told of the massacring of his people during the first years after the war, of the deportations, of the lack of understanding abroad as to the gravity of the situation, of his sorrow at not being allowed by the government to go to the Holy Father for his ad limina visit, and of his fear that Rome might wish to come to a compromise with Com munism: "A treaty with the devil is impossible. We must faithfully follow the heroic way in which the great martyr-bishops, especially Cardinals Mindszenty and Stepinac have preceded us."

Then he invited us to inspect the seminary. The bare chapel, the primitive refectory, the communal washing arrangements consisting of a row of taps above a piece of gutter. The dormitories full of old bent iron beds, litter from hospitals and camps. Twenty senior seminarists sleep together in one dormitory. For the junior seminarists there are fifty beds in one room. The young priests sleep six in a room and the professors two in a room. Not a foot of space is wasted because the number of new vocations decreases with every yard of space that is lacking. There are no cupboards but only planks along the wall running the whole length of the room. There are no chairs and no washing-stands. On the beds are worn-out straw mattresses lovingly patched and re-paired by the nuns in plain clothing who look after the housekeeping. On the walls there are a cross and the compulsory portrait of the red ruler of the country. "Christ died for him too," said the bishop with a smile.

In the daytime the seminarists lived in the high, gloomy halls where their courses are given. There are old-fashioned night desks on long legs with a lid two feet wide. That is the living space of a seminarist for ten years while he is being trained for the priesthood. Downstairs in the basement the nuns live and work. Along the walls are numbered pigeonholes with the students' under-wear. Every Saturday a nun distributes the clean clothes. But many pigeonholes are empty because the parents are too poor. They are often deprived of their livelihood because their son is studying at the seminary.

It is a miracle that there are still so many vocations—most of them have to be refused on account of lack of space. For some years the children have only been allowed to enter when they are fifteen, after they have finished the atheistic state schools with their Communist educational system. They have to interrupt their studies for their military duties, which often last three years. Almost all of them persevere in their vocation.

The bishop knew the faults and shortcomings of the past. He frankly admitted that the Church with all its privileges and earthly security was in a state of spiritual corruption. He could well understand that many older priests were not able inwardly to overcome the present difficulties on account of their education and traditions: "In the tempest of this persecution an epoch and a generation are lost. Only my young priests, who have been purified in fire and water are a guarantee of the future of the Church in this country."

These young priests, the best assistants of the small bishop in his overalls, are being trained by God Himself in this proletarian seminary. They are a legion of true apostles detached from all material wants and prepared for everything. They are amused at the measures that the government invents to harass them. Even without our aid they will persevere until the fall of Communism or until their own death as a martyr. But we, on our side, must fear the punishment of God if we leave these bravest of the brave to their fate and if we are not prepared to help them whatever it may cost.

The third bishop is seventy-three years old. Kindness and goodness shine from his thin, transparent face. He is extremely modest and courteous. He lives in an annex of his palace with three aged relations. He has no domestic staff. His day begins with an hour's meditation. At half past five he celebrates Holy Mass. After breakfast, consisting of water and dry bread, he works from seven o'clock at his desk. He has no secretary. Almost every Sunday he is off to administer Confirmation in the villages. He has no car. Unaccompanied he walks for hours through the deserted lanes of his diocese, uphill and downhill, in scorching heat, through rain and snow, to preach, to confirm and to encourage his poor priests and Christians. His priests live on the alms of their parishioners. But the bishop has no parishioners of his own, so that he is the poorest of the poor.

This bishop wept when I was with him. He, too, was concerned for the existence of his seminary, for which he had no revenues at all. He would very soon need a considerable financial subsidy. Hesitatingly he mentioned the sum of 20,000 dollars.

Otherwise he would be compelled to close the seminary. There is no food for the seminarians and the people are no longer able to help. They have reached the extreme limits of their capabilities. The buildings are on the point of collapse. There is no bedding. There is one glass for two seminarists. There are no dinner things . . . they have to eat from old food tins. Starvation and disease threaten the vocation of ninety-three seminarians. Many parishes no longer have a priest so that the Church cannot do without these vocations.

The seminarians themselves are ready for any sacrifice. In this country, too, they have to do years of hard military service after their schooling. The bishop considers it a special favour of the Mother of God that not a single one of his students has as yet lost his vocation and that all of them returned from the army unscathed in soul and morals. The Holy Ghost compensates with exceptional gifts of grace for what the souls are deprived of by religious persecution. The parents of the seminarians, too, are heroic in their self-denial and the number of vocations has more than doubled in the last few years.

Open persecution is now less violent, but by means of economic force, loss of livelihood, the prohibition of church collections, unjust taxation and starvation the government endeavors to undermine the loyalty of the faithful and the constancy of the priests. Help can only come from abroad. It would be a calamity for the Church and a shame for the West if God's work in the souls of these seminarists were allowed to be destroyed because Christians in the free world did not give the help that was so indispensable.

The fourth bishop uttered an explicit warning against the dangerous temptation to search for a compromise between Church and Communism. Actually not a single Communist government—neither Polish nor Yugoslavian—is willing to meet the Church on co-existential grounds.

For the Church behind the iron curtain no *modus vivendi* with Communism is possible, only a *modus moriendi*, a long and certain death-struggle in the grasp of a system that is in its deepest being materialistic, godless and devilish. Therefore there is no point in trying to propitiate the authorities by concession or by a slavish "legality" to prove that the Church is prepared to adjust itself to the new conditions. The spirit and letter of all Communist laws are in their very essence aimed at the destruction of the Church. If the Church should obey these laws according to their spirit and letter—which are in conflict with God's inalienable rights—it would sign its own death-warrant. It is useless to try and conceal the fact that the Church in many countries of Central Europe was affected by a certain decay. Liberalism and Josephinism had struck deep wounds especially in the former Austrian-Hungarian Danube monarchy. The material security that fell to the State Church was not always advantageous for the spirit of independence with which bishops and priests ought to resist abuses. Especially where Iron Curtain Church Relief's chapel-truck mission is concerned, working among the refugees from those countries, it appeared how superficial and inadequate was the pastoral care in some of the present-day satellite states.

It is, therefore, easily understood that some of the clergy and great masses of the population were not able to withstand the persecution of the Church and that there are also bishops who only hesitatingly follow the defiant example of Cardinals Mindszenty and Stepinac. The tragedy of the unfortunate peace priests who serve with the Communist regime mostly from fear or for material gain, or to prevent worse things happening, is a proof of the confusion reigning behind the Iron Curtain.

It is not for us to throw stones from our safe position of liberty at these brethren, struggling with God and their consciences and with their own human fears, and who do not always have the strength to choose the most heroic path. They are partly the victims of their upbringing and of circumstances over which they have no control. If we can ever apply Jesus' command not to judge it is here. We must pray for them and think of them only with love and mercy. And we may wonder whether we ourselves would be prepared to sacrifice everything for our Christian convictions. But in no case may we allow ourselves to be influenced by the compromise that they have made. And it would be dangerous to allow ourselves to be tempted in the name of "legality" as they do, to consider the steadfast resistance of the Church behind the Iron Curtain as wrong and exaggerated.

There are countries in Eastern Europe where 80 or 90% of church collections and gifts have to be passed over to the state as taxation. There are countries where bishops and priests owe millions to the fiscal authorities and where time and again sums of money, cheques, chairs and cupboards, typewriters or motor-cycles are confiscated to pay these debts. Legality at all costs in such countries would mean ecclesiastical suicide.

In numbers of "show-trials" bishops and cardinals were condemned for having irregularly accepted financial support from abroad. This was called violation of currency control regulations. The unsinning West was dismayed every time a bishop, accused of this crime, admitted that he was guilty. Afterwards this admission was an incentive to mud-throwing at martyrs and confessors, representing them as reactionary and political-minded clericals and to besmirch the purity of their spiritual conflict. This fate was not even spared to Cardinals Mindszenty and Stepinac. They were called fools because they ignored regulations that infringed the rights of the Church. They were disavowed by Catholics claiming to practise pure Christianity. But the oppressed peoples of the East are grateful to them for the risks they dare to take. And more than three years after the death of Cardinal Stepinac his tomb, still covered in flowers in the cathedral of Zagreb is surrounded all day and deep into the night by throngs of praying people, who, in his example, find strength not to betray God and the Church.

The Church is fighting a battle for life or death. Legality in the Communist sense can never become the highest principle of its actions. In persecution new heroes and saints, who are prepared to obey God rather than men, are growing to full stature. They act according to their consciences and are prepared to bear the utmost consequences of it. Of course, there are victims but life continues irresistibly. Therefore we would express our confidence and respect for the bishops, priests and laymen, who in dungeons and concentration camps behind the iron curtain, are atoning for "illegal" acts. Hence we call it a shame that heroes condemned by a sham justice in the East are disapproved of by some Catholic circles in our safe West for not respecting the arbitrary and unjust laws of the red reign of terror. For this reason Iron Curtain Church Relief is feverishly seeking ever new ways and means of bringing Western aid in the first place and especially to the hard, unyielding fighters who risk their livelihood, their freedom and their lives that the Church in the East may survive the Communist terror.

Poland

Centuries ago, the Vatican had hopes that Poland would be able to "convert" the Russians to Catholicism. But the decline of Poland thwarted that hope. Poland was partitioned among several countries in 1795 and ceased to exist for more than a century.

One author commented on the situation in these words:

> The Vatican naturally followed the rise of Russia and the decline of Polish power with great interest. It recognized that it would no longer be possible to conquer Russia. . . . As a result, Poland as a factor in the expansion of Catholicism was written off, and the various partitions of Poland were not objected to by the Vatican.

At the beginning of World War II, a situation analogous to the Polish-Lithuanian one, centuries earlier, developed. Pius XII recognized Hitler's conquests in Poland. "He kept hoping that Hitler's troops would open the way for Catholicism's advance into Russia."

Germany's capitulation in 1945 terminated this hope also.

Poland, wholly Western in culture, is the East's strongest link with the West. Although the Hungarians are also a Westernized people, they do not speak a Slavic language and their culture is inaccessible to Russians, save for a sprinkling of scholars.

The Westernized Lithuanians live inside the Soviet Union itself, but they too speak a non-Slavic language. In addition, they are hardly more numerous than the two million and more Poles living in the Soviet Union from the Black Sea to the Baltic and as far east as Siberia.

It is so easy to forget. That sometimes seems to be the fate of those who are in a very real sense held captive by the Soviet Union. The August, 1974, issue of *East Europe* recalls that there are two million forgotten Poles in the Soviet Union. It says:

> There is some knowledge about the Poles in Lithuania, primarily in the Wilno region; in Byelorussia ; in the Ukraine, especially in the former Polish areas, such as Lwow, Tarnopol and Stanislawow, and in Moscow and Leningrad.

The article points out that in Moscow, St. Louis parish has about 3,000 parishioners, with more than 70 per cent of them Polish. This is a "show" church, because among those attending church services there are Catholic members of the diplomatic corps—and heads of state visiting Moscow often attend services at St. Louis Church.

Basically the parish has no financial problems. Economically, the Poles in

Moscow fare fairly well. Their standard of living, although substantially below the one in U.S.A., seems to be fairly good. In fact, almost twice as good as of their counterparts in Poland.

But in other parts of the Soviet Union, it is a different story. In Byelorussia, "all signs of Polishness were eliminated." In the Ukraine, "there are three Polish schools and three Polish churches in Lvov but only one elderly priest, attached to the Cathedral."

In Lithuania, however, *East Europe* estimates there are about 200,000 Poles; there are Polish schools, a Polish daily in Vilnius and about 10 regional papers, a large number of books in Polish but most of them represent Communist literature.

One great need of Poles attending Polish churches in the Soviet Union is prayer books. *East Europe* points out that the Soviet authorities do not permit publishing Polish prayer books, nor even importing them from Poland. When a tourist from Poland tried to bring in Polish prayer books, customs officials confiscated them at the border. As a result of this ban, there is a considerable number of handwritten copies of the old books among the faithful.

In the vast area of the Soviet Union, from the Urals to Valadivostok there is only one Polish priest to care for the spiritual needs of more than a million Poles. Thousands of Poles are in Soviet prison camps in Siberia.

East Europe says that many Poles in the Soviet Union, faced with discrimination because they are Polish, do not state their true nationality and list themselves as Russians.

There is still little information about the vast majority of the Poles living in Russia, but there is no question that their condition is very difficult, and their spiritual needs are both ignored and hindered by the authorities.

For the average Russian, Poland represents Western culture. So long as Western ways and ideas flourish in Poland and among Poles in the Soviet Union, so long as this symbiosis of East and West survives in the Soviet camp, no basic misunderstanding about the West is likely to arise in the Soviet Union.

No matter how secularized the West may have become, in Poland the biggest and perhaps the only vehicle for the Western ethos is Christianity.

The moral sense of almost all Poles is bound up with their religious sense. They have no ethical theory beyond the Christian code. Their folk culture and popular literature are also impregnated with Christianity.

Polish history was born at the baptismal font a thousand years ago, and Poland's distinctive culture grew in the air of Western Christianity.

Polish nationhood survived a century and a half of oppressive German and Russian occupation, and the Polish language survived its banishment from public and cultural life by the occupiers.

For this, Christianity can take the lion's share of the credit.

That, added to the universally-admitted fact that Marxist philosophy has fallen to low estate even among Communist Party officials, would seem to leave Christian philosophy a monopoly in Poland.

One can ask whether the country's development will be better with or without the Church's participation and one can ask the same question regarding education. We believers in Christ think that the answer is "with."

Poland's Christian faith is not merely a relic from the past which twentieth-century secularism has not succeeded in eliminating. On the contrary, the Roman Catholic Church is now stronger than at any time during the past 150 years, and statistics indicate very considerable growth during the past 30 years:

	1937	1972
Number of dioceses	20	25
Number of parishes	5,170	6,376
Number of priests	11,239	18,151
Number of churches and chapels	7,257	13,292
Number of monks and nuns	24,000	30,162

While churches in almost every part of the world bewail the decline in the number of men offering themselves for the priesthood, ordinations in Poland have for some time been double the pre-war figure. Ordinands are trained in 24 higher diocesan seminaries and 23 monastic seminaries, where at the end of 1971 there were 4,130 students in residence. There is now one priest for every 1,750 people in the country.

In Poland in the year 1974 there were 638 new priests ordained, consisting of 486 parish and 152 religious priests. From the given information by the secretary of the Polish Bishops Conference it appears, that it was the highest number of ordination in the six-year period. Recently in Poland there were 4,216 priest-candidates: 116 Franciscans, 75 Jesuits, 67 Minorits, 89 Salesians, 88 Steyler Missionaries, and 82 Pallotinians.

Although the Roman Catholic Church now dominates the Christian scene

there are about 700,000 non-Catholic believers in the country, of whom the largest number are members of the autonomous Orthodox Church which has approximately 460,000 members, four dioceses, 216 parishes, 300 church buildings and just over 200 priests. These Orthodox Christians are Polish citizens but are not of Polish nationality—their numbers being determined by the shifting frontier between Poland and the Soviet Union. On the whole they have benefited from the Communist regime and gained greater freedom than they enjoyed prior to 1945. The Polish National Catholic Church is Old Catholic—it identifies with those Catholics who at various times and in several places have separated from Rome—and has about 25,000 members, three dioceses, 41 parishes, 59 churches and chapels, 33 priests, several monasteries and one publication.

In March 1972 the Methodist Church in Poland celebrated the 50th anniversary of its foundation and reported a total membership of 4,133 in 45 congregations and preaching stations. These are served by 30 full-time pastors, of whom one is a woman, and a number of local preachers and deacons. The Lutheran Church is a good deal larger, with about 95,000 members and is divided into six dioceses. Within the dioceses are 125 parishes, 368 churches and chapels, 107 pastors and 40 deaconesses. In 1970 Lutheran religious instruction classes had 10,143 pupils. The Baptist Church had about 10,000 members in 1939 but after the war this went down to 1,800 owing to the departure of German-speaking people and the ceding of the eastern areas to the USSR. Even so, the Baptists now have about 2,300 baptized members, 1,000 children and youth, and 650 adherents. A new Baptist headquarters has been opened in Warsaw and an English-language school in Warsaw is very popular. The Baptist community is served by about 70 pastors who are working in 124 centres. There are also 4,000 Calvinists and a number of small evangelical churches.

The only significant religious minority which, for political reasons, has been denied legal status in post-was Poland is the Eastern-rite Catholic (Uniate) Church embracing the majority of Poland's estimated 200,000 Ukrainians who now live dispersed among the Polish population in the former German territories in which they were forcibly resettled in the late 1940s.

. . . At the outbreak of World War II there were 3,250,000 Jews in Poland. During the next six years some 2,900,000 of these were killed by the Nazis, and of those who survived the war a large proportion have now emigrated to Israel. . . . Now there are only 7,000 Jews in the whole of Poland, and there is organized Jewish life in only 20 towns. Warsaw and Wroclaw each have one synagogue, there are two in Cracow, several in Lodz and a number of prayer houses in other towns. There have been no rabbis since 1965.

To understand the difficulties of the Church in Poland, you need only consider that the country's whole economic and cultural life is atheistic.
Everybody must depend upon the government's atheistic institutions. The Church has only two institutions: the parish and the family.

It can hardly be a coincidence that both institutions, parish and family, have come under heavy fire from the Communists at some point or other in their quarter-century reign in Poland.

Apart from a brief interlude during the short-lived "liberalization" of 1956, relations between Catholic and political leaders in Poland were frozen in hostility for nearly two decades.

Mr. Gierek started moves in the direction of a "thaw" soon after he became Polish Communist Party chief, who on Church-State relations stated:

One can be a good Catholic, like most Poles, and be an active participant in the construction of a socialist society at the same time—as most Poles are. We have never considered the church a challenge to the Polish Communist Party or our system, and in fact the church has never tried to endanger the system or the party. We, on our part, have never tried to endanger the church. In both our practice today and our endeavors for the future, we will not attempt to minimize the role of the church in Poland. It is a basic assumption of our government that the church is a substantial force in this nation (that) can participate in keeping moral values and virtues that are common to all people irrespective of their faith.

First he set two major national priorities: improvement of the economy and living standards, and conciliation between the regime and Polish society, which was then dissatisfied at all levels. The latter goal included reconciliation with the Roman Catholic Church.

Early gestures in this direction included an easing of taxation and the writing off of large unpaid back taxes previously levied on church assets. It also included restoration of church titles to hundreds of sequestrated buildings and lands.

On its side, the Vatican appointed six long-time Polish "administrators" as full-fledged bishops of dioceses in the western territories.

This, in effect, was recognition of Poland's western (Oder-Neisse) frontier, already acknowledged by West Germany in the treaty concluded with Poland earlier in 1972.

The Polish government was miffed at the Vatican for creating new dioceses within former German territories now governed by Poland because the government wanted the Vatican only to place the old original dioceses under Polish bishops. Previous recognition by West Germany of Poland's control over those territories, the Vatican had named Polish bishops to be only administrators of the dioceses in those areas.

In fact, Church officials both in Poland and in the Vatican had been expecting the Polish regime to protest the creation of the new diocesee, but a statutory three-month period passed without a protest by the government and the new dioceses acquired legal status before Polish law.

For the Polish government, this was a major step, satisfying, in fact, its principal condition for opening formal relations with the Vatican.

Both the Polish Communist regime and the Holy See still regard each other with caution and skepticism, which is not surprising after all the years of mutual intransigence.

"We are not the Church of silence," the Polish bishop said. "We are the Church of hard work."

Although bishops and priests can speak loud and clear from the pulpit, the Church in Poland remains a Church of silence; insofar as all ordinary means of communicating with the broad Catholic public are denied it.

And although the vast majority of Catholics in Poland belong to the working class—and indeed make up the very working class which is supposed to rule in Communist Poland—there are plenty of Catholic professional people and scholars.

Polish priests, almost to a man, are working from early morning till evening, and in many cases till late at night. Committed lay Catholics work with the priests day and evening in Poland's numerous marriage guidance centers.

Other lay persons are at the Church's catechetical centers early in the morning to welcome the children. Virtually all these lay people are unpaid volunteers.

Because printing presses and even mimeograph machines are forbidden to the Church in Poland, dozens of nuns in every diocese are busy all day typing hundreds of carbon copies of the most innocuous material such a catechetical sylabuses and parish assignments.

To get a copy of one bishop's pastoral letter into every pulpit in his diocese, some 400 copies were typed by nuns working day and evening. This is far from an isolated instance. It is wholly commonplace.

Poland seems, like ancient Egypt, to echo with Pharaoh's rude command: "Let them be oppressed with works."

Father Wladyslaw Piowarski, a professor at the Catholic University of Lubin, placed Polish priests into three groups: the highly educated, conscientious ones ("unfortunately, this group of priests is not numerous in Poland, and in general they are young priests"); the "routine priests" of traditional mentality ("really constituting and enormous mass"); and "the third group, the priests—pardon me for saying it—who are materialized and laidized."

Father Stanislaw Glowa, a Jesuit theology professor in Warsaw, commented on Father Piowarski's second group.

> When one speaks with the priests making up this group the picture which unfolds is indeed tragic. They believe that Western Catholicism is in the process of seeking new religious forms; that the vernacular is introduced into the liturgy because Catholicism there is in a state of decomposition. Since so many people still attend church these priests believe no innovations are necessary in Poland, not even desirable. This conviction is deep-rooted.

Poland's primate is criticized by some of the clergy and the laity for being slow in introducing council reforms.

> People from abroad are naturally impressed by the dynamism of the faith here. But there are problems. The post-conciliar period is here, yet the liturgican movement is practically dead. The canon still is in Latin. This is saddening for us. Our cardinal is a traditionalist. He says his own Mass in Latin, with his back to the faithful. He does not concelebrate either.

Poles familiar with the primate's views and problems insist that the Polish Church's postcouncil record is much better than it sometimes is made to appear.

As for the liturgical movement, they admit that Poland lags behind some other countries but they assert that this is beyond the primate's control. With printing and paper under strict government rationing, plans were made to have new missals printed in France. They were printed and all could have been delivered to Poland in a big truck. Instead Polish Church authorities were told the missals would have to be sent one at a time to names on a series of lists provided by the government.

A seminary professor noted that there is much more to the spirit of the council than a change in liturgical forms.

> Remember too that the communications available to the primate are primitive compared to the supersophisticated systems in your country. He has no daily newspaper, no radio, no television. All he can do is speak from the pulpit. But he speaks well and bravely.

The primate's sermons encourage Catholics and anger those who seek the Church's demise.

The Polish priest's day usually begins at 5 A.M. Within half an hour he is in church, where he and his colleagues alternate saying Mass and hearing Confessions, weekday or Sunday. (Frequent Confession remains rooted in Poland's Catholic life). The last morning Mass on weekdays is at 8 o'clock.

Before the last Mass is over, some priests have breakfasted and are at work preparing catechetical instruction or even, in some cases, giving it. In most parishes, the teaching of religion goes on morning, afternoon, and (for older children and adults) evening.

Then there is the normal parish work as well.

In one diocese, priests and nuns, plus a sprinkling of lay persons, give a total of 12,759 hours of catechetical instruction weekly. About half the priests living in that diocese are engaged in catechetical work, most of them for 20 or 25 hours a week. Some priests in the diocese teach catechism about 40 hours a week, and some say this holds true throughout Poland.

Catechism lessons are virtually the only means allowed the Church in Poland to reach the young. But coverage is almost total.

In the Warsaw archdiocese, well over 90 per cent of the primary school children attend catechism classes. In another diocese the figure is 95 per cent for primary school children and 77 per cent for youths in secondary and trade schools.

Such high attendance at religious studies should be a constant source of concern for Poland's Communist authorities, since atheistic Communism regards religion as a diminution of man and of society.

Attempts by the authorities to control the curriculum of catechism classes met early shipwreck on the same shoals of Church authority and Catholic solidarity. Every year the state asks parish priests how many students they have when they meet, and who teaches them. On firm orders from the bishops, the pastors refuse to give that information.

State education officials who seek to examine the catechism classrooms are refused admission, although fire inspectors and health department officials are admitted.

The latest stratagem of Communist authorities has been to switch the schedules of catechism classes. One pastor, in confirming that this had happened to him already, said one of his assistants had to adjust to nine such switches in a single school year at another parish.

Polish Communist law restricts organized religious activity to churches or parish houses. But there are just not enough churches and parish houses in Poland to accommodate nine out of ten of the nation's children, wholly because government policy prevents the construction of churches and parish houses.

As a result, catechism is taught not only in the churches and rectories but in private houses as well. In one diocese, one-third of the catechism classes are held in private homes.

When religion was banished from the schools in 1961, nuns and male religious were forbidden by law to teach catechism. The law was ignored, again upon instructions from the bishops.

Some religious were in fact fined, and lost clothing or radios to the police in lieu of ready cash. But in many cases parents of children they were teaching came forward to pay.

That same principle obtains to this day in Communist Poland. It is the parents, principally working-class, who support the parishes and through the parishes support what may be the most formidable system of catechetical instruction in the world.

The Polish bishops have regarded the government's new education law as the most formidable threat to the Catholic religion since Communists took power in the wake of World War II.

The government's education reform law, according to Church officials, would make it humanly impossible for Polish priests to continue their catechetical work or, more exactly, for children to attend catechism classes. The work of religious instruction has been the most time-consuming task of Polish priests, keeping them in makeshift classrooms for as much as 40 or more hours a week.

Poland's bishops have urged the nation to resist—whatever the consequences—the official atheism that the Communist regime imposes daily through the mass media, the schools and numerous channels of economic and social life.

A pastoral letter of the Polish bishops on government-imposed atheism marked a startling reversal in the outwardly conciliatory policy both Church and State seemed to have been pursuing in Poland recently:

> We must defend ourselves, our families and the Whole nation against the secularism and atheism that are being imposed upon us. We must rally courageously to defense of the life of religion.
>
> Have the courage to confess Christ and His Church publicly, in school, at the university, at work, in the office. Do it without thinking of the consequences

you might suffer.

If you believe deeply within the four walls of your home, don't lack the courage to confess Christ in public, even when you must pay the price and undergo some sacrifice.

It sometimes happens that religious people lack the courage to go to Church, to marry in Church, to baptize their child, to have him make his First Communion, to admit a priest on a pastoral visit. Sometimes they are afraid to hang on the wall of their own home a cross or a picture of the Blessed Virgin.

Why? Are they afraid of what their colleagues may think? What the neighbors or their acquaintances may think? Are they afraid of endangering their social or economic situation?

Believers are treated as second-class citizens for the simple reason that they believe.

If some have the right to atheize the nation against its will, against the will of Catholic parents and of young people themselves, against the constitution which guarantees everyone freedom of conscience and of confession, then Catholics have all the more right to defend themselves against this abuse of the law!

We have not only the right, but the moral and religious duty to defend the faith, Christ's Church, Christian morality, our traditions and our Polish culture.

But this isn't all. We must become apostles of our surroundings. In the family, at work, we must remember Christ's words "Go into the whole world and announce the good news to all creation."

The bishops reminded parents that they have the right to decide the religious education of their children, but that atheism 'is imposed by school programs.' They urged parents to protest against movies and television programs that 'by their subject or by their tendencies make fun of God Himself, ridicule the Church, mock Christian morality.'

'We must react with courage for the truths of faith are presented falsely, turned to ridicule or criticized.'

Recalling the defeat of Sweden's anti-papal armies by Polish defenders at the monastery of Jasna Gora in 1655, the bishops said: "We need only remember that they teach us, above all, fidelity, courage and valor in the struggle to preserve our nation's most sacred values."

The bishops called divorce, abortion and alcoholism "a deluge a hundred times more dangerous than the Swedish deluge," which had all but submerged Poland in the 17th century.

... You well know where these perils come from. They come from the propagation of atheism and of secularism. Alas, spiritually weak men are succumbing to them.

A programmed atheism is spreading, although not always with success. We must be aware of this. It is growing in school instruction, as in the whole system of materialistic education, which arrogates to itself full exculsivity of rights in this domain, paying no attention to the rights of the Catholic family and of the Church.

Atheism is pursuing its march in social contacts. There is an attempt to convince society, by every means, that the atheist is the very personification of progress.

The style of life is secularist; the family, education and the school are secularist;

art and culture are secularist; the press, books movies and television are secularist. In sum, everything is secularist.

In the joint pastoral letter the bishops voiced their fear that legislation to prolong the school day is designed to prevent attendance at catechism class and create "a monopoly for atheistic education."

If the bill to lengthen the school day is passed, it would bite deeply into the high-powered catechetical program to which Poland's bishops have given priority for years. Communist officials on a local level have tried to upset the catechetical program by switching students from morning classes to after-noon classes and vice versa, but catechetical officials have simply adjusted their own rosters accordingly. The new legislation would make such adjust-ments much more difficult.

The country's bishops, after warning that the bill was designed to drive out religious education and give atheistic education an unchallenged monopoly, urged Catholic parents:

You must not, you cannot, allow this! They are your children!

Education belongs to the nation, to the family, to society and not to a simple party, to a clique or group whose action is deplorable, even destructive and inimical.

The bishops asserted that the legislation has been drafted as if there were no believing Catholics in Poland, as if our country had no Christian history, as if there were no Church in the history of our nation or in education, as if Catholics played no part in the life of contemporary Poland.

As far as Poland's problems are concerned one has to have a general view of Poland and Polish history stressing the deep religious faith that permeates the thousand years of Polish national life, the spirit of tolerance and Poland's dedication to freedom.

Medieval Poland opened her frontiers to the Jews. Persecuted in other lands they found protection under the Polish crown. Later when other countries led religious wars, Poland was known for her tolerance. These are glorious pages of history!

Instead of conquest Poland had a freely accepted union with Lithuania; she was a pioneer of the parliamentary system of government; she had defended Europe from the onslaught of the Tartars and Turks. These were wonderful *Gesta die per Polonos*.

The old Polish motto: "For your liberty and ours," was the battle cry under which Poles fought in their many uprisings after Poland's partitions, under which they also fought many battles on so many fronts of the Second World War. The spirit of independence still lives among the Polish people.

The great majority of the Polish people are Catholics and deeply attached to their religious faith, therefore, one cannot talk about Poland without speaking about the Church, about Cardinal Wyszynski who has played and is still playing such an important role in the land of Polish forefathers.

He knows how to defend the Polish faith and Church with dignity and strength in the best interest of the Polish people. He also knows how to seek better relations with the state, relations based on mutual justice and respect.

Stefan Cardinal Wyszynski, who has become a true spiritual leader of his people, would gain a new title of greatness. But any improvement of mutual relations calls for good will on the part of the State

The Polish constitution proclaims religious freedom and says that the

Roman Catholic Church and followers of other religions "may freely dis-
charge their religious functions." Yet two jeeps of uniformed militiamen are
parked around-the clock at the exit of the national Marian shrine at Czestochowa. The policemen halt and search all cars to make sure that no one is
smuggling out a replica of the "Black Madonna" image for use in diocesan
processions elsewhere in Poland.

One of the most striking instances of the idea of "separation" as understood behind the Iron Curtain is provided by Poland. The Polish Constitution of July 1952 provides, in Article 70, par. 2, as follows: "The Church is
separated from the State. The principles of the position of religious bodies,
are determined by laws." There is, first of all, an obvious contradiction
between the first and the second sentences. This contradiction was pointed
out by the Polish bishops in a commentary of theirs dated February 11, 1952.
But under date of February 9, 1953, a decree was issued which confirmed
their suspicions that the second sentence concealed an intention of ham-
stringing the church. By the terms of this decree, the Polish Communist-
controlled regime made all ecclesiastical appointments dependent upon the
approval of the government's own agencies. This decree also authorized the
state agencies to remove priests from their posts without even giving any
reason. It also laid down that any act of ecclesiastical jurisdiction was dependent upon the approval of the secular authority. These ecclesiastical acts
could therefore be declared void.

In any non-Communist regime such a law clearly is incompatible with the
concept of "separation." At one point even in Poland it was supposed that the
constitution of 1952 preserved the Catholic Church and other religious
bodies from the kind of government meddling envisaged in the decree of
February 9, 1953. In their protest of the following May 8, the Polish hierarchy were able to cite President Bierut himself against it. The President of
Poland had taken a leading role in drafting the constitution, and at the time
of the debates he declared that the separation clause signified "the Church
has its own autonomous organization and structure." How, asked the
bishops, can this be reconciled with Art. 70, par. 2 of Bierut's constitution?

The contradiction was too obvious to be faced down even by the Communists who are past masters at ignoring uncomfortable facts. They argued
in rebuttal that the constitution could not tolerate the misuse of religion for
purposes endangering the state. This being the case, it was held, the Government has the right to exercise over-all supervision of ecclesiastical appointments, including the right to remove those church officials it found
objectionable. This at least was the stand taken by the government radio.
The informational program "Wavelength 49 Replies" frankly admitted on
the Warsaw Home Service of April 14, 1953 that it had received many letters
on the subject of freedom of religion in the new popular Polish democracy.
It hastened to point out the limitations of this freedom:

> Our people's state insures freedom of religion for all its citizens and in no way
> hampers the activities of the church which serves to meet the religious needs of
> the population. But in guaranteeing these rights, our people's state must also
> closely watch that they are not exploited for political work hostile to the state
> and the nation—espionage and diversionary activities which have nothing to
> do with religion, work which even insults religious feelings.

In other words, the religious-freedom clauses, and notable the separation provisions, offer feeble, if any, defense against the anti-religious policies of the regime. The ordinary general laws protecting a state against spies and revolutionaries are deemed insufficient. The Catholic Church and other religious bodies are viewed *a priori* as centers of reaction and as such permanent natural menaces that special legislation is necessary. The broadcaster continued, referring specifically to the decree of February 9, 1953:

> The Council of State decree on church appointments was aimed at making impossible the exploitation of religion for anti-state work. This decree does not hamper the priests in fulfilling their religious duties. It merely reduces freedom to harm the nation and the state and hampers traitors who are unworthy of fulfilling the duties of a priest. This is not interference with internal church matters. Our state neither interfered nor intends to interfere with internal church matters. But guarding over the interests of the nation and taught by sad experience, the state has the duty to insist on the right of checking on and approving candidates put forward by the Church hierarchy.

This interpretation of Article 70 virtually nullifies the value of the constitutional guarantees of religious freedom, as implied in the "separation" clause. This argumentation can be applied at will to any other phase of the religious life of the nation. If such a decree is possible, what other decrees having the force of law are not possible, equally nullifying religious freedom?

It should be added that interference in internal church matters is not confined to the Catholics, or only to Poland. The Orthodox and Protestants also have experienced this interference, perhaps to a greater degree. State decrees have usually been followed and supplemented by the "free" decision of the church communities. In Hungary, for instance, both the Lutheran and Calvinist communities were reorganized in this fashion. New regulations were pushed through by government pressure to facilitate the removal of opposition churchmen and their replacement by more docile personalities. It is, of course, denied that this domination by the Communist government in any way violates "separation."

One of the differences between the constitutions of the satellite governments and that of the Soviet Union of 1936 is the absence of the provisions of famous Art. 124, which guaranteed "freedom for anti-religious propaganda," while pointedly neglecting to concede the corresponding right to religious propaganda. However, echoes of this idea are not entirely absent in several constitutions.

Art. 70, par. 1 of the Polish Constitution of 1952, after guaranteeing the freedom of religious bodies to perform their religious functions, goes on to say, on the other hand: "It is forbidden to coerce citizens from participation in religious activities or rites. It is also forbidden to coerce anybody to participate in religious activities or rites." This sounds innocent enough, but what does "coercion" mean? Any positive effort on the part of the bishops or priests to stimulate the faithful in the exercise of their religious duties and in manifesting their religious convictions runs the risk of being called "coercion" and therefore illegal.

During this discussion of this article in Parliament, Deputy Jodlowski made a surprising interpretation. He declared:

> Any activity, from any quarter, restricting religious cult, would be contrary to the new constitution. But at the same time, any activity to draw people into religious practices would also run counter to the constitution. Here we have in

mind any attempt on the part of the clergy to evoke in people's minds a demand for religious schools, or for religious ceremonies, services or celebrations.

This is a curious definition of religious freedom, but it corresponds faithfully to Art. 124 of the Soviet Constitution. Though in Poland the Communists did not dare to say it in so many words, it is clear that for them it is not "coercion" when the government inspires violent press attacks against the religious convictions of believers.

The Communist idea of "coercion", when applied to certain activities of religious groups, fits in with their central policy of striving to limit religion's role in the life of the nation to purely liturgical matters. Marxism has accorded to religion the domain of liturgical worship as its last sanctuary. Every other aspect of human life and culture it reserves to itself. When religious leaders step out of their alloted sphere, uninvited by the government, they are likely to be charged with using religion for political purposes.

Many of the present Communist-controlled regimes have aided in the reconstruction of damaged churches and in the building of new ones. They have even authorized and supported seminaries for training students for the ministry. But it is "coercion" when the priests so trained try to educate the youth in the traditional Christian virtues. It is even worse "abuse" when the religious leaders fight for religious instruction in the schools. "The abuse of freedom of conscience and religion for purposes endangering the interests of the Polish People's Republic," says paragraph three of the Art. 70, "is punishable." As the interests of the people's democracies is the construction of a Marxist society and the creation of a Marxist culture, it can be understood how wide an application this provision can have.

Externally, Polish Catholicism seems to be thriving as much as ever.

Religious orders have not been suppressed. There are 41 men's orders and congregations and 101 women's. Friars and nuns in religious dress are encountered along the street, on buses and in shops.

Some churches have as many as 18 Masses on Sunday and drop-in visitors often so crowd a church during the week that one would think a major religious service was taking place.

Religious instruction has been taken out of the schools, but is permitted at some 17,000 officially certified "catechism points' throughout the country after school hours.

There are nearly 50 diocesan and religious seminaries where 4,000 seminarians are studying for the priesthood. In Warsaw, the Ministry of Public Instruction and Higher Education finances the Catholic Theological Academy which was established after the government eliminated the theological faculties at the state universities of Warsaw and Cracow. In the eastern part of Poland the Catholic University of Lublin, financed and operated by the Church, celebrated its 50th anniversary in 1968.

In an information bulletin the official Polish news agency, *Interpress*, after giving a lengthy if necessarily incomplete review of religion both before and during the communist era, concluded on an optimistic note. For one thing, the agency declared that the Polish United Workers Party (Communist) believes that "full settlement" of church and state relations is indispensable in the interests of each. The agency also said there are no "basic differences of interests between the Roman Catholic Church as a denominational institution and the ruling Marxist-Leninist party."

All of these external signs give an encouraging impression of the Church's situation two and a half decades after it was confronted with a Communist-governed Poland. They do not automatically mean that all goes well for the Polish Church. Nor do they mean that Communism has given up trying to dominate Catholicism in Poland.

"We Poles have a saying that Cracrow was not built at once" an attitude towards the layman from Lower Silesia remarked. "The communists remember this in their attitude towards the Church. They realize that 25 years is too short a time for Catholicism to die in a country which has been Catholic ever since the nation was born 1,000 years ago."

> Their strategy is the same, but communist tactics have become more sophisticated in keeping with the times. Arrests, the threats of firing squads, Siberia—all that is passe. Everything is subtle now. The main tactic is the classic divide-and-conquer—to split Catholics into opposing groups; to separate the clergy from the episcopate, diocesan priests from the religious, the bishops from one another, lay people from the hierarchy; most of all, to isolate the primate from everyone else.

The primate of Poland, Stefan Cardinal Wyszynski, has been the spearhead of the Polish Church's struggle for survival in the Communist era. Handsome and vigorous, he looks and acts like a leader of the Roman Catholic Church. In 1953 he was arrested by the Communists and confined to a monastery in the mountains at the southeast corner of Poland until freed during the "Polish October" of 1956, a kind of "minirevolution" against the oppressions of Stalinist times.

Cardinal Wyszynski's popularity with the Communist government has not improved noticeably. At the end of 1968 he was permitted to travel to Rome for a brief visit after being denied a passport by Polish authorities for three years. The Communists consider him inflexible and unbending in the face of "political realities."

In one of those Polish paradoxes, Cardinal Wyszynski is losing popularity with some of the Catholic clergy and laity. His Catholic critics admire him for his defense of the Church. But they argue that he actually is hurting the development of Catholicism by being overly slow in permitting Vatican II reforms to be applied to the Church in Poland.

The entire episcopate, including Poland's second member of the sacred college, Karol Cardinal Wojtyla of Cracow, remains united around the primate defending him from both attacks from Communist quarters and from criticism by some Catholics. But anti-Church elements seek out and magnify the differences of opinion among Polish Catholics, endeavoring to spread them into a picture of disunity.

For example, the two-week visit at the end of May, 1969 by Father Pedro Arrupe, general of the Society of Jesus, was seized upon by those interested in splitting the ranks of Catholics. They encouraged the impression that dissension exists between the Jesuits and the primate—and maybe even between Rome and the primate.

As a matter of fact, the Polish Jesuits do have a problem with getting the primate's full endorsement on a catechetical project of theirs: a series of catechisms for different age groups and a separate book of instructions for catechists.

Writing catechisms is nothing new for Poland's Jesuits. In pre-Communist times, Jesuit Father Joseph Siryek of Cracow wrote a catechism that was used widely. Along with 4 million other Poles, he died in the Nazi extermination center of Auschwitz, about 25 miles from Cracow. He was one of nearly 100 Jesuits and 2,000 priests, who were victims of World War II in Poland.

In 1969 the Jesuits of Cracow completed part of their new catechetical project. They produced first- and second-grade catechisms, whose preface contained a dedication to the Jesuit priest who died at Auschwitz. Each catechism is a handsome booklet with an easy-to-read text and attractive line drawings.

The two catechisms were approved by Cardinal Wojtyla, archbishop of Cracow, and by the Polish episcopal conference. Approval then was obtained from the government for the printing of 10,000 copies of each one. These have been printed and are in use, and the Jesuits are seeking permission from the government to print 10,000 more.

But the primate held up publication of the supplemental book which gives detailed instructions to catechists on how to teach each lesson. He also blocked the third- and fourth-grade catechisms while in preparation.

It is not a matter of a Polish version of a Dutch-type catechism. There are no theological questions involved in the Jesuit project. It is theologically sound.

Cardinal Wyszynski's reservations are based on the Western methodology and approach used in the instruction book. He told the Jesuits that, for psychological reasons, it would not be appropriate to publish the instruction book at this time.

The catechism problem was blown out of proportion by *Pax*, a self-styled Catholic lay organization which has been a helpmate of the Communist government since 1945. *Pax* did its best to make the Jesuit's catechetical effort appear to be a major issue in the Polish Church. As a result, the exploitation of the catechism problem by *Pax* "gave some tension to the Jesuit general's meeting with the primate," according to a reliable source.

Paradoxical as it might seem, *Pax* used elaborate and extensive coverage of Father Arrupe's visit as the other principal means of seeking to bring discord within the Church.

Father Arrupe was given VIP treatment. The general of the Franciscan friars, Father Constantine Koser, was in Poland at about the same time as the Jesuit general but he passed practically unnoticed.

Pax correspondents followed the Jesuit general's entourage in their car. Each day they provided detailed reports on what he said and did in the *Pax* daily newspaper, *Slowo Powszechne (Universal Word)*.

The subtlety of *Pax's* activity was explained this way by a Polish Jesuit:

> Father Arrupe always made clear in his public pronouncements that there was no disagreement between the Jesuits and the episcopacy. But in nuances and in between the lines the Pax reports tried to indicate there was a conflict. It would refer to Father Arrupe as being *progressive*, for instance. Pax always makes little holes like this which it can deepen in order to split the Church.

Pax itself is a paradoxical organization.

It describes itself as an association of Catholic laymen but it has been condemned by the hierarch and has been aided and comforted by the government. When *Pax* celebrated its 20th anniversary in November, 1965, its principal officers were received by Wladyslaw Gomulka, the first secretary of the Polish United Workers Party.

Pax was formed by a group of wartime underground fighters who came primarily from a paramilitary organization commanded by Boleslaw Piasecki. The Soviets, on entering Poland from the east, arrested Piasecki and sentenced him to death. After eight months in prison in Lublin, he was released in mid-1945.

"His freedom probably was tied to a promise to collaborate," according to a Warsaw Catholic resident whose leg was crippled in one of the three war-time anti-nazi uprisings of the city's civilian population. "But at the same time, Piasecki probably was convinced that collaboration with the communists was a good idea."

Piasecki, father of a son and three daughters, a deputy in the *Sejm* (Parliament) and a wealthy man, has headed *Pax* since its founding. A Stalinist hardliner, he (and *Pax*) ran into difficulties during the de-Stalinization epoch, but quickly rallied to become stronger than ever.

Pax's propagandizing technique is as smooth as a new typewriter ribbon and as pious as the sales pitch of a Bible salesman. In July, 1945 when *Pax's* founding fathers were preparing to go into business, they presented the new, Communist, Soviet-backed government with a memorandum of their beliefs and aspirations. In the memorandum they declared:

> We stand for the Christian *Weltanschauung* (outlook on the world). We assume there exists absolute and everlasting criteria of good and evil, of truth and falsehood, of beauty and ugliness; and we set up the following hierarchy of aims to be pursued by the individual: God, humanity, nation, family. As a belief in man's life for extratemporal reality lies at the foundation of our view of the world, we strive to provide such material and cultural circumstances that the human personality might thrive in them and we profess it our main concern.

Pax's founding fathers at the same time gave a blanket endorsement to all the "radical, social and economic reforms" of the fledgling Communist government. They also acknowledged that "relations between the Polish nation and the nations of the Soviet Union should feature a neighborly friendship and a policy of the mutually outstretched hand.

> We are for the socialist system, so in that sense we are pro-government. But we have proposed alternative programs. We believe socialism should not be an instrument of communist atheism. We are fighting for a neutrality, a laicism of socialism. We are fighting for equal rights of Catholics in the sense of equal opportunity in government offices, in promotions, etc.

Boleslaw Piasecki, the chairman and founding father of *Pax* regularly attends Mass with his family at the Dominican church of St. Hyacinth in Warsaw's Old Town district. From time to time he arranges solemn novenas for himself and his associates.

"Maybe he does this for appearance sake," a Warsaw resident says. "But I can't be sure. I can't see inside his conscience."

Pax has 10,000 members and a network of 100 regional and local offices. Stefanowicz says 100,000 people regularly attend meetings, including 2,000 of the 17,000 priests in Poland. No priests are members of *Pax*, he admits.

> "About 400 to 500 priests have associated themselves with *Pax* in one way or another," a Polish prelate estimates. "Some of them have been black mailed by the communists. Perhaps during the war they collaborated or, while in concentration camps, they were not particularly heroic. Others do it for the money. Some want to build or restore their churches.

"These 'peace priests' do not make any offense as such against canon law.
The Church could impose warnings or suspensions, but that might do more
harm than good. In any case the influence of the 'peace priests' is marginal."

As for the *Pax* members, the prelate says: "There are some idealists in *Pax*
who think collaboration is good for the Church, for the Polish people, for the
nation. But most of those in *Pax* are there because they think it is good for
themselves."

Pax has gained political power by its religious activities and has grown rich
by its business operations.

It dominates the Catholic publishing field in Poland. *Pax* publishes three
weekly newspapers and a monthy periodical as well as *Universal Word*, the
only Catholic daily newspaper in the country. *Universal Word* has a circulation of 80,000 to 90,000 on weekdays and around 200,000 on Sundays. It is
sixth in circulation of all Polish newspapers. The Communist Party daily,
Trybuna Robotnicza (Workers Tribune) in Katowice is first with a 700,000
circulation.

Pax also is the largest publisher of religious books, making available the
thinking of prominent Catholic writers and theologians of the West. This is
one activity which gets great praise from Catholics who otherwise have few
good words for *Pax*.

"In religious efforts and activities in Poland," a theology professor says,
"the *Pax* people are quite orthodox and many fine books have been trans-
lated by them. Without *Pax* the printing of books would be very limited."

Pax sends researchers and scholars abroad on completely legitimate study
projects. A cynical layman says such activity is only window-dressing. "*Pax* is
like a botanical garden. It has some beautiful flowers to show off under glass.
But there is a lot behind the scenes no one gets a peek at."

The Ministry of Finance allows *Pax* and the two other Catholic lay organizations to operate commercial and industrial enterprises and to use the
profits (after 30 per cent state taxes) for financing their activities.

Under the name of *Veritas (Truth), Pax* operates more than 40 religious
article shops throughout the country. In nearly 50 industrial plants *Inco*, a
Pax holding company, produces consumer goods ranging from cosmetics to
Christmas tree lights. One of four *Pax* plants is the Cracow area for instance
makes shoe polish and has 220 employees.

It is big business. An informed source estimated annual production of the
Pax enterprises at more than a billion zlotys ($250 Million at official rate).
This compares with 200 million zlotys for the output of the Christian Social
Association, a second lay organization, and 140 Million zlotys for the Libella
enterprises which are run by laymen associated with *Znak (The Sign)*.

All these commercial and industrial operations of the lay organizations are
part of the national plan. Raw materials are bought from the state; the
output, when exported, is handled by the state. Without state approval such
operations would not be possible. Similarly, everything from the formation
of an association of laymen to the publication of a prayer book requires state
permission.

The three lay organizations call themselves independent but two; *Pax* and
the Christian Social Association lean in the direction of the state while *Znak*
leans toward the Church.

Nearly 90 per cent of the seats in the Polish *Sejm* are allotted to the three
political parties (United Workers, Farmers and Democrats). The remainder

are distributed among social groups, such as the League of Polish Women and trade unions. Twelve of the 49 seats available to the social entities have been assigned to the three Catholic lay organizations, with *Pax* and *Znak* getting five each, and the Christian Social Association, two.

The allocation of seats to the Catholic lay organizations has taken place only since 1957.

> "Twelve seats in such a large Parliament of a Catholic nation is not much," a *Znak* member observed. "Still it is better than nothing. Besides when the allocation first started there were 15 Catholic seats and all were given to *Znak*. *Pax* was having its troubles with the Communist leadership at the time and the Christian Social Association just was being formed."

Janusz Makowski, vice president of the Christian Social Association and a Catholic deputy for many years, says there are 800 laymen in the organization, including some who are Protestants and Orthodox. There are no priests. The association publishes the monthly *Zai Przeciw (For and Against)* with a circulation of 50,000. "We could sell more, " Makowski says affably, "but there's no paper and no permission." They also publish a monthly for Poles overseas. It is said in Polish Church circles that the chief *raison d'etre* of the Christian Social Association is to weaken the hostility of overseas Poles to the Communist regime in Poland.

The Christian Social Association shares the religious articles market with *Pax*. Its *Ars Christiana* (Christian Arts) company has 60 shops which sell everything from vestments to "hundreds of thousands of prayer books a year," and publishes high-quality books about Poland's artistic and historic churches. The *Ars Christiana* income is the association's main financial source.

Makowski says the association is established in 14 large cities and each month arranges discussion groups in nearly 50 Polish cities on social questions such as emigration from country to city, social assistance and civic education.

> The aim of our association is to organize Christians for work in the public life of a Marxist-governed Poland. We accept the political, economic and social principles of Marxism, but we cannot accept the materialist doctrine and Marxist philosophy. In religious questions we submit to the hierarchy but only in matters of dogma and morals. We are independent of the Church in political and social questions.
>
> Not all relations with all bishops are cordial. We are criticized by the cardinal-primate and some bishops. In the West, Catholics exist in many parties. We are committed to the building of socialism in Poland and we with the Church to be neutral in political questions. But laymen can be committed.
>
> When Pope John received the Polish bishops for the first time in 1963, he made a speech in which he said Wroclaw (called Breslau by the prewar Germans) was a Polish city which had returned to the mother country. This was a political act on his part and the Germans quickly protested.
>
> Pope John spoke warmly of Poland to the bishops. He said he found in Polish History an inspiration for his own vocation as a priest. He said that he had read Polish literature as a boy and was a compatriot of Col. Francesco.

After the "Polish October" of 1956, *Znak* established Catholic Intelligentsia Clubs in some 20 cities but only five were registered officially by the state—Warsaw, Cracow, Wroclaw, Poznan and Torun. Registration was a means used by the state to limit the movement's activity. In 1959 a monthly publication, *Wiez (The Bond)* was started in Warsaw. *Wiez* also publishes books which deal more with social economic questions than religious ones.

The nonpublishing activity of the *Znak* movement involves the operation of a certain number of small businesses which, through a company called *Libella*, produce chemicals, precision metal parts and a few other things.

There are approximately 3,000 members in the *Znak* movement. The weekly newspaper has a circulation of 50,000 but it was "fined" 10,000 copies not long ago when its editor, along with 33 other persons, signed a very general declaration calling for cultural freedom. Thus, *Tygodnik Powszechny* may print only 40,000 copies but it is estimated that at least four persons read each copy.

The monthly *Znak* has a circulation of 7,000; *Wiez*, 6,000.

Waclaw Aulaytner, secretary of the Catholic Intelligentsia Club in Warsaw, describes the purposes of *Znak* this way:

> We have a purpose that is strictly educational in the universal sense—to develop the education of our members universally; to form members not only in religious and philosophical attitudes, but also in social, economic and even political ones. We are not a political group. But we have political attitudes and take positions on political questions.
>
> Our first principle is to develop our activity on our own responsibility, without involving the hierarchy but in liasion with them. We do not think it can be otherwise. Many times we are "in dialogue' with the hierarchy, but we always are in liaison. The primatate comes here and discusses things with us.
>
> Our second principle is that we accept all economic and social reforms since 1944 which have been made by the communists in Poland as long as they are in accord with Catholic morality. Therefore many times our deputies vote against certain projects in the *Sejm*; for example on questions of divorce, abortion— matters which are unacceptable to Catholics. We criticized another parliamentary project, which limited activities of social organizations. As a result we often are "in dialogue" with the government. We have differences of opinions as in a family.
>
> The third principle is that our attitude must be open, always ready to collaborate with people in a positive way. Thus our attitude before Vatican II was in keeping with the conciliar attitude and we deepened this after the council.

In a meeting with Wladyslaw Gomulka a few years ago, the primate made two requests. "You and I, " he told the Communist chieftain, "are making history. Let us do it in a good way." Then, noting that divorce and abortion are prohibited in Russia, he made his second request: "Give us, please, what they have in Russia."

From time to time, as he did right after parlimentary elections, the primate (with the unified backing of the episcopate) has a letter read in Poland's churches enumerating existing problems in church-state relations.

The principal problem, as he noted in the letter, is the slowness with which permits are given for the building of new churches. The government says it is moving as fast as it can. Alexander Merker, head of the section for the Roman Catholic Church in the State Office for Religions and Cults, says:

> We have less homes than we need, and not enough schools and hospitals. From 1945 to 1965, 479 new churches and chapels were built; 530 were rebuilt; 44 were under construction. In Gostynin, a Warsaw district, the nazis blew up the church there and it now is being rebuilt. Until now they have been using a temporary chapel.

It is a long time since the end of the war. But we have a lot to build. Naturally people want things to be faster. But when we're building churches, we can't build houses. If steel is used for a house, we can't use it for a church. There is a building program and everything must be in proportion.

At Nowa Huta, the postwar steel center established outside of Cracow for more than 100,000 residents, the foundation stone for the new Mary, Queen of Poland parish church was not laid for a very long time because the government had not granted a permit. There is another parish in the general area which has been built around an ancient Cistercian monastery; in neighboring villages there are two chapels.

But Mary, Queen of Poland parish, with 80,000 parishioners is one of the largest in the nation. Ten Masses are said on Sunday in the outdoor chapel which has been serving as the church. The foundation stone came from St. Peter's and was blessed by Pope Paul. He gave the first offering for the building fund of the church, and the people themselves (as well as Poles abroad) provided the remainder.

In Ochota, a new residential development in Warsaw's outskirts, it seems likely that the 20,000 parishioners of Divine Providence parish will have to be content with their jerry-built barracks chapel for some time. The government shows no sign of easing the crisis which not only has blocked a building permit but resulted in the jailing of the pastor.

The conflict is an old one. In 1956, during the short period of Communist relaxation after the bloodless "October revolution," the state made available to the Church a block of land in the newly developing area. Then in 1959 the state took back half of the land, put a fence around it, built a kindergarten and effectively barred the pastor from building a church. The land already had been consecrated and a church started.

Nonetheless the pastor did not stop building.

He built a chapel, quarters for himself and four other priests, and several rooms which serve as the parish offices. This building effort brought in the police and led to his arrest. He again faces arrest if he does any more building. He has the full backing of Cardinal Wyszynski and one evening the primate was present at Benediction in the tiny chapel. The area was mobbed with parishioners. There are 14 Masses on Sundays.

Government refusal to grant building permits also is a problem for the Catholic University of Lublin, which has to use scattered, cramped and improvised quarters.

Many students are forced to live on the outskirts of Lublin because of the lack of facilities. This keeps them from using the 12th century church on the campus. But this has a bright side. On Sundays four-fifths of the students from the nearby State University and the state-operated Academy of Medicine attend Mass in the church on the Catholic campus. The Catholic university students meanwhile go to churches near their residences.

Five times a year a collection is taken in all the parishes of Poland for the university's support. There is also a Society of Friends of the University with 120,000 subscribers.

The Catholic university is permitted by the state to have an enrollment of 2,000 students. Almost all are laymen. There are four faculties: canon law, theology, Christian philosophy and literature.

In all state universities there is a quota because in a planned socialist society a job must be waiting for each graduate. The Catholic university has been given a quota in two of its schools for other reasons. The Christian philosophy school is limited to 30 new students each year; the literature school, 80.

At Czestochowa, a copy of the sacred image of the Black Madonna remains imprisoned behind the grille of a side altar in the national Marian sanctuary. The copy was made by Cardinal Wyszynski in 1957, after his release from prison, and brought by him to Rome where Pope Pius XII blessed it in preparation for a visitation of Poland's parishes.

The visitation was halted abruptly in 1966 in Warsaw. The primate was in one car and the image in another when the militia stepped in, seized the copy of the Black Madonna and brought it to the cathedral where it remained for the rest of the Warsaw visitation period. The scheduled visits to parishes were made in name only.

When the time came for the official visitation of Katowice in Silesia, its bishop journeyed to Warsaw and collected the replica. On Sept. 2, 1966, the bishop's car was stopped on a road outside Katowice. The replica was seized by the police and taken to the national shrine. Two jeeps of militia-men now make sure it stays there.

All primary and secondary education is in the hands of the state.

There are less than a dozen Catholic schools. The school of the Sisters of Immaculate Conception, west of Warsaw, is popular with Communist officials. They like to send their young daughters there, apparently because they believe their training and education will be excellent. Religion, of course, is taught at the school but it is an optional subject.

Before the war there were 15,000 nuns in Poland. The figure has nearly doubled. Many nuns work in state hospitals and in state-financed health centers and old people's homes. Those in state jobs are insured and have old-age pensions, but there is no government insurance or pension coverage for the others. Most of the nuns work in parishes, doing everything from cleaning to teaching catechism.

Catechism teachers have to be certified as "qualified" by a government school inspector. When a priest gives the lessons the certification is not needed. Once a year a report has to be made to government authorities on attendance at the catechism lessons and when and where they were given.

Theoretically the pastor receives 1,000 zlotys from the state for religious instruction. But Cardinal Wyszynski has asked priests not to accept it.

Many parents hesitate to send their children to catechism lessons, a Warsaw prelate says. Particularly reluctant are Party members, government jobholders and teachers in public schools. They are afraid of losing their jobs.

Catechism attendance drops off sharply after First Communion. Of the 7 or 8 million school children in the 6-to-18 age group, the prelate estimates, only 4 or 4½ million receive religious instruction.

The Church was a unifying, national force for the Polish people up to World War I, when their nation was partitioned among Russia, Prussia and Austria. Since the end of World War II the Communists have been trying to unify the country on their own terms and using their own methods.

In 1945 the new Communist government declared that the Holy See had broken the concordat of 1925 by appointing Germans, rather than Polish citizens, as bishops in Poznan and Chelmo. After the break with the Holy See, state-church relations worsened, culminating with Cardinal Wyszynski's arrest. A general agreement between church and state was signed in April, 1950 and this was followed by a more specific one in 1956.

The 1956 agreement set up a General Government-Episcopal Commission to deal with current questions. It was composed of two bishops, a government minister, and a member of Parliament. The commission has not met since December, 1966. The two bishops have died. The government representatives no longer hold the same posts. In effect, the commission is dead.

"But both sides could name new members" Alexander Merker notes.

A daily working relationship remains. Bishop Bronislaw Dombrowski, secretary of the episcopate, meets with government officials in the State Office for Religions and Cults, when necessary, and the office has branches in each province.

From the Vatican there have been emissaries in recent years. Franz Cardinal Koenig of Vienna visited Poland in 1963. Polish Bishop Wladyslaw Rubin, secretary general of the Synod in Rome, made a visit in February, 1968. Msgr. (now Archbishop) Agostino Casaroli, then attached to Vatican Secretariat of State, made two trips, the second in March, 1967.

The visit of Archbishop Casaroli was described by the bishops' communiques as an "event of the greatest importance for the Church as well as for the Polish state." The document said it would cary with it "advantages both for the Church and the nation."

The communique, however, also pointedly thanked Pope Paul VI for his decision that in negotiating the reestablishment of normal relations in Poland "no decision is to be taken without the participation of the Polish episcopate."

The communique noted that the Polish bishops "want to cooperate closely with the delegation of the Holy See, in which it has full confidence." At the same time the Polish bishops intend to continue their conversations with Polish government officials seeking "to find a solution to fundamental problems of the fulfillment of the mission of the Church in Poland."

The communique said also that the bishops "are opposed to a loyalty oath to the Polish state that new pastors are required to take." That ceremony imposes an old law that should have been abolished, the bishops said, because "it places in doubt the civic loyalty of priests and could appear as a form of discrimination."

On his return from talks in Warsaw, Archbishop Casaroli told newsmen he was optimistic about the possibility of "normalizing Vatican-Polish relations." He added that both sides had shown interest in the "speediest and most comprehensive solution possible," and that the Warsaw talks "had brought positions closer on some fundmental points."

A particularly thorny question keeping the Holy See and the Polish government apart is the ecclesiastical status of dioceses in what are called "the former German territories." There are four such dioceses—Wroclaw in Silesia and Olsztyn in Prussia, which existed before the war; Opole and Gorzow, which were created as new jurisdictions by the Polish primate in 1945.

The Pope has named bishops for these jurisdictions and the bishops were at the Second Vatican Council. But they do not have full Vatican recognition as dioceses and the bishops are known as apostolic administrators. The Holy See has been holding off recognition until a German peace treaty is signed by the Allies. The territorial issue is so complex that the Wroclaw diocese has four different addresses in the Vatican directory—one in Germany; one in Czechoslovakia; two in Poland.

A 1933 concordat with Germany, meanwhile, specifies that diocesan boundaries must coincide with state borders. Thus any move by the Holy See would bring a swift reaction from either Poland or West Germany—and the Polish government realizes this.

Is a new Vatican-Polish concordat in the offing? "For a concordat," said Marker, the Polish government official, "We must negotiate. But we have not even got to the stage where we are having negotiations over negotiations."

Poland's government took the first step in its proposed "normalization of Church-state relations" when the Polish Primate, Stefan Cardinal Wysznski of Warsaw, met with Premier Piotr Jaroszewicz.

The first such meeting between top-level Church and government leaders in 11 years, the discussions lasted three hours and ran the gamut of problems centering on more Church freedom in a variety of areas.

The Cardinal and his secretary, Father Hieronim Gozdiewicz, went to premier Jaroszewicz' office for the March 3 meeting. Reportedly, the discussion was a preliminary one aimed at sounding out each other's views on various subjects. Other meetings were expected to follow.

At the time the Polish Primate conferred with a top Polish Communist leader in January, 1960, when he met with the deposed Wladyslaw Gomulka, then they discussed Church-state relations which were badly deteriorating. Church-state relations have been extremely poor since then.

The present Polish leadership presumable believes that a solid Church-state understanding would help bolster the new regime's position and make it more popular with Poland's heavily Catholic population

Church support could also assist the government in motivating Polish workers toward greater productivity in order to revive and stimulate the nation's sagging economy.

Moves to improve Church-state relations got underway in Poland after Edward Gierek replaced Wladislaw Gomulka as Polish Communist Party leader, following food riots in Polish coastal towns.

ьpeaking to hundreds of worshippers, Cardinal Wyszynski said Poles "understood that normalization would not be a departure from God, but a recognition of the Church's rights."

If the state would admit the Church had been wronged, he said, attempts at sound normalization would not be so much a corrective measure but a "non-repetition, non-multiplication and non-prolongation of the present state of harm."

"But as long as this state of harm continues," he said, "we shall not be able to overcome the feeling that the denial of full human and political rights is being prolonged."

He appealed to the Polish government to allow Catholics not only to study and work in their own buildings, but "also to pray, at least, in modern tents."

Assailing reports in the state-controlled press that "unity" and "normalization" can only come when the Church accepts Polish political realities, the Cardinal declared "real Polish unity can be achieved only through the faith. It is neither comprehensible nor justified when attempts are made to destroy unity by luring workers away from the unity with Jesus Christ."

First talks between official representatives of the Polish government and the Vatican were held in Rome, opening direct negotiations between Warsaw and the Vatican.

But the much advertised normalization of relations between Church and state inside Poland does not seem to be proceeding smoothly.

Shortly after the Vatican and Warsaw announced the conclusion of their conversations, a communique issued in Czestochowa by the Polish bishops complained about obstructionist tactics by the middle and lower Communist Party apparatus.

For both the Vatican and Poland, the opening of negotiations was of historic importance.

Vatican sources said discussion centered on the question of Church administration in Western Poland. There were recurrent and denied rumors about the possibility of a papal visit to Poland, and information that taxation of the Church in Poland, facilities for building new churches and licensing of the Catholic press were discussed.

The communique published in Czestochowa at the end of the Polish bishop's conference revealed substantial differences between the regime's approach to the Vatican and that toward the Polish clergy. The latter point was expressly reflected in the following passages of the Czestochowa communique:

> The bishops stated that local administrative authorities have still been acting according to the policy of the former period, which has been expressed in a negative handling of the motions forwarded to them by Church authorities concerning the construction of churches in new districts of the cities and in establishing parishes.
>
> The conference expressed the hope that the top state authorities will issue new regulations to the officials which will take into account the needs of the Church and of the society of believers. It is indispensable to calm down society, especially where efforts have been made for several years to get permission.

On the face of it, the Czestochowa communique seems to suggest that an immediate end to the "tangible" problems of the Church is of primary importance to the Polish Episcopate.

Compared with the optimistic press comments on the Vatican communique, the Czestochowa statement seems to stress the much advertised "regularization" of Church-state relations inside the country is a task on which hardly any progress at the ground level has been made.

The opposition of elements of the Polish intelligentsia to the government has little if anything to do with foreign policy. A typical criticism from one of those involved in the events that surrounded and followed the expulsion of Professor Kolakowski from the Party would be that the style is wearyingly and unnecessarily dogmatic; but the fundamentals are not challenged. The Catholic bishops, especially Cardinal Wyszynski, are, however, thought by some to present such a challenge—focused in the celebrated letter to the German bishops, and elaborated at intervals during the strained acrimony of the Millennium commemorations of State and Church.

Yet the balance of evidence suggests that the Cardinal is first and last a Polish churchman, not a serious, systematic right-wing political thinker in the manner of Bonald or de Maistre, nor a reactionary like the fixed tenant of the US Embassy in Budapest, Cardinal Mindszenty. His conservatism is theological and ecclesiastical, with a strong dash of chauvinist patriotism. As the believers pay their deep respect to him—no one can doubt his following, especially among peasants—he is encouraged to conceive the church as the true embodiment of the Polish nation.

A buttressing factor is his belief that an "atheist" government is neither genuinely Polish, nor much to be trusted; he is perhaps more opposed to their atheism than their socialism. In Rome in 1957, after his release from prison (two years after Gomulka's own release), Wyszynski was conducted through the splendors of the Basilica by rather self-satisfied Cardinal, and he said at the end: "A beautiful building, but tell me, where are the faithful?" The style and stiffness and glitter of the Vatican does not suit him; he is a churchman of the Polish masses.

The clash with the state arises not from clearly formulated ideological irreconcilability, but from Wyszynski's rash, and finally indefensible, aspiration to "speak for the nation." Not for "the Catholic community of Poland" does he pretend to speak, but for "Poland," which infuriates the government. A Catholic who knows Wyszynski well said he had never heard the Cardinal enunciate anything remotely like an alternative foreign policy for Poland: "Its's just that to him 'Poland' and 'The Church' are two sides of the same reality, and an atheist government is an outrage."

What will happen to the blend of proletarianism and sheer pragmatism in the foreign policy thinking of the present elite of old Communists, when the young professionals, who have had all the advantages of education and stability that the old elite lacked, and have little of their doctrinal conviction, arrive at the helm? "The great change since the war," observed a leading sociologist, "is from messianic attitudes, including the notion that Poland has a special calling, to a fascination with technology and a concentration upon economic development." The replacement of "heroes" by "citizens" has some way still to go, and Gomulka is increasingly said to be out of date, and failing to take a really long view, facing the future on its own terms.

The passing of the old Communists, however, will remove a strong ingredient of dedication and public-spiritedness from Polish government.

A recent survey found among the young "a conspicuous absence of public ambition, desire for power, or readiness to serve others;" none of these things Gomulka lacked. Can Poland face the international future in all its potentiality when quite a lot of the young are disengated, distrustful of what has been offered them in the realm of ideas, bent single-mindedly upon private goals?

The striking fact is that the very success of Gomulka's policies has given Poland a period of growth and consolidation that has, in turn, produced the professionalism, practicality, and political disengagement of the young. The lack of challenge to the present government is due both to the subsiding of the romantic spirit in Poland, and to the satisfaction that is widely felt with the adjustment Poland has made to a world she never made. Whether the "soul of Poland" is fulfilled is imponderable, and few seem to ponder it. The reality is that the body of Poland, dismembered and tortured so often in the past, is tending its own needs in a climate of peace and quiet.

When the Communists took over Poland, an estimated 95 per cent of the populace was Roman Catholic. For the most part, the Poles have stubbornly continued practicing their religion, even in the face of pressure and outright persecution. One of the Catholic leaders, Cardinal Wyszynski, said that "there is not enough room in the churches for the faithful."

Tensions between the Church and the Communist government in the late fifties and early sixties prevented any dialogue. Now things are looking up.

The Vatican has refused to accept the post-war German-Polish frontiers as basis for the boundaries of bishoprics and maintained this question could be solved only after the signing of a German peace treaty. The Polish bishops, in recent years, pressed for a change of this position.

In January, 1971, the Vatican made moves to recognize the border between East Germany and Poland as the Oder-Neisse river, following the Polish-West German agreement. This has been one of the sore points between Poland and Rome. Later in the year, the Polish chief of state, Gierek, granted 4,700 chapels and other parish buildings of the former German territories to the Polish Church.

The Polish Bishops' Commission for western and northern territories at the meeting at Wroclaw in a declaration for ratification of a 1970 West German-Polish non-aggression treaty stated:

> This will have momentous importance for the future relations between the two nations, marking as it will a forward step toward the reconstruction of mutual confidence and a reconciliation between the two nations.

The declaration added:

> The Polish Church reiterates its hope that the Apostolic See will take the long-awaited decision on the status of Polish bishops in Poland's western and northern territories.

Since the end of World War II, the Vatican has appointed "apostolic administrators" rather than resident bishops to the former German dioceses.

The Polish government, in an effort to re-establish "normal relations" with the Polish Catholic Church, already has given the Church full title to Church property in the former German territory.

However, reports of gradually improving relations between the Church and Poland's Communist government were interrupted during Holy Week by a police raid on a chapel in suburban Warsaw that included confiscation of a tabernacle.

Meanwhile, Stefan Cardinal Wyszynski said in a sermon Polish authorities still disregard pledges for freedom of religion. He complained that police tore down a chapel in Zbrosza-Duza, 20 miles from Warsaw, because the chapel was built without consent of town authorities.

"Such things never happened in Poland before," the Cardinal said.

"I have to speak about them even at the Easter Holidays, because silence would be interpreted as weakness."

Stefan Cardinal Wyszynski, addressing a Lenten service in St. John Cathedral, denounced the raid as an "irresponsible act" and an unprecedented sacrilege, and demanded "satisfaction" from the government.

According to reports, 150 policemen surrounded the chapel in Zbrosza

Duza, charged in and made off with a tabernacle containing a consecrated Host.

The report came soon after Premier Piotr Jaroszewicz informed members of the newly elected *Sejm* the government would continue to "normalize" relations with the Church in Poland.

> We expect the Church and its hierarchy to meet these efforts half way. I am convinced that the Church hierarchy will make a constructive contribution to the process of normalization of relations with the state.
>
> As is well known, the government has undertaken talks with the Vatican. We expect the talks to result in guarantees that the Church in Poland will confine its religious activity within the framework determined by our national interest and by our laws.

Polish authorities often take as long as four or five years to grant permission to build a new church, according to reports. Of the 361 applications for church buildings filed in 1975 by 28 dioceses, 22 were granted.

Clearly dramatizing this situation, Cardinal Wyszynski delivered his Easter sermon in a prefabricated temporary church.

> I pray for the time when Poles can live in the hope that, on the basis of the new constitution, methods like that used at Gorky will be abandoned. I pray for an epoch in which attacks like this will no longer be organized in Poland.

The Easter declaration was intended as a summary and a clarification of the bishops' stand on the new constitution, due to confusion and misunderstanding in the nation about an apparent endorsement by them of the regime's final charter. Intellectuals who had publicly criticized it had been persecuted.

In fact, the recent document supported the dissenters in an important final paragraph.

> We expect that due consideration will be given to those citizens who have expressed their opinion through legal channels in writing to the special constitutional commission.
>
> They have taken advantage of this right as free citizens, and have performed their moral and political duties whereby they gave evidence of their civic maturity.
>
> Respect for the inviolable rights of man, of the human person, is the basic obligation of a just administration in social and national affairs. Such respect goes hand in hand with the recognition of the legal rights of the Polish nation.

There is no doubt that the 1,000-year-old Polish Church—by far the strongest local Church in Eastern Europe and perhaps even in the entire world—has thrived under subtle Communist persecution.

After 30 years of Communism, the Church can claim the support of about 80 per cent of Poland's more than 30 million people. Almost all Catholic youth attend catechism classes held at a church or rectory. There are no Catholic elementary or high schools.

The government will not permit new churches in vast new residential areas. So the people respond by worshipping in snow or rain in open fields.

Chartered buses for a religious celebration are mysteriously canceled at the last moment. So Catholics fill horse-drawn wagons or walk miles to the Mass site.

The heroism of Catholic Poles crosses age and social lines. Risks are run equally by the young man or woman who, defying the current antivocation drive in the state schools, enters a seminary or convent, and the parents who are threatened on the job for permitting their child to choose full dedication to the Church.

Chances are taken by a group of women doctors, lawyers and university professors who form a secret secular institute which collaborates with Stefan Cardinal Wyszynski.

Church-state relations differ from region to region and often from parish to parish. But several obstacles are universally put in the way of the Church's ministry.

Most Bishops agree that the major block is the lack of churches.

Since World War II, which practically leveled Warsaw and left much of the country in ruins, the government has embarked on a massive and impressive construction program.

The plans have included whole new cities, like Nowa Huta near Cracow which has more than 100,000 people.

For 25 years as permission to build a church was sought in vain, the people of Nowa Huta stood outside to hear one of 18 Sunday Masses regardless of the weather.

A huge church now stands at Nowa Huta in the shape of a ship—thanks to protests of the people and pressure from visitors from outside Poland.

But Nowa Huta is an exception. "We've asked the government since World War II for permission to build 1,000 churches," a Polish bishop said. "We've received permission for about 100."

But even with permission, building materials are hard to obtain. The vast oval church of the Holy Rosary in Gdansk opened on Holy Thursday, 1976, but a month later the parish's young pastor was hauled before the magistrate.

In good faith he had purchased building material a contractor had illegally acquired. Church officials fear that the pastor, who, with four other priests, serves 50,000 Catholics, will be jailed.

One recently consecrated bishop was granted permission to build one church as a consecration present from the government. But he reports that taxes of 300,000 zlotys will have to be paid on purchase of the land for the church. The land cost the pastor 380,000 zlotys.

The issue of government foot-dragging in the matter of permits for new churches and chapels has long been a bone of contention the Church and the Communist regime.

In an official communique, Bishop Jerzy Modzelewski, and auxiliary bishop and vicar general of the Warsaw archdiocese, announced in October, 1977 that in Warsaw itself, new churches were being built in six parishes, while permits had been granted for building of two other churches and the rebuilding of one.

Permission had also granted for drawing up plans for new churches in 10 other areas of the Warsaw archdiocese.

Money is not a problem for the Polish Church, which is generously supported by the free-will offerings of the people. But government taxation is.

The Church is regarded legally as a profit-making industry. Taxes on the Church and on priests are steep. Most priests are currently joining in a tax boycott, and it appears that an agreement with the state is near on new tax provisions.

To prepare seminarians for what they will be up against as priests seminaries offer courses called "Church-State."

The subtlety of the Communist persecution in Poland must be emphasized. There are no Russian soldiers blocking entrance to churches, nuns are not being slapped aroung.

There are a few faint signs, however, that the government is tiring of the anti-Church battle it hasn't been able to win.

Officials sometimes turn the other way when Catholics smuggle altar missals into the country. The law which slapped a fine on those who display religious images in public has been left to languish after too many people set up May shrines to Mary in their windows in defiance of the statute.

Another pastor boasts that the first secretary of the Party in his rural town of 2,000 is a daily communicant during October and attends May devotions. The same priest is saluted in public by the Communist mayor and was even invited to address a parent-teachers meeting which he opened with a prayer.

When he needed two tons of cement for building, a woman Party member and parishioner came back with six tons.

He is the first to admit that his situation is exceptional. Even so, other priests report that Party members often travel to another town to attend Sunday Mass. Many more of them take advantage of the anonymity offered by huge religious celebrations, attracting thousands, to confess and receive Communion.

Part of the limitations imposed on the Church by the country's Communist government includes no access to the major mass media.

Since World War II, Poland's once extensive Catholic publishing outlets have dwindled. Those remaining must print in small quantities for lack of paper.

Plants, like the one begun by Blessed Maximillian Kolbe before the war, were shut down completely by the government because of the Franciscan's strong anti-Communist stance.

Several Church-sponsored Catholic papers still print, but paper shortages prevent an adequate press run.

Yet, drawing from ancient Church tradition as well as from modern technology, the Polish Church has been able to meet creatively the challenges of communicating in a socialist system.

In many parishes, for example, the absence of hymnals is compensated for by an overhead projector that flashes hymn words and tunes on a screen.

In a country where one bishop claims he cannot even get visiting cards printed without government approval, holy cards are not available for sale. A costly but legal substitute, however, is found in photographs of sacred images, printed holy-card size.

More serious problems arise for communications between the Polish Bishops' Conference and its 75 members, and between bishops and their flocks.

Neither the conferences nor the dioceses can legally possess photocopying or reproduction machinery, so pastoral letters and conference communiques are typed by nuns and other secretaries using stacks of carbon paper.

Partially because of the communications problems, the Polish Bishops' Conference meets six times a year in plenary session—more than any other national bishops' conference in the world.

Laity get together much more often, too. Lay Catholic organizations are outlawed, but pilgrimages and outdoor festivities are not. At such manifestations, crowds stand patiently, often for more than three hours, to hear a sermon by the Polish Primate, Stefan Cardinal Wyzsynski of Warsaw, or other bishops.

The sermon has taken on greater importance as a support of faith in Poland than elsewhere.

And partially because of the media ban, Church externals—those things sarcastically called "trappings" by many Western Catholics—are revered by Poles.

With the media blackout, a procession with relics becomes a way of communicating a lesson on saints. Kissing a bishop's ring becomes a way of communicating solidarity with the Church.

A priest walking Warsaw's main shopping street in a cassock becomes a statement that Communist materialism is not the only way offered man, and so on.

Be it through overhead projectors, gold-encrusted relics, photography or signs that others might term outmoded or triumphalist, the Polish Church is communicating, and doing it well.

According to some observers of Vatican-Polish affairs, Cardinal Wyszynski, who visited Pope Paul VI privately three times, has asked that the Polish bishops be consulted before any formal agreement between the Vatican and Poland is reached. Vatican dipolmats have visited Warsaw, and Polish representatives have had exploratory talks in Rome in recent years in attempts to work out a new state-Church arrangement in Poland.

However, even as the Polish foreign minister was visiting the Vatican on November 12, 1973, the government was pushing educational reforms that could restrict the rights of the Church in providing religious training to the young.

Pope Paul VI and Soviet Foreign Minister Andrei Gromyko met privately for more than 50 minutes February 21, 1974 to discuss "the major problems regarding peace in the world, and especially that of the Middle East with particular reference to Jerusalem."

Also discussed during the meeting were the International Conference on European Security and Cooperation and the "of the church in the Soviet Union's territory."

As for Church-state relations within the Soviet Union, the field of discussion—at least from the viewpoint of the Catholic Church—is vast. The Catholic Church in the Soviet Union has no freedom and Catholics in the Ukraine have been forced to go underground or to embrace the state-tolerated Russian Orthodox Church.

In the former Baltic Republics of Lithuania and Latvia, Catholic bishops labor under severe handicaps. In Lithuania, most of the bishops of the seven dioceses are not permitted by the government to carry out their pastoral duties. Some of the dioceses are governed by apostolic administrators in place of regular bishops because of the difficulties encountered.

The meeting of Pope Paul and the Soviet foreign minister—the fourth since 1965—took place during a general easing of tensions between the Catholic Church and Communist-dominated Eastern Europe.

The Polish people are under no illusions regarding political change. While the Church remains the only effective opposition, Poles liken their country's position to that of the Auschwitz Concentration Camp where 100,000 people were held captive, and liquidated, by 300 German guards.

The Church in Poland is persecuted: priests are still beign arrested and imprisoned; the faithful are subject to continuous harassment, loss of jobs and income and educational frustration. All Church printing is in the hands of *Pax*, the collaborators organisation; government permission is required for all Church printed literature including letter headings and memorial cards. With sugar rationed, priests receive no sugar ration at all, even though more sugar is available for those with coupons and money at uncontrolled prices. A typical parish priest's level of taxation (levied against all inhabitants of his parish including atheists and Party members) is about three-quarters of a working man's wage. There is, moreover, very little meat in Poland since it has been sold to East Germany. The radio has announced "it is the will of the people."

In a strongly worded pastoral letter read in all churches in Poland November 28, 1976, the Polish bishops have appealed to Catholics to oppose their government's "hateful, brutal campaign" against the Church.

The letter, released by the Rome press office of the Polish bishops, was the strongest yet in a series of recent public statements by the bishops or their leader, Stefan Cardinal Wyszynski, expressing disagreement with government policies.

In the frank 10-page letter, the bishops listed the principal elements in what they called a stepped-up program to "politically atheize" Poland.

Among these elements, the bishops cited:

Government failure to permit building of churches and other Church-related buildings,

Discrimination in hiring and professional advancement against practicing Catholics,

Anti-Church propaganda in films, plays, on television and in the print media, and

A program in schools to discredit religion, and to dissuade students from attending church and religious instruction classes.

The bishops also alerted Polish Catholics, who make up about 90 per cent of the national population, that they will sponsor soon a national day of prayer "in defense of the faith."

The pastoral letter came at a particularly delicate moment for Poland's Communist government. Following the 1976 worker strikes to protest steep government price hikes on consumer items, Party leader Gierek has been trying to enlist the Church's help in his efforts to keep a lid on national unrest.

In its pastoral, the bishops' conference clearly warned Gierek that "new methods" in the campaign against religion "are also blocking social and economic reforms since they stir unrest and opposition toward the government."

"Embittered men do not make good workers," the bishops warned.

At the top of the list of complaints, the bishops underlined government reluctance to grant building permits to the Church.

A chronic shortage of churches has resulted, especially in huge new residential areas which have sprung up around the nation since World War II. In such areas it is not uncommon to find parishes where as many as

100,000 Catholics are forced to attend Sunday Mass in crude shelters, constructed with trash.

In 1976 alone, Poland's 27 dioceses have asked permission to build about 500 churches and chapels, but most of the requests have been refused.

The pastoral letter also severely condemned religious discrimination on the job.

The bishops pointed out further that many believers who have lost their posts because of their religion had won awards for excellence on the job.

The pastoral letter accused the mass media of presenting the "history of the Church in a false light, deforming the content of the Bible and deriding religious practice."

It asserted that the greatest efforts in the government's campaign against religion are aimed at youth.

"Children in many places", charged the bishops, "are blocked from attending catechism class or Holy Mass and other religious functions."

In 1976 some Catholic youths attending state-run summer camps were forced to remove religious medals and crosses they were wearing.

The letter condemned government attempts to draft seminarians into the armed forces, a move which is against existing Church-state agreements, according to the bishops.

It also charged that university students are being dissuaded from seeking out services of Catholic campus ministry. The fact that young workers are offered tourist outings or made to work on Sundays was seen by the bishops as a further attempt to curb religious practice among youth.

The Vatican's willingness to go along with the dropping of several religious feasts from Italy's overloaded holiday calendar has caused problems for the bishops in Comunist Poland.

The Vatican announced that it would not object if Italy abolished from the National holiday schedule five of the ten religious holidays recognized by Italy in its 1929 concordat with the Holy See. Italy is seeking to reduce civil and religious holidays as a move to improve the economy.

The Polish bishops, who for years have been fighting against attempts by the Communist government to purge society of any signs of religion, indicated that the Vatican's action in Italy was almost an open invitation for the Polish government to erase from the civil calendar the few remaining religious feasts officially recognized.

The Polish bishops stated that from their own experience the abolition of Church feasts serves to secularize social life in a communique following their February general meeting in Warsaw.

In Poland, the communique continued, economic reasons have been cited for the suppression of religious feasts. But, the bishops pointed out, suppression of mid-week religious holidays have often been followed by the granting of holidays on Saturdays.

Saturday is a work day in many European countries.

The communique stopped short of directly criticizing the Vatican's decision in the case of Italy. It pointed out that even if the Italian proposal for dropping the five religious days off is accepted by the Italian parliament, Italy will still have many more religious holidays than Catholic Poland has.

> We beg you to confess your faith in Christ courageously and faithfully. Watch over the catechesis of children and youth. Cultivate the holy faith in families,

and above all, defend the faith with fervent prayers. We urge you to pray in community.

The Catholic faith has strengthened and united Poland for over a thousand years. So today, too, as throughout the centuries, we consider it our essential, fundamental tie of a national-religious character.

Our greatest treasure, the Catholic faith, is continually threatened. The skillfully masked programme of making the nation atheistic is becoming an ever more serious matter, since it tries in every way to deprive the life of our social community of the spirit of Christ's Gospel.

A superficial glance at the life of the Church in Poland may give the illusion that the activity of the Church in our state meets with no obstacles. Everyone, in fact, desires normalization. In actual fact, however, the hateful, brutal struggle against faith in God and against the Church of Christ, has not yet ended. A mysterious conspiracy against God is felt everywhere, at all times. The programme of making the nation atheistic is being undertaken and carried out on an ever vaster scale also by institutions of formation and by social and political institutions.

The struggle against religion, carried out by means of pressure of a juridical and administrative character, is difficult and risky, since it arouses reactions and it compromises the State authorities in the eyes of world public opinion. It cannot be carried out universally and radically. Therefore another system has been applied: to appeal to the mass media, that is, to culture. A vast sector of Polish theatre, television and even publishing has been mobilized in anti-religious propaganda. This struggle, well concealed to begin with, has now become open and aggressive. Atheistic propaganda often presents the history of the Church, in Poland particularly, in a false light, distorts the content of Holy Scripture and presents religious practices in a way that hurts the feelings of believers.

Liturgical and sacramental life is replaced by a lay ceremonial, which is often very shallow.

The political programme to implement atheism is being carried out more and more energetically. Its introduction into practical life proceeds in stages, so that our society will not realize easily that it has been subjected to the mannoeuvred process of the destruction of faith.

Poland and the Holy See are nearing a rapprochment which will be the most striking step yet toward church-state harmony in a Communist country.

"The Roman Catholic Church will be able to cooperate more fully in solving Poland's problems only when the church is granted the freedom it requires," Pope Paul VI told Edward Gierek, head of the Polish Communist Party, at the Vatican meeting December 1, 1977.

In response Gierek stated that "between the church and the state, there will not recur a situation of conflict."

The Polish government maintains a diplomat with the rank of minister in its Rome Embassy for Vatican contacts; the Vatican maintains a permanent working group headed by Archbishop Luigi Poggi that occasionally visits Poland.

Gierek himself, in his address to the Pope, referred to the cardinal and to the meeting he had with Cardinal Wyszynski October 29, 1977, a meeting that may have changed the course of the relationship. It was not only their first meeting since Gierek took command of the Party in 1970, but it also led to a communique that acknowledged that the discussion covered national as well as church affairs.

The recent visit to the Vatican of Polish foreign minister Stefan Olszowski, and his audience with Pope Paul VI capped previous negotiations.

And the prospect is that Poland—where the Roman Catholic Church wields its biggest influence within the Communist area of Europe—and the Holy See will establish diplomatic relations at an early date.

Poland would thus become the first Warsaw Pact power to admit Vatican representation in the form of a papal nunciature with full, normal diplomatic status.

In fact, Warsaw made its first moves in this direction following the change of power in Poland when the oppressive Gomulka regime was replaced by the relatively "liberal," and certainly more flexible leadership headed by Edward Gierek.

It made a number of concessions, including restoration of legal ownership of church properties in the former German lands, the so-called Western Territories, which since have been formally acknowledged by West Germany as part of Poland and recognized as such by the Vatican in its administration of the church.

The move clearly was intended to win Polish church support and goodwill among Poland's still predominantly Catholic population for the new regime's bid to conciliate and unite the nation after a political crisis which brought it to the brink of civil war in the winter of 1970.

Talking with Mr. Olszowski, the Pope raised other issues, including the Polish episcopate's desire to build more churches—for which government sanction, including appropriations for materials, is required. The foreign minister noted that, since taking office, the Gierek government had approved applications for 120 new churches.

Currently, a more actual cause of church uneasiness is the educational reform voted by Parliament. The Polish bishops have professed fears that it may handicap the church's religious teaching of children. The bishops allege, among other things, that a new school hours system could impede religious instruction conducted—in accordance with law—outside the schools and in the churches or the homes of priests.

But unbiased observers regard the reform as a necessity, prompted by requirements of modern education and more efficient use of existing resources. Official assurances have been given of full respect for Catholic feeling.

"Polish conflict has theological basis," thus writes Patrick Riley in *The New World*.

> "Our biggest problem," a Polish bishop said, "is lack of churches."
>
> This death of churches is, of course, the work of Poland's Communist party and the government it controls. But if the Polish Communist regime has created the Catholic Church's biggest problem, the biggest problem of the regime is probably the Catholic Church.
>
> That helps explain why for two decades the regime adamantly denied permission for construction of churches. But that is not the only reason for the state's policy.
>
> The struggle over churches is only a microcosm of the conflicting forces in Poland. These forces are political, cultural, historical and even military as well as religious.
>
> There is also an economic factor, though it has very little to do with the

economic pretext often advanced by government officials to explain why churches cannot be built: that Poland's pressing need to forge ahead on the industrial front does not leave enough materials for churches.

The problem is at root theological, as some maintain all problems are. It is Communism's dogmatic atheism, the noting that religion diminishes man's dignity, destroys his intellectual independence and dulls his sense of indignation at economic and social inequity.

This Communist dogma comes into conflict with the powerful religious feeling of the great mass of Poles. For them, the Catholic faith is inextricable bound up with the things they hold dearest in life: their sense of personal worth and integrity, their family, their patriotism. It has been this way for a thousand years.

Poles are a volatile and romantic people, ready to brave death not because they hold life cheap but because they hold it less dear than the things that make it worth living.

And for Poles, once again, these are the things most powerfully bound up with religion: personal worth, family, patriotism.

Obtrusive anti-religious propaganda only antagonizes. Furthermore, all mockery of religion is in theory punishable by five years' imprisonment. (This does not however discourage newspapers from dropping casual but ubiquitous remarks about religion as backwardness or obscurantism.)

An attempt by the government a decade ago to put a stranglehold on religious instruction by making it financially dependent upon the state was parried effortlessly by Stefan Cardinal Wyszynski of Warsaw. He simply forbade any priest to accept a state salary for catechetical work.

How about jailing recalcitrant bishops, such as Cardinal Wyszynski? That was tried and didn't work. It only created martyrs, men of enhanced authority. Cardinal Wyszynski's three years' detention in mid-1950s is considered one reason for his immense prestige and unchallenged authority in the Polish Church.

The government also has tried exploiting differences within the Church publicizing Catholic criticism (sincere or otherwise) about the conservatism and authoritarianism of the bishops but without noticeable success.

The only strategy left seems to be the one the regime has actually been pursuing. This strategy has two stages:

First, declare politics strictly off limits to the Church, and at the same time define politics so broadly and all-inclusively that nothing is left for religion except praying and preaching.

There is no Catholic press, no access by churchmen or committed Catholics (save those openly favorable to "socialism") to the mass media, no widespread Catholic cultural, social or relief organizations or activity except for pastoral car and so-called Catholic organizations fostered by the regime but disavowed by the bishops.

That keeps the Church inside the churches, with the solitary and (in Poland) highly important exception of pilgrimages.

The next stage in the strategy is to hold down the number of churches, on the principle that people without churches become people without religion.

According to some observers in Poland, this strategy is beginning to show signs of paying off. A progressive if barely noticeable secularization is taking root among the working classes. The Church is gearing up to forestall the approaching crisis through the religious education of adults. For the past two years, since the fall of communist chieftain Wladyslaw Gomulka, the regime has allowed the construction of a few churches. During 1971, about 20 new churches were allowed, and that tempo seems to have continued in 1972. Nine churches were rebuilt in 1971, and half a dozen were enlarged.

But this hardly begins to meet the need. Cardinal Wyszynski has said "several thousand" new churches must be built. In Warsaw alone, he has said, at least 40 churches must be built, whereas only two have been allowed.

In December, 1970, the country stood on the brink of civil war, according to Communist party first secretary Edward Gierek. When new leadership took over from a disgraced Gomulka, one of its first acts was to declare through Premier Piotr Jaroszewicz that it wanted to normalized relations with the Church.

The reason for such willingness to bargain was evident: the Communists were walking a knife-edge and could hardly afford to be unfriendly with anybody, least of all with the spiritual (and even cultural) leaders of the mass of Poland's working class.

Negotiations between the two hierarchies, Communist and Catholic, have proceeded since then, but results thus far have been minimal—such as the building of a few dozen churches and the abolition of an obligatory but unenforceable inventory on parish goods.

The bishops' conference, held in the Prezemsyl diocese in southern Poland in honor of the See's 600th anniversary, primarily assessed the situation of the Polish Catholic Church with respect to the continuing efforts for "normalization" between Church and state.

In their concluding statement, the bishops expressed "great concern" over the pastoral care of children, teenagers and university students, particularly during summer holiday camping periods which are organized by the government.

The bishops also referred to the recent visit to Poland by Archbishop Luigi Poggi, a special papal envoy to the Polish government. The statement said the visit had "positive results" and expressed hope that there be further meetings and contacts between the Vatican and representatives of the Polish government, "which can . . . bring about the full normalization of relations."

The high level of religious practice among Catholics in Poland and the loyalty of the people to the bishops have their roots in the difficulties Poland has experienced in the last 200 years.

From the late 18th century until the end of World War I, Poland was partitioned among Prussia, Austria and Russia. After 20 years of independence the country was occupied by Germany from 1939-45. Since then, Communist governments, backed by the presence of more than 70,000 Soviet troops in the country, have ruled Poland.

Having no alternative by virtue of geography and recent history, the Poles give unswerving loyalty to Moscow's desires and dictates in the field of politics and foreign policy.

In return for this loyalty, the Soviets have shrewdly permitted Poland to express its own true self in the broad areas of culture and economics. Polish nationalism is a very powerful force, more so than elsewhere in the East bloc and Moscow realizes it must be safely vented.

As a result, it is not Communist ideology but nationalism reinforced by religion that animates Polish society.

The Roman Catholic Church constitutes the most powerful religious body anywhere in the Communist world. At times it is referred to as "the other government in Poland." Nearly four-fifths of all Poles attend Mass every week; nearly all children are baptized and subsequently receive after-school religious instruction—including the children of many Communist Party members.

Poland is conspicuously free of the "sloganitis" one finds in other East bloc countries, where buildings are strewn with red banners proclaiming the virtues of socialism and pledging "eternal friendship" with the Soviet Union.

The country's number one citizen, Communist Party boss Edward Gierek—even refuses to allow his portrait to adorn government offices. Poland's traditional symbol, the eagle, is invariably displayed.

"We admit it, in Poland Wyszynski is more Pope than Paul," a high Vatican official recently confided.

In Poland, the Cardinal is head for life of the bishops' conference which meets six times annually—more often than any other conference. The Vatican will name no bishop in Poland without prior consent of the Primate.

It is Poland's situation which makes the Primate's power necessary and his own unswerving devotion to the papacy which makes it tolerable, even desirable.

There is no doubt that the Primate's personal strength and the "cult of personality" build up around him are major factors that have kept the faith in Poland strong while the Church in some other Eastern European nations is dying.

Polish Church leaders admit that there are strong nationalist overtones in the image which the Primate projects.

> For centuries the Polish Primates ruled when there was no king. We often joke that Wyszynski still believes in this concept of 'interrex.'

In the mid-1960's the Primate was a staunch defender of Poland's right to disputed territories in German hands on the Oder and Neisse Rivers.

In sermons, the Primate, who grew up in the town of Zurela under Czarist Russian rule, has warned Poles against Russian influence.

In the winter of 1975, he successfully led Poland's bishops in a fight against a government-sponsored amendment to their national constitution which would have recognized a special bond between Russia and Poland.

In 1956, when he emerged from three years of house arrest for not endorsing the government's imprisonment of another bishop, the Cardinal attributed his release to the Black Madonna.

Getting off the train in Rome on his way to receiving the red hat promised while he was under arrest, the Primate told the West, "I bring you the blessing of Our Lady of Czestochowa."

Despite vestiges of triumphalism, a fierce Marian devotion and strong nationalist feelings, the Cardinal is not an immovable conservative.

On the political front, he tried early to reach a *modus vivendi* with the Communists. In 1950 he signed an agreement in which the Church recognized the Communist government in return for liberties (never fully granted). With Wladislaw Gomulka's rise to power in 1956, Cardinal Wyszynski emerged from arrest and initiated a similar agreement, with a similar lack of results.

Even critics say that his hard-line stance against the government, clearly voiced in his periodic hour-long homilies, is the fault of the authorities.

And doubtlessly the Cardinal is still convinced of what he said about Poland's future during a Church-state crisis several years ago: "I can assure you that Jesus Christ will be the master of the coming century."

Czechoslovakia

Few political reforms in history have aroused as much popular support as Dubcek's ill-fated liberalization in Czechoslovakia. Dubcek pleased everyone in Czechoslovakia except the Russians. Even religious leaders joined hands with long-time Communists and workers with long-haired students in unqualified support for their besieged leader and his programs.

Everyone feared a purge, with the betrayals and calumnies that are always part of that institution. But a few days after the invasion, an *ad hoc* meeting of religious leaders throughout the country issued a joint statement on the crisis. It opened with words expressing the churches' support for the Czech leaders, to whom they affirmed allegiance. Next came a paragraph of support for democratic socialism and the values it espouses. The remainder of the letter outlined a set of moral guidelines for Christians. Christians were admonished to retain the bonds of love with every person, no matter what his political conviction: to befriend, help and guard one's neighbor against wrong. The letter was signed by major Protestant figures and every Catholic bishop in the country.

Before Dubcek, the Church in Czechoslovakia was properly described as a *Church of Silence*. This does not mean that churches were closed. They were open and functioning all through the Communist period, but the Church had no voice in public affairs and no influence on society. All Church property had been nationalized in 1949, and by way of indemnification the State paid the salaries of priests and maintained the churches. But the Church was an employee of the State and subject to intervention and control at every turn. Religious orders were disbanded, and their priests sent to work. Only those few priests who gained the approval of the Minister of Religious Affairs could do priestly work.

Since most bishops were not acceptable, Czech sees remained vacant, administered by a chancery official or a vicar general.

All the seminaries were closed except two—one for Czechs, one for Slovaks—and the government controlled the number of applicants. Each year about seventy applications were made, but twenty candidates received government approval; of the twenty, usually about twelve finished. Over the years this has caused a shortage of priests, which Bishop Tomasek called "one of the most pressing problems facing our Church today."

The Catholic press was not totally shut down, but it was effectively stripped of any real influence. Censorship worked directly and indirectly. The editorial boards received very precise directives. There were rules defining what kind of news could or could not be reported. Full-length articles, often highly critical of the Pope, bishops and religion, were forced on Catholic papers. The Church was silent because it had no voice of its own.

Dubcek returned to the Church both its voice and its self-esteem. Press censorship was removed—which immediately restored new life to the Church. Freed from an exclusive preoccupation with its own intramural problems, the Church addressed itself to public issues in order to bring a Christian perspective to the pressing questions of the day. Public announcements were permitted. Conferences and public lectures were organized. In a word, the Church again began to make a difference.

Every aspect of Church life improved under Dubcek. Instructions for children were permitted on church premises, and the fear of reprisal disappeared. The restrictions on seminary applicants were removed, and the number of students jumped immediately from 20 to 135 in one seminary; it went to 120 in the other. "We have plenty of vocations," said Bishop Tomasek.

> The challenge is to give them the best possible education, to make them men of the times, not just parrots of tired old platitudes. They must understand the moment in which they live if they are to be effective priests.

Bishop Tomasek was no longer alone in Czechoslovakia. There were now six other bishops governing dioceses in every part of the country. Seven sees were still vacant. Under Dubcek, presumable, they would have been filled before long. Now no one is sure what will happen.

In a recent issue of *Via (The Way)*, a theological review, was this editorial comment:

> These last years we were, in our country, in a sort of interior emigration. The underground, persecuted Church became transformed more and more into a personal, private one. Today, as we appear openly again, we become a Church both personal and public. Circumstances have changed; we are no longer a state Church; the Constantinian era is over. We have much to do, much to rebuild. But after all, it is God's grace, our faith, that will bring the final response.

Czechs make up about 65 per cent of the population and Slovaks 30 per cent. The Slovaks regard themselves as a group distinct from the Czechs, although a majority favor working with the Czechs in a common state with extensive autonomy for Slovakia. The remaining 5 per cent of the people are Hungarians and Ukrainians in Slovakia, Germans in Bohemia and Moravia, and Poles close to the border in northern Moravia. There are also about 250,000 Gypsies, who live mainly in Slovakia, and are the fastest growing ethnic element in the population.

At the time of the 1948 coup there were more than nine million Roman Catholics in Czechoslovakia, including about 500,000 of the Eastern-rite (Uniates). They were served by 5,779 secular priests and 1,163 priests who belonged to religious orders; of these clergy about 400 were Uniates. By 1965 the number of Roman Catholics had fallen to eight million. Detailed figures obtained from a Czechoslovak Catholic source indicated the following position at the end of 1972:

In the 13 dioceses and administrations of the Latin-rite

Number of parishes	4,489
Number of non-parochial cures	1,602
Number of active clergy	3,335
Number of retired clergy	442
Number of convents	327
Number of nuns	7,169
Number of ordinands	542

In the one diocese (Presov) of the Eastern-rite

Number of parishes	201
Number of non-parochial cures	14
Number of active clergy	197
Number of retired clergy	65
Number of convents	5
Number of nuns	78
Number of ordinands	19

In the course of just over 20 years the number of active Roman Catholic clergy has fallen by about 50 per cent.

The largest Church after the Roman Catholic is the Czechoslovak National Church, or the Czechoslovak Hussite Church, as it is now called. In 1970 its membership was said to number about 650,000, located in about 350 parishes and served by a rather smaller number of priests, of whom about 80 are women. There are six bishops, headed by a Bishop Patriarch (Novak), who is *primus inter pares*.

Figures relating to the Evangelical Church of Czech Brethren have about 270,000 members who meet in 521 places of worship and are served by 278 ministers, whose number includes 20 women.

The Slovak Lutheran Church has 430,000 members, 384 places of worship and 350 ministers. The Reformed Church in Slovakia, which embraces a Calvinist theology and is of Hungarian origin, has 100,000 members, about 300 places of worship and about 150 pastors. The Silesian Lutheran Church has 50,000 members, 41 places of worship and 25 pastors. The Church of the Brethren has 8,000 members, 29 churches and 30 pastors, while the Unity of Brethren (or the Moravian Brethren) has 8,000 members 18 churches and 20 ministers. The Baptist Church has only 5,500 members on its rolls but probably twice as many as this attend its worship regularly. There are small numbers of Old Catholics, Methodists, Seventh Day Adventists and Unitarians.

At the end of World War II, and after the Sub-Carpathian Ukraine were about 48,000 Jews in the country, and when the Communists seized power, more than half of these emigrated to Israel. By the time of the "Prague Spring" in which some Jews played an important part, Jewish population is only 8-10,000. There are about 10 congregations in Bohemia and Moravia and about 20 congregations in Slovakia. There are two rabbis—one in Prague, the other in Bratislava. Before World War II there were 320 synagogues and prayer-houses in Slovakia alone, but now only 20 of these remain.

A strikingly clear and comprehensive summary of the sufferings of the Roman Catholic Church over a period of almost 20 years was given in a petition signed by 22,317 Catholics and sent to Alexander Dubcek on March 17, 1968. It read:

> After a number of unsuccessful negotiations between Church and State, an attack was mounted in the 1950s against the Catholic Church in the CSSR by the public authorities then in power. This upset both the life of the Church itself and good mutual relations (with the State):
>
> 1. The dioceses were robbed of their bishops, who were interned or imprisoned.
> 2. The legal authority of those bishops who remained was reduced to a minimum.
> 3. Hundreds of priests were imprisoned—simply because they fulfilled their duties conscientiously.
> 4. Religious and ecclesiastical superiors were involved in show trials for which force was used to extort confessions of guilt that referred to alleged facts that had no basis in reality.
> 5. In the course of the single night of 13-14 April, 1950, all the religious orders and congregations in the entire republic were dissolved in a manner in which no parallel can be found in the history of European civilization.
> 6. Relations with the Holy See were broken off.
> 7. "Church secretaries" were established to whom in effect was transferred all episcopal authority in the administration of Church affairs.
> 8. For this office people were chosen who made no secret of their attitude of hostility towards the Church.
> 9. Under the pressure of threats and discrimination religious instruction has until recently been almost completely abolished in the schools. Even today, though religious instruction is given here and there, in many places the same methods of intimidation are applied as in former years.
> 10. Many priests affected by measures described above, such as imprisonment, were not given the opportunity of returning to pastoral work, although the number of priestless parishes has been increasing.
> 11. For years incredible difficulties have been put in the way of young men wishing to devote themselves to the priestly vocation and to enter the seminary.
> 12. At the present time these restrictions remain for the most part in force. This gives rise to the remarkable situation that the condition of the Catholic Church in the CSSR probably represents the last enclave in which to an undiminished extent those measures of coercion are still most strongly applied which at one time were applied to citizens in general during the period of the so-called cult of personality. Five dioceses in Bohemia and Moravia and five dioceses in Slovakia have been without a bishop for several years. It is difficult to understand that such a state of affairs is possible in the heart of Europe, among peoples with a highly developed civilization.

The following decade offers only a depressing commentary on the serious grievances referred to in the petition. All but two of the seminaries were closed, and during the early part of 1950 the religious orders were ruthlessly attacked. After a show trial in which the superiors of ten religious orders were accused and pronounced guilty of subversive activities against the State, soldiers and policemen were sent to every monastery and convent in the country during the night of April 13-14, 1950. The monks and nuns were forced into lorries and taken to a number of "concentration monasteries." Here they were supposed to be free to continue the religious life, but gradually they were secularized. Recruitment ceased and, although many monks and nuns remained faithful to their vows in factories and on the farms where they were driven to work, the institutional expressions of monasticism were virtually eliminated.

A fortnight after the assault on the seminaries, it was the turn of the Uniate Church in Slovakia. This Church had a single diocese, Presov, and just over 585,000 members who were served by about 400 priests, but on April 28, 1950, a council attended by five priests and 300 lay people declared themselves in favor of the Uniate Church returning to the Orthodox Church under the Patriarchate of Moscow. Once this decision was announced, the government moved to enforce it. Within a short time the Uniate bishop (Gojdic) and his suffragan (Hopko), together with about 100 priests were arrested and given prison sentences. Bishop Gojdic died in prison in 1960.

Since 1969 there has been a limited breakthrough in the production and distribution of Bibles. Prior to the "Spring" there was very little Bible production in Czechoslovakia but between 1969 and 1973, 120,000 copies of Czech and Slovak Scriptures were produced. An ecumenical committee is working on a new Czech translation of the Bible and 30,000 copies of the Gospels were printed in 1973. It will be a few years before this project is completed, but a new translation of the Slovak Bible was ready for production in 1973. Distribution of Bibles takes place in the churches and copies are also on sale in church bookshops in Prague.

The main churches of Czechoslovakia all have their own newspapers and magazines, the chief of which are published in both Czech and Slovak.

Yet the fate of Marxists ready to enter into ideological dialogue has also been harsh. So thorough was the purge of philosophers, sociologists and psychologists that after 1969 the faculties teaching these subjects in Prague and elsewhere had to suspend almost all their work. Many of those dismissed are now taxi-drivers and waiters. Officially, the links forged in dialogue remain.

Is there a "persecution of Christians" under East European Communist regimes? Marxist-Leninist exponents are offended at the question. They point out that churches are still open and clergy not imprisoned—only "enemies of peace and detente" would make such "unfactual" statements.

An objective picture of actual conditions in Czechoslovakia has just become available through the arrival in the West of a secret program for the annihilation of Christianity.

It concerns Orava, the most northern part of Slovakia, little visited by tourists but a land of beautiful scenery and rich cultural tradition. Christianity still has strong roots there. Since "85% of the population are still influenced by Christianity" the document reveals that the government has sent especially trained atheistic ideologists to the area. These are some excerpts from the program:

Religion is not a matter of educational level but concerns the emotions. The mother has the child in the decisive formative years. Women also work on their husbands and influence them to participate in at least some church functions. The trade unions are delegated to the task of influencing women. "The threat of losing their jobs or being forced into more menial employment should afford effective means of moral pressure." Since sick people are vulnerable, Christian girls are not to be accepted at nurses' training schools or schools of medicine.

The liquidation of the church must begin with the irresolute, those having two faces. There are some who have an ambiguous or hypocritical attitude to religion. Their true feelings come to the surface in exceptional situations, such as the Dubcek era. Most of them are intellectuals.

Police informers are to be increased in number, so that clergy and active laymen in every neighborhood can be kept under surveillance. In the last two or three years the activity and influence of the church has been noticeably curtailed. The state now requires a permit before clergymen can perform ministerial functions. This has served to eliminate clergymen who spread anti-socialist views and by their actions and attitudes contradict the socialist constitution.

Splitting the Catholic clergy by playing up to the "Pacem in Terris" group helps confuse the faithful. This minority group favors cooperation with the Marxist-Leninist state in humanitarian service. They will also appear on the platform at state functions and issue statements praising the government for programs of social betterment. These leftist clergy can be called the speech choir of the State Secretariat for Church Affairs. We must support every priest who does not want to be drawn into the counter-revolutionary camp.

Also, the Slovakian Evangelical Church from now on must be better watched. Its activities and worship services are not to be underestimated, especially since many laymen participate. It has progressive tendencies theologically, which weaken the socialist ideological battle spirit.

The conditions for a successful outcome in the anti-religious campaign involve granting psychological, social, political and financial favors to those who abandon their faith.

The outline of an atheistic political platform is followed by these concluding remarks:

Our immediate goal in Orava is to increase the number of atheists from 13% to 25% by June, 1976. In the current school year the percentage of children taking religious instruction must be reduced by half. The responsibility for this rests on school superintendents, the Party chairmen, the trade unions, and all classroom teachers.

Individuals in higher positions of whatever kind, who do not grasp the leading role of the Party in society, are to be discharged. In such cases an investigation is to be made as to whether these parents are securing socialistic training for their children. If not, such children are to be expelled from middle and high schools.

Prosecution of the church in Slovakia began before the end of World War II.

Communist agents parachuted into the state during the summer of 1944, set up a pro-Communist National Slovak Council through which they mounted an early offensive against bishops, priests and religious, many of whom were hindered in the performance of their duties, and a

STATUS OF RELIGION IN EASTERN EUROPE   311

number of whom were killed.

On April 16, 1945, church schools were nationalized on the basis of an order issued by the Council the previous September 7. Thus the regime seized elementary schools, secondary schools and colleges. By the end of the month the confiscation of all church property was ordered.

On April 25, 1945 Catholic youth organizations were disbanded and their property taken over. Severe restrictions were placed on the availability of Catholic books, and the Catholic press. The training of students for the priesthood was crippled.

In 1947, a year following elections in which more than 60 per cent of Slovak voters opposed Communist state, all church property was confiscated. In December, Msgr. Jozef Tiso, president of the Slovak Republic, went on trial for "treason;" he was executed the following April.

Between April and June, 1945, some 20,000 persons were confined to concentration camps. Two bishops—John Vojtassak of Spis and Michael Buzalka, Auxiliary of Trnava and 170 priests were jailed. Between 1945 and 1947, it is estimated that 120,000 Slovaks spent time in jail. During the first year following the coup of February 25, 1948, between 120,000 to 150,000 were imprisoned. Between 1945 and 1949, approximately 10 per cent of the Slovak population spent some time in jail or a concentration camp.

In the summer of 1948, in what might be called the last dramatic public demonstration by Catholics in the country, Slovak peasants rose to the defense of priests and religious, clashing with police and other government agents seeking to enforce restrictive measures against them.

On February 26, 1948, orders were issued for the prohibition and restriction of Catholic publications. More than 53 of them were suppressed by the following January.

In the same year, church-run hospitals and ecclesiastical real estate were nationalized. All primary and secondary schools and junior seminaries were placed under state administration. Within a year, Catholic schools were forced out of existence. The Catholic Action organization was liquidated in November 1948, in a preliminary step toward the formation in June, 1948, of a puppet organization designed to infiltrate the Church.

The regime took the first steps toward ending diplomatic relations with the Vatican in April, 1948, and completed this action by March 16, 1950, eight months after the Holy See condemned active and willing membership in the Communist Party. A state bureau of Ecclesiastical Affairs was set up under a law passed in October, 1949, for the purpose of tightening control over the Church.

Between April and May, 1950, the Eastern-rite Diocese of Presov in Slovakia was dissolved, and pressure was applied to 341 priests and 327,000 faithful to make them an Orthodox Diocese.

All religious houses were taken over between March 14, 1950, and the end of 1951. Men and women religious were expelled, assigned to work brigades and camps, or detained in concentration monasteries under government surveillance. In 1951, about 3,000 priests were deprived of their liberty as the government attempted to force "patriot" priests on the people.

A number of theatrical trials of bishops and priests were held in 1950.

In the following year, in Slovakia, three bishops were tried and sentenced to prisons: Vojtassak, 24 years; Buzalka, life, and Paul Gojdic, Byzantine-rite of Presov, life.

In 1958 from 450 to 500 priests were in jail; an undisclosed number of religious and Byzantine-rite priests had been deported; two bishops released from prison in 1956 were under house arrest; one bishop was imprisoned at Leopoldov and two at the Mirov reformatory.

In 1960, a new Constitution gives no recognition to the Church and implicitly aims at the suppression of any traces of religious freedom.

Despite the Communist government's claims that it is tolerant of religion, over the past few years a consistent campaign has been mounted against religious freedom.

Demands by the bishops to be allowed to carry out their religious functions in freedom to run their seminaries without state control and to enjoy the right of giving instruction freely, have been interpreted as examples of their anti-socialist, anti-Communist attitudes.

In the early 70's, public officials moved in on the Catholic Church to restrict freedom. The Slovak Socialist Republic made it a requirement that priests get government permission to celebrate even a private Mass. Such is the life of the Catholic Church in enslaved Slovakia.

Bishop Dominik Kalata said in an interview that religious persecution of Catholics in Slovakia has been renewed with vigor by the Communist regime in Czechoslovakia.

The Bishop, who was secretly consecrated in his homeland so that others could be ordained, said the old-style religious persecution was carried out "with an iron hand and brutality."

> Today they are trying to achieve the same ends with much more refined methods. This way, for the benefit of the outside world, an impression of democracy is presented. The less this fight against religion is noticeable, the more radical it is and the more thorough.

> However, because the state ideology is uncompromising and intolerant, this is only an empty phrase on paper and it can be cleverly used for propaganda purposes abroad.

These hardest hit in the regime's campaign against religion are teachers and state employees in influential positions.

> After the removal of Dubcek, they were all carefully scrutinized and their files updated. Only teachers and professors who are considered reliable Marxists can teach in the high schools and universities. It is required of them to sever their affiliation with their church. . . .

> The teaching of religion is forbidden in Slovakia's high schools, and in elementary schools it can be taught only if both parents of the child request it. Headmasters are obliged to warn parents about "grave consequences" if they persist in asking for religious classes for their children.

Diplomatic relations between Czechoslovakia and the Holy See were broken off in 1950.

At present, less than half of the country's 13 dioceses are administered by full-time residential bishops or apostolic administrators.

For the first time since 1946, the Vatican has been allowed to nominate and consecrate four new bishops in Communist Czechoslovakia.

The Vatican's "foreign minister," Archbishop Agostine Casaroli, presided over the ordination of the new bishops, an unprecedented step that stresses its importance for the Church.

Three of the four nominated bishops are former leaders of the *Pacem in terris (Peace on Earth)* group, a priests' movement that is accepted by the regime and has been openly accused in the official Vatican newspaper of allowing indirect Communist rule of the Church in Czechoslovakia.

One of the new bishops, who for years headed the priests' group, is Msgr. Josef Vrana, named bishop of Olomouc in Moravia with the title of apostolic administrator.

The other new bishops were for dioceses in Slovakia. The Rev. Julius Grabis was named to the See of Trnava, the Rev. Jan Pasztor was made Bishop of Nitra and Msgr. Josef Feranec, Bishop of Banska Bystrica.

Previously, 10 out of Czechoslovakia's 13 dioceses were provisionally filled by "Pacem" appointees. Only one residential bishop, one auxilliary bishop, and two apostolic administrators (substitute bishops) remained of the original church hierarchy to minister to the needs of Czechoslovakia's estimated 11 million Catholics, who comprise 70 per cent of the population.

The attachement to religion is weakest in Bohemia, somewhat stronger in Moravia, and strongest in Slovakia. No reliable figures have been published on religion since 1948.

Czechoslovakia's Communist regime has quenched any smoldering hope that its tireless campaign against religion had slowed down when it allowed four of the country's 11 vacant dioceses to be filled.

According to *Prague Radio*, Bishop Josef Vrana has assured the regime he will continue as president of the government-sponsored movement of "peace priests," *Pacem in terris*. The Vatican had agreed to his nomination as apostolic administrator of Olomouc only on condition he resign as president and cease active participation in the organization.

The Czech-language and Slovak language Catholic newspapers, which have different editorial staffs, both quoted government sources as expressing satisfaction at the nominations on the grounds that two of the four bishops were favorable to *Pacem in terris*. This however is strongly denied by Church sources.

The ordination ceremony at Olomouc was crowded by about 6,000 people, including many who had to remain outside the church. Seven bishops distributed Communion to the crowds, and an eyewitness described the distribution of Communion as "seemingly endless."

A Slovak Jesuit, secretly consecrated a bishop after being imprisoned for his opposition to Communist rule, now has a menial job in a storehouse in Bratislava, Czechoslovakia.

Earlier in 1975, Bishop Joseph Korec was deprived of the state license he needed for any sort of priestly activities as a Jesuit. He contracted tuberculosis while in jail, yet was forced to work in a chemical factory which made his condition worse. He is now store clerk in the same plant.

The education of seminarians and the functioning of newly ordained priests has been severely restricted by authorities of the Slovakia region of the country.

Of the 90 seminarians scheduled to be ordained in 1974, 41 have been ordered into military service for two years, despite the fact that students are exempt.

In addition, only 20 of 80 applicants were permitted to start seminary studies. Authorities said there are not "a sufficient number of openings" available for the future priests. About 70 parishes in Slovakia, however, are without pastors, and many other parishes need more priests.

Also, many of the 80 newly ordained priests are unable to function as priests, not even to say Mass. The only Mass many of them have said was one at their ordination.

In ceremonies of consecration of new priests in Pressburg, of 47 candidates, 7 were not consecrated because they had not taken part in *Pacem in terris*-organized Red Army's celebration. However, the reason was given as "lack of respect towards their dean."

The newly ordained priests who do have pastoral posts have been warned not to try to promote priestly vocations among altar boys and to refrain from using any teaching aids of any sort except the catechism in religion classes.

Vatican Radio reported on August 29, 1974, that courts in the Ukraine and in Czechoslovakia have jailed Catholic priests for violating laws restricting religious freedom.

Quoting the Italian news agency ANSA, which in turn quoted the Lvov newspaper *Lwowskaya Pravda*, Vatican Radio said Father Bernard Mitskevicg, 44, had been sentenced for repeated violations

The newspaper lamented that atheists in the Ukraine "had not taken sufficient note of the priest's influence on youth."

Three columns in the newspaper's August 20 issue, said Vatican Radio, reported the trial and the charges, which involved: drawing the villagers to church, repairing the church, organizing group excursions in the Carpathian mountains, exhorting parents to bring their children to church, organizing prayer groups for youth and distributing crucifixes and other religious objects.

The newspaper did not report the length of the sentence imposed on Father Mitskevicg. Vatican Radio quoted the Center for East European Studies as reporting a three-month solitary confinement sentence passed January 22 by the Czechoslovak Lipt Mikulas district court on Father Jozef Gazda. The 41-year-old priest had been accused of giving catechetical lessons to his nephews and some of their friends.

Father Gazda, added Vatican Radio, had been deprived of his state permit to act as a pastor on November 28, 1971.

According to the study center's report of the court finding, as broadcast by Vatican Radio, the priest "confessed, and in his defense declared that he saw no criminal activity in his actions."

However, the court found he had committed a crime because ministerial activity may be carried out only with government permission.

Monks and nuns are either sent back to the only institutions they are allowed to manage—asylums and psychiatric hospitals or kept in old convents, living under conditions resembling those of concentration camps.

In the village of Bila Voda, which is located in the northern part of Czechoslovakia, there are three nuns for each inhabitant. In this village, in one of the sisters' monasteries in Czechoslovakia, live about 300 nuns. They belong to nine different orders. The religious receive State pensions.

Religious life in Czechoslovakia is being liquidated, according to superiors of Religious communities who have asked their country's bishops in a letter and an accompanying "Memorandum on the Situation of Religious Communities in CSSR" to aid in this "grave situation."

In their letter dated in summer of 1977, the superiors told the bishops that "further silence concerning the present situation would mean acquiescence to the factual liquidation of Religious life among us."

In 1950, there were 12,570 Religious—1,910 men and 10,660 women— in the country. That year, "the Religious were driven out from their convents. The greater part of the Sisters were forced to work in other than their own institutions or in factories."

Although the bishops had discussed the problems at a conference (1972) and later approved a document that was sent to the Ministry of Culture, "five years have passed since that time and our situation became worse; besides discrimination against us, about 1,000 Religious have died."

In their four-page memorandum, the superiors protested 10 current situations which they said violate national or international laws. Among them:

Religious have been forbidden to congregate freely for community living or to receive new members since March 1, 1971;

Religious are not permitted to pursue studies at the university level or in special fields, and women Religious are barred from administrative posts in almost all areas;

Travel to foreign countries is denied to Religious persons more than other citizens;

Today we are not concerned about the past, but mostly about the present and tomorrow. If we plead for your help, we declare that for us it is not a question of returning to us the property of the Religious, but of insuring the right of Religious life and the possibility of living this Religious life in our socialist society.

The letter stated the superiors' belief that permission to accept new members into the religious orders

would not affect the situation of the work force among us; the members of religious orders would continue to work in their calling with the awareness that they could realize their God-given charism.

In the response to the memorandum, four Dutch associations of religious priests, sisters, and brothers have appealed to the Prague government to end its stranglehold on religious life in Czechoslovakia.

The declaration was sent in late October, 1977, to key Czechoslovakian government officials.

Actual state of the religious sisters is a state of dying out. According to the State rule, novices can not be accepted any more. There are in the country still some 7,000 sisters, but one can clearly foresee when the monasteries will cease to exist. Occupations of the sisters are strictly limited by the government. The religious sisters who were working previously in schools, hospitals, orphanages and old peoples' homes, now are permitted at the best to take care of retarded children and old invalids. When they reach retirement age themselves, they are sent to one of twenty-nine old peoples' homes for nuns and priests, run by a Catholic organization and supported by the State.

Nuns working in hospitals for the incurable in Czechoslovakia must now wear civilian dress if they joined their communities after 1968.

In addition, the nuns are salaried like civilian employes.

Also, according to reports, all priests licensed to function by the country's Communist government have been ordered to renew their licenses.

Only a relatively small fraction have so far been permitted to continue functioning, and many are being scrutinized by the government for "loyalty to the state."

Czechoslovak priests are being forced to retire at the age of 60, while nuns are sent to "concentration convents."

A memorandum by Slovak nuns to the Prime Minister of the Slovak Socialist Republic is characteristic of the present situation. In this memorandum the nuns protest against a vast limitation on their activities.

The activities of the nuns in Slovakia are restricted to the following areas: a) sanatoriums and nursing homes for feeble-minded people, b) charitable homes for aged priests and nuns, c) health care according to the rules of the Ministry of Health—probably only in lunatic asylums.

On the other hand, the nuns are forbidden to engage in the following: a) activities in institutions for the aged, b) social work in families and communities, c) teaching of religion, d) handling of parish households, 3) accepting novices (while young people who were already accepted are to be released), f) acquiring property for the order.

Only a very limited number of students of theology is admitted to one seminary for six dioceses of Bohemia and Moravia and one Slovak seminary, and so the situation reached the stage where more priests have been dying per year than new ones have been ordained. The situation is so serious that in some areas one priest is in charge of eight or even ten parishes and it will soon be like that everywhere. All priests, pastors, and ministers of religion must have a special government permit for performing normal priestly duties and the permit must be regularly renewed. At present about six hundred Catholic priests and seventy Protestant pastors were refused the permit. Any priest who says the Mass—even privately at home—without the government permit, shall be sentenced to one year of prison, and any priest who permits his church to be used for those "illegal masses," shall be sentenced to two years of prison. The permit was refused to two priests in Prague just because they were too successful in their pastoral activities among young people.

Of course, foreign tourists can see in Prague that churches are full, but they do not know how many churches are closed and how many sacrifices and sufferings it costs those who practice their religion.

It has been forbidden to build new churches and so new settlements with fifty or eighty thousand people are without a church. Some churches were turned into art galleries (in Cheb), into concert halls (in Opava), and into storehouses (in Karlovy Vary).

A group of protestant students of theology sent a petition to the government authorities complaining that in the most cases the necessary permit for normal pastoral duties had not been granted to the graduants of the Evangelical Faculty of J. A. Comenius, and asked for a more tolerant policy. The result was that the initiator of this petition, F. Matula, was sentenced to fifteen months of prison.

No priest is permitted to administer any sacraments to the sick in hospitals; no confession, no holy communion, and no anointing of the sick is possible in hospitals, and no pastor or a minister of religion can console those who are dying in hospitals and assist them by his prayer.

When the new liturgy was introduced by the Catholic Church, no missals could be printed in Czechoslovakia and missals printed in Rome could not be sent as a gift or brought by tourists into the country, so duplicated sheets have been used by priests in churches.

There are no Church schools in Czechoslovakia, no religious books can be printed and only one Catholic weekly for the whole territory of Bohemia and Moravia with a limited number of pages and copies have been tolerated until now. Monasteries and convents were closed and only a small number of communities of sisters, who care for retarded children and old people, have been in existence but no novices can be admitted.

Czech daily *Prace* complained in a long article that "enemies of the regime" were smuggling Bibles, holy cards and rosary beads into Czechoslovakia and that tons of that hostile propaganda was confiscated by the border police. "Disruptive elements, spies, criminals, refugees, tourists-smugglers, these are those individuals, who have been always trying to smuggle those weapons of imperialistic ideological arsenal into our country," so concluded *Prace*.

The criminal methods of the Czechoslovak Communist regime can be illustrated by the martyrdom of Cardinal Trochta, Bishop of Litomerice, who was visited by the Communist district secretary for Church Affairs and interrogated by him. The district secretary knew about the Cardinal's illness and that his doctor ordered that the patient must not be disturbed, but despite that, the district secretary roared at the Cardinal and used crude insults and threats and subjected him to sharp interrogation and mental torture for six hours. After the secretary's departure, Cardinal Trochta went to bed completely exhausted, suffered a stroke and died the following day on April 8, 1974.

Pope Paul VI, meeting with Czechoslovak bishops who were making their five-year *ad limina* visits to Rome in 1977, told:

> This Apostolic See has not failed to do everything and will not fail to do anything to insure that the 13 dioceses of Bohemia, Moravia and Slovakia have sacred pastors who are known for piety and zeal for souls, and who are bound to the Church and have generous love for their country.

During the Pope Paul's 14-year pontificate, the Vatican has repeatedly received an icy "no" from Czechoslovak Communists to its request for permission to appoint bishops to the eight vacant dioceses.

Vatican officials say that the situation of the Church in Czechoslovakia is one of the worst in Europe.

Lately Communist officials have intensified a broad program to spread atheism, especially among youth.

By all known facts it is clearly documented that Communism is a deceitful, aggressive, and criminal type of atheism which has been using all positions of power to destroy religion, freedom and democracy by all means of government administrative machinery, police courts of law, economic sanctions, schools and exclusion from higher education and from advancement in career.

To a certain degree, an internal peace returned to Czechoslovakia in 1975: the purges and political processes belonged to the past, the living standard continually rose, and for decades the low birth-rate increased significantly. However, many of "Prague's Spring" representatives from 1968, in their explicit declarations, said that people ruled by fear can be easily swayed to care for their private matters and leave the politics to the politicians.

Indirectly there can be noticed a lack of existential security among the Czechs and Slovaks, and also a constant increase of spirituality among the adults and young people since 1971. The State is trying to eliminate churches institutionally, while the Party of the neo-Stalinist faction has a strong opposition to any religious expression. The keen anti-Church policy of the objectors is pronounced in the magazine *Atheismus*, which is of a low intellectual profile, in obvious disgusting form, an exact copy of the fight against the Church from the times of Stalin. There are many indications that this verbal-radicalism will affect the concrete measure very little because Husak's leadership from a higher point of interest within a reasonable space of time has, after much difficulty, nearly reached internal pacification.

The Russian "liberation" which ended Dubcek's career did not seem to dampen his renewal of religious freedom. The Czech government expressed an interest in normalizing relations with the Vatican in July, 1970. In March, 1971, the Vatican dispatched a delegation to Prague for a new round of talks to accomplish this end.

However, the thaw was followed by bitter frost. This statement applies not only to the political developments in Czechoslovakia after the crushing of the "Prague Spring" in 1968, but also to the situation of the Church.

Experts agree the situation—after the short bright spell of 1968— is similar to that in the Stalinist period. The Church has become the butt of concentrated attacks from two directions—through administrative measures and ideological arguments.

The Communist regime is attempting to curb religious activities slowly but effectively by administrative action. The "truce," which held until talks between the government and the Vatican failed in the spring of 1971, no longer exists.

More than half of all parishes in Bohemia lack priests, and there is no chance to overcome the shortage. At the moment only 12 students study for the priesthood in the entire Archdiocese of Olomouc. As a result of administrative chicanery, the number of children attending religious instruction in school is sharply declining.

At the same time, the regime has endorsed increased ideological attacks on the Church. Jozef Lenart, first secretary of the Slovak Communist Party, charged the Church with having misused the situation in 1968 "to create a political basis for clericalism and Catholicism."

Lenart claimed religious sentiments were misused by the Church to promote "anti-Sovietism and anti-socialism."

The regime has increased its atheist propaganda. The magazine for teachers, *Ucitelski Noviny*, urged abolition of any "liberal attitude toward religion and the Church in our society." The journal also pledged increased atheist education of young people by the Party, mass media, schools and major organization.

It also suggested the Academy of Science should devise the best methods to promote atheist education.

Party officials have said repeatedly at recent meetings, that religion "has a negative influence on the formation of Socialist conscience."

The Bratislava Communist newspaper, *Pravda*, demanded that religious ceremonies—christenings, weddings and funerals—should be replaced by Socialist ceremonies, because "the Church has misused the most important stages of human life for its own purposes."

> After rightists and counterrevolutionaries are removed from the party and government, we must concentrate in working a platform to cope with the reactionary policy of the Church. Our task is very difficult, but we shall solve the problem.

While its Eastern European neighbors seem to be trying to reach an accommodation with the Catholic Church, Czechoslovakia has taken several steps backward.

The campaign against the Catholic Church began early in 1972. The program was increased in May and June, after the Central Committee of the Communist Party published a 140-page report showing a marked increase in the practice of religion in 1968 and 1969, when Alexander Dubcek was in power.

The situation in Czechoslovakia may perhaps be pictured by this:

Only one diocese, Litomerice, still has a resident bishop recognized by both the Vatican and the government, Bishop Stepan Trochta, 67 years old. He served a 10-year prison term, then worked eight years as a plumber before he was allowed to resume his position as bishop in 1968.

The government has begun the selective retirement of priests at 60 years of age, which adds still more to the critical shortage of priests.

Kathpress in Vienna, the well informed Austrian Catholic news agency, reports the regime in spring of 1972 suspended 33 priests without explanation, most of them young.

The Czechoslovakian government is making every effort to reduce the number of priests. In April, 1972, the government excluded 50 of 80 new applicants at one of the two remaining seminaries, and expelled seven students about to be ordained.

With this background, it is almost laughable to read in *Rude Provo*, official Communist newspaper in Prague, accusations of "church propaganda in the west" telling "malevolent lies" in pointing out that Czechoslovakia is persecuting the Catholic Church.

In 1949 the government demanded that all priests sign an oath of loyalty to the regime. Although Bishop Beran refused to sign, he allowed his clergy to do so. Otherwise they would not have been allowed to function as priests. In a short time, however, inevitable conflicts arose in a state where the Church was considered inimical and contradictory to the very idea of Communism.

The outcome of these conflicts was a priesthood divided into a spectrum. At one end stood the total collaborators—whether opportunistic, fearful or honestly convinced that state control of the Church is good. Shading off from these men were the priests who had compromised themselves during the years—not out and out collaborators, but men forced to violate their consciences. Next in the spectrum stood those who were stunned by the change to Communism from the beloved old order. Many just pulled their heads in and waited out their years, apathetic and antiseptic in their ministry.

At the brighter end of the spectrum were priests who had mastered the art of walking the tight rope, practicing as devoted priests at the dangerous boundary of the no man's land that the government calls anti-socialist activity. Other priests who had stepped over into the mine-laden no man's land soon found themselves moved from areas where they had had influence on Czechoslovakian life to some small, quiet village far from Prague, Bratislava, Brno or Pilsen.

Finally, at the far end of the spectrum were those priests who had made the mistake of speaking out on controversial topics, or of having joined religious orders, and who now work as bus drivers and factory workers. These latter, most of whom had spent many years in Communist jails, may not function as priests.

A brighter aspect of the picture of the priesthood was the situation among the younger priests who had not lived as priests through the 1949-1960 period. Having grown up under Communism, they seemed far more capable than the older men to do effective work while avoiding difficulties with the police.

In 1968, during the famous "liberalising" spring in Czechoslovakia, there arose possibilities for the restoration of the Greek Catholic Church. On April 10, 1968 a meeting of 133 priests and faithful, with the participation of Bishop Hopko, took palce in the town of Kosice in East Slovakia. The meeting set up an Action Committee for the restoration of the rights of the Greek Catholic Church in Czechoslovakia. As a result of its activities, the government of Czechoslovakia, on August 13, 1968, issued an official permission for the restoration of the rights of the Greek-Catholic Church. Since that time reorganisation of the Church has begun. About 170 priests have joined Bishop Hopko and have begun to serve their parishes of which there should be about 300.

The church of St. Clement in Prague, which for the last 18 years was in the hands of the Russian Orthodox metropolitan Dorotey, was restored to the Greek Catholics and Bishop Hopko celebrated Mass there in 1968. The remains of the martyred bishop, Pavlo Goydych, were transferred from Leopoldovo prison and buried with all the reverence due to a church dignitary in Priashiv.

The Czechoslovakian Communist Party considers without any doubt that religion has no prospects of any place in Socialist society because it is absolutely incompatible with Marxist-Leninist ideology, which supports a global conception of the world, absolutely atheistic, which it is indispensable to adopt in order to generate the "new man," the protagonist of his future in the new society. "Religious survivals," though hard to die, have no future and their disappearance must be actively promoted. In education, the key sector of society, there must be no space for any alternative to a formation consistent with the ideology of the regime.

Believers in Czechoslovakia, both Catholics and non-Catholics are therefore exposed every day to the hard struggle which the omni-present apparatus of the State is waging tenaciously against their convictions, in particular against aspirations for a religious formation of their children.

The persecution of the Church in Czechoslovakia is being continued. This is not an empty allegation made by "revengers" but a matter of fact having become widely known. The persecution by the Red regime of Prague starts with vexing the few nuns still allowed to practice and ends with a complete surveillance of the bishops. It further consists in hampering religious welfare in the parishes and the training of future priests. However, the persecution of other groups of undesirable persons has recently also been intensified.

Official circles being afraid of the political influence of the Church within the country, of the organizations in exile and the emigrants, the Central Committee of the Communist Party of the CSSR has convened a confidential meeting at the highest level at Bratislava to diliberate on how to fight against the influence of the Church and the emigrants.

The secret talks carried on in Bratislava have led to the following results:

> The methods of persecuting Christians in the CSSR are getting worse and worse. Numerous clergymen are imprisoned, and the nuns are obstructed in their charitable activities. The Church is "run" by the Church Secretariates created by Government and Party. The bishops exert hardly any influence on the running of the Church since they are—just like other clergymen—only employees of the State Church Secretariates. Theological literature sent to the CSSR is confiscated.

> The addressee is interrogated by the police and questioned about alleged "returns." No priest is allowed to say mass without official permission. Transgression of this prohibition is punished by two years of imprisonment. Formerly convicted priests who were rehabilitated under Dubcek are now sent for trial again. They not only have to pay the costs of the new trial which is compulsory, but also return the indemnity received upon their rehabilitation. This applies to all CSSR citizens who were rehabilitated in 1968 and have now again been subjected to Socialist justice.

> The effect of the Church press which is censored anyway has been considerable reduced in Czechoslovakia. By refusing to allot paper the state thwarts the edition of books and publications. The importation of religious literature from the West is punished in principle. Clergymen are even not allowed to have duplicators or visit families; bishops must not publish pastoral letters. Even the most insignificant publication must be authorized by the State, for instance a reference to confirmation lessons.

> There is one exception to all this: a small group of priests whom Moscow is prepared to present to Rome at any cost. Monasteries no longer exist nor hardly any church educational institutions. The Church in the CSSR is exposed to a pressure menacing the roots of its existence. The large number of clergymen dismissed by the regime of Prague from Church life during the past months are now doing any work just to subsist. However, these persecuted priests have only a limited choice of alternative jobs. According to Party functionaries they are suited for subordinate jobs only.

The Catholic Church in Czechoslovakia is still persecuted by the Communist government there despite guarantees of religious freedom contained in the Helsinki agreement and the country's constitution, *Vatican Radio* reported.

Citing a 150-page "white paper" issued by the Swiss national commission on justice and peace, *Vatican Radio* said that the Czechoslovak Church is persecuted as much today as it was during the late 1940's and 1950's, when suppression of Catholicism was at a peak.

According to *Vatican Radio*,

> among the new forms of oppression are fines for and imprisonment of priests who exercise their priestly functions after retirement; various kinds of pressure, psychological and otherwise, to discourage parents from providing their children with religious education, and the refusal to advance qualified children with religious training to higher grades in school.

The report also criticized the government-sanctioned movement, *Pacem in terris*, an organization of priests considered "safe" by the authorities. This group succeeded the "peace priests" movement, which was disbanded in 1968.

Reports reaching the West from Czechoslovakia portray religious groups in a quiet struggle to keep balance in the face of government policies designed to thwart their influence.

Government authorities recently pressured all religious organizations to issue their own statements denouncing the human-rights manifesto Charter 77, according to the New York-based Research Center for Religion and Human Rights in Closed Societies (RCR). The resulting statements use many phrases in common, which the center feels were supplied by the government.

Only seven clergymen are reported to be public signers of Charter 77, which has been endorsed by about 500 Czechoslovaks of various walks of life. But this figure of seven may not reflect the discontent of the some 500 churchmen who have been banned from their pastoral duties since 1968.

According to information, more than 100 Roman Catholic priests have been arrested since the 1975 Helsinki declaration, which pledged 35 signatories to observe certain standards of human rights.

Anti-religious propaganda directed against school children has promoted fears that holding religious beliefs may reduce a child's prospects of receiving higher education. Attendance at religious classes has declined about 40 per cent in Bratislava, Trnava, Kosice, and Piestany (cities in the southeastern part of the country closest to the Soviet Union), since children have been required by schools to fill out questionnaires on their religious beliefs and activities.

In the fall of 1976 four leading rock musicians, both Protestants and Catholics, were sentenced to prison terms ranging from 8 to 18 months for anti-social and anti-socialist conduct. One of the musicians, Scatopluk Karasek, was apparently a graduate of the Protestant Theological Faculty in northwestern Bohemia, and had argued at his trial that belief in religious liberty could not be interpreted as anti-socialist.

Ironically, the measures designed to restrain the influence of the human-rights movement among church circles may be promoting publicity of that cause. Says the RCR, while some churches had heard of Charter 77 via official news media, many of them had never actually seen its provisions until the government pressed them to issue statements about the charter.

The reason more churchmen have not openly signed Charter 77 may be the hardships endured by church circles in recent times. In addition to threats that children of religious families might lose their access to higher education, clergy have faced the constant possibility of dismissal by the

Czechoslovak government, which has the final say on appointments to church offices. Many churchmen have been dismissed and reassigned to manual work, driving trucks, operating elevators, and gravedigging, according to the RCR.

The small group of clergy who did sign Charter 77 apparently are more or less organized and maintain close ties with one another. Several of the Protestant clergy signers were followers of a leading figure in the movement to promote better understanding between East and West, the late Prof. J. L. Hromadka. Mr. Hromadka, former professor at Princeton Theological Seminary and prominent member of the World Council of Churches in the 1960's, had worked in Czechoslovakia to promote Christian-Marxist dialogue and founded the so-called Christian Peace Conference, an alliance of churchmen in Eastern European countries.

Followers of Mr. Hromadka who signed Charter 77 were expelled from their congregations by Communist authorities three years ago "because of their critical attitude to the church policies of the Czechoslovak Government."

Frantisek Cardinal Tomasek, a prelate who has known imprisonment and harassment through much of his ministry as priest and bishop under a government committed to atheism, said that the Catholic Church in Czechoslovakia is strongly committed to its tradition, but is having difficulty carrying out its pastoral ministry: Catholic schools are not permitted to function, religious communities cannot accept members, and government permission must be obtained for all priest appointments. Even the admission of candidates to the two remaining seminaries in Czechoslovakia and the issuing of pastoral letters require state approval.

> The cross is our light, our strength and our hope. We are not afraid, but we are concerned about how to reach our people more effectively, about how to strengthen them in their faith.

The general secretary of the U.S. Catholic Conference (USCC) has urged the U.S. government to take into account "blatant violations" of human rights in Czechoslovakia in any negotiations with it on trade and financial matters.

In a letter to Secretary of State Henry Kissinger, Bishop James Rausch described the Czechoslovak regime as

> one of the most repressive in Eastern Europe in regard to the exercise human rights. The right to defense counsel in criminal trials is virtually abrogated, as is the right of *habeas corpus*. The press is heavily censored, intellectuals are treated with suspicion and creative artists are almost completely stifled.

He was particularly concerned about "the issue of the right to freedom of religion."

> Czechoslovakian policies and practices violate Article 18 of the UN Universal Declaration of Human Rights, which recognizes the individual's right to manifest his religion or belief in teaching, practice, worship and observance.

Listing examples of the regime's "systematic efforts to suppress the practice of religion" Bishop Rausch cited a government ban against Czechoslovakian citizens entering Religious orders of women. If the "present strategy" is allowed to prevail, it will mean "the liquidation of the 22 Religious orders within the next several decades."

Another example illustrates the nation's perverse attempt to dominate the clergy. Seminarians are prohibited from all contact with lay people other than their immediate family or close friends and are forbidden to have radios and to read any literature from abroad, including theological books.

There are strong indications that the government applies intimidation and discrimination against parents who have children enrolled in religious education as well as against the children themselves.

Religious life in Czechoslovakia is illustriously described by Jiri Horak as follows:

During the last three years the persecution of churches and religious societies in Czechoslovakia has deepened to such an extent that informed observers speak of quiet liquidation of spiritual and religious life in the country. The daily press and the so-called professional journals in Czechoslovakia publish an ever increasing number of articles denouncing religious worship and different churches as an expression of primitive attitudes, antithetical to scientific knowledge, obstructing the road toward happiness, and undermining the principles of socialism.

Systematically planned anti-religious propaganda is conducted under the direct control of Moscow and is based on the most recent Soviet experiences. The Czechoslovak Government established new centers for the teaching of so-called scientific atheism with Soviet lecturers.

It is characteristic for the communist system whose constitution incidentally guarantees the freedom of religious expression that religious journals are not allowed to defend religious faith or to dispute the so-called scientific anti-religious approach.

The present anti-religious policies of the Czechoslovak government and of the Communist Party of Czechoslovakia pursue the following course:

1) In spite of great popular interest, churches and religious societies are allowed no independent publishing activity. All such activity finds itself under strict governmental control. Moreover, all decisions of the governmental institutions in charge of religious and church affairs are taken without the participation of church representatives. Import of religious books and journals is prohibited. All contact of religious organizations with abroad is controlled by the regime. These controls apply to the participation of Czechoslovak delegates to the World Council of Churches and its organs.

2) The Czechoslovak regime makes difficult, if not impossible, the pastoral work of priests, especially of those who are most dedicated to their vocation. The most talented among them are simply deprived of the right to serve their church. Czechoslovak bishops and other church functionaries, to the extent to which they are allowed to occupy their posts at all, are also hindered in the performance of their functions. This persecution takes place without being publicized and it is, therefore, virtually impossible to ascertain how many priests have been sentenced and imprisoned. The government has also drastically reduced the opportunity for the education of new priests, while at the same time systematically forcing into retirement all the priests who have reached the age of sixty. As a consequence of these measures, the number of parishes and congregations without a priest or a spiritual administrator keeps growing constantly.

3) Religious orders have been brutally suppressed, and during the re-

cent period, their members were allowed to serve only in those health and social welfare institutions in which, as a rule, the lay workers refuse to work.

4) The Czechoslovak government discriminates severely against all active Christians. It persecutes those parents who attempt to provide their children with religious instruction, and children who have received religious education are, as a rule, excluded from access to institutions of higher learning.

The Czechoslovak government has engaged in all those measures in order to liquidate religious life in that country in a manner that would not provoke too much criticism abroad. It is well known that on their visits abroad, the representatives of different churches in Czechoslovakia do not speak of this state of affairs and of the conditions under which they have to work in their country. They cover up for the regime and may even praise its attitude toward religious life in Czechoslovakia in order to save for themselves the minimum opportunity for contact with their fellow believers in foreign lands.

The Czechoslovak regime which tries to eliminate the churches and religion from public life denies that religion plays any social function. On the other hand, however, it forces the clergymen of all denominations to support all domestic and foreign policy goals of the Czechoslovak government. The government was instrumental in establishing an organization called *Pacem in terris* composed of the so-called patriotic Catholic priests. As far as Protestant ministers are concerned, the Government created the so-called ecumenical committees which are a member organization of the Czechoslovak Protestants in the so-called World Christian Peace Conference whose seat is in Prague.

At the meetings of the *Pacem in terris* Association and of ecumenical committees, the clergymen approve various resolutions expressing support and loyalty for the regime and under a disguise of the protection of world peace pass resolutions in support of Soviet foreign policy. These religious organizations, either Catholic or Protestant, have nothing in common with the goals and mission of churches. The activities of these organizations serve as a means to have clergymen occupied and to keep them away from their pastoral duties.

Religious freedom is internationally recognized as one of the basic human freedoms and the freedom of conscience and worship is one of the basic human rights. From that reason they have been incorporated into all international documents—the U.N. Charter, Human Rights Charter, etc. However, in spite of the fact that these freedoms or rights to religious life are considered as something quite natural, one finds little indication that the Western powers and their religious organizations are upset over the violation of these rights in Eastern Europe. To state it briefly, one has an impression that the violation of these freedoms and rights was not considered as an international issue. Only recently, at a Helsinki Conference in 1975, a certain change took place: freedom of religion and freedom of conscience were stressed as basic human rights. And this step has changed the situation also for the defense of religion in Czechoslovakia. While until now the Czechoslovak religious representatives were not in favor of having various international gatherings pass resolutions in defense of religion because of fear that the reaction of the

Czechoslovak regime would be to tighten the screw, such an apprehension on the part of religious leaders in Czechoslovakia is valid no more. The West and the world's religious institutions have an obligation to demand from the government of East European countries observation of the provisions of the Final Act of Helsinki concerning the respect for religious life.

The present religious persecution concerns also the Jewish religious communities, although only in a restricted way because the Jews had already been subjected to a severe persecution during the Nazi occupation of Czechoslovakia in the spring of 1939. Numerous reports are reaching from Prague indicating that Judaism, which had played a highly significant role in the intellectual and cultural life of the Republic before 1938, may completely disappear within the next twenty years. Works by such important authors as Kafka, Werfel, Brod, Kisch, Langer, Torberg, Wechsberger, Polacek, Bass and Vamos will become unknown in the country.

At the time of the 1930 census, 254,288 Jews in the religious sense ("practicing Jews") were living on the territory of present-day Czechoslovakia. The 102,542 Jews who had lived in Ruthenia at that time, and their losses, are left out of the scope of this discussion since that part of pre-war Czechoslovakia became part of Hungary in March, 1939 and was annexed by the Soviet Union in 1945. Out of the more than a quarter million Jews on present Czechoslovak territory, about 135,000 perished as a result of the Nazi extermination policy: over 77,000 in Bohemia and Moravia, and more than 57,000 in Slovakia.

After World War II, thousands of Jews returned to liberated Czechoslovakia. They were the survivors of Nazi concentration camps, pre-war civilian emigres, as well as thousands of Jews who had served with the Czechoslovak armed units in East and West. Thus, in 1946, the number of Jews in Czechoslovakia was estimated at some 55,000. This situation did not last long, however. Many of the repatriated Jews were soon dissatisfied with the conditions they found upon return,

Thus, a trickle of Jewish emigres again began to flow West or to Palestine as early as 1946, to join those tens of thousands who had emigrated in 1938-1939 and never returned. Many of the emigres, as well as many of those who had remained in Czechoslovakia, discared the Jewish faith and attempted one or another form of assimilation.

Figures on legal and, especially, illegal Jewish emigration after 1945 are hard to come by. It appears that, from the end of World War II to August 1947, some 5,000 Jews had emigrated, half of them to Palestine and 15,589 in 1949, when legal emigration from Czechoslovakia was stopped.

Simultaneously, persons of Jewish origin continued to emigrate to other Western countries. After the Communist take-over, everything except personal effects had to be left behind, and emigration fees of up to 50,000 Kcs had to be paid to get emigration permits. For those who were emigrating from Czechoslovakia for the second time, the involved bureaucratic procedures were reminiscent of the emigration scenery from the Protectorate of Bohemia and Moravia in 1939. Jewish emigration to the West gathered after February, 1948, until this avenue was closed for all practical purposes in late 1949.

In view of the fact that less than 20,000 Jews remained in Czechoslovakia after 1949, it may seem surprising that the authorities deemed it
necessary to pursue not only aggressive anti-Zionist propaganda but often
thinly camouflaged anti-Semitic policies as well. Latent popular anti-
Semitism apart, such behavior was obviously a product of Stalin's virulent
anti-Jewish and anti-cosmopolitan feelings in the last years of the Soviet
dictator's life. Popular anti-Semitism was further nourished and methodi-
cally reinforced by regime propaganda through the circumstance that
Slansky, Reicin, Geminder, and other prominent Communists sentenced to
death in 1952 were of Jewish origin; those unpopular figures were conveniently blamed for the many negative aspects of life under totalitarian
socialism of those times. The official anti-Semitism of the regime relaxed but
never disappeared in subsequent years—a phenomenon which was caused
by more factors than the pro-Arab stance of the regime's foreign policy
alone.

The last—and final—mass Jewish exodus took place after the 1968 invasion. By then not only Jewish anti-Communists and apolitical people but also
Communists who had become disillusioned decided to leave the country. A
large percentage of this new Jewish emigration was made up of intellectuals,
professionals, physicans, economists, and others. The total number of Jews
who escaped after the August, 1968 invasion was estimated at 4,000 to 4,500
people. Now the practicing Jewish community in Czechoslovakia consists of
only 5,000 people, of whom some 1,200 live in Prague.

There is no pressure from the few remaining Jews to emigrate; there
are no appeals to the West; no underground journals.

Most of the rest are old people, pensioners who do not want to leave to
face an uncertain future. Still, the community is closely watched, and its
members know it. A prominent member is believed to be an informer of
the Ministry of the Interior, a fact which cannot but reinforce the general
apathy of the religious community.

In spite of the steady diminution of the Jewish community in Czechoslovakia, the authorities have never allowed it unhindered development.
Not only did the State Security Service have its informer within the Council of Jews, but any genuine defense of Jewish interests or even an assertion of simple historical truth evoked regime reprisals.

Jewish religious life proper was a reflection of the situation sketched
above, aggravated, of course, by the general atheistic stance of the regime,
which "permits" churches more for optical than for substantial purposes,
trying to use them for its own ends. Since Czechoslovakia's Chief Rabbi,
Dr. Richard Feder, a person of authority, died at the age of 95 on
November 18, 1970, there has been no successor in the top religious office. Thomas E. Salamon, who had been trained at the Budapest Rabbinical Seminary and was supposed to have taken over rabbinical duties in
Czechoslovakia, remained in London after the invasion. A study of the
Czechoslovak Jewish monthly *Vestnik Zidovskych Nabozenskych Obci v Cesko-
slovensku* shows that rudiments of Jewish religious life are still in existence
in a number of Czech and Slovak towns, but this appears to be more out
of tradition, habit, and the need for togetherness than out of genuine
religious feeling, to say nothing of hope.

Under these circumstances, Jewish religious life in Czechoslovakia is
doomed within a generation.

Bulgaria

The study of Bulgaria points out that under Communism "the formal separation of church and state spells the full subordination of the church to the state." Reporting on the persecution of the church in Bulgaria and on the subordination of the Bulgarian Church to the state, both official publications and abundant secondary source material show that when the Communists seized power they immediately staged mock trials of the clergy and confined about 200 priests to forced labor camps. Some church leaders, including the metropolitan of Nevrokop, Bishop Boris, were killed, and others, such as the administrator of the Rila Monastery, Egumenus Kalistrat, were sentenced to long imprisonment. Churches and monasteries were profaned.

The Communist government proceeded to purge and replace churchmen Protestant pastors on charges of espionage for the United States and Great Britain. On March 8, 1949, the Sofia district court sentenced all these pastors to imprisonment and heavy fines.

As in the case of the Protestant churches, the Catholic Church was suppressed on the allegation that it was engaging in espionage. In September, 1952, a trial against 40 leading Catholic priests and laymen opened in Sofia. The trials ended on October 4, 1952, with the death sentence for one bishop and three priests and prison terms for the remaining defendants. Soon after the trial the church was obliterated. Catholic schools were closed and Catholic priests, monks, and nuns were forced to leave Bulgaria in 1952. Today, no Catholic clergy would subordinate itself to Communist policies.

The churches still in existence are under constant pressure by the present government which has been applying different methods to curtail church activities in the country. Thus, for instance, publications of religious communities were deprived of printing paper and their distribution was jeopardized; priests have been sent to labor brigades every year and church buildings have been transformed into public homes; theological schools have been closed and their buildings used for other purposes.

The Bulgarian Orthodox Church embraces over 80 per cent of the population; in addition, there are four minority denominations which, according to an estimate made in 1956, counted 930,000 Mohammedans (750,000 Turk-Moslems and 190,000 Bulgaro-Moslems, known as Pomaks); 56,000 Catholics; 28,000 Protestants; and 6,000 Jews (prior to the establishment of the Communist government, the number of Jews in the country was over 50,000 and they maintained about 30 synagogues).

According to the official organ of the Bulgarian Orthodox Church, *Tsurkoven Vestnik,* in 1950, there were 11 dioceses, 2,940 houses of prayer; 100 monasteries; 9 bishops; 7 episcopates, 47 archimandrites; 52 prelates; and 2,900 priests. In Sofia, there were 234 church employees.

Prior to the seizure of power by the Communist government, there were in Bulgaria: one theological faculty at the University of Sofia; two theological seminaries (academies), i.e., one in Sofia and one in Plovdiv, and one school for training priests. The theological faculty was detached from the university in 1950 and organized into a higher religious school of the Bulgarian Orthodox Church; both theological academies were merged in 1950 into one semi-higher theological school and transferred to the village of Cherepish, but in 1951 it was closed.

At present there is only one Higher Religious School of the Bulgarian Orthodox Church and one intermediate higher theological school in existence. The Communist government admits that it is its aim to do away with religion.

However, the Communist regime in Bulgaria has established pseudo-Orthodox, Moslem, Protestant, and Jewish churches and synagogues in spite of the fact that the basic principles of these religions are hostile to the Communist ideology. Moreover, a certain degree of religious tolerance has been maintained for the purpose of attracting religious devotees to Communist policies. These churches serve as vehicles for propaganda whose main theme is the peaceful intentions of the Communist world as opposed to the aggressive imperialist plans of the West. The patriarch of Bulgaria and the Holy Synod are always participants in "peace congresses" and signers of "peace appeals."

The present position of the Bulgarian Orthodox Church (as well as other churches) may be best illustrated by the following facts and events.

On the occasion of the 70th birthday of Stalin all churches in Bulgaria had to hold special services.

Through the Circular Letter No. 3478-19 of May 3, 1963 the head of the Holy Synod of the Bulgarian Orthodox Church, Patriarch Kyril, made a declaration defending the policy of the Communist governments concerning the preservation of world peace.

The declaration of the Holy Synod of the same church concerning bacteriological weapons was ordered to be read by the priests in all churches.

The official organ, *Tsurkoven Vestnik,* very often carries articles and editorials with titles such as "Aggression Against the Freedom and Independence of Cuba," "Let Us Help Korea," and the like.

One of the recent blows against the church was the abolition of Sunday as a day of rest (holiday). According to Resolution No. 825 of November 16, 1963, of the Council of Ministers, Sunday was declared to be a regular workday and a day of the week was designated as a day of rest. Under the pretext of saving electric power, the day of rest is different in the different administrative districts of the country. This change became effective as of December 1, 1963, just before the greatest religious holidays. This decision may well completely paralyze church life, and those who had the courage to attend church services on Sunday will be deprived of that possibility since they cannot absent themselves from their jobs for that purpose.

Recent reports show that, after subjecting the church leadership in Bulgaria to its dictatorship, the Bulgarian Communist government turned to the Bulgarian church organizations abroad, especially in the United States, Canada, and Australia, with the intention of extending its influence and control over them. The visit of Bishop Pimen of Nevrokop in the United States during March, 1963, the restoration of Bishop Andrey in New York as administrative head of the Bulgarian diocese in the United States, Canada, and Australia, and the establishment of the spiritual council of the diocese in New York were among these efforts of the present government in Bulgaria.

This produced an open split in the Bulgarian Orthodox community in America and Australia: members of the Bulgarian Orthodox faith voted for and carried a resolution calling for spiritual unity with the mother church in Bulgaria but for independence from its hierarchial control. For that reason, considering the precarious position of the Bulgarian Orthodox parishes which have been reluctant to remain under the leadership of the representatives of the Communist-dominated Bulgarian Holy Synod, the archbishop's synod in America, by an ordinance of April 25, 1963, took over the Bulgarian Orthodox diocese in the United States and Canada and placed it under the protection of the Russian archbishop's synod which acts independently from the Soviet-dominated Russian Orthodox Church in the U.S.S.R.

The constitution of the People's Republic of Bulgaria provides general guarantees on religious freedom to all citizens. Yet Catholics must get permission to build a church, to hold a procession in the street surrounding the church, or to assign a priest from a country parish to a vacancy in the city—and permission rarely is given.

No bishop can be named without the government's approval. This is much more than a formality. In 1958, after the de-Stalinization period had gotten under way, the Vatican named bishops to succeed one who had been condemned to be shot and one who had died in prison. It was two years before the bishop of the Plovdiv-Sofia diocese could be consecrated. Nikopol, the other Latin diocese in Bulgaria, was without a bishop until 1975.

Article 3 of the Religious Denominations Law assigns a favored place to the Orthodox religion, declaring that Orthodoxy is the traditional religion of the Bulgarian people. Catholics and other minority religious groups are not mentioned.

Catholics also are ignored in the title of the government office which regulates the activities of all religious groups. It is called "The State Committee on the Orthodox Church and the Religious Denominations."

When Nikita Khrushchev visited Sofia as Russia's Red chieftain he suggested that the government gild the huge domes of the Alexander Nevski Orthodox cathedral. It would make a spectacular tourist attraction,

he predicted. But permission to rebuild the city's Catholic cathedral of St.
Joseph, destroyed by a bomb in March, 1944, still has not been given.

Neither Catholics nor Protestants have been recognised juridically by
the government since the Communist-staged show trials of bishops,
priests, ministers, nuns and laymen in 1952. In the case of the Catholics,
all their property was confiscated.

Many Protestant, Jewish, Moslem and Orthodox religious leaders were
jailed by the Communists, along with Catholics. But the small Catholic
Church of Bulgaria was the hardest hit. Practically all of the 72 priests in
Bulgaria today have served time in Communist jails or concentration
camps.

About 200 men are studying for the priesthood at the Orthodox
Academy of Theology in Sofia. Catholic seminaries—together with orphanages, schools, hospitals and kindergartens—were confiscated 20
years ago, and replacements never have been authorized.

Orthodox Patriarch Kyril told that he has visited Russia 11 times, did
historical research in the diplomatic archives in Paris for several weeks in
1969 and has made numerous journeys to Bulgaria's neighbors.

But Bulgarian Catholic leaders are stay-at-homes. They were allowed to
go to Rome for the Second Vatican Council, but had to take turns—only
one for each session.

The Russians under Czar Alexander freed Bulgaria from five centuries
of Turkish domination in 1878 and the Catholic Church began to develop
in the midst of the Orthodox majority.

When Catholic Uniates were expelled from Greece, Turkey and
Macedonia following World War I, they took refuge in Bulgaria. The
Vatican, deeply concerned, sent Msgr. Angelo Roncalli to Sofia in 1925 as
an apostolic visitor to help the refugees of the Oriental-rite.

Uniate sees in Salonika, Edirne (Turkey) and Istanbul had been
abolished so a new one was established in Sofia. In 1926, a year after his
arrival in Bulgaria, Msgr. Roncalli went to Rome with Archimandrite
Cyril Kurteff, a 36-year-old priest, and had him consecrated as the bishop
for the Oriental-rite. Although arrested several times by the Communists,
Bishop Kurteff still heads Bulgaria's Oriental-rite Sofia diocese.

By the start of World War II, Bulgarian Catholics had nearly 150
churches, close to 200 priests (including approximately 50 of the Oriental-
rite), a few dozen teaching brothers, several hundred nuns, and a number
of schools, hospitals and orphanages.

A half-dozen international congregations of priests—Jesuits, Passionists,
Capuchins, Conventual Franciscans, Assumptionists and Resurrec-
tionists—and the Brothers of the Christian Schools were represented in the
country. The priests of most of these orders were of both the Latin and
Oriental-rites. There were 10 congregations of nuns, including international communities of Carmelites and Sisters of Notre Dame of Sion, active
in the country.

After seizing power in 1944 the Communists proceded step by step to
destroy the Catholic Church in Bulgaria.

First religious instruction in schools was halted. Feast days, including
Christmas, were made regular work days. Those who worked on Sunday
were given a day off during the week. Not only was permission denied for
rebuilding St. Joseph's cathedral, but the money collected for the project

was seized by the government. Catholic seminaries and other institutions were shut down.

Diplomatic relations with the Vatican were broken in an undramatic way. While on a visit in Italy early in 1949, the representative of the Holy See was informed by the Bulgarian legation in Rome that his return to Sofia was not desired.

A comprehensive Law on Religious Denominations, which went into effect March 1, 1949, legalized some of the anti-religious measures already taken by the government and smoothed the way for others.

The law's language, while oblique and even obscure, was nonetheless effective. The international congregations of priests and nuns, for example, were not banned specifically. However, the new law prohibited all organizations which were "directed from abroad." That meant the expulsion of foreign priests, nuns and brothers.

The native clergy was dealt with after the foreigners were expelled.

In February, 1950 the pastor of St. Joseph's parish in Sofia, a Capuchin friar, was arrested and after beign "investigated" for nearly two years was given a long prison sentence. His successor received the same treatment a few months after becoming pastor.

The most spectacular anti-Catholic action was the mass arrest in July, 1952 of 40 priests, a number of nuns, and Bishop Eugene Bossilkoff of Nikopol.

They were charged with such crimes as espionage, sabotage and plotting against the state. The evidence presented at their public "show trials" was by no means consistent with the charges, but the sentences were. Bishop Bossilkoff and three other priests were condemned to be shot. The other accused priests, nuns and laymen were sentenced to prison.

The 20th anniversary of Communist power in Bulgaria in 1964 was the occasion for granting an amnesty to those priests still in prison who had not died meanwhile.

About the same time the Bulgarian government, which till then had isolated itself behind the Iron Curtain, stepped up relations with its Communist neighbors as well as with western Europe and Africa.

In 1953, following the mass arrests and show trials of the Catholic priests and the Latin archbishop of Sofia-Plovdiv, police burst into the Carmelite cloister before dawn and took the nuns to prison.

Eventually the foreigners in the community were expelled, while some of the Bulgarian nuns were sent to concentration camps. The others were sent to their home villages with orders to stay there.

Meantime, a Bulgarian Oriental-rite congregation of nuns known as the Eucharistines also was being hounded by the police.

Worse than poverty is the life of inactivity to which the Bulgarian clergy have been condemned.

Even something as basic as catechism teaching is limited. Catechism lessons are restricted to the sermons at Sunday Masses. Priests can preach in church, but not outside. As in the days of the early Christians, families hand down the religion to their children, giving them their spiritual formation at home.

But young people are not going to church the way they used to, a priest complains.

Earlier in the year of 1970, the weekly newspaper of Sofia Press, the

government information agency, published the results of a study on religion among Bulgarian farmers. The study was conducted by a member of
the Bulgarian Academy of Sciences.

He found that the religiousness of the villagers, while strong among the
older people, was weak among the young—80 per cent for those over 68
held strong religious convictions; but only 15 per cent of those in the
18-23 age group.

> The connection between religion and age is proof that religious faith is not
> an inherent feature of the everyday life, culture and spiritual makeup of the
> Bulgarian peasant, but a product of specific social conditions—the disap-
> pearance of which also means the disappearance of religion.

The academician's theory, while comforting to hard-line atheists,
nonetheless leaves unanswered some aspects of religiousness which must
make Bulgaria's Communist leaders wonder at times.

It does not explain why seven women who would seem to have many
good reasons to forget about their Carmelite vows and return to a relatively easy civilian life prefer to live in crowded, inconvenient quarters in
the choir loft of a small chapel.

Probably no member of the Bulgarian Academy of Sciences knows the
explanation, but any Catholic in Bulgaria does.

Archbishop Agostino Casaroli, on the invitation of the Foreign Minister, Peter Mladenov, paid a visit to the Peoples Republic of Bulgaria from
November 3 to 10, 1976, concerning relations between "the Holy See and
the Bulgarian state." The meeting with the foreign Minister was marked
by an open and cordial atmosphere. Various questions of current international interest which concern, each in its own domain, Bulgaria and the
Holy See were discussed. In particular and among other matters, consideration was given to the problems with regard to the faithful application,
both in the letter and in the spirit, of the final part of the Helsinki Conference on Security and Cooperation in Europe, as well as to the follow
up to that conference and to the problems of the third world, for which
both parties showed a lively interest. The situation of the Catholic Church
in Bulgaria and its relations with the state were the subject of attentive
consideration.

Bulgaria takes a special place among the East European states ruled by
Communists in its church-religious relation. On the one hand, the Church
is gratefully acknowledged; the Church has been for centuries the last
bastion of national-cultural continuity against the foreign rule of Byzantine and Turkey. And this criterion moderately affects official atheistic
rites. On the other hand, Bulgaria pursues classical Communist Church
policy, i.e., Church and religion become indeed as only one in-
stitutionalized counterpart tolerated, although attacked.

In Bulgaria since February, 1974, there has been noticeable intensification of atheistic propaganda and oppressive endeavor in order to introduce "social ritual"—replacement of Church ceremonies, but it has been
without success. Numerous sources report that atheistic indoctrination is
conducted on a low level and is unfit to serve as protection to the ideological education.

Religious—socialistic inquiry, which has been more strongly carried out
in Bulgaria than in the rest of East Europe, attests that religious aware-

ness of adults since the '60's had remained unchanged while the religious awareness of young people has recently increased distinctly. The theorists in an interesting way admit this as a sign of "protest."

Since 1945 no Bible texts have been printed in Bulgaria. The only exceptions to this are several copies used for liturgical purposes.

A new translation of the New Testament and of the Psalms is now waiting to be printed. Given as the reason for the delay is that the Church wants to publish an entire Bible. The translation of the Old Testament will take about another two years.

As far as the Orthodox is concerned, the Patriarchate in Moscow immediately after the end of the war made efforts to gain increased influence on the Orthodox churches in the countries of Eastern and Southeastern Europe. Only in Bulgaria, however, have these efforts actually resulted in the far-reaching organizational change of an Orthodox church outside the Soviet Union. In Article 3 of the Church Law of 1949 it is, among other things, explicitly stated that the Orthodox Church is "inseparable linked with the history of the Bulgarian people and, as a People's Church (National Church) is in its form, substance and spirit a people's democractic church." Today, Orthodox Christians in Bulgaria are completely Moscow-oriented and thus Russia, and that country, was able to strengthen its influence also through the policy of the Orthodox Church. In Romania and Yugoslavia, however, the Orthodox churches are more noticeable national and independent. From this position, even as servants of state power, they have been able to derive some advantages.

The Muslim part of the population of Bulgaria, Albania and Yugoslavia initially was subjected to much Communist persecution. Recently, however, the men in power have become somewhat more tolerant of their Muslim citizens' right to worship.

There are no official figures available for the membership of the Bulgarian Orthodox Church, but informed observers usually speak of about six million or 75 per cent of the total population. More precise details concerning other aspects of the Church's life are given in a publication issued by the Bulgarian Orthodox Church in 1966. This indicates that at that time there were 3,700 churches and chapels served by 1,785 active priests. (In 1938 there were 2,486 priests.)

The same publication also provides a certain amount of information about the other churches and religions of Bulgaria. In 1966 there were said to be about 50,000 Roman Catholics worshipping in 30 churches and served by one bishop and 46 priests. According to *Annuario Pontificio* the number of priests had increased to 48 in 1969, and a government official said in 1972 that there were four Catholic monasteries with 36 priests and 113 nuns.

Uniates total approximately 10,000, grouped in 25 parishes of quasi-parishes, and served by one bishop and 21 priests. Of these priests, 13 are monks. There are 21 nuns. In contrast with the Communist policy in most other parts of Eastern Europe, no attempt has been made to absorb the Uniates into the Orthodox Church. The Baptists are a very small community of about 800 members. These are distributed among 23 congregations, each with its own pastor. Recent reports indicate that the replacement of ageing pastors is proving very difficult. The Pentecostal Church is somewhat larger with 6,000 members, 25 places of worship and 36 ministers, while the

Armenian Church has 22,000 members, 12 churches and 12 priests. There are also minority Congregational and Methodist Churches.

After the Orthodox Christians, the Moslems are easily the largest religious group in the country. In 1966 they numbered about 650,000 or 8 per cent of the population. The great majority of these are Moslem Turks, who have 1,180 mosques and 460 imams. The Moslem Bulgarians (Pomaks) have 120 mosques and 100 imams. Some indication of the recent decline of organized Moslems is provided by the fact that in 1956 the two Moslem communities were served by 2,715 imams. In pre-war Bulgaria there were about 50,000 Jews, the majority of whom survived the war, thanks mainly to King Boris who had the Bulgarian Jews scattered into remote villages. However, between 1948 and 1955 over 40,000 of them emigrated to Israel and today there are only about 6,000 left, of whom 4,000 live in Sofia, 600 in Plovdiv and the rest are distributed throughout the country. There is a central synagogue in Sofia and two others—at Plovdiv and Ruse—but there are no rabbis; lay people carry out their functions.

Still in 1952 priests and religious have suffered harsh persecution. Thirty priests, among them all three of the country's bishops, were violently imprisoned. In one of the recent trials, Bishop Bosilkoff with three priests were sentenced to death "because of espionage and hostile attitude toward the State." Many priests received prison terms between twelve to twenty years. Finally, Pope John XXIII, who was for many years Vatican's nuntius in Sofia, succeeded; the lasts priests were freed in 1964.

Following the trials of the post-war period, the Catholic Church in Bulgaria is only now showing signs of re-emerging. The Bulgarian Catholics were the first to come to Rome for Holy Year pilgrimage from the Communist nation where the Catholic Church had been harshly suppressed following World War II. Currently, there are about 70,000 Catholics in Bulgaria. In all, there are about 50 religious orders and ten diocesan priests.

Five weeks after the visit of Bulgaria's President to Pope Paul VI, appointments of bishops to the Apostolic vicariate of Sofia and Plovdiv and diocese of Nicopolis were announced. In August, 1975, the Vatican announced that Msgr. Bogdan Dobranov, reportedly secretly ordained a bishop 15 or 16 years ago, was named vicar apostolic of Sofia and Plovdiv, and Father Vasko Sayrekov was appointed Bishop of Nicopolis. Both installations were held in the Plovdiv Cathedral and were attended by Archbishop Mario Brini, secretary of the Congregation for Eastern Churches.

Also, after Zhivkov's visit, the fate of Bishop Bosilkoff, who had been sentenced to death in 1952, was cleared. In an official announcement it was said that "he had died in prison."

After the death of Bishop Simeon Kokov, apostolic administrator of the Bulgarian apostolic vicariate of Sofia and Plovdiv, only one bishop remained in Bulgaria, Apostolic Exarch from Sofia, Bishop Metod Stratiev. As a result of Bulgaria's and Vatican talks, great progress has been achieved.

After Bishop Eugenio Bosilkoff died in prison in 1952, Bulgaria was without a bishop until 1975 when President Todor Zhivkov visited the Vatican and agreed to allow the appointment of bishops in his country. One chosen was Bishop Vasco Seyrekov of Nicopolis, a diocese which takes in all of Bulgaria north of the Balkan Mountains. He lived a hard life trying to cover his diocese, sleeping in railroad stations and on trains. He was on one of his long trips when he came down with a pulmonary ailment and died early in January, 1977, at the age of 56.

Hungary

The evidences of the Catholic Church mark every skyline in Budapest, and in the countryside as well. A few a scattered red stars are on top of some buildings, to counteract, one imagines, the cross of Christ which tops so many churches.

Undoubtedly many of the churches have been turned into museums, or are used for other purposes, but one is surprised to find, in some, religious goods being sold—rosaries, little statues, and the like.

They are inexpenisvely made, true—but they are being sold openly and right inside the church entrance. This was true at the famous Church of Our Lady in Buda.

Alongside the cathedral at Esztergom, excavations have uncovered remnants of a royal castle built in the 12th and 13th centuries. Interestingly, paintings found on the walls show the religious beliefs of the members of the royal family.

There is no question that Hungary is a Communist country, but one wonders whether there may be a little easing of the attitude toward religion—perhaps not toward the Church officially, and maybe only as concessions to the people of the country. For instance, how else would one explain the crucifixes occasionally seen along the main roads, just as in Austria? Not as many, perhaps, but even seeing some makes one wonder how effective the Communist crackdown has been.

Perhaps, however, the government is working for the long pull, letting the older people have their religious symbols, their religious beliefs and trying to educate the young away from them.

Of the three main Christian churches in Hungary, the Roman Catholic is easily the largest. At the last official census, in 1949, there were 6,240,427 Latin-rite Catholics and just under 250,000 Uniates, who together constituted just over 70 per cent of the total population of the country.

In 1964 there were said to be about 3,700 Catholic priests and a report in *Informations Catholiques Internationales* mentioned 2,188 Latin-rite parishes and 157 Uniate parishes. The same report referred to 3,517 priests of the Latin-rite and 452 Uniates priests, of whom 90 per cent are married.

The Reformed Church of Hungary has, according to its official, published figures, two million baptized members with 1,250 self-supporting independent parishes. The parishes are grouped in 17 seniorates and four church districts. There are 1,250 parish ministers and 250 assistant ministers. The Church runs sixteen charity institutions and several rest homes for the elderly. It also has two grammar schools.

The Hungarian Evangelical Lutheran Church, again quoting its own official figures, has 430,000 baptized members, i.e., just over 4 per cent of the total population. There are 320 parishes grouped in 16 presbyteries and served by 400 pastors. The Church has 18 charity institutions, which include homes for the elderly, orphans and people with incurable dieseases. In common with other Hungarian churches, the Lutheran Church suffered serious losses of buildings during World War II, and since 1945 it has reconstructed 227 church buildings and 140 parsonages, and erected 30 new churches.

Hungary's Council of Free Churches represents 50,000 Protestants, who are not only overshadowed by the major Reformed and Lutheran bodies in Hungary, but very much a minority in a country that was two-thirds Catholic at the time of the Communist takeover.

The Hungarian Baptist Church, which began to function in its present form in 1873, is variously estimated. Published figures speak of 50,000 adherents. Other reports mention only 20,000 members. At the 1949 census there were just under 19,000 Baptists, and indications are that the number has not decreased since then. This Church has 500 congregations spread throughout the country and these are served by 96 pastors.

The Methodist Church now has about 2,000 members and 2,500 adherents who attend services in 41 places of worship; 13 of these are prayer rooms or chapels, the remainder are the homes of church members. There are eleven pastors and six lay preachers, and one Methodist charity home.

A conflict which had been simmering for months has just flared up within the Hungarian Methodist Church. The dispute sets a group of pastors of this faith against their hierarchy and the country's authorities.

Three pastors are currently waiting to be charged for "abusing the right of assembly." They risk a minimum sentence of 2 years' imprisonment. On August 28, 1977, in the company of a few believers, they gathered in the street and prayed outside their usual place of worship, which the police had closed a few hours earlier.

The origins of this affair date back to 1973, when Mr. Frigyes Hecker, following in the footsteps of his father, Adam Hecker, was named superintendent of the Hungarian Methodist Church. The circumstances surrounding this handover of power evoked criticism from five preachers. They criticized the hierachy for accepting the introduction into the church statutes of an amendment stipulating that in the future the annual General Assembly would not have the right to meet without the consent of the office for church affairs.

The five rebels were removed from their pastoral function, but they disregarded this decision, which cost them a 5-month suspended prison sentence in 1975 for "abusing the right of assembly" and " falsifying official documents." (They had reinserted the title "clergyman," which authorities had removed, in their identity papers).

There was a further development in December, 1976: The five dissenting clergymen, joined by seven others, wrote a declaration addressed to "people of good will." They proclaimed, in part: "By remaining attached to our civic and human right to pursue a collective religious life we are convinced that we are acting in accordance with our loyalty to the state."

This document, which was not made public at the time in hope of some arrangment being reached with the hierarchy and the authorities, was sent by the rebels in mid-August, 1977, to several Hungarian newspapers and various personalities, particularly Janos Kadar, first secretary of the Hungarian Socialist Workers Party. This move resulted in a tightening up: Between August 17 and 22 the police cleared the places of worship which the rebels had been using until then in Szeged, Wyirgyhaza, and Budapest. This affair contrasts with the current policy of normalizing relations with the churches pursued by the Hungarian Party and government. Kadar's recent visit to Vatican and Baptist preacher Billy Graham's very successful tour of Hungary have been the most spectacular recent signs of this desire for a loosening up.

In 1941 there were 725,000 Jews in Hungary. Today there are about 80,000, of whom 60-70,000 live in Budapest. In 1956 there were about 150 synagogues, 70 congregations and 89 rabbis, but with the decrease in size of the Jewish community there are now only 30 synagogues and places of worship, 60 congregations and 30 rabbis. Twenty of the synagogues and places of worship are in Budapest, where the largest has a meeting capacity of 5,000. The National Rabbinical Seminary is also in Budapest; in 1970 it had nine students and six professors. A number of Jewish secondary schools are still open in different parts of the country—including a co-educational grammar school in Budapest—and religious instruction is given in 17 Talmud Torahs by resident or itinerant rabbis and teachers. About 1,000 people attend the Budapest Talmud Torah. There is a Jewish hospital (240 beds) and eleven old-people's homes, the largest of which provides accommodations for 800. Seven of these homes are financed by the State, while the other four are supported by the Central Board of Hungarian Jews—the body which unites the local communities.

Joseph Cardinal Mindszenty, former primate of Hungary, made an appearance on Capitol Hill on May 20, 1974 where he declared that Communist policies have turned Hungary into "the most orphaned, most lonely nation in the world"—a nation of the "old and dying."

The Vatican press office has confirmed that Joseph Cardinal Mindszenty did not resign voluntarily and that Pope Paul VI himself removed the 81-year-old Cardinal as Archbishop of Esztergom.

Cardinal Mindszenty issued a statement in Vienna February 7, 1974 denying reports that he had voluntarily resigned from office. The Cardinal lived until his death in Vienna, after a short stay in Rome, since he left Hungary.

The Cardinal's statement issued in Vienna said the appointment of bishops and apostolic administrators in Hungary following his removal "does not solve the problems of the Hungarian Church." The statement charged that naming government-approved priests to important Church positions had been agreed to by the Holy See while the Church is suffering restrictions in its freedom, especially in the schools.

The Vatican press spokesman, obviously replying to those criticisms, stated:

> The pastoral concern which inspired the decisions cannot certainly signify that there was lacking a conscious and full evaluation of the particulars, that is, the well-known circumstances in which ecclesiastical life is carried out.

> Even less, is it to be interpreted as an acquiescence to principles or compromises which the Church could not approve or accept. On the contrary, the pastoral concern, precisely because it takes into account these conditions, aims at responding to the primary need of the life of every ecclesial community to be able to enjoy the guidance and active presence of the normal rule of canonical administration, encouraged and fortified by its own pastor.

Joseph Cardinal Mindszenty, exiled Primate of Hungary, in an exclusive interview in the U.S.A., spoke of his memoirs, his imprisonment in Hungary, and his wish that St. Stephen's crown, symbol of authority in Hungary, be preserved for "all Hungarians."

The cardinal spoke of his seven years in solitary confinement, before he was freed in the 1956 uprising, as "not just imprisonment, but the worst kind of imprisonment, the very worst kind."

The greatest need for Catholics in Hungary today is "human rights and religious freedom."

Of the need for priests in Hungary he said, "This is the internal affair of the priests and of the Church. And we do not ask this from the authorities, because they are diminishing rather than increasing the number of priests."

He described the situation in Hungary since he has left as "deteriorated," and said this was also true of the "outside world."

In the last 15 years in a country of 10 million people, there have been an estimated 3.2 million abortions, in effect a method of genocide for the country. Abortion for any reason runs strictly against Catholic teaching.

From 1945 until now

> of the 3,163 Catholic elementary schools none remain; of the 2,459 priests and 7,525 nuns about 400 remain. Of the 30 seminaries 2 remain, of 187 monasteries there are 6 left and of the 456 cloisters 2 survive. Persecution of the religious since 1945 continues. Church life is commanded by the "Bureau of Religious Business" in the hands of the atheistic Communists. In 1945 the Catholic Church in Hungary had 6,900 priests,—in 1956, 4,500 and at the moment there are no more than 3,600; 283 of these priests are between 20 and 30 years of age. Their average age is about 60.

The Roman Catholic Church has played an enormously important and decisive role in Hungary. In addition to its role in government, the Church maintained and operated, before 1945, about 75 per cent of the elementary schools in the Hungarian country-side; Benedictines, Cistercians, Dominicans, Franciscans, Piarists, Premontrarian Canons and Jesuits were responsible for an important part of Hungarian education and literature, among them, first of all, the Jesuit Peter Cardinal Pazmany, Archbishop of Esztergom in the 17th Century, one of the founders of Hungarian literary language and also the founder of the Budapest University, established in Nagszombat in 1635.

Before 1945 the Hungarian Catholic Church also possessed great wealth emanating from the donations of King Saint Stephen of Hungary (997-1038) and was able to maintain numerous charitable, social and cultural institutions for the benefit of the Hungarian people using its own resources only. It could be safely said that the fate of Hungary and its Catholic Church were inseparable during their entire history.

The arrival of Soviet troops in 1945 made radical changes in the life and social sturucture of Hungary. Although some contacts with the West survived until 1948, a *de facto* totalitarian Communist regime has been in power since the arrival of the first Soviet military units to Hungary. Despite the fact that Latin-rite Hungarian Roman Catholics, with their small community of Byzantine-rite Roman Catholic brethren, made up 70 per cent of the entire Hungarian population, the situation of the Church became very precarious indeed.

The result of this tyrannical rule in Hungary can be best measured by some statistics:

Between 1945 and 1965 the number of ordained priests declined from 6,900 to 4,500. Seminarians declined from 994 to about 300.

Of the 2,459 monks and of the 7,525 nuns in 1945 about 400 or less were left in 1965, less than the 5% of the original number.

Seminaries declined from 30 to 6, monasteries from 187 to 6, convents from 456 to 2.

Of all the 3,163 Church-related elementary schools and the 32 Church-related teachers' colleges in 1945 none survived in 1965. Between these dates Catholic high schools dropped in number from 49 to 8, Catholic periodicals and newspapers from 68 to 4, Catholic publishers from 50 to 2 and lay organizations from about 4,000 to 2.

... But the greatest tragedy which struck the Church was the relentless persecution of the bishops and the clergy, and the burning of a great percentage of existing religious literature in Hungary. From the mock-trial of Cardinal Mindszenty, which resulted in his sentencing for life-imprisonment in 1949, the persecution of bishops and priests did not really stop until the outbreak of the Revolution in 1956. In this period of time, many bishops, leading Catholic priests and laymen were condemned or forced into exile.

Almost all members of the religious orders were deported, compulsory religious instruction was abolished and all Catholic schools were closed in 1949.

Amid such circumstances and by means of shameless intimidation, the Board of Hungarian Bishops was forced to sign an agreement with the government on August 30, 1949. All religious orders were disbanded except the Benedictines, Franciscans and the Piarists and also the School Sisters of Kaloscar each of which could maintain 2 high schools only. Altogether, 8 high schools were returned to the religious orders by agreement, with the understanding, that only a restricted number of religious teachers handpicked by the government could be retained for teaching; the rest of them had to find jobs in civilian life, mostly in factories and were forbidden to live in religious communities. The government also assured a meager financial subsidy for the Church and—stopped the deportation of the religious.

For these so-called "benefits" the bishops had to recognize the Communist regime, and let priests take an oath of loyalty to the Communist government.

To make things worse, there was also danger that the vacant or *de facto* vacant sees would be filled by totally unworthy government appointees. This consideration led to the Vatican-Kadar "protocol" of September 30, 1964.

The "protocol"—not a treaty—does not mention Cardinal Mindszenty, but in it the Church received government permission, first to appoint five bishops to vacant sees and one bishop to an archbishop see; second, to send few Hungarian priests to Rome for higher ecclesiastical studies.

There were also some general promises made by the Kadar government about the freedom of episcopal government, of priestly ministry and of religious instruction of the youth. The Vatican also succeeded in preventing the appointment of government-selected members of the *Opus Pacis* to diocesan sees, a demand orginally presented by the regime.

At the same time, the Vatican had to acknowledge the Budapest government's veto power over the appointments of Roman Catholic prelates and accept the fact of oppressive government interference with and full control of the day-to-day administration of the Church in Hungary.

As Cardinal Mindszenty stated in his February 6, 1974 message:

> ... the Church is not free today in Hungary. It is in chains and is being humiliated day after day by an atheistic, totalitarian regime.

> The seminaries are also in very deplorable situation. Instead of the original 30, only 6 regular seminaries are now in operation. According to the latest reports, there are about 300 seminarians permitted by the Office of Church Affairs to be prepared for priesthood, and about 40 to 45 seminarians are ordained as priests every year.(As a small comparison: In 1938 we had about 2,000 seminarians and ordained 230 to 240 young priests a year). And this is not the result of a lack of priestly vocations: not at all! As always in a desperate situation, as now in Hungary, the grace of the Holy Spirit is flowing freely among young Hungarians and in the first decade of the Communist terror we had more applications for admission to seminaries than ever before. The reason for the decline is simply the *numerus clausus* or closed number of seminary admissions, a limit imposed not by Church authorities, but by the Communist officials of the Office of Church Affairs. And while the admissions are limited to a very small number among the many who apply, according to very reliable reports those applicants, who are sent by the Government—youngsters with Party or secret police connections—have to be accepted by the seminary. These characters serve as informers for the Government and for the police and also form a reliable nucleus—reliable from the point of view of the Communist Party—in the new generation of Roman Catholic priests.

> All of this has resulted in the biological aging of the Hungarian clergy. According to the latest report there are only 3,663 Catholic priests in Hungary (please recall the fact that we still had 4,600 in 1965!). Out of the 3,663 only 283 of the priests are under 30 and more than 1,700 are over 50. Today the average age of a Hungarian priest is near to 60! No question: if the strict state limitations in seminary admissions are continued, it is evident, that within 10 or 15 years there will be a further dramatic decline in the number of ordained priests in Hungary.

Each of the three remaining orders for men, the Benadictines, the Piarists and the Franciscans, and the only remaining order for women, the School Sisters of Kalocsa, allowed to accept only *two* novices a year, and not more. It is a well-known government-initiated practice in today's Hungary that the young novices are immediately called for military service: one upon his acceptance by the religious order, the other one three months later. They have to serve three consecutive years in the Army as privates and are exposed to all kinds of physical and mental pressure in order to discourage them from their religious vocation.

Another intolerable fact is the State's shameless meddling into the internal affairs of the religious orders.

Hundreds of former monks and nuns are still working in civilian jobs and are forbidden to live in communities. And the new Vatican policy has not been able to help them.

Religious instruction is allowed on paper, but in practice it has all but disappeared in Budapest and in the cities of Hungary. The pressure is so tremendous, the intimidation is so shamelessly strong, that most parents simply do not dare to risk their jobs by sending their children to religious education.

Religious education is dead now in Hungary. Dead in the cities and dying in the villages where the last vestiges of the ancient Hungarian village social structure are being systematically demolished. In the new order, with a quickly changing village population, the defense of religious education is weared to a point of total annihilation. The right of spiritual self-defense is deprived from the Churches in Hungary.

The result is a totally uneducated young generation of Hungarians, as far as God, religion, and churches are concerned. They still have a strong desire to know God and to have answers to the basic human problems: life and death. Instead of the official teaching of the churches—which is not available to them—many young people create their own "private" religions put together by a wide variety of books read and by impressions received. The Communists failed to turn them into atheists; but they do not belong to the organized churches either.

Perhaps the most characteristic example of the ecclesiastical situation today is an article published on March 31, 1974 in the *Katolikus Szo (Catholic Word)*, a State-sponsored so-called Catholic periodical. The reporter, in a long article, presents his findings on the state of affairs of country parishes and pastors in Hungary.

The reporter, who wrote this article for a "Catholic" periodical and who supposedly should be promoting faith, religion and priestly vocations, finds that the Hungarian Catholic Church's greatest problem is to retain the 99 lambs in the fold without worrying about the one lamb which has been lost. He visited several county parishes.

> In one rectory the pastor—a Doctor of Sacred Theology—was cooking some squash, his only plate for dinner. The kitchen was loaded with unwashed utensils. The priest's study was loaded with books, but he had not cleaned his quarters for at least a month. The pastor was very proud of having up to 15 children in his religious class, but, the reporter tells us no one opens his door on weekdays. There are 4 or 5 weddings, 8 to 10 baptisms and 15 to 20 burials a year, apart from the Sunday Masses, and that's all. If he feels himself alone, he goes to the organ, sings a "Tantum ergo...," or an "Ave Maria." After that only a few bottles of wine remain for him. Some priests write for their own deskdrawer, others desperately try to have retreats organized for their flock, even more, simply drink. And almost

all of them sooner or later, have ulcers. They cannot hire a cook, cannot afford to eat regularly in a restaurant, and so the ulcers are unavoidable. The pastor has more and more empty wine-bottles, and he, himself, slowly, but surely is being covered with dust. . . .

This is how a Hungarian, state-sponsored "Catholic" periodical "promotes" the idea of priesthood and Church for the general public in Hungary. And there is no protest from the Hungarian Board of Bishops or from anyone else. There is none, because, it would be an exercise in futility.

At the 17th Congress of the *Pax Romana* section of exile-Hungarians, Imre Andras, the chairman of the Church-socialistic institute in Vienna, gave the following facts: since 1948 in Hungary 150 men's and 450 women's monasteries were liquidated and the Catholic associations dissolved. Twenty Catholic printing presses, which were supplying more than 2,000 Catholic schools, were nationalize. Later on, 8 junior high schools and a gymnasium were returned to religious orders. Of 22 priest-seminaries, only 6 exist, which are under strict governmental control. A majority of the religious are not allowed to take part in church activities. The shortage of priests is becoming increasingly more critical.

In fact, Hungary probably has the most liberal church policy among Warsaw Pact countries. Sunday schools and youth retreats are permitted. Bibles, though expensive, are available. Even so, open evangelism and freedom of church publication in the Western sense are unknown. Evangelical Christians are customarily excluded from the universities and the professions.

Romania

When the Communists came to power in Romania they were very weak and played also the role of being friends of religion. Now, being so weak, the Communists have convened in Romania in the building of the Parliament, a congress of cults. There were 4,000 priests, pastors, rabbis, mullahs, of all kinds of religions. The Prime Minister of the Communist government, Petru Groza, delivered a speech and said, "Oh, yes, in olden times in Russia there have been bad things about religion. These have passed away long since. You should be on our side." That was in '45. "You should be on our side. We will support religion." And the Minister of Interior Affairs, Teohari Georgescu, an old Communist, made big crosses and kissed the icons. And priests believed them; 4,000 priests and pastors cheered the Communist Prime Minister. There was only one pastor out of the 4,000 who protested there on the spot. One pastor out of 4,000. This one, Rev. Richard Wurmbrand, went to prison.

Everywhere the Communists, until they have the power, say that they are the friends of religion.

Religious allegiances generally follow ethnic lines with about 80 per cent of all Romanians nominally belonging to the Romanian Orthodox Church. The Greek Catholic or Uniate Church, to which about 10 per cent of the populace belonged, was incorporated into the Romanian Orthodox Church by *fiat* in 1948. Roman Catholics, largely Magyar, constitute about 9 per cent of the population; Calvinists, Jews, and Lutherans the most numerous of the remaining 11 per cent of the population.

There is no other country in the East Bloc today as Romania representing such an erroneous opinion. This country with its entire internal Stalinistic policy and with the most cunning informer system of the Communist world, is often considered relatively a free country on account of Ceaucescu's maneuvers of foreign policy for Western observers and Ceaucescu biographies of internal politics have presented a wrong interpretation. These false pretenses also can be applied to the status of the Church in Romania.

The mixed picture of this country's nationalities is also reflected in the composition of various confessions. From about 21 million inhabitants there are approximately 16 million Orthodox believers.

Mostly non-Romanians adhere to Latin-rite Catholics. The Bulgarians make up around 60 per cent of the 1.2 million Catholics, while the Germans take second place with a quarter of a million faithful. They are mostly Donau Schwabes in Banat, who at the time belong to the vacant Temeschwar Diocese. To their 164 parishes besides Hungarians and Germans, Bulgarian and Croat parishes, including Slovaks and Czechs, also belong.

The Catholic Church of Romania at the time of Communist takeover had almost over three million believers. From this number there were more than one and a half million Byzantine-rite Catholics. In 1948 this Church with six dioceses and 1,810 priests was forcibly incorporated in the Orthodox Church. All the bishops died in imprisonment. The last one to die was bishop Julius Hossu. Pope Paul VI elevated him to cardinal in *petto* in 1969. Until today the Uniate Church in Romania is forbidden, while the State and Orthodox Church uphold a fiction of its "voluntary return in the Orthodox Church."

From the five Latin-rite dioceses, according to the Vatican Yearbook, only one is occupied by a proper ordinarius: Diocese of Karlsburg (Alba Julia) where Bishop Aaron Marton with his lawful successor Msgr. Antal Jakob live.

In Jassy just one titular Bishop, Peter Plesca, resides. The rest of the dioceses: Satu Mare—Grosswardein, Temeschburg and Bukarest are without a bishop, whereby in Bukarest an ordinarius-substitute administers the Metropole. Except for Bukarest, these reprimanded dioceses have never been recognized by the State.

The education of Catholic priests is permitted only at Karlsburg and Jassy seminaries. In Karlsburg the official teaching language is Hungarian while in Jassy it is Romanian. Until the year of 1948 there was a seminary in Temeschburg for German-speaking priests, which does not exist any more and there is no other institution in the German language for new priests.

From the million Romanian Protestants, 800,000 belong to Hungarian Calvinists, 180,000 to German Lutherans in Siebenburgen, and 100,000 to Hungarian Lutherans. In addition, there are 120,000 Unitarians, who deny the Holy Trinity, and a number of various sects. The Gregorian Armenian National Church has a diocese with 30,000 believers.

The Orthodox Church and various Protestant denominations as well as the Jews have at their disposal the least religious media available, while the Catholics do not have any Church newspapers nor any Church literature.

In Romania as in Czechoslovakia some religious orders are forbidden. Religious instructions are permitted only on the church premises: church halls and rectories, and are submitted to various kinds of vexations. The religious instructions are not permitted to use any kind of instructional material, nor Bible, and the children are not allowed to take any kind of notes at the religious instructions. Besides, there is an unescapable fear and mistrust of the presence of secret police. The public is required to inform the police within 24 hours of conversation or other contact with Western visitors. This requirement is especially strictly requested from believers and clergy. Non-observance is punishable.

Thus the Catholic Church in the country is a real "church in need!" Nevertheless, Article 30 of the Constitution guarantees every citizen freedom to confess one's religious belief or not. Both are assured as stated: "Religious cults are organized by themselves and they function in a free manner." However, the Communist State harasses each religious denomination, discriminates and hinders Latin-rite Catholics and denies the existance of one-and-half million Uniates.

Of the 21 million Romanian citizens, 88 per cent are Orthodox believers, 16 per cent Catholics, 69 per cent Protestants, and a small number of Jews and Moslems. The figure for the Catholics is approximately 1.3 million. Another 1.3 million belonged to the Greek-Orthodox Church, which was forcibly, in 1948, united with the Orthodox Church. Officially it does not exist anymore.

In 651 parishes there were 900 priests in the year of 1975. Even though the Church is oppressed there is continuously active life in it. The Catholics have established a true brotherly love.

In the Vatican's Yearbook there is missing information about the occupancy of the diocesian assignments. Only the Diocese of Alba Julia is indicated as to be entrusted to Bishop Aaron Marton. Besides that, the Catholic Church in Romania is served by secretly consecrated bishops. In the West only two are known: Bishop Adalbert Boros and Msgr. Duma consecrated by the papal nuntius. Both of them are working as plain clergymen in the district of Bukarest.

President Nicolae Ceausescu of Romania called on Pope Paul VI at the Vatican, marking a recent improvement in relations between the Communist government in Bucharest and the Roman Catholic Church.

In a long talk, the Pope and Mr. Ceausescu reportedly discussed the status of about a million Catholics in Romania—mostly Hungarian- descended residents of Transylvania—and of the country's 1.5 million Byzantine-rite Catholics who are in communion with Rome.

President Ceausescu's visit to the Vatican came at the end of a six-day tour of Italy, during which time he had talks with government leaders, inspected industrial plants in the northern part of the country and made a side trip to tiny San Marino.

Legally, no Romanian may belong to the Eastern-rite Catholic Church in Romania; legally, that Church does not exist.

After the suppression of the Eastern-rite Catholic Church in Romania 30 years ago, those of its priests who refused to join the Orthodox Church were declared "vagrants" in a decree of the Romanian ministry of the interior. Any priestly activity on their part made them liable to severe penalties and imprisonment.

All five Eastern-rite diocesan bishops in Romania were imprisoned, as were all their principal aides. Also imprisoned were all seminary professors. None of the bishops survives.

Shortly after their arrest, five other bishops of the Eastern-rite were secretly consecrated by the papal envoy in Romania, the late Archbishop Gerald P. O'Hara, an American. Their identity was discovered almost immediately by the Romanian police, not through informers, but by simple observation of a number of priests who approached the new bishops for consultation.

The new bishops were imprisoned. After terms that varied from man to man, they were released—all in condition that they not carry out any religious ministry.

Now they live privately in various parts of Romania, supporting themselves by work in offices or institutions. They are Bishops Joan Ploscaru, Joan Dragomir, Juliu Hirtea, Alexander Todea and Joan Chertes.

All Eastern-rite Catholic priests in Romania are under constant police surveillance. So far as can be determined from abroad, this surveillance has not in any way been relaxed since Romanian President Nicolae Ceausescu visited Pope Paul.

The Stalinist-inspired suppression of the Romanian Eastern-rite Catholic Church also remains in full force despite Romania's virtual declaration of independence from its Soviet masters.

One of Ceausescu's strong cards in his difficult game with the Soviet Union, however, has been rigorous internal policy, however liberal his foreign policy may have become.

In 1959 the Holy Synod under Patriarch Justinian's leadership drew up new regulations organizing monasticism. Prior to that there had begun between 1948 and 1958 a monastic renaissance. According to the new regulations, one wishing to become a monk must have finished eight years of elementary schooling and the course in one of the six seminaries. The number of monks is fixed by the state for each given monastery and there is a waiting list of aspirants. The monks and nuns are all required to know a trade and work at it. The level of spirituality, however, is nothing that could qualify as a renaissance except in the two monasteries for men at Sihastria and Putna. But it is precisely there that a definitely rigid limit has been placed on the number entering.

The Orthodox nuns are more numerous. The monasteries of Agapia and Varatec number 325 and 300 nuns, respectively, giving the impression of a whole village of nuns. Here too they must work at a trade, usually on the farms, and during winter, indoors at embroidery, painting, printing and in general at the production of artifacts that are contracted for by the government agencies and exported to ready markets abroad.

The visitor to Romania is struck by the numerous Orthodox churches that are everywhere open and well-attended, not only by the old but by the young as well. To staff the 8,568 parishes there are 9,400 priests, one for every 1,500 of the faithful, and there seems to be no dearth of vocations. Although no church organizations are allowed and no religious teaching can take place outside church walls, nevertheless catechetical instruction is given to the young on Saturdays and to the adults by way of an extended sermon on Sundays, accompanied, by order of Patriarch Justinian, with readings from the Greek Fathers and the lives of the saints during Communion and after the liturgy. Although there is no open anti-religious instruction in the public schools, believing parents still complain that their children have been greatly weakened in their faith by an education that is totally indifferent to religion on principle and by law.

The Romanian Orthodox Church is organized into five metropolias. Each of these metropolias has also one or more suffragan dioceses for a total of twelve. The Church is governed on the deliberative level that deals with the spiritual and canonical matters by the Holy Synod, composed of the Patriarch and all the active metropolitans, archbishops and bishops as members. It usually meets twice a year.

All the various church groups enjoy a very friendly relationship with each other. Whenever a Catholic or Reformed Hungarian or Unitarian bishop comes to Bucharest, he knows that the Patriarch has a room for him in his palace. In the circumstances perhaps nothing of a more serious ecumenical nature can be hoped for.

Since the Romanian Orthodox Church's entrance with the Russian Church into full participation in the World Council of Churches in 1962, the Romanians have begun to take a more active part in international conferences. Metropolitan Justin of Jassy is the Patriarch's spokesman in all Church foreign affairs. A former professor of Holy Scripture, Justin has maintained a hard line toward dialogue with Rome. He has opposed the setting up within united Orthodox of an organ of dialogue with the Roman Catholic Church since he argued at Chambesy: "Rome is not mature enough for a serious dialogue. It must be further studied and we must use great prudence." Like the Greek Orthodox, the Romanian Orthodox mistrust Rome and its past history of Uniatism.

The Romanian Orthodox Church has a militant anti-Roman history, and considers itself a bulwark against the Papacy. But there are indications that this attitude is changing. Although the government has suppressed the Catholic Church in the past, perhaps even more so than other religions, it has made gestures that in some ways have not been very well received locally. However, the Vatican itself has seemed willing to overlook any reluctance on the part of the regional Catholic hierarchy, thus showing its willingness to cooperate with a nation's internal affairs.

In 1948 Latin Catholics numbered 1,174,000, while the Byzantine Catholics numbered 1,573,000. The latter Church was totally suppressed in that same year, while the Latin-rite Catholics suffered harsh persecution, imprisonment and confiscation of practically all their church property.

In the 1960's, the conditions became somewhat better, until today a *modus vivendi* has been worked out that allows all the former Latin churches to be opened as well as allowing the Roman-rite priests to function properly.

Two major seminaries offer the full course in philosophy and theology at Jassy for the Romanian-speaking seminarians and at Alba Julia for those preparing to serve in the Hungarian-German speaking parishes. The Latin churches seem to be well frequented by fervent Catholics. They are served by dedicated priests of a basic conservative bent. The Romanian priests are reluctant to introduce the vernacular into the liturgy for fear that the government might take the same sort of step it took to suppress the Uniate Church.

This is one of the saddest pages in recent religious history in Romania. The Uniates were in origin Orthodox who in 1698-1700 united with Rome while retaining their own Byzantine liturgy and religious way of life, identical with that of their fellow Orthodox. The Romanian State, following the example of the U.S.S.R., which in 1946 liquidated the Uniate Church of the Ukraine, violently suppressed the Uniate Romanian Church on December 1, 1948. Numbering nearly 1.6 million faithful, the 1,800 parishes and 2,588 churches and all adjoining property were turned over to the Orthodox; 1,834 priests were given the option either to become Orthodox or be secularized. All six bishops were put into prison, where five of them died.

The majority of Uniates continue their religious practices in the Orthodox Churches. Most of these were their former Uniate parishes, so they see very little changed.

The Orthodox Church leaders still feel Rome should recognize the fact and encourage those who resist to give up any hope of a restoration such as occurred in Czechoslovakia. Those who have remained faithful to Rome do so as a matter of conscience, and Rome feels it cannot do violence to their convictions.

Protestants in Romania are divided into four major groups: the Calvinist Reform, the Evangelical Lutheran (Augsburg Confession), the Evangelical Church of the Presbyterian Synod and the Unitarian Church. The Reformed Calvinists represent the largest Protestant body, 700,000 faithful, and are found predominantly in Transylvania.

The Lutherans of German nationality, numbering about 180,000, are found also in Transylvania as well as in Banat. Bishop Albert Klein of Sibiu is their leader.

The Presbyterian Evangelical Church numbers only 30,000 faithful of predominantly Hungarian nationality and live also in Transylvania. Bishop Gheorghe Argay of Cluj governs this Church.

The Unitarian Church, world-wide now in scope, actually originated in the city of Cluj when a group of Hungarians under David Ferenc denied the Trinity as well as the divinity of Jesus Christ. Bishop Eleck Kiss of Cluj is the only Unitarian bishop in the world, a position that has come down from the 16th century. There are about 65,000 Hungarian Unitarians, mostly in Transylvania.

These Protestant Churches, including the Unitarians, have a joint monthly journal called *Reformatus Szemle*. Other Protestant groups with a proper constitution approved by the state, and hence granted religious freedom, are the Pentecostals, Baptists, Seventh Day Adventists and Evangelists. As with the Orthodox and Catholics, the salaries of these instructors and ministers are paid by the state, the same as a corresponding professor in the state universities.

The two non-Christian religious groups, constituting quite small minority groups, are given equal religious liberty with all the Christian Church bodies. Dr. C. Segal, president of the Jewish Community in Bucharest, explained the situation of the Jews in Romania. Under the German occupation up to 1944, thousands of Jews were shipped to Germany and there exterminated. Other thousands migrated to Israel, America and other free countries, since today the Romanian government still allows freedom of emigration only to the Jews and Muslims. Today, Dr. Segal estimates that there are about 100,000 Jews still in Romania, of whom over half are living in Bucharest itself. Although they possessed in Arad the Yeshiva Theological Institute, the lack of vocations to the rabbinate forced the Jewish community under Rabbi Moses Khoren to close its doors. This constitutes the greatest difficulty for the Jews in Romania: lack of rabbis and cantors to serve in the synagogues that already are functioning.

The Muslims number about 30,000 and are under the direction of Muftiu Iacub Mehmet. They are the remnants of the Tatars and the

Turks who inhabited the Eastern part of present-day Romania around the Black Sea, called Dobroudja. There are about 25 mosques open, including the beautiful one in Constanta seen by most tourists.

In spite of the "Iron Curtain," certain information, sometimes contradictory, regarding religious life, foreign tourists or officially invited guests believe that they can report news affirming the existence there of religious freedom. Furthermore, the country's authorities do not fail to advertise the existence of religious liberty in the country since the churches are open to practice religion and, moreover, the clergy is paid and the constitution guarantees such practice of religion.

Unfortunately, other evidence, collected recently based on facts, reveals another truth which one can neither ignore or conceal; that persecution continues in the Romanian People's Republic due to the absence of any real religious freedom—persecution less violent certainly, but persecution nevertheless. During the Stalin period the persecutions in the Romanian People's Republic were bloody and unusually brutal. Although the Orthodox Church—the majority of religious organizations—was persecuted less, it nevertheless did suffer, while the Catholic Church of both rites—the minority—suffered cruelly.

As a matter of fact, after the Orthodox Church was neutralized by appointing a patriarch as its head, the Communists wanted to make the United Catholic Church disappear, at any price, by national-religious expedients. Since the union with Rome in 1700, a part of the Romanians of Transylvania, members of the United Romanian Church, rendered great service to the nation in the religious, cultural, and other national fields. Aware that this church constituted a serious obstacle to the total enslavement of the country, the present regime of the Romanian People's Republic disguised its (process of) destruction under the pretext of the "religious reunification" of the country and love of the nation, (for the regime) cannot tolerate the influence of a foreign power—the Holy See—in the country's internal affairs. This is why the Uniate Catholic Church was "legally" suppressed by the decree of December 1, 1948.

If there really had been liberty in the Romanian People's Republic, the regime could, on the occasion of the Ecumenical Council of Churches, have freed the two Romanian Uniate bishops and allowed them to go to Rome. The regime, of course, denied permission to the only Catholic bishop of the Latin-rite—who is kept under surveillance at his domicile—to attend the Council. The other five died in prison. The situation of the Catholic Church of the Latin-rite during the Stalin period was very precarious for the regime wanted to separate it from Rome. However, it was unsuccessful.

During the "peaceful coexistence" of the Khrushchev period, the Uniate Church of Romania was always a persecuted "Silent Church." The church of the Latin-rite, with its leaders dead, subsists for better or for worse. The Orthodox Church, which suffered during the Stalinist period, is tolerated under "peaceful coexistence." However, contrary to some allegations, at the present moment the regime conducts an underhanded and persevering, but all the more perceptible, fight against religion itself and Christianity, and equally against the Orthodox Church. No doubt, the Orthodox churches are open as are many of those of the Latin-rite and their members are praying there. The state pays the clergy and has even reestablished some monasteries and churches, which are more than 500 years old. However, at the same time, it has permitted the cathedral of Blaj, which is 200 years old, to collapse, and for good reason.

The article, "Ways of Providing Atheistic and Scientific Education in Schools," by Predescu said intense atheist propaganda should be carried out both inside and outside schools. He held that atheistic concepts should be spread not only by social science teachers but by those in all fields— "botanics, zoology and anatomy, physics and chemistry, history and geography."

The vigor with which the campaign to combat religion and promote atheism has been pursued since July, 1971 may be partly explained by the fact that, according to Constantin Pirvulescu at the November session of the Romanian Communist Party's central committee, "manifestations of mysticism have been detected even among party members who have not yet completely renounced their religious concepts."

Western political observers believe that, mindful of the 1968 Soviet-led invasion of Czechoslovakia, the Romanian Communists acted against liberalization at home lest they might be accused by Moscow of delivering Romania into the "capitalistic camp" as the liberal Communist leaders were accused in 1968 in Czechoslovakia.

The Vatican has taken issue with a statement by Romanian Orthodox Patriarch Justinian in Brussels recently that the Roman Catholic Eastern-rite Church of Romania had "dissolved itself."

In an unsigned article, *L'Osservatore Romano*, Vatican City newspaper, said categorically, the "Greek-Catholic Church of Romania is in fact suppressed."

The Vatican City daily noted that in his Brussels press conference, the Romanian Patriarch made his statement without indicating the shock it has "aroused among those present and which was taken up by a large part of the press in Belgium."

According to this article, Patriarch Justinian had told reporters that the period of persecution and imprisonment of members of the Greek Catholic Church in Romania had ended. He also alleged the existence of this Church, known in Romania as the "Uniate Church," "is an impediment and an obstacle on the road to unity with the Catholic Church."

The Vatican newspaper commented:

> Apart from this last affirmation which we cannot share, insofar as regards the so-called self-suppression, this is what has been told us by well-informed sources
>
> The Greek-Catholic Church of Romania was in fact suppressed. The act had a formal initial date: October, 1948. That day, in fact, 38 Catholic priests of the Oriental Rite (of about 2,000 priests then in existence) were coercively called for a synodal meeting which would decide on the integration of the Uniate Church with the Orthodox one—at the meeting only 36 of the 38 were present. . . .
>
> The meeting was supervised by the police, and the speech by Traian Belascu had been prepared by the authorities. . . .
>
> The meeting could not have the value of a synodal meeting . . . nonetheless despite this invalidity the resolution approved by the meeting was presented on October 3, 1948, to the Orthodox Patriarch of Bucharest, Justinian.

L'Osservatore reported the protest made by the apostolic nuncio, Msgr.

Gerard Patrick O'Hara:

> The diplomatic step, however, had no practical effect and on the basis of the Cluj document, pressure was exerted on the other priests and on the people to endorse this union with the Orthodox Church.
>
> In many cases the transfer was effected summarily. In others, when priests and faithful, despite the pressure on them, even through local administrative organs, refused to sign, they had to support the consequences. Many resisting priests were deported and very many faithful, who had refused their adherence, were forced to leave their jobs.

The Vatican newspaper wrote that this continued until October 28, 1948, when the six bishops of the "Uniate Church," with all their chief assistants, were interned. Eventually, they died in prison.

On the basis of these facts, "consecrated by history," one cannot therefore talk of self-dissolution of the Oriental-rite Catholic Church and its voluntary integration into the Orthodox Church.

It added that Latin-rite Catholics in Romania had joined with the Uniate Church in protesting, but to no avail.

> Thus, about 3 million citizens of the Romanian People's Republic, sons of the Catholic Church, were treated by law and authority as though they were enemies of the people, guilty of crimes against the people, they (citizens) who were sons of this land, which they had worked for centuries with the sweat of their brows.

Some 250,000 Scripture portions were produced for the Romanian Orthodox Church during 1968-72, more than three times the number going to that Communist country in 1945-68, it was reported by United Bible Societies.

This phenomenal growth is considered a "break-through" for Scripture production in the country whose president, Nicolae Ceaucescu, has frequently stressed a need to "increase and intensify atheistic propaganda."

Of the 250,000 Scripture portions published in the recent four-year period, there were 100,000 Bibles, 30,000 selected texts for teaching, 60,000 New Testaments with Psalms, 10,000 editions of the four Gospels, 10,000 copies of the Book of Acts and New Testament Epistles, and 40,000 Books of Psalms.

Romanian Baptists are under pressure to take an oath of allegiance to party as well as state required of all Romanians.

The Baptists are confined by law to small congregations, and their often clandestine Bible readings in private homes are punishable as illegal assembly. Members declare themselves loyal Romanian citizens, but they resist taking the oath as a matter of Christian conscience.

The only apparent reason for all this tightening up in the intensely puritanical party line demanded by President Ceausescu in recent years.

In 1973 there were 8,185 Romanian Orthodox parishes and 11,722 places of worship, served by 8,564 priests and 78 deacons. Bucharest itself has nearly 250 parish churches, with just over 400 priests and about 20 deacons. Parishes, naturally, vary considerable in size. In general, approval is not given for the formation of a new parish unless there are at least 500 Orthodox families in a town area, or 400 families in a village, though exceptions to this rule are made in special circumstances.

In 1972 it was reported in an official release by the Romanian Orthodox Church that there were 114 monastic foundations with a total number of 2,068 religious, of whom 1,493 were nuns and 575 were monks. These figures may be compared with those for 1956 which indicate that there were at that time 200 monasteries with over 7,000 members of religious orders.

The liaison between the government of the Socialist Republic of Romania and the various church bodies is centered in the Ministry of Cults, under the direction of a Secretary General who has succeeded in bringing about a tight control or surveillance on the part of the government over each religious group, while at the same time obtaining fairly high degree of good will and co-operation and dialogue between State and Church did not always exist in Romania, even in the recent past. An attempt to live with religion began in some degree in 1948, at least in regard to the state's attitude toward the Orthodox Church, which then numbered about 14 million faithful.

In 1948 the government allowed the Holy Synod to draw up a new constitution, which the National Assembly promulgated on February 23, 1949, giving a more ample organization and assuring new freedoms to the Orthodox Church.

It is a fact that Petru Groza, who was president of the Romanian Republic from 1952 to 1958, was on most friendly terms with Patriarch Justinian. Groza had served as a lay member of the Holy Synod from 1919 to 1927, and during his presidency aided greatly to create a relationship between Church and State unknown in any other Communist country.

An abrupt change took place in 1958 that mirrored the hard line of the Party in the USSR. In June, 1958 , a wave of arrests of bishops, priests, ministers, rabbis, monks and laity took place, and the prison camp of Baragan and the prisons of Mercurea-Ciuculiu, Dej, Gherla and Pitesti were overflowing with Orthodox, Catholics, Protestants, Jews and Muslims. The Communists had become alarmed by the expansion of religion under Groza and their own inability to effect their socialistic aims. Monasticism was especially hard hit. More than 2,000 Orthodox monks were unfrocked, and half the monasteries were closed. All Catholic religious orders and congregations of men and women were dissolved, and all non-Romanian Catholic religious were deported. A similar persecution hit the Protestant Churches and other believing groups. In the years 1963 and 1964, however, an amnesty was declared, and most religious prisoners were "rehabilitated" back into society.

When Gheorghiu Dej died on March 19, 1965, Nicolae Ceausescu took over and has continued a realistic program of openness to all factors that would make Romania a strong nation. One major factor, in his eyes, is still religion. Ceausescu recognizes the power of religion for the Romanian people.

To show good will on the part of the state, all ministers of 15 approved religious groups receive salaries paid them by the state along with pensions and other social benefits equal to what other citizens receive, such as free hospitalization, etc. Clerics and seminarians are exempt from military service. The government, not always totally uninterested in tourism, has spent in the last few years enormous sums of hard currency to restore and conserve ancient religious monuments. These include some of the Moldavian monasteries, such as Succevita and Voronet, the 14th-century Roman Catholic Gothic cathedral of Alba Julia and the Hungarian Reformed Church of the 16th century in Cluj.

As in most predominantly Orthodox countries, it is difficult in Romania to know where the Orthodox religion ends and where nationality begins. Out of its 20 million inhabitants, it is estimated that about 12 to 13 million still adhere to the Orthodox Church, making the Romanian Church the second largest Orthodox Church in the world, next only to that in Russia.

Much of the credit for a strong Orthodox Church in Romania must be given to Patriarch Justinian. He has brought to his church administration since 1948 a discipline and order mingled with a desire to take religion out of the dark churches and bring it into the market place by a new awareness of Orthodoxy's social obligations. Much of his success with the socialist leaders and within his own hierarchy is due to his personal charm and skilled diplomacy, plus his ability to adapt his Church to the actual situation at hand. He declared in his address at his enthronement in 1948 that he wanted especially to elevate the spiritual and intellectual level of the Orthodox clergy as well as to reform and renovate Orthodox monasticism.

In 1956 he obtained a decree that allowed for high-level theological formation in the seminaries. There are now three levels of seminary formation. The basic two-year course is one offered in the six preparatory seminaries in Bucharest, Neamt, Cluj, Craiova, Caransebes and Buzau to train parish cantors. This is followed by three more years in the same schools to prepare priests for the smaller villages. The better qualified students go then to the two theological institutes of university standing at Bucharest and Sibiu, where a most intensive four-year course in theology is offered.

East Germany

The West German Bishops Conference at meeting in Fulda, West Germany, said that more members of the Church are persecuted today than at any other time in history, and those who are free should come to their aid.

The bishops issued a statement which surveyed persecutions in Africa, Asia, Northern Ireland and Lebanon, stating that some of these had their roots in economic, social, racial and anti-colonialist, rather than religious attitudes.

Turning to their own country, the bishops said:

> We are thinking in particular of our brothers and sisters in the German Democratic Republic, who must show constant and special courage in everyday life in order to profess their Catholic faith. Parents especially find themselves in deep anguish of conscience as regards the religious education of their children, particularly at the age of development; the young people are often exposed to difficulties and obstacles in their general and professional formation.

> In nearly all countries where totalitarian ideologies dominate, and not only in areas under Communist rule, Christianity is combatted. This occurs through open persecution, or by means of vexations, or at least through limitations of religious and ecclesiastical freedom.

> Religious freedom in the Soviet Union and in the Eastern bloc countries, consists in the fact that adults can participate in liturgical worship. While atheism is supported by the whole State apparatus, even the dialogue between Christians and non-believers is forbidden. In some countries, where visits to the sick and the administration of the sacraments to the dying are not directly forbidden, official permits must be obtained beforehand. Charitable activity is widely forbidden. The Polish Bishops are continually in the necessity of protesting against the monopoly of Communist opinion, the censorship of the press and the attacks on the activity of Catholic institutions. In the Soviet Union parish communities are directed not by parish priests, but by ecclesiastical councils, which are made up partly of Communist officials. These councils control the parish priests. The situation is different in each Communist country. In general, however, no member of a

Christian community can become a teacher, a civil servant or official. In some countries religious instruction is forbidden. Even the parents are sometimes not allowed to bring up their children in a religious way.

Among the thousands of persons who are obliged to live in special work camps, in the Soviet Union, there are a good many who have been exiled for religious reasons: Orthodox, Baptists and Catholics.

The DDR government has been relatively mild in its dealings with the Roman Church in East Germany, even though only a small minority of the people are Catholic. No clergymen have been imprisoned.

On the whole, the bishops have followed instructions from the West German church. In fact, considering the comparatively lenient attitude of the government, the church hierarchy in the DDR has been criticized for not working more closely with the secular authorities. But the Vatican appears to be moving toward recognition of East Germany; it has already given *de facto* recognition of the Oder-Neisse line.

There is no prohibition against public worship. The government has not closed down the churches or made it an offense to assemble publicly for religious reasons. But the struggle against religion is there and constitutes a genuine threat to one of the last liberties not yet entirely suppressed.

The Communists are engaged in a slow but deliberate campaign to destroy all vestiges of religious liberty. It is waged in the following manner.

In schools, youth movements, the press and over the radio, religion is set in a bad light. Historical events with their dire consequences are unearthed to show how religion has been the "opiate of the people." Through this means the younger generation is taught to abhor and despise religion—to regard it as a "superstition." Many of the kindergartens formerly run by the church are either cut back or taken over by the state.

But not all. Some schools are still administered by the church. But once parents send their children to the parochial schools, the fate of their offspring is sealed. From that moment on, their children are doomed to become second-rate citizens, with no chance of ever climbing the social ladder. They are shunned and discarded from fulfilling any worthwhile function in the nation. Life is hard for those resisting the state's reforms for a "Socialist Utopia." Their aspirations of being someone when they grow into adulthood are forever shattered, the best they can hope for is a steady factory or clerical job.

The Communists know that most of the younger generation will traverse the easier course. Only the older generation will want to hold on to religion—and they are allowed to. But in the government plan it will merely be a matter of time before the older generation will die and with it, religion.

Secularization, lamented for years by West German church leaders, has gone much further in Communist East Germany where atheism dominates as the official state religion.

On paper, East Germany's constitution guarantees freedom of conscience and religious belief as well as the right to engage in religious practices. But as a result of years of political pressure, most citizens now are Christians in name only.

Discrimination particularly affects the young.

Opportunities for a higher education are practically nil unless youths prove their worth to the state through membership in the Communist youth organization and take part in other political activities, including paramilitary training.

"Active participation in shaping the Socialist society," rather than good grades, determine admittance to a high school or university.

East Germany is predominantly Protestant and before the Communists took over in 1945, the children of Lutheran parents passed through religious confirmation which marked their acceptance into the community of the faithful.

This traditional observance has long been substituted by an atheist "youth dedication" ceremony to which practically all pupils submit now. At this rutual, boys and girls pledge to "work and struggle for a happy life in our workers and peasants state" and to "dedicate all strength . . . to the great cause of Socialism."

Refusal to participate would forego from the start any chance for further education and professional advancement.

What concerns the church leaders is that the number of those who attend religious confirmation after the Communist ceremony has been going down steadily.

At first, both Lutheran pastors and Catholic priests refused to confirm children who had gone through the Communist youth dedication. But they had to compromise on this as well as on other principal issues.

There are no recent statistics on the number of Christians remaining in East Germany. During the 1964 census, 60 per cent of the 17 million East Germans professed to Lutheranism. Pastors say, however, that no more than 5 per cent of the population, and then mostly elderly people, still attend religious services.

An estimated 10 per cent of the infants born in East Germany are still being baptized. Church weddings are equally rare.

In its systematic drive against the church, the Communist government has tried, and not without success, to deprive such high Christian holidays as Christmas and Easter of their religious meaning and turn them into atheistic celebrations.

Many East Germans, worn down by the pressure of meeting production targets, by incessant political propaganda, and the daily struggle for some of the amenities of life, obviously found the conflict too great and succumbed to the demands of their rulers.

Yet, despite its precarious position, the Protestant Church was the last major institution in East Germany to end resistance and sever organizational ties with Protestants in the West.

The split between Protestant Germans in East and West finally was sealed in 1972 after the Communist authorities had refused for five years to allow the bishop of Berlin-Brandenburg to visit the eastern part of his diocese.

New pressure is on the smaller Catholic Church to disassociate itself from the four dioceses in West Germany to which the 1.3 million Catholics in East Germany belong.

In the country-wide census of 1964, about 67 per cent of the population of the DDR described themselves as either "Protestant" or "Catholic."

Incidentally, it is only on census forms that it is legal in the DDR to make official enquiry as to a person's religious belief; otherwise it is regarded as purely a personal question.

The great majority of those describing themselves as members of one of the Christian denominations are Protestants—about ten million in number, or 59 per cent of the total population.

The vast majority of the Protestants belong to the Evangelical Church, which has 7,800 congregations, 6,000 pastors, 5,500 catechists, and 5,500 deacons and deaconesses.

In addition there are a number of free churches, most important of which are the New Apostolic Church (80,000 members); the Evangelical-Methodist Church (45,000 members); and the Seventh Day Adventists (27,000 members).

The number of Catholics is about 1,300,000 or 8 per cent of the total DDR population. There are more than 1,400 regular and secular priests, and 2,700 nuns in 14 different orders, including the Benedictines, Ursulines, Cistercians and Grey Sisters.

Financial support for the churches comes from various sources, largely from church levies on the incomes of congregation members and collections. In addition, the church is a considerable landowner (200,000 hectares), and this land was not affected either by the land reform in 1945-46, or the transition to cooperative farming in 1960. The churches run a total of 50 agricultural enterprises.

Though there is no state obligation to give financial support, a contribution of over 12 million marks annually is made to both the Evangelical Church and the Catholic Church as a supplement to the salaries of pastors and priests. Apart from this subsidy the state gives grants for church restoration.

The DDR Constitution guarantees the right to profess a religious creed and to carry out religious activities. Most religious activities take place in the churches, but there are traditional church processions in some places on Corpus Christi Day, or other high festivals.

A number of the main, traditional Christian holidays are legal holidays in the DDR: Good Friday, Whit Monday, and Christmas, and Sunday is for most people the day of rest.

Apart from services, many of the other auxiliary activities pursued by churches in other countries are also usual in the DDR: mothers' circles, Bible study, preparation for confirmation, etc.

A very considerable amount of charitable and social work is done by both the main churches. The Evangelical Church maintains 54 hospitals with 12,500 beds, and provides accomodation for over 13,000 persons in old age homes. It also has day nurseries with room for 20,000 children, and children's homes for 3,000 children.

The 830 parishes of the Catholic Church in the DDR (with 1,372 priests in 1973) are administered by 62 deanaries, and 7 juridicial offices. The Catholic Church in the DDR still has at its disposal:

Pastoral offices and places for worship	1,046
Student chapels	30
Retreat homes	13
Educational Institutions for priests and church servants	13

Church Social Centers	11
Publishing houses	2

In the area of social and health care the Catholic Church has:

Old peoples homes and infirmaries	103
Hospitals and clinics	34
Nurseries and kindergartens	56
Recreation, nursing homes, sanatoriums	26
Maternity hospitals	3

According to the Berline's estimates, approximately 50 per cent of the DDR citizens belong to a Christian Church. Some 10 per cent of the population belong to a small group of "conscientious Christians" because of their regard for their significance in political involvement.

Both churches have their training schools at which hundreds of nurses are trained according to the standard state study plans.

There is good cooperation between the church social institutions and the state. The state pays the standard rates for the hospital and other services provided by the church installations, a sum amounting to about 60 million marks annually. Under an agreement with the Free German Trade Union Federation, the church authorities pay the doctors and nurses in the church installations the full union rates, the excess being made up by the state.

A new generation of pastors is trained at the theological sections at the universities of Berlin, Leipzig, Halle, Jena, Rostock and Greifswald. The state bears the full cost of the training. Between 500 and 600 students are generally in training, nearly all of whom receive the state grant of 190 marks monthly, plus special extra grants for good work; about half the theology students get the good-work grant. At present the theological sections cost the state about 4.3 million marks annually.

Theology students enjoy the same rights and duties as all other students, and a study of social sciences forms part of the curriculum.

Catholic priests mainly receive their training at a seminary in Erfurt.

There is plenty of theological and religious literature available in the DDR; about 12 per cent of all titles published in the DDR fall under these headings. In 1968 a total of 325 books and booklets in this group were published in a total edition of over 4,500,000. In addition there are 31 different church newspapers and magazines. The books published include Bibles (154 printings between 1962 and 1969), theological works, art books and fiction.

Every Sunday the DDR radio devotes one hour to a church service and church music; participation in the program is granted in accordance with the size of the various churches.

Among the young people of the DDR, a new religious revival is spreading. Apparently it is not imported from the West, but, formed by official youth work. The young people gather in groups to read the Bible and meditate for hours. The movement is not a youth protest against the world of adults. The beginning of the movement goes back to '60's where it gained recognition in the Berlin Youth Festival of '73. The DDR youth are making references to Biblical quotations during discussions, singing pious songs and praying together.

The Communist authorities in East Germany claim that young people who are Christians should not get jobs if other equally qualified people are available—because they cannot be trusted. The governing body of the Evangelical Church is determined to discuss this type of discrimination:

> Several motions presented to the Church's governing body allege that even highly educated young Christians are not allowed to take up further training for the careers they want to follow.
>
> Christians who do not belong to the political youth party are particularly discriminated against. Similarly, those who have not been "confirmed" as young Communists in the *Jugendweihe*.

The Lutheran Church of East Berlin held a synod in April, 1975, in which it gave a clear guidance on Christian responsibility in a Communist society where contradictions emerge.

The Synod decided to publish the full facts about State discrimination against young Christians both in education and in employment. It also regretted that, with one exception, it had been impossible to get permission to build any new churches or community centres in new housing areas. With West German financial help it had, however, been possible to embark on a comprehensive program of rebuilding and restoring historic churches.

On the conclusion of *Berliner Bischofskonferenz*, on October 26, 1976, the director of the Press Office of the Holy See, Fr. Romeo Panciroli, read the following statement:

> 1. With the decree of 25 September 1976 the Sacred Congregation for Bishops approved—with the usual clause "ad experimentum, ad quinquennium"—the Statutes of the *Berliner Bischofskonferenz*.
>
> This Conference, which takes the place of the *Berliner Ordinarienkonferenz*, which functioned as regional Episcopal Conference within the *Deutsche Bishofskonferenz*, will have the functions and the competences that the canonical dispositions in force attribute, for their respective territory, to the autonomous Episcopal Conferences.
>
> 2. The constitution of the *Berliner Bischofskonferenz* responds to necessities of an ecclesiastical nature.
>
> The Motu Proprio *Ecclesiae Sanctae*, in fact, established in art. 41, 1 that "the Bishops of the Nations or territories in which an Episcopal Conference does not yet exist, in accordance with the Decree *Christus Dominus*, will take steps to set it up as soon as possible and to draw up its Statutes, which are to be approved by the Apostolic See."
>
> The Episcopal Conferences—which are "a kind of council in which the bishops of a given nation or territory jointly exercise their pastoral office" (Decree *Christus Dominus*, art. 38, 1)—are therefore considered, after the Second Vatican Ecumenical Council, organs necessary for the regular development of the life and the pastoral action of the Church. In some cases, specific ones, they are accorded the authority (also by canonical dispositions) to take decisions which, under the conditions established, "have the force to oblige juridically" within their respective territory.
>
> There are no absolute criteria for defining the territorial sphere of the individual Episcopal Conferences. Normally this sphere corresponds to that of the respective State. The Decree *Christus Dominus* and the Motu Proprio *Ecclesiae Sanctae* mentioned above, use the word "Nation", but in the sense obviously of "State", as happens, moreover, also in the Code of Canon Law. Special motives, however, may lead to a different territorial delimitation:

thus, for example, within Great Britain there are two autonomous Episcopal Conferences (Bishops' Conference of England and Wales, and Bishops' Conference of Scotland); vice versa "wherever special circumstances require and the Apostolic See approves, bishops of many nations can establish a single conference"(Decree *Christus Dominus*, art. 38, 5), of which there are, in fact, various examples.

Generally speaking, it can be said that the criteria for the delimitation of the territorial sphere of the Episcopal Conferences are, without neglecting other elements (of a historical or political character) essentially and preeminently those of pastoral necessity or usefulness.

3. Bishops exercising their ministry in the territory of the D.D.R. (German Democratic Republic) did not have the possibility of taking part in the Assemblies and activities of the German Episcopal Conference of which they were theoretically members.

The German Episcopal Conference thus found itself in the necessity of making its decisions without the Bishops of the D.D.R. being able to contribute directly their experiences, opinions and proposals. Therefore the decisions of the German Episcopal Conference referred mainly to pastoral conditions quite different from the ones prevailing in the D.D.R.

Then, too, the *Berliner Ordinarienkonferenz*—though of great help for the coordination of pastoral activities and cooperation among the Bishops who belonged to it—did not have, being a regional Conference within the German Episcopal Conference, either the authority or the competences that the canonical dispositions in force attribute to autonomous Episcopal Conferences.

Keeping in mind in particular what precedes, the Holy See felt that determinant reasons of pastoral necessity and utility, made it necessary not to delay further the constitution of the *Berliner Ordinarienkonferenz* as an autonomous Episcopal Conference: all the more so in that the problems of the Church in the territory of the D.D.R. require that the Conference of those Bishops be able to tackle them with full authority.

The decision of the Holy See was communicated to the Bishops of the *Berliner Ordinarienkonferenz* on 10 April 1976, with the request to proceed, as the law indicated to draw up the new Statutes and then send them to the Holy See for approval: which has been done.

4. From what precedes it is clear that the existence of two parallel Episcopal Conferences does not interfere in the unresolved questions between the two German States, including the national question, referred to in the introduction of the "Treaty on the basis of the relations between the Federal Republic of Germany and the German Democratic Republic" on 21 December 1972.

The Holy See looks, as always, with benevolence and understanding to the German people and hopes that, also in conformity with the letter and the spirit of the Final Document of the Helsinki Conference on Security and Cooperation in Europe, it will be possible to arrive at a peaceful and satisfactory solution of the problems still unresolved between the two German States, to the advantage of the inhabitants of the two parties also at the ecclesial level.

SILENT CHURCHES

Albania

The anti-religious campaign in Albania bears no special stamp to differentiate it from the anti-religious attitude in any other country where Communism has seized power.

There is, however, one novel item of information because of the large Moslem population in Albania. The Moslem religion has been persecuted as have all other religions, so that of the 530 mosques which used to function there, only a few dozen are still open. But, despite this, the remaining Moslem clergy have been exploited by the Communist government in various Communist-supported peace conferences or by sending them abroad for propaganda purposes to the Moslem countries of the Middle East and northern Africa.

In the first three years of Communist domination, the legitimate leaders of the churches were deposed, jailed or killed and Communist-dominated hierarchies were set up in their stead. Church property was confiscated and religious communities were persecuted to the point that none of the three Albanian churches, Moslem, Orthodox, and Catholic, can be said to exist today in its true form. Thus, although the institutions of religion may remain, they are manipulated for Communist political ends.

Despite the persecutions and martyrdom of the church leaders and the destruction of places of worship, the people often flout the regime's anti-religious progaganda at great peril to themselves. Some time ago the main organ of the Communist Trade Union reported that a teacher dared to keep the Koran in school and asked that he be punished for being influenced by the bourgeoisie ideology.

> This man has forgotten that he should be an example to his pupils. . . . In fact all the students, following this teacher's example, began to take crosses and pictures of Christ to school and went so far as to talk about religion among themselves.

> Despite the merciless persecutions there are still many faithful who remain true to their church. They fill the Franciscan Church on Sundays, and they stream into the village churches up in the mountains.

The Jews of Europe have suffered a cruel fate, first through the extermination policy of the Nazis and later through discrimination of varying degrees by the Communist rulers of Eastern Europe.

Yet the small rugged country Albania, China's inaccessible ally on the Adriatic Sea, seems to be the only country anywhere that even today withholds any kind of information about its Jewish citizens.

The news blackout goes back to 1946, when the People's Republic of Albania was proclaimed and the Balkan nation began isolating itself from the rest of Europe.

Squeezed between Yugoslavia and Greece, Albania claims it is the first truly atheist country in the world. And its veteran leader, Enver Hoxha has proclaimed on more than one occasion that the only religion for its 2.5 million people is Albanism.

Following a ruthless anti-religious campaign, the more than 2,100 mosques and churches in Albania were closed in the 1960's and converted into youth centers, movie theaters, or storage houses.

Observation of religious rites and possession of prayer books is forbidden by law. Religious edifices have disappeared even from picture postcards.

Before the eradication of religion the majority of Albanians professed to the Muslim faith. But there were also about 300,000 Greek Orthodox and 200,000 Roman Catholics in the country.

According to private sources about 300 Jews live in Albania today, about half in the capital, Tirana, and 60 in the port of Valona, while the rest are scattered throughout the country.

In 1952, 50 Jewish families were given permission to emigrate to Israel. They never got there. A year later, several Albanian Jews tried to cross the border into Greece. They are said to have been shot.

Persecution of the Catholic Church was indicated in a special article about Albania published in the official Vatican newspaper *L'Osservatore Romano* on April 26, 1973:

> Places of worship either no longer exist or have been transformed into dance halls, gymnasia or offices of various kinds. Scutari cathedral has become the "Sports Palace;" a swimming pool with showers has been constructed in place of the presbytery and sacristy; the artistic bell-tower that soared above it has been razed to the ground. The ancient canonry chapel at Scutari, used as a baptistry, among other things, has become a warehouse for tires. The church of St. Nicholas in the Catholic district of Rusi has been transformed into flats for factory workers. The church of the Stigmatine Sisters has become a lecture hall, the one of the Institute of the Sisters of St. Elizabeth is used as the headquarters of the political police. The national sanctuary of Our Lady of Scutari, "Protectress of Albania," has been pulled down. On its ruins there now rises a column surmounted by the red star.

The head of the Orthodox Church of Albania, Archbishop Damian, died at the age of 80 years in a state prison. The Archbishop of "Tirana and all Albania" died in November, 1973 after about six years of imprisonment.

Officially, the Orthodox Church of Albania is composed of an archbishopric and three dioceses. The Albanian Church was recognized as autocephalous by the Ecumenical Patriarchate in 1937. The Ecumenical Patriarchate states that there were about 250,000 Orthodox Christians, 29 monasteries and two seminaries for priests in Albania. Since 1967 the Orthodox Church of Albania has been severely persecuted. At that time not only all churches were closed down, but the entire hierarchy and part of the Orthodox clergy were imprisoned. Any religious manifestations have since been punished by prison and other severe sanctions. These steps are taken not only against those practicing Christian religions but also against Moslems. According to statistical data, there are about 160,000 Orthodox Christians and 124,000 Catholics in Albania. According to these data the percentage of Moslems ranges between 50 and 60 per cent of the total population.

A new Bible translation for the first atheist state, Albania, is being prepared by the approximtely one million Albanians who live in Yugoslavia.

In Albania proper such a project is impossible, because all ecclesiastical establishments have been closed or even destroyed since the seizure by the Albanian Communist Party in 1967. All decrees on religion have been invalidated. Although the organization of the Moslems, Orthodox, and the Catholics has been destroyed, one must still entrust the "Albanian Democratic Front" with the extermination of the "religious leftovers." Angered Party functionaries turn to the fact that icons and crosses are still being kept in homes and that women still wear white bridal gowns, unequivocally of religious origin. Often one sees engraved crosses on palms and fingers. The Moslems are said to secretly continue the custom of circumcision.

Information concerning religious congregations and related matters is no longer published in Communist Albania. Even the demographic statistics reported in the yearly book of statistics of the People's Republic omit all information as to the population distribution from a religious viewpoint. Therefore there is no possibility of establishing from the available sources the number of congregations for each religion or the number of the followers of each church. The only information available with regard to the organization of churches and their hierarchy is that contained in the various statutes. Thus, the statute of the Catholic Church of Albania in article 9 states that the church consists of two archdioceses headed by two archbishops and four dioceses headed by four bishops.

The Orthodox Autocephalous Church of Albania is headed by an archbishop and is divided into four dioceses, each headed by a bishop (art. 8 of the statute of the Orthodox Church of Albania).

The Moslem religious community is divided into two major groups, the Sunni and the Bektashi, the first of which may consist of four first-class muftis and two muftis of the second class, in accordance with the religious districts over which they are supposed to preside.

Under these muftis there are 22 deputy muftis residing in the major towns of Albania. The Bektashi group consists of six religious districts, each headed by a grandfather, all under the guidance of and headed by a chief grandfather who is the universal head of this religious branch (art. 7 of the Statute of the Bektashi movement).

However, this organizational setup does not exist in practice, or if it does, its offices are not filled with the required personnel. No Catholic bishop or archbishop performs diocesan duties today. Since the purge of the high Catholic clergy these positions have remained unfilled and their functions are performed by vicar capitulars.

To a lesser degree the same seems to apply to the Orthodox and Moslem Churches, although a leadership does exist for both of these religious communities. The head of the present Orthodox Autocephalous Church of Albania is "Msgr." Paissi, a defrocked priest who is an active Communist. His son is one of the leading members of the Central Committee of the Communist Party of Albania. The situation is similar in the case of the present heads of the Moslem religious communities.

The leadership of both the Orthodox Church and the Moslems have been exploited by the Communist government in the various Communist-supported "peace" conferences, or by sending them abroad for propaganda purposes. This is especially true of the Moslem community's leadership who are sent very often to Moslem countries of the Middle East and north Africa. Albanian Moslem and Orthodox Church leaders have also been sent to countries behind the Iron Curtain and the Bamboo Curtain.

In pre-Communist Albania the religious population was divided as follows: 826,000 Moslems constituting circa 70 per cent of the population, 212,000 Orthodox or circa 18 per cent, and approximately 142,000 Catholics making up the remainder of the population of the country in 1941. Since then, however, the population growth has been steady and, according to the most recent Communist statistics, has amounted to 50 per cent since before the war. It is not known to what extent this population increase has been reflected in church membership.

At the time of the Communist takeover the Catholic religious community was bereft of all its bishops. The only bishop to survive the purge was Msgr. Bernardin Shllaku, 80 years of age, and in 1951, at the moment of the proclamation on the Catholic Church of Albania, he was appointed by the government as its head without his knowledge, although he was kept in confinement and under strict surveillance by the Communist police until his death. Of 62 secular deacons, 4 were shot, 14 were thrown into forced labor camps, and the remainder were drafted into the army. Of some 364 religious Catholic laymen of both sexes, 13 were shot, 18 were imprisoned for long terms, 149 are missing, and 184 were expelled.

The Catholic school system was wiped out en bloc. This included 5 high schools with 570 pupils and 10 elementary and vocational schools with 2,750 pupils. At that time there were also 13 orphanages with 465 inmates. All these schools and orphanages were suppressed and their furniture, equipment and property, and other supplies were confiscated. All Catholic associations with approximately 3,000 members were similarly suppressed.

These operations were carried out in a little less than 3 years and only later was a law dealing with these matters passed.

The National Committee for a Free Albania published a document in 1953 showing the all but total confiscation of Catholic institutions for Communist use or, in many instances, their actual physical destruction. These figures, broken down for the period 1945 and 1953, are as follows: churches and chapels were reduced from 253 in 1945 to 100 in 1953; seminaries from 2 to none; monasteries from 10 to 2; convents from 20 to none; orphanages from 15 to none. Of 16 church schools, 10 charitable institutions, 2 printing presses, and 7 religious periodicals none existed when a survey was made 7 years later.

The document shows that out of the 93 Catholic priests in Albania in 1945 only 10 were left in 1953; 24 of them were murdered, 35 imprisoned, 10 were missing or had died, 11 were drafted, and 3 reached the free world.

Although the Catholic religious community was undoubtedly the hardest hit for a variety of reasons, but above all because it was better organized and more active than the other churches and also because it was a minority and easier to deal with, the other religious communities did not fare much better. Both the Orthodox and Moslem leadership were replaced or eliminated.

Comprehensive data have not been published concerning the Moslem communities of Albania. However, it is reported that of the 530 mosques which used to function only a few dozen are still open. The remainder were closed or transformed for other uses.

The same fate befell the Orthodox Church: its leadership was deposed, and its bishops were arrested and replaced by persons loyal to the Communist cause. It was directed to enter into relations with Moscow's Patriarchate and other Orthodox churches behind the Iron Curtain. Most of the churches, after being deprived of their property, were closed or transformed into museums or restaurants as in the case of the old Church of St. Prokop on a hill overlooking the capital city.

Holy days sacred to the Christian and Moslem calendar are ignored by the regime and have become mere working days. According to Decree No. 1600 of January 8, 1953, published in the official gazette of the People's Republic of Albania No. 2, 1953, some of the most important religious holidays such as Christmas and the Kurban Bajram of the Moslems have ceased to be recognized as legal holidays. Until 1953, even Sunday was a working day for the Christians, but the above decree reestablished it as an official holiday and also recognized the Catholic and Orthodox Easter, and one day at the end of the holy month of Ramadan for the Moslems. However, the measures did not bring any relief to the majority of Albanians of the Moslem faith who are not allowed time off to worship in their mosques on Friday, their weekly sabbath.

Religious persecution in Albania began in the early years of the Communist takeover. But even then, except for one case, known as the "trial of Jesuit Seminarists," in 1946, tried by a revolutionary court which inflicted death penalties and life imprisonment on a number of Catholic clergy, there have been no other cases involving religious personnel alone. Throughout the terror then and later the clergy and religious personnel were tried together with other Albanians or subjected to repressive measures without due process of law.

During the third congress of the Albanian Communist Party in 1955, Secretary General Enver Hoxha stated that, although the Communists did not believe in religion, it was not true that they burned churches. Of course he failed to say that these churches were transformed and used for other purposes. He further stated that it was also not true that the clergy were mistreated, and that the law dealt with them only when they failed to respect the laws of the people's government in which case "they were handed over to our people's courts, tried and punished the same as anyone else." This contradicts what the secretary had said during the second congress of the party. Then some of the Communists themselves appeared shocked over the extreme policies of the regime against the Catholics and wondered if they had not gone too far with such persecution. On that occasion Comrade Hoxha berated one of the leading members of the Central Committe of the Party, and later eliminated him. He stated that:

> In contradiction to the political line of the party and of the state concerning religion generally and the Catholic clergy in particular, he has not properly understood and has not acted as he should against the Catholic clergy; Comrade Tuk Jakova has not hated them in sufficient measure.

The secretary general's statement also contradicts the fact that in 1945-48 the leading newspaper of the regime, *Bashkimi*, demanded in its daily caption that "all Fascists in clerical clothing be shot in the head without trial."

Persecution of the Church and of Christians in Communist-dominated lands has not ended and it is an error to believe so, according to an article in the Rome Jesuit magazine *Civilta Cattolica*.

In "Let Us Not Forget the Martyr Church," the magazine gave as an example of the continuing persecution some details of the execution of an Albanian Catholic priest for having baptized a baby in a prison camp.

In 1973 the Catholic press informed the West about the Catholic priest Kurti who was sentenced to death and executed—this news was confirmed by official authorities.

Shtjefan Kurti, a former parson of Tirana, had baptized a child, when imprisoned in the labor camp of Lushnje, south of Tirana. The child's mother had asked the priest to baptize her child. Although Kurti performed the ceremony secretly, he was observed and denounced. He was immediately sentenced to death and shot.

According to an eyewitness to the trial of Father Shtjefen Kurti, he was brought to the people's court at Milot, Albania, in December, 1971. The witness, a woman, identified only by her initials, G. T., recently escaped from Albania to Austria.

According to the woman, the people's court was held in a former church. She described the scene as follows:

> The church was filled with people and the judge ironically invited the accused to stand in front of the place where the altar had once stood and say Mass. The reply was a dignified silence.

> Then the judge asked him if he had baptized a baby. Father Kurti did not deny it. He replied: "I am a priest and it is my duty." The unanimous verdict was death.

In citing the trial of Father Kurti, the Jesuit magazine declared: "The agony of Christ is in the agony of the Church; this is the deep meaning of what is happening in Albania and in other countries where for whatever reason the Church is persecuted."

Similar situations are to be found in other Communist countries, the magazine declared:

> Undoubtedly, the situation is improved as compared to the first years of power when the communists came in, even if every once in a while violence of the past repeats itself . . . it would be an error to believe that the oppression of the

Church in these countries has ended. It continues, whether under more refined systems or not, but systems which are nonetheless efficient.

Six years after destroying most of Albania's 2,000 mosques and churches, Albanian leaders have made an unexpected admission about the survival of religious beliefs in the "atheist state" they had proclaimed:

"Openly in some places, clandestinely in others, in new forms and in old . . . religious vestiges are still alive," said the authoritative Albanian newspaper recently.

"Religious opinion remains," continued *Zeri I Popullit*, the Communist Party daily.

Saints' days are still being observed in Vlores and Gjirokaster. In Korce, people stay away from work at Easter. (All three towns are in the traditionally Orthodox south, where a small Greek minority still lives.)

Surreptitious pilgrimages are made to the sites of former churches, and people still visit holy shrines in the towns of the formerly Roman Catholic north.

Muslim festivals are observed, even by people living in Tirana, the capital, and Durres, major port and second largest town.

Ex-priests continue to visit houses for private worship. Icons are kept hidden at home, and women wear crosses in their necklets.

"We have by no means achieved complete emancipation from remnants of religious influences," wrote another newspaper, *Bashkimi*.

This paper rebuked local Party organizations for slipping into an easygoing attitude that religion persists now only among the very old and therefore will disappear of itself. The paper urged the Party to be more vigilant.

These disclosures in the press indicate a new target in a campaign the Communist leadership started in mid-summer against various political deviations, "liberalism," and other "foreign influences."

To the visitor to this isolated, secretive land, the move would seem to have succeeded. There is no evidence of religion whatever—except perhaps for the few old men who sit daily outside the few mosques saved as showpieces for Albania's trickle of tourists.

Clearly, however, the regime's new drive against religion is aimed at the young people.

"Religious rites," said *Zeri I Popullit*, "were still being passed on to the younger generation. Even in big towns some students still were influenced by their parents' inbred devotions."

SILENT CHURCHES

Yugoslavia

Tito may yet score another first in history—by being the first Communist ruler to officially visit the Holy See for an encounter with a Pontiff of the Catholic Church.

Such an encounter would not be something extraordinary. It should surprise only those who have not closely followed the tremendous improvement in Vatican-Yugoslav relations over the past decade. It was this change that led in 1966 to the signing of a protocol agreement, regulating Church-State relations in Yugoslavia, and providing for the exchange of diplomatic representatives between Belgrade and the Vatican. On that occasion, Tito sent Pope Paul an appropriate gift—a wood carving of Christ and the Samaritan Woman by the sculptor Ivan Mestrovic.

In fact, Church-State relations began improving for a variety of reasons as far back as the late 1950's. With the decline of Marxist ideological militancy, Yugoslav Party leaders were no longer eager to wage a destructive war of attrition against the Catholics who make up 37 per cent of the country's population—all the more so since persecution of the Church created unfavorable publicity for Yugoslavia in the United States and elsewhere in the West at a time when Belgrade wanted to improve relations, expand trade and obtain hard currency credits.

The protocol, in effect, confirmed the internal *modus vivendi* that had gradually evolved in Yugoslavia under the patient and moderate leadership of Cardinal Seper and in an atmosphere of steadily increasing religious toleration. But many Catholic priests were not satisfied by the protocol. They object particularly to the passage that confirms by implication the government's contention (used earlier to justify persecution of the Church) that many Catholic priests were involved in wartime terrorism on behalf of the local Fascist authorities in Croatia.

In a broader sense, the significance of the protocol lies in the fact that it creates a precedent for a possible general normalization of Church-State relations in other countries under Communism, on condition that the Church accept the "permanence" of the Communist regime and that the clergy act as "loyal" members of Communist societies. The protocol also contributes to the over-all endeavor to promote the Christian dialogue with Marxists and atheists, which has been so ably championed on the Communist side by the French ideologue Roger Garaudy.

The protocol undoubtedly brought numerous practical benefits to Catholics in Yugoslavia. Catholic bishops and priests are now free to travel abroad, maintain normal contacts with people abroad, receive foreign books and other publications. Local officials, who earlier often harassed the Church and impeded its religious activities, have, after the signing of the protocol, showed a much greater willingness to meet justified Church demands for the return of confiscated seminary buildings and for the granting of construction permits for new churches, particularly in the urban communities, which have expanded tremendously because of an influx of hundreds of thousands of people from the farms.

As Church-State relations improved on the official level, rank and file Communist Party members were no longer punished if they attended Mass or baptized their children, and soldiers dared to show up in church in uniform.

Similarly, the clergy have been allowed a greater participation in the life and activities of the community.

The normalization of relations has made it possible for the Church to develop a phenomenal publishing activity. In a joint effort of Catholics and Communists, a new Croation Bible was published, which instantly became a best-seller. The weekly newspaper of the Zagreb Archdiocese, *Glas Koncila (Voice of the Council)*, has attained a circulation of over 200,000, far exceeding most Yugoslav publications. In addition, the Church publishes many magazines; perhaps the most intellectually rewarding is *Crkva u Svijetu (Church in the World)*.

The popularity of the Church newspapers is largely due to their liberal and progressive militancy. They discuss openly the right of the Croats to separate cultural and linguistic identity, criticize the massive unemployment plaguing Yugoslav industry and seek to help and maintain contact with the 400,000 workers who have gone abroad, particularly to West Germany, to find better-paying jobs. The Church publications also discuss frankly the problem of religious relevance in a materialistic world and speak with alarm about the exceedingly low birth rate among Catholics, except in economically backward areas.

The normalization of relations has enabled the Church in Croatia to emerge from its post-World War II isolation and parochialism. Once again it has rejoined the mainstream of European Catholic development. This in turn has created some severe stresses and serious problems, whose existence had not even been suspected by the hierarchy in the days of the Church's struggle for physical survival.

The opening of the Yugoslav Church toward the world also came at the time of the reforms of Vatican II, which challenged many old practices and traditions. Without doubt the Council has had a profound and often revolutionary impact, particularly on young priests, who had joined the Church at a time of its greatest tribulations out of idealism and a desire to make all things new.

Though the protocol establishes the strict separation of Church and State, its effective working depends on cooperation between the two parties, which in turn means that Church authorities in practice must consider the views of secular officials in matters that might seem of a purely administrative ecclesiastical character.

The archdiocese, with over 2,000,000 Catholics, is by far the largest in Yugoslavia, but it remains without a resident archbishop. Bishop Franjo Kuharic of Zagreb has been named temporarily the administrator of the archdiocese.

Yugoslavia, because of its multi-religious character—with Croat and Slovene Catholics, Serbian, Maccedonian and Montenegrin Orthodox, and two million Muslims—is a good place to examine the possibility of Christian ecumenism between Catholic and Orthodox Christians. Because of national rivalries, ecumenism has not made any noticeable progress despite a formal improvement in relations between the Catholics and Orthodox hierarchies. Thus, curiously, insofar as ecumenism has made progress, it has been in strengthening cooperation between the Catholics and the Bosnian Muslims, whose intellectual leadership is Croat in national sentiment.

The strength of Catholicism among the Croats and Slovenes, as among the Poles, for instance, resides in considerable measure in the identification of religion with nationalism. But this tie-in does not, of course, provide an answer for other issues that are increasingly concerning thoughful ecclesiatics and laymen; for instance, the relevance of a Christian outlook and values in a society that is becoming increasingly oriented toward material ends. This spiritual crisis, long apparent in the non-Communist Western community, the Church is trying to deal with through its current *aggiornamento*. It has now spilled over into the Communist half of Europe.

Of course, the most astounding news which commanded the headlines in 1971 was the meeting between Yugoslav President Tito and the Pope. There are, of course, full diplomatic relations between Yugoslavia and the Vatican. The Yugoslav leader served the Soviet Union directly for a quarter century, initially as a soldier in the Red Army and subsequently as an agent of the Comintern. Despite the subsequent differences he had with Moscow, President Tito remains a product of Soviet political indoctrination.

The uniqueness of Tito's government among the Communist nations is a major contributing factor, no doubt. But the renewed relations are nonetheless quite significant, in light of the slaughter of Orthodox Serbians by the Catholic Ustachi government in Croatia during World War II, and the fact that Catholics are a religious minority.

Church-state relations in Yugoslavia continue to deteriorate; experts in the East European affairs report increasing anti-religious propaganda in the government-controlled press, and legal measures against the Catholic press and clergy. Both the Roman Catholic and the Serbian Orthodox Churches have been accused of engaging in "nationalistic propaganda" and of trying to create centers of "political clericalism."

It is also asserted by observers in the West that the Yugoslav government may be attempting to limit the Churches' social and educational activities and restrict them to the sole performance of religious duties.

Religious activities within the Serbian Orthodox Church have also come under sharp attack. In 1974 the regular sessions of the Holy Synod of this

Church expressed its concern over difficulties hindering religious education because it was not possible to obtain authorization and sites for the construction of new churches, and because of the "hostile and negative" reporting on church activities in some Yugoslav press organs.

Two priests, editors of a religious magazine in Split, of the Republic of Bosnia-Herzegovina, have been arrested on charges of fostering "nationalist" sentiments.

According to the report, they were arrested on orders of the Split public prosecutor's office for publishing in their journal a poem, "A Croatian Prayer." According to the prosecutor, the poem depicted a Croatia-hotbed of strong nationalist feelings—as "alone, distressed and nameless."

More than 700 members of Croatia's Communist Party have resigned, been expelled or relieved of their duties in 1971 in a continuing purge of nationalists.

Catholic papers have expressed displeasure over the school authorities' frequent and systematic propagandizing against religious instruction and over a number of what they call illegal administrative measures taken against young seminarians and parish priests. Perhaps the most serious has been the measures taken by the Slovenian authorities against the two largest local Catholic periodicals— *Druzina* and *Ognjidce*.

The editorial boards of both journals were charged with financial irregularities and with having contacts among anti-Communist exiles in Western Europe. These actions had been preceded by a month long political campaign involving leading Slovenian Communists who repeatedly attacked the Catholic Church in Slovenia for its alleged atempt to revive political clericalism.

In trying to determine the reason behind this campaign, Western analysts note that between 1966 and 1972, church-state relations in Yugoslavia were developing satisfactorily. After the 1966 agreement between Yugoslavia and the Holy See, high-ranking Catholic prelates frequently expressed their loyalty to the Yugoslav state and its socialist system. Conversely, Communist officials then expressed similar satisfaction with the development of relations with the Catholic Church.

But these analysts also note that the activity of the Catholic Church increased considerably as a result of the 1966 accord although, as stipulated in the accord, it was still forbidden to interfere in political life.

The Serbian Church, although numerically the strongest in Yugoslavia, clearly fell behind the Catholics in respect to activity, religious education, and general influence in the 1966-72 period.

The consolidation and increased activities of both Churches started to be regarded with suspicion by the Yugoslav Communist Party and government some time in 1972.

The timing coincided with nervousness over an internal Communist Party struggle at the time and increased nationalistic agitation within the six-republic Federation. Political purges culminated this campaign in the Croatian and Serbian parties. The new policy aims at tightening controls over the activities of various social groups—a policy which has not bypassed the church communities in Yugoslavia.

As a result, attacks on the churches for an alleged nationalistic attitude in domestic affairs have become more frequent. Western analysts feel that the Yugoslav establishment may fear that the Catholic Church, being predominantly Croat, and the Orthodox Church, being overwhelmingly Serb, must eventually support local nationalistic trends.

The authorities may also suspect that the Churches, while defending the religious rights of individuals, would become in effect the defenders of other constitutional and individual rights. These suspicions have been mirrored in the Yugoslav press, which frequently accuses both Churches of engaging in "nationalistic propaganda" and of interfering in non-religious affairs.

This coordinated campaign against the two Churches in Yugoslavia has resulted in increased cooperation between them. Instead of stressing differences, both Churches have of late been stressing their common ideological stand, and have engaged in coordinated public activities.

Both churches have increased their efforts to achieve better mutual understanding and cooperation in pastoral activity. One of the most recent evidences of this was the ecumenical symposium on theological problems in Maribor, Slovenia, October, 1974.

Knowledgeable observers of the Yugoslav scene say that in such a situation it has become more difficult for the Communist authorities to maintain that the Churches are advocating nationalistic agitation.

Nevertheless, in a November, 1974, interview in the student monthly, *Ideie*, the influential Croatian leader Jure Bilic said that the Communist Party would not tolerate "religious feeling to be exploited in order to combat the socialist self-management system." He added that from the historical perspective, "the church has always served every class system, but it is still refusing to serve the working class."

To analysis in the West, this message seemed to indicate that the Yugoslav authorities may no longer be satisfied with the loyal but neutral position adopted by the Churches with regard to the socialist system. What they apparently would like is "active" support of the system.

This is a demand which goes beyond the 1966 Yugoslav-Vatican accord, and the situation in church-state relations remains therefore at an impasse.

> The church's power to settle religious questions must be taken away; from now on these must be discussed only within Communist commissions. . . . The Church's influence among Yugoslavs working abroad must be impeded. . . . The real leaders of the country are the neo-Stalinists. Their intransigent line of conduct leads Yugoslavia into greater dependence on Russia because economic development is stagnating. The Soviets have included Yugoslavia as an integral part of their Mediterranean strategy, and it matters to them that it also be an ideological certainty.

Increasing anti-religious propaganda and some recent incidents in Yugoslavia have provoked a sharp reaction on the part of Catholic press and Church spokesmen.

The Church is stressing the individual and constitutional rights of believers to adopt freely any religion or philosophy whatsoever, and to educate their children in it. The latest developments obviously indicate a further deterioration of state-Church relations in Yugoslavia.

Persistent and increasing criticism of religious and church activity in the press, trials of priests and repeated bans of religious publications in Yugoslavia are testifying to a deterioration of relations between the Communist Party and state authorities and the religious communities.

The Catholic fortnightly *Glas Koncila* recently reported some striking details about the practice. In describing the life and work of a Catholic priest in a parish in Croatia, the paper noted that some people in his parish are afraid to send their children to religious instruction, since they believe "this could harm the children's further instruction, reducing their chances of getting state scholarships."

The priest, who because of complicated circumstances in the Croatia area during World War II, fought actively on the side of the partisans, even mentioned evidence proving that the state school authorities and teachers are exerting pressure on pupils and their parents. In "some school classes the pupils were called up by name, and those who were receiving Communion (or who had been confirmed) were registered."

"This is well known. However, it cannot be proven in a legal proceeding, since the children are afraid," said the priest. Recently, even propaganda against attending church services had become evident. For instance, at the entrance to one parish church, there was a sign saying, "Entrance forbidden for men in particular." At this the priest laughed bitterly, concluding that he had seen similar signs "only in Dachau" where he was deported "during the war."

Glas Koncila did not, however, limit itself to reporting. In the same issue, an editorial comment sharply condemned such anti-religious practice on the part of the state and Communist Party authorities. It said that anti-religious and anti-Church propaganda is no longer waged covertly under the pretext of the Church's alleged "politicization and nationalism," but directly and openly against the believer's faith.

This was the gist of a series of installments on religion written recently by a respected "federal official" and specialist on religion. While rejecting such interference in the citizen's private lives, *Glas Koncila* emphasized that Catholics are believers and will continue to believe. And they say openly that "we are not Marxists, and we don't ever want to become Marxists."

> If the schools continue to divert believers' children from religion, we will then consciously and systematically oppose by all legal means such an interference by the schools or anyone else. We say this openly. If Marxism did not include atheism, then it would be the free choice of every believer to adopt this philosophy. However, even in such a case, we are convinced that the state authority cannot impose any philosophical system on its citizens.

Glas Koncila said other obviously anti-religious incidents had occurred recently, and stressed particularly the anti-religious program carried by Sarajevo TV during the Christmas holidays. In a short program telecast on Christmas Eve, the birth of Jesus was ridiculed, something which aroused indignation among Catholics, Orthodox and Moslem viewers.

On January 1, 1973, Archbishop Smiljan Cekada of Sarajevo and Bosnia protested publicly, saying that this TV program was "an offense to millions of Orthodox brethren . . . and an offense to millions of Moslems who consider Jesus Christ as the greatest prophet after Mohammed."

Archbishop Cekada also protested in a letter sent to the Commission for Religious Affairs of the Republic of Bosnia and Herzegovina:

> Millions of believers would not allow Jesus to be offended publicly. In these and similar questions we cannot be "neutral," as Pope Paul VI said recently. Therefore we demand that we be respected as men and as citizens as well, that our faith be respected and that we be allowed to educate our children in our faith. This should be understood by all, particularly by those who appreciate our endeavors, i.e., the endeavors of the Church for peace, justice and international cooperation.

To local observers, this reaction by the Catholic Church and Catholic believers in defense of their religious, individual and constitutional rights indicates the strong position of the Catholic Church in its confrontation with the state and Communist Party over such activity.

As a matter of fact, the Catholic Church, and the Serbian Orthodox Church as well, have in recent years considerably improved their positions in society. Many political and social factors have contributed to this.

Conscious of their improved position, both Churches, and the Catholic Church in particular, are using it when necessary in defense of religious, individual and constitutional rights. This is why the Catholic Church took a firm and uncompromising position on this latest case. Thus, the present anti-church and anti-religious offensive on the part of the Yugoslav Communists may take an extremely risky and uncertain course, informed observers believe.

After the World War II the Greek Catholic Church in Eastern Europe was almost completely suppressed. In the Soviet Ukraine, and also in the Carpatho-Ukraine, which belonged to Czechoslovakia before the World War II, in East Slovakia and in Romania, Uniates were forced to join the Orthodox Church and by this action the Uniate Church was dissolved.

Only in Ungaria, Bulgaria and Yugoslavia the Uniates survived. In Ungaria they suffered and still suffer because of over-all bad situation of Churches; in Bulgaria they are weak because of a small membership. Only in Yugoslavia they can operate freely.

About 60,000 Uniate Catholics in Yugoslavia form the largest diocese, Krizhevci, in the territory of Yugoslavia thus being the largest diocese in Europe.

Since 1950 at the head of this diocese was Gabriel Bukatko, who in 1964 became Archbishop of Belgrade, and since then Apostolic Administrator of Krizhevci. The Auxiliary Bishop Joachim Segedi resides in Zagreb, from where a long time ago a large number of Uniates had left for Croatia's capitol, and now Krizhevci has a cathedral without a flock.

The Uniates in Yugoslavia belong to five different ethnic groups with their own languages. There are 30,000 Ruthenians, making up a half of the Eparchie; 13,000 Ukrainians, who migrated from Galicia before the turn of the century; in addition to those, there are 11,000 Croatian Serbs in Zhumberak, 5,000 Macedonians and just about 1,000 Romanians in Banat.

The figures for the Serbian Orthodox Church show 2,404 parishes organized in 20 dioceses. Although the Orthodox dioceses are generally larger than the Catholic dioceses, most are reasonably-sized units of just over 100 parishes. In 1971 there were 1,598 priests, of whom 200 were monks. This meant that no fewer than 769 parishes were without a priest, and there was in fact only one priest to every two church buildings.

There are a reported 120 students at the Orthodox theological faculty in Belgrade, and there are 647 students in five seminaries. The Orthodox religious houses have been numerically weak in Yugoslavia since the days of the Ottoman Empire, and there are still only 200 monks in the entire country. Since 1945, however, the women's religious houses have shown signs of revival, and there are now 650 nuns and 187 female novices.

In 1971 the Roman Catholic Church had a total of 2,634 parishes organized in eight archdioceses, 13 dioceses and three apostolic administrations. Most of these are, by Western standards, quite small. The diocese of Kotor, for example, has 27 parishes, three monasteries, 18 nunneries, 18 secular priests, five priest-monks and 120 nuns. The archdiocese of Belgrade has only 14 parishes, five monasteries, 14 nunneries, ten diocesan priests, 19 priest-monks and 395 nuns. In Kosovo province and in Macedonia, where there are large Albanian communities, there is an Albanian bishop and the Mass is celebrated in Albanian. The Little Sisters of Charles de Foucauld are working among the Albanian peasants. There are, in all, 3,582 Catholic clergy; this number includes both secular priests and members of religious houses, some of whom serve as parish priests. There are 6,539 nuns. No figures are given for the total number of Catholics in the country but according to *Annuario Pontificio 1976*, published in Rome, there are just over six million Catholics in Yugoslavia, representing 32 per cent of the total population.

The two Catholic theological faculties at Zagreb and Ljubljana had 403 students in 1971, while the eight major seminaries had 477 students and the 22 minor seminaries 1,535 students.

The Protestant churches claim the allegiance of only 0.8 per cent of the population. There are four Evangelical Churches, which are members of the Lutheran World Federation, each serving a separate national minority. The largest of these is the Slovak Lutheran Church which has one bishop, 27 parishes, 12 smaller units, 20 ministers and preachers and 30 church buildings. The Evangelical Church in Serbia has a mainly Hungarian membership, while the Evangelical Christian Church of the Augsburg Confession in Slovenia, which was established in 1945, serves Slovenes in 13 parishes and two smaller units. The Reformed Church (Calvinist) is largely Hungarian and it is organized in three seniorates, each of which has between 10 and 20 parishes, plus a large number of preaching posts. In 1971 there was a total of 26 ministers, and six students were training in Vienna, Budapest and Debrecen.

There are now 54 Baptist parishes, each of which has a "prayer home," and these are served by 12 full-time and nine auxiliary ministers. Fifteen other "prayer homes" are located in more isolated communities where the numbers are small.

Adventist groups have been active since the beginning of the present century, and they are now organized as the Adventist Church in Yugoslavia, with 120 full-time ministers serving about 300 local churches.

The Old Catholic Church, established in 1923, is very small with about 12 parishes and the same number of priests. The Church of the United Brethren has no full-time ministers, but supports 24 local churches, while the Methodist Church has 40 preaching stations and a secretariat in Novi Sad. There are also the Church of the Nazarenes and a small Pentecostal Church.

Moslems have 2,037 mosques and 1,573 imams. Imams are trained in two schools: the Gazi Husrevbeg madrasah (Koranic school) in Sarajevo has about 250 students, while the Alaudin madrasah in Pristina (where the teaching is in Albanian) has about 130 students.

At the outbreak of the Second World War there were about 76,000 Jews in Yugoslavia, but no fewer than 60,000 of these were murdered in concentration camps and of those who remained about 8,000 have moved to Israel. The rest are now organized in 36 Jewish communities which belong to a National Association. They have no full-time rabbis; the functions of the rabbis are carried out by laymen as far as possible.

In 1967 Macedonians took the ultimate step and declared their complete independence from the Serbian Orthodox Church. The Macedonian Orthodox Church has 953 churches served by 250 active and about 50 retired priests. There are 86 monasteries.

The Catholic Theological College in Zagreb has announced, that in the winter semester of 1974-75, 375 students were enrolled. In Zagreb, people of Yugoslavia study theology. On the faculty there are 11 teaching areas and 5 institutes. The teaching staff consists of 25 instructors.

10

Destruction of Other Religious Groups

Baptists

The development of flourishing Russian Protestant groups in the nineteenth century was considerably aided by the work of the Russian Bible Society, working in conjunction with the Orthodox Church to make Bibles widely available in Russian for the first time.

Although Protestantism was foreign in origin and only tolerated among foreign immigrants, there was a vast potential among the peasants and town workers. People often were neglected by the monopolistic, state controlled Orthodox Church. Village priests were largely unable or unwilling to cope with their desire for a deeper spiritual commitment coupled with an urge to handle the scriptures in their own way. There were differing strands: Lutherans and Mennonites, foreign in origin; the "native" Molokani; Stundists, a sturdy native peasant development in Southern Russia, Ukraine and Caucasus, inspired originally by German protestants, and gradually adopting adult Baptism, and the Evangelicals of the north, who originated in the fashionable society of St. Petersburg. There, it spread through the "good works" started by the aristocracy, who went off to summer houses, so that the continuity of the new congregations had to depend on able people like Prochanov, and of the "lower" classes themselves.

The "Living Church" contained genuine Christians who longed for reformation of the Orthodox Church and closer contact with Protestants. The very impressive list of specific activities forbidden by the notorious 1929 legislation on state and religion provide a guide to and attack on Protestant outreach activities, which had flourished during their few years of freedom, and had little relevance to the Orthodox Church, decimated by fierce persecution.

In 1944 the basic continuity of state religious policy was shown in the government controlled amalgamation of most Protestant churches in the All Union Council of Evangelical Christians and Baptists. Centralisation and control and exclusion and persecution of "outside" sects was a fundamental in Communist policy as it has been under the Czars. It is ironic that, of all groups, Protestants, with their tremendous emphasis on individualism, should now be expected to maintain the Party line. Many groups had joined because of self preservation rather than out of loyalty or commitment to a central federal body. The release of those who had not compromised from prison in the 1950's added a new element to the religious ferment which was to result in schism in the 1960's.

The Russians have no experience of a pluralist society and the free confrontation of different values. The struggle of the Reform Baptists is now not primarily against the official church but against stifling claims of the totalitarian regime itself.

Some religious and political "dissidents" have recently expressed hope that the election of Jimmy Carter, a devout Baptist, as the American President will result in a relaxation of religious repression and persecution in the Soviet Union.

This feeling appears to be strongest among Russia's one million Baptists, particularly those belonging to an evangelical sect that is outlawed by the Communist authorities, and among the 200,000 Russians who profess the Pentecostal faith.

The Pentecostals are Protestant fundamentalists who share some doctrinal similarities with Baptists. Like the Evangelical Christians, their belief in gaining converts through proselytizing has brought them into head-on conflict with the Communist Party, which is still committed to spreading atheism throughout the Soviet Union.

The Evangelical Baptists have recently challenged the Kremlin by establishing a clandestine press that publishes a professionally bound magazine called the *Herald of Truth*. It describes the activities of the sect and details the persecutions that members of the group have undergone.

The publication was previously put out in mimeographed booklet form, but it began to appear as a magazine since October, 1976.

> They have thrown down the gauntlet by establishing the press. The authorities can't let it go on, but for the sake of their image abroad, they may be reluctant to crack down, especially with a Baptist for a U. S. President.

The Baptists are seeking to change Soviet laws that prohibit proselytizing, even the teaching of children in Sunday schools, as well as regulations that require congregations to register with the state. They charge that the latter violates the principle of separation of church and state laid down in the Soviet constitution.

The dissidents are also protesting the arrests and imprisonment of Baptists, the most recent of which took place in August, 1976.

Six men and women, some in their late 60's and early 70's, were sentenced to terms ranging from 2½ to 5 years, with additional sentences of 5 years in Siberian exile.

One of the more well-known cases of religious persecution was that of Georgi Vins, secretary of a Baptist organization that broke away from the official Baptist church in 1961.

In February, 1975, Vins was given 5 years in prison and 5 in exile for "damaging the interests of Soviet citizens under the pretext of religious activity."

Vins has been subjected to harsh treatment, which he has protested by staging hunger strikes.

In contrast to the Baptists, the Pentecostals are not seeking reformation of the nation's internal policies regarding religion. Their position is that reform is impossible in this country, and that emigration is the only answer for those who want religious liberty.

Although hundreds have applied for exit visas only three have been granted in recent times. In December, 1976, an entire Pentecostal community of 500 people presented the government with applications to emigrate.

> To emigrate, we have to pay between 800 and 1,000 rubles for a visa and for papers renouncing our citizenship. But we have large families and little money. Because of our beliefs, we can't get decent educations or good jobs.

The Kremlin has stepped up repression of the Evangelical Baptists, the minority wing of the long-established Russian Baptist Church. The Evangelical Baptists, representing a population group of about 2½ million, often refuse to comply with registration and regimentation laws imposed by the government.

An appeal for religious tolerance signed by more than 500 Evangelical Baptists, addressed to General Secretary Leonid I. Brezhnev, has reached the West. It states the number of ministers arrested has increased steadily since 1970. In the first five months of 1973, the appeal declares, ministers were arrested a month or two after returning from 10 years exile. Tape recorders and Bibles have been confiscated, Scripture texts ripped from the wall.

Evangelical Baptists noted as being devoted and alert church members have underground duplicating machines and even printing facilities which most other religious groups lack. This is one reason for the regime's ire. Political dissenters often are motivated by religious inspiration. By hitting hard at Evangelical Baptists the Kremlin may hope to close a source of dissent.

The Soviet Constitution guarantees every citizen the right to practise his religion and states that anyone who prevents him from doing so is liable to punishment. *Samizdat* sources, however, not only provide evidence of religious persecution but also show that Soviet laws are so framed as to enable the authorities to imprison believers for nothing more than the normal practice of their faith.

Modification of the Constitution is one of the believers' chief demands because it prevents real freedom of worship. Since May, 1929, when the Constitution was amended to bring it into line with the still-valid law of April 8, 1929, "Concerning Religious Associations," "freedom of religious propaganda" has been excluded. Believers do not have the right to teach religion to children or to adults (other than in officially recognised seminars). Soviet believers have also appealed for their Constitutional rights; petitioned the officially approved religious authorities to allow a democratically elected hierarchy; appealed for the registration of illegal sects (such as the dissident Baptists), for the reinstatement of dismissed churchmen and against the closure of churches.

Some very limited successes from these protests have been reported. The officially recognised Baptist Church has gained a small measure of independence in the appointment of its churchmen—for example, since 1966 its Moscow headquarters has been staffed solely by Church members. And a few churches have been saved from closure or conversion into atheist museums.

The continuing existence of the Evangelical Christian Baptists despite increasing persecution may also be regarded as a success. Indeed, the activities of believers and the circulation of clandestine publications have not been reduced by retaliation; rather, the religious issue has been brought before a wider audience and more Soviet citizens, especially young intellectuals, are now taking an interest in religion.

The Baptists, who have been in Russia for a century, have seldom had it easy. From 1905-1917 and after the Revolution until Stalin began to cement his control, they were left alone.

During World War II as a matter of need Stalin relaxed his persecution of all faiths. Khrushchev also persecuted the religious, and as can be seen things, are not much better under Brezhnev. However, there is a steady flow of material on Christian religious activities at the grassroots level coming out from behind the Iron Curtain and helpful material going back in. The latter, of course, is to encourage those who are willing to risk imprisonment, deprivation, social ostracism and ridicule to spread the Christian Gospel where people hunger for a faith that transcends the sterile dictates of little men.

The official position of the World Council of Churches, the National Council of Churches and the Baptist Alliance is to maintain that there is no religious persecution of Christians in the Soviet Union. All of these bodies have accepted verbal assurance from Eastern churchmen, refusing themselves to investigate the situation. After all, Soviet churchmen joined the Baptist Alliance in 1954 and the World Council in 1961. To question their position might anger them and make them resign, and that would never do, for the underlying rationale is that a little religious freedom is better than none at all. But the Kremlin needs the respectability of these organizations far more than they need the Soviet churchmen.

In spite of the insistence of these churchly bodies—not in turning the other cheek but in turning a deaf ear and a blind eye to the reviled state of Christianity in the Soviet Union—the word is beginning to make itself felt. And in that regard, *Radio Liberty* is doing a tremendous service in reporting to the Russian people what is going on and what is being said in their own country.

As to the repeated liberal cant that there is a dialogue going on between the church and the Communist state—there is no dialogue except in the Western minds of the duped. In Poland, Romania and East Germany where the Church still remains strong, no mention is made of such theoretical nonsense; it simply does not exist. In Hungary, Czechoslovakia, Bulgaria and the Soviet Union, where the Church has been brought under firm state control, the church leadership maintains there is nothing antagonistic between Communism and Christianity.

On the 10th of July there was a convention of the Lutheran Church,

Missouri Synod. It was attended by Dr. Mihalko, chairman of the Commission on Worship and Spiritual Life of the Lutheran World Federation. He is a Czechoslovakian. This man declared previously in a dialogue, "Socialism represents high moral values and pursues honestly humanistic goals. Socialism has not liquidated the church and has not persecuted it."

And then again, "It has not misused the church for its purposes."

Mihalko asserted that socialism has not persecuted the church. Then Kosygin and Brezhnev are liars because they say in the Soviet press, "We persecute the church." They say, "We have created the atheistic school of the irreconcilable." They say, "We have taken away children from their mothers only because they are Christians." And Mihalko, Hromadka, and Nikodim come to tell that there is no persecution. Niemoeller has been there, the vice chairman of the World Council of Churches. He came to Norway, having a schedule to preach. On the first day, he said in an interview that Communism has made no more martyrs since 1920. Niemoeller was asked in the press: Have you ever heard about Cardinal Mindszenty?

> Was he arrested before or after 1920? Have you ever heard about Cardinal Beran? Have you not heard about Eastern German Protestant pastors, pastors of your fatherland, arrested after 1920? Why do you lie?

The "essential dilemma of Soviet atheism" is that persecution of religion tends to increase the number of believers, a report published in London said. "There is in the U.S.S.R. an Evangelical Christian Baptist Church under the supervision and authority of the Pan-Soviet Synod of Evangelical Christian Baptists (V.S.E.C.B.)," explains the Chairman of the Council on Religious Affairs of the Cabinet of the U.S.S.R. Several years ago a group of so-called "reformers" rebelled against the leadership of V.S.E.C.B. and tried to replace it.

> Having failed in their adventurous attempt to seize the leadership of the V.S.E.C.B., the ringleaders of this group proceeded to lead an organized struggle against Soviet religious legislation. They began to spread among Evangelical Christian Baptist societies libelous leaflets, letters and appeals of all sorts, attacking the Soviet state for its policies toward religion, distorting the tenets of the cult legislation, and exhorting believers to resist it. They also attempted to organize religious processions in the streets of a number of towns. They conducted prayer meetings in public places, institutions and parks, and gave children religious instruction in violation of existing ordinance.

> The Council of Religious Affairs of the Cabinet of the U.S.S.R. and other official government and local authorities tried in vain to point out to the leaders of the group the illegality of their demands and conduct. That was why some of these ringleaders had to be prosecuted.

> When referring to the reformers, one must differentiate between the ringleaders and the ordinary Baptists who in their vast majority are loyal Soviet citizens. Therefore it is imperative that Soviet cult legislation, which gives the believers full guarantees to fulfill their religious needs, and protects their civil rights, be patiently and carefully explained. Only when this has been done will believers understand the illegality and the real danger of an underground nucleus like the so-called "Synod of E.C.B. Churches," whose leaders try to deceive their members for their own selfish interests.

> Many Baptists have already grasped the situation by breaking off with these
> latter-day ringleaders.

Since 1960, seven Baptists have died in prison and about 500 have been arrested at various times. But they are the only religious group in the Soviet Union to have won the right to hold regular national congresses.

More recently one Protestant group, the Council of Churches of the Evangelical Christians and Baptists, was totally outlawed.

Paradoxically, Baptists are among the most favored and the most persecuted religious groups in the Soviet Union, though no clear division exists between those who are state-recognized and those who are not.

In October, 1944 two major evangelical groups, the Evangelical Christians and the Baptists, united to become the one legally-permitted Evangelical church body in the Soviet Union. Now other groups began to join this All-Union Council of Evangelical Christians and Baptists (AUCECB) as the one alternative for existence open to them. One Pentecostal group joined in 1945, another in 1960 and one group of the Mennonites known as the Brethren Mennonites joined in 1963. Since this union also includes Baptists in Estonia and Latvia who even today rely on interpreters when meeting at the All-Union level, the use of the name "Russian Baptists" is a rather arbitrary shorthand to refer to this mixed national and denominational union.

The Baptists are indeed now scattered throughout most of the Soviet Union, although their main centers are the Ukraine, Byelorussia, Latvia, Estonia, Moldavia, central Russia, the Caucasus, south-western Siberia, Soviet Central Asia and the Soviet Far East. They have a widespread reputation for hard work, clean living and practical concern for other people.

With the creation of the All-Union Council of Evangelical Christians and Baptists in 1944, the Baptists were able to lead an open, though restricted, existence. Conditions worsened again in 1959 when Khrushchev launched a campaign against all churches which was more severe in some ways than that of the 1930's. This involved a massive atheist campaign using literature, lecturers on atheism and the creation of mandatory courses in atheism. It also involved administrative measures. No statistics are completely reliable, but some sources suggest that there may have been 5,400 congregations registered before 1960, of which over half were abolished soon after.

One direct result of the Khrushchev persecution has been a schism which deeply affects the life of the Russian Baptist Church. In 1960 the State authorities imposed new *Statutes* and a *Letter of Instructions* on the All-Union Council—the faithful were instructed to keep their children away from services, to stop those under 18 being baptized and to suppress so-called "unhealthy missionary tendencies." Some believers would not accept this. They insisted on the illegality of this interference by the authorities and reacted by rejecting the authority of the All-Union Council. They formed an Action Group in 1961 and demanded a congress at which disagreements could be discussed. A congress was held in 1963 but it did not resolve all the difficulties, even though the *Letter of Instructions* was annulled and the *Statutes* were modified. By 1965, when no agreement had been reached, the Action Group formed their own governing body, the Council of Churches (CCECB) and became widely known as *initiativniki* or "reform Baptists."

Among Evangelical Christian Baptists, the process of bowing to the new demands of the state did not include the refinement of a national assembly of ECB church leaders. In 1960, the officials of the AUCECB in Moscow, which since August, 1945 also had included representatives of the Pentecostalist churches, merely adopted and distributed a new "constitution" *(polozhenie)* and 5-page "Letter of Instructions" to district superintendents (senior presbyters) of the ECB churches. Unlike the Russian Orthodox Church, the reaction of local Baptist churches was immediate and vigorous. A grassroots protest movement took shape involving Baptist pastors and laymen who objected to both the content of these documents and the procedure by which they had been adopted. As early as May, 1961 delegates from a number of local Baptist churches met to discuss these documents and in August, 1961 they began to write official protests in the name of a new body which they had founded, the "Initiative Group for the Convocation of an All-Union Congress of the Churches of Evangelical Christian Baptists." When their demands for an All-Union meeting showed no signs of being met, they took the initiative, beginning in April, 1962, of converting themselves into an "Organizational Committee" to arrange such an All-Union congress and they appealed directly to the Soviet government and personally to Khrushchev to recognize their right to do so. The procedural aspect had a great deal of merit, especially in the light of the universal Baptist principle of local church autonomy; this was implicitly acknowledged by the next major step, which was permission by the Soviet authorities to the AUCECB in Moscow to hold, for the first time since 1944, a congress of more than 200 ECB delegates in October, 1963. Like the Russian Orthodox "synod" of 1961 it was not properly convened and the voice of the protesting *initsiativniki* was not heard, because their delegates were not allowed to participate and some of their leaders were already under arrest. The protesting, or a better disignation, the "Reform" Baptists refused to recognize the revised by-laws *(ustav)* adopted by the AUCECB Congress of 1963; and the compromises which it made toward the *initsiativniki*, as well as the formal withdrawal of the offensive "Letter of Instructions" of 1960, did not satisfy their basic demands. In September, 1965 the Reform Baptists adopted their own constitution *(ustav)* and established a rival nationwide representative body known as the "Council of Churches of Evangelical Christian Baptists" (CCECB) which thereafter has claimed to be the true spokesman of Baptist churches in the USSR (and, indeed, it apparently had twice as many affiliate churches as the AUCECB, at least in the mid-1960's). This is the story in a nutshell of the "schism" which has existed among Baptist churches of the USSR for more than a decade.

There have been attempts at re-unification between the two groups. In 1969 the All-Union Council set up a Unity Commission and it took its task of finding a solution very seriously. Meetings between the All-Union Council and the reform Baptists took place on April 19 and May 17, 1969. As it later became clear, Sergei Golev, one of the leaders of the reform movement, was negotiating under severe duress. He had only recently been released from prison and on April 3 a new investigation had opened against him. He may well have been threatened by this means of force to find a solution to the problem. It seems that relations between the two sides were very friendly at the first session. Each side put forward its own case and it seems that some verbal concessions at least were made by the All-Union Council. Unfortunately, these relations soured in the interval between the two meetings. Mutual recriminations were made about breaking the agreement of silence on what had been said at the first meeting. One can do no more than speculate whether or not state pressure was brought to bear on the All-Union Council during the intervening month. At any rate, the second meeting dissolved without concrete agreement. The All-Union Council appeared to show less pessimism about the situation and produced a draft of a text of agreement which they said they would sign. The reformers then said they would need to consult their brethren about this. Two months later Golev was arrested and quickly sentenced to three years in a strict regime camp. Already an old and sick man, he was so weak that he had to be helped into the dock during his trial.

Despite this, attempts at a reconciliation did continue. Further consultations took place on October 29 and December 4, 1969. Representatives of the All-Union Council again expressed willingness to repent publicly for having adopted the controversial *Statutes* of 1960, but only if the reform Baptists would repent of sins on their side—which the latter refused to do. The All-Union Council put forward another draft agreement, which the reformers found quite unacceptable. Later, in February 1970, the reformers accused the registered Baptists of circulating this draft as an agreed "Joint Declaration" and deceiving many congregations. Such an action, the reformers said, showed that the official body was still capable of betraying its flock.

Preparatory to the Congress (December, 1974) the registered Baptists announced new efforts towards a reconciliation. The All-Union Council sent a letter to the reform Baptists in 1972 without success. Then in March, 1973 they sent another letter of invitation to come to a meeting, stating that they would set no pre-conditions for it. Having received no reply by July, the All-Union Council decided to make public the letters, declaring that by refusing to reply, the Council of Churches showed its unwillingness for reconciliation. Instead, the Council now invited all believers of Evangelical Baptist persuasion to join in the Congress, specifically naming adherents of the Council of Churches, Brethren Mennonites and two groups of the Pentecostals. The announcement then went out to the churches specifying the procedures for delegate selection. These procedures required these non-union participants to seek election through local and regional registered groups, thereby presumably blocking a contribution at the All-Union level.

But whatever the future of the Baptist schism in the Soviet Union, with the agonizing problems of conscience and judgement which it must inevitably face for all concerned, the activity of the reformers will surely go down in history as an original and remarkable form of challenge to the state's authority in the sphere of church self-government, just as in a wider sense the regular preaching of the gospel in registered churches is a challenge to the spiritual totalitarianism of the Communist system.

Some areas of the Soviet Union were less affected by the schism than others—places where Baptist pastors quietly buried the two disruptive documents from the start and avoided friction, while risking state reprisals.

From the first the reform movement has been totally outlawed by the authorities and at no time in the past thirteen years have there been less than 150 of its members in prison or labor camp. Its leaders have proved themselves to be men of great integrity and courage. They have driven for reform, come into conflict with the authorities and been imprisoned for their efforts.

The reform Baptists have sought to establish their right to teach religion privately to their children—and it was probably with their activities in mind that one clause of the March, 1966 revision of the Penal Code made the organization of any kind of Sunday School more explicitly illegal than ever before. Yet illegal Sunday schools do continue. A recent Soviet book entitled *Children and Religion* gives the following account:

> Particularly active in children's work are the so-called "initiativniki" Baptists, who split off from the great mass of Baptists in 1961. Contrary to Soviet law, they have begun to create, for example, illegal religious schools for children. The main aim of these schools is to educate these children in a spirit of religious fanaticism, tearing them away from "worldly" and "satanic" life. Such schools have been discovered in Rostov, Petrozavodsk, Zhitomir, Alma-Ata and other towns and villages in our country.
>
> In the village of Sokoluk, Kirgizia, an underground religious school was discovered, where eighty children of school age and under were being taught. Activities commenced with prayer. Then the teachers handed out to the children the text of a special oath: "I shall sing to the Lord all my life, I shall sing to my God as long as I live." Soon you could hear this from the children: "the aim of our life is faith in Christ and union with Him in the world beyond." All such religious schools which have been uncovered in our country in recent years have been closed and their organizors sentenced for breaking Soviet law on the separation of Church and state.

Undoubtedly as a result of continuous pressure from the reform Baptists, registered Baptists have now gained a number of significant privileges. In 1968 they were able to print 20,000 Bibles plus another 20,000 New Testaments with Psalms in late 1974. Hymnbooks were printed (also in completely inadequate quantities) and the circulation of their journal, *The Fraternal Messenger*, was increased to 6,000. Theological education for the ministry was re-introduced after a gap of forty years in the form of a correspondence course. More than 300 people applied for the course, but a limitation of 100 was set by the authorities. Since it was introduced in 1968, two classes, totalling 179 people, have graduated. The director of the course is the Rev. Artur Mitskevich, Assistant General Secretary and Treasurer of the Union. A number of young Baptist ministers have also been permitted to study abroad—currently there are six in London and Hamburg Baptist colleges.

The Baptist *samizdat* has a distinctive manner, presenting a wealth of circumstantial detail about the oppression of believers by the Soviet authorities and displaying a sound knowledge of constitutional law. The documents are marked by a complete integrity and objectivity, while often bearing moving witness to the joys and suffering of a church under per-

secution. Another remarkable feature of the documents is the attitude of
the writers towards the authorities—an attitude based on love and prayer-
ful concern.

The collection of documents from the 1970 conference of the CPR
could be seen as the forerunner of the first issue of the *Bulletin of the
Council of Prisoners' Relatives*. This appeared in April, 1971, setting the
pattern for subsequent ones, which have continued to appear regularly
since then.

In June, 1971 the reform Baptists announced that they had set up their
own publishing house, *The Christian*, and since that time it has had great
success in producing many pieces of religious literature—despite attempts
by the state authorities to track it down.

In the context of the general evolution of Soviet society, the Baptist
church has great significance. Over recent years a grass-roots human
rights movement has slowly evolved in the Soviet Union and it is a significant social phenomenon that a dedicated band of believers should
have been, by example, among the founders of this movement and should
have forged several new lines of action before others devised or perhaps
even dared think of them.

In the context of the world-wide Christian Church also, the Russian
Baptists have great significance. In many instances, their faith has been
enriched through persecution. They understand more fully the joy of the
resurrection since they have experienced more vividly the suffering of the
crucifixion. Christians in the West have much to learn from them, much
to share with them, many ways in which to help and re-assure them.

Baptists in the Soviet Union have frequently asked that their situation
be made known in the West in order that public attention be drawn to
their plight and that other Christians may share in their suffering and
join together with them in prayer.

On December 12-13, 1970 the second secret meeting of relatives of the
imprisoned Evangelical Christians-Baptists (ECB) was held in Kiev. The
meeting published 13 important documents—statements, appeals and reports which expose the terrible persecution of innocent people by the
Russian barbarians. Among these documents are the following appeals:
"To All Christians of the World," "To the Secretary General of the UN,"
"To the President of the World Council of Baptists" and to the leaders of
the Soviet Russian government. The meeting informs the whole world
about the inhuman and high-handed persecution of Christians in the
USSR.

In one of these important documents the second all-union meeting of
relatives of the imprisoned Baptists, condemning Russian tyranny, heroi-
cally demands complete religious freedom:

> We would like to remind you that to date, beginning with 1961, 524
> persons—among them 44 women, have served or are still serving prison
> terms in prisons and camps for their belief in God. Eight persons—Church
> attendants, have not returned home to their families for they were tortured
> to death for their profession of faith in God during investigations or in
> prisons. In the raids by militia and the prosecuting organs 2,840 religious
> books—Bibles, Gospels, hymn books, etc.—were confiscated from the faith-
> ful during searches. Albums, musical instruments and texts with religious
> contents were also taken.

Seven hundren ninety-one persons spent 15 days in prison each for participating at prayer meetings—altogether 11,865 days, 986 pogroms by militia and the prosecuting organs were held during prayer meetings at which the faithful were beaten; 1,380 persons were called out a total of 8,648 times for questioning. When one adds to this the questioning during the raids, then their number is infinite . . . children of religious parents, besides being questioned in school, were also questioned and intimidated by the militia and the prosecuting organs. The amount of "fines" for going to meetings totals 94,300 rubles. Dozens of faithful were expelled from universities or were not allowed to enroll in schools for belonging to those believing in God. Everything cited here is only 50% of all facts about which we received information.

Beginning in 1960 hundreds of articles in central, oblast and regional papers and magazines of the Soviet press showered with insults and mocked the Christian faith, while the believers were portrayed as fanatics, idlers, barbarians, the sowers of dope, hypocrites, obscurants, etc.

Everything mentioned above had been done and is being done with your approval, for the Council of Relatives of Prisoners has sent you 38 special reports, statements and express telegrams in the period between 1964 to 1970, but you have not replied to any of them. This confirms once more your calculated course in the treatment of believers.

Five thousand baptisms have been officially registered by the All-Union Council of Evangelical Christians and Baptists in Moscow.
Nationwide the Baptists number more than 500,000.

Getting baptized is not against the law. But those who are willing to come forward have made the decision that life in the hereafter is more important than their lives on earth today. They are not afraid. They are in league with God. They are loyal to their motherland and they work hard at their jobs. Even the Communists have to recognize this.

So zealous have been the Baptists in Soviet history that they have been among the more persecuted of Russian believers. Their numbers have swelled the labor camps and prisons, wherein they still insist on delivering the message and preaching the Word.

The message is: In spite of Communist opposition, a religious revival is taking place in the Soviet Union, the fatherland of world Communism.
That revival is underway, under conditions that would be regarded as intolerable in the Western world and by Western churches:

Religious activity confined to church buildings, prohibition of "religious propaganda," no access to the media, rigid suppression of religious publications, state recognition and licensing of every congregation, no public religious instruction in Sunday Schools, no Protestant seminaries and only three seminaries for the Russian Orthodox Church, heavy penalties for unauthorized activities, and a steady program of public ridicule of religion.

I simply say that after a lapse of 25 years, it's high time they implement the Universal Declaration of Human Rights, which the United Nations adopted. It says, among other things, that a person shall have the right to leave a country freely. I would hope that the Soviet Union would permit people who want to leave to leave. . . .

I'm disappointed in the President's position in all of this. I've been reading some statements that he made back in 1963. The United States, he said, should be willing to sell wheat to the satellite countries as a business deal

provided that the government involved gives some greater degree of freedom to emigrate. Well, I couldn't agree more.

Soviet Russia is discovering, to its annoyance, that belief in God and
human freedom cannot be liquidated out of the man. He can be hunted
and haunted, tantalized and tortured, scorned and scandalized, but he
will not give up his God or his ideals.

The bulletin of the All-Union Council of Evangelical Christians-Baptists recorded that in 1976 over fifty new churches were opened in various
parts of the USSR. There are twelve new Mennonite churches: six in
Podolsk, Pretoria, Kanenka, Petrovsk, and elsewhere in the Orenburg region, and six in Leninogorsk, Lugovaya, Chkalov, and other towns in
Kazakstan. New Pentecostal churches were opened in Minsk and Vitebsk
in Byelorussia. In the Bryansk region four new ECB and Pentecostal
churches were established, and others were opened in the Novosibirsk,
Perm, and Vologda regions and in the Altai Krai. More than twenty new
Pentecostal churches were opened in the Ukraine, and Zaporozhe, Cher-
novtsi, and other Ukrainian cities have new ECB churches. There is also a
new ECB church in Aleksandrovka-Nikolaevka in the Krasnoder Krai.
More than 100 persons were baptized in the Crimea, thirty-seven in Voronezh, sixty-four in Lutsk, and about 100 in Kiev. New pastors were ordained for work in more than 100 churches. From reliable sources it is
also understood that more than 1,000 ECB conversions took place in the
Ukraine in 1976.

However, on August 30, 1977, a force of 300 police and KGB security
men battled six hours to break up a protest by Soviet Baptists over closing
their prayer house in the town of Bryansk.

The trouble started when police told the Baptists that their new prayer
house, nearly completed at a cost of more than $66,000, was being taken
over by the local authorities.

The Christian Committee for the Defense of Believers' Rights said the
order coincided with police actions that day in the city of Rostov-on-Don
and the east Ukarinian town of Gorlovka, in which Baptist prayer meetings involving hundreds of believers were dispersed.

Baptists of the Soviet Union hope to open a seminary in Moscow within
a couple of years, according to officials of the Baptist World Alliance.

This is considered a highly significant development for a religious
group that has suffered from a dearth of opportunities for the formal
education of church leadership.

Though they have some 500,000 members in 5,000 congregations. The
Baptists have had no institutions for training clergy since another Moscow
seminary was closed in the 1930's.

The official denominational body in the Soviet Union, the All-Union
Council of Evangelical Christians-Baptists, offers correspondence courses,
and a few Soviet Baptists have studied at Baptist seminaries in Scan-
dinavia, West Germany, Britain, and Canada. But most congregations depend on untrained, lay leaders.

Soviet Jews, who also have no seminary, received permission a few years
ago to start sending rabbinical students for training in Budapest.

The Soviet Union has allowed the importation of 3,000 German-
language Bibles, which have been distributed among this country's ethnic

German Baptist communities.

Alexei Bychkov, secretary-general of the All-Union Council of Evangelical Christian Baptists, told *Reuter* the Bibles were sent in February, 1976 at his organization's request by the Brussels-based United Bible Society.

"We were very grateful because it was the first contact with the Bible Society in the years of Soviet power," Bychkov said.

The council which represents more than 500,000 registered Soviet Baptists, is planning to ask for more Bibles in other languages spoken in the Soviet Union.

The same Alexei Bychkov and his associate Michael Zhidkov, servants of the Baptist ministry are "famous agents of the Soviet Intelligence establishment, who have been identified as KGB agents" by various authorities behind the Iron Curtain. In fact, Bychkov is very well known as an atheist among the Christians of the Soviet Union.

The former pastor, Eugene Bachman, of the Evangelic-Lutheran community in Czelinograd talks about the religious life in the Lutheran communities of the German population in the Soviet Union.

According to Bachman, for 1.4 million Evangelists, Soviet citizens of German descent, today have only 8-10 Lutheran communities registered in the U.S.S.R. As a center for religious life of the German Lutherans is the Czelinograd community to which the members of the faith often undertake the 1,000 km. long route in order to take part in the divine serviced or other church activities.

In its effort to exercise control over religious life through the instrumentalities of the Moscow Patriarchate and the AUCECB, the Soviet government has been confronted with two diametrically opposite problems. The Russian Orthodox Church has always been a highly-centralized, hierarchical church which, before 1917, was the state church. The Over-Procurator of the Holy Synod was one of the Czar's closest advisors. During the first 25 years of the Soviet regime all efforts were directed at breaking the hierarchical discipline of the Orthodox Church, at isolating local churches from the authority of the Moscow Patriarch was re-established to a limited degree, but certainly not to a degree which permits the Patriarch or the Holy Synod to rule independently and supreme over the formal church hierarchy which still exists. Soviet policy toward the Russian Orthodox Church has been basically anti-hierarchical and remains so even to this day.

With regard to the Baptist and other Protestant denomination, the Soviet government was faced with the opposite problem, no existing hierarchy whatsoever; the basic unit of the Christian comity among Baptists is the local congregation itself, in which every single believer has an equal voice, not excluding the pastor and deacons whom they may choose to elect on the basis of their spiritual qualities. The only superior bodies which may exist according to this principle of local church autonomy are those created by delegates from the various congregations who meet for purposes of fulfilling a common cause or need, for example the creation of theological seminaries, the publication of religious literature, or other similar functions. Even when these inter-church bodies have been created, however, they are not invested with powers to dictate to the local churches. They may not, for example, appoint pastors and other church officials not accepted by the local congregation; and they naturally have no right to prescribe general church rules and regulations. These are powers which no Protestant church will delegate to the organs of any church federal union. Faced with this state of affairs, the Soviet government had a difficult problem: it had to create a rudimentary hierarchy where none existed in order to enforce its control of such a Protestant denomination from the top. The Reform Baptists of the USSR understand this all too well; and it is for this very reason that they refuse to join the AUCECB. In their own eyes, the Reform Baptists are fighting for the principles which have been basic to the Baptist movement throughout history; to sacrifice those principles of church government would be tantamount to abandoning the Baptist faith, which they identify with Biblical commandment. The requirements of the Soviet government since 1960 posited before the Baptists, as it did also before the Russian Orthodox churches, the ancient problem of just how they should "Render unto Caesar that which is Caesar's, and unto God that which belongs to God." The present split between adherents of all religious denominations in the USSR may be seen as essentially a division of opinion among believers over this question: Just how far can a true believer yield to the unreasonable claims of Caesar to things which biblically and traditionally belong only to God?

Moslems

The Moslems of the USSR have been adherents of Islam since the ninth century. For the most part they are of Turkic origin. Their homes were in Eastern Europe, Tatary (the Kazan Empire), Siberia, Turkestan, and the Caucasus. The conquest of these areas, which began with the overthrow of the Kazan Empire by Ivan the Terrible in the sixteenth century and ended at the beginning of the twentieth century with the annexation of Khiva and Bukhara, encountered fierce resistance, rooted in the characteristics which distinguished the Moslem areas from Russia proper. No small part was played in this resistance by Islam, which forms and develops the personality and prescribes opposition to regimes of another faith or of other national and cultural interests.

The February Revolution was greeted by the Moslems of Russia with great sympathy and high hopes. However, the Provisional Government, which lasted only a short time, did not fully meet their national demands, although it did permit some democratic freedoms, including freedom of religion and freedom for schools throughout the Empire to use the local national languages.

Islam and Communism came face to face for the first time after the October Revolution and after the Bolshevik seizure of power in the former Russian Empire. Lenin approved Marx's theory concerning religion by saying: "Religion is the opium of the people. Religion is a kind of spiritual brandy in which the slaves of capitalism drown their human nature."

Lenin denounced religions as a whole and called for a decisive campaign against all cults: "We should fight against religion. This is the ABC of all materialism and consequently of Marxism. . . . The struggle against religion must be connected with the class movement, which aims at removing the social roots of religion."

The campaign against Islam included the closing of mosques and their conversion into clubs, places of amusement, and storehouses. In Turkestan 14,000 mosques were closed, in Idel-Ural 7,000, in the Caucasus 4,000, and in the Crimea 1,000. In all, 26,000 mosques were closed. By 1938 there was not a single mosque in the Crimea.

Serious outrages against the religious customs of Islam were committed. In 1950 the newspaper *Kzyl Tataristan* declared proudly:

> A conference of women held on March 8th discussed the problem of pig-breeding. Previously Tatar peasant women, in accordance with the Koran, did not engage in pig-breeding. Now Tatar women no longer fear God and are being freed from their prejudices. The Tatar woman has conquered Allah the Prophet, the mullahs, and the kulaks. The pigs have triumphed over Islam.

The Moslem schools (medresses) ceased to exist. Moslem priests (mullahs) and scholars (alims) were killed or deported. In the large cities anti-religious museums were established.

During World War II there was some relaxation in the persecution of religion, including the campaign against Islam. On June 29, 1941, Metropolitan Sergei appealed to the people to pray for the Fatherland, and the League of Militant Atheists was dissolved. In September of the same year the magazine *Atheist* was closed down. Radio Moscow began to broadcast a "Christian Hour." The Patriarchate was revived by the elevation of Metropolitan Sergei to the post of Patriarch, and he was given an audience by Stalin. Almost simultaneously a Muftiate for the Moslems of the entire Soviet Union was established. However, on September 8, 1943, the Soviet government officially declared that it had changed its religious policy. A month later a declaration providing freedom of religion was published, although this did not prevent Kalinin, the President of the Supreme Soviet, from stating that Communist teaching considers religion to be a superstition and "fights for the liberation of man from religion."

Kalinin's words proved to be correct even before the end of the war. Approximately one million Caucasian and Crimean Moslems were done away with at the end of 1943 and the beginning of 1944. Some Moslem peoples, such as the Chechens, the Ingushes, the Karachai-Balkars and the Crimean Turks were completely deported from their own territories.

In 1946 anti-religious propaganda, actively promoted by officials, was renewed.

A network of Moslem Religious and Territorial Administrations was created, adapted for internal and external propaganda uses. Within the country these administrations strive to undermine the foundations of religion and to distort it in accordance with instructions from the Soviet government and the Communist Party. For example, on May 11, 1956, the Moslem Easter, the Iman of the Moscow mosque called on Moslems not to observe the festival, since its observance was not prescribed in the Koran. Anti-religious exhibits were displayed beside the mosques in Azerbaidzhan, the North Caucasus, Turkestan, and Tatar-Bashkiria and anti-religious museums, in numbers many times greater than before World War II, were opened. In the capitals of the Moslem republics anti-religious propaganda was organized to compete with the mosques: such propaganda was conducted by a Society for the Dissemination of Scientific and Technical Knowledge, which trained propagandists in special courses under the supervision of the Communist Party.

At the same time, for the outside world the Soviet government has made use of the Religious Administrations to convey the impression that Islam is thriving in the Soviet Union. In 1956 it was announced that the

Religious Administration for Moslems of Central Asia and the Religious Administration for the Moslems in the European Part of the USSR and Sibiria. For purposes of foreign policy Moslems are sent to Mecca, obviously by the government, since no Moslem can obtain a visa or undertake such a journey at his own expense.

In 1955, Radio Moscow broadcast a speech by Mufti Babakhan, the chairman of the Religious Administration for Moslems of Central Asia and Kazakhstan, who in the course of a prayer service appealed to a gathering of 3,000 Moslems to take an active part in the campaign launched in the Soviet Union for signatures to the appeal of the World Peace Council against the threat of atomic war. The radio reported that on the same day services were held in the mosques of Khiva and Bukhara at which similar speeches were delivered by prominent Moslems.

In a broadcast in Arabic in 1957, Mufti Babakhan stated that "there is full religious freedom for Moslems in the Central Asiatic republics in the USSR."

The fact that such claims are intended for foreign propaganda and have no relation to reality is obvious to anyone who has studied even casually the history of the treatment of Islam in the Soviet Union during the 60 years since the revolution. It is a history of an unrelenting effort to destroy a religious group as a group. Nor is the campaign of genocide against the Moslems of the Soviet Union likely to be soon concluded. In spite of all measures of force and propaganda, the campaign against Islam is never-ending, for as a Soviet author admitted in 1956,

> Islam, or Mohammedanism, is one of those religions, survivals of which still remain among a portion of the population in the republics of Central Asia and Kazakhstan, in the Caucasus, Tatary, Bashkiria, and several oblasts of the RSFSR.

As in the case of the Uniate Church and Judaism, Islam has close ties with nationalist aspirations. Clandestine Islamic documents have not reached the West, but their existence was revealed by the Soviet party organ *Pravda*, when it spoke of one called *Extracts from the Decision of the Congress*. This had been compiled by Murids in the Chechen-Ingush Republic at a secret congress held in the Nazranov district. The document instructed "every person of Ingush nationality to comply strictly with the 'ten commandments' or else break all contacts with other people.". Following the Soviet custom of attacking religion by smears or exaggeration, *Pravda* accused the Murids, who have fought for national and religious freedom since the mid-19th century, of favoring the kidnapping of young girls, "*kalym* (bride money) and blood feuds"—customs virtually obsolete among Soviet Muslims.

Despite 60 years of Soviet rule, traditional practices and attitudes persist among the mostly Moslem Central Asians.

Soviet rule was established in 1924, when Tadjikistan was part of ancient Turkestan, then one of the most inaccessible and backward parts on Earth.

Since that time—at first by force, later by persuasion, propaganda, and example—the Russians have attempted to eradicate tribal and religious customs incompatible with Socialism and the Soviet way of doing things.

Nevertheless, some traditions have hung on in Central Asia, especially in the craggy vastness of this republic, whose Pamir Mountains—the high white range known as the "Roof of the World"— border on Afghanistan and China's Sinkiang Province.

One of these is the *kalym*, the dowries a groom's parents must bestow on the bride's family. Soviet authorities have made repeated attempts to stop the practice. The *kalym* is so expensive that it often bankrupts a family.

Officially, Soviets will tell you that the custom has vanished, while Tadjiks know differently.

Sundays, Wednesdays, and Fridays are usually the days when the boy's parents ask the girl's for her hand. Her family then discusses the arrangement with her.

About a week later the family of the prospective groom is invited back. If the girl's parents cook pilaff for them, it means they have agreed to the marriage. If there is no pilaff, the wedding is off—it's a diplomatic way of saying no.

The wedding usually takes place the following Saturday, beginning with the state ceremony in an official "wedding palace." In spite of Soviet efforts to secularize marriage, almost all Tadjik families insist on a religious ceremony afterward. It is conducted by a *mullah*, a Moslem priest.

Wedding celebrations are huge. As many as 400 guests are invited to the feast, which goes on all day and half the night to the throb of Asian tribal drums and the blare of the long brass horns called *karnai*.

A bonfire burns at the gate of the husband's house, symbolizing the couple's bright hopes. He walks around it three times, carrying his bride. When he sets her down, her mother lays down a strip of white cloth that she walks on. Single men then race to pick up the cloth. The winner will be the next man to get married, according to the custom.

The next day, Sunday, is the showing of the new bride. The girl wears a thin veil—probably the only time a modern Tadjik woman will wear one—which has been sewn by a young mother. The woman's child lifts the veil to wish the bride fertility.

Islam

Few variations exist among the sources of Soviet hostility toward the 24 million Soviet citizens professing the Islamic faith, except perhaps a greater determination to destroy the religious life of Soviet Moslems. According to Geoffrey Wheeler, the Soviets regard Islam as a way of life far "more dangerous and objectionable than any branch of Christendom." Looked upon as backward doctrinally, institutionally, and from a total societal point of view, and regarded as a counter-revolutionary force militating against material progress, having been promoted and perpetuated first by feudal potentates and later by imperialists for selfish ends, Islam is considered to be totally incompatible with the Soviet way of life. Incompatibility has been a persistent theme in Soviet anti-Islamic criticism, and attempts by Soviet orientalists to establish a common, syncretic basis for Islam and Communism have been unequivocally condemned. Opposing Islam more an materialistic grounds than on the ideological, the Soviets generally regard it as an obstruction to establishing Soviet cultural and economic influence. The Soviets have always held that Communism, and even socialism, has had practically no roots in the Moslem community.

Another source of Soviet hostility derives from the universality of Islam which binds the Moslem communities both inside and beyond the U.S.S.R. into a spiritual unity based on common religious beliefs and larger social and cultural shared values. Since the early days of Bolshevism, the Soviets have been concerned about potential dangers inherent in pan-Islam and pan-Turanian movements.

Finally, the essential connection between Islam, as a religion and a way of life, with Soviet Moslems and its vast and powerful resources for shaping the personality and life of the Moslem peoples, renders the task of destroying this nexus highly important, indeed vital, in achieving the ultimate goals of fusion.

Propaganda has probably been one of the most powerful weapons used by the Soviets to destroy the Islamic connection to the Soviet Moslem peoples. The institution mainly concerned with the anti-religious cam-

paign is the Society for the Dissemination of Scientific and Political Knowledge. The scientific-atheistic propaganda section of the society seeks to
promote its objectives by organizing atheistic lectures and publishing
atheistic pamphlets. In 1954, as many as 120,179 lectures were given on
anti-religious subjects; in 1958, the number increased to 300,000. The
general focus of criticism and ridicule of the Moslems is on such religious
concerns as ritual, customs, festivals, and the like. Illustrative of anti-
Islamic propaganda is the following excerpt from *Sovetskaya Kirgiziya* of
Frunze:

> Islam, with its Koran and the Shari'ah founded upon it, popularizes a soci-
> ety of exploiters, intensifies the oppression of the workers, serves the prop-
> ertied class. . . . Islam has always played a reactionary role, tended to per-
> petuate the impotence of people before the forces of nature . . . and ap-
> peared as an implacable enemy of progress and science. By means of its
> absurd legends, it has demanded, and still demands, the ecstatic expectation
> of miracles, a belief and the supernatural aid of Allah. . . . It imposes upon
> its followers ignorance, intolerance of the heterodox, and the possibility of
> the Ghazavat, or holy war against the infidel.

Soviet propaganda attacks on Islam are persistent and all embracing.
The extent and intensity of the campaign can be seen by the study in
depth of Kazakhstan in the post-Stalin period from March, 1953 to July,
1957. During that period, 26 anti-religious publications, numbering
311,000 copies, were printed, 24 of which were in Kazakh (304,100 copies), 1
in Russian (3,000 copies), and 1 in Chechen (4,000 copies). What makes
these statistics particularly significant is the fact that of all the Moslem
peoples, the Kazakhs are said to be the least "worked over" by anti-religious
propaganda efforts. During the 2½ years from January, 1955 to August,
1957, for example, 49 anti-religious tracts were published in Soviet Central
Asia as a whole and 670,000 copies in the local language. Other publications
appeared in Russian and other languages.

According to a lengthy article that has recently come to light entitled
"Neutrality Is Harmful" and carried in the Tataristan republican daily
Sotsialistik Tatarstan, the older generation as well as the young people are
practicing the religion widely and openly.

Basing his article on a letter received from citizens of the village of
Krasny Vostok in the rayon of Biektav, the paper's special correspondent
F. Jalay reports:

> Despite remarkable social progress, Islam shows an amazing vitality. This is
> the result of the believers' efforts to adapt Islam to our modern times. The
> custom of circumcision is stubbornly continued by many parents, despite the
> fact that the circumcision is illegal. There is hardly a child in our own vil-
> lage, as well as in other villages, who is not circumcized.

> In the Tatar villages of the Biektav rayon fasting and Qurban Bayram (holi-
> day on sacrifice) are observed rather widely. Cases of slaughtering of sacrifi-
> cial animals are likewise numerous.

> Believers are especially active on religious holidays. They perform prayers at
> the cemeteries and in houses of private citizens. They try to attract to these
> prayers as many people as possible. Therefore, in some places, they carry
> out mass prayers in the village streets. For example, such public prayers
> were carried out in the villages of Aldermesh, Saya, and Obra. After the
> prayers people gather in private homes for festive meals. These gatherings

turn into a favorable forum for talks on religion. During a recent religious holiday, the Mullah of Aldermesh was at gatherings in dozens of homes. It is not difficult to imagine how many people listened to his religious lectures and how much he collected in alms.

The efforts of the believers to influence the women and girls in this rayon are quite obvious. Although it is prohibited by the Shariat (Moslem law), they invite women and girls to perform the prayers together with the men. The number of young people participating in prayers and religious ceremonies is considerable.

The local Soviet authorities remain neutral. They pretend to know nothing about this. They don't want any quarrels with the villagers.

Atheist education is practically nonexistent. In 1971, out of 3,465 lectures given in the rayon, only seventy-two were on atheist themes. In 1972, the situation remained about the same. In the first quarter of that year, only twenty-two lectures were given on atheist themes, out of a total of 1,022. Because of a lack of skilled propagandists, the atheist lectures given were on a very low level.

The term "Muslim" designates various national groups which belonged before 1917 to the Islamic faith. It does not necessarily imply that "Muslims" still practice their religion. Soviet authorities continue to use this expression, however, because it corresponds to a reality. While it is impossible to confuse today the terms "Russian" and "Orthodox," in the case of Islam a confusion between religion and nationality is still valid.

According to the Soviet statistics, Islam occupies second place among the religious communities of the USSR as regards the number of its adherents. In the absence of any official assessment, the total number of people who can historically be regarded as Muslims is between 25 and 30 million. Officially there are said to be 400 mosques and about 1,000 unregistered groups practising religious observances in their own homes.

The position of Islam in the USSR is unique in more respects than one: it is the sole religion practiced by over 30 or more or less compact but distinct nationalities, among whom it serves as a cultural bond of union; the traditional Islamic way of life, especially in the towns, remains as a whole far more distinct and particularist than that associated with any other religion or ideology; the Muslim peoples of the USSR have much closer cultural, social, and biological affinities with the non-Soviet Muslim peoples living adjacent to them than with any of the non-Muslim Soviet nationalities.

There is no biological symbiosis between Russians and Muslims. Mixed marriages are exceptional even if it is a Muslim who marries a Russian girl. Cases of such marriages permitted by the *shariyat* law are rare, and as a rule, if the mixed family lives in a Muslim territory, the Russian wife is assimilated by the new family milieu. The contrary—the marriage of a Muslim girl with a Russian, formally forbidden by Muslim religious law—is still practically unknown in Muslim territories.

There is no cultural assimilation of the Muslims either. The present-day cultural life of Soviet Muslims is characterized by passionate attempts to resuscitate, rediscover and revitalize the traditional national patrimony. The movement called *mirasism* (from the Arab *miras* "patrimony") tends to restore in the Muslim territories the ties with a thoroughly Islamic past, more or less severed in the late 1920's when the Latin script replaced the

Arabic. This tendency does nothing to facilitate the emergence of the so-called "Soviet culture," which according to Soviet propaganda is supposed to be the blending of the best cultural elements of all Soviet nations, but which in reality represents merely the traditional Russian culture rendered even less acceptable because of certain specific features with which the Soviet regime has endowed it.

The *mirasism* often assumes a purely "nationalistic" aspect, inasmuch as it selects for heroes the "Great Ancestors," objects of national pride, who fought the Russians: Shamil in the Caucasus, Kenesary Kasymov in Kazakhstan, Madali Ishaṇ in Uzbekistan, Edighe in Tatarstan and above all the Great Timur, who among other feats succeeded in reducing Russia to ruins.

Nationalism is no longer a Russian monopoly: all major, and probably also minor, Soviet nationalities are acquainted with the same phenomenon and with its accompanying symptom: xenophobia in a more or less virulent form.

Right from the beginning, the Soviet government considered the anti-religious campaign as exceptionally important. It never relented in this respect, except during the war years. The effort is just as intense today, as under Khrushchev, during the rule of Stalin, or under Lenin in the first years of the Revolution. It finds its expression in the publication of books, pamphlets and periodicals in all the languages used in the Union, in the organization of atheistic museums, fixed or travelling exhibitions, anti-religious schools and even of universities, special atheistic conferences, talks, movies, plays, television programs. . . .

According to an editorial in *Uzbekistan Kommunisti*, during the two years 1969 and 1970, 42,000 conferences have been organized in Uzbekistan alone (with a Muslim population of less than ten million) on the special subject of scientific atheism. There were in that Republic 20 anti-religious "universities," and 218 schools with 3,000 students specially trained to become future senior staff of professional propaganda and agitation workers.

In 1951, that is twenty years earlier, the number of conferences devoted to atheism in the same republic of Uzbekistan was 10,000. It would therefore seem that in spite of the political rapprochement between the USSR and the Arab world, the anti-Islamic effort, far from relaxing has rather increased.

An article published in the anti-religious magazine, *Nauka i religiya*, gives an idea of the intense effort displayed by the authorities in this connection. In an Uzbek kolkhoz of medium importance in the region of Samarkand the anti-religious *agitkollektiv* comprises "over a hundred agitators" working on full-time or part-time schedule.

Every year this kollektiv organizes "three or four seminars" with the participation of professors of Samarkand University, the object being to train anti-religious militants. The agitators organize every year "several thousands of conferences on different scientific subjects, one third of which are devoted to anti-religious topics." If "several thousands" means a minimum of three thousand, this represents a thousand anti-religious conferences a year—and this for a population which, excluding infants and invalids, cannot number much over a thousand. This absurdly high figure must certainly include "private talks" with the believers and non-believers in the *chay-khanehs,* the "cultural parks," and even at homes, during the evening meal, or on rest days. Needless to say, agitators specialized in such "home talks" must enjoy particular popularity, especially if they happen to be non-Uzbeks and non-Muslims!

The anti-religious arguments used against Islam religion are well known. They have not changed since the late 1920's, when the first anti-religious campaign was launched in Central Asia, and they repeat, often word for word, the rich anti-Islamic literature composed in the nineteenth century by the Organization of the Missionaries of Kazan.

Anti-religious arguments may be divided into two categories:

A. General arguments used indiscriminately against all religions, which are denounced as relics of the capitalist era and barriers to progress, as the "opium" that prevents people from participating actively in the construction of socialism, as phantasmagoric superstructures doomed to disappear automatically in the new socialist society. Nevertheless, it is deemed useful to speed the process by means of scientific propaganda agitation and, if need be, by coercion.

B. Specific—more bitter—arguments used against Islam, for instance:

1. Its "anti-scientific," "primitive" character.

2. Its "anti-social" features, in particular its anti-feminist stand.

3. Its "fanatical xenophobia" and, especially in the past, its hatred of Russia and the Russians.

4. The extreme conservatism of the Koranic law *(shariyat).*

5. Its foreign origin—for Islam was "enforced" by the Turkish, Arabic and Persian invaders upon the peoples of the Caucasus and Central Asia.

6. The "cosmopolitan," "anti-national" nature of Islam, a supra-national religion which tends to erase national differences and thus prevents the formation of "modern nations."

One may wonder at the enormous, heavy, costly and seemingly useless effort directed against a religion with a practically nil intellectual religious life, strictly limited to the performance of religious rites, whose leaders show a most rigorous and certainly sincere loyalty to the Soviet establishment. The official chiefs of the Muslim religion take utmost care to persuade the Soviet authorities that, far from opposing Communism, Islam aims at contributing to its development. They continue today to eleborate the old themes of "Mohammed—percursor of Karl Marx" and of the "fundamental similarity between Islam and Communism" so popular in the 1950's among young radical intellectuals of the Middle East, though universally abandoned today. It would seem that under the circumstances the Soviet government has doubtless much less to fear from the various innocuous ecclesiastical hierarchies than from the dissenters, liberals, anarchists or radicals, representatives of the Soviet intelligentsia, originating in the ranks of the Communist Party itself and in the Komsomol. An yet the struggle against the shadowy and abusive enemy goes on.

The official Muslim hierarchy takes great care to avoid anything that can be interpreted as ostentatious opposition to the policy of integration. But the penalty for the passive attitude to which it has thus been reduced by its struggle for survival is that it can in no way help the Soviet authorities in this respect in spite of all professions of faith to the contrary. More than any other ecclesiastical organization in the USSR, the official Islam is but an empty shell. The religious administrations of the four Muftiates (Ufa, Tashkent, Baku and Makhachkala) are all that is left to create a certain illusion and present a certain sham appearance for the benefit of foreign tourists, but there is nothing much behind the scene: two *medressehs* with maybe sixty students, probably less than five hundred official "working" mosques, perhaps a maximum of a thousand registered *mullahs*.

As to the internal situation of this official Islam, the little is known of it discloses a deep intellectual decadence. The Islam of the Tatars and the Azeris, in its bold and modern character so far in advance of the Islam of the Arabs, the Turks and the Iranians in the early twentieth century, finds itself today exactly where it was at the moment when the October Revolution stopped its progress.

In many ways, it appears even more conservative than it was at the beginning of the century. Thus in 1970, the Mufti of Ufa, whose jurisdiction extends over the most "progressive" regions of Soviet Islam (Tatarstan, Bashkiria and the Tatar colonies of the large Russian towns) deemed it necessary to proclaim in a special *fetwa* that it was permitted to use musical instruments and to attend cinemas and theaters.

Thus, one finds in the USSR and official high Muslim hierarchy, which like all other ecclesiastical hierarchies there, has a spiritual life strictly limited to public worship and a very conservative intellectual life, without a trace of reformist tendency and above all no expression whatsoever of the religious dissent or opposition to the Soviet establishment which can be found in other religions.

In order to solve the paradox a person must take into consideration the existence on one hand of the "parallel," unofficial, clandestine or semi-clandestine Islam and on the other, the social and national aspect of Islam religion.

The existence of "parallel religions" is a general phenomenon in the Soviet Union. The official Church with its skeleton structure, cannot give satisfaction to the still important proportion of the population practicing religion or simply reluctant to break away completely from the faith of their ancestors. Thus the unavoidable happened, and side by side with the official hierarchy appeared a "non-official" Church, impossible to keep under control and endowed with its own, more or less clandestine organs, no longer possessing the purity of the original faith but deeply embedded within the masses.

This is a universally known phenomenon in the Soviet Christian world. The Orthodox Church is losing a certain percentage of its believers who join various radical conservative sects opposed to both the establishment and the Church.

The "unofficial" Islam may be compared to these heterodox sects originating in Russian Orthodoxy. Like them, it reverts to old cults: pre-Islamic rites and practices of Zoroastrianism, Manicheism, Buddhism, Nestorianism or simply paganism, such as the worship of the *pir*, pilgrimages to *mazars*, to local holy places, springs, groves, etc., which orthodox Islam always viewed with distrust. At its extreme, this return to the past leads to confusion between Islam and primitive shamanism, where the Muslim cleric turns into a witch-doctor.

This "parallel Islam" is characterized by its secrecy and dynamism. It represents a little-known, closed world, escaping the observation not only of foreign visitors but also of Soviet specialists.

For years, the Soviet authorities paid little attention to the existence of this parallel Islam, obviously underestimating its "danger" and sincerely believing that it represented a simple *perezhitok*, a manifestation of popular superstition, condemned to die out on its own. Today, Soviet specialists begin to accept the idea that they are faced with a real danger from this semi-clandestine and most vigorous organization. It has its own "prayer houses," officially forbidden but tolerated in practice by local authorities. In Azerbaizjan alone, with its sixteen official mosques, there were, in 1967, three hundred places of pilgrimage. It has also its net of clandestine Koranic schools, which maintain the elementary knowledge of Arabic needed for worship purposes.

The "unregistered" mullahs that direct them are numerous enough to accomplish the essential rites: marriages, circumcision and funerals, and also to carry on very active preaching, counteracting victoriously the dull bureaucratic propaganda of the official *Agitprop*.

To understand the efficiency of the parallel Islam, one must remember that as a rule the "non-official" mullahs belong to various Soufi Brotherhoods (*tariqa*). The most dynamic and powerful among these, the *Nagshbandyyah*, founded in the fifteenth century, has a five-hundred-year-old tradition of organization and "political engineering." Since the eighteenth century it has been the hard core of the Muslim resistance to Russian conquest. Towards the Soviet regime it has an uncompromisingly hostile attitude. *Tariqa* are closely united, decentralized bodies, bound by iron discipline and a rigorous loyalty to the Brotherhood.

It can be added that the Soviet authorities' ignorance of the activity of this "unofficial Islam" may be explained not only by the clandestine character of its organization, but also and more simply by the absence of well-trained specialists in Islamology.

Most of the specialists of *Agitprop* are half-educated "failures," and as long as they confuse the active *tariqa* preachers with simple "idlers," "parasites," "whose main interest lies in profiteering by every possible means," the *tariqa* do not need too much effort in order to flourish.

It is basically thanks to this semi-clandestine Islam that a diluted but nevertheless powerful religious feeling survives in the major part of the Muslim population. As soon as the adults reach what the Soviet authorities call the "critical age" (between 45 and 55 for men, and 35 to 45 for women), the former atheists revert to faith in God, not so much by religious conviction but because the expression of non-belief would exclude the unbeliever from the national community.

It would be wrong to think that the attachment to religious beliefs of whatever creed means necessarily an open and active hostility to the regime. There are probably numerous cases of believers for whom "all authority comes from Above"—be it only as a form of punishment for sins, and who are ready to "render unto Caesar what is Caesar's." This is the usual lukewarm mass that rejects all fanaticism and asks only for a minimum of freedom in the performance of religious rites. Their motto is that one may be an excellent Soviet citizen and a practicing believer provided one succeeds in avoiding the clash between dialectical materialism and the religious *credos*, which can be achieved by limiting one's activities to the purely external rites of both disciplines.

But the radical Christian sects and the Muslim *tariqa* are made of a different stuff. The world forced upon them is to them the world of evil, which it is their duty to fight. They are aging a "holy war" in which there might be a truce but no lasting peace, the enemy being the Establishment.

But while in the Christian world the heterodox sects are violently hostile not only towards the regime but also, and even more so, towards the "compromised" official Church, there is no rift between the official and the "popular" Islam. Both belong to the same realm—that of the Muslim faith. The official Islam represents the peaceful face of the *Dar ul-Islam*; the *tariqa* are living in the *Dar ul-Harb*, the "World of War." It could even be said that the first is the protective mask of the second, and it is because the Establishment senses this fact that it deems it necessary to develop its efforts even against the harmless official institution, since it cannot locate the *tariqa* which spring from it.

Muslim *tariqa* seem to exist everywhere, in the rural areas of Central Asia and in the urban centers of the Middle Volga, but their basis is still in the North Caucasus, especially in the original bastion of Muridism, the Daghestan and the Chechen-Ingush country. According to recent information, in one district (raion) of the Chechen-Ingush Autonomous Republic there exist "a number (meaning at least three) of Islam sects."

The Soviet authorities consider the persistance of various traditional customs more dangerous than the activity of the *tariqa*. Actually, in a less outspoken and aggressive, but much more insidious and irreductible form they are but another facet of the "Holy War," its defensive stage so to say. Aggressive Holy War is waged by Islam in many places throughout the world and under different names and pretexts. It has taken on different aspects, starting from preachings in official and unofficial places and ending with the occupation of airports. But much more effective is its passive stage: the clinging to what constitutes the very core of Islam: the intermingling of religion with everyday family and individual life, the constant reference to what the West patronizingly calls "customs," and the Soviets, disdainfully, *perezhitki*. It must be remembered that though not even half of the Muslim population has access to rites and celebrations (women and children excluded), every Muslim is governed in all his activity by religion, which does not mean necessarily the same thing as faith. A Muslim can give up participation on public prayers, but nothing will persuade him to view with less than disgust the sullying of his daughter by a marriage with an infidel or to consider it his duty to denounce his father to the authorities for nonconformist behavior, to give but a few examples. Since, on the other hand, the Soviet credo is also by essence all-penetrating and interferes in every aspect of psychological life, the clash between the two sets of beliefs is unavoidable. And, as Russians had opportunity to learn from a long history, you can flog people into reluctant obedience but not into belief, which alone would ensure a possibility of the rapprochement (*sblizhenie*) and its final stage, the merging (*sliyanie*) of nations. One cannot count for the biological symbiosis (one of the theoretical dreams of the regime) on individuals who occasionally stray from their community, such as the rare Russian girl who agrees to enter an alien family governed by strange and complicated rules.

There are many forms of resistance to the emergence of the *homo sovieticus* in that particular domain: the persistence of the patriarchal structure of the family, undisputed authority of the elders (*aqsaqalizm*), the inferior status of women, the segregation of sexes, traditional matrimonial customs (*kalym, amengerstvo*), exogamic and endogamic taboos. Some other forms are "static," purely passive, often unconscious. The Soviet authorities—and not the fanatical Party doctrinaires alone—consider this passive resistance as obnoxious. Very often the Soviet press insists on the danger of the almost general practice of circumcision among the Muslim, including the members of the Communist Party. Thus in 1968 the very official and serious *Izvestia Akademii Nauk Turkmenskoi SSR* declared that,

> ... the result of the investigations show that almost all boys in rural areas and the majority of boys in the town are subjected to circumcision. The only exceptions are those whose father or mother are not Muslims. It was established that circumcision today is carried out by the older generation. They subject their grandchildren to circumcision and the parents of these children adopt a position of compromise.

The resistance may be also active, though not yet openly violent. This form of resistance is multiform and among the Muslim the "unofficial" Islam represents certainly only an infinitesimal aspect of the general anti-Russian feeling which characterizes more and more the new generation of Muslims. Broader and deeper is the purely secular "nationalist" aspect of the resistance, centering around the interpretation of history, the right to have access to national patrimony, the desire to oust the Russians out of the Muslim territories, the *mestnichenstvo*, etc.

However, even in this "secular" form of resistance, the importance of the religious factor is steadily growing, which is easy to understand.

In the 1940's and even in the 1950's, the nationalist movement was already strong among Muslim intelligentsia, but its arguments were based not on Muslim religion but rather on the theories of national Communist leaders of the 1920's: Sultan Galiev, Turar Ryskulov, Faizulla Khodzhaev. The older generation, born before 1917, still remembered the time of the Mangyt dynasty in Bukhara or the Khanate of Khiva, and this recollection was in no way attractive. Nobody then wanted to go back to the past. Today nobody remembers the evil side of the pre-Revolutionary period, and even the incessant criticism by Soviet propaganda does not succeed in reviving memories. On the contrary, today there is a new curiosity about Islam. The new generation, especially the young intellectuals, tend to over-idealize the past and they feel that there must be something in Islam, otherwise the government and the Party would not oppose it so vehemently.

> It is difficult to remove the poison of religion and old customs from the minds of the young. All of us Communists and intellectuals must strive to increase our atheistic propaganda, for the influence of the clergy and of Islam is very strong ... young people continue to flock in large numbers to the Mosque of Tilla Quash, celebrate the *quarbam*, and keep up antique religious practices. Till now these things have been tolerated ...

> However, actually it is doubtful whether stepping up persecution will work. In the past, armies of trained propagandists were sent into Muslim Republics to 'destroy God.' But God refused to be destroyed. Instead, as Tadjikistan's

Rasulov had to admit some time ago, the anti-God preachers were 'afraid to go among the people.'

For the benefit of the world outside, the Soviets maintain a pretence of complete freedom for every religion. In actual practice not only is the Orthodox Church and Islam being destroyed, but strenuous efforts are made to destroy religious beliefs in general.

Yet the drive has failed. In Moscow, the small number of churches that still exist are filled to bursting with worshipers—not just old people but young people who were born after the Revolution.

And in the Muslim regions of Central Asia, although mosques have been shut down and turned into museums, stables, and defiled in other ways, the faith of the ancestors is still being kept alive by the love and devotion of the common people.

"Is there any one more unfair than that who prevents the mention of His name in the mosques of God and seeks to undermine them?"

But the Communists were not satisfied with the level their oppression of the Islamic peoples reached and their attempts to undermine the Islamic religion, being the strong obstacle against the establishment of the Communist state which gives all the authority to few members of the Communist Party. As a first measure in this direction, they restricted the freedom of the Imams of the Mosques, in their speeches from the platforms of the mosques and their preaching of Islam, especially in those directives of Islam connected with the freedoms of man and human rights. As a second measure, the Communists applied a novel scheme to undermine all the existing mosques, wholesale.

The Communist authorities allocated a limited sum of money to pay for the needs of the various religious administrations, including the religious administration of Moslem affairs. But the allocation was so little as to be inadequate to face the simplest expenses of the repair and maintenance of those mosques, leave aside the costs of lighting, water supply and salaries of the Imams of the mosques and other personnel.

Mosques began to close their doors, one after another, until there remained only one mosque in the big cities including the city of Bukhara. Before the Communist rule, that city had fifty mosques. Gradually, those mosques disappeared, except one which now has no second.

Under the Communist rule, 29,000 mosques in the various parts of the Islamic lands in the Soviet Union were abolished. They were as follows:

—14,000 mosques in Central Asia and Turkistan
— 7,000 mosques in the Urals and Southern Siberia
— 4,000 mosques in northern Caucasus
— 3,000 mosques in Azerbaidjan
— 1,000 mosques in Crimea

Some of these mosques were turned to ruins and stables for horses. Those mosques that were not ruined were turned to clubs for the Communist youth. When some Moslem individuals tried to collect contributions to finance the repair of some mosques, they were prevented from using these contributions for the purpose they were collected for, since the repair of the mosques was considered "an unfruitful deed."

Thus, the Moslems lost their mosques. Furthermore, about 80,000 Moslems or more, who were working as Imams, reciters of the Koran and teachers, lost their means of living in the name of the religious "freedom" under Communism.

Despite the fact that the remaining mosques were few, the Communists imposed a price to keep those mosques in existence. The price was that the Imams of the mosques should follow the orders of the Communists and become trumpets of Communist propaganda. In fact, Communism, with all its defects, has mastered the art of propaganda as to turn the meaning of words upside-down and present its oppression of the Moslems and its attempts to put an end to the Moslem entity as religious "freedom" chanted by Communist emissaries in every meeting and every conference.

For this purpose, the Communists frequently delegate some Moslem religious leaders to conferences and meetings of religious nature held in other Islamic countries, such as the United Arab Republic, Saudi Arabia and Indonesia to speak, as strictly instructed, about religious freedom in the Soviet Union and praise the attitude of the Communists towards the Moslem and the good care given to the Moslems by the Communist regime.

The case is the same when foreign visitors from the countries of the free world come to the Soviet Union.

Many of the delegates from among the Imams and Moslem scholars and jurists are helpless people who ceased resistance after suffering long years of exile and persecution in Siberia and then brought back and given the highest positions in the religious administrations to become the humble servants of the Communists. This is clearly demonstrated in the speech which chief jurist Abshan Baba Khan, head of the religious administration for Central Asia and Kazakhstan, was forced to broadcast from Radio Moscow to Arab peoples on February 25, 1959, and in which he praised the Communist system, stressed the religious freedom in the Soviet Union and described the Communists as "the enemies of imperialism."

Then there was the case of Ahmedyan Mustafain, the Imam of the Mosque of Moscow. During the fasting month of Ramadan, in 1956, he addressed his Moslem brethren in the Soviet Union, under orders from the Communists. In that speech, he tried to convince the Moslems that they should not celebrate the Islamic Holiday of al-Fitre. Thus, that Imam found himself forced, under pressure from the Communist authorities, to openly call for an action that constituted a clear-cut violation of the dictates of a religion which, by the nature of his job, he should have protected.

Until the present time, some Moslems go secretly to special meetings where religion and the Koran are taught. There are very rare cases where some Moslems reject their religion. This shows that the spirit of Islam is deep-rooted in the hearts and souls of those peoples.

However, the Islamic peoples did not surrender to the measures aimed at weakening them and putting an end to their religious foundations. They revolted against those tyrannic measures, one time after another. But on every such occasion the Communists used to suppress the revolution with all kinds of violent means, the well-known measures used by the Communists to suppress revolutions. On many occasions, they left the job of suppression to the Red army which used its heavy artillery, armored cars, tanks and the air force to completely annihilate whole Islamic tribes. That was the fate of the remaining part of the Moslems of Crimea and the Kalmuk who were living in Astrakhan plains. Those who remained alive from these tribes were moved to the remotest ends of Siberia. Their properties were confiscated. Russians and Slavs were settled in their places.

Then the Communists took another step in the carrying out of their program to put an end to the entity of the Islamic peoples and weaken the Islamic religion. The step was taken in two stages. The first stage represented the complete obliteration of the Islamic organizations and institutions, such as the humanitarian associations and the religious endowments administrations. In the second stage, they outlawed the use of Islamic law in matters concerning the daily life and dealings of the Moslems, such as matters of inheritance, marriage, divorce and other matters considered as important distinguishing features of the Islamic society.

The way the Communists used to put an end to the influence of Islamic law had a story behind it. On December 28, 1922, the central executive committee of the Republic of Turkistan issued a decree placing the various Islamic institutions and institutes under the supervision of the commissariat of education and transferring the management of their properties from the hands of Moslems to the hands of the local governmental authorities. The decree also gave the local government the right to appoint and dismiss the directors of the Islamic endowments. In other words, the Islamic organizations were placed under the absolute mercy of the Soviet authorities.

Other Islamic republics of the Soviet Union met with the same fate that befell the Republic of Turkistan. By 1930—eight years after the issuance of that decree—the Communists had succeeded in dwarfing the Islamic endowments and in diverting them from their objective. They had put an end to Islamic institutions in all parts of Central Asia and the Caucasus lands.

Undoubtedly, the Islamic law is the basic foundation of the Islamic society because it governs many of the special affairs of the Moslems such as inheritance, marriage and divorce. If the Czarist Russia had not dared to abolish the Islamic law except those articles that were incompatible with the procedures of the Russian administration, Communist Russia went beyond combatting Islamic law and was not satisfied with less than abolishing the law, itself, which governed the affairs of the Moslems.

For a period of time, the Soviet peoples' courts and the Islamic courts remained, each doing their particular job. The first were concerned with criminal and some civic cases and the latter were concerned with Moslem affairs. But later on, the government began to issue one decree after another to tighten the grip of the Communist authorities.

The conditions in which the Moslems live under the Communist rule are very well described by the reverend Abdelwahed al-Bakistani in his article published in the Pakistani daily *The Observer*, following his visit to the Soviet Union:

> The Moslems living in the Soviet Union are not deprived of practicing their religion and teaching their children the principles of Islam and yet the Islamic culture itself is disappearing in a systematic way.

Even the Soviet magazine *Ethnographic* itself, with reference to the situation of Islam in the Soviet Union says, in clear-cut words that can never be misunderstood: "The leaders of the Islamic religion have lost their autonomy and become no more than a tool in the hands of the communist government."

The religious leaders in the Soviet Union do their job under the constant surveillance of the Communist authorities. They cannot appear in public meetings without the permission of the authorities. Even, the political police attend the prayers in the mosques to listen to all what may be said and see what can be seen and report them to the authorities.

In the Soviet Republic of Uzbekistan 218 schools exist for the training of atheist agitators. In Tashkent a school exists for the training of lectors for atheism. At the moment 29 universities of atheism are at work in this Soviet republic. In Tashkent the "House of Atheism" is also to be found. Between 1969 and 1970, 42,000 lectures were held against religion.

In Bokhara there is a school for priests which is attended by about 30-40 people, but in whose program of studies most attention is given to the doctrines of Marxism-Leninism.

This religious administration, just like the others, was previously unable to publish even a newspaper in defence of Islam. They must all be silent for the Soviet laws tolerated no organized religious activity. The upholding of the spirit of Islam has become an affair of the individual believers. The religious administrations of the Muslims must not attempt to coordinate the individual efforts of Islam either. They exist principally as instruments of Soviet foreign policy. Their role has particularly grown in the age of "fraternization of the Soviet Russians with the Arab countries."

The Soviet regime shows two faces towards Islam: inside its own sphere of power it is radically anti-Islamic, and towards Islam abroad, pro-Islamic. It understands wonderfully how to balance one attitude against the other. One example can make this even clearer. The religious administration of the Muslims in Tashkent has published a book on the "Islamic monuments in the Soviet Union" and distributed the copies to leading Islamic figures abroad. It was well presented with color photos. The famous monuments included the mosques and the famous mausoleum of the important Islamic mystic Khodzha Akhmed Yasavi and the mausoleum of Pakhlivan Mahmud from the city of Khiva, dating from the 17th century. The editor, however, does not mention that both monuments are already being used as "Houses of Atheism."

Finally, it can be mentioned that Soviet Russian atheism will need generations in the struggle against Islam before it reaches the last phase, for within the Muslim community in the Soviet Union, especially in Turkestan, two kinds of ideas have at present become widespread:

(1) "The social revolution took place after Islam came into existence. Therefore the social revolution of the Communists means nothing."

(2) "As long as a single copy of the Koran is to be found, Islam will continue to exist even under the regime of atheism."

Therefore, the Soviet anti-Islamic movement is concentrating its efforts against the teachings of Islam, in order to discredit it in the eyes of the believers.

Buddhism

Among the many different peoples of the USSR, two, the Buryats and the Kalmyks, are adherents to Buddhism. They belong to two different branches of the Mongol family. The Kalmyks are a subdivision of the Oriots, i.e., they are West Mongols, and both in language and customs are closely related to the inhabitants of the People's Republics of Mongolia and Inner Mongolia.

The original religion of the Buryats, the Kalmyks, and all the Mongol peoples was Shamanism. According to the historic beliefs of the Eastern, i.e., the Transbaikal Buryats, there were individual lamas serving in felt yurts by the end of the seventeenth century, i.e., by the date of subjugation of the Buryats by Russia, but Lamaism only began to spread widely in Transbaikalia after a group of about 15 lamas arrived from Tibet in 1712, joined the Buryat tribes, and began to preach Buddhism.

The first felt temple was built in 1741 in the town of Khilgantai on the Chikoi River, and in 1780 the first wooden temple was erected.

The number of Buddhist temples and monasteries in Transbaikalia increased rapidly. In 1786 the Tungni Datsan Monastery was transferred to a new site; in 1775, the Khudun Monastery, which had burned down, was rebuilt; in 1795, the Anin Monastery, in 1811 the Agin, and in 1821 the Tsugol Monasteries were built. By 1846, the number of monasteries had risen to 34, with 4,509 lamas. The census of 1858 showed 32,214 Khorin and Agin Buryat "souls," registered adult males.

Since more than half of the monasteries were located in the territory of the Khorin and Agin Departments, it may be assumed that half of the lamas in 1846, that is 2,254, had lived in these Departments and that there was thus an average of one clergyman for every 14-15 persons.

This large percentage of clergy undoubtedly constituted a heavy burden on the rest of the population, and the local Russian authorities were much concerned about their ever-increasing number. For this reason, a "Law on the Lama Clergy in Eastern Siberia," approved in 1853, fixed the upper limit for the number of monasteries at 34; positions were approved for one Pandit Khambo and 216 lamas, as well as 34 bandi, or servants. Arbitrary building of new monasteries over and above the approved number was forbidden, but there was no penalty for exceeding the legal number of clerical positions, and the only action taken was the imposition of a poll tax on unofficial and self-styled lamas, from which the approved lamas were exempt.

The purpose of the law of 1853 was only partly achieved: it is true that after 1853 only three new monasteries were added, so that by the time of the revolution in 1917 there were still only 37, but on the other hand the number of lamas continued to increase steadily. It is difficult to establish accurately the number of lamas in Buryatia in the years 1917-20. The Buryat scholar B. Baradiin estimates that of the largest monasteries, Khambiyu Kuri had more than 1,000 lamas, Atsagat Monastery about 300, Anin Monastery up to 1,000, Egetuev Monastery up to 700, Agin Monastery more than 1,000 and Tsugol Monastery more than 1,000, making a total in these monasteries of approximately 5,000. The number of lamas in some of these larger monasteries alone was thus almost 25 times the legal number. According to observations made in the country itself in 1928-32, the total number of lamas in the Buryat-Mongol ASSR was about 10,000, or one twenty-fifth of the entire Buryat population.

The Civil War was the first serious trial for the Buddhist Church. It struck the Kalmyk people in the lower Volga valley (the former Stavropol Province) and in the territory of the Army of the Don. The majority of the Kalmyks joined the Volunteer Army, rising to defend their country against Bolshevism. Some of the monasteries, and the Kalmyk clergy, who in any case were not numerous, suffered heavy casualties. Among the Kalmyk priests who perished was the spiritual head of the Don Kalmyks, M. Bormanzhinov, who died in 1919 at the age of 65 in a refugee camp in the Kuban. Nevertheless, in 1921 the majority of the monasteries still existed. However, the anti-religious campaign of the Bolsheviks was so intensive that by 1925 there were no longer either monasteries or clergy in the Don Valley.

However, the situation in the Mongolian People's Republic changed fundamentally after 1936. The policy of mercilessly uprooting the "remnants of feudalism" resulted in a number of show trials of representatives of the top and medium-ranking lamas. Such trials included those of the Yugodzer khutukhta, the Mandzushri khutukhta, etc. (a total of 38 prominent religious and lay personalities) in 1930; the trial of "feudal theocratic elements" (Tegus Buantu Khure) in 1930; the case of the dean of Gegen Monastery in 1935; the trial of more than 100 senior lamas of 17 monasteries in 1935-36; the case of "counter-revolutionary senior lamas headed by the dean of Ulan-Bator Monastery and heads of 48 other large monasteries" in 1937-38. The last named trial affected more than 2,000 senior lamas.

At the present time there is not a single large monastery in the Mongolian People's Republic. The repression of the Buddhist clergy in Mongolia logically stemmed from Soviet policy regarding this satellite, since the Bolsheviks could make no use of the lamas in achieving their objectives. The religious center of the Buddhists was in Tibet, an inaccessible mountainous country, isolated from the rest of the world and therefore almost completely without influence on neighboring countries. For this reason the Kremlin ceased completely to take the lamas into account. Even during the war, when the Communists had to compromise with the Orthodox Church and temporarily to repudiate their anti-religious policy, such a weakening was not necessary in Mongolia. The temporary retreat from the policy of persecution of the Church in the USSR was necessary both from the point of view of internal and foreign politics. It was essential to obtain the sympathy of the Orthodox population in the Balkan countries and to appease the Allies, who believed that there was freedom of conscience in the USSR. Concessions were also made to the Mohammedan clergy with the aim of obtaining the sympathy of the Moslems in the Near East. There could be no such policy in the Buryat-Mongol ASSR, where the attack on the lamas had begun during the period of the first Five-Year Plan.

In 1930-31, almost all the larger monasteries were still in existence, although a harsh taxation policy had been introduced against them. However, as a rule, the faithful paid the taxes for the monasteries in full, since collectivization was only in its initial stages and the Buryat herdsmen still had money to pay the taxes.

Most of the monasteries began to close down during the second Five-Year Plan, although some were liquidated in 1929-30. Thus the Alar Monastery, a small one which had never had more than 112 lamas, was closed in 1929. The large monastery at Gusino Ozera (in the village of Tmocha, 25 kilometers from the city of Novoselenginsk), which was famous for its learned teachers and its wonderful annual *tsam*, was closed in 1930. (The *tsam* includes performances of mystery plays, pantomines, and masked dances devoted to scenes taken from the lives of the Buddhist saints.)

Some of the monasteries still existed in 1935, but the last were closed in 1936-37. The end of the Agin Monastery, which was liquidated in about 1934, was particularly tragic. At first it was simply closed, and the lamas were for the most part arrested or sent to the concentration camps in Turukhan Krai. A few months later, the film "Descendant of Genghis Khan" was being made in this area. One of the episodes in the film showed a procession of lamas carrying sacred books. The 108-volume work, *Gandzur*, was withdrawn from the monastery library for this purpose. After the filming was over, when the books were no longer needed, they were thrown into a ditch beside the road.

Lamas virtually ceased to exist in Buryatia in 1936. In that year, when a reception for representatives of the working people of the Buryat-Mongol ASSR was being in the Kremlin, Molotov commented on the liquidation of the "parasitical lama class" as one of the "achievements of the policy of government organs in the Buryat-Mongol ASSR."

In 1937 all the lamas in Leningrad were arrested and executed. Dorzhiev was also arrested, and despite his great age (he was about 85) was deported to Ulan-Ude where he was imprisoned. He died there at the beginning of 1938.

This was the end of organized Buddhism in the USSR, of which not a single memorial remains. In Asia Minor and in Greece the ruins of ancient temples have been preserved, making it possible to study the ancient culture of Hellas. Nothing remains of the Buddhist temples in Buryatia and Kalmykia. The fate of Lamiasm in the USSR deserves attention as an example of the complete destruction of a religion and the destruction of a religious group as a group.

In the '30's Buddhism was almost liquidated in the USSR. After the Second World War, Buddhism began to manifest itself again, and even became the subject of research works. These works are now the object of persecution.

According to Western newspapers, arrests were conducted in August, 1972, among scholars who dealt with Buddhism.

During court proceedings on November 21-23, 1972, they were convicted and confined to a psychiatric "clinic."

In the course of the court proceedings, it was decided to charge eight more persons. Their trial was to have been held in December, 1972, but it is not known whether it was held or not, nor when or where. In line with rumors, the "socialist verdict" was to have been oral not written, as a consequence of which the accused allegedly lost their jobs. At the same time, house searches and interrogations were carried out in various localities, and the "objects of the cult"—statues, pictures and correspondence with the Buddhist sect— were confiscated. It so happened that from many persons all correspondence, including that having no connection whatsoever to the Buddhist sect, was confiscated.

During the interrogations and inquiry various tricks and brutal methods were used in order to force the accused to talk. From the proceedings of the interrogations, an accusation was fabricated to the effect that the accused belong to a fanatical sect, which demands bloody human sacrifices and engages in murder.

It is assumed that since Stalin's death the position of Buddhism in the USSR has not been as endangered as it is today.

The Kalmyk inhabitants of the Russian Empire were divided for administrative purposes into the Astrakhan Kalmyks, who formed the majority; the Stavropol Kalmyks; and the Don or Salsk Kalmyks. The last had the same legal status as the Don Cossacks and formed part of the "Army of the Don." The Astrakhan and Stavropol Kalmyks had statutory rights which differed from those of other "non-autochtonous" peoples.

The Kalmyks of Czarist Russia were highly religious. Their spiritual longings were satisfied by the Buddhist appeal to moral perfection and the practice of the "Ten White Paths." Also, freedom to practice the Buddhist faith gave the Kalmyks, whose civil rights were otherwise limited, a means of satisfying their national aspirations. The Buddhist clergy were able to perform a particularly important role in this respect.

At the time of the 1917 Revolution, the Astrakhan Kalmyks had 87 khuruls, or monasteries, and the Don Kalmyks 13. These, as in the case of the Buryat Mongols, were cultural as well as religious centers, repositories of valuable books and historic examples of art and architecture. Each khurul was headed by a *baksha*, or incumbent, who was elected by the clergy and laity, and enjoyed universally recognized authority.

The February Revolution stirred the Kalmyks. Two congresses were held, on March 25 and July 24-25, 1917, at which the leading elements of the Kalmyk people were represented. Plans for the spiritual, cultural, and economic development of the people were proposed at these congresses and Lama Chimid Balzanov was elected religious head of the community.

Lenin's "Declaration of the Rights of the People of Russia" of November 15, 1917, like his "Appeal to the Kalmyk Working People" of July 22, 1919, distorted the true state of affairs, passed over in silence the bloody events that had preceded the grant of national status, and contained promises that proved untrue.

From the very beginning, whenever Red Guards entered the Kalmyk *aimaks*, or settlements, they immediately broke into and devastated the sanctuaries, and vied with one another in defiling the holy places. For miles around, the steppe was strewn with the torn pages of sacred writings. Precious images painted on silk were burned. Statues of Buddha and Buddhist saints were used as targets for rifle practice. Lenin's revolutionary followers conducted anti-religious propaganda among the people to "prove by sober facts that God does not exist." Public defilement was accompanied by the taunt, "If your Buddha is all-powerful, let him punish me!"

The beginning of collectivization proved to be the beginning of the end for the Buddhist clergy. The people were drained by the Bolsheviks of everything they possessed and were therefore unable to continue to assist the clergy to pay taxes. As a result, the temples and houses of the priests were publicly sold for non-payment of taxes. The temples were turned into clubs or into barns and stables for collective farms. The priests were accused of opposing collectivization and classed as vagrants. They were sent to collective labor camps in droves. For instance, the last head of the Chora Monastery, Rab-Dzhamba Sandzhiev, had over one hundred Buddhist monks in his charge. All were sentenced without formal trial by an NKVD tribunal to various terms of imprisonment. The majority died in concentration camps of hunger and sickness. Sandzhiev survived his deportation in Camp Kozhikov near Novosibirsk, where he worked at timbering and excavating.

As has been said, there were about one hundred khuruls in Kalmykia, each with an average of 25-30 *gelyuns*, or priests. All were gradually liquidated. The last two monasteries, the Mochazhnensk and Zaga-Amansk, held out until 1936, after which there was not a single monastery remaining in Kalmykia and, officially, not a single Buddhist priest. In isolated cases, a few priests carried on an illegal existence and secretly catered to the religious needs of the population. Among them was Dordzhi Burmetov, baksha of Novo-Alekseevsk Khurul. He was a Buddhist scholar and beloved priest. He remained in concealment for many years, protected from the NKVD by the entire Kalmyk population, including some Communists. In the end, however, he was tracked to his hiding place and killed in 1940.

The Soviet authorities dealt very shrewdly with Tepkin, the spiritual head of the Kalmyks. He was respectfully called to the NKVD offices, where some concern was expressed about the fact that his diplomatic passport would soon be running out. He was offered assistance in obtaining an extension and was confiding enough to accept the offer and hand over his passport; he vanished soon after. Not until several months later did it become known that Tepkin had been sentenced without formal trial by an NKVD tribunal, to ten years' imprisonment. He died as a deportee.

The fate of the sentenced priests and their movements from one labor camp to another were almost identical in all cases. Few survived.

The Buddhist monasteries and clergy of the Don area had been liquidated considerably earlier, in 1918-20 during the Civil War. An insignificant portion of the clergy were able to reach countries of the free world through Turkey. The rest were massacred on the spot.

Menko Bormanzhinov, the spiritual head of the Don Kalmyks, deserves special mention. One of the most eminent of the Kalmyk clergy, he died as a fugitive in 1919.

The fates of all the heads of the 13 Don monasteries are known. Six fled into exile abroad as a result of Communist persecution. Lylin, the baksha of the Kuvud-Chorabg Khurul, was killed by the Bolsheviks in 1919. Five others died as a result of hardships undergone in years of illegal existence in the USSR. Tsedna, the baksha of the Tsevdyanken Khurul, was still alive and in hiding at the beginning of World War II.

In the light ot the history ot the Bolshevik destruction of the religious life of the Kalmyk Buddhists, the claims of religious freedom in the USSR are ridiculous. While at formal receptions for official visitors from abroad some individual garbed as a Buddhist lama may be exploited to describe in the name of the Buddhist community the revival of Buddhist religious life, in fact the Buddhist religious community has been completely destroyed with not a single religious or historical relic left to mark a once flourishing existence.

Judaism

Horrible things are happening with the Jews in Russia from a religious point of view. In Kiev there are something like 300,000 Jews who have only one synagogue, with one rabbi 80 years old.

In Vilnius there is also only one synagogue.

The chief rabbi of Georgia has been hanged with the head down.

In Tashkent there has been recently a pogrom. Jews have been driven to suicide in Russia, being called to the secret police and asked to organize anti-Israel meetings.

Now, they could not organize them, first of all because Israel is right, and then they belong to Israel. And they were driven to suicide, because otherwise they would have gone to prison.

Lastly in Soviet Union, officers of Jewish background have been dismissed from the army.

The attitude of the Communists towards the Jews has been seen in the recent Middle East crisis, when they were entirely on the side of the Jews.

The official attitude of the Communist International towards the Jewish question is fixed in a book of Heller, an official book of the Communist International, and it is called *Der Untergang des Judentums (The End of Judaism)*. It was first published in Germany. In it they say that Communism means the end of Judaism.

Communism has been anti-Semitic from its beginning.

The Jewish Communists are very few, but noisy, giving thus the wrong impression that they are many.

"What is the main ideology of the Jewish national revival of the Soviet Union?" concluded Zand. "It can be stated in four words: 'Let My People Go!' "

Judah L. Graubart, in an article, confirmed Zand's remarks. He said Russian anti-Semitism is "a tool of statecraft . . ." and that "Soviet Jews have begun to demand above all the right of emigration to Israel."

Graubart pointed out the great increase in numbers and percentages of Jews being allowed to emigrate: and unprecedented rate of 750 per week, or a rate of 3.3 to 1 of visa applications to visa recipients.

"Few of us can remain unmoved in the face of such facts as these. Yet there is a great responsibility that comes with such information. What are we going to do about it? Are we merely going to shake our heads or shall we do something?"

Sen. Jackson believes in action. In an interview with *U.S. News & World Report* he said:

> ... I believe that our economic power at this point in history can be far more effective than our military power alone. It is our trump card. ...,
>
> We're on notice now that there are millions in Russia who went to concentration, forced-labor camp in Russia. ...
>
> I would put top on the list the freer movement of people, the freer movement of ideas across frontiers. ...
>
> I'm speaking now of my insistence that the Russians open the way for Jews or others to migrate out of Russia as a condition of the trade concessions—most-favored nation treatment and U.S. government credits and guarantees—that the Russians are seeking and that require congressional authorization.

Soviet hostility toward Judaism derives from multiple sources. Conventional Communist attitudes toward religion constitute a primary source and inevitably imposes upon religious minded Soviet Jews a tremendous burden. A basic incompatability exists between all religions and Communist doctrine. The historic tradition of anti-Semitism, rooted in Russian life and never really eradicated in the Soviet era, has had a lasting influence on shaping Soviet attitudes. In addition to the intellectual, economic, and social phenomenon inherent in the causes of anti-Semitism is the idea, seemingly never accepted by the Russians, that adherence to Judaism could be compatible with loyalty to the state. "Judaism kills love for the Soviet motherland" is a typical slogan in the Soviet press. Another is the charge that Judaism is a "servant of bourgeoisie nationalism, Zionism, and Israel." Reinforcing this notion of "disloyalty" is the universality of Judaism with its ties to the outer capitalist world—Western Europe, United States, and especially Israel. All of these factors converge in creating a general attitude of open and undiluted hostility toward Judaism, its doctrine, and its institutions. Soviet policy and Soviet action are directed toward the goal of destroying this nexus of faith binding the religious Soviet Jew to the universal Judaic community.

Propaganda attacks and acts of violence against religious Soviet Jews have been especially severe. Published literature, even from leading Soviet academies, has been designed to discredit Judaism and its institutions. The Yiddish theater, such as it is, touring Soviet towns, concentrates its attention on ridiculing the Jewish religion and customs. The ancient superstition of Jewish ritual murders, which entailed drinking the blood of victims, has been resurrected, apparently with passive Soviet acquiescence, and used as a weapon to discredit Judaism and enflame anti-Semitic riots.

Direct attacks on Jewish religious life have been frequent, persistent, and harsh. The public baking and sale of matzah, the unleavened bread indispensable for the religious observance of Passover, has been forbidden. Soviet Jews, some synagogue officials, have been arrested and imprisoned for illegally selling matzah. Severely discriminating actions have been taken against Jewish religious leaders. The arrest, trial, and death sentence imposed upon B. Gavrilov, a rabbi, on charges of alleged speculation in foreign currency and gold, aroused the Rabbinical Council of America to lodge a formal protest with the Soviet Embassy in the United States. Jewish leaders in other parts of the world added their voices of protest in denouncing the Soviet action. Raids on private prayer meetings *(minyanim)* have also taken place. Synagogues have been vandalized and reduced to poverty by restrictive administrative actions. Reporting on his journey to Jewish Birobidzhan in 1959, Max Frankel of the *New York Times* referred to "the shack that serves as a synagogue" where Sabbath services were conducted without a rabbi. Synagogues have been closed in cities where the Jewish population numbers into the thousands. A report in May, 1963 stated that the closing of Jewish places of worship in 10 cities during 1962 brought the total number of synagogues closed since 1959 to more than 60 and substantially reduced the total of 150 the Soviet claimed existed in July, 1963.

More subtle means of discrimination, but means equally effective, have also been resorted to in the Soviet anti-religious campaign against the Jews. Publication of religious material is forbidden. No Jewish religious book of any kind has been published since the early 1920's. No Hebrew Bible has been published since 1917. The study of Hebrew has been outlawed, even for religious purposes. Production of indispensable religious objects such as the *tallis* (prayer shawl) and *tefillin* (phylacteries) and other religious articles has been prohibited. Until 1957, Soviet Jews had no *yeshiva* to train their religious leaders. That year, one was permitted in Moscow, but with a severely restricted enrollment. Preference appeared to be given to training older men, thus reducing the tenure of their religious ministry. In April, 1962, students from Jewish communities in Georgia and Daghestan were prevented from studying in Moscow, leaving only four students in the *yeshiva*, thus transforming it, in Moshe Decter's words, "into a virtually empty shell."

Soviet Jewish religious life is no doubt in jeopardy; for the dimension and depth of the Soviet campaign to eradicate its influence is considerable and distinctively multifaceted and all encompassing. As Ronald Hingley, the British specialist on Soviet affairs, observed: "Practicing Jews are more severely impeded than any of the other main religious communities in the Soviet Union." The purposes and effects of all the acts of persecution and discrimination against Judaism was probably best summed up by Moshe Decter who concluded that

> critics in the West worry that Jews and Jewish culture in Soviet Russian are doomed to extinction because of assimilation and inter- marriage and a deliberate neglect of religious traditions and rituals. But many Jews in Birobidzhan insist that Jewish and Yiddish culture is not dying out. They claim the opposite is true. They admit that intermarriage is brisk, but call this "normal" and "progressive."

> If you stand on the idea that Jewish culture means simply Jewish religion, going to the synagogue, learning how to read the Talmud and other religious books, then certainly Jewish culture is dying out. But most Jews in Birobidzhan are not religious. We don't believe in God. We don't go to the synagogue any more than most Russians here go to church. We do have a small synagogue here, but its attendance is no more than 18 or 20, and they are quite elderly persons.

Besides the Jewish People's Amateur Theatre of Birobidzhan, other approved signposts of Yiddish culture are eagerly shown to the visitor. For example, bookstores contain dozens of titles of novels and other works in Yiddish. A Yiddish newspaper, *Birobidzhaner Shtern*, is published five times weekly. There is a daily radio program in Yiddish. A monthly Yiddish literary journal, *Sovietish Heimland*, published in Moscow circulates widely. All publications, of course, are screened by the local Communist leadership.

No schools in the region teach Yiddish but officials explained that anybody who wanted to study it could do so. Teachers of Yiddish were available, and language lessons were given in the monthly literary magazine.

When Yiddish schools existed, many Jewish children objected to them and preferred to attend ordinary Russian schools. It is nevertheless true that Stalin's so-called "anti-cosmopolitan campaign" struck a direct blow at Yiddish culture and, in Stalin's days, Yiddish schools were shut down.

The first issue of the clandestine Jewish journal *Exodus* in April, 1970, described how the synagogue had become the center of Jewish spiritual life in the Soviet Union. But it had been unable fully to answer the people's needs and questions, partly because "the active hostility of the State towards all religions in the country is strongest perhaps against Judaism, the 'religion of the enemy from within,' " and fearing repercussions, the synagogues had been meekly agreeing to all the authorities' demands. It was also partly due to "advanced assimilation" which had caused linguistic and cultural alienation between the synagogues and the Jews (many of whom cannot speak Hebrew and are not permitted to receive instructions in it from the rabbis or study with them the Jewish observances and traditions). Some, seeking religion, have been turning to the Orthodox Church—"one more step on the road to assimilation."

> Since there is no registering of the believers in this country, the only evidence can be gained from selective sociological surveys. These have shown, for example, that as few as two per cent of the Jews polled in the Byelorussian city of Bobruisk said they considered themselves to be believers.

> In Novosibirsk, which has a Jewish population of 11,000, synagogue solemnities in recent years have had an attendance of 100-200, or 1-2 per cent of the total. In Kuibyshev, where the Jewish population is 16,000, the attendance has ranged between 150 and 450, that is, 1-3 per cent. In Leningrad, 2-2.5 thousand at the most, or about 1.5 per cent, out of the Jewish population estimated at 160 thousand by the 1970 census. The attendance of religious festivities is at the same low level among other confessions existing in the USSR, such as Orthodox Christianity, Islam, Buddhism or Baptists. Sociologists explain this by the rising educational and cultural standards of the population and also by the fact that several Soviet generations have been brought up in a spirit of atheism.

> There are 92 syangogues operating in the USSR today, 80 of them being housed in public buildings placed at the disposal of the believers free and for all time. In addition to synagogues, there are small groups of believers *(minhahs)* consisting of 10-20 or sometime 30 believers who get together irregularly, mostly on major holidays.

> The Moscow choral synagogue may be regarded as a kind of national centre of Judaism. This congregation regularly publishes religious literature (church calendars, prayer books). The synagogue runs an Ecclesiastical school *(eschibot)* to train rabbis.

> Because of the disestablishment of the church in the USSR, the number of temples (Orthodox churches, mosques, synagogues and other prayerhouses) is

fixed not by the state authorities, but depends on the needs and material possibilities of the congregation and parishioners. This is a matter of each congregation's internal competence.

The Jews are still regarded as a distinct nationality, and this is entered in their passports and identity documents. According to a census carried out in 1959, some two and a quarter million Soviet citizens registered as Jews, and if it is assumed that a sizeable number of people of Jewish origin registered as members of other nationalities a total of three million Jews seems reasonable. Moscow itself has almost a quarter of a million registered Jews.

In 1957 Khrushchev began an anti-religious campaign directed against all religious bodies. Many of the remaining synagogues were closed, and by 1964 only 92 were open in the entire Soviet Union. The usual method employed in securing their closure involved a local press campaign in which it was alleged that illegal or pro-Israeli activities were taking place in a certain synagogue; letters from readers, some of whom were said to be Jewish believers, were then published. These invariably asked for the "corrupt" synagogue to be closed. Finally came an official announcement from the authorities to the effect that they had closed the synagogue in response to local demand. The buildings were then generally converted into warehouses or secular meeting places. At this time the building of new synagogues was forbidden and any Jews who applied for permission to build were likely to be interrogated by the police and threatened. Meetings for prayer in private houses were also forbidden by the authorities.

There are, however, increasing signs of "a Jewish renaissance" in the Soviet Union. This includes a totally unexpected revival of Jewish religious life. Though the number of synagogues and prayer houses has now been reduced to about 60, more than half of which are in Georgia, and though there are less than 20 active rabbis, it seems that increasing numbers of young Jews are attending the synagogues.

> Young Jews, who have only recently discovered their Jewishness, while brought up in an atheistic atmosphere and therefore dismissing religion as reactionary and unscientific, nevertheless express their Jewish identity by turning to the synagogues as the last visible symbol of Jewish culture and as the only Jewish address. Probably unconscious of following a traditional Jewish pattern, they look upon the synagogue as a House of Assembly rather than as a House of Prayer. They gather there on Jewish Festivals in large masses, particularly for the celebration of *Simhat Torah* ("Rejoicing in the Law"), which marks the annual completion of the synagogue reading of the Pentateuch.

Despite the ferocity of the attack upon it, the Jewish religion continued to be an important factor in Soviet Jewish life. Even the *kehillas* showed remarkable resilience, though they had been officially stripped of all their social welfare functions and remained no more than congregations of worshippers. In 1925 there were 418 *kehillas* registered in the RSFSR, and in 1926 there were 1,003 registered in the Ukraine.

In many small town the religious community was still the main welfare agency. There were still about five hundred synagogues and Houses of Study in Byelorussia. In the Ukraine the number of synagogues had declined only from 1,034 in 1917 to 934 in 1929-30. The number of rabbis in the Ukraine had fallen from 1,049 in 1914 to 830 in 1929-30. All in all, 646 synagogues had been seized since the Revolution.

But some Western observers claim that today the Jewish religion is being pursued more zealously than other religions, particularly the Russian Orthodox faith. There are only about sixty synagogues functioning in the Soviet Union; there is a dearth of religious articles and of religious functionaries; there is not a single Jewish theological seminary or academy. When this situation is compared with that of other faiths, it is often concluded that the Jewish religion is beign discriminated against as part of an overall policy of anti-Semitism.

Religious life of the Bulgarian Jews in characteristic to the rest of Soviet Jews:

> A small prayer room with a tall stovepipe as its center pillar is large enough, with places to spare, to gather in on the Sabbath eve all the Bulgarian Jews who pray. The splendid high-domed synagogue next door, long out of use, gives evidence of how many prayed here once, and it was only one of several.

> The voices that joined the elderly cantor who leads the Sephardic rite— switching now and again from Hebrew into Ladino, the medieval Hebrew-Spanish mixture that was the daily language of most Bulgarian Jews, whose ancestors were expelled from Spain 500 years ago—are cracked with age. The faces of the men and women are worn.

> The oldest of the worshippers is 94, and except for a couple in their thirties and a boy accompanying his grandmother, no one looked under 70. . . .

> The service opened with a prayer for the dead. The roster of those who died in recent weeks was long, and no new generations replace them. Occasionally there is a circumcision of a new-born, done by a Jewish doctor who comes in from the provinces. No one could recall the last bar mitzvah, the receiving of a boy of 13 into the religious community.

> The community has been without a rabbi for many years. The only kosher meat is an occasional chicken slaughtered by the cantor. Some of the religious have become vegetarians.

> The offices of the social, cultural and educational organization of the Jews in the People's Republic of Bulgaria presents occasional cultural evenings, featuring music or programs devoted to Jewish writers deemed progressive. It publishes a biweekly newspaper in Bulgarian and a yearbook of articles of Jewish and Communist interest.

11

Religion Under Communism in World's Politics

Vatican's Ostpolitik

The Catholic Church had always vigorously opposed Communism up to the time of the Second Vatican Council in the early 1960's. In 1937, for instance, Pope Pius XI could say "Communism is intrinsically wrong and no one who would save Christian civilisation may collaborate with it in any field whatsoever."

Pope Pius XII who followed was just as resolute. In 1949, he warned against the dangers of detente with Communism: "Out of respect for the name of Christian, compliance with such tactics must cease, for, as the Apostle warns, it is inconsistent to wish to sit at the table of God and that of His enemies." At the time of the Hungarian Revolution, he issued no less than three encyclicals in three days condemning the Russian invasion. He died in 1958 and a whole era died with him.

He was succeeded by John XXIII whose policy of "peace and goodwill" was intended to put an end to the Cold War and inaugurate a period of brotherly collaboration with the Communists. Vatican diplomacy was put into reverse gear. At all costs the Russians must be won over.

In 1962, two weeks before the great Second Vatican Council was due to start, a cardinal was sent from Rome to Moscow. His mission was to persuade the Russian Orthodox Church to send observers to the Council. Hitherto they had obstinately refused to have anything to do with it. But Cardinal Willebrand was a very determined man. He would not take no for an answer. His mission succeeded. How did he win over the Russians? Peter Nichols, *Times* correspondent in Rome, explains: "There cannot be much doubt that the Vatican gave assurances of some kind that the Council would not breathe a spirit of anti-communism."

"Peace and goodwill" were bought . . . at the price of silence. But the Pope's policy of detente was soon to be tested.

During the course of the Council, 450 bishops—one quarter of the world's total—prepared a petition to the Council asking it to issue a condemnation of Communism. It pointed out that if the Council were to remain silent about the danger of Communism this would be equivalent to disavowing all that previous popes had said against it. But this did not seem to bother those who ran the Council. The petition was deliberately blocked by Council officials— indeed, the name of the priest who was chiefly responsible is available. The petition ended in the wastepaper basket and the architects of the Church's new policy of detente with Communism were able to breathe again.

While the Council was still in session Cardinal Willebrand made another visit to Moscow. He went with one of the Russian observers to the Council. They went at night to a small cheap hotel where they were introduced to another Cardinal—Cardinal Slipyj head of the Catholic Church in the Ukraine. The Cardinal had just been brought from a prison camp where he had spent the past 18 years. The Soviet authorities had agreed to release him on condition that he was not "exploited as anti-communist propaganda." The Church readily agreed. Slipyj, who was not well enough to fly, was taken by rail to Vienna where he was made to change into a dark civilian suit so that no sign of his ecclesiastical office was visible. In Italy the train was stopped before it reached the Rome terminus and, unnoticed by other travellers, the Cardinal was whisked away in the car of the Pope's personal secretary.

What very strange behavior! Why the night journeys, the change of clothes, the James Bond secrecy? Is the Church ashamed of her living martyrs? Had not Cardinal Slipyj seen his Church officially liquidated by the Soviet state in 1946, its five million members forcibly absorbed into the Russian Orthodox Church, half of his 2,000 clergy put in prison and the other half driven underground? Had not most of his bishops died in Russian labor camps? Should not this man have been welcomed in daylight on the steps of St. Peter's? Had he not earned the public acclamation of his Church?

In 1971 Slipyj spoke to the World Synod of Bishops in Rome:

> Ukrainian Catholics have sacrificed rivers of blood and mountains of bodies because of their loyalty to the Church and they still suffer severe persecutions. But what is worse, there is nobody to defend them . . . Ukrainians who have suffered so much and so long as martyrs and confessors are ignored as inconvenient witnesses of past evils. We have become an obstacle to Church diplomacy.

Could anything be more plainly put? And this betrayal by the Church of her own bravest defenders of the Faith was seen again in 1974 when Cardinal Mindszenty, Primate of Hungary, was demoted and humiliated by his own Church at the behest of a Communist government! Mindszenty was just another "obstacle to Church diplomacy."

Perhaps this is the most shameful consequence of dentente: that the western Churches are prevented by the very terms of detente from offering any support to the victims of Communist persecution. In a country such as Soviet Russia where human rights are treated with contempt, where there is no appeal to government, courts or church, the dissidents' only hope lies in arousing the conscience of the Western churches. What he does not know is that those churches have, by their policy of "peace and goodwill" entered into an agreement with the persecutors—an agreement which binds them to silence. No matter what injustices, atrocities and uncivilised acts are committed in Communist countries the Western churches will maintain their discreet silence.

The Vatican's foreign minister once asked,

> Do people really think that I don't notice the bitter taste of the champagne we drink to conclude another compromise? Have they ever stopped to think what the Church's position would be in those countries if the Holy See had not done what it did?

As the Vatican's foreign minister for the past twelve years, the Archbishop has been instrumental in shifting the Church's relations with the Communist world from the hostility of the 1950's to the detente diplomacy of the 1970's. Because of his central role in the planning and execution of the Vatican's detente, Casaroli is often referred to as "Pope Paul's Kissinger." The comparison is not limited to the two men's frequent travels or summit style of diplomacy, however. Like Kissinger, Casaroli and his detente diplomacy have come in for increasing criticism within the past year or two. Disappointment with detente has been a growing political trend in many Western countries, and it is probably not surprising that even the special brand of reconciliation the Vatican pursues has not escaped the critics' scrutiny. The Vatican, though, represents not only a sovereign nation, but also a major religion, and is thus expected to reflect that religion's moral principles in its diplomatic activity.

Internationally, the Vatican has a certain moral stature, but its negotiating palette holds little more than episcopal appointments, diocesan boundary changes and limited Church-State agreements. This narrows the Vatican's diplomatic options considerably, especially with the Communist countries of Eastern Europe. Should the Holy See "refuse to negotiate with atheists" and restrict itself to religious and moral exhortations to Catholics around the world? Should it do all in its power to aid Catholics in Communist countries but draw the line at cooperation with their governments? Or should the Vatican be open to negotiations with the local governments if they offer the promise, however slight, of improving the lot of believers in that country and expanding the rights of the local Church? Pius XII preferred the first option, whereas John XXIII and Paul VI made clear decisions for the third. The recent re-examination has brought the first two options back into discussion and left a question mark as to the future path the Vatican *Ostpolitik* will take.

Pius XII's comment about negotiating with "Why speak when there is no common language?"—seems to be the motto of Casaroli's most vocal critics. Strongly anti-Communist, these observers feel that the Vatican has been confusing the basic difference between Communism and Christianity by accepting the Eastern European governments as negotiating partners. Furthermore, critics such as the Austrian Catholic journalist Erik von Kuehnelt-Leddihn argue, these talks are bound to fail because the Vatican enters into the negotiations in good faith while the Communists retain their goal of destroying religion. This view has received reinforcement from the ranks of the exiled Soviet dissidents. Alexander Solzhenitsyn, who has denounced the West for maintaining contacts with the Soviet Union, has been equally critical of the Vatican for doing the same. Anatoli Levitin-Krasnov, the founder of religious *samizdat* in the Soviet Union, thinks that Casaroli's efforts to promote his *Ostpolitik* have only compromised the Vatican in the eyes of the Soviet people. They have also encouraged the Soviet authorities to take a more cynical attitude toward religion. According to Levitin-Krasnov, the Soviet Union has not complied with a single demand put forth by the Vatican. If, however, the Church were to take "fundamental positions," he feels, "its authority would increase immediately."

Some skeptics disagree not so much with the need for a Vatican *Ostpolitik* as with its present execution. Their doubts are well expressed in an editorial which appeared in 1976 in the West German monthly *Stimmen der Zeit*.

> Rome is compelled to stake all to preserve the life of the Church. There is no reason to believe that Catholics would gain greater freedom if the Vatican were to set out on a confrontation course.

After this initial affirmation, the editorial went on to ask a crucial question about Casaroli's diplomacy.

> Has the Vatican let itself be misled by wishful thinking? Is it not rendering service to the other side without a corresponding return?

This is where Casaroli's critics sound most like Kissinger's. The main objection to the archbishop's diplomacy, according to these skeptics, is its overtly diplomatic nature. Casaroli, they say, puts too much emphasis on "summit diplomacy" and agreements with government officials and not enough on the problems of the local Church in question. This view's most persistent supporter is probably Poland's Stefan Cardinal Wyszynski. An astute politician, Wyszynski has long understood the need for some sort of understanding between Church and Communist State. But he objects to agreements between Warsaw and the Vatican which do not directly improve the Church's position at the local level. When Bishop Luigi Poggi, the Vatican's special nuntius for Poland, made a month-long visit in 1976, the Polish episcopate took exception to his frequent talks with government officials which ended with communiques about peace, detente and mutual respect. "When a representative of the Holy See comes to Poland," Wyszynski commented dryly in a sermon during Poggi's visit, "it is not enough to discuss peace among nations." Rather, he felt, the Vatican diplomat should devote more time to the concrete issues confronting the local Church, such as building permits for new churches, religious instruction for children and job discrimination against believers. Poggi's fact-finding tour in 1977, which concentrated heavily on travel through the country and discussions with the clergy, seems to have been a response to Wyszynski's complaint.

The Vatican *Ostpolitik's* best spokesman is undoubtedly Archbishop Casaroli himself. A charming man in his 60's, Casaroli occasionally gives speeches and interviews to explain his diplomatic approach. His guiding force, Casaroli explains, is what he calls "the Roman tradition of thinking in centuries." In this view, the primary goal of the Vatican *Ostpolitik* is the preservation of Church hierarchies, since only they can guarantee the survival of the Church at the local level. Bishops, because of their power to ordain priests, are thus the "pillars" of Casaroli's policy, and he often spends months negotiating with local officials to find episcopal candidates acceptable to both Church and State. Beyond this *sine qua non*, the archbishop feels, the Vatican should limit itself to agreements which, if even vaguely, expand the rights of the local Church. "Pope Paul's Kissinger" is wary of seeking broader-based agreements such as full diplomatic relations or concordats. In most cases, they would require far more Church-State consensus than presently exists, and would probably illuminate rather than alleviate the problems the two sides now have.

Support for East-West detente is a crucial and sometimes controversial element in Casaroli's approach. With the trend toward better relations between the superpowers has come an improved climate for the Vatican and its goals. To show its support for detente, the Vatican has been active in several areas of international diplomacy. Vatican negotiators took an active part in the wrangling at the Helsinki Conference, arguing with particular emphasis for Basket Three with its sections on human rights and religious freedoms. The Holy See has always commented favorably on Kissinger's detente diplomacy, Willy Brandt's *Ostpolitik*, and disarmament negotiations such as the SALT talks, often to the dismay of these policies' opponents abroad. Casaroli even traveled to Moscow in 1970 to add the Vatican's signature to the Nuclear Non-Proliferation Treaty. Of course, Vatican City is not a nuclear power and shows little interest in becoming one. But the Vatican felt the treaty was important enough for world peace that the Church's *imprimatur* had to be on it.

Finally, the archbishop likes to ask, does the Vatican have an alternative to detente? Statements like those of Pius XII, denounce godless Communism or examples like Joszef Cardinal Mindszenty in bitter opposition to the Hungarian government might satisfy Western critics demanding a tougher stand on Communism. But, Casaroli replies, while the Cold War bloomed, the Church in Eastern Europe suffered. Vatican diplomats were banned from the Communist countries. Mindszenty's self-imposed exile in the American Embassy in Budapest blocked the consecration of a new generation of bishops. The atmosphere has been changing since the early 1960's, and there is some increased freedom for Church leaders and a dialogue between the Vatican and the local governments. "We know that the atmosphere alone cannot solve the problems," Casaroli has commented. "But it can contribute to a further examination of these problems and bring them closer to a solution."

How close is the Holy See to a "solution" in Eastern Europe? That depends on the country. Vatican-Yugoslav relations are generally considered a model for the Vatican *Ostpolitik* . Diplomatic ties were resumed in 1966 when the two sides signed an agreement guaranteeing the complete separation of Church and State. In the text, Belgrade accepted the Church's jurisdiction in all religious and pastoral questions, while the Vatican promised to limit Church work to those areas and discipline priests whose activities take on a political character. Under the circumstances, the agreement was rather tolerant, and bilateral relations have been satisfactory. But Yugoslavia is generally more liberal than the other Communist countries, so Casaroli can hardly expect to reach similar agreements elsewhere in Eastern Europe.

The Holy See does not have diplomatic relations with Warsaw, but the Polish Church is certainly the most influential in Eastern Europe. Almost 90 per cent of all Poles are Catholics, a fact which makes Cardinal Wyszynski one of the most powerful men in the country. Until recently, Edward Gierek's government had been conducting a subtle drive to undermine the Church's position in Polish society. But, with his own power weakened after the price riots June, 1976, Gierek has now turned to the Church for cooperation. The episcopate replied with an appeal to the people to work for the good of the country and a demand to the government to release workers jailed for their strike activity. After Wyszynski repeated the amnesty demand in two sharply worded sermons, Warsaw complied by releasing some of the sentenced strikers. Because of his local power base, the Polish primate is reluctant to allow the Vatican to become too active in its dealings with the Gierek government. But despite any disagreements they may have with the Cardinal, neither the Vatican nor Warsaw wants to see him go. As a 75th birthday present, the Polish government sent Wyszynski a bouquet of flowers and Pope Paul rejected his obligatory letter of resignation.

Slow progress is being made in East Germany and Hungary, East Berlin, careful not to antagonize the large West German Catholic Church, has been rather tolerant of the Catholic 10 per cent of its population. In return, the Vatican, while mindful of the West German Catholics' distrust of detente, has been making slow adjustments to postwar reality. In 1972, diocesan boundaries were redrawn to conform to the post-1945 border between Poland and East Germany. Late in October, 1976, the Vatican announced the creation of a separate bishops' conference for East Germany, a halfway step before informal papal recognition of that country. The East German bishops had formerly belonged to the German Bishops' Conference centered in the West, but contacts had become increasingly difficult to maintain after the Berlin Wall was build. In Hungary, Church-State relations began to improve after Cardinal Mindszenty left Budapest for Viennese exile in 1971. In 1974, the Hungarian government permitted all Vatican bishoprics to be filled, and eased restrictions on religious instruction, seminary admissions, and catechism and Bible printing. In March of 1977, Bishop Laszlo Lekai succeeded Mindszenty as primate of Hungary; in May, he was appointed to Mindszenty's long unused seat in the College of Cardinals. Since then, Lakai has appeared in public with Party leader Janos Kadar and has sought to promote Christian-Marxist cooperation in Hungary.

Today, regime and church relations are more harmonious in Hungary than anywhere else in the East bloc, even in Poland.

Catholic, Calvinist, and Lutheran churches and Hungarian Jews all have their seminaries for training priests and rabbis. There are six Catholic high schools with substantial enrollments.

But not all is "sweetness and light." The Catholic Bishops' Conference recently recalled Party leader Janos Kadar's declaration of a decade ago that public office is open to patriotic Hungarian believers and that no one should be at a disadvantage in job or career because of religious faith.

Bishop Joszef Cserhati reiterated the church's sympathy with "society's interests," but Catholics, he protested, are still treated as "second-class citizens" when it comes to responsible public posts. Or they are subjected to other pressures.

The government has recently re-emphasized its interest in continued "Christian-Marxist dialogue." Its spokesmen conceded that its church policy is often ignored at local levels. The head of its religious affairs office, Imre Miklos, has written of efforts to "hammer home" that differences of outlook cannot be met by "arbitrary measures" and that religious freedom cannot be confined to participation in liturgical events.

Elsewhere in Eastern Europe, Church-State relations are rarely as civil. The "normalization" introduced after the Soviet invasion of 1968 brought to Czechoslovakia a reintroduction of the atheist campaigns of the 1950's. Just such a campaign seems to be on the upswing now, with reports of official chicanery against priests and believers appearing more frequently in the

Western European press. Bishop Poggi visited Romania in October, 1976, and Archbishop Casaroli spent a week negotiating with the Bulgarians in November, 1976, but it was the simple fact that the meetings took place rather than any special agreements resulting from them which made a slight improvement seem visible.

But even more important than these temporary problems is the larger question of where the Vatican *Ostpolitik* goes from here. In East Germany, Hungary, Poland and Yugoslavia, most of the major barriers to Church-State dialogue have been overcome; although still at a disadvantage, the Church has at least been accepted as a legitimate representative of a certain segment of these societies and allowed a limited freedom. In the other countries, even this is far off. The question arises whether, after more that a decade of detente, this is as far as the Vatican diplomacy can get in Eastern Europe. Could there be, short of full diplomatic relations, no further concessions Casaroli can make to his negotiating partners? Might other developments, such as the recent criticism of Casaroli's diplomacy or the Vatican's drive against the Italian Communists, be creating in-house barriers to closer cooperation with the Communist leaders?

The answer to these questions might not be yes, but it tends in that direction. Until now, Casaroli has been working on the initial stage of the Vatican's detente. He has made the first visits, signed the first agreements, and consecrated some of the first bishops. Thanks to his efforts, it is now normal in Eastern Europe for Church and State to discuss their differences and, to a degree different in each country, to strive for a solution. But now that Casaroli has helped to lay down the guidelines for these negotiations and even had some success at them, it seems to be getting more difficult to progress with specific local problems. Like Kissinger, Casaroli has probably found out that it is easier to visit Moscow for the first time than negotiate there for the fifth.

With the initial barriers overcome in several countries, the emphasis of the Vatican *Ostpolitik* will probably shift to the local churches. It will be up to them to deal with their governments within the framework Casaroli has helped to erect. Their success will depend partly on the policies of their governments and partly on their own ability to define, as Cardinals Wyszynski and Lekai are trying to do, the role of Catholics in a Communist society. As for Casaroli, he will probably continue his activity in Eastern Europe, especially in those countries where the Church is farthest from a solution.

At a time when the Communists are extolling the importance of ideological struggle and faithfulness to the materialistic manifesto set down in 1848 by Marx and Engels, and later refined into harsh doctrine by V. I. Lenin (Marxism is materialism . . . it is . . . relentlessly hostile to religion), a small but substantially influential number of supposed guardians of Judeo-Christian teachings and ideals has adopted a policy of unilateral ideological disarmament in the face of Red agressiveness.

The use of phraseology such as "a decade that is gone" and "Communism of yesterday" infers that Communism has, through the years, mellowed toward religion. It ignores the writings of Lenin himself who declared in "Socialism and Religion" (1905) that "Christians and those who believe in God" should not be denied membership in Communist ranks simply because they "still cherish certain relics of the old superstitions." Once within the ranks, however, a good Communist is expected to purge himself of these "superstitions."

Cardinal Alfredo Ottaviani, recognized for years as a prominent expert on matters of Communism and the Church, recently restated the Vatican's position in an exclusive interview in the Catholic periodical *Relazioni*. Asked to comment on the impression that the Catholic and Communist worlds are moving closer together, Cardinal Ottaviani replied as follows:

> There is no cause for wonder that, on the Communist side, there is a wish to have it thought that the attitude of the Church concerning Communism has actually changed . . . it is therefore very necessary to state definitely that there has been no change in the position.

> Communism was declared by Pius XI to be "intrinsically evil," and in the Decree of 1949 the Holy Office explained clearly the reason for its condemnation. To the question "if it was permissible to enroll in the Communist Party or to assist it," it replied in the negative stating: "in reality Communism is materialistic and anti-Christian." Although by twisting their words the leaders of Communism may claim that they are not opposed to religion, in fact both in their teaching and actions they frequently show that they are opposed to both God and Religion.

Noting that the Vatican decree on Communism issued by Pius XII ruled that any Catholic who "knowingly and freely" joined the Communist Party or aided it in its goals could not be admitted to the Sacraments, Cardinal Ottaviani pointed out that a similar decree was issued by Pope John XXIII—whose Encyclical, *Pacem in terris*, has been so severely distorted and misused by the Communists—in an April 4, 1959 ruling that Catholics could not vote

> for those parties or candidates who, although professing principles not opposed to Catholic teaching and even calling themselves Christian, in fact however associate themselves with the Communists and with their methods and support them.

The advocates of ideological disarmament have been cleverly conditioned by Red propaganda to reason incorrectly that, in opposing Communism, one is also opposing such things as social justice for the poor, better cooperation between the races, and fair wages for workers. They have forgotten—or never studied—Pius XI's Encyclical, *Divini Redemptoris*, which not only condemns Communism but reemphasizes the Church's teachings on social justice, racial harmony, and the rights and duties of workers and employers. With good reason, Pius XI was able to remark how "outstanding statesmen have asserted that, after a study of various social systems, they have found nothing sounder than the principles expounded in the Encyclicals" and the teachings of the Church in modern times.

As Cardinal Ottaviani pointed out in his *Relazioni* interview, there are some in the Church who are erroneously leading their followers "along paths which, instead of guiding the Catholic Social Movement towards the goals laid down by the Supreme Magisterium of truth and justice, carry it away to swell the ranks of Communism."

There is no need "to run after other systems" such as Communism, he added, "When in the Supreme Magisterium of the Church there is the teaching and the spur to satisfy every just requirement of modern man" such as Leo XIII's *Rerum Novarum*; Pius XI's *Quadragesimo Anno* and Paul VI's *Populorum Progressio*.

On the 13th anniversary of his elevation Pope Paul VI made a solemn appeal to Marxist regimes and other anti-Church governments to give the Church its "legitimate freedoms."

The Pope, who traditionally makes a major address on Church problems to Cardinals at the end of June, told them June 21, 1976:

> We would only like to make known the pain we have felt in our heart because vast sections of the world ruled by Marxists still remain closed, not only to understandings but even to contacts with this Apostolic See.

Pope Paul in his 13-year reign has launched a series of diplomatic exchanges with Communist governments. This *Ostpolitik* (a policy seeking accommodation with Eastern Marxist governments) has had limited success in some nations and almost none in others. It has been highly criticized especially by emigrants from Communist countries and also by some Catholic leaders in those nations.

> The Church does not ask special protection for itself or privileged treatment. The Church only needs and desires its legitimate freedoms.

The Pope's reference to Marxist regimes which have refused even to talk with the Vatican seemed to be aimed especially at the People's Republic of China. Since the early 1950's the Vatican has had almost no contact with the more than three million Chinese Catholics.

While the Pope did not name specific countries, he said that his appeal for religious freedom was made to governments in "vast regions of Europe and Asia" some governments in the Americas and Africa.

> In these nations Church-state problems have stemmed from the accession to power of political forces which have written into their ideological foundations and their practical and so-called strategic programs what they call the liberation of humanity from "religious alienation."

The Pope called on all Christians to join him in prayer for the achievement of religious freedom.

He told the Cardinals that he is continuing on the diplomatic level

> a dialogue conducted by our close and valiant collaborators who are active and tireless, patient and frank, and those carrying out the Vatican's *Ostpolitik* are as firm in affirming principles and rights of the Church and of believers as they are ready for an honest understanding which is faithful and reconcilable with these principles.

In reply to the critics of his policy, the Pope denied ever having forgotten the "passions and heroisms" of the victims of religious intolerance.

> The fidelity of those who have been and still are victims (of religious persecution) is not unknown to us and we have in mind always their sufferings, just as we share with them their hopes and prayers.

The Pope charged that governments have sometimes made the Church suffer for reasons which have nothing to do with religion.

Pope Paul VI at the general audience of June 2, 1976 said:

> Even if we are not all able to analyse the anti-religious phenomenon of our time, we all know, however, how radically it opposes our spiritual tradition, especially the Christian and Catholic tradition, even in countries historically imbued with religion, and we feel, to some extent, how atheism threatens, within the soul, the solidity of the motives that justify and demand the religiousness of our rational and spiritual being.

Once atheism was judged negatively by public opinion, as an absence of the
common faith; now, on the contrary, it is judged positively, erroneously and
unfortunately, we think, as progress, as liberation from a mythical, primitive
mentality, as a banner of the new times. Science is sufficient. Reason shuns
mystery. But is is not true; on the contrary, those who love science and perceive
its depth and precision cannot, must not block the way of thought in its
metaphysical and mystical explorations. Those who desire not to restrict reason within the limits of its conventional treatises must admit the necessity and
the joy of transcending them to seek at least, or to experience, and enjoy if
possible, the meeting with a Wisdom, with a Word, which while it bows them to
religious worship, raises them to the preludes of a suprarational and intoxicat-
ing dialogue, prayer.

For Rome the Iron Curtain was not novelty. There had been an iron
curtain, spiritually speaking, screening Russia in the days of Gregory XVI
and the Czar Nicholas I. Nor had other powerful rulers hesitated, elsewhere,
to impose prohibitions upon the Church's free communication with Rome.
Such iron curtains had been erected by Napoleon, by Bismarck, and by some
of the revolutionary governments of Latin America. But the iron curtain
around eastern Europe after 1945 was more impenetrable, and behind it
whole Catholic populations became, in the Pope's phrase, the "Church of
Silence."

The persecution was naturally most rigorous in those territories which
were incorporated within the Soviet Union proper, namely the eastern
provinces of Poland which became part of the Soviet republics of the Ukraine and of Byelorussia; the Carpatho-Ukraine, a territory seized from
Czechoslovakia and incorporated in the Soviet Ukraine; and the three
incorporated Baltic republics of Estonia, Latvia, and Lithuania. A large
proportion of the Catholics in these territories were Uniates, using the
Greek-rite; by dint of imprisoning the Uniate bishops and finding pliant
parish priests, the Soviet government secured the separation of these bodies
of Catholics, once more, from Rome, and their union with the Orthodox
Church; in this way nearly four million Catholics in Poland alone were lost.
This was a technique less easily applied to those of the Latin-rite, but the
Latin priests, particularly in Lithuania, were expelled in hundreds on fabricated charges. Many were taken to Siberia; the more fortunate found their
way to the West, and Pius XII founded the Lithuanian Ecclesiastical Institute
to minister to their needs and to confirm them in their Faith.

The technique of separating the Uniates from the other Catholics and
merging them with the Orthodox Church was also pursued in Romania,
which lay outside Soviet territory proper. It was facilitated by the Orthodox
Patriarch of Romania, who worked in close collaboration with the restored
Patriarch of Moscow. By restoring the patriarchate of Moscow in 1943 the
Soviet government had effectively provided itself with an instrument which,
despite its own atheist principles, it could use to advantage in its endeavors to
weaken the influence of Rome in eastern Europe. Not only would it facilitate
the transfer of the Uniates, but it would tend to prevent the Orthodox from
allying with the Catholics in a common defence of Christianity.

By 1950 the Pope, on account of what was happening in Romania, was
obliged to withdraw his acting nuncio from Bucharest. Meanwhile the persecution of the Church was proceeding in all the countries nominally independent but behind the Iron Curtain. In Yugoslavia, under Marshal Tito,

and especially in the Catholic province of Croatia, priests were executed, imprisoned, or driven into exile or into hiding, and religious education ceased. The popular Archbishop Stepinac of Zagreb was accused, on account of his impartial assistance to all refugees, of collaboration with the Germans and was sentenced to sixteen years' imprisonment; the hope of better days for the Church when Tito subsequently quarrelled with Stalin was not realised. In Hungary, a Catholic country, the primate, Cardinal Mindszenty, was arrested in January, 1949 and condemned in February to life imprisonment as a result of a trial which attracted the horror and amazement of the whole world.

When the Communists acquired control over Czechoslovakia in 1948 the Archbishop of Prague, Joseph Beran, was put under house arrest, and the government tried to institute new bishops without reference to Rome. But Beran, like Mindszenty and Stepinac, could rely upon the Pope who continued to recognise him as the lawful ruler of his see and refused to recognise any appointment, in substitution, by the government.

In Poland, the largest and most Catholic of the quasi-independent countries behind the Iron Curtain, the Communist government, set up by the Russians and recognised, perforce, by the allied powers, concentrated its efforts upon trying to drive a wedge between the Vatican and the Church. In the delicate matter of the western territories awarded to Poland after the war, at the expense of East Germany, Rome was represented as supporting the Germans, although she remained neutral in the matter of the political boundaries, and the Pope's only offence was to express his sympathy with those who found themselves forcibly evacuated on account of the changes.

Since 1950 the battle has continued. In that year the apostolic delegate was expelled from Moscow and his church was entrusted by Stalin to a compliant nominee from Latvia. Archbishop Stepinac, released from prison by President Tito, but kept under house arrest, was not allowed to attend the Consistory of January, 1953 to receive his cardinal's hat, and the Yugoslav government made the dignity conferred upon him the opportunity to break off diplomatic relations with the Vatican. The primate of Poland, Archbishop Wyszynski, created a cardinal on the same occasion, was likewise prevented from attending, and a few months later he was arrested. Cardinal Mindszenty remained in prison. In Hungary there was a brief break in the clouds at the time of the revolution of October, 1956, and Cardinal Mindszenty was released. A few words of peace, and of pardon for his enemies, and the clouds from the Carpathians descended once more, in the shape of Russian tanks, and the Church of Hungary became once again a part of the Church of Silence.

Bishop Myroslaw Marusyn, apostolic visitor for Ukrainian-rite Catholics in Western Europe, scored dissenting members of his rite during a sermon in Rome March 21, 1976 commemorating the 30th anniversary of the liquidation of the Catholic Ukrainian-rite in the Soviet Union.

This liquidation took place at the so-called "synod" of Lvov in the Ukraine, March 3-10, 1946, when more than 200 priests voted to renounce the Pope and swore allegiance to the Russian Orthodox Patriarch of Moscow.

There were three factors in the liquidation of the Church in the Ukraine:

The atheistic agents of the Soviet government, like the troops of Pontius Pilate, had no pity for believers.

The Russian Orthodox Church called for the Catholics to return to the

(Orthodox) fold and showed no sympathy for the persecuted Catholics.

Among the group of priests who collaborated in the so-called "synod," two of the three leaders had already been consecrated secretly as bishops by the Russian Orthodox Church. All later died under mysterious circumstances.

How could the Church coexist with Marxists according to whom religion is just a myth, promising him after his death on earth a happy, peaceful, eternal life and the end of his sufferings. According to the Marxists this is just opium. God and the other world do not exist. The only reality is the material in constant evolution. Communists have to fight against all religions. They have to close churches; to eliminate the clergy and to forbid all kinds of religious cults.

The problem which the Church has to solve is what to do in countries in which the Communist rulers change their tactics and try to show indifference or even tolerance towards the Catholic church. As an example can be mentioned three countries: Yugoslavia, Poland and Soviet Russia. The Christians had to choose: either to accept the *modus vivendi* offered by the State, or to refuse it and work underground. Where the Church has accepted the first solution, it was because it thought that it could help to avoid a war between East and West. This, however, is not very convincing because the political influence of the church in Communist ruled countries is without importance. It is very modest in Russia and Yugoslavia. The situation in Poland is not quite the same. But even if certain concessions are granted to the Church today, there is a great risk that they will be cancelled tomorrow. The main argument, however, against collaboration between the Catholic Church and the Communist State is the following: One of the important tasks of the Christian Church is teaching. It has to teach the full truth and to condemn false doctrines. It cannot limit its activity in the field of teaching, and thus cannot avoid criticising and contesting the dogma of the Communists. They simply cannot remain silent when they hear and read in their country the praise of atheism and materialism. Catholics must fight against Marxist theories; a compromise is not possible, and if realised, it would not last long and would have pitiful consequences.

These arguments are not new. The Vatican's present policy does not seem to accept them fully. Mgr. Lekai, the new Primate of Hungary, appointed recently by Pope Paul VI after the previous consent of the Hungarian government, declared himself to be a "realist." And Hungary is not alone among the Communist ruled countries having realist priests with the blessing of the Holy Seat.

Perhaps in a few years, one will see the results of co-existence as well as of the intransigent refusal of it. There is no doubt that the Church, by accepting a certain co-operation with the Communist ruled state, renders a great service to the Communist Party. Among other things it facilitates the decision of leftist Catholics to join the Communist Party. On the other hand, there is a French saying: *Les absents ont toujours tort* (Those who are absent are always wrong). The presence of the clergy in a Communist state can have a certain importance in critical situations. Results might not be the same in different Communist ruled states at different periods. Much depends also on the leading ecclesiastical personality of the Catholic Church in the respective country.

With the great Catholic turn to the left executed by John XXIII, the expression "equidistance" became fashionable. It meant exactly what "non-partisanship" had meant to Pius XII. There can be no doubt Pius XII would have sought an arrangement with the East European states had Stalin not blocked all possibilities of a *modus vivendi* by his persecutions of the Church. This diplomat par excellence among the Popes explained in September, 1955 at the 10th International Congress of Historians that the Catholic Church was not bound to any single civilization. This proposition, one of the results of the Reform Council, created a stir because the Congress was the first time Soviet scholars had come to the Vatican.

Although the Holy See strives to stand "above the contending parties," the Church, like every other community, is plagued with political forces unleashed in our "age of revolutions." East Europe's 60 million Catholics did not fall under Communist dictatorship because they willed it. It happened as a consequence of the division of Europe which was signed and sealed at Yalta. The Catholic Church is also a victim of Yalta, and while no Curial diplomat will say so, the truth is that this causes a certain resentment.

There are incidents that say more than many words. In 1962 John XXIII received pilgrims with whom he joined in the *Angelus.* He explicitly stated that the prayer was for one of the Soviet astronauts who had been shot into outer space just a few hours earlier. He was visited several weeks later by Lyndon Johnson, then U.S. Vice President, who handed the Pope a model of an American space rocket. This was regarded in the Vatican as a polemic gesture because John XXIII had never prayed for an American cosmonaut—at least not publicly.

The Soviets had announced their readiness to begin a dialogue with the Holy See as far back as 1957. One day the Soviet ambassador in Rome phoned the Apostolic Nuncio at the Quirinal and transmitted his government's surprising proposal that Rome be declared an "atom-free zone" in case of war because it was a "holy city." This feeler was not followed up since it was obvious that the neutralization of Central Europe, not Rome, was the Soviet goal.

However, the passports granted the two Russian Orthodox Council observers marked the real beginning of a diplomatic "escalation" between the Kremlin and the Vatican. In May, 1963 banner headlines announced that Pope John XXIII had received Khrushchev's son-in-law, Adzhubei, and his daughter. Three days later journalists asked Adenauer for his opinion. He replied: "Perhaps you can tell me when the Pope is going to visit Moscow?" Subsequent visits by Gromyko and Podgorny to Paul VI have settled that point.

What real interest does the Soviet Union have in beginning a dialogue with the Vatican? An East European expert with exceptionally good contacts in the capitals behind the Iron Curtain stated that the present planning staffs in Moscow believe Communism has no chance of success either in Latin America or in black Africa south of the Sahara if it openly opposes the Catholic Church. In addition, the Kremlin values highly the Vatican's position among the Arab states. The Italian Marxists, eager for a dialogue with the Catholics, think that the East European regimes are becoming aware that the religious impulse cannot be crushed and that, therefore, they should tolerate religious communities provided they accept "socialism's" political and social order.

The maximum that can be achieved today is probably represented by the treaty signed in June, 1965 between the Holy See and Yugoslavia. Under it Yugoslavia's Catholic bishops swore loyalty to their country's Communist constitution. Tito had sent emissaries to Rome ten years earlier. He had a special reason for resuming relations with the Vatican: he wanted to pacify the Slovenes, and even more so the Croatians, and so consolidate his multinational state. Clearly the Catholic Church was well suited as a moderator in this linguistic dispute with its nationalist overtones.

German experts on East Europe consider the legal position of Yugoslavian Catholics to be almost as favorable as that of German Catholics in the Third Reich. A basic difference is, of course, that the German government allowed religious instruction in the schools. The treaty with Tito does not go that far. However, practicing Catholics can send their children to the parish house for religious instruction. There is also a Catholic press in Yugoslavia, and after some initial difficulties the authorities are now faithfully observing the treaty. Since the Titoist constitution proclaims the division of the state and church, official, not full, relations were established between the Vatican and Belgrade. Tito's representative is officially described as a "plenipotentiary," but in person he is actually accorded ambassadorial rank.

The treaty with Yugoslavia is the model being offered to the eastern satellite countries, the example of coexistence between the church and the Communist state. Thanks to it, the Holy See has intensified its diplomatic activities in Hungary, Czechoslovakia and Poland. The Vatican yearned most of all for a treaty with Poland, which has always had a reputation as the "most faithful daughter of the Catholic Church."

The first and highly secret meeting of an official Polish representative with the Pope occurred at the end of November, 1964 when the Chairman of the Catholic *Znak* parliamentary group visited the Vatican. Later, the deputy reported his impression that the Germans, especially Cardinal Dopfner, had great influence with the Pope (at the time there was a rumor in Rome that Paul VI wanted to appoint Cardinal Dopfner to the Curia) and that the Pope was merely interested in seeing what the Poles wanted.

The Polish parliamentarian may have been mistaken. Even then, Paul VI was probably thinking of his participation in the 1966 celebration of Poland's one thousand years of Christianity. It is true the international press reported that Cardinal Wyszynski's circle had proposed the invitation to the Pope. But it is not at all unlikely that the real initiative originated with the Pope and his entourage, especially Cardinal Dell'Acqua, who was at that time Monsignor.

In any case, Dell'Acqua sent intermediaries to Warsaw, one of them the left-wing Catholic La Pira, former mayor of Florence. The Catholic gobetweens negotiated with the deputy Party secretary, Kliszko, and the conversations seemed headed in a positive direction. The Polish government ordered the Czestochowa airport fixed up so that it could receive the Pope's four-motor jet plane in a worthy fashion. In the meantime the Papal state secretariat was busy preparing a public reconciliation between German and Polish Catholics before the planned pilgrimage at the beginning of May, 1966. The Curial diplomats realized that the Pope's Polish trip might provoke nervous reactions in Germany, so they also considered having the Pope stop off in a German city in the Ruhr, or even West Berlin, on his return.

The situation became dramatic when Gomulka seized on the readiness of the German and Polish bishops to reconcile as a pretext for unrestrained attacks on the Catholic Church, with Cardinal Wyszynski in the first line of fire. Not only was Wyszynski deprived of his exit visa, but he was informed that the Pope's journey would not be approved. Gomulka probably feared that the thousand year celebration might become an unparalleled demonstration of Polish Catholicism. Undoubtedly these fears were heightened by comments in the western press.

The Pope swallowed this affront and continued seeking further opportunities for a *detente*. At the end of 1966 Paul VI's personal secretary, Monsignor Pasquali Macchi, flew to Warsaw. The trip led to a resumption of talks on a treaty with the Holy See. The Vatican's traveling diplomat, Monsignor Casaroli, has visited Poland several times. In these discussions Poland has sought to wring concessions from the Vatican on the question of the Oder-Neisse dioceses. The administrator of these Polish episcopates had died and the Poles demanded the appointment of a regular Polish bishop.

On Easter, 1967, the head of the German Christian Democratic parlimentary group, Raines Barzel, convinced the Curial diplomats of possible negative German reactions to such a step. A month later the Vatican appointed the Polish administrator of the East German dioceses as Apostolic administrator. The Germans, including Bonn, publicly accepted this solution because it did not entail official Church ties. However, Polish President Ochab demonstrated Warsaw's dissatisfaction by reversing the precedent set by Podgorny, Soviet head of state, a short time before, and not seeking an audience with the Pope.

Because each Communist nation has a separate history and background, it is important that one briefly surveys the major countries in Communist Europe and their relations with the Vatican. The strategies of the present become much more significant when viewed against the record of past centuries.

It is very important to realize that the religious background of Russia is predominantly Russian Orthodox, with connections to the Greek Orthodox Church of Constantinople. The Roman Church has had very little influence in Russia.

Up until 1917, the basic Eastern policy of the Vatican was simply to bring the Orthodox Churches, including the Russian Orthodox, back into the "wider embrace" of the Church. Despite Communist persecutions of the Orthodox, and the forced acceptance of state control, Russian foreign policy cannot ignore the Russian Church. That Church, and religion in general, still has a surprising influence, even after three generations of indoctrination. Likewise, the Vatican's dealings with Moscow must take the Russian Patriarch into account.

One historical fact, which the Russians may not have forgotten, is that the Vatican once promoted the military conquest of Russia by Catholic powers, notable Poland. A Polish-Lithuanian alliance actually captured and held Moscow for two years in the early seventeenth century.

In spite of that fact, relations between Moscow and the Vatican are warming up.

"Religion is the opiate of the people," wrote Lenin, the founder of Soviet Communism. His religious antagonist, Pope Leo XIII, stated in 1891 that Socialism, including Communism, leads to "an odious and unbearable state of servitude for every citizen."

These seemingly irreconcilable positions between Catholicism and Communism have been maintained—at least to the casual observer—for decades. But note the very surprising recent moves on both sides of the ideological fence:

The Vatican's *Ostpolitik*—policy toward Eastern Europe—has obviously changed very drastically. So has Communist thinking about Rome and its "opiate." In actual fact, the recent moves are not at all surprising, as veteran observers are quick to point out. They are simply the latest moves in the globe-wide and millennia-long chess game of world politics.

The term "Vatican politics" might sound incongruous. Most people think of the Vatican as only an ecclesiastical establishment. This is especially true of Americans, who have historical traditions of the separation of church and state.

But the Vatican is not just Church—it is also state. In fact, Vatican City is geographically the smallest state or nation in the world, occupying an area of only 109 acres, with, a population of about 1000. Nevertheless, it sends and receives envoys and ambassadors as any other sovereign nation. In fact, for several centuries, the Vatican controlled a vast teritory—the Papal States, which included the city of Rome and other lands in central Italy. All these were lost by 1870.

The Vatican is willing (for various reasons, including its lack of military strength) to cooperate with any secular government that will reciprocate. The semi-official newspaper of the Vatican, *L'Osservatore Romano*, once commented, "The Holy See deals with States as such to guarantee the rights and freedom of the Church, without regard to any other consideration and appraisal." This same article observed that people have the freedom to choose the form of government which they believe to be best.

Therefore, if it appears that the Vatican has not cooperated with the East, it is because the East has not cooperated with the Vatican! In fact, the U.S.S.R. and the Vatican did carry on mutual collaboration soon after the Bolshevik takeover.

Pope Benedict XV organized a relief program to help the Russians during the 1921 famine. Pius XI, who came into office in 1922, continued the efforts, which included trying to establish contacts with the U.S.S.R. Just a few days after the Pope's coronation, a cardinal declared on behalf of the Church at the start of an international conference in Genoa:

> The ultimate principles of the Church imply no objection on its part against a Communist form of government. . . . The Church merely demands that the organization of the state, whatever nature it may be, must not interfere with the freedom of religious worship, nor with the freedom of the priests to discharge the functions of their office.

So even a half century ago, the Catholic Church declared its willingness to work with Communist governments, if they would allow religious freedom. Only the recalcitrance of the Communists prevented this. In spite of the Kremlin's brusque treatment, the Vatican has periodically attempted to approach various Communist nations in Eastern Europe.

The Vatican has good reason to be concerned about Eastern Europe. Over 10 per cent of the Catholics in the world are behind the Iron Curtain. One estimate puts the present total number at 60 million. At the time of the

Russian Revolution, there were only about 4 to 6 million Roman Catholics in Russia (the predominant religion was Russian Orthodox). But in other Eastern countries taken over by Communism, a great number of Catholics naturally came under persecution. There were an estimated 20 million Catholics in Poland before its partition; Hungary and Czechoslovakia together had 15 million more Catholics.

Another calculation put the total number of Catholics, at the beginning of Communist rule, around 45 million. If this figure is correct, one out of eight Catholics went behind the Iron Curtain (many of those have since been killed in "purges" or "persuaded" to give up their religion).

With such an enormous number of Catholics, former Catholics and potential Catholics under Moscow's influence, it is no wonder that Rome is interested in Eastern Europe. It has a vital interest at stake in the area.

So one of the prime reasons for rapprochement attempts by the Vatican is obvious: freedom of Catholics to practice their religion without interference. But many observers consider that purpose secondary to the expansion of Vatican influence in world politics.

Like all political and religious organizations, the Vatican wants *pacem in terram*—peace on earth. By such a quest for peace, it seeks to extend its influence over secular areas.

Such a campaign would give world prestige to the Vatican as an international mediator and peacemaker. It would establish the Pope as the chief agent in bringing about worldwide tranquility. Pope Paul himself recognizes the importance of such a quest. No other pope has even begun to match his unprecedented travels. For example, Pope Paul has gone to Jerusalem, India, Constantinople, the U.N. and Geneva. All these trips have certainly created an image of the Pope as a seeker of peace among the nations of the earth.

One of the biggest roles desired by the Vatican is that of mediator between East and West. Any man who could fulfill such a role would certainly go down in history. Pope Paul assuredly would like to be the one who is credited with bringing about peace between the Communist bloc and the Free World.

As part of the worldwide unity quest, the Vatican has directed strong efforts to bring Eastern Europe into the fold.

Tying right in with the search for peace is the role of the European Common Market or European Economic Community (EEC). The nucleus of the EEC is its Catholic majority. Britain will be the first country in the union with a Protestant majority.

One of the greatest hopes for a united Europe is its ability to serve as a balance of power between East and West. The fact of having Europe united religiously under the banner of Catholicism could well offset political and national animosities—and make the union a doubly more powerful entity.

Realizing this critical point, the Vatican established diplomatic relations with the six Common Market nations in November of 1970, nominating Igino Cardinale as nuncio or ambassador to the Common Market Commission in Brussels. The story in *L'Osservatore Romano* emphasized that the Vatican has always supported efforts to unify Europe without any political reservations.

One of the major arguments for a politically united Europe is that this "Third Power Bloc" could serve as a balance and "referee" between the United States and the U.S.S.R.

If Europe is "united" under a common religion, then the Vatican would have more than just its prestige to help bring about a reconciliation. It would also have the political and economic power of a United States of Europe to back up its efforts.

No such political-religious entity has existed since the Holy Roman Empire. But there are many who would not view a new "Holy Roman Empire" as such a bad innovation. Certainly, for many Europeans, and definitely for the Vatican, a union such as this would have a great many advantages.

A question which still remains is: How can Europe be united if a significant portion of it remains outside EEC jurisdiction and behind the Iron Curtain?

Some very definite trends are clearly visible and with predictable results, unless something unusual occurs. For one thing, a politically united Europe seems inevitable. How long it will take or exactly in what form it will emerge remains to be seen. In spite of the pessimism expressed by some authorities as late as two years ago, the hopes and dreams set down in blueprint for the union continue to take shape in reality.

The exact size of this "United States of Europe" is still undetermined, though some have already suggested the reasonable number of 10 nations. Others would be closely associated. But any final European union seems incomplete without the traditionally European countries of Poland, Hungary, Romania, Czechoslovakia, or Yugoslavia—and of course, East Germany. Will some or possibly even all of these Eastern countries eventually find their way into some sort of European federation? Only time will tell.

De Gaulle's dream of a united Europe from the Atlantic to the Urals seems out of the question, even for the future. Although Russia may be European geographically, it just does not fit in with the rest of Europe. In contrast, some of the Eastern European countries have historically had their ties with the countries of Western Europe. That is why Russia is having a hard time keeping them under control. Only superior military might has held the rusting Iron Curtain from disintegrating.

The Vatican, you can be sure, will continue to do its part in courting the Eastern European countries. Its *Ostpolitik* has been to bring them back into the "fold" for a long time. And that is certainly the path it must continue to travel.

On 22nd December, 1967 Pope Paul VI in the sacred college of cardinals once more expressed his anxiety and care "for that part of Christ's flock still deprived of freedom and of the exercise of the normal rights claimed by Church and religion." He repeated with emphasis the appeal the Council had made to all governments: "The Church asks nothing more of you than freedom. Freedom to believe and to preach its faith, freedom to love God and to serve Him, freedom to live and to disseminate its message of life among the people." Pointing to the many steps taken by the Holy See during the last few years—sometimes with a little success—to alleviate the fate of the persecuted Church, the Pope expressed his bitter disappointment that the result of these attempts was in general not what could be expected.

Here the Pope undoubtedly had in mind the agreement with the Hungarian government signed by Mgr. Casaroli at Budapest on 15th September, 1964. This agreement, greeted with enthusiasm especially in the West, has in reality been of very little use to the Church. This is confirmed by the following passages from a letter recently received from Hungary:

Reports that new bishops' appointments are imminent cause great anxiety both to the interned bishops and those who are unable to carry out their duties, and to the priests and Christians. Seeing that the candidates for the bishoprics must have the absolute approval of the government before they can be appointed, the choice will have to fall on those priests whose reputation is not very high among the people, who are in an overwhelming majority anti-communistic. The best bishops and most of the priests feel such compromise appointments as a slap in the face and a want of appreciation for their twenty years' loyalty to the Church. The ordinary people are indignant or indifferent. It is ascertained with bitterness that in spite of the agreement of 1964 Cardinal Mindszenty and the courageous bishops Shvoy (recently passed away), Endrey, Kisberk, Petery (dead) and Bard have not been rehabilitated, might not take part in the Council nor carry on their duties; that Mgr. Bellon, appointed by the Holy See in 1959, is not consecrated bishop; that the excellent priests, numbering about a thousand, who were forced by the state to leave their pastoral work or were exiled to unimportant parishes, have not been restored to their rights; that the thirty priests who were condemned in a secret trial, after the agreement between Rome and Budapest, for having worked among the youth, are still in prison; that none of the wishes of the Holy See laid down in the protocol added to the agreement have been complied with; that there is no freedom in the administration of the dioceses, no freedom of religious teaching, no freedom of admission to the seminary, no freedom to print religious texts and books in a sufficient number.

The Christians who for twenty years have had to pay for their allegiance to Christ and the Church with heavy sacrifices and the greatest personal disadvantages, are only interested in a true freedom of religion and not in the extension of a pseudo-hierarchy desired by the Communists, which can be nothing else but an instrument in the hands of the government.

For an extension of the hierarchy in the present circumstances can benefit only the Communists who have at their disposition the means to missuse the new bishops for a propaganda to which even in the West too many people are falling victim. For the rest, the Church does not only consist of a hierarchy but in the first place of God's people. These people of God do not ask for new puppet-bishops but for freedom of religion. If the Church of tomorrow is to be saved, everything should be avoided that can cause such discouragement to the faithful Catholics that they will soon have no more strength left to remain faithful. . . .

These then are the high points of Eastern Europe today: there is a Communist satellite zone in a condition of flux and change, as it enters a distinctly new phase of ideological evolution. Old techniques of repression have been abandoned, new recognition has been given to normal human aspirations and desires, new opportunities for trade and tourism present themselves, and an older generation of doctrinaire Communists is yielding to a new wave of youth and experimentation.

How the West reacts to these changes and what are their implications for the long-range evolution of East-West relations? It seems plain that there is a great opportunity and that if we conduct ourselves with wisdom, imagination and restraint, it perhaps will go a long way toward resolving the great ideological cold war of the twentieth century.

There have been heard of the revolution of rising expectations in the

developing countries of the world. The Communist countries of Eastern
Europe are caught in a counter-revolution of rising expectations .

All men have certain natural drives in the political and economic spheres,
including the desire for political expression, for human contact and for
property. As standards of living improve in Eastern Europe, as adequate
housing, health care and education become generally available, as communications and direct exposures with Western societies increase through
tourists who visit from the West—these drives become stronger. They force
Communist governments to change, to adjust to these drives. The first
demand may be freedom to choose one's work. The inevitable result is
freedom to choose how to dispose of the gains of work—more choice, in
other words, in what to buy and where to travel. And eventually, although
this end is certainly not yet in sight, there will undoubtedly be a demand for
freedom of choice in politics.

One can be convinced, therefore, that time is on our side in Eastern
Europe. The trend there is toward freedom—and not away from it. Communism is changing to accommodate this trend, changing more slowly in
some countries—and more rapidly in others. It seems obvious that one can
best hasten this erosion within the Communist world by increasing contact at
every level, and in every sphere of activity, between the countries of the West
and those of Eastern Europe.

There are some definite political steps which one should be prepared to
take in response to the situation. A person should lose no time in ratifying
the Soviet Consular Convention, which might in time be a model for similar
agreements with the nations of Eastern Europe. And one should enact
legislation to promote East-West trade, granting to the nations of Eastern
Europe the non-discriminatory, or so-called most-favored nation tariff
treatment they so much desire.

There may be other clear opportunities for political and diplomatic action
on our part as time goes on, particularly if one is fortunate enough to be able
to take steps in such areas as arms control. But the essential, continuing
challenge is a philosophical one and it is one which one will have learned to
anticipate and respond to effectively if he fully appreciates what is now
transpiring in Eastern Europe.

In July, 1975, all ecclesiastical and political circles of Rome found themselves confronted with Rome's tragic figure and the human tragedy surrounding him. The Supreme Metropolitan of Lvov, Cardinal Joseph Slipyj
was once more faced with the dilemma:

> —either to follow the call of his Church and the request of ten million Greek-
> Catholic Ukrainians or to obey the Pope; either to join the protests of the
> Ukrainian *Anno Santo* pilgrims from the American Diaspora against the Vati-
> can's *Ostpolitik* or to keep silent—and only pray in secret for the national
> Catholic Church of West Ukraine, since thirty years doomed by the Soviets to
> nonexistence and forcibly united with the Great Russian Patriarchate of Mos-
> cow.

The spokesmen of the Ukrainian Rome pilgrims request the Eastern-rite
Cardinal to insist on his being nominated Patriarch of the Ukrainian
Church, i.e., claim the same rights as the Patriarchate of Moscow. Since May
24, however, the Metropolitan has certainly read again and again Paul VI's
letter imploring him to renounce such requests and not to incriminate

Church politics vis-a-vis the Soviet Union.

However, the diplomats of the Vatican may argue that for the first time since 1945 their *Ostpolitik* has recently succeeded in laying down altogether the existence and vital interests of Eastern-rite Catholics vis-a-vis a Communist, Slavic and Orthodox state, in a common document—the communique issued on the occasion of the visit of the Bulgarian State and Party Chief, Zhivkov, on June 27, 1975, mentioned "the problem of the Bulgarian Catholics of both rites."

On the other hand, those criticizing the Vatican *Ostpolitik* argue that it was easy to have the Bulgarian, inexperienced in these matters, discreetly mention these problems; the Russians, however, would certainly know how to censure and correct this in practice.

The Vatican-Moscow detente since the early 1960's and the development of increasingly close ecumenical relations between the Holy See and the Moscow Patriarchate has radically changed the Vatican's overt treatment of the Catholics in the USSR and its public attitude to the Soviet religious policies.

While the Holy See has since Vatican II suspended its public criticism of Soviet religious policies, accepted the principle that henceforth all appointments of Catholic bishops or diocesan administrators within the USSR must be made with prior consent of the Soviet authorities, and has come close to a *de facto* recognition of the Soviet liquidation of the Ukrainian Greek Catholic Church —little has been offered in return by the Kremlin. To be sure, the Soviet government ceased open attacks on the Holy See in its foreign propaganda, but it hardly moderated the tone of its anti-Catholic agitation at home; and it allowed the Russian Orthodox Church to respond positively to the Vatican's ecumenical approaches. It permitted selected Roman Catholic bishops and clerics to attend the Ecumenical Council and to pay occasional visits to Rome; it gave its *placet* to the appointment of several new Latin-rite bishops; and it allowed the publication of a few church books in Latvia and Lithuania; but in very limited printings—"concessions" which amounted to the partial lifting of arbitrary restrictions imposed by regime upon the Church's rights "guaranteed" by its own Constitution.

These fruits of the Vatican-Moscow detente benefited to some extent the Roman Catholic Church in Latvia and Lithuania, though not without some less desirable consequences: the danger of infiltration of the Church leadership by "progressive" bishops and canons enjoying the support of the authorities but lacking confidence of believers; and the Vatican's diplomatic silence in the face of the continuing Soviet violations of the rights of the Catholic clergy and faithful. The apprehension that "the Vatican is being deceived" in its "dialogue with the Soviet government," that Roman Catholics have been "betrayed" and abandoned by the Roman Curia, has been repeatedly voiced by the underground *Chronicle of the Catholic Church in Lithuania*:

> . . . while defending victims of discrimination all over the world, (the Holy See) barely recalls the "Church of Silence and Suffering," does not bring up and does not condemn covert and overt persecution of the faithful in the Soviet Union.

The *Chronicle* noted the demoralizing effects of such actions of the Roman Curia as the conferring of ecclestiastical distinctions on "certain priests 'loyal' to the Soviet system" and the nomination as bishops of "the handpicked candidates of the government." "The most deadly thing for the Catholic Church in believers" it had "reunited with the Russian Orthodox Church." This apparent *de facto* recognition of the liquidation of the Ukrainian Catholic Church with the USSR was strikingly exemplified in the failure of the Vatican's official representative at the 1971 Local Sobor of the Russian Church, Cardinal J. Villebrands, to protest against the Sobor's resolution (read in his presence) which ratified the so-called "reunion" of the Uniates with the Moscow Patriarchate. Neither was there any official protest issued by the Vatican against this "unilateral act" after its delegation returned from the Moscow Sobor. Such attitude of the Holy See, the fraternization of its representatives with the persecutors of the Uniate Church, and its negative response to demands for greater autonomy of the Ukrainian Catholic Church abroad—have embittered and divided the Uniate Church both inside and outside the USSR, while strengthening the position of those formerly Uniate priests and laymen who had abandoned the persecuted Church. To the anti-Uniate propaganda in the Ukraine, this seeming "betrayal" of the *Catacomb Church* by the Vatican has offered a potent weapon to demoralize this Church's following.

The "unofficial" Vatican position has been less conciliatory to Moscow, than suggested by the official pronouncements and actions, or by the silence and inaction of the Roman Curia. *Annuario Pontificio* continues to list the Greek Catholic dioceses in the USSR (as well as those in Poland and Romania) despite repeated Soviet protests, the Vatican Radio continues its religious broadcasts for Catholics in the Soviet Union, including Ukrainian Uniates, which are not "jammed" by the regime; and, privately, the Roman Curia keeps reassuring the Uniates abroad that it has not forgotten their brethren in the Western Ukraine, that it is powerless in the face of the adamant Soviet refusal to reopen the Uniate issue; and that "the time is not ripe" for the realization of the aspirations of the Ukrainian Catholics in the West to have all their dioceses and those in the Ukraine unified in an autonomous "Patriarchate of Kiev and Halych."

There are, nevertheless, some powerful forces within the Roman Catholic Church that would apparently be willing to "sacrifice" the Ukrainian Uniate Church to the cause of a lasting reconciliation between Rome and the Russian Church and which may be inclined to accept the agreement of the Moscow Patriarchate that the "anachronistic" Uniate "bridgehead" is the most important "obstacle" to the truly ecumenical relations between the two Churches, and that once this "obstacle" has been removed even a reunion of the Christian East and West may become a real prospect.

Church-state relations in Poland and Hungary, the two most Roman Catholic countries in East Europe, are improving.

Elsewhere in the Communist bloc, however, the Vatican's *Ostpolitik* has been less successful. Although the tough repressions that prevailed until the 1960's have abated, most denominations are still restricted. The Communist regimes have set the terms on which they tolerate the churches.

In Hungary, relaxation began 10 years ago with a first "normalization" accord with the Holy See. It culminated in February with the installation of the first primate of Hungary in active office for nearly 30 years.

With the appointment of a new Hungarian Bishop and an Auxiliary April 12, 1976, the Vatican has at last achieved its aim of filling all of Hungary's long-vacant dioceses.

It is the first time all eleven Hungarian dioceses have had Bishops since the Communists took power after World War II.

The two appointments in the dioceses of Gyor and Veszprem were made after the usual consultations between the Hungarian government and the Vatican.

Pope Paul VI has named Bishop Kornel Pataky to fill the last vacant diocese in Hungary as Bishop of Gyor, and named Father Laszlo Toth Auxiliary Bishop of Veszprem.

Father Toth was formerly a parish priest in Ajka, a mining center in the Veszprem diocese.

Bishop Pataky has been apostolic administrator of Gyor since January, 1975, when—after a long series of negotiations—the Vatican named five new bishops and transferred four others to fill all but two of Hungary's dioceses.

In Poland, where Communist officials blithely admit a majority of the population is or calls itself Catholic, compromise began in 1970 with the relatively tolerant leadership of Edward Gierek. Since then, church-state conflict has lessened.

Recently, the government made striking—even surprising— concessions to church opinion in modifying amendments to the Constitution. Contacts with the Vatican are not far short of a formal diplomatic relationship.

In both Poland and Hungary, this acceptance of a more substantive role for the churches has meant considerable gains for their governments. It has enhanced their standing with Western countries with which they seek greater economic cooperation in trade and technology. It also has aided them in the process of domestic conciliation and stability.

In each country, the Catholic hierarchy includes bishops in the "liberal" mold of the late Pope John XXIII. As one Hungarian bishop put it, they are independent clerics who believe the churches of today can be "moderately progressive" and cooperate with the state on common social projects without weakening their religious commitment.

At his recent enthronement, the new Hungarian primate, the Archbishop of Esztergom, Laszlo Lekai, said the "grinding pressures" of the past were gone. He spoke of "a sense of reassurance and calm thanks to which bishops and faithful now can serve in a harmonious way our faith and our country."

Such "assurance," however, has yet to reach most of the churches in other Soviet bloc countries.

Promising talks between the Vatican and Czechoslovakia broke down in 1968 after the ouster of Prague's liberal regime. Only five years later did they resume, and the appointment of four bishops followed.

Now the talks are suspended again. Nine bishoprics remain vacant, and several hundred priests are barred from performing their office. A campaign to make atheist teaching an integral and obligatory part of the educational system has intensified.

The Protestant churches in Czechoslovakia are under constant pressure. Although the Orthodox church, which is linked to the Moscow Patriarchate, and the Czech Hussite church suffer less harassment, the enrollment at their seminaries has been limited in recent years.

Romania, whose foreign economic policy requires Western goodwill, has made some small moves toward better relations with the Roman Catholic and Anglican churches abroad. At home, however, both are subject to highly restrictive "regulations of religious cults." The Uniate Church, which recognizes the Pope as its leader, was dissolved by the Communists in 1948.

Recently, Romania has put pressure on its Baptists. They are limited by law to small and even clandestine congregations because they balk at making the oath of allegiance to the state demanded of every Romanian citizen. Although they protest their patriotic loyalty, the Baptists decline to take such an oath as a matter of Christian conscience.

Outside the bloc, Yugoslavia resumed diplomatic ties with the Holy See in 1966 with considerable gains in religious toleration in the Catholic republics of Croatia and Slovenia.

There is some concern that new legislation may reduce the "social" activities of the churches there, but the bishops are being consulted by the governments of the republics. The draft legislation includes the substantial guarantees embodied in the protocol with the Vatican.

This *Realpolitik* with its delayed effect is also based on a Christian, pastoral and apostolic vision which precisely the last two Popes, John XXIII and Paul VI, cannot be denied. In their view all means of diplomacy, protocol and *Realpolitik* have always served the purpose to widen, step by step, pastoral freedom within the Communist sphere of power, to have the connections between Catholics and Rome authorized and to make the ecumenical dialogue possible with the Orthodox East European Churches, on the one hand and with the spontaneous movement of religious revival in Russia, on the other.

The tragedy of the Pope and his East European Church leaders resides precisely in this dilemma: Unless John XXIII—the Ukrainian Church having been exterminated—had taken up relations with Khrushchev the Supreme Metropolitan, Cardinal Joseph Slipyj, would not have been released six months later, after 14 years of imprisonment in Soviet prisons and concentration camps, and expelled to Rome where, since that time, he bears witness to the living Ukrainian Church but must simultaneously live in a permanent moral conflict with Pope Paul VI.

> Even in the most secularized countries of western Europe, secularism is being questioned by sophisticated Christians. Secularism simply represses too many things—suffering and dying, for example.
>
> What I think is happening is that people are discovering that faith comes alive in suffering. Many are talking here about the cost of discipleship, and the fact is that many delegates are paying a high price in their home countries to be faithful to the gospel. It's an old cliche but it's true—the nearer we are to the cross, the closer we come to one another.
>
> Once again suffering is uniting Christians. I sense there is an enormous desire here to find a community stronger that the forces that divide us. Even a year ago, at committee meetings, some were lost in a kind of provincialism, using the banner contextual theology. Now, we are coming out of that. We are discovering together a textual theology, that what we have in common is the biblical message.

Attacks on the Vatican which have recently been appearing in the Soviet ecclesiastical and secular press indicate that the Moscow Patriarchate has joined the World Council of Churches not only to promote the basic theses of Soviet foreign policy but to promote the formation of a common front against Russian Catholicism as an irreconcilable opponent of the materialist world outlook and Communist doctrine. This is apparently one reason why the Moscow Patriarchate is so active in defending the concept of a federative ecclesiastical union in the ecumenical movement as a counter to the concept of a centralized union as proposed by the Roman Catholic Church. Anti-Catholic activities in the USSR had been stepped up with the approach to the Catholic Church's 21st Ecumenical Council, which the Soviets feared may provide a platform for official ecclesiastical condemnation of Communist theory and practice, a fear well justified by proposals addressed to the Central Commission for convening and conducting the Catholic Ecumenical Council.

Outstanding examples of the current sharp anti-Catholic attacks have appeared in two articles, one in the *Journal of the Moscow Patriarchate* and the other in the Authoritative Journal, *World Economics and International Relations*. In the article in the former journal, "The struggle of Orthodoxy with the Catholic Union," the Moscow Patriarchate labels the Vatican as an unquestionable enemy of Orthodoxy.

The Vatican has not been yielding to atheistic ideology in dealing with Church-state affairs in Eastern European countries, according to the Rome Jesuit magazine *Civilta Catolica*.

The removal of the heroic figure of Cardinal Mindszenty from his last ties with his native land has caused criticism of the *Ostpolitik* of Pope Paul, that is, the continuing policy of reducing long standing tensions between the Catholic Church and the Eastern European Communist regimes.

> The *Ostpolitik* of the Holy See . . . cannot be understood as a yielding to an atheistic ideology nor as a choice in favor of a government or regime. It is only to be understood as a rightful and respectful effort to guarantee in the best manner possible the life and action of the Church.

Rejecting charges that such decisions as the dismissal of the Hungarian cardinal constitute

> a violation of the rights of the human person or are Machiavellian, however, the norm in those cases has been the need to act quickly before it might be too late.

Prolonged absence of bishops from dioceses and the attendant evils this poses for the faithful require the Church to ask "personal, yet legitimate and even sometimes rightful sacrifices" for the good of souls.

> The article also rejected the contention that the Pope's decision showed less respect or diminished consideration for the person of the Cardinal.

> Before it (the Pope's decision) was made public and effective there was a respectful, open, understanding and patient dialogue between him (the Cardinal) and the Holy Father. And indeed it was a sign of regard (on the Pope's part) not to insist on a renunciation which (the Cardinal) did not wish.

> Holy See has taken on itself the responsibility for the step, notwithstanding . . . the anticipation of criticism and hate. Given the need for a concrete solution of the problems in many eastern European nations, it concluded, the Holy See holds it to be its duty to do what is possible in an honest and Christian way to assure in these nations room for the life and action of the Church.

SILENT CHURCHES

World Council of Churches

One of the most important acts of the third General Assembly of the World Council of Churches held in New Delhi, India, in November and December, 1961, with more than 600 delegates from Protestant and Orthodox churches, was the admission to membership of the Russian Orthodox Church, whose delegation of the Moscow Patriarchate, consisting of 16 members, was headed by Archbishop Nikodim, Chairman of the Department of the Patriarchate. The official admission of the Russian Orthodox Church, and of the Orthodox churches of the Soviet satellite countries of Romania, and Poland, took place on November 20. This controversial action by the World Council of Churches makes fresh interest attach to the question of the present status of religion in the Soviet Union and the relation between the Russian Orthodox Church and the Soviet regime.

The decision to seek admission to the World Council was adopted at a Russian Orthodox Synod on March 30, 1961 and ratified by a council of Russian Orthodox Archbishops on July 18, 1961. In his speech at the latter Synod, Patriarch Aleksei gave the following description of the relation of the Russian Orthodox Church to the ecumenical movement and its future role in this movement:

> At the present time we have changed our position in relation to the World Council of Churches. However, even previously, we Orthodox Christians had an attitude to Western Christians that was not cold and certainly not scornful. . . . Now, when those who have fallen away from the church are themselves seeking unity with it, we should meet them halfway in order to facilitate their seekings. . . . When the Russian Orthodox Church is admitted to the World Council of Churches, our representatives will witness in it to the truth preserved in the Orthodox Church. . . . Under the present circumstances we cannot help but see indications of the need to encourage a spirit of Christian community and to link the Christians of the East and West. . . . Our mission under present conditions is to show Western Christians the light of Orthodoxy.

In view of the degree to which the official actions of the Moscow Patriarchate are under the control of the Soviet authorities, it is clear that the decision to enter the World Council reflects a change in state policy. In 1948 at the first General Assembly of the World Council of Churches in Amsterdam, the Moscow Patriarchate had refused to enter the World Council of Churches on the grounds that the Council "mainly pursues anti-democratic and not ecclesiatical aims," and that the entire ecumenical movement, "having lost its ecclesiastical character, has turned into a weapon for creating a single front of Protestant Churches against atheism and Communism." The Moscow Patriarchate is now softening its previous categorical formulations and, without repudiating its former refusal to enter the Council, explains that at that time the ecumenical movement was too much under the influence of "religious groups interested in solving or formulating political problems agitating public opinion in the West," and that the Moscow Patriarchate could not avoid regarding this attitude as "an encroachment of the vanity of this world upon the sphere of religious relationship."

In spite of this criticism of the encroachment of politics on religion, the message from Patriarch Aleksei of Moscow and all Russia which Archbishop Nikodim read to the Council Assembly consisted of political statements of proposals of an obviously political character. For example, it expressed a wish that the Assembly call upon the governments of the great powers to convene a conference on the highest level to solve the problem of reducing international tension and begin negotiations at once "on universal and complete disarmament," both of which demands are in line with the present Soviet government policy. The same effort to direct the day-by-day activities of the World Council of Churches into political channels was also evident in the ideas on this subject put forward in the official journal of the Moscow Patriarchate:

> It would merit surprise if Christians strove for mutual understanding only in the field of understanding of religious values, paying no attention to the field of international and inter-personal relations. . . . The question of peace throughout the world has been raised with particularly great acuteness just in our time and this, of course, is not a question of politics alone. . . . The world wars could not but be regarded by Christians as a very great evil. And Christians could not avoid undertaking a struggle against this evil.

Rather oddly in view of the more than 40 years of Soviet struggle with religion, the delegation of the Moscow Patriarchate at the World Council repeatedly supported its proposals with the claim that at least two-thirds of the Soviet population are members of the Russian Orthodox Church. (The leaders of the ecumenical movement estimate the number of believers at approximately thirty million, or about one-seventh). The Moscow Patriarchate supplemented its claims of strength by presentation of a "gift" of money, building materials, and even carpets for the new World Council of Churches building in Geneva.

The political efforts of the delegation of the Russian Orthodox Church were crowned with some success. In its report on foreign policy, the Assembly opposed the arming of West Germany with nuclear weapons, demanded the immediate renewal of disarmament talks and warned against "further acts of provocation" in Berlin.

The World Council of Churches, with headquarters in Geneva, Switzerland, is a vast ecumenical organization. Its aim is the reunion of communities of Christians, long split into a chaos of denominations and sects and cults: an end devoutly to be desired. But the WCC has become involved in political attitudes and commitments that have much reduced its reputation and diminished contributions of funds from various churches and many individuals.

The World Council of Churches at its founding assembly in Amsterdam in 1948 laid down this:

> It is part of the mission of the Church to raise its voice of protest wherever men are the victims of terror, wherever they are denied such fundamental rights as the right to be secure against arbitrary arrest, and wherever governments use torture and cruel punishments to intimidate the consciences of men.

A noble statement of aims . . . yet the WCC has said hardly a word in all its 29 years about the total suppression of liberty in Soviet Russia.

In the summer of 1973 the WCC's Central Committee met in Geneva. It discussed "the violence of social structures" and it drew up a list which was later published of examples of oppression and discrimination drawn from several countries. In the USA, it said, Christians in civil rights movement were fighting against "a systematic oppression armed with weapons both brutal and subtle;" in Northern Ireland "Christians oppose Christians . . . atrocities are committed by groups wearing labels inherited from the Church's past. . . ."

However, the World Council seemed to have overlooked the fact that several hundred million people in Soviet Russia and Eastern Europe are kept in place by electrified fences, trip-wire operated mines and guard dogs. That intellectuals are subjected to "psychiatric" treatment to cure them of their anti-social tendencies. That Russia keeps a slave population of over a million in labor camps living on starvation rations and forced to do long hours of heavy labor. That Soviet citizens are under constant surveillance by the secret police and are punished for any deviation from the ideological norm. That there is no free press or radio since every word that is made public must first be approved by the state censor. And that its citizens lack the basic right of religious freedom: a man may be sent to a labor camp for holding a prayer meeting in his home and a mother may be forcibly deprived of her children for teaching them their prayers.

There was one very brave man at that Central Committee meeting. He got up and asked if a reference to the suppression of human rights in Eastern Europe could be included in the list. His suggestion was voted on and heavily defeated: only two out of 120 members supported him. Yet only the previous year at its Utrecht meeting the WCC had rededicated itself "to assist in the implementation of human rights wherever they are being violated seeking to avoid all ideological prejudice."

During the 1970's the most dismaying action by the World Council was the granting of subsidies to various African terrorist organizations operating against the Republic of South Africa.

In Angola, on the Atlantic shore of Africa, 21 children were massacred along with five women and four men, at the village of Rivungo. The terrorists who slaughtered them were guerrillas of the "Movement for the Liberation of Angola," based in the Congo. This MPLA is one of several fanatic groups intent upon bringing to Angola the ruin which fell upon the Congo for several years.

They are said to receive funds from the Communist powers. It is certain that the MPLA, or *Movimento Popular de Liberacao de Angola,* is to receive

$20,000 from the World Council of Churches.

That's right—the World Council of Churches, which in September, 1970, through its Executive Council, voted this grant to the child-killers of the Angolan frontier, along with similar grants to 18 similar African and Asiatic organizations allegedly concerned with "racial justice."

The World Council's bureaucracy makes no effort to conceal such benefactions; indeed, they are proud of their generosity, even though they have begun to worry that it might produce a reduction of gifts to the WCC from old-fangled obscurants who thought that Christians were supposed to love their neighbors.

The WCC functionaries describe their gifts to the MPLA and to two other Angolan revolutionary groups as "intended for economic, educational, health and social welfare programs." The dead of Rivungo did not benefit from these humanitarian undertakings. The WCC claimed that these three gangs of atrocity men control about a third of Angola—which is like asserting that the Black Panthers control a third of America.

"It is true that the World Council action has some risks attached to it," a release by the WCC's Information Office runs; "it is even conceivable that history will judge it to have been a mistake." But why worry about it? It gives the WCC's Executive Council a warm glow to think of the grateful terrorists. You can buy a lot of ammunition with $20,000, and shoot more reactionary children.

That the terrorist gangs along Angola's frontiers represent "racial justice" is a notion that can be advanced only by liars or fools. Most of the victims of these terrorists are black Africans. For that matter, Portugal's African provinces already are more thoroughly and successfully integrated, racially, than any other regions in the world. Nearly all the inhabitants of Angola would be classified in America as Negroes. The dominant element in that land consists of people of mingled African and European ancestry. There is no racial discrimination of any kind, and anyone can vote who has a rudimentary education.

So what kind of "racial justice" are MPLA and other fanatics bringing to Angola? The "racial justice" of Soviet Russia, which persecutes Jews and other minorities? The "racial justice" of the government of the Sudan, which slaughters black Christians?

At the Last Judgment, perhaps the murdered children of Rivungo may appear to testify against the bureaucracy of the World Council of Churches. But, of course, the Executive Council of the WCC does not believe in any Last Judgment: that's merely a myth of the primitive church. What does the World Church believe in? Why, pass the Lord, and praise the ammunition.

Those guerrilla gangs actually have been diminishing in numbers and effectiveness during the past year, in part because they have outraged African tribes in the regions where they operate. But the WCC, by giving money to this failing fanatic cause, in effect prolongs the struggle and the killing. How ecumenical!

A gentleman long associated with the World Council recently remarked that the great majority of the WCC's supporters look upon the organization as devoted to ecumenical labors; if they understood how deeply involved the World Council has become in international politics—including the politics of terror—they would be deeply shocked. And he suggests that one sees at work the subtle influence of Soviet Russia upon the World Council.

How can a Christian organization become the dupe of an atheist and totalist regime? Why, in part because the Russian Orthodox clergy in the council claim that they represent by far the largest single body of Christian communicants among all the 200-odd churches affiliated with the council.

The WCC defers to the Russians proportionately. But the Russian Orthodox Church is a mere puppet of the Soviet regime which permitted the Orthodox hierarchy to join the WCC only because this might enable the men in the Kremlin to influence world opinion through the WCC's bureaucracy and propaganda apparatus.

The Russian Orthodox people in the WCC claim that there exists in the USSR some 22,000 functioning churches, an extravagant assertion which nobody in the WCC challenged. Actually, according to Russian government sources, at the time Khrushchev fell from power there were only 7,500 churches still functioning in the Soviet Union; there may be fewer now; moreover, the congrgations of many of those churches are dismally small. But the WCC bureaucracy finds it prudent to ignore these facts.

Also the WCC has found it best to sweep under the carpet the undoubted fact that the Soviet Union engages in persecutions of Christians, Jews and Moslems.

In 1967 Baptists in Soviet Russia appealed to the WCC for aid, sending proof that more than 200 Baptists were in Soviet prison camps, in consequence of deliberate persecution. The council merely acknowledged receipt of these documents, and has done nothing whatever, it appears, to intervene in favor of these brothers in Christ although at the next meeting of the WCC's executive committee, the WCC dignitaries endorsed protests against Greece and South Africa for imprisoning political opponents.

Opposition to domination of undue influence by Soviet Russia exists within the WCC. Yet the Russian Orthodox hierarchy—wholly subservient to the Soviet state—moved their way gradually toward more positive power in the WCC, feeling confident that the council's general secretary was Dr. Eugene Carson Blake, an American citizen—no Communist, but in effect a person who sees no enemies to the left.

When, early in 1967, Dr. Blake was chosen as the WCC's new chief officer, the Moscow Patriarchate enthusiastically applauded his selection. Well they might. In contrast with his independent (if self-opinionated) positions when he was a power in American Protestantism, he differed almost servilely to Russian Orthodox attitudes.

It is much in the Soviet interest that terrorism should continue in southern Africa—dividing Western allies, seriously draining the slender resources of Portugal and embarrassing richer South Africa, diverting attention from Soviet imperialism, opening a way for massive Soviet influence in Africa generally.

Without openly demanding that the WCC support guerrillas in Africa, the Soviet-dominated Russian Orthodox clergy in the WCC can use its votes and influence for that grim purpose. In several other instances, the WCC has issued pronunciamentos on world crises which favor Soviet interests—one during the Cuban missile crisis of 1962 being expecially notorious.

It is significant that the WCC does nothing to assist the Negro Christians of southern Sudan, for years slaughtered by the troops of the Moslem government at Khartoum. Those victims of the upper Nile mean nothing to the

Kremlin. As matters are drifting, the WCC may become increasingly the dupe but also the instrument of Soviet foreign policy.

With Communist forces gaining control of Portugal and her overseas Provinces, the international Left is stepping up its attack upon the Republic of South Africa—a bastion of anti-Communism and Western Civilization on the African Continent. Taking a leading role in this assault is the World Council of Churches.

At its outset the WCC stated that it wanted to bring about "Christian unity" and heal the "scandalous divisions" within Christendom. In this regard, the WCC has made overtures to the Catholic Church and there have been recently-expressed hopes of a possible "reunion of Christendom."

The true radical character of the WCC surfaced in the early 1960's. In 1961 the Russian Orthodox Church and other Eastern European Satellite churches joined the WCC. The Russian Orthodox and other Satellite Churches are not independent religious institutions, but are instead mere departments of the ruling Communist governments. As the Senate Judiciary Committee pointed out in its exhaustive study, *The Church and State Under Communism*, "the church is needed for selling Soviet foreign policy and propaganda." Since the Russian Orthodox Church joined the WCC, many Protestant Church delegations have visited the Soviet Union and almost without exception write favorable reports on the religious situation in that country. Interestingly enough, the USSR has been trying to use bogus "Moslems" for similar propaganda purposes in the Middle East.

As some of the European nations released their African colonies and formed synthetic mini-states, the WCC began to preoccupy itself with social, political, and economic problems and demonstrated a growing sympathy with international socialism and a hatred for Western capitalism. In 1962 the WCC condemned the U.S. for its "anti-Communist" handling of the Cuban Missile Crisis. Finally, in 1966, the WCC committed itself to revolutionary change and in 1970 established a fund to assist U.S. deserters and draft dodgers seeking asylum in Sweden and Canada. It also sent medical supplies to North Vietnam and started a fund for the support of terrorism in South Africa. In 1972 the WCC established a Special Fund to Combat Racism, with South Africa, Rhodesia and the Portugese Provinces being the principal targets.

The WCC today has a totally non-religious look and employs numerous radical sociologists, economists and political activists. Under a new definition of "missionary work," the WCC publicly claims that the terrorists it now supports are "Christian freedom fighters" and attempts to convince sincere Christians that the terrorists are engaged in a holy crusade and thus perform a "sacred duty."

African Christian Churches have roundly condemned the WCC since it first gave monetary grants to terrorists in 1970. The Anglican Bishop of Johannesburg, the Rt. Rev. Leslie Stradling, accused the WCC of having "almost forgotten its aim of promoting love and unity among Christians" and of being "so occupied with activism as to have little time left to spare for Christ as the Savior of the world." Criticism has mounted during the past years, but the WCC has responded with even more radical measures and pronouncements.

The director of the WCC's program to combat racism is a Netherlands sociologist, Dr. Baldwin Sjollema. Speaking in London in the summer of

1973, Sjollema attacked the idea of bringing about economic or political reforms in Southern Africa. Instead, he talked of "radical reform" and supports wholesale terrorism as the better alternative. Sjollema and other WCC leaders are most concerned about the rising standard of living enjoyed by black South Africans. Sjollema has recently argued that improving the standard of living and economic growth will lessen agitation and inhibit revolutionary change.

While the WCC has been claiming to be a "world's conscience," this has not stopped it from overlooking real humanitarian problems in other parts of the world. The WCC has failed to address itself to the mass slaughter that has taken place in Burundi and Rawanda. Idi Amin's Uganda, where the most blatant kind of racism is government policy, has not been the subject of WCC criticism. Nor has the WCC shown much concern for the victims of the West African drought that has affected over ten million lives in the ministates of Chad, Mali, Mauritania, Niger, Upper Volta and Senegal. The WCC was also silent in 1968 when the Soviet Union invaded Czechoslovakia, finally expressing some "regrets" only after the Soviet objectives had been achieved. The 1972 political trials of dissidents in Czechoslovakia and Yugoslavia were treated with silence and the exiled Romanian Christian leader, the Rev. Richard Wurmbrand, has testified to the fact that persecuted Christians behind the Iron Curtain have never received any meaningful assistance from the world body.

The WCC has given money to terrorists aiming to destroy the Kunene Dam on the border of Angola and South West Africa. The dam can generate much hydro-electric power to benefit underdeveloped areas and improve living standards. Yet, the WCC's Sjollema has viewed the dam as "disastrous," and reaffirmed the WCC's support of the saboteurs.

Now Dr. Philip Potter from West India is the general secretary of the WCC and has admitted that the organization has no effective control over the way the "liberation movement" spend the grants donated by Christians. He has said that while he abhors violence, the terrorists "are fighting against oppression which is violence of a differend kind."

The Communists are making impressive gains around the world and hope to achieve control of the key strategic areas of the world. One of these primary targets is South Africa, which has the largest Free World deposits of gold and is master of the Cape of Good Hope. The WCC is playing an increasingly critical role in the demise of South Africa by providing moral and financial support of the Communist terrorists.

The World Council of Churches has made a third set of grants totaling $200,000, through its Program to Combat Racism.

More than half the sum will go to black "liberation movements" in white-controlled areas of Africa. These movements are aligned with revolutionary and terrorist groups.

The largest of the 25 allocations is $25,000 to the Mozambique Institute of FRELIMO and $25,000 to the African Independence Party of Guinea and Cape Verde Islands (PAIGC), whose leader, Dr. Amilcar Cabral, was assassinated in mid-January, 1973.

The new grants, approved by the WCC Executive Committee, meeting in Gangalore, India, bring to $600,000 the amount distributed by the controversial effort.

Referring to an upsurge in guerilla raids in Rhodesia from across the Mozambique border, the Salisbury Radio said:

> This is the nature of the unholy war to which the WCC is contributing. It is a war waged by stealth, with modern weapons, with the object of striking terror into the hearts of peaceful and defenseless people.

Shortly before Christmas, a band of raiders—armed with Soviet-made AK-47 Kalashnikov rifles, rocket launchers and land mines— crossed into Rhodesia through the northeastern border of Mozambique.

The black guerillas shot up two farmhouses 90 miles north of Salisbury, wounding a white farmer and his two daughters. Three weeks later, another band of terrorists killed two white land inspectors near Mount Darwin.

> Behind the rockets, which were fired in the night at farmhouses, behind the land mines and the other weapons, stands the money from the World Council of Churches.

Revolutions may be a regrettable necessity under some sets of circumstances but for the Christian Churches to provide money that can easily be used to purchase guns does seem to be a bit at odds with the Gospel—particularly when the money comes, for the most part, from members of American congregations who could have the odd notion that Jesus came to preach love and not hatred.

The argument in favor of the World Council's involvement with "liberation" movements is that this is the way to become socially relevant, but the sorry history of 2,000 years offers melancholy evidence that whenever the Churches as organized bodies become involved explicitly and officially with political movements, both the Church and the movements suffer in the long run.

In October and November, 1971, *Reader's Digest* published two devastating articles on the World Council of Churches. In April, 1972 the World Council responded with "Should Churches Play it Safe" through J. Irwin Miller, past president of the National Council of Churches.

The substance of Miller's retort is that the World Council is merely fulfilling its "prophetic role." He says that the "role of prophet is active, often disruptive and always painful," and concludes, "I believe that the World Council of Churches is only practicing what Christianity has always been about."

Undoubtedly, the major criticism of Miller's approach (apart from the fact that he never quite speaks to the issue) is his failure to distinguish between false and true prophets, thus leading to maintain that the ruling hierarchy of the World Council of Churches is the very embodiment of wolves in sheep's clothing.

The former false prophets, wolves in sheep's clothing, denied the God of Holy Scripture much like their present-day counterparts. And even Billy Graham admitted, "There is no doubt that secularism, materialism, and even Marxism not only have invaded the church, but deeply penetrated it."

Christian Century once wrote, "The God of the fundamentalist is one God, and the God of the modernist is another." The modernist's God is a humanistically contrived God, and it is this kind of God the hierarchy of the World Council of Churches worships.

Indeed, it was G. Bromley Oxnam, one of the first presidents of the World Council who referred to the God of the Old Testament as a "dirty bully."

And Arthur Ramsey, another past president of the World Council of Churches not only denied the historicity of Adam (something neither Christ nor Paul did) but further argued, "Heaven . . . is not a place for Christians only. Those who have led a good life on earth but found themselves unable to believe in God will not be debarred from heaven. I expect to meet some present-day atheists there." Ramsey might be meeting some atheists, but, as one might gently put it—not in heaven!

The Digest in November, 1971, wrote,

> Nowhere has the World Council been more delinquent than in its refusal to champion the tens of thousands of persecuted religionists in the Soviet Union—those minority religious groups outside the Soviet approved churches. In the WCC Geneva files are exhaustive documentations from these groups who have refused to bow to Moscow; evidence abounds of wholesale closing of churches, of thousands of Christians harassed or sent to slave labor camps for nothing more than having Bibles, opening their homes to religious services, instructing their children in religion.

J. Irwin Miller did not deny the charge! Instead, he chose to remain silent and talk instead of the WCC's need for "the prophetic role." One would think, however, that speaking out against such religious repression would be part of the "prophetic role." Indeed, it is fortunate Miller did not deny the charge for the Russian author Solzhenitsyn loudly condemned the Russian Orthodox Church and the Soviet government for its part in closing churches, banning religious instruction, etc.

Solzhenitsyn said, "A church dictatorially directed by atheists is a spectacle that has not been seen for 2,000 years." Solzhenitsyn told more truth about Communism and the Russian Orthodox Church in one Lenten Letter than the World Council of Churches since 1948!

In 1962 J. Irwin Miller led a group of Americans to Russia. He said, after returning from his three-week tour,

> In many ways you find that Russia possesses an almost old-fashioned government, conservative, almost to the point of being Victorian. Many of their individual and corporate standards of morality are taken whole directly from Christianity with only the Christian terminology dropped.

What Miller forgot to mention was that when the Communists took over Russian in 1917, divorce, free love and abortion were free to overflowing. But after the Communist "experiment" threatened to collapse the state, the Soviet authorities found it necessary to make laws which placed sanctions upon all three.

In a word, the Communists found it necessary to return to approximately the same moral code found in Christian-oriented countries. It seems that the Communists discovered that a nation must more or less generally observe the basic principles of the nautral law—or perish.

Then, too, Miller's naivety certainly would not have fooled Solzhenitsyn who is undoubtedly aware of the 83 million human beings who paid with their lives for the establishment of Russian Communism! But Miller, no doubt, fooled those who wished to be fooled (whose numbers sometimes appear to be legion).

According to Miller, the WCC has a "concern for human beings," but he did not say if the WCC had any concern for those millions still suffering under Communist dictatorships. In fact, the WCC has had personages such as John C. Bennett who finds in Communism "many things to approve in it."

Other WCC leaders, including K. H. Ping and T. C. Chao, have praised

Communism and some of the WCC leadership have even been awarded the Lenin Peace Prize. Professor Will Herberg (Drew University) admitted, "It is a scandalous fact that many churchmen are soft on communism. All you have to do is look at the World Council of Churches."

The Reverend Richard Wurmbrand, a former representative of the World Council of Churches in Romania, was in prison in 1948 for "illegal preaching," released after eight years, but imprisoned again from 1959 through 1964. When he was released the second time, his captors told him he could "preach about Christ, but not against communism."

> I came into the Free World to find many clergymen voicing the same advice. I found the World Council of Churches urging an end to attacks on communism. I'm very sad. The church can never have peaceful coexistence with atheism. Communism is poisoning the minds of our children.

When the WCC met in Uppsala, Sweden, in 1968, the *Digest* pointed out that problems relating to race, violence and oppression were discussed freely and passionately. "But as soon as prevailing conditions behind the Iron Curtain became the order of the day, stony silence reigned."

One participant, the Reverend Knut Norberg, president of the consistory of the Lutheran Church in Sweden observed,

> How can an ecclesiastical universal assembly refuse to take notice of the ever-growing appeals from deportation camps, prison cells and torture chambers where fellow-Christians are suffering and even dying? Is it a matter of tactics? If so, it means a total capitulation to the Soviet Union and its Marxist-Leninist religion.

Christianity Today's editor, Harold Lindsell, answered Norberg's question when he wrote,

> A deep current of anti-Americanism ran beneath assembly deliberations. It seemed to be based on opposition to the war in Vietnam and to America's affluence as well as on a preference for socialism and communism over capitalism.

If these churchmen preferred socialism and Communism (Communism is socialism, economically) it should be obvious why these churchmen can not bring themselves to criticize the fatherhood of socialism and Communism!

The weakness of Miller's defense and the chicanery of the World Council of Churches is also noted in an editorial which appeared in the *Christianity Today*. It stated,

> Despite all the WCC says about the necessity of being involved, and being controversial, and taking a stand for justice, it consistently refuses to speak out against injustice when to do so would entail a major ecumenical risk. WCC leaders know full well that a candid announcement condemning the lack of religious freedom (the supreme injustice) in the Soviet Union would alienate all member churches in the Communist bloc. So they keep silent on this and host of other world issues.

It further said,

> Miller manages to avoid all the major issues brought to light in two earlier articles critical of the WCC. The arguments he answers are not the main ones in which sincere Christians call the WCC to account. . . . One is tempted to conclude that Miller's superficial appeal is a screen to hide the ecumenical movement's theological bankruptcy.

Churches should not "play it safe," but neither should they deny the Lord that brought them nor give aid and comfort to the anti-Christ.

However, the persecuted Church is not so much impeded by the Communists as by those who, at each smile or tactical concession of the red rulers, believe that the end of the persecution has arrived. They are poisoned by the slogan of peaceful co-existence. Since the day when this expression was invented by the wily Khrushchev, they underestimate the mortal danger of Communism and flirt with dubious peace movements, with progressive conceptions and with the wolves in sheeps' clothing who have entered the fold of the Church. Of course their consciences have to be salved. So the inherent evil of Communism is minimized and reports of Communistic moral constraint are set aside as exaggerated and fanatical. For this reason they are endeavouring in the name of co-existence and in the interests of peace, which is no peace, to turn the Church of the free world into a silent Church, too. At the same time they are disseminating diligently the theory that Communism has developed and altered.

This theory is false. It is quite wrong that convinced Communists are wanting to make peace with God and are prepared to give the Church its freedom. Those who declare that conditions have essentially improved for the menaced Church in Communistically-ruled countries are mistaken. In Yugoslavia or in Czechoslovakia during the "Prague Spring" where the position of the Church had undergone some temporary improvement, there is or was no question of an authentic Communistic regime. That is why Moscow is doing everything it can to restore the *status quo*. In the Communistic countries with Russian observance nothing has changed. Freedom of religious instruction is still greatly curtailed. Control of church attendance and the punitive measures against practising Catholics have not been cancelled. The separation of Church and State is a farce. The interference of party and government in purely ecclesiastical fields of government and jurisdiction has not come to the end. The training of new priests has been reduced to a minimum or abolished. The parents have been deprived of the right to educate their children. Compulsory atheistic education is unavoidable. The scandal of the puppet pastors and Quisling prelates upon the Church is still undiminished.

The Fifth General Assembly of the World Council of Churches took place in Nairobi, Kenya, in November and December of the year 1975. At the assembly delegates from the countries of the Third World, irrespective of race and nationality, broadly indulged in emotional attacks on the world's major democracies, accusing them of practicing "neo-colonialism" and "racial discrimination." In contrast, the political program of the delegations from the countries of the Soviet bloc was, though not lacking in offensive tactics, of a more defensive orientation; coldly calculated and closely co-ordinated to support the Moscow Patriarchate, it proved to be considerably more effective—even in the face of resistance.

Of the delegations from the 286 churches and religious bodies taking part in the assembly in Nairobi, that of the Moscow Patriarchate was impressive because of its size and the standing of its members in the ecclesiastical hierarchy of the Russian Orthodox Church. Led by the President of the Commission of the Holy Synod on Christian Unity and Interdenominational Relations, Metropolitan of Leningrad and Novgorod Nikodim, the delegation was made up of thirty representatives of the Moscow Patriarchate, including: the Metropolitan of Kiev and Galicia, Exarch of the Ukraine Filaret; the head of the Department of Church Foreign Relations of the Moscow Patriarchate, Metropolitan of Tula and Belev Yuvenaly; Archbishops Valdimir and Makary; Bishops Mikhail, Iriney, and Nikolai; Archimandrites Kirill and Yosif; Protopresbyter Professor Vitaly Vorovoi; Secretary of the Patriarchate Matvei Standnyuk; Secretary of the Department of Church Foreign Relations A. Buevsky; N. Zabolotsky, professor of the Leningrad Theological Academy; and G. Skobei and N. Bobrova, members of the Department of Church Foreign Relations.

The delegation of the Moscow Patriarchate took an active part in the plenary sessions of the assembly and in the work of special committees and sub-groups. Its members also met and held personal talks and informal discussions with the delegates from other churches and religious bodies. From the speeches of its representatives, it becomes clear that the principal aims of the Moscow Patriarchate at the assembly were: (1) to propagate the advantages of the political and social system of the Soviet Union over the systems of other countries: (2) to fend off criticism of the Soviet Regime for its anti-religious policies and for the persecution of religious persons; and (3) to get Metopolitan Nikodim elected to the Presidium of the Central Committee of the World Council of Churches, thereby gaining more influence in this body.

Propaganda for the Soviet Union was conducted primarily in connection with the question of human rights, which was on the agenda of the fifth session of the assembly. This subject aroused great interest among the participants in the assembly, and over two hundred delegates took part in the work of the session. Metropolitans Yuvenaly and Filaret, Archbishop Valdimir, Bishop Iriney, Secretary of the Department of Church Foreign Relations A. Buevsky, and the representative of the journal *The Moscow Patriarchate*, V. Kulikov, presented the views of the Moscow Patriarchate. The majority of the delegates who spoke at the session were representatives of churches in the developing countries. All of them expressed grievances against the so-called Capitalist world, spoke of the racial and political persecution of those who shared their religious convictions, and told of prisons, torture, and poverty in the countries of Asia, Africa, and Latin America. Their speeches alternated with speeches by the representatives of the Socialist countries. The delegates from Romania, Hungary, Bulgaria, Czechoslovakia, and the USSR called for equality, justice, and legality, repeatedly asserting that in practice these virtues exist only in the Socialist countries. The statement made by Metropolitan Yuvenaly at the meeting on November 29 is typical:

> I have listened very attentively to all the speeches of the delegates, and I have been thinking: How do I see it as a representative of a Socialist country? Not only has no light been thrown on the conditions of life in a certain part of the world by these speeches; no criticisms have been leveled at this part of the world. It is as if it did not exist. Though we as representatives of the Socialist commonwealth at this session are in a minority, I am nevertheless deeply convinced that without some testimony about this part of the world it is impossible to conduct a discussion about the situation in the world at large.
> When the question of the exercise of power was touched upon, the thought came into my mind that the people of Russia—regardless of whether they were a poor people or a wealthy people—were the first to demonstrate, several decades ago, how to achieve liberation and build a new life based on principles

of social justice. Today there is already a great brotherhood of such peoples united in the Socialist commonwealth, and I would like to say that it is a simple matter when we discuss the problem of equality of labor, of liberation from poverty, since it is already being realized in our countries. As I listened at this morning's session to talk about the liberation of women in Capitalist countries, it was quite clear to me that such liberation had already been accomplished in practice in our country. Of course, it is impossible in the space of the three minutes alloted to speakers to paint a picture of our society. We often come up against the fact that, as a result of the Cold War, there is a great deal of prejudice and distorted information that prevents us from freely approaching the discussion of these problems in a Christian and brotherly way. It seems to me that our duty as Christians is to bring clarity and mutual understanding to the discussion of the problems that face us.

Such ideas invariably received unflinching support from the representatives of churches in the other Socialist countries. To cite but one example, Dr. I. Gromadka, a delegate from Czechoslovakia, who spoke at a meeting of the session on human rights on December 3, declared:

> I champion the observance of human rights. Freedom of religion is part of this. I assure you that we in Czechoslovakia do not remain silent when the question of religious freedom is raised. But it must be understood that we do not find it possible to fight against a Socialist regime that is more just than other regimes. We do not wish to receive Bibles illegally from abroad, especially when political proclamations are slipped into them. This harms us. Our country is closely allied with the Soviet Union. The Soviet Union liberated us from the Fascists and helped us to restore the standard of living in our country.

One cannot escape the impression that the proponents of the theology of revolution know very little history. Or maybe they just do not remember the Crusades or the holy wars of the past.

> This assembly of the World Council of Churches, unlike its predecessors, is not likely to make major headlines. But for serious Christians, I think this will prove to be a very important meeting.

That assessment was given at the midway point in the WCC's fifth assembly by the Rev. Dr. Juergen Moltmann of West Germany, widely regarded as one of the world's leading contemporary theologians.

Dr. Moltmann, an early champion of the "theology of hope" and the author of a major recent book titled *The Crucified God*, is a member of WCC's Faith and Order Commission and is secretary of the assembly section, "Confessing Christ Today."

To the surprise of many church leaders, accustomed to think of WCC solely as a politically activist body, a majority of the delegates preregistered for the section on faith, giving it priority over other sections dealing with human rights, church unity, and social injustice.

Dr. Moltmann refuses to read this as a sign that the WCC is "retreating from social and political issues."

> Christians want to know what it means to be a Christian today. There is a search for the certainty and the boldness of faith.

> In the 1920's many of the early modern ecumenists believed doctrine divides, service unites. Now doctrines aren't that divisive.

> In the 1960's the church was preoccupied with faith and action. Many thought theology was irrelevant and would be replaced by psychology, sociology or

some other ideology. This no longer is a threat.

Since Uppsala churchmen and women have regained some of their self-
confidence and no longer stand in awe of secular authorities.

Leading up to this declaration was an unforeseen obstacle that was put in
the way of the propaganda activity of the representatives of the Moscow
Patriarchate and their supporters. On November 25, "An Appeal to the
Delegates of the Fifth Assembly of the World Council of Churches," written
by the Russian Orthodox priest Gleb Yakunin and the Russian Orthodox
layman Lev Regelson, was published in the newspaper *Target*, which is the
local organ of the Christian churches of Kenya. The authors of the appeal
sought to draw the attention of the assembly to the persecution of believers
in the Soviet Union and called upon the World Council of Churches to
demonstrate "genuine Christian solidarity" in coming to the aid of brother
Christians who are suffering for the faith. The appeal states:

> The Russian Orthodox Church joined the World Council of Churches in 1961.
> For the Russian Church, this year was marked by a growing wave of anti-
> religious excesses and the forced closure everywhere of churches, monasteries,
> and theological schools. Protestant communities suffered no less cruel persecu-
> tions at the same time. The Twenty-second Congress of the CPSU declared
> that 'the present generation of Soviet people will live under communism.' It
> was probably in order to bring this event closer to fruition that more than
> 10,000 Orthodox churches were shut down on the territory of the USSR
> between 1959 and 1965. Recurrences of this kind of persecution also took place
> in the following years. The last such act was the closure and subsequent
> barbaric destruction (in August 1975) of the Orthodox church in Zhitomir—a
> church considered to be an architectural monument. The church was blown up
> before the very eyes of a crowd of stunned parishioners. Believers within the
> Russian Church had no particular illusions about the Moscow Patriarchate
> joining the World Council of Churches. This act, which was sanctioned by the
> state organs at a time of the cruelest persecution of religion, evidently pursued
> aims of a tactical nature having little to do with the task of strengthening the
> position of Christians in the contemporary world. Despite this, Orthodox
> believers still hoped that Christian solidarity and the desire for genuine unity
> would prove stronger than the influence of anti-Christian forces, and looked
> with expectation for the World Council of Churches to give energetic support
> to its new member, to initiate an international movement to defend Chris-
> tianity under persecution.

For the past 29 years of its existence, the WCC has managed to avoid
making almost any adverse criticism of Communist countries. Christians
may be persecuted in Soviet Russia and there may be millions in labor camps
but the WCC remains massively and imperturbably silent. Consider then the
effect of a letter from two Russian Christians, smuggled into the Assembly
and circulated amongst delegates, denouncing the Assembly for remaining
silent while "half the Russian Church is being destroyed" and demanding
that the WCC does something to draw the attention of the world to what is
happening in Soviet Russia.

The letter was written by Lev Regelson and Fr. Gleb Yakunin of the
Russian Orthodox Church. Yakunin is a brave Moscow priest who in 1965
addressed a letter to Patriarch Alexei in which he said:

> Today the bitter truth is obvious to everyone who loves Christ and his Church.
> It is clear that the Russian Church is seriously and dangerously ill, and that her

sickness has come about entirely because the ecclesiastical authorities have shirked from fulfilling their duties . . .

Yakunin went on to accuse the Church leaders of conniving with the government to reduce the Church to servile dependence on the state. For his outspokenness, he was barred from his altar.

The council could help by obtaining permission for "exhausted Christians" to emigrate "somewhere where they would be allowed to work and observe their religion in peace," and asked for help in the "unrestricted distribution" of the Bible.

The letter ran to more than 11 pages and was signed by Father Gleb Yakunin and Mr. Lev Regelson, who are both well known for their protests at world church meetings.

Father Yakunin was the co-author of an open letter in 1965 which described the internal situation of the Russian Orthodox Church. Earlier in 1975 he published a protest against a decision to declare Easter Day a work day. For this he was threatened with dismissal.

Having been forbidden to serve as a priest in 1966, he had a job as a watchman in the Church of the Ineffable Joy in Moscow. On July 12, 1975, the new churchwarden, N. G. Klyutina, informed him that he was being made redundant "because of reductions of staff."

Knowing that redundancies were not in fact envisaged, Father Yakunin warned that he was prepared to take the matter to court, as was his legal right. Soon after this, something quite new for a Moscow church occurred. Burglar alarms were installed, and amplifiers appeared at the front of the church. Then the churchwarden announced that all the watchmen, including Father Yakunin, were no longer needed, and were dismissed as from July 10.

Father Yakunin was refused a transfer to other work, though there was a serious need of choristers.

Soon after his dismissal, the amplifiers and then the burglar alarms were removed, and the other watchmen were re-engaged.

Father Yakunin then found work as a reader in church in the Moscow region, but held the job for only a month and a half. The churchwarden, A. A. Solovyova, told him that she had been ordered to dismiss him by A. A. Trushin, the Moscow regional commissioner of the Council for Religious Affairs. This happened just after his letter to the WCC Assembly, and Father Yakunin believes "can be considered only as a reprisal against me" and "an attempt to stifle every free word in the church."

Besides serving to introduce the question of the persecution of Christians in Socialist countries at the assembly, the appeal of Yakunin and Regelson effectively compromised the delegation of the Moscow Patriarchate, for it suggested that the Patriarchate not only leaves believers defenseless, but actually plays into the hands of a godless regime by concealing the fact of religious persecution in the Soviet Union. At the meeting of the session on human rights on December 3, this idea was trenchantly vented by one of the Bishops of the Estonian Church in Exile:

> I do not wish to insult the Moscow Patriarchate or its body of priests, nor the Estonian Church in the USSR. Only I maintain that the situation in the Baltic countries is very grave. I find it hard to imagine that The Holy Church could possibly identify itself with an unjust regime that oppresses the faith. My

brothers in Christ! I cannot imagine that you would agree with this. It is your
duty to fight for the Church of Christ, or, more precisely, it is the duty of all
churches within the territory of the Communist bloc.

Evidently in the belief that criticism from an individual emigre bishop was
of little importance, Metropolitan Yuvenaly sought to brush it aside with a
single, dogmatic utterance: "As a Christian and citizen of the Soviet Union, I
cannot accept this speech and consider it offensive." But to deal in the same
way with the appeal of Yakunin and Regelson was patently impossible,
particularly since Yakunin is an Orthodox priest known in the West for his
probity and judiciousness. In fact, it took the delegation of the Moscow
Patriarchate several days to come up with a reply to the appeal of Yakunin
and Regelson. The reply took the form of an open letter published in *Target*
and signed by Metropolitan Yuvenaly. Obviously intended to be brought to
the attention of the assembly at large, the letter sets out to minimize the
standing of Yakunin and disparages Regelson for holding parochial views
on ecumenism:

> We note that the first of the two signatories, the priest Gleb Yakunin, has for
> some time been at odds with his own church authorities. The second of them,
> Lev Regelson, is well-known for his anti-ecumenical views. In a statement that
> he sent to the Local Council of the Russian Orthodox Church in 1971, he
> strongly criticized the ecumenical approach and the ecumenical activities of
> Moscow religious leaders who are authorities in the field of theology. In the
> same statement Regelson maintains that the ecumenical movement and every-
> thing connected with it represents a danger to Orthodoxy as such and con-
> sequently should be considered a modern heresy.
>   The letter then goes on to argue that instances of religious persecution in the
> USSR are not the result of an anti-religious policy on the part of the state but
> the result of infringement of the laws on religion by religious persons: We
> make no secret of the fact that various kinds of complications have arisen and
> will continue to arise in the life of the Church in the Soviet Union. This comes
> about because of the infringement of the laws pertaining to religious bodies.
> On the one hand, the guilty parties are representatives of the local state
> authorities; on the other, they are themselves members of church parishes.
> Nevertheless, we must testify to the extremely positive activity of the Council
> for Religious Affairs under the USSR Council of Ministers, whose business it is
> to solve misunderstandings of this kind.
>
> Often rumors of such infringements of the laws come to the attention of
> Christians in the West in a somewhat exaggerated and sometimes even in a
> distorted form. This leads to a mistaken reaction on the part of these Christians
> and thereby complicates our internal problems. Each country has its own laws
> for the regulation of life. Infringement of these laws entails certain consequ-
> ences. As loyal citizens of our country, we are against the actions of those who
> violate these laws—whether in the political sphere or any other.
>
> At the same time we cannot avoid making mention of the fact that our society
> has embarked on the path of an ever growing evolution of democratic princi-
> ples. The Church has found its place in this process and furthers it insofar as it
> can. It is for this reason that we contemplate the future with faith and hope in
> our Lord.

The letter signed by Metropolitan Yuvenaly was supported by a similar
statement published on the following page of the same newspaper and
carrying thesignatures of four representatives of the All-Union Council of

Evangelical Christians and Baptists, a joint body formed in the Soviet Union in 1944 for the purpose (never fully realized) of co-ordinating and administering the activities of all religious communities of a generally evangelical character. Designated "The Reply of the Russian Baptists," this statement maintains that the information of Yakunin and Regelson gives a misleading impression of the Baptist movement in the USSR. According to the authors,the complications of the Baptist movement in the Soviet Union are primarily attributable to the sectarian group that has become known as the "Baptist Action Group" (*Baptisty-Initsiativniki*):

> In 1961 a new sect was formed in our country. The leaders of this Baptist sect began to condemn us for co-operating with three other Protestant groups and for taking part in the World Council of of the necessity of reuniting. We have already achieved some good results in this area. Many of those who left us have returned to their former parishes, but thirty other congregations that broke away have officially registered with the authorities as autonomous religious bodies.

> Only some of the Baptists who broke away from us have been convicted after repeated warnings from the local authorities that their activities must conform to existing laws. The leaders of the All-Union Council have repeatedly expressed their desire for a reconciliation and their wish to hold church services together. The delegates of the Congress of the All-Union Council of Evangelical Christians and Baptists sent two appeals to the leaders of our country requesting that mercy be shown in the cases of convicted Baptists. Many of those sentenced have been released, including a group of five persons convicted for illegal printing activities in Latvia. The process of reunification continues. But it is a question of our internal affairs, and with God's help we will see it through.

> We are very disturbed that the activity of the Baptists who have dissociated themselves from us has become the object of a political game in the West, in which some churches have also joined. To this, it must be added that the role of our separatist brothers is often exaggerated, which harms peace and friendship between churches and peoples.

The official statements by Metropolitan Yuvenaly of the Moscow Patriarchate and the four spokesmen for the All-Union Council of Evangelical Christians and Baptists, published in *Target* on November 28, failed to keep delegates at the assembly from speaking out against the persecution of religious persons in the USSR. On December 4, Pastor Richard Holloway, a representative of the Scottish Episcopalian Church, informed the press that on the basis of Paragraph 14 of the Basic Rules of the Assembly he would seek to introduce the question of what the World Council of Churches ought to do to ease the fate of individual Christians or even whole churches that are being persecuted because of their religion or prevented from practicing their religion. In his speech, Holloway expanded on the proposal made by the Dutch representative Dr. A. van den Heuvel that the General Assembly, the legislative organ of the World Council of Churches, should entrust the General Secretary of the Council with the responsibility for ensuring the protection of persecuted Christians throughout the world.

Council spokesmen disputed the charge that it has failed to pay attention to religious persecution and noted the council's protest in 1974 at the trial and conviction of Russian Baptist George Vins, and other consultations in Russia in behalf of religious rights.

The stir over the Russian letter came as the keynote speaker of the assembly declared that of many gripping qualities of Jesus, the most urgent, timely trait at present is "Jesus as liberator."

> For this time and this place the claim of Jesus to bring freedom, and the cry of oppressed peoples for freedom, converge and cannot be separated,

declared Dr. Robert McAfee Brown, a prominent American theologian, promoter of Christian unity and social activist.

The World Council of Churches temporarily dissolved a tempest over religious liberty in the Soviet Union.

A relatively calm debate on a resolution urging implementation of the 1975 European-American Helsinki (Finland) agreement on security and cooperation became stormy and briefly threatened East-West ecumenical detente after Dr. Jacques Rossel, a Swiss delegate, introduced an amendment stating:

> The WCC is concerned about the restrictions to religious liberty especially in the U.S.S.R. to apply Principle of the Helsinki agreement.

> Principle 7 calls for respect of human rights and fundamental freedoms, including the freedom of thought, conscience, religion or belief.

Seconding Dr. Rossel, the Rev. Richard Holloway heated the debate when he stated:

> I have observed there is an unwritten rule operating that says the U.S.S.R. must never be castigated in public. Nevertheless, it is well-known that the U.S.S.R. is in the forefront of human rights violations. To mention this fact appears to be unsporting. I think this tradition should end.

> The U.S.S.R. should take its place in the public confessional along with the rest of us from white neo-imperialism.

At that point, Metropolitan Yuvenaly of the Russian Orthodox Church said that many countries could be faulted if a serious debate were begun on religious liberty.

Apart from the obvious embarrassment of the Russian delegates at the question of persecution in Russia, there were also according to Mr. Holloway, "bullying and blustering voices, one of which was reliably reported to have come from a KGB agent masquerading as a Baptist minister, accusing the West in a terrible, offensive kind of way . . ."

During the heat of the debate, a delegate asked the moderator of the session to rule that TV cameramen and other photographers be asked to refrain from photographing the Assembly while a vote was being taken. As a result TV lights were turned off and cameras removed.

When a motion to close the tense debate was defeated, Archbishop Edward W. Scott, primate of the Anglican Church in Canada, introduced a conciliatory statement asserting:

> The WCC is concerned about restrictions on religious liberty in many parts of the world including the U.S.S.R. We are grateful for Russian leadership in the Helsinki agreement and call upon all governments to live up to principle 7.

The resolution was then referred to a committee which would bring it back in its final form.

The World Council of Churches decided not to point an accusing finger at the U.S.S.R. Instead, delegates to WCC's fifth assembly approved by overwhelming majority a compromise resolution hammered out overnight by a three-man drafting committee that included William P. Thompson, president of the National Council of Churches in the United States; Alexei Buyevsky, a Russian Orthodox lay theologian, and Gen. Tahi Bonar Simatupang of Indonesia.

Rossel withdrew his strongly worded criticism when it became apparent that a committee of an American, an Indonesian and a Russian had reached a compromise agreement on just how far the WCC would go in criticizing the U.S.S.R.

Rossel later said:

> We have put a foot into the zone of silence, and since this has never been done before, you must see this as a beginning.

The Russian Orthodox delegations abstained, objecting to the "emotional climate" of the debate.

The resolution stated:

> The general assembly recognizes, that churches in different parts of Europe are living and working under very different conditions and traditions. Political systems, constitutions and administrative practices vary from nation to nation. . . .

> In spite of these differences, Christians in both parts of Europe, and throughout the world, are one in Christ. The solidarity that results from faith in our common Lord permits the mutual sharing of joys and sufferings and requires mutual correction.

> Christians dare not remain silent when other members of the body of Christ face problems in any part of the world. But whatever is said and done must be preceded by consultation and must be an expression of Christian love.

Given an opportunity to directly confront the Soviet Union for its restrictions against religious freedom, the general assembly chose to back away and work instead within the polite procedures dictated by the religious detente that characterizes the WCC.

After passing critical resolutions against South Africa for its intervention in Angola, and for building nuclear energy plants, the assembly admitted that a double standard exists whereby South Africa, the United States, and Latin American countries are fair game for WCC criticism while the U.S.S.R. is still off-limits.

Supporters of this double standard maintain that the Russian Orthodox delegates at the assembly might have been forced to walk out if the WCC persisted in passing a proposed resolution that singled out the U.S.S.R. in connection with a human rights principle of the Helsinki Agreement, signed by the U.S.S.R. and 34 other European nations.

"This is not the United Nations," United Methodist delegate Tracey Jones said after the assembly had passed a much milder resolution that had originally been introduced. Jones, who heads his church's Board of Global Ministries, pointed out that the World Council is held together by a common Christian commitment which requires members to relate to one another in a spirit that unites rather than divides.

It was Jones' belief that from within the perspective of the WCC members, the language of a resolution that alluded to "alleged" violations of religious freedom within the U.S.S.R. was strong enough to put that government on notice that the WCC would be investigating charges of religious oppression during the next 10 months.

Prior to the assembly, representatives of the Patriarchate at the headquarters of the Council in Geneva had circumspectly but unambiguously let it be known that they were hoping for the election of Metropolitan Nikodim. After all, so the reasoning went, the representatives of other churches in the Orthodox community had already occupied this post in the past. And on what basis could the largest of all these churches, the Russian Orthodox Church, be refused this right, particularly at a time of the emergence of a detente, with continuing efforts being made to improve relations between the West and the Soviet Union? At the same time, the purveyors of these thoughts hinted that the Moscow Patriarchate might face unpleasant consequences at home if its bid for greater recognition in the Council through the election of Nikodim were to go unheeded: the Russian Orthodox Church might have to forfeit the opportunity of extending its ties with the West, and persecution of religious persons in the Soviet Union might be stepped up.

It was clear from the start of the Assembly that the lobbying of the Moscow Patriarchate was having success, and there seemed little chance of anyone protesting against the election of Metropolitan Nikodim to one of the six seats on the Presidium of the Central Committee of the Council. This outlook was reinforced by the inclusion of Nikodim on the list of candidates prepared by a special commission of the Council on nominations. But after the delegates to the assembly became acquainted with the appeal of Yakunin and Regelson, the election of Nikodim suddenly appeared to be less of a certainty. Many of the delegates wondered whether a man who fails to defend members of his own church against religious persecution and who leaves an impression of collaborating with an atheistic regime and supporting it politically ought to hold one of the highest offices—a position of international prestige and authority—on the World Council of Churches. The delegation of the Moscow Patriarchate was, however, not to be denied in its determination to strengthen the position of the Russian Orthodox Church in the Council and it set about achieving this end in three ways:

1. By exerting *political* influence on all the East European Churches that are members of the Council. Acting in accordance with instructions from Moscow, the delegation of the Patriarchate could presume that the representatives of the East European Churches, wishing to avoid conflict with their own authorities, would not dare to jeopardize the interests of the Moscow Patriarchate and would support it at all international conferences. If there were any doubts about this at the assembly, they were dispelled by the consistent pattern of voting: *all* the delegates from the East European counties *always* voted in such a way as to support or second the Moscow Patriarchate.

2. By exerting *religious* influence on the other Orthodox churches—e.g., the Eastern Orthodox (Monophysite) churches. Towards this end, the delegates of the Moscow Patriarchate repeatedly spoke of themselves at the assembly as "defenders of the Orthodox" in the face of "pressure" from the Protestants.

3. By exerting *political and economic* pressure on the developing counties. For example, at a reception given on December 5 by leaders of the Christian Peace Conference (CPC), many of whose members were participating in the assembly, a great deal was said about the economic

aid provided by the Soviet Union and other Socialist states to the countries of Asia and Africa and also about the contribution of the USSR towards the struggle of these countries for liberation from colonialism, imperialism and, capitalism. At the same time, attention was drawn to the role of the Moscow Patriarchate as an intermediary between the government of the Soviet Union and various political and religious movements in the developing countries.

Apart from this, whenever the question of the election of Metropolitan Nikodim to the Presidium of the Central Committee of the World Council of Churches came up, the representatives of the Moscow Patriarchate did not hesitate to make clear that there might be certain drawbacks for the Council if Nikodim were not elected. For one thing, the Patriarchate might use its influence to increase the cooperation of the Orthodox community with the Roman Catholic Church, at the expense of the participation of the Orthodox churches in the ecumenical movement, which consists primarily of Protestant groups. For another, it might promote the activities of the Christian Peace Conference in the developing counties, which would serve to distract their attention from the World Council of Churches. Following this, it might work to raise the level of work of the Christian Peace Conference, so that it would be possible for this organization to compete for influence with the World Council of Churches, which in turn could lead to many members leaving the Council. These were not idle threats. It is well known, particularly to members of the Council, that Metropolitan Nikodim has for some years now been at the head of the Christian Peace Conference and that the churches of the East European countries have been taking an active part in this organization. The politicking of the Moscow Patriarchate's delegation to the Fifth General Assembly of the World Council of Churches was thus successful: Metropolitan Nikodim was unanimously elected, and a principal objective of the delegation in Nairobi was realized.

Finally it remains to note the appointment of Metropolitan Nikodim of the Russian Orthodox Church as one of the WCC's six presidents. Nikodim was largely responsible for bringing the Russian Orthodox Church into membership of the World Council in 1961 and he has always led the Soviet delegation. Nikodim has always denied that his Church suffers from any state interference and when 10,000 churches were closed under Khrushchev, he claimed that it was due to shortages of church funds. Anatoli Levitin who was put in a labor camp for criticising the subservience of the Church to the state once described Nikodim as "an odious personality" and referred to his "lying statements about persecutions of the Church." But that is not how the Western world sees Nikodim: U Thant presented him with a United Nations medal of peace and now he is accorded high office in the WCC. Acknowledging his election to the presidency Nikodim said:

> The role of the Church is in giving moral support to people fighting for liberty . . . as one of the presidents of the WCC I now feel even more concern for this kind of work.

No signs of increased religious liberty have appeared in the Soviet Union since the signing of the Helsinki agreement. However, the agreement said that according to interpretations of the Soviet Union, it had been granting full religious liberty all along.

But the agreement includes a process of review and this gives Western governments a basis from which to pose questions.

The agreement already had proved useful in activating the World Council of Churches to begin investigating how well the Soviet Union, as well as other countries, was respecting human rights.

At the WCC's General Assembly in Nairobi, Kenya, in 1975, delegates called for a study of whether signers of the Helsinki agreement were abiding by it. And machinery for following up on that action was established at the WCC's Central Committee meeting in Geneva in summer of 1976.

Public opinion in the outside world does carry influence in the Soviet Union, for instance, the Jewish campaign won emigration rights for a large number of Soviet Jews.

WCC, which includes most of the larger Protestant and Eastern Orthodox churches, has often been charged with directing fire only against non-Communist countries in its statements on religious liberty and other human rights issues.

Conservatives have been particularly vocal on this point, but some others as well have expressed concern that an international voice of Christian conscience appeared to ignore repression in the Communist world.

Communist authorities, defenders of the WCC explained, might crack down more severely on national church officials who attended an international meeting and tolerated criticism on their goverment. And Soviet bloc churches might well be forced to withdraw from WCC membership.

Not that anybody who has had knowledge of the organization gives it any credibility or prestige anyway, but there are still a few people in the country who think that the WCC stands for something and perhaps will finally be touched by reality. One does not have to go over the whole distressing history of the WCC to appreciate how morally bankrupt this international, inter-denominational organization has degenerated on a top priority moral issue, religious freedom, especially as it pertains to Communist-dominated lands.

> Cynicism with the WCC is understandable when one considers their manipulation of the human rights issue on a double-standard basis. The long silence by the WCC on the religious freedom aspect of human rights as violated by Communist regimes is but another explanation for the increasing spread of Communist tyranny among the forces of freedom in our time.

The implementation of Soviet religious liberties as practiced on a day-by-day basis might be the only means of bringing the World Council of Churches back to reality.

The World Council of Churches' Fifth Assembly ended on December 10, 1975. The 2,300 participants have returned to their own countries to reflect on the value of this ecclesiastical circus which is held at great expense to the member churches every seven years.

No sooner had the Anglican eleven-strong delegation returned than they sent a letter of protest to Dr. Philip Potter, General Secretary of the WCC. There were about 750 delegates from the 271 member churches at the assembly, but there were about 1,500 other "participants." The letter said:

> We do not regard it as satisfactory that the official delegates of the member churches should be outnumbered more than two to one by supernumerary persons, many of whom participate fully in the proceedings, save for voting, sometimes to the exclusion of other delegates.

The letter also indicated a reason for the presence of these super-numeraries; "they were always," it said, "more sympathetic to the radical and unorthodox approach."

A WCC press hand-out which purports to give a breakdown of the 2,300 participants, in fact accounts for only 1,600 and that includes stewards, translators and interpreters. Who were the remaining 700, who invited them and what was their function are questions that Dr. Potter is unlikely to answer.

The WCC held a consultation at Montreaux, Switzerland, in July, 1976, to consider how the resolution would be implemented. And then in an August meeting of its Central Committee, it set up two committees to advise Mr. Potter and the Council's international affairs unit on handling future human rights issues.

A report in the conservative journal *Christianity Today* indicated that some critics remained unimpressed; and still skeptically awaited the day when an official WCC unit would speak directly on the question of Communist violations of religious liberty.

At the present time the World Council of Churches is still in process of taking up the main emphases given it by its Fifth Assembly at Nairobi in 1975 and incorporating them into its program.

Chief among them is the concern to enable the member churches to express better the unity between them and to work more earnestly to overcome their divisions. For this reason the Fifth Assembly stressed that all of its programs must be conceived and implemented in view of the goal of unity which was described as "a truly conciliar, ecumenical fellowship of local churches which are themselves truly united." In the 1976 meeting of the Central Committee the General Secretary, Dr. Philip Potter declared that it is the calling of the World Council of Churches to enable the member churches to grow into such a fellowship and that the concern for this must be the mark of all World Council programs.

As it seeks to continue and intensify its relation of "fraternal solidarity" with the World Council of Churches the Catholic Church, working through the Joint Working Group, which is just now taking up its new program, is promoting a joint study on the unity of the Church. The study calls for reflection on the nature and extent of the real but imperfect bond of communion between the Catholic Church and the member churches of the World Council of Churches. Equally the study will try to envisage ways which may be taken in the future in order to overcome the divisions which still exist and to prepare for the perfection of this communion. Although all of the work of the Joint Working Group is directly concerned with unity and its completion, this will be the first time it has been possible to take up a joint study between the Catholic Church and the World Council of Churches on the theme of unity in such an explicit fashion. Whether this direct approach will be the most fruitful one remains of course to be seen.

During the 1976 Central Committee meeting Dr. Potter described the World Council relation with the Catholic Church as "far more intense than with many member churches." It is envisaged that this can be fruitfully sustained and that signs of the relationship, rooted in the grace of Christ, can be multiplied between the World Council of Churches and the Catholic Church in all places.

A new Joint Working Group between the Catholic Church and the World Council of Churches was announced simultaneously in Rome and Geneva on July 1, 1976.

The Joint Working Group was formed in 1965 to facilitate collaboration between the world bodies and to elevate together the development of the ecumenical movement. The Fourth Official Report of the Joint Working Group was approved at the Fifth Assembly of the World Council of Churches in Nairobi in December, 1975. It also received the approval of authorities of the Catholic Church.

The Report recommended the setting up a re-structured Joint Working Group of approximately 16 members to meet normally once a year and a small Executive Group of six members to be responsible for the ongoing work between meetings. Its task is to discover and assess promising new possibilities for ecumenical development. In so doing it will facilitate the exchange of information about the progress of the ecumenical movement, especially at the local level.

12

Religious Movements in the Soviet Sphere

The rapidly-growing Christian movement in Eastern Europe coincides with, and indeed is the same as, the individual national movements for independence and freedom in all of the Christian nations of Eastern Europe. It is neither Pan-Slavic—for it embraces as equals non-Slavic Georgians, Armenians, Romanians, Hungarians, Lithuanians, Latvians, Estonians and Finns—nor Pan-Orthodox—for it embraces as equals Catholic Croats, Slovenes, Hungarians, Slovaks, Czechs, Poles and Lithuanians and Protestant Latvians and Estonians— but elements of Pan-Slavism and Pan-Orthodoxism, in their best sense, are found within the Pan-Christian framework.

Every Slavic nation—Orthodox Russians, Ukrainians, Byelorussians, Cossacks, Bulgars and Serbs and Catholic Croats, Slovenes, Slovaks, Czechs and Poles—has suffered tragically from the most materialistic of Western diseases, atheistic Marxism. It is the common suffering from that disease that has encouraged a revival of Pan-Slavic sentiments, but on the principle of self-determination of nations, not domination by one or another Slavic nation.

In 1959 the Croatian Catholic priest, Juraj Krizanio, visited Orthodox Moscow to propagate Pan-Slavism and the Union of the Greek and Roman Churches. The Slavs well know that narrow Pan-Russianism is not real Pan-Slavism, witness Ukraine and Poland; nor narrow Pan-Serbianism, witness Croatia and Slovenia; nor narrow Pan-Czechism, witness Slovakia.

Today's Russian Christians recognize that Russia's past view of Pan-Slavism is erroneous. Thus exists the desire expressed by such as Alexandr Solzhenitsyn for Russia to develop Siberia and Russia's North-East and give independence to the non-Russian nations. Only in that way can Slavic solidarity be achieved as an Alliance among free, independent and equal nations. And that Alliance cannot entail Slavization of the non-Slavic nations, for that would destroy the entire moral basis of the Slavs gained through the martyrdom of all of their nations at the hands of Nazi and Communist tyrannies.

The Pan-Orthodox currents have a similar origin. Only Greece, the

Mother of Orthodoxy, has been spared among the Orthodox nations from the Marxist disease. And even Greece has had to endure a bitter and sanguinary war against armed Marxist bandits and the current Christian tragedy in Cyprus. All of the Orthodox consider the Russians to be the most deeply spiritual people among the nations. But the Orthodox of all non-Russian nations, Slavic and non-Slavic alike, do not want to suffer from Pan-Russianism in a Pan-Orthodox guise. Fortunately, today's Russian Christians recognize that the long-awaited re-unification of Christendom will be accomplished through Russian spiritual inspiration, and not through the concept of "Moscow as the Third Rome." Thus their emphasis on pure Christian Saints such as St. Sergei of Ratdonezh and St. Nil Sorksy.

Christians in East Europe know that the new Pan-Slavic and Pan-Orthodox currents are but tendencies to assist in a truly great goal: the Union of Christianity after centuries of disunity and fraticidal conflict, first between Greek and Latin, then between Catholic and Protestant.

Christian manifesto first became organic in the program of the Croatian national movement and its Croatian liberation army. The same concepts motivate the Christian resistance in every other East European nation.

The Brezhnevs and the Titos represent the rapidly dying past. The Christian manifesto represents the real, imminent future.

The battle being waged in the world is materialism versus spiritualism. Whether the cross or barbed wire prevails depends upon Western attitudes and support of Christians behind the Iron and Bambo Curtains. The choice for the world is quite clear.

Communist governments for many years have been trying to drive religion out of the souls of their subjects, and for years their efforts have been conspicisously ineffective. It is true that the Communist governments have many ways to shut down churches and harass people trying to attend church services—but the flame of Christianity still burns in Communist countries, sometimes a bit fitfully, but never completely out.

In 1974, Easter was an illustration of this point. Across the vast expanse of Russia, thousands of candlelight processions circled churches at midnight, and attracted literally millions of people to participate in and watch the traditional Russian celebration of Easter.

> Religious tradition and belief remain deeply imbedded in the life of this officially atheistic nation. Churches claim more than twice as many followers as the Soviet Communist party does members.

> Interestingly, it is not just the older Russians, but groups of curious young people crowded the church yards at Easter time. *Pravda* noted "a notable increase" in religious interest among young men and women. The paper said: "The dying off of religion under socialism is not an automatic process," but requires increasingly sophisticated anti-religious propaganda.

Party members are participating in religious ceremonies at weddings, baptisms, funerals, etc. One paper reported that recently while one Communist Party official was lecturing on atheism, his wife and mother-in-law were takig his children to be baptized.

In 1973 Alla Tarasova, a world famous actress at the Moscow Art Theater, member of the Communist Party for 19 years and a deputy in the Soviet parliament for 12 years, shocked Party officials and friends by leaving a will demanding she be given a religious funeral.

There are many restrictions and official pressures against the churches in Russia, but the Spirit still lives in the hearts and souls of the Russian peoqle—and the Communist Party will not be able to drive it out.

> The church in Russia is not merely a church of old women. Anyone who continues telling that story neglects the facts and repeats propaganda. In the churches in Russia, one sees many young people and middle-aged people. There are many baptisms in the churches. The church in the Soviet Union is in great difficulties but there are several active congregations with a deep religious life.

> There are still 35 million members of the Russian Orthodox Church in the Soviet Union. In Moscow, 45 Orthodox churches are still open, in a city which has 1,000 church buildings.

> In the churches that are open, there is an intensive liturgical life with two well attended religious services every day. Every priest baptizes about 1,000 persons each year.

> In the Soviet Union there is no freedom of religion but only freedom of worship. The church can be active only within its own buildings. The State's position is that the church exists for the satisfaction of religious needs and the state is able to provide for all other human needs and desires.

Since 1917 all religious publishing has been rigidly controlled and censored by the government, so that today the U.S.S.R. produces less religious literature per capita than any country in the world— except for China and Albania, where for several years there has been no religious literature at all. During the decade following the Soviet revolution, the Russian Orthodox Church was under more severe pressure than were the religious sects (Pentecostals, Seventh-day Adventists, Baptists), which had been outlawed under the czars until 1905 and therefore were now enjoying advantages similar to those of other groups which had formerly been repressed. During the 1920's several Protestant journals were permitted: *Golos Istiny* (*The Voice of Truth,* published by the Seventh-day Adventists), *Khristianin* (published by the Evangelical Christians), *Baptist* and others. The so-called "Living Church," a government-supported minority within the Orthodox Church, was the only Orthodox body which could publish anything at all. But by 1930 all this activity was forcibly stopped. During the Stalin purges the name "Church of Silence" could have been applied to all Christian denominations in the Soviet Union.

During World War II both the Russian Orthodox Church and the united Protestant church, the All-Union Council of Evangelical Christians and Baptists, came to an agreement with the state which allowed them more freedom than previously was the case. Each was permitted to begin publishing a religious periodical in a small edition. The *Journal of the Moscow Patriarchate* became well known, since a high percentage of the copies of each issue have always been sent abroad. It appears in monthly unnumbered editions and is probably the stiffest, most formal religious journal published anywhere today. By the time it is distributed its news is always at least three months old. The Baptists' *Bratsky Vestnik* (*Fraternal Herald*) is published only once every two months, but since the time of the schism in the Baptist denomination, it has sometimes published more controversial material than its Orthodox counterpart. Although there are no officially-marked circulation copies, the Moscow Baptist leaders recently claimed that the periodical's previous circulation of 5,000 doubled in 1968.

In addition to these two regular journals published in Moscow, there is a small amount of publishing by churches in places other than the capital. For example, in Tallinn, the Armenian Church publishes a journal, *Echmiadzin*, and the Estonian Lutheran Church a yearbook (actually no more than a calendar). Apart from two printings of the Bible (which, according to the maximum estimates, would have provided no more than two copies per parish), the only publishing of religious books since World War II has been an occasional edition by the Moscow Patriarchate. An examination of *The Russian Orthodox Church* (Moscow, 1958), published in several European languages, clearly shows that the primary purpose of such books is to demonstrate to foreigners the supposed freedom of the Russian church. There have also been two or three theological titles designed for church use and printed in minuscule editions. But it is likely that the volume of religious literature published in the U.S. in any given week exceeds the total output of the churches of the Soviet Union in the six decades since the revolution.

In Russia, religious writing is censored as rigidly as any other sort of literature. To compensate for such tight control, a flood of religious *samizdat* (private publishing) has been circulating in the Soviet Union since 1960. The first sign of such activity reached the West about in 1962 and consisted of a number of handwritten sheets of paper—sometimes semiliterate, often almost illegible. Most of these came from poorly educated people who were complaining about the attempts to close such places as the Pochaev monastery in the Ukraine.

Today the many underground religious publications are much more sophisticated—for example, the fine handprinted 1967 volume, complete with photographs, which the *initsiativniki* Baptists produced for the centenary of the Russian Baptist movement. Seventh-day Adventist underground publishing activity has drawn so much attention that its typewritten editions are quoted in all recent Soviet books about the Adventists.

The other religious denominations are engaging in similar activities. So much is being published clandestinely that the authorities appear powerless either to put an end to the activity of to prevent its products from leaving the Soviet Union.

> Religious dissent is widespread in the Soviet Union and growing. If Western governments press the believers' case persistently in the years ahead, there is reason to hope for a real, gradual and extremely reluctant retreat by the Soviet government.

While mistreatment of Jews has captured world attention in the last few years, Soviet Christians are speaking out increasingly against what they call despotic and brutal conditions.

Most Soviet Christians wishing to emigrate are members of the Pentecostals, whose religious practices are similar to Baptists, generally refuse to register with the government and live an outlawed religious life.

The same year of the Helsinki Accords, the Soviet Union published new restrictions on religion, harsher than those legalized in 1929.

About 1,500 Pentecostals have applied to emigrate, and many more would do so if they thought they could leave. So far only a few have been allowed exit visas.

Despite the signing of the accords, the Soviet governmnet continues to persecuted believers both physically and morally.

There isn't a single official prayer house for the Pentecostalists in the USSR. The meetings take place in private homes. Those who attend are regularly fined and prosecuted.

Soviet power is great. It does not fear international opinion. Thousands of you have been killed in the past, and if it is necessary, thousands more will die.

A community of 520 Pentecostalists appealed to President Carter as "our brother in Christ" to help them leave the Soviet Union for the United States and religious freedom.

"President Carter is our brother in Christ," elder Nikolai Goretoy told Western correspondents. "We ask him to help us in our efforts to leave the Soviet Union and enter the United States."

A five-member delegation led by Goretoy filed petitions with the Supreme Soviet asking Communist Party Gen.-Sec. Leonid I. Brezhnev, Prime Minister Alexei N. Kosygin and President Nikolai V. Podgorny to permit all 520 members of the religious community to emigrate.

The Soviet constitution guarantees freedom of religious worship, but efforts by Stalin and Khrushchev to stamp out religion caused widespread persecution and the closing of churches. In 1961, the Soviet Communist Party Congress set a goal of eliminating religion by 1980 .

This goal appears to be forgotten and not a word is mentioned of it today.

Soviet newspapers constantly report that the number of religious believers is dwindling, but experts on religion report the number of baptisms appears to be growing.

Some Russian priests report an increasing number of requests for requiem Masses by families of deceased Communist Party members and officials who were given atheist burials.

First of all, abundant new evidence has come to light in recent times that the religious situation in Soviet society has undergone a historic change which challenges some of the assumptions and working hypotheses of western analysts of that situation. There is evidence, for example, of a quantitative increase of interest in religion among Soviet citizens, which contrasts starkly with the opposite phenomenon in the non-Communist world. There is much evidence that religion in the Soviet Union has jumped the generation gap, that significant numbers of Soviet young people and students find religion more attractive than atheism—thereby confounding the official assumption that the dying-out of religion in the USSR is merely a matter of time, a matter of awaiting the coming of a new generation. On the qualitative side of the picture there is abundant evidence that religion in the Soviet Union has an intellectual vitality and even a profundity which has no real equivalent anywhere else in the world, that some of the best thinkers, writers, artists, scientists and even state office-holders are increasingly interested in religious ideas and customs, thereby challenging the easy assumption that religion survives only among the backward masses of the Soviet population. There is evidence, moreover, that religious intellectuals in the Soviet Union have succeeded in overcoming the official handicap imposed by hard and fast juxtaposition of religion and Communist ideology, a posture which automatically makes religious belief anti-Communist and anti-Soviet; many of these religious intellectuals reject that juxtaposition outright, arguing that a Soviet citizen can be both religious and communist—and in any case, religious belief does not make a citizen automatically disloyal to his country. Christian socialism is not unknown in the Soviet Union, it would seem. There is much evidence also that religious thought and interest in the Soviet Union is as firmly oriented toward the future as it is toward the past, that concern for traditional religious values has been augmented by intelligent concern about adaptation and recombining these values to the benefit of Soviet society, perhaps even of a new Communist society. Here the anti-thesis between religion and Communism disappears completely, as does also to some extent the gulf between the religious intellectual and the simple religious believer in the mass population. Finally, there is abundant evidence of indomitable courage and a willingness to suffer, if necessary, on the part of religious believers in the Soviet Union of a magnitude and intensity not seen in the world for several centuries.

The sources of evidence are manifold and diverse, however, only three seem to be most important. First, there is the Soviet press itself, which day by day—and clearly not intentionally—provides example after example from the local scene supporting and even confirming some of the general statements. The various research organizations in the western world which systematically study Soviet publications for information about religious affairs are constantly calling attention to this source material, which they feel no student of Soviet affairs should ignore.

Secondly, the emergence in the USSR during the last decade of the unofficial literature known as *samizdat* has thrown much light on the facts of religious life and thought in Soviet society, showing it to have a vitality which was virtually unknown and not even suspected among most western observers. As specialists who study these *samizdat* materials are aware, fully one-third to one-half of all *samizdat* documents which reach the West are directly concerned with religious matters. Approximately 40 per cent of the 50,000 manuscript pages registered in the *Arkhiv samizdata* in Munich is material which falls into the category of religious dissent. And much of the remainder, dealing more broadly with problems of human rights in the Soviet Union, is indirectly concerned with questions of religious freedom.

Thirdly, the emigration to the West within the last years of a large number of articulate Soviet intellectuals—some of whom prevously wrote in *samizdat* and some who did not, some who are themselves religious believers and others who are not—are living witnesses about religious realities in Soviet society today. They have enriched understanding of religion in the Soviet context by the very diversity of their information and their views; they have shown the complexity and the inter-relatedness of many factors on the religious scene in the USSR which none of the one-dimensional or even two-dimensional pictures could encompass.

More and more churches and mosques are being closed in Russia, but religion still keeps the Communists worrying.

The Party line has long been that religion is the consolation of the uneducated. But lo and behold, as Soviet education has increased, so has the interest in religion.

The Party is seriously disturbed.

Pravda carried a five-column article about the best methods of fighting religion in industrial Bashkiria, an autonomous Tatar territory southeast of Moscow. In the past 10 years, the article boasted, 23 churches and 15 mosques have closed their doors.

Yet *Pravda* complained that even some Party officials, for whom militant antheism is a must, observe religious practices.

What makes this trend so dangerous, according to *Pravda's* editorial, is its link with nationalist tendencies. The Russians themselves brought up this angle several years ago by interpreting the Orthodox crosses around the necks of many bathing youngsters as an expression of pride in their national heritage. The crosses, supposedly, had no religious significance.

There is an increasing interest among students in Russia's past and its continuity with the present. They have only to go to a film like *War and Peace* to see that past recreated for them. This inevitably includes an examination of the importance of religion, and the assessment is often so positive that many students spend their summer searching the Siberian *taiga* for "lost" groups preserving ancient religious customs. Or they may try to find forgotten old churches that still preserve magnificent icons. Today's Soviet student may be cut off from much vital information about world affairs, but he will inevitably return from such expeditions with a greatly increased sympathy for his national past and its relevance.

The Orthodox Church undoubtedly attracts those interested in Russian tradition. Such was the case with Stalin's daughter, Svetlana. By her upbringing she should have been a model of the new Soviet atheist; yet in 1963 she received baptism from a Moscow priest.

> Now I began to read Tolstoy and Dostoevsky in a different way. What a profound meaning revealed itself in *The Possessed*, in the teachings of Starets Zosima. Tolstoy became closer to me, and I understood now why.
>
> In the spring of 1962 I was baptized in an Orthodox church in Moscow, because I wanted to be in communion with those who believed. I felt this need with all my heart; dogmas meant little to me.
>
> Nikolai Alexandrovich Golubtsov baptized me, gave me a prayer book, taught me the simplest prayer, taught me how to behave in church and what to do. He brought me into communion with millions of believers on earth.

The secret baptisms of children have been done in the Soviet Union already for a long time, even in the years of the fiercest religious persecutions. Mass-baptismals of adults and children were observed in the territories occupied by German troops. Baptisms also increased inside the Soviet borders during the times of idealogical relaxation. With the renewal of atheistic hate-campaign to infiltrate family, schools, higher learning institutions, places of work, factories and collective farms with professional propagandists, baptisms of adult ceased. The people, from self-denial, in order not to hurt the family's future, either broke the ties with religion bringing up their children and grandchildren in the spirit of godlessness or they hid their beliefs not only from their schoolmates and working fellows, but also from their neighbors and even from their own families.

Since the beginning of the sixties, baptisms have been on the increase again. The intellectual part of youth started to become interested in the history of the country, analysing the ideals of the revolutionaries. They came to the conclusion, that in Russia in 1917 "a fatal and tragic mistake" had been done. Parallel with it a complicated process of revision in their own disposition towards the religion had begun.

The process and motives of the young *intelligentsia* of that time towards baptism is so eloquently told by Svetlana Alliluyeva in her book *The First Year* (1968). The baptism of adults and children is related by Father Dmitri Dudko in his diary (1961-1974) which appeared under the title *Baptism in Russia* in the Russian language.

The experiences of Svetlana Alliluyeva are recognizable. An echo of her poetic story has found assertions in the other neophythes, who have received baptism in today's Moscow. From the excerpts of Father Dudko's diary *Baptism in Russia* it is not possible to determine the exact number of baptisms performed in the period from 1961-1974. Now and then Father Dmitri notes:

> At first I have marked how many I have baptized, but now I have lost the count. ... Now I have lost count entirely, whom I have baptized. Sometimes I must baptize two or three adults, without counting children.

Assuming that Father Dmitri baptized two adults on the average per day then, he has baptized 730 persons per year.

Briefly Father Dudko dwells in his notes of merely 199 baptisms (adults-81; pupils of older age—11; children up to 9 years of age—107 baptisms).

He often speaks about group baptisms without indicating whom he has baptized:

> The first group baptized;
> In the afternoon of May 2, 22 people baptized;
> The children of a family from Vladivostok baptized, because there is no church; a family from Magadan baptized;
> six adults baptized;
> few adults baptized, a.s.o.

From the concrete evidence of the baptisms it is possible to obtain a certain notion about sex, age, education or the profession of the baptized, degree of preparation for the Sacrament of Baptism and the motives which have led to baptism. From the records of Father Dmitri about the baptism of babies, whom the godparents were can partially be seen.

From the mentioned 199 baptisms, the following statistics can be obtained:

Sex		Age	Education	Job
men	34	22-35	most of men have secondary school	Architect; Engineer, lt. colonel; scientist, a poet and "many artists." Engineers; writers; journalists; film regisseurs; TV clerk; philolog, artists.
adol.m.	6	11-17	1 with 4 grade education	
women	47	20-33	4 with university education	
		65 (2)	most of women have secondary	
girls	5	11-17	education. 3 - techn prof. school	
children	107	0-9	6 - university education	

Preparedness for the baptism by the adults and pupils of both sexes:

asked of their own accord, after they have believed in holy Baptism	76 persons
with religious knowledge	21 persons
with some knowledge of religion	33 persons
with no knowledge	17 persons
under pressure from relatives	13 persons
an unbeliever, to avoid family conflict	1 person

Motives, that have led them to baptism:

- found the faith while alone in the desert.
- without Christ, life is not worth living.
- the Christian commandments have attracted me.
- I would like to become Christian.
- three persons gave up Buddhism to become Christians.
- the death of a comrade brought me to the faith in God.
- I believe the love of men brought me toward God.
- as a sequence of the repulsive reality 'where only fraud rules,'
  by the search of absolute Truth.
- from belief in the power of the prayer
  that I have noticed in myself.
- in a dream I heard bells, song, I saw a monk, who inspired
  the necessity of baptism in a certain time of crisis in me.
- in order to repent for sins.
- to be cured from a disease.
- in order to start a new life.
- it is alarming not to be baptized.
- in order to have a godchild.
- the saving of Russia lies in the Orthodox Church, etc. . .

Father Dmitri reports that many Jews wanted to be baptized. They explained their becoming Christians as follows:

- I believe in God, without Him everything is senseless, I have to
  come to the recognition that Christianity is an absolute necessity.
- for a long time I have had faith in Christianity. Now the Jews
  must sojourn with Christ.
- I have taken recognizance of the eternity of the Christian Church.

Father Dmitri also has baptized a Mohamedenian woman from Bashkiria and an Ossetian who have become conscientious about Christianity.

To those persons intended to be baptized who do not have any conception about the faith, who doubt about it, Father Dmitri reminds them to approach Holy Baptism with the following words: "Lord, I believe, help my unbelief." By that he puts God above everything else.

Father Dmitri begins every baptismal with a dialogue about faith, and he establishes a degree of preparation by reading the confession of faith to everyone. He makes sure that the infant to be baptized has been properly prepared to receive the Christian truth.

The infant's parents usually choose young adults, who are friends and relatives, to be the godparents. On the question if they are believers, frequently mockingly and boostingly they answer: "Certainly, we are unbelievers!" On the question why they have brought the infant to baptism, they answer with equal assurance but embarrassed: "In order to have rites. . .; so that it may be baptized, everybody is baptized!"

In some instances one tries to find an excuse by saying: "How shall I believe when my parents are Communists." Father Dmitri says it is all right, if the godparents tell the truth, but if they consider themselves as unbelievers, categorically he forbids them to take part at the Sacrament. He chooses a church janitor or a person from his parish instead.

Articles in the issues of *Komsomolskaya pravda* and the *Literary Gazette* report cases of mass baptism by immersion of groups of young men and women who have reached the age of eighteen. *Komsomolskaya pravda* recounts that a "presbyter" in Tashkent recently baptized forty young men and women, while the *Literary Gazette* reports that in a district of Moldavia more than twenty young men were baptized in Bolshevik Pond.

The problem of church christenings and weddings in the USSR is of such pressing interest in Party and Komsomol meetings at which Komsomol members are transferred to Party membership that it has become customary to ask the question: "Have you had your child christened or were you married in church?" It has been proposed that there be introduced into the new Party statutes a clause to the effect that Party membership is incompatible with the observance of Church rites. *Pravda* indicates that Communists themselves have been observing religious rites:

> A kolkhoz Party organization which includes 34 Communists conducts atheist propaganda poorly, without love and without inspiration. . . . The Communists themselves do not set an example in the upbringing of their families, are not ashamed to keep ikons in their houses, and observe Saints' days. Images of 'saints' adorn the huts of Communists.

Admitting that the propagation of religious beliefs among the youth is increasing in the USSR, the Soviet ideological press has been attempting to define the concept of a "believer" and make a "scientific" categorization of various types of believers. An article entitled, "Concreteness in the study and definition of religious survivals" classifies believers as follows: (1) Believing fanatics actively propagating and defending their views, sincerely convinced of the truthfulness of religious belief, and striving to follow their principles in their lives: (2) Soviet citizens professing to be believers but not thrusting their convictions on others, regarding atheism with tolerance: (3) People observing religious rites and customs, celebrating religious holidays, marrying in church and christening their children, but doing this not from deep religious conviction, but "from fear of condemnation on the part of believing people:" (4) Representatives of the young generation "who, although they do not observe religious rites, do not have firm convictions in relation to religion. If they are not reeducated and not given a scientific world outlook, they may become believers."

This classification gives some idea of the extent and intensity of the propagation of religious beliefs in the USSR, and of the degree to which it is possible that they may increase. Soviet theorists refuse to state tne approximate number of believers in the Soviet Union on the grounds that there was no question on this subject in the last population census.

The struggle against the propagation of religious beliefs hampers the development of good relations with the Church and religion on the part of local Party officials and social and administrative institutions. It is reported that even important Komsomol officials fail to take action against the propagation of religious beliefs among youth, but often say: "Tell me, what is wrong in a person's believing in God? He will not cease to be a Soviet person because of this." The editorial board of *Young Communist* makes the following comment:

> Of course, it cannot be assumed that once a person has become a believer, he has ceased to be a Soviet person. That would be incorrect. But belief in God,

along with a reactionary world outlook and piles of religious relics, considerable reduce the energy of a believing person. . . .

"A spiritual renaissance is under way in the Soviet Union," said Franz Cardinal Koenig of Vienna, president of the Vatican Secretariat for Non-Believers.

This rebirth is characterized by a new and authentic religious self-questioning among leading personalities as well as small, private groups. And the revival of religious belief is occurring despite the official death sentence under which religion in the Soviet Union has been for the past 58 years.

The survival of religion after 58 years of propaganda and atheist discrimination, especially when the complete change in the system of production is taken into account, poses a serious problem for Marxist-Leninist theory.

Efforts of Marxist intellectuals to establish new stand in relation to religion, however, have still not had any concrete effect on Christians in the USSR and the other socialist countries.

There is no true separation of church and state in the USSR and the Soviet Union is the kind of ideological state typical of past centuries, of the era of absolutism, for instance.

Official doctrine, states that religion must wither away, and that therefore the fight against "religious vestiges" is the duty of every good citizen. From this point of view, Marxism-Leninism is not a political doctrine but a world view which explains reality and, much more important, claims to possess the sole valid explanation.

In its claim to absolute truth and its messianic bias, the Marxist-Leninist system, particularly in its sociological and philosophical aspects, takes on a religious cast. The Communist party is the church in which that "religion" is incarnated.

The Marxist-Leninist world view occupies the position of an established church. The situation gives rise to what amounts to two classes of citizens: those who follow the "state religion" (official atheism), and those who do not because of their personal faith.

The Soviet Constitution excludes the Church from education and guarantees freedom of religious worship and freedom of antireligious propaganda.

Under Soviet law belief in God and atheism cannot be considered on the same basic footing. In fact, the process of building communist society—that is, the goal of the Soviet Union—presupposes the gradual disappearance of religion. Soviet theory leaves no doubt that even the limited freedom of worship conceded to the faithful is only temporary in the face of an eventual "total disappearance of the traces of religion."

Religious believers in the Soviet Union cannot enter the civil service as teachers or officials, and are either denied entrance to universities or given difficulties in entering. They remain excluded from all civic activities except voting and military service, unless they keep their convictions to themselves.

In the Soviet Union churches and religious furnishings are state property leased by contract to religious associations, which must pay for maintenance. The associations do not have the right to set up aid and assistance funds or to organize religious meetings. Priests are excluded from the administration of the associations.

These restrictions have resulted in the decrease in Moscow in the number of churches open for worship from 657 for a population of 1.9 million in 1917 to about 40 for a population of 7 million today.

Soviet ideologists have sought to explain the persistence of religious belief despite such obstacles by attributing it to men's need for comfort in difficulties or to remnants of the old regime.

But the men behind today's new religious awakening are not nostalgic for the old days, nor are they men with personal problems which spur them to mysticism. For the most part, they are men who have lived in a socialist state since infancy but who have not sidestepped the problems of the origin, and purpose of life, and who have found the answers in Christ.

Those behind the religious revival have practically no living link with the past and have been screened by the government from any religious murmurings from abroad.

Nevertheless a report from an Orthodox priest that he baptized 5,000 adults in a two-year periods suggests that the revival is definitely a movement which affects the masses.

Calling the Soviet fight against religion a useless waste of enormous energy just because of its scientific claims, Marxism-Leninism should reflect on whether the axiom according to which religion is only the product of a socio-economic system and must die of its own accord when that system falters, can any longer be maintained.

When the Soviets seized power, their goal was to mold a man with a scientific, non-religious, world outlook and socialist morality— a man, well balanced and harmoniously developed.

Now after more than 60 years, socialist morality has been accepted as the official yardstick of good behavior, but whether Soviet man is more harmonious than his predecessor is a moot question.

A scientific outlook is there, but so is religion. Its comeback is a phenomenon which the ideologists of Communism cannot explain and about which they prefer to remain silent.

Outwardly the comeback of religion shows in many ways:

Internal opposition against the state-controlled hierarchy of the Orthodox Church.

The rising number of baptisms and conversions.

The spreading of sects uncompromisingly opposed to Party and state.

An underground religious literature with better technical facilities than the secular civil-rights movement.

A religious mood pervades the works of some of the best young poets and is evident in the monumental novels of Nobel prizewinner Alexander Solzhenitsyn. Also religious themes come to the fore in other literary works which cannot be published.

Recordings of liturgical music are produced and in demand. Historians study the role of the church in the unfoldment of Russian civilization.

Revival of religion among the young baffles the Kremlin. Not since the early days of the Bolshevik revolution has the regime displayed so much concern about the influence of religion, and religious oppression once again is in evidence. Yet it is different from both that of the early days of the revolution and the massive administrative oppression during the last years under former Premier Nikita S. Khrushchev.

Today's oppression is more selective, more subtle; it is not directed against the official church not even against established minority churches, but against believers who refuse to come to terms with the establishment and seek spiritual freedom in underground worship.

What worries the Soviet authorities most is the young. Surveys of high-school students show that many young Russians think intelligently about religion.

In Leningrad one student in his final year wrote: "Religion gives people hope for something in life. What a man believes may be mythical, but without faith one cannot live."

Another student wrote: "Why does religion exist? Obviously because man yearns for something pure and exalted. Religion satisfies this yearning."

According to this survey, published in the journal *Questions of Scientific Atheism*, what interests young people most is the principle of morality, suffering for the sake of one's faith and the role of religion in the development of mankind's spiritual treasure.

In an attempt to understand what is going on in these youngsters, a subsequent issue of the same journal distinguished between various types of believers: those with "a profound faith in the existence of supernatural forces—God, angels, the soul—and the conviction . . . that these supernatural forces always influence . . . the entire life of a man."

"Another group has faith in a world beyond and its help in one's daily life."

"The religiosity of this group results from long and intensive influence of a religious environment and is strengthened by unfavorable life experiences of the young people themselves."

The group with which the Communist investigators are most concerned

> is the one whose basic core of religiosity is participation in religious observances by their families. . . . As the young people grow older and acquire their own families, traditions become increasingly important. . . . This religious type is the least studied in our literature.

What are some of the ideas influencing this deep-seated faith? Among them

> is the idea that only religion is the mainstay of morality. . . . Studies of life histories of many young people have revealed that turning to religion is linked with the belief in its beneficial influence on personal morality.
>
> Prominent in the religiosity of some young people are the ideas of "love thy neighbor . . . comforting the needy and the burdened. . . ." These ideas strike a chord among young people. . . . In a 1965 study of religiosity among Evangelical Baptists in the cities of Anapa and Krasnodar (in the rich Kuban region), 19 per cent cited the need for solace and compassion as the reason which brought them into religion.

The Communists clearly lean over backward to understand the upsurge of religion among the young, but so far all their analyses have been unable to make them understand the elementary need for a spiritual underpinning to one's life.

For Communist analysts, religion is either an outgrowth of environment, which can be changed; a mental error, which can be corrected; or a device of internal or foreign enemies to misdirect the people.

The established churches which have gone through alternating periods of toleration and persecution are sharply controlled and viewed with suspicion as purveyors and custodians of religion. From the Communist point of view, the churches are dangerous because they are the most effective in spreading numbers of people in an emergency such as the war.

The big churches, moreover, are older than the Soviet state and the only organizations which were not set up or taken over by the Party.

The main body of Soviet believers is in the ancient Orthodox Church, which in 1967 claimed 30 million adherents and 22 million regular churchgoers. According to more recent estimates about one-quarter of the adult population are of the Orthodox faith.

Such figures do not mean much under present conditions. What matters is the dynamism of religion—how religion, muzzled, reviled, ridiculed by a militantly atheist state, has phoenix-like risen from the ashes.

Anatoly Levitin-Krasnov, an Orthodox Christian, who has contributed copiously to the religious underground literature, has defined the attitude of three generations toward the Orthodox Church.

The author writes that the most progressive and energetic representatives of the generation which lived at the time of the revolution, despised the Orthodox Church as the mainstay of the Czar. With them, hatred of the church frequently turned into anti-religious fanaticism.

The second generation, the parents of today's young, grew up at a time when organized religion was driven underground and was ignored by a large majority of the people.

The third generation, the young people of today who seek culture and knowledge and are intently concerned with the meaning of life, has been stirred up and quickened as never before. In this group the breakthrough to religion, when it occurs, is of extraordinary intensity and power. Moreover, such breakthroughs no longer are isolated events.

The initiative always comes from the individuals as the church is not supposed to proselyte, and its priests are warned against seeking to win over nonbelievers.

"The philosophy of dialectical materialism does not satisfy me. I would like to know the viewpoint of believers," says a young engineer-physicist.

Another young physicist, a Jew, son, grandson, and nephew of Communists, had been searching from Freud to Nietzsche, to Berdiaev (Nikolai Berdiaev, a onetime revolutionist and associate of Lenin, became a prominent Orthodox philosopher after his emigration). This young man joined the Orthodox Church and married the baptized daughter of a fanatical atheist. Others have been converted under the influence of Dostoyevsky's novel The Brothers Karamazov or through the study of Russia's ancient religious art.

The religion of these newcomers to Orthodox Christianity usually is not that of the institutional church. In the course of a journey to Russia, a traveler had an opportunity to talk with young people baptized into the Orthodox Church, who later had received an atheist education. Learning that they were speaking to a believer, one of them quipped facetiously: "The cosmonauts have not seen God." When told that God is Truth and cannot be seen and reminded that Jesus had said: "God is spirit," one after another came around and said: "In this sense we all believe in God."

These young people admitted that they prayed and that prayer gave them strength. Most of them attended church services more because they were mystically inclined than because they understood what was going on. They were attracted by the church as a guardian of Russian national tradition.

Such confused motivations are typical of the problems facing the Orthodox Church. The liturgy in Church Slavonic is no longer understood. The sermons, which must not offend Communist ideology, have become monotonous. Even in Moscow lively sermons are rare. Most bishops are tied up with the regime and have lost moral authority.

But behind the institutional ceremonies of Orthodox there are the young people, supported by independent searchers and younger priests—the latent church—who ultimately may transform the official church's ancient institution. But there is another aspect to the religious upsurge—the evangelical churches.

Evangelical churches, originally alien, are historical newcomers. The two most important established evangelical groups are the Baptist and Lutheran churches—the latter mainly a national-majority church in the Baltic countries just as the Roman Catholics are a national-majority church in Lithuania and other western territories.

The Baptists are different. Their church is a product of a genuine religious reformation among the Orthodox, which began to spread in the 19th century. In 1942 the Baptists claimed 4 million Russian brothers and sisters. There are about 5,000 Baptist communities.

In contrast to the Orthodox Church, which until about 10 years ago was predominantly a church of older people, Baptist services always have attracted the young.

Whereas most Orthodox churches are crowded only on high holidays, Baptist churches and houses of prayer are never big enough to hold the faithful. Baptists usually are skilled tradesmen, farmers, mechanics and engineers, well-balanced, self-respecting people who seek a link with a religious community. Their religiosity is simple and intense.

Baptist pastors and deacons frequently have technical diplomas and take a lively interest in secular affairs.

When the regime clamped down on the Baptists in the late 1950's, some communities split. The secessionists, who called themselves evangelical Baptists or *initiativniki*, formed communities of their own and actively propagated their faith. Many evangelical Baptists refuse military service and remain aloof from the atheist state.

These evangelical Baptists have been severely persecuted. In 1968, 80 of them, in the industrial Donetsk province, were confined in a mental asylum. Thousands of *initiativniki* are in jail or in labor camps; their children are taken away from them.

Equally hard is the fate of the Pentecostals, Adventists, and Jehovah's Witnesses who have made many proselytes since the war. Next to the non-registered Baptists, the Pentecostals have the largest number of communities.

One learns about the activities and the religious fervor of these dissident Protestants from court sentences meted out to them, which are published in the press, and from the polemics against them in atheist journals.

The fearless underground work of religious dissidents is amazing. In contrast to the secular civil-rights movement, they have gained access to printing presses and duplicating machines. Some of the equipment and the literature is sent in from abroad. The pamphlets, hymnals, and Bible texts of the *initiativniki* and other such Protestant churches enable them to hold Sunday schools and to train deacons and pastors.

Since most Protestants are hard working and often educated people, they have money which allows their pastors to travel widely.

For Party and state these dissident Protestants are an anathema, and the secret police are after them with everything they have. But movement apparently cannot be suppressed.

In 1968 evangelical Baptists marched, singing hymns, with homemade posters through the streets of Krivoi Rog, a Ukrainian city of about half a million, and scuffled with the police. The incident was reported in the Ukrainian press.

Another outlet in the Soviet Union for latent religious feeling is the many smaller sects, especially in Kazakhstan and in the western Ukraine. Most sects predate the 1917 revolution.

Except for such violent ancient sects as the Russian *skoptsy* who mutilate themselves, an ecumenical spirit of mutual tolerance reigns among the Protestants and is spreading among the younger members of Orthodoxy.

Russians, and most of the non-Russian peoples living among them, always have felf a deep need for religion. Communism at the beginning of the revolution had struck many observers as a religion against the grain. Communism's militant atheists of today may have become self-satisfied oppressive bureaucrats, but at least they are not indifferent toward religion.

The men in the Kremlin know that the growing religiosity of the people—especially of the young—is a serious matter, which more than anything else erodes the ideological, albeit not necessarily the political, foundations of the regime.

The rise in the USSR since 1965 of a significant grassroots human rights movement was helped by the widespread circulation of *samizdat* documents and literature. *Samizdat*-like writings have a long tradition: Radishchev in 18th-century Russia; Pushkin, Chaadayev, Herzen, Dostoyevsky and Leo Tolstoy in the 19th century; and from the first years of the Bolshevik regime such clandestine works were constantly written, including books, plays, essays, poetry and novels by such famous figures as the Russian Orthodox priest Pavel Florensky, literary giants such as Bulgakov, Mandelshtam, Pasternak and many others.

It was in 1966, for example, that the Reform Baptists saw the advantage of presenting a complete record of their five-year struggle against the new anti-religious policy of 1960. They did this by laboriously copying by hand all the documents, petitions, letters and telegrams which the CCECB and its predecessor bodies had sent between 1961 and 1966, and compiled these into a 280-page volume (*sbornik*) which they made available at home and abroad through *samizdat* channels. This is a book of considerable interest ot church historians and, although a copy came to the West as early as 1967, it has never been published. Lithuanian Catholics discovered the advantage of *samizdat* about 1970; members of the Georgian Orthodox Church began to use *samizdat* in a regular and large-scale manner only in 1974. Russian Orthodox *samizdat* has been appearing steadily since the early 1960's and the Orthodox religious *samizdat* is one of the largest in volume, about equal in this regard to the *samizdat* of the Evangelical Christian Baptists.

During the last ten years more than 50,000 manuscript pages of *samizdat* has come abroad from the Soviet Union, by the most diverse means and through many channels. The *Arkhiv samizdata*, located in Munich, has been carefully collecting and registering these documents since 1968. On the base of the thousands of documents now contained in this archive, it can be stated with some assurance that roughly 40 per cent of all *samizdat* material from the USSR is concerned directly with religious questions and church-state relations. The religious dissenters in the USSR come from all parts of that vast country and they represent all churches and faiths. It is due to the existence of this voluminous religious *samizdat* that western observers know more about religious life in the USSR today than they ever knew before. And they also know from the content of this material that religion in the USSR is not dying but is in fact, to repeat Metropolitan Yuvenaly, experiencing a genuine "spiritual revival."

The Russian Orthodox authors of *samizdat* have created a fund of literature which in many respects differs from that of the other religious faiths. It includes more philosophical treatises and essays, complex discussion on culture, history, society, as well as, of course, religious themes and protests about the dire condition of church-state relations in the USSR. This more intellectual type of writing is perfectly natural for Russian Orthodox thinkers. After all, the whole history of the Russian people, their society, culture, traditions, philosophy, ways of thinking—all these are inextricably tied to and have deep roots in Orthodoxy. Thus, the best writers and thinkers in the USSR today pore out their works with continual reference to the spiritual heritage of the Russian Orthodox Church. To name only a few: Bulgakov, Sinyavsky, Maximov, Galich, Maramzin, Tendryakov, Shimanov, Agursky and—best known of all—Aleksandr Solzhenitsyn. Large numbers of Russian Orthodox believers write for *samizdat* under pseudonyms such as Ustinov, Altaev, Chelnov, Denisov, Gorsky, Polyakov and some even give only initials; their works can be found regularly, along with named authors, in the quarterly journal, *Vestnik of the Russian Christian Movement*, which is printed in Russian in Paris. For instance, the issue No. 115 of this journal devotes more than 70 per cent of its 268 pages to articles written in the USSR, a fact which has caused the editors of the *Vestnik* to add Moscow, to Paris and New York, as the editorial home of the journal.

The Russian Orthodox Church is historically a passive church, and the traditional rules of hierarchical discipline have worked against any schismatic movement such as occurred among Soviet Baptists. Nonetheless, it would be a mistake to think that Russian Orthodox *samizdat* has not contained a host of documents of vocal protest about state persecution of the church. Whole congregations of Orthodox believers have signed petitions, with as many as 1,500 names on some of them, to protest the refusal of the governmental organs to permit the opening of a new church (e.g. in Gorky, Perm, Naro-Fominsk and Novgorod) or to protest the closing of an existing church (as happened in November, 1973 in Zhitomir). Within the Russian Orthodox priesthood itself the voice of protest also has not been entirely subdued. One only had has to mention such names as Archbishop Yermogen, and the priests Boris Talentov, Sergei Zheludkov, Pavel Adelheim, Svevolod Shpiller, Nikolai Gainov and Dmitri Dudko to recall the wide extent and the fervor of this inner-church dissent. And, of course, one must not overlook the extensive *samizdat* literature created by Russian Orthodox laymen, the most prolific of whom has been Anatolv Levitin-Krasnov.

Not so important is *samizdat* volume or even its quality, but the fact that this voluminous literature has thrust the religious dissenters of all faiths and churches in the Soviet Union into the broader human rights movement. It has made it possible for Soviet dissidents with no strong personal religious commitment themselves to join in the call for the right of religious freedom. The Moscow Human Rights Committee, under Academician Sakharov, has frequently added its voice of protest to those of religious people. Igor Shafarevich, Valery Chalidze, Andrei Tverdikhlebov and many other "legalist' human rights defenders have spoken out vigorously in cases where religious rights were violated. More than this, however, religious believers have tended to see their own cause and interests in a broader light; one encounters documents in which Russian Orthodox support the protests of Baptists and vice versa. There is little wonder, therefore, that the KGB campaign against all aspects of the *samizdat* and the human rights movement (a campaign which has been greatly intensified since early 1972) has also brought a more repressive atmosphere into the Soviet state's battle against the church and against religious belief in general. Religion can no longer be treated as a separate or isolated issue in Soviet politics or in Soviet society.

The Soviet KGB, besides fighting underground literature, *samvydav,* is compelled also to reveal the underground radio stations. At least in five republics the underground stations are operating. The *Komsomolskaya pravda* is drawing attention to this protest action. There were articles in this newspaper that police in Ukrainian town Donetsk uncovered illegal radio stations. "Pirate Radio Stations" stand in particular against intensified Russification in Ukraine. Other illegal radio stations are operated in Lithuania, in Caucasian republics, Azerbaijan, Georgia and recently also in the Soviet Asian republic Uzbekistan.

There is no significant example in history, before our time, of a society successfully maintaining moral life without the aid of religion.

Karl Marx taught that man may improve himself spiritually by means of improving his material environment.

Jesus Christ taught precisely the contrary—that man's material environment may be improved only as a result of spiritual rebirth and continuing growth.

The search for individuality in a machine-made setting takes interesting forms. One is the fad of icon collecting, which the *Literary Gazette* has criticized not merely because that atheist newspaper suspects that it is a disguise for religious impulses, but because, like other disapproved fads, it has given rise to a thriving black market.

One illicit dealer was found to have assembled 400 icons, crosses, and other objects of religious art. The *Literary Gazette* contrasted such gainful collectors with those who "in the age of technology and the domination of material goods seek spiritual riches."

In the era of standardization, it conceded, an icon adorns existence and creates a link with what is eternal and unique. Nevertheless, the newspaper came down hard on what it called the snobbery and corruption surrounding the newfad.

In all the talk of the new benefits showered on the young generation, one of the new topics has been education. As one writer in the magazine *Novy mir* put it, the age-old concern over the means of existence is gradually giving way to a new concern over the means of individual development.

Young Russians still are told what a wicked thing religion is but they appear more curious than zealous about the fight against God.

Although religion is on the decline, as much through natural social change as through official suppression, a strange new phenomenon appears to be developing. This is what is known as the "third-generationers." Their grandfathers survived the revolution and helped to build Stalinist Communism. Their parents survived the Second World War and built up prosperous, influential careers which enabled them to give their children a first-class education and all home and vacation comforts.

These sophisticated young men and women now entering adult life often seem to question the values of a purely materialistic society, and look for some better reason for human existence.

What strikes many people most sharply in the reawakened interest in religion is the crowds of curious young people who cram the courtyards outside the onion-domed churches at Easter time to glimpse the gilded robes of priests, the ornate church interiors, the colorful rites and to catch an exotic whiff of incense or to hear the chanting of the choir. However, a large majority of church-going Christians are older people.

Pravda and other Party publications acknowledged their concern over what *Kommunist*, the Party's ideological publication, termed "the vitality and tenacity" of religion.

Foreigners run into evidence of aroused interest in religion in many places. A foreign churchman is told by a Moscow priest that he has little time to counsel young people because he is so busy doing 1,000 baptisms a year, like many other priests. An Intourist guide asks an American businessman for a Bible. Another young guide joins a foreign group in lighting a candle at the Zagorsk Monastery.

For the first 40 years after the revolution, the only religious people in Russia were uneducated and of simple faith.

The educated had turned against the church. But now they are becoming interested again. Intellectuals in increasing numbers, especially students, are turning to religion.

> Russians are looking for personal integrity and it's being denied by the cynicism of the government. They are told what to believe. They're taught dialectic materialism in school, but its application in Russia changes so frequently that children are sometimes told one answer to give the teacher and another for a government inspector.

The only valid measure of religiosity in modern Russia is whether or not an individual considers himself to be religious. There exists at the present time no objective method of determining the extent or nature of religioas affiliation. Official religious statistics, when not kept secret, are distorted. In any case, even if all available religious statistics were published, they would fail to shed light on the true situation. On the one hand, these statistics exclude believers whose names do not feature on official lists of persons attending sacraments (weddings, funeral services, christenings, confirmation, etc.), and on the other hand, they overlook the fact that many people who do not consider themselves believers, but who are simply following cultural traditions or their own aesthetic inclinations also attend sacraments and visit churches. Statistics also ignore the small number of people who conceal their membership of permitted churches or sects, as well as those (even fewer) belonging to unregistered churches or sects. Finally, they pass over the so-called "individual believers," i.e., people who consider themselves religious, but who cannot or do not want to identify themselves with any known church or sect, and whose numbers and influences are continuously increasing.

When the status of the official churches was restored in the "late Stalin" period, some former believers returned to the fold, but relatively few young converts were attracted until the "early Khrushchev" period of liberalization. The young intelligentsia of the mid-1960's were particularly open to conversion, and the trend continues to this day at an ever increasing rate.

It engendered a parallel resurgence of spiritual themes in both permitted and unpermitted literature. This renaissance concerned mainly Orthodoxy, and only to a lesser extent Catholicism and Protestantism.

The newly converted Orthodox intellectuals exert an extremely strong influence on the dissident movement, by giving it a culturally religious orientation. At the same time, they have an unconscious and unwitting influence on the official Orthodox Church, especially where their ideas are taken up and passed on by capable young priests. It is no accident that these recent intellectual converts have almost no connections with the growing semi-chauvinistic Slavophile movement. Characteristic of this group is both a fundamental preoccupation with Orthodox theology, and an active and profound interest in religious metaphysics and the study of other religious teachings, inspired by their scientific and academic training as well as their general erudition and intellectual outlook. Young people have shown that they are beginning consciously to oppose the spirit of the official church and to propose instead a positive line, notable for its greater universality, spiritual freedom and philosophical approach. Both in content and tone, this line tends towards abstract Christianity which, in their opinion, is what genuine Orthodoxy should ideally strive for. This attitude is partly explicable by the attraction of these people to Russian religious and philosophical literature of the "Silver Age."

The most active section of Orthodox believers is composed of newly converted intellectuals and artists, aged between twenty-five and thirty-five, in Moscow and Leningrad. In the mid-1960's, in this same narrow milieu, a growing interest in Buddhism (especially in its northern, Mahayana form) became evident, and brought devotees into contact with the Buddhists of Buryatia. Although Buddhists are only a few dozen in number, as against the tens of thousands of young Orthodox believers, the Buddhist conversions seem to be extremely symptomatic, for they offer in principle the possibility of a spiritual choice and of spiritual pluralism, which is by no means a usual phenomenon in mofern Russia.

From the viewpoint of an outside religious observer, the position of young Orthodox intellectuals can be summed up as being syncretic, abstract-Christian and "generally religious," and construed as a spiritual-intellectual reaction against the narrow sectarianism of official faiths and related organizations. Many of these Orthodox believers (and certain Buddhists) are coming more and more to deny the conception of religious hierarchy, on the grounds that it goes against the mystical grain of each and every religion. It is worth stressing that non-organized religion is objectively less susceptible to administrative, ideological or social control, while at the same time it exerts a more effective influence on the most diverse strata of the population, including convinced atheists.

Sooner or later, official churches and permitted sects will be permeated by these ideas, or will, at the very least, be forced to react to them, whether in a positive or negative sense.

The mentioned phenomena are symptomatic of a trend which, although still obscure, is nevertheless extremely powerful and promising for modern Russia, namely the emergence of new cultural alternatives. At the end of the 1950's, and during the early 1960's, the basic alternative was the choice between the "official" and the "dissident" standpoints, with an additional choice between "believer" and "non-believer" status (in the sense of an organizational and confessional affiliation). Now, however, the main alternative is between a "religious approach to life" and "life without religion." In the future, this will be the cornerstone of all manifestations of Russian cultural-social life, although it does not exclude the possibility of conflict with the official atheist ideology, as well as the ecclesiastical opposition movement, and perhaps even with the Russian dissident movement as a whole.

Religious stirrings throughout the Soviet Union once again have the Kremlin worried.

In April at a trial in Dushanbe in the central Asian republic of Tadzhikistan, a Soviet official named Reiner was found to be an organizer of the local Baptist movement. He converted the young as well as the old and even managed to form a Baptist choir from local schoolchildren. With the help of a typewriter brought in from Switzerland, he published a whole series of religious writings.

Lithuania's Roman Catholics and their clergy are demanding new rights.

The Muslims too are stirring. In central Asia a sect which calls itself "Rebirth of Islam" has appeared, but because of their commitment to fostering friendship with the Arabs, the Soviet authorities have avoided a showdown. (While Mr. Reiner was sentenced to five years of hard labor for his Baptist activities, the restive young Muslim clergymen were only exiled to distant Muslim settlements).

But what concerns the Soviets most is a religious revival within the Russian Orthodox Church—especially among the young.

In the small Church of the Miraculous Nikolai on the outskirts of Moscow, the Rev. Dmitri Dudko, a veteran of the war and of Stalin's concentration camps, has held free-wheeling question- and-answer sessions about religion on Saturday evenings ever since December, 1973.

The gray-bearded Russian Orthodox priest looked up from the sheaf of papers he was holding and asked: "Why should we be imprisoned—because we wish each other good?"

The priest, the Rev. Dmitri Dudko, was speaking at one of his regular question-and-answer sermons which have attracted growing numbers of people, both atheists and believers, to his small suburban Moscow church to hear discussions of almost every aspect of spiritual and social life.

From explaining the meaning of resurrection or why Easter falls on a different date each year, he touches on his own attitudes to atheists and to the more conformist Orthodox clergy.

The young, middle-aged, and elderly pack the candle-lit church, whose walls are covered with icons, to stand through a further two hours of discussion. He said at one sermon that he had started the question-and-answer sessions at the request of the congregation.

Each sermon is punctuated by anecdotal material and letters from people describing their conversion to Christianity or their problems some of which bring tears to the eyes of many present.

But frank discussion of religious themes in an officially atheist state must inevitable cause a stir as it cannot help but involve politics—and some questions, apparently posed by the skeptical, are evidently considered sinister by both Fr. Dmitri and his congregation.

At his eighth sermon in March, one questioner invited Fr. Dmitri to "admit that you don't like your country and your people."

Fr. Dmitri replied: "You probably wanted me to say that I am simply anti-Soviet. It would be easier, in order to concoct a case and imprison me."

The priest's answer caused gasps of shock and surprise among the congregation and many of them crossed themselves fervently. Many political dissenters have received long prison and labor camp sentences for "anti-Soviet" activities.

But Fr. Dmitri continued: "You are wrong. I love my country and my people and I pity those who have strayed. I particularly pity atheists."

Believers should not reproach atheists for their errors but "behave towards them with sympathy, see in them a belief in God. They believe, but are going toward God by the back door."

Some of the most interesting statements come in answer to questions about the Orthodox high clergy who are often accused of a soft line towards the atheist authorities.

One questioner said a true intellectual was ashamed of going to church because of the stand of its hierarchy who only express opinions which coincide with state views.

> Learn to be objective. You see faults in the modern clergy and point to the Patriarch himself, but do you know that you are looking too superficially?
>
> Who else is in such an arbitrary position as the Patriarch? They say he is surrounded by thousands of informers. He sighs and it is heard by all the organs.

In Russian, the word "organs" is frequently used to describe the authorities, particularly the KGB (security police).

Letters from believers, explaining why they began to believe in God or how religion has helped them through difficulties are followed carefully by the congregation.

Fr. Dmitri, who occasionally himself refers to time he spent in a Stalinist labor camp after World War II in his sermons, once quoted from a letter by a woman who said her religious belief helped her stand up to the rigors of an interrogation.

Her interrogators handed her over to a hypnotist, but she said a prayer to herself and managed to resist him to the point where he admitted: "I can do nothing with her." At this, most of those listening crossed themselves.

After the eighth sermon in April, someone told Fr. Dmitri in a letter: "What you say is frightening. Nobody spoke like that before and we are afraid that you will be misunderstood."

The priest answered: "I am also afraid of that . . . but if I am misunderstood that does not mean I should be silent, I am doing God's work. . . ."

His reply was greeted with cries of "Thank you, Fr. Dmitri," while many members of the congregation again crossed themselves.

Such active meetings could not continue unnoticed in the Soviet Union. Fr. Dmitri encountered opposition from those attending the meetings and even from the church hierarchy.

Then on May 18 he suddenly announced his resignation from the clergy saying that he was forced out because of "the illegal interference by the godless in the internal affairs of the church." As he left the church, he told his congregation: "I again appeal to you to stand by me. This is all I can do."

When Valdimir Maximov, the famous Soviet novelist, arrived in Paris in mid-March, he was asked by a correspondent of the emigre journal *Posev* if interest in religion among Russia's youth was merely a fact.

He replied: "In today's Russia, youth seeks God with a clean heart and an inquisitive mind. Many of them have paid with their lives for their faith."

The correspondent also asked Mr. Maximov whether the state's control of the church unfavorable influenced the clergy.

He replied: "The great majority of the priests are selfless and courageous and seek to strengthen the faith of their flock."

Mr. Maximov, who attended some of Fr. Dmitri's talks while he was still in Moscow, was asked if there really were Marxists within the Soviet Union who had become Christians.

His reply: "Perhaps there are not yet so many, but they are becoming more and more. The religious movement is the most powerful social movement in Russia."

The Soviets claim that only uneducated and backward people are attracted by religion. But a survey published in 1974, in the second issue of the Soviet monthly *Nauka i religiya*, disputes this. This was conducted by the department of atheism of the University of Kiev together with Party organizations in several provinces of the Ukraine. Those surveyed were selected young workers in some of the most modern factories.

Surprisingly, of 1,048 workers questioned, 433 refused to say that religion had a negative influence on one's spiritual outlook. "One should not force one's convictions on others," wrote 237, and 110 answered, "If the believer believes in God, let him."

This may sound very sensible to a Westerner. But in the USSR, where atheism is preached to everyone from childhood, while religion is denounced as anti-social and a harmful superstition, this refusal of about 40 per cent to denounce religion is astonishing.

Nauka i religiya attributed the unsatisfactory result of the survey to indifference, but the organizers admitted that most of these "allegedly" indifferent workers had graduated from high school or from a technical institute.

"This shows," concluded the journal, "that a considerable part of our students do not acquire a sufficiently solid world outlook, even though they may gain the knowledge which they need for their work."

For the Party's militant atheists, who attribute the survival of religion usually to the influence of superstitious grandmothers, the result of the survey conducted by the University of Kiev must have come as a shock. Moreover, the Party must know that of the some 500 young workers who replied as they were expected to respond, many must have had mental reservations. It is an old Russian saying that one does not let outsiders look into one's heart.

Everything considered, the survey confirms Mr. Maximov's view that religion today has become an important trend among young Soviets, although it may not yet be "the most powerful social movement in Russia."

Many young members of the intelligentsia have turned to the church, and Orthodoxy has become fashionable in some circles. There has been a new wave of interest in icons and other religious artifacts.

The future of this revival is uncertain. The official attitude toward the church is ambivalent at best. On one hand, the church is allowed to maintain the monastery at Pechori (where from 60 to 70 monks now live) and 11 others around the country; it is permitted three seminaries for the training of priests (about 1,100 young men are now pursuing the four-year course); and because they are "architectural monuments," the state helps preserve some of the oldest churches. In Moscow, a city of more than seven million, is permitted about 45 working churches.

On the other hand, the state strictly forbids Sunday schools or any form of organized religious instruction for children. It effectively prevents most of the brightest youths who apply for the priesthood from pursuing that vocation. (A heavy percentage of priests in training are farm boys). In new industrial cities—some with populations of a million or more—it is unusual to find even one church.

The state also has compromised the church hierarchy to such an extent that many believers ridicule its subservience to the official line and its huge "donations" to official causes.

In a bitter open letter to the patriarch of the church, novelist Alexander I. Solzhenitzyn, himself a believer, accused the church of betraying all its own values, and called it "a church dictatorially ruled by atheists," a reference to the State Council for Religious Affairs, which has the ultimate say in all religious matters.

A Lenten letter to the All-Russian Patriarch Pimen.

Your Holiness!

> What this letter is about is pressing like a tombstone upon the head and shattering the breast of the not quite dead Orthodox Russian people. Everyone knows it, and there was a loud outcry, but they then remained forebodingly silent. And now another pebble must be placed on the tombstone, so that silence may no longer be possible. I was weighed down by just such a pebble when on Christmas night I listened to your Encyclical.

> I felt a pang at that passage where you spoke, at last, about children—perhaps for the first time in half a century from such a height: that side by side with love for their country parents should instil in their children love for the Church (and, evidently, for faith itself?) and should strengthen it by their own good example. I listened to that—and my early childhood, spent at many church services, rose up before me, together with that primitive impression, uncommon in its freshness and purity, which later no millstone and no intellectual theories could eradicate.

> But—what is this? Why do you direct this honorable appeal only to Russian emigres? Why do you urge that only those children be brought up in the Christian faith, why do you warn only the distant flock to 'discern calumny and falsehood' and to be strengthened in justice and truth? And we—should we be discerning? And what about our children—should we instil in them love for the Church or not? Indeed, Christ did command to go out and seek even the hundredth lost sheep, yet, only when the ninety-nine are in their place. But when even the ninety-nine near ones are missing—should not one's first concern be for them?

Why must I present my passport when I come to church to have my son baptized? What canonical requirements govern the Moscow Patriarchate in the registration of those being baptized? One ought still to be amazed at the strength of spirit shown by parents at the dimly perceived spiritual opposition inherited from olden times, with which they submit to that talebearing registration, exposing themselves to persecution at work or public ridicule on the part of nincompoops. Yet their persistence dries up with this, for the baptizing of infants is usually the totality of the children's connection with the Church, the succeeding paths of religious upbringing being tightly shut to them, access to participation in church services is likewise shut off, sometimes also to communion, and even to attendance at services. We are robbing our children when we deprive them of the never-to-be-repeated, purely-angelic perception inspired by divine worship, something which cannot be made up in adulthood, so that they do not even know what it is that they have lost. The right of perpetuating the faith of their fathers has been riven, as well as the right of parents to raise their children according to their own understanding of the world,—and you, the church hierarchy, have come to accept it calmly and you promote it, finding an authentic characteristic of freedom of belief in this fact; in the fact that we must give up our defenseless children, not into neutral hands, but into the clutches of atheistic propaganda, of the crudest and most unscrupulous kind; in the fact that youth torn away from Christianity —so as not to become infected by it!—and its moral upbringing has been confined within the narrow defile between the agitator's notebook and the criminal code.

Already half a century has slipped by, I no longer speak of liberating the present, but of how we shall save the future of our country?—the future, which will be made up of today's children? In the end, the true and profound destiny of our country depends on whether the right of power will become firmly embedded in the national consciousness, or whether this will be cleared of that eclipse and the *power of rights* will again shine forth? Will we succeed in preserving in ourselves at least some Christian traits, or will we lose them all completely, and give ourselves up to considerations of self-preservation and comfort?

The study of the last few centuries of Russian history leaves one with the conviction that it would have advanced in an incomparably more humane and harmonious manner if the Church had not renounced her independence, and the people would have listened to her voice as, for instance, they do in Poland. Alas, we are far from that. We have been losing and forfeiting the shining moral Christian atmosphere in which for a millennium our mores, our style of life, outlook, folklore, even the very name of the people—*Krest'iany*–have stood firm. We are losing the last characteristics and traits of a Christian nation—and can it be that this is not the chief concern of the Russian Patriarch? The Russian Church has its impassioned opinion, on any kind of evil whatsoever in far-off Asia or Africa but in domestic troubles she never has any. Why are the pastoral letters that come down to us from ecclesiastical summits so traditionally unruffled? Why are all Church documents so placid, as if they originated in the most Christian of nations? Harrying from one unruffled epistle to another, does not the need to write them vanish completely in one bad year? Outside the patriarchal chancery there will not be anyone to address them to.

It is already seven years since the two upright priests, Yakunin and Eshliman whose self-sacrificing example confirmed the fact that the pure flame of the Christian faith has not died out in our land, wrote a well-known letter to your Predecessor. They confronted him with abundant evidence of that voluntary interior enslavement, to the point of self-destruction, to which the Russian Church has been reduced; they requested that any untruth in their letter might be pointed out. But every word of theirs was the *truth*, yet not one of the hierarchy sought to refute them. And what answer did they receive? The simplest and coarsest: they were punished, for speaking the truth they were deprived of church ministry. And *you*—up to this day you have not set it right. And the terrible letter of the twelve citizens of Viatka also remained unanswered and only brought oppression upon them. And to this day the only fearless Archbishop, Ermogen of Kaluga, who did not allow a belatedly enraged atheism, which achieved so much before 1964 in the other eparchies, to close his churches and to burn icons and service books, similarly remains imprisoned in monastic confinement.

It is seven years since that resounded loudly and plainly—and what has been changed? For every church in use there are twenty razed and irreparably damaged and twenty more in desolation and profanation—is there a more heartrending sight than these ruins, left to the birds and storehouse keepers? How many populated centers are there in the country without any church within 100 or even 200 kilometers? And our North is left without any churches whatsoever— that North which from ancient times has been the repository of the Russian spirit and, one can expect, will most faithfully show it forth again, in the future. Workers, almsgivers, donors meet with obstacles at every attempt to *restore* even the smallest church, because of the one-sided laws of the called *separation* of church and state. We do not even dare to ask about the ringing of church bells—but why is Russia deprived of her ancient adornment, her finest voice? But why speak of the churches?—we cannot even get the Gospels anywhere, even the Gospels must be brought in from abroad, just as our missionaries at one time used to bring the Gospels to Indigirka.

Seven years—and does the Church make a stand for anything whatsoever? All ecclesiastical administration, the appointment of pastors and bishops (and even of unprincipled ones, to make it that much easier to deride and demolish the Church), everything is carried out secretly according to the directives of the *council on religious affairs*. A Church directed dictatorially by atheists—is a sight unseen for Two Millennia. All administration of church business, as well as the use of church monies—those coppers dropped in by pious fingers—are given over to their control. In grand gestures 5 million rubles at a time are donated to outside causes, while the lowly are driven from the church entrances, and there is nothing with which to repair a leaking roof in a poor parish. Priests are without rights in their parishes, only the conducting of divine worship is still entrusted to them, and that only within the churches, while before stepping outside to visit the sick or to go to the cemetary it is first necessary to ask permission of the city council.

On what evidence can one convince himself that the systemic *demolition* of the Church body and soul at the hands of the atheists is her best way of *preservation*? Preservation—for whom? Certainly not for Christ. Preservation—by what means? By *lying*? But after lying what shall be the kind of hands offering the Eucharist?

Your Holiness! Do not totally ignore my unworthy outcry. It may be that you will not have to hear things like this every seven years. Do not give us reason to suppose, do not make us think, that for the arch-pastors of the Russian Church earthly authority is higher than heavenly, earthly responsibility more terrible than accounting to God.

Neither before men, and all the more, not a prayer, shall we pretent that material forces are stronger than our spirit. Things were not easier at the inception of Christianity, yet it survived and flourished. And it showed us the way: *sacrifice*. If one is deprived of all material powers—in *sacrifice* he always achieves victory. Many of our priests and co-believers within living memory accepted just such a martyrdom, worthy of the first centuries. But then they were thrown to the lions, today all one can lose is his comfortable well-being.

In these days, falling on your knees before the Cross carried into the center of the church, ask the Lord: what other purpose does your ministry have in a nation which has almost lost the spirit of Christianity and even its Christian image?

Aleksander Solzhenitsyn

Lent,
Week of the Veneration of the Holy Cross,
1972

In sum, the church survives, but only by accepting restrictions on its behavior which may prove fatal a generation or two from now. This is probably the hope of Communist Party ideologists, many of whom have obviously concluded that it is counterproductive to try to extinguish religion when a natural, if drawn-out, process may eventually accomplish this goal painlessly.

The history of church-state relations since the Bolshevik Revolution has been erratic. The Bolsheviks assumed (correctly) that the church would oppose them and in the first years after the revolution relations were hostile. In 1922 the authorities improved relations, although the church had relinquished its independence.

The church survived Stalin's collectivization and purges in the 1930's, but only with difficulty. The dictator closed all the seminaries and monasteries, had many rural priests arrested and otherwise harassed the church. But the outbreak of war forced him to reverse his position. The church became Stalin's staunch ally on the home front and he allowed it a period of unprecedented official blessing in return.

This era of good feeling did not last long, but while it did the church was able to train thousands of new priests in eight seminaries that Stalin allowed to reopen. The priests trained in this rush now compose the bulk of the clergy.

In the late 1940's, Stalin turned on the church again. His successors allowed a period of relative freedom, but Nikita Khrushchev conducted a harsh anti-religious campaign. Khrushchev's successors have been more tolerant. Official anti-religious propaganda is now rare.

Throughout Russian history until the Revolution, church and state were intertangled. Many essentially political arguments in old Russia were conducted in theological terms.

If a young Russian wants to establish some personal connection with his cultural heritage today, one Western student of Orthodoxy has noted, he must turn to the church. Churchmen, believers and outsiders agree that this has drawn many younger and better-educated Russians to the church in recent years.

Apart from a connection with their past, the church gives its adherents something to believe in, which must also help explain its adherents something to believe in, which must also help explain its continued appeal. "You might call this country an ideocracy," one practicing Christian said recently, referring to the official Communist ideology. "But there isn't much left in the idea, and people want something more."

So, the Orthodox church appears in no danger of losing its special place in the hearts of the Russian people. A widely accepted estimate is that at least 30 per cent of the babies born in Moscow are christened.

A poll taken in the large industrial city of Gorki showed that 60 per cent of the babies were baptized, despite a half-century of official atheism in the Soviet Union.

Most of the parents listed themselves as non-believers. But their answers indicated the continuing strength of religious feelings and traditions in this country.

Sixty-one per cent said they decided on baptism because of the urging of the family. Another 23 per cent said they regarded the ceremony as an old Russian custom.

Of the parents polled, 20 per cent belonged to the Young Communist League, whose members are supposed to be militant supporters of official doctrine.

The League's magazine, *Molodoi kommunist*, reported the poll results and expressed concern about the continuance of religious traditions. It noted that 56 per cent of the parents of baptized children also celebrate Christmas.

Molodoi kommunist said a stepped-up struggle to spread atheism was necessary. It pointed out unhappily that only 12.6 per cent of the parents who opted for baptism declared themselves to be convinced atheists.

The number of avowed believers was small, 3.5 per cent. But the great majority simply listed themselves as non-believers, with some of these wavering between an acceptance or a rejection of religion.

Molodoi kommunist warned that the young parents covered in the poll had received good educations by Soviet standards. The authorities there usually dismiss religion as something that only ignorant, old peasant women still observe.

"This is a reproach to our schools and atheistic propaganda," the magazine declared.

Molodoi kommunist did not disclose the number of persons questioned or give complete results on all answers.

The poll was confined to Gorki, which with a population of 1.2 million is the seventh largest city in the Soviet Union. Other reports have indicated that religious practices are much more widespread in the small towns and country than in the big cities.

In the countryside, priests still perform many of their traditional functions, particularly christenings and funerals.

There has been an amazing interest among young people recently in the energetic and missionare-minded movement of the Evangelical Christians and Baptists. Here is how the press described a baptism at Rostov-on-Don in 1966:

> During the May Day celebrations a great meeting was held at Rostov-on-Don, at which about 1,500 believers were present. Naturally they could not all fit into the small private house, and so the meeting took place on the road beside it. A great many non-believers, in fact a whole crowd of them, watched the meeting and listened to the word of God. . . . About 80 souls repented (of whom, moreover, the majority were young people); amongst them were apparently, 23 members of the Komsomol.

The following day a baptism was held in the river Don. The police wanted to arrest the organizers, but "the brothers and sisters formed a tight cordon round the church officers and gave the police no chance to seize them."

Even more impressive is the latest list of Baptist prisoners, compiled by a council of their relatives, which has been formed for their defense. This shows that the most active *initsiativniki* or "Action Group") are in their early forties.

Of the two hundred prisoners whose ages are known, 146 were born since the Revolution, 84 since 1930 and 20 were in their teens or twenties when sentenced. This list should be required reading for those Soviet propagandists who, through fear, ignorance or censorship state that religion is "dying out" in the Soviet Union.

The nub of the religious problem that confronts Soviet is how to mold a completely atheist generation. To campaign against baptism, as such, scarcely scratches the surface, and the authorities probably realize this. Nevertheless, the matter of baptism has always loomed large. Soviet statistics on baptism are so scattered and contradictory as to be meaningless, but the number of times the practice is attacked in the press suggests that its incidence is high indeed.

The chief difficulty here is with the Russian grandmothers. Those who kept the economy of the country going during the "Great Patriotic War" are not now going to relinquish meekly the religion so many of them hold dear. It is no longer legal for them to carry their grandchildren off to the priest for pre-emptory baptism, but very often they lay down their own law to their sons and daughters: "Get your infant baptized or I won't baby-sit for you."

Religious studies are apparently attracting more new students in Eastern Europe. One possible explanation may be that Communist theoretical opposition to religion may actually increase religion's appeal.

In Poland, for example, 604 priests were consecrated in 1972 compared to 418 in 1971. Although Polish theology students, in contrast to students in other studies, must do military service, only 2 per cent of the recruits did not return to their studies after their release from the Army.

In Czechoslovakia there were 112 ordinations in 1972 compared to 59 in 1971. Numerous clauses limiting the number of admissions to seminaries have been reintroduced to curtail the trend.

In East Germany (DDR), the number of ordinations has declined but the number of Protestant theology students has increased from 549 in 1961 to 642 in 1965. In 1972 the DDR had nearly 500 theology students, all of whom have free tuition and receive fellowships.

Soviet and other East European newspapers are complaining more and more frequently about growing religiousness and piety among all classes of Soviet society.

In the USSR 60 million people, i.e., 20 per cent of its total population, are organized in 20,000 Christian and other religious congregations. In Ukraine the proportion of believers is the highest.

Official circles are particularly disturbed about the fact that the formerly given explanations for this phenomenon seem no longer to be correct. Whereas formerly mostly older people, especially old women, were concerned about religion and went to church, which fact was considered and done with as a "vestige of superseded far-off ages," *Pravda* now complains about a growing interest in religion among the young. "There are many young priests and popes." *Pravda* states that alone in Kalinin about 30 per cent of the priests are younger than 40 years. The number of 20- to 30-year-old people who are interested in religious matters and attend church-services is steadily growing. Even members of the Komsomol are participating in religious ceremonies. In Moscow, 60 per cent of all newborn children are being baptized. Young believers are distributing religious pamphlets and organizing religious meetings even in public schools. The thesis that religious "superstition" is due to insufficient intellectual education of the population is no longer true either since the number of religious intellectuals is growing. Well-known physicians, teachers and other experts believe in God and take part in religious rituals. Furthermore, the argument that religion is unmasked as "opium for the people" by the workers in particular is not true to reality. *Pravda* states that in some factories of Moscow the number of pious workers is especially high. Even ideology cannot deter young people from religion. Yepishev, head of the political department of the army, is very much concerned about the fact that uniformed soldiers are increasingly attending church services.

No one can imagine the range and intensity of religious life in the USSR. There is no doubt that it is a question of the greatest volcano in Christianity. This is affirmed by Archbishop Roger Etchegaray of Marseilles, President of the Episcopal Conference of France, in an article published in his diocesan bulletin, and Archbishop speaks with admiration of what he saw and heard during his contacts with many Orthodox communities. "If we think of the recent past of this Church it must be admitted that its survival has something miraculous about it." He recalls some data of his past: in 1938 there were only 4 bishops at liberty out of over 160; with the exception of only 160, the 50,000 or so priests were all in prison; not one monastery was open out of 1,052; and all 57 seminaries were closed.

After a short period of respite during the second world war and in the years immediately following, the Orthodox Church was subjected to new vexations ordered by Khrushchev, particularly from 1959 to 1964. The closure of 10,000 churches and other restrictions still remained in force.

> The life of the Church, stripped of all its activities, even in the field of education (religious instruction for the young is forbidden), has been reduced and restricted to worship. However any Christian who has a social function cannot practise openly and, for many people, going to the nearest church can be a long pilgrimage. For example there are only 9 churches in Kiev, a city with two million inhabitants. There are none at all in the new districts, such as the large Darnitsa complex, with its 600 thousand inhabitants.

Archbishop Etchegaray goes on to say that the strength of the Russian Orthodox Church is the serenity of this people of God which is continually rising from its own ashes and which succeeds in imprinting the mark of its faith on an everyday reality which is tainted by militant atheism.

Also a group of Swedish Lutheran churchmen reported that there are signs of a spiritual revival among youth in the Soviet Union.

Lutheran Archbishop Olaf Sundby of Uppsala, who led a delegation on a two-week tour of the Soviet Union, said Soviet churchmen attribute the apparent interest in religion to three factors: a reaction against materialism, a discovery of the religious traditions in Russian history and the aesthetic appeal of churches.

The Soviet Union's non-Russian nationalities, eager to assert their national identity, occasionally also turn to old religious customs, which goes smack against Communist efforts to whittle down national differences.

Even more disturbing from a Communist point of view is the stubborn survival of religion in the armed forces.

On a front-page editorial of *Red Star*, the armed forces' daily, complained about "Survivals of the past in the consciousness and practice" of Army personnel.

Earlier, the same journal carried a long article according to which a "Baptist sect" had been able to win over wives of officers and enlisted men.

In another case, crosses made of aluminum were found strewn on the floor of the barracks of a military unit whose commander was a staunch Communist.

The *Red Star* carried an article naming several soldiers— apparently Byelorussians—who had refused to carry arms or take the military oath. These conscientious objectors belonged to the so-called *initsiativniki*, or unregistered evangelical Baptists, who, in contrast to their registered cor-religionaries, oppose many institutions of the Soviet state.

When political officers ultimately persuaded the recruits to take the oath and to carry arms, the soldiers' parents arrived, or members of their sect, and very soon the young men again became conscientious objectors.

In 1970 Anatoly Levitin was a school teacher, a Russian Orthodox layman writing under a pseudonym. He sent a 24-page letter to Pope Paul VI revealing a tremendous spiritual awakening in the USSR.

Levitin stressed that the revival among the young people (like the Jesus Movement in the United States) "in intensity and strength is no less than the feeling of fiery enthusiasm of the earliest Christians."

Young people were even being wed in cathedrals instead of the official "wedding palaces," Levitin said. Conversions were happening through the witness of other Christians; also through the reading of the Bible or the writings of Dostoyevsky and Berdaev.

> Modern youth in Russia is a disturbed youth; it seethes and passionately seeks for something. . . .
>
> . . . more and more frequently there are cases in Moscow where the sons of Communists and even of old *tchekists* are baptized. . . .
>
> There is an authentic ecumenism, in living religious practice, and this ecumenism takes place without conference, official speakers, or great banquets. . . .

At about the same time a visiting lecturer from India to Russian Orthodox theological academies confirmed Levitin's words. In a later article for *Christian Century*, Paul Verghese said there are 40 Orthodox Churches in Moscow; 14 in Leningrad, a city about the size of Chicago; and a total of 30,000 parishes in Russia. Some of the city churches pack as many as 9,000 inside and have large crowds standing outside.

Thus the revival becomes more open and obvious to all. *Christianity Today* tells of a young painter, Yuri Titov, who used to depict themes of the Communist line. Now he portrays the conflict between good and evil; religion and atheism. Titov is quoted as saying, "Our forgetfulness of the truth revealed to us by the Holy Scriptures has brought the modern world to the brink of chaos."

Yet to their amazement, the Soviets cannot extinguish faith, however many of the faithful they destroy.

A NOTE ON SOURCES

This book is based upon the most recent research and current sources. However, because of the voluminous nature of this work, the footnotes have been omitted. The reader is kindly asked to overlook this shortcoming. On request for specific information, sources of re – ference will be supplied.

APPENDIX A

The peoples of the Soviet Union and their religious beliefs [1]

Nationality	Numerical strength (unless stated otherwise according to the 1970 census)	Geographical distribution	Majority religion or church	Minority religions
Great Russians	129,015,000	In all 15 Soviet Republics especially in RSFSR (107,748,000), Ukraine (9,126,000), Kazakhstan (5,500,000), Uzbekistan (1,114,000).	Russian Orthodox Church	Old Believers, Baptists, Dukhobors, Molokan and other sects.
Ukrainians	40,753,000	Ukraine (35,284,000), RSFSR (3,346,000), Kazakhstan (930,000), and Moldavia (507,000).	Ukrainian Orthodox Church	Catholics of Slavo-Byzantine rite (dominan among western Ukrainians) Baptists, Seventh-day Adventists, Pentecostalists, and other sects.
Uzbeks	9,195,000	Uzbekistan (6,026,000), and Tadzhikistan (666,000).	Sunnite Moslem	
Byelorussians	9,052,000	Byelorussians (7,290,000), RSFSR (964,000).	Byelorussian Othodox Church	Strong Catholic minority, Baptists, Pentecostalists, and other sects.
Tartars (including Crimean Tartars expelled from the Crimea in 1944).	5,931,000	In many parts of the USSR, especially in the Tartar and Bashkir Autonomous Republics and in Uzbekistan (Crimean Tartars).	...do...	About 100,000 Tartars, the so-called Kryashens are Orthodox Christians.
Kazakhs	5,299,000	Kazakhstan (4,161,00) and USSR (478,000).	...do...	
Azerbaidzhani Turks	4,380,000	Azerbaidzhan (3,777,000), Armenia (148,000), and Georgia (218,000).	Shiite Moslems	Sunnite Moslems (30 percent).
Armenians	3,559,000	Armenia (2,208,000), Georgia (452,000), Azerbaidzhan (484,000), RSFSR (299,000).	Armenian Church	Small groups of Catholics and Baptists.
Georgians	3,245,000	Georgia.	Georgian Orthodox Church	Shiite Moslems (Inghilo), Sunnite Moslems (Adzharians), Pagans (Khevsurs), small groups of Catholics and Baptists.
Moldavians	2,698,000	Moldavia (2,304,000) and Ukraine (266,000).	Russian Orthodox Church	Baptists, Innocentists, Jehova's Witnesses, and other sects.
Lithuanians	2,665,000	Lithuania	Roman Catholic Church	Lutherans, Calvinists.
Jews	[2] 2,151,000	RSFSR (808,000), Ukraine (77,000), Byelorussia (148,000), Uzbekistan (103,000), Moldavia (98,000) Georgia (55,00), and Baltic States (66,300).	Judaism	Insignificant groups of Evangelical Christian converts in the Ukraine, and converts to Islam, the so-called Chala in Central Asia.

1. Source: Pravda, April 17, 1971.

2. About 3,000,000 according to unofficial Jewish estimates.

The peoples of the Soviet Union and their religious beliefs—Continued [1]

Nationality	Numerical strength (unless stated otherwise according to the 1970 census)	Geographical distribution	Majority religion or church	Minority religions
Tadzhiks (including Pamir nationalities).	2,137,000	Tadzhikistan (1,630,000), and Uzbekistan (457,000).	Sunnite Moslems	Ismailites.
Germans	1,846,000	About half in Siberia and the other half in the central Asian Republics, especially Kazakhstan.	Lutherans	Strong minority of Roman Catholics, also Mennonites, Baptists, and smaller groups of Seventh-day Adventists.
Chuvash	1,694,000	Chuvash ASSR	Russian Orthodox Church	Strong minority of Roman Catholics, small groups of Orthodox and Baptists.
Turkmenians	1,525,000	Turkmenistan	Sunnite Moslems	
Latvians	1,430,000	Latvia	Evangelical Lutheran Church	
Mordvinians	1,263,000	In the eastern parts of European Russia, especially in the Mordvinian ASSR. Estonia	Russian Orthodox Church	
Kirghiz	1,425,000	Kirghizia	....do....	
Bashkirs	1,240,000	Bashkir ASSR	....do....	
Poles	1,167,000	Byelorussia (383,000), Ukraine (259,000), Lithuania (240,000).	Roman Catholics	Orthodox.
Estonians	1,007,000	Estonia	Evangelical Lutheran Church	Fairly strong Orthodox minority, smaller groups of Baptists and Methodists.
Peoples of Daghestan	1,365,000	All in the Daghestan ASSR there are about 137,000 Lezghins in Azerbaidzhan.	Sunnite Moslems	
Including:				
Avars	396,000			
Lezghins	324,000			
Darghinians	231,000			
Kumyks	189,000			
Laki	56,000			
Tabasarans	55,000			
Nogay Tartars	52,000			
Rutuls	12,000			
Tsakhurs	11,000			
Aguly	8,800			
Udmurts	704,000	Udmurt ASSR	Russian Orthodox Church	Small Moslem minorities, remnants of pagan beliefs, especially Kugu Sorta sect among the Mari.

Group	Population	Location	Religion
Mari	599,000	Mari ASSR	...do...
Chechens	613,000	Chechen-Ingush ASSR	Sunnite Moslems
Ossetins	488,000	About 3 in Georgia, 5 in RSFSR (north Caucasus).	Religious allegiance divided between Orthodox and Sunnite Moslems. Remnants of pagan beliefs. Small Baptist groups.
Komi and Komi Permyaks	475,000	Komi ASSR, Komi-Permyak, National Okrug.	...do...
Circassians (Soviet statistics divide them up into Cherkess, Adyge, and Kabardinians).	400,000	Northern Caucasus region (Kabardinian-Balkar ASSR, Karachai-Cherkess, and Adyge Autonomous Provinces).	Sunnite Moslems
Bulgars	351,000	Ukraine and Moldavia (151,000).	Russian Orthodox Church
Koreans	357,000	Uzbekistan, Kazakhstan (78,000), and RSFSR.	...do...
Greeks	337,000	Ukraine, Georgia (89,000), RSFSR, and Kazakhstan.	Russian Orthodox Church.
Buryats	315,000	Buryat ASSR, Chita, and Irkutsk Provinces of RSFSR.	Buddhists... In the Irkutsk Province, Orthodox Christians and Shamanists.
Yakuts	296,000	Yakut ASSR.	Russian Orthodox Church. Shamanist survivals.
Karakalpaks	236,000	In Uzbekistan, especially Karakalpak ASSR.	Sunnite Moslems.
Gypsies	175,000	About half in RSFSR, half scattered over other Soviet Republics.	Nominally Orthodox. Central Asian Gypsies (5,000) are Moslems.
Hungarians	166,000	Transcarpathian Province of Ukraine.	Calvinists.
Karelians	147,000	Karelian ASSR, Kalinin Province RSFSR.	Roman Catholics, small Baptist groups.
Peoples of the north	151,000	European Arctic, northern Siberia, Far East, especially Amur Valley, Kamchatka, Sakhalin Island and Aleutian Islands.	These nationalities practice or practiced until recently every kind of worship characteristic of primitive peoples anywhere in the world—adoration of the sun, ancestor worship, cult of inanimate objects (fetishism), cult of animals (totemism). Usually the peoples of the north are referred to as Shamanists in view of the important role played by the Shaman, the Siberian witch doctor. At the time of the establishment of Soviet power, the peoples of the north found themselves in various stages of Evangelization. The Lapps (Kola Peninsula) and the Itelmeny (Kamchatka) may be considered as Orthodox Christians, Certain groups of Evenki have been under Buddhist, others under Orthodox influence.
Including:			
Nentsy	29,000		
Evenki	25,000		
Khanty	21,000		
Chukchi	14,000		
Eveny	12,000		
Nanai	10,000		
Mansi	7,900		
Koryaks	7,500		
Nivkhi	4,300		
Selkupy	4,400		
Ulchi	2,400		
Saami (Lapps)	1,900		
Udege	1,500		
Itelmeny	1,300		
Kety	1,200		
Orochi	1,100		
Eskimos	1,100		
Nganasany	3 1,000		
Yukagiry	1,000		
Aleuts	600		
	400		

3. Kolarz, Walter, Religion in the Soviet Union, New York, St. Martin's Press, pp. 490-497.

The peoples of the Soviet Union and their religious beliefs [1] —Continued

Nationality	Numerical strength unless stated otherwise according to the 1970 census)	Geographical distribution	Majority religion or church	Minority religions
Uigurs	173,000	Kazahstan, Kirghizia, and Uzbekistan.	Sunnite Moslems	
Ingush	158,000	Chechen-Ingush ASSR.	Sunnite Moslems	
Gagauz	157,000	Moldavian ASSR and Odessa Province of Ukraine.	Russian Orthodox Church	Baptist groups.
Kalmucks	137,000	Kalmuck ASSR	Buddhists	
Rumanians	119,000	Transcarpathian and Chernovtsy Provinces of Ukraine.	Russian Orthodox Church	
Karachai	113,000	Karachay-Cherkess Autonomous Province.	Sunnite Moslems	Shamanists;
Tuvinians	100,000	Tuvinian Autonomous Province	Buddhists	
Kurds	89,000	Armenia (57,000); Georgia, and Azerbaidzhan.	Armenian Kurds are Yezidis and Sunnite Moslems; Georgian Kurds are Yezidis; Azerbaidzhani Kurds are Shiite Moslems.	
Finns	85,000	Leningrad Province, Karelian ASSR.	Lutherans	
Abkhazians	83,000	Abkhazian ASSR (21,000).	Religious allegiance divided between Sunnite Islam and Georgian Orthodox Church.	
Talyshi	77,000	Southern parts of Azerbaidzhan Soviet Republic.	Shiite Moslems	
Turks	79,000	Scattered mainly over Transcaucasia.	Sunnite Moslems	
Khakassians	67,000	Khakassian Autonomous Province.	Russian Orthodox Church	Shamanist survivals.
Balkars	60,000	Kabardino-Balkar ASSR.	Sunnite Moslems	
Altaitsy (Oirots)	56,000	Autonomous Province of the High Altai.	do	Remnants of 'Burkhanism', a nationalist-messianic faith and Shamanist survivals.
Dungans	39,000	Kirghizia Kazakhstan.	Sunnite Moslems	
Persians	28,000	Scattered over towns of Transcaucasia and Central Asia.	Shiite Moslems	Bahai.
Czechs and Slovaks	33,000	Ukraine.	Their religious background is Catholic and Protestant, but many may have adopted the Orthodox faith.	
Chinese	25,000	Presumably scattered all ove USSR.	Their religious background is Confucianism and Buddhism, but nothing is known about an organized Chinese religious life in the U.S.S.R. Half of the Soviet Chinese do not speak the Chinese language and they are bound to be estranged from their national and religious traditions as well.	
Abaza	25,000	Karachay-Cherkess Autonomous Province	Sunnite Moslems	
Assyrians	24,000	Armenia.	Nestorian Christians	
Taty	17,000	Azerbaidzhan.	Shiite Moslems	
Vepsians	16,000	Karelian ASSR, Leningrad Province.	Russian Orthodox Church	Orthodox.
Shorians	16,000	Kemerovo Province (southern Siberia).	do	Shamanist survivals.
Arabs	8,000	Uzbekistan.	Sunnite Moslems	
Baluchi	7,800	Southern Turkmenistan.	do	
Karaites	5,900	Lithuania, Ukraine, and scattered over other parts of USSR.	Karaite religion	

APPENDIX B

THE ROMAN CATHOLIC CHURCH IN THE BALTIC REPUBLICS PRIOR TO SOVIET ANNEXATION

	Status[3]	Bishops	Churches	Parishes	Priests (Diocesan and Regular)	Monasteries	Monks	Convents	Nuns	Seminaries	Seminarians	Believers	Pop.
Estonia [1939]	AA	1[a]		6	8+2					1[b]	28	2,000	1,525,000
Latvia [1944]													
Riga	AD	2	166	126	120+17	3	36	1	11	3		476,963	1,930,502
Liepaja	D	1	50	40	46+7	3	9	15	15			89,617	592,028
Lithuania [1944]													
Kaunas	AD	1	240	120	27+34	12	93	31	326	1	48	560,000	640,000
Vilnius 1	AD	1	(60)	60	245+4	2	13	24	198	1	32	280,484	354,792
Panevezys	D	1	207	125	245+4	2	7	10	95		6	418,950	450,000
Telsiai	D	1	143	135	268+16	4	37	8	60	1	32	358,872	401,306
Vilkaviskis	D	1	120	101	214+12	3	26	15	91	1	33	350,000	365,000
Kaisiadorys	D	1	104	66	102+7	4	19	6	46		5	224,700	228,026
Klaipeda 2	P		(9)	9	12							85,000	160,000

NOTES TO TABLE B

1. Portion of the former Ploish Archdiocese of Vilnius (Wilno); another part of the Archdiocese was annexed to Byelorussian SSR.

2. Prelatura Nullus, presently administered jointly with the Diocese of Telsiai.

3. AA Apostolic Administrator; AD Archdiocese; D Diocese; P Prelatura.

a. Apostolic Administrator of Estonia (bishop Edward Profittlich, missing since 1941), Auxiliary of Archbishop of Riga

b. Until 1940, theological faculty of the University of Riga.

Sources: Annuario Pontificio, 1939-46; Mailleux, loc. cit.; Kolarz, op. cit.

APPENDIX C
THE ROMAN CATHOLIC CHURCH IN THE U.S.S.R. IN THE 1970's

	Active Bishops	Parish Churches	Active Priests	Seminaries	Seminarians
Lithuania	4	609[a]-622[b]	620[c]-761[d]	1	48[e]
Latvia	2[f]	178[g]	145[h]	1[i]	18[j]
Estonia	—	2[k]	2[k]	—	—
Byelorussia	—	65[l]-100[m]	40[n]-65[o]	—	—
Ukraine	—	50-75[p]	30-35[q]	—	—
Russia and Kazakhstan	—	2[r]	5[s]	—	—
Kirghizia	—	1[t]	1[t]	—	—
Georgia	—	1[u]	2[u]	—	—
Moldavia	—	1[v]	1[v]	—	—
Estimated total:	6	902-982[w]	846-1017	2	66

NOTES TO TABLE C

a. **Annuario**, 1973-76.

b. (Krasauskas & Gulbinas, loc. cit., pp. 32-33.

c. **Ibid.**, pp. 33-34.

d. **Annuario**, 1973-76.

e. CCCL. No. 8, 1974, p. 26.

f. Not including banished bishop K. Dulbinskis.

g. **Annuario**, 1973-76; "about 150 parishes," acc. to Mirski (loc. cit., p. 57)

h. **Annuario**, 1973-75.

i. Acc. to Mirski (loc. cit.), serving also the Church in the Ukraine.

j. **Annuario**, 1973-76; "over 20" students, acc. to Mirski (loc. cit., p. 56).

k. Subordinated to the Archdiocese of Riga. Mailleux, loc. cit., p. 366.

l. **Ibid.**; in 1960, Haroska estimated that there were only about 30 parishes left in Byelorussia (loc. cit., p. 100).

m. "Over 100" churches, acc. to the official **Akademiia nauk Belorusskoi SSR, Prichiny susschestvovaniia** (p. 107), published in 1965.

n. Mirski, **loc. cit.**, p. 58. Haroska's 1960 estimate was 30-35 (loc. cit.).

o. Mirski, **loc. cit.**, p. 366. A Russian bishop spoke of some 75-80 priests.

p. A very rough estimate, incl. also Hungarian parishes in Transcarpathia (26 in the late 1960's, acc. to Mailleux, loc. cit., p. 366).

q. A rough estimate, incl. also Hungarian priests (22, acc. to Mailleux, loc. cit.).

r. Moskow and Leningrad.

s. Incl. 3 Lithuanian priests said to be active in Siberia (Krasauskas and Gulbinas, loc. cit., pp. 33-34).

t. In Frunze.

u. In Tbilisi (Mirski, loc. cit., p. 62).

v. Kishinev, with a Polish priest (ibid.).

w. The 1966 **Spravochnik propagandista i agitatora** (p. 1) listed a total of "about 1000" Roman Catholic churches in the USSR.

APPENDIX D

THE ROMAN CATHOLIC CHURCH IN LITHUANIA IN 1971[a]

Diocese	Parishes	Clergy[b]	Seminarians	Baptisms	Believers
Kaisiodorys	65	79	5	1,972[d]	224,700[c]
Kaunas	122	188	6	5,061	560,000[c]
(Klaipeda)[e]	11	14	?	1,343	90,000[d]
Panevezys	120	161	5	3,498	418,950[c]
Telsiai	134	148	6	4,338	385,000
Vilkaviskis	94	122	5	4,689	365,000[c]
Vilnius[f]	63[g]	249	?	5,610	286,845

NOTES TO TABLE D

a) Unless other dates are indicated below.
b) Including active, retired and "impeded" clergy.
c) 1944 figures.
d) 1970 figures.
e) Prelatura Nullus, administered by the Diocese of Telsiai.
f) All data for the Vilnius Archdiocese are from 1969.
g) Including three quasi-parishes.

Sources: Annuario Pontificio, 1969-1976.

APPENDIX E

THE UKRAINIAN GREEK CATHOLIC CHURCH PRIOR TO SOVIET ANNEXATION OF THE WESTERN UKRAINE [1]

	Status	Bishops	Churches	Parishes	Priests [Diocesan and Regular]	Monasteries	Monks	Convents	Nuns	Seminaries	Seminarians	Believers
Galicia [1943]												
Lviv	AD	3	1,308	1,267	1,004+57	9	57	59	284	1	106	1,300,000
Stanislav[2]	D	2	886	455	495+36	8	101	58	246	1	26	1,000,000
Peremyshl[3]	D	2	1,268	640	657+58					1	12	1,159,380
Lemkivshchyna[3]	AA		198	129	128							127,580
Carpatho-Ukraine [1944][4]												
Mukachiv	D	1	459	281	354+13	5	35	3	50	1	85	461,555

NOTES TO TABLES E

1. The Table does not include data on the small Ukrainian Greek Catholic Church in Bukovyna.

2. Also known as Stanislaviv, the city was renamed Ivano-Frankivsk in 1962.

3. As a result of redrawing of borders between the USSR and Poland in 1944-45, the western portion of the Peremyshl diocese including the city itself (in Poland: Przemysl), as well as the entire Apostolic Administrator of Lemkivshchyna, were annexed to Poland. The smaller, eastern portion of the Peremyshl diocese which found itself under Soviet rule was placed under two vicar generals, one for the southern part, the other for the northern part of the diocese.

4. Though occupied by the Red Army from October 1944, the Carpatho-Ukraine was formally transferred from Czechoslovakia to the USSR only in June 1945. The Table does not include the Priashiv (Presov) Diocese of the Ukrainian (Ruthenian) Greek Catholic Church which has remained within Czechoslovakia.

Sources: Annuario Pontificio, 1943-1945

List of works cited

Books

Acta Baltica, Haus der Begegnung, Konigstein/Taunus.
Albania's Empty Handed Freedom, European Christian Mission, Rosendale, England, 1976.
Alekseev, V., Russian Orthodox Bishops in the Soviet Union, 1914-1953, New York, 1954.
——, The Foreign Policy of the Moscow Patriarchate, 1939-1953, New York, 1955.
Alliluyeva, Svetlana, Only One Year, Harper & Row, New York, 1969.
Annuario Pontificio, Vatican City.
Aspaturian, Vernon, The Soviet Union in the World Communist System, Stanford, 1966.
Assembly of Captive European Nations, New York.
Babris, Peter, Baltic Youth Under Communism, Research Publishers, Arlington Heights, 1967.
Bardizian, A., The Crisis of the Armenian Church and Those Responsible for It, Boston, 1934.
Beeson, Trevor, Discretion and Valour, Collins, London, 1974.
Bennett, John C., Christianity and Communism Today, Association Press, New York, 1967.
Berdyayev, N. O., Russkaya ideya, Paris, 1930.
Bourdeaux, Michael, Religious Ferment in Russia, Macmillan, London, 1968.
——, Patriarch and Prophets, Macmillan, London, 1970.
Bundy, Edgar C., How the Communists Use Religion, Wheaton, Illinois, 1970.
Burko, D., Na Khresny puti, Munich, 1955.
Ciszek, Walter J., With God in Russia, McGraw-Hill, New York, 1964.
Conquest, Robert, ed., Religion in the USSR, London, 1968.
Cuibe, L., The Lutheran Church of Latvia in Chains, Stockholm, 1963.
Cutler, Donald R., ed., The Religious Situation: 1969, Beacon Press, Boston, 1969.
Decker, Nikolai K. and Lebed, Andrei, eds., Genocide in the USSR, Institute for the Study of the USSR, The Scarecrow Press, Inc., New York, 1958.
Delaney, Edward L., Harvest of Deceit, 20th Century Factfinder, Sacramento, 1971.
Deutscher, Isaac, Stalin, Pelikan Books, Great Britain, 1970.
Die ersten Opfer des Kommunismus: Weissbuch uber die religosen Verfolgungen in der Ukraine, Munich, 1953.

Dubinaitis, Evalds, *Der Kampf gegen Religion und Geistlichkeit in den sowjetisierten baltischen Landern Estland, Lettland und Litauen,* Konigstein/ Taunus, 1966.

Fedotov, G. N., *Svyatye drevnei Rusi,* Paris, 1931.

Fletcher, William, *A Study in Survival: The Church in ̉Russia, 1927-1943,* Macmillan, New York, 1965.

—————, *The Russian Orthodox Church Underground, 1917-1970,* Oxford University Press, London, 1971.

Golombek, Oskar, ed., *Die katolische Kirche und die Volker vertreibung,* Wienand Verlag, Cologne, 1966.

Grabbe, Georgii, *Pravda o russkoi tserkvi na rodine i za rubezhom,* Jordanville, New York, 1961.

Graham, Robert A., *The Church of Silence,* American Press, New York, 1961.

Grossu, Sergiu, ed., *The Church in Today's Catacombs,* Arlington House Publishers, 1975.

Grousset, Rene, *Histoire de L'Asie,* Paris, 1950.

Grunwald, de Constantin, *The Churches and the Soviet Union,* Macmillan, New York 1962.

Gustafson, A., *The Catacomb Church,* Jordanville, New York, 1960.

Hales, E. E. Y., *The Catholic Church in the Modern World,* Image Books, New York, 1960.

Handbuch des Weltkommunismus, Munich, 1958.

Hayward, Max and Fletcher, William C., eds., *Religion and the Soviet State: A Dilemma of Power,* Frederick A. Praeger, New York, 1969.

Hebley, J. A., tr. by John Pott, *Protestants in Russia,* Belfast, 1976.

Heyer, Friederich, *Die Orthodoxe Kirche in der Ukraine von 1917 bis 1945,* Cologne, 1953.

Higley, Ronald, *Under Soviet Skins: An Intourist's Report,* London, 1960.

Inkeles, A. and Geiger, K., eds., *Soviet Society: A Book of Reading,* Houghton Mifflin, Boston, 1961.

Iwanow, Boris, ed., *Religion in the USSR,* Institute for the Study of the USSR, Munich, 1960.

Kaval, Prakop, *Bielarus u datach, likach i faktach,* Paris, 1953.

King, Robert K., *Religion and Communism in the Soviet Union and Eastern Europe,* Bringham University Press, Utah, 1975.

Klimovich, L., *Islam, ego proizkhodenie i sotsialynaya suchnost,* Moscow, 1956.

Kolarz, Walter, *Religion in the Soviet Union,* New York, 1961.

Konstantinov, Dimitri, *Gonimaia tserkov,* All-Slavic Press, New York, 1967.

Kovalevsky, M., *Opozitsiyni rukhy v Ukraini i nationalna polytika SSR (1920-1955),* Munich, 1955.

Large Soviet Encyclopedia, Moscow, 1954.

Lately, Maurice, *Tyranny,* Penguin Books, England, 1972.

Latvijas PSR Mazā Enciklopedija, Zinātne, Rīgā, 1968.

Levitin, Anatolii, *Monasticism and the Modern World,* Paris, 1966.

Lietuvos Tarybu Socialistines Respublikos Baudziamasis Kodekas, Vilnius, 1970.

Likholat, A. V., *Razgrom natiionalisticheskoi kontrarevolyutsii na Ukraine (1917-1922)*, Kiev, 1954.

Lisavtsev, *Religiya v borbei idei*, Polizdat, Moscow, 1975.

Lochman, John M., *The Church in a Marxist Society*, Harper & Row, New York, 1970.

Marchenko, Anatoli, *My Testimony*, Dell Publishing Co., New York, 1971.

Marshall, Richard H., ed., *Aspects of Religion in the Soviet Union 1917-1967*, Chicago, 1971.

Martin, Andre, *Buried Alive in the Soviet Hospital-Prison*, Fayard, Paris.

Maser, Werner, *Genossen beten nicht*, Wissenschaft und Politik, Cologne, 1963.

Mindszenty, Cardinal Jozsef, *Memoirs*, Macmillan Publishing Co., New York, 1963.

Morality and Religion, Institute for Philosophy of the USSR Academy of Science, Moscow, 1964.

Mourin, Maxime, *Der Vatikan und die Sovjetunion*, Nymphenburg, Munich, 1967.

Mykula, W., *The Gun and the Faith*, Ukrainian Information Service, London, 1969.

The New Communist Propaganda Line on Religion, U.S. Government Printing Office, 1967.

Nichols, Peter, *The Politics of the Vatican*, Federick A. Praeger, New York, 1968.

Noble, John, *I Found God in Soviet Russia*, St. Martin's Press, New York, 1959.

O religii i tserkvi: sbornik dokumentov, Moscow, 1965.

Oliveira, de Plinio Correa, *L'Eglise et l'Etat Communiste — la coexistence impossible*, Sao Paulo, Brazil, 1963.

Pallas, P.S., *Reisen durch verschiedene Provinzen des russischen Reiches*, St. Petersburg, 1776-1778.

Pascal, Pierre, *The Religion of the Russian People*, Oxford, 1976.

Patriarkh Sergii i ego dukhovnoe nasledstvo, Moscow, 1947.

Payne, Robert, *The Life and Death of Lenin*, Simon and Schuster, New York, 1964.

——————, *The Rise and Fall of Stalin*, Pan Books Ltd London, 1968.

Platonov, R., *Vospitanie ateisticheskoi ubezhdenosti. Propaganda nauchnogo ateizma v sisteme ideologicheskoi deiatelnosti partiinykh organizatsii Belorussii v 1959-1972 gody*, Minsk, 1973.

Polsky, M., *Kannonicheskoe polozhenie vysshei tserkovnoi vlasti v SSR i zagranitsei*, New York, 1948.

——————, *Novye muchenniki Rossiskie*, Jordanville, New York, 1949.

Report on *The First Assembly of the WCC*, SCM Press, 1949.

Robottom, John, *Modern Russia*, McGraw-Hill Co., New York, 1971.

Rothenberg, Joshua, *The Jewish Religion in the Soviet Union*, KTAV Publishing House, New York, 1971.

Russkaya Pravoslavnaya Tserkva v SSSR, Central Union of Political Emigres from the USSR, Munich, 1962.

Rutkis, J., *Latvia: Country and People*, LNF, Stockholm, 1967.

Salo, Vello, *Die Kirchen von Finnland, Estland und Lettland*, Rome, 1965.

Savasis, J., *The War Against God in Lithuania*, Manyland Books, Inc., New York, 1966.

Shapiro, L. and Boiter, A., eds., *The U.S.S.R. and the Future*, Institute for the Study of the USSR, Munich, 1962.

Schwarz, S., *The Jews in the Soviet Union*, Syracuse, 1951.

Shafarevich, I. R., *Zakonodatelstvo o religii v SSSR*, YMCA Press, Paris, 1973.

Sheinman, M., *Vatikan vo vtoroi mirovoi voine*, Moscow, 1951.

Simon, Gerhard, *Church, State and Opposition in the USSR*, London, 1974.

Situation der katolischen Kirche in der Tschechoslovakei, Schweizerische National Kommission *Justitia et Pax*, 1976.

Solzhenitsyn, Alexander, *The First Circle*, Fontana Books, London, 1972.

——————, *The Gulag Archipelago*, Harper & Row, New York, 1974.

Spravochnik propagandista in agitatora, Moscow, 1966.

Spuler, B., *Die Gegenwartslage der Ost Kirchen*, Wiesbaden, 1948.

Staat und Kirche in der DDR, Quell Verlag, Stutgart, 1975.

Straaten, van Werenfried, *They Call Me Bacon Priest*, Spaarnestad Haarlem, 1961.

——————, *Where God Weeps*, Keston, England, 1976.

Struve, Nikita, *Christians in Contemporary Russia*, Harvill Press, London, 1967.

Studies on the Soviet Union, Institute for the Study of the USSR, Munich, 1965.

Theodorovich, Nadezhda, *Religion and Believers in the USSR*, Institute for the Study of the USSR, Munich, 1965.

Till, Barry, *The Churches Search for Unity*, Penguin Books, Great Britain, 1972.

Time Capsule/1929, Time, Inc., New York, 1967.

Titlinov, B., *Novaya tserkov*, Petrograd, 1923.

Torma, A., *The Church in Estonia*, London, 1944.

Tsinava, L., *Vsenarodnaya partizanskaya voina v Belorusii protiv fashisthikh zakhvatchikov*, vol. II, Minsk, 1951.

Valentinov, A., *Chernaya kniga*, Paris, 1925.

Vidler, Alec R., *The Church in an Age of the Revolution*, volume 5, Penguin Books, London, 1965.

Wheeler, Geoffrey, *The Peoples of Soviet Central Asia*, The Bodley Head, London, 1966.

Williams, Julian, *The World Council of Churches*, Christian Crusade Publicants, 1973.

Wurmbrand, Rev. Richard, *Underground Saints*, Fleming H. Revell, New Jersey, 1968.

——————, *Today's Martyred Church Tortured for Christ*, Cross Publishing Co., California, 1967.

Zatko, James, *Descent into Darkness: The Destruction of the Roman Catholic Church in Russia, 1917-1923*, Notre Dame, Indiana.

Zlatkin, Ya., *Mongolskaya Narodnaya Respublika — Strana novoi demokratii*, Moscow, 1950.

Articles - Papers - Pamphlets

"The anti-Western Aims of the World Council of Churches Exposed,"
East-West Digest, January, 1976.

Antic, Oxana, "Assistant Chairman of Council on Religious Affairs Comments on Churches in the USSR," *Radio Liberty Research,* April 20, 1977.

Balinov, Shamba, "The Kalmyk Buddhists," *Genocide in the USSR,* The Scarecrow Press, Inc., New York, 1958.

Balkunas, John, "Silent Church Behind the Iron Curtain," *The Immaculata,* June/July, 1969.

Barnover, Herman, "Judaism in the USSR," an unpublished paper presented at a symposium on "Religion in the USSR, 1975," Munich, April 16-18, 1975.

"Beleaguered Fortress," *American Committee for Liberation,* New York, 1963.

Benningsen, Alexandre, "Islam Today in the Soviet Union," a paper presented at a symposium on "Religion in the USSR, 1975," Munich, April 16-18, 1975.

Bociurkiw, Bohdan R., "Catholics in the Soviet Union Today," a paper presented at a symposium on "Religion in the USSR, 1975," Munich, April 16-18, 1975.

———— , "Religious Dissent in the U.S.S.R.: Lithuanian Catholics," *op. cit.*

Bourdeaux, Michael, "Baptists in the Soviet Union Today," a paper presented at a symposium on "Religion in the USSR, 1975," Munich, April 16-18, 1975.

———— , "Monasticism in the Soviet Union," *Radio Liberty Research,* October 10, 1975.

Brizgys, Bishop Vincent, "Religious Conditions in Lithuania under Soviet Russian Occupation," Chicago, 1968.

Brodin, Eric, "Religion Under Communism," *Christian Economics,* September, 1972.

Brownfeld, Allan C., "The Continuing Soviet Persecution of Religion," *Human Events,* June 26, 1971.

Buckley, William, F., "Russia Contra Naturam," *National Review,* February 20, 1976.

Caputo, Philip, "Folk myths still color Russ culture," *Chicago Tribune,* January 25, 1977.

Contons, A. J.,"Religious persecution in Lithuania — Soviet Style," *Litaunus,* No. 2, 1972.

Cottier, G., "A Date to Remember: 19 March 1937," *L'Osservatore Romano,* March 31, 1977.

Dalima, Alfons, "La Ostpolitik del Vaticano," *ABN Correspondence,* Munich, September/October, 1975.

Encyclical *Caritate Christi compulsi,* Vatican City, 1932.

Encyclical *Divini Redemptoris,* Vatican City, 1937.

Encyclical *Mater et magistra,* Vatican City, 1937.

Encyclical *Mit brennender Sorge,* Vatican City, 1937.

Encyclical *Pacem in terris,* Vatican City, 1963.

Flaherty, Daniel, "Of many things...," *America,* May 4, 1968.

Fletcher, William C., "On the Eve of the Fiftieth Anniversary of the October Revolution: Promise and Realization," *Institute for the Study of the USSR,* International Conference, Munich, October 24-28, 1966.

General Report On The Communist Persecution Against the Catholic Church in Soviet Russia From November 1917 to January 1953. Balance of the Losses of Persons and Material, Collegium Russicum, Rome, 1953.

Gorskii, V., "Russian Messianism and a New National Consciousness," *Vestnik Studencheskogo Khristianskogo Dvizheniya,* July, 1970.

Grabbe, Lester, L., "The Vatican Looks Toward Eastern Europe," *The Plain Truth,* February, 1972.

Groier, Ruvin, "Soviet Jews Enjoy Full Equality," *Soviet Panorama,* February, 1977.

Gruliow, Leo, "Russians challenge paper-work weddings," *The Christian Science Monitor,* May 21, 1973.

Gubanov, N. I., "Atheistic Propaganda in the USSR in 50 years of Soviet Power," *Problems of Scientific Atheism,* 1967.

Haroshka, L. "The Roman Catholic Church in the Byelorussian SSR," *Religion in the USSR,* Institute for the Study of the USSR, Munich, 1960.

Hayit, Baymirza, "Islam and the Anti-Islamic Movement in the Soviet Union," *ABN Correspondence,* May-June, 1972.

Heneghan, Tom, "The Vatican's Ostpolitik, *Commonweal,* March 4, 1977.

Hoffman, Nikolai, "The Mass Closure of Monisteries in the USSR after the Twenty-first Congress of the CPSU, *Radio Liberty Research,* May 20, 1976.

Hoffner, Cardinal Joseph, "Horst du nicht ihr Schreien?" Presseamt des Erzbistums Koln, May 23, 1976.

Horak, Jiri, "Religious Oppression in Czechoslovakia," *Congressional Record,* April 28, 1976.

Ilitschev, L. F., "Die Formierung der wissenschaftlichen Weltanschauung und die atheistische Erziehung," *Nauka i religiya,* Moscow, No. 1, 1964.

Jackson, James O., "The ritualism of Moscow's atheist burials," *Chicago Tribune,* January 13, 1975.

"Kirche in Not am Beispiel Romanien," *Koningsteiner Jahrbuch 1977,* Koningstein/Taunus, 1977.

Kirk, Russel, "World Council of Churches Gives $20,000 to Terrorists," *Human Events,* June 26, 1971.

Klesment, Johannes, "Church and State in Estonia," *The Church and State Under Communism,* U.S. Government Printing Office, Washington, 1965.

Koretskyi, D., "V kostioli ta navkolo nioho," *Liudyna i svit,* No. 1, 1974.

Krausauskas, R. and Gulbinas, K., "Die Lage der Katholischen Kirche in Litauen," *Acta Baltica,* Vol. XII, 1972.

Krivickas, Domas, "Church and State in Lithuania," *The Church and State Under Communism,* U.S. Government Printing Office, New York, 1965.

Levitin-Krasnov, A. "V oboroni Ukrainskoi Katolytskoi Tserkvy," *Suchasnist,* No 1, January, 1975.

Lombardi, Frederico, "Atheistic Education in the East beginning from Youth," *L'Osservatore Romano,* March 24, 1977.

McNaspy, C. J., "Atheism and the Working Class," *Catholic Mind,* New York, 1962.

Madden, Daniel M., "The Paradox of Poland," *Columbia,* April, 1970.

——————— , "Pope John's Bulgaria Today," *Columbia,* December, 1970.

Mailleux, Paul, "Catholics in the Soviet Union," *Aspects of Religion in the Soviet Union 1917-1967,* Chicago, 1971.

Manifesto of-the Slovaks for Independence of Slovakia, New York, 1975.

Marin, Yury, "The Failure of the Party's Campaign against Religion," *Soviet Affairs Analysis Service,* No. 39 (1961-1962), Munich, 1962.

Markus, Vasyl, "The Suppressed Church: Ukrainian Catholics in the Soviet Union," a paper presented to the International Slavic Conference at Banff, Canada, September, 1974.

Martin, John M., "The Bacon Priest," *Our Sunday Visitor,* Huntington, February 21, 1971.

Mestrovic, Matthew M., "Renewal in Yugoslavia," *America,* November 22, 1969.

Miano, Vincenzo, "Essential continuity of the Doctrine of the Church," *L'Osservatore Romano,* October 7, 1976.

Muthig, John T., "Cardinal Wyszynski Force Behind Polish Catholicism," *The New World,* July 30, 1976.

Mydans, Seth, "Soviet Union Saves Its Religious Past," *International Herald Tribune,* Paris, July 21, 1976.

Mydlowsky, Lev, "Bolshevist Persecution of Religion and Church in Ukraine 1917-1957," Ukrainian Publishers Ltd., London, 1962.

Namsons, Andrivs, "Die Lage der Katholischen Kirche in Sowjet Litauen," *Acta Baltica,* Konigstein/Taunus, 1962.

Neerskov, Hans Kristian, "To Cry Out for All the World," *ABN Correspondence,* July/August, 1976.

"Padre Dimitrij Dudko — Porroco A Mosca — Conversazioni Seriali," *Centro studii Russia Christiana,* Milan, 1976.

"Patriarch Aleksii of Moscow," *Eastern Churches Review,* Autumn, 1970.

"Peaceful Co-existence," *North American Voice of Fatima,* September 15, 1970.

Pell, Claiborne, "Eastern Europe the Changing Climate," *Vital Speeches of the Day,* April 15, 1967.

Pogany, Andras H., "The Plight of the Catholic Church in Hungary," *Congressional Record,* September 24, 1974.

Poppe, N., "Buddhism in the USSR," *Vestnik,* No. 5, Munich, 1954.

—————— "The Buddhists," *Genocide in the USSR,* The Scarecrow Press, Inc. New York, 1958.

Pospielovsky, Dimitry, "The Kaunas Riots and the National and Religious tensions in the USSR," *Radio Liberty Research,* Munich, May 31, 1972.

Pozdeeva, Elena, "The Report Card of the Moscow's Patriarchate's Delegation in Nairobi," *Radio Liberty Research,* Munich, 1976.

"Press Conference of Moslems in Munich," *Institute for the Study of the USSR,* Munich, 1956.

Prichyny sushchestvovanii i puti preodoleniia religioznykh perezhitkov, Minsk, 1965.

Raisupis, Matas, *Dabarties kankiniai,* Chicago, 1972.

Register of Documents, *Arkhiv samizdata,* Munich, 1975.

"Religion and the Soviet Intelligentsia," *Radio Liberty Research,* March 2, 1973.

Resolution on the Religious Situation in Czechoslovakia, *Congressional Record,* September 2, 1976.

Riley, Patrick, "We're Church of Hard Work: Polish Bishops," *The New World,* November 24, 1972.

"Roman Catholics in Latvia Petition USSR Government," *Radio Liberty Research,* Munich, 1976.

Rusis, Armins, "Church and State in Soviet Latvia," *The Church and State Under Communism,* U.S. Government Printing Office, Washington, 1965.

"Russian Orthodox Church and the Soviet Leadership," *Institute for the Study of the USSR,* Munich, 1961/1962.

"Samizdat Sources Reveal Religious Persecution," *Radio Liberty Research,* April 23, 1971.

Sawatsky, Walter, "Secret Soviet Lawbook on Religion," *Religion in Communist Lands,* Winter, 1976.

Schilling, Joachim, "The Vatican Looks East," *Atlas,* March, 1968.

Seeger, Murray, "A Burning Faith, Underground — Lithuanian Catholics Defy Russ," *Congressional Record,* March 14, 1974.

Sipkov, Ivan, "Church and State in Bulgaria," *The Church and State Under Communism,* U.S. Government Printing Office, Washington, 1965.

Slavnyi, P. P., "Obchestvennoe mnenie i nauchnoateisticheskaya propaganda," Moscow, 1976.

Stoicoiu, Virgiliu, "Church and State in Rumania," *The Church and State Under Communism,* U.S. Government Printing Office, Washington, 1965.

Theodorovich, Nadezhda, "The Byelorussian Autocephalic Orthodox Church," *Genocide in the USSR,* The Scarecrow Press, New York, 1958.

————— , "The Roman Catholics," *op. cit.*
————— , "The Russian Orthodox," *op. cit.*
————— , "The Catacomb Church in the USSR,"*Bulletin of the Institute for the Study of the USSR,* April, 1965.
————— , "Religion und Ateismus in der USSR — Dokumente und Berichte," Munich, 1970.
————— , "Religion and Believers in the USSR," *Analysis of Current Development in the Soviet Union,* Munich, 1965.
Turner, Ewart E., "Czechoslovakia Increases Campaign Against Churches," *The New World,* Chicago, August 1, 1975.
Vikopola, Kemal, "Church and State in Albania," *The Church and State Under Communism,* U.S. Government Printing Office, Washington, 1965
Wiejek, Joseph, "The Church in Czechoslovakia," *America,* June 8, 1968.
Williams, Julian, "The World Council of Churches and Revolutionary Violence," *Christian Crusade Weekly,* October 20, 1974.
Willoughby, William, "No Compromise With Reds, Mindszenty Insists," *Congressional Record,* May 21, 1974.
Wohl, Paul, "Religion in Russia," *The Christian Science Monitor,* December 22, 1970.
Wolf, John B., "Islam in the Soviet Union," *Current History,* March, 1969.
Yurchenko, Alexander, "The Ukrainian Autocephalic Orthodox Church," *Genocide in the USSR,* The Scarecrow Press, New York, 1958.

Journals, newspapers, and other news media

ABN Correspondence, Munich.
Agitator, Moscow.
America, New York.
Arkhiv samizdata, Munich.
Atlas, New York.
Baltic Review, New York.
Baptist Times, London.
Beleaguered Fortress, New York.
Bezbozhnik, Moscow.
Bolshevik, Moscow.
Butu Ukis, Kaunas.
Catholic Mind, New York.
The Chicago Catholic, Chicago.
The Chicago Daily News, Chicago.
The Chicago Sun-Times, Chicago.
The Chicago Tribune, Chicago.

Christian Century, Chicago.
Christian Crusade Weekly, Tulsa.
Christian Economics, Buena Park, California.
The Christian Science Monitor, Boston.
Christianity Today, Washington, D.C.
Chronicle of the Catholic Church in Lithuania, Maspeth
Chronicle of Current Events, London.
Church of England Newspaper, London.
The Church and State Under Communism, Washington.
Columbia, New Haven.
Commonweal, New York.
Contemporary Civilization, Chicago.
Darbininkas, Brooklyn.
Dergi, Munich.
Digest des Ostens, Konigstein/Taunus.
Dzmintenes balss, Riga.
The East Turkic Review, Oxford.
Echmiadzin, Erivan.
Elta — Press, Rome.
Expulsus, Konigstein/Taunus.
Figaro, Paris.
Gaisma, Leuven.
Georgian Opinion, New York.
Glas Koncila, Zagreb.
Glaube in der 2. Welt, Zurich/Kuesnacht.
Human Events, Washington.
Hungarian Church Press, Budapest.
Immaculata, Kenosha, Wisconsin.
The Intercollegiate Review, Philadelphia.
International Herald Tribune, Paris.
International Kirchliche Zeitschrift, Munich.
Izvestia, Moscow.
Journal of Moscow Patriarchate, Moscow.
Jubilee, St. Paul, Minnesota.
Kathpress, Austria.
Katolicke Noviny, Prague.
Kazakhstanskaya pravda, Alma-Ata.
Kizil Uzbekistan, Tashkent.
Komjaunimo Tiesa, Vilnius.
Kommunist, Moscow.
Kommunist Ukrainy, Kiev.
Komunistas, Vilnius.
Komsomolskaya pravda, Moscow.
Komsomolskaya zhizn, Moscow.
Komunists, Riga.
Krasnaya zvezda, Moscow.
Kultura, Paris.
Kzyl Tataristan, Tashkent.
La Nation Roumaine, Paris.
Laiks, New York.

Latvian Information Bulletin, Washington, D.C.
Latvija Amerika, Toronto.
Leninskaya smena, Leningrad.
Lietuvos Pionierius, Vilnius.
Liguorian, Liguori.
Litaunus, Chicago.
Literaturnaya gazeta, Moscow.
Literaturnaya Rossiya, Moscow.
L'Osservatore Romano, Vatican City.
Los Angeles Times, Los Angeles.
March of the Nation, Bombay.
Mokslas ir Gyvenimas, Vilnius.
Molod Ukrainy, Kiev.
Molodezh Moldavii, Kishiner.
Molodoy kommunist, Moscow.
Moscow News, Moscow.
Munchner Katolische Kirchenzeitung, Munich.
Nasha Tserkva, London.
National Catholic Register, Fort Worth, Texas.
National Review, New York.
Nauka i religiya, Moscow.
Neue Zuricher Zeitung, Zurich.
New Leader, New York.
New Republic, Washington, D.C.
New World, Chicago.
New York Times, New York.
Newsweek, New York.
North American Voice of Fatima, Youngstown.
Noukagude Kool, Tallin.
Novosti, Soviet press agency.
Novoye Russkoye Slovo, New York.
Novy mir, Moscow.
Observer, London.
Ogonek, Moscow.
Ostprobleme, Bad Godesberg.
Our Sunday Visitor, Huntington, Indiana.
Padomju Jaunatne, Riga.
Partiynaya zhizn Kazakhstana, Alma-Ata.
Plain Truth, California.
Posev, Frankfurt.
Poslednye novosti, Paris.
Prace, Prague.
Pravda, Moscow.
Problems of Communism, Washington D.C.
Questions on Leninism, Leningrad, 1932.
Questions on Scientific Atheism, Moscow.
Radio Free Europe, Munich.
Radio Liberty, Munich.
Radio Liberty Research, Munich.
Radio Moscow, Moscow.

Rahave Haal, Tallin.
RCDA — Religion in Communist Dominated Areas, New York.
Reader's Digest, New York.
Red Line, St. Louis.
Red Star, Moscow.
Referrativnyi zhurnal, Leningrad.
Religion und Atheismus in der USSR, Konigstein/Taunus.
Religion in Communist Lands, London.
Reuter, Moscow.
Ridna Tserkva, Munich.
Rude Pravo, Prague.
Russkaya mysl, Paris.
Sacrum Poloniae Millennium, Rome.
Skola un gimene, Riga.
Sodalis, Detroit.
Sovetskaya Estonia, Tallin.
Sovetskaya Kirgiziya, Frunze.
Sovetskaya kultura, Moscow.
Sovetskaya Latvia, Riga.
Sovetskaya Litva, Vilnius.
Sovetskaya Moldavia, Kishinev.
Sovetskaya pedagogika, Moscow.
Sovetskaya Rossia, Moscow.
Sovetskaya yusticiya, Moscow.
Soviet Affairs Analysis Service, Munich.
Soviet Life, Washington, D.C.
Soviet Panorama, Canada.
Soviet Union Today, Ottawa.
Soviet War News, London.
Spiegel, Hamburg.
Studies on the Soviet Union, Munich.
Suchasnit, Munich.
Sunday Telegraph, London.
Survey, London.
Tablet, London.
Tarybinis Mokytojas, Vilnius.
Tass, Moscow.
Tiesa, Vilnius.
Time, New York.
Times, London.
Toronto Star, Toronto.
Trud, Moscow.
Trybuna Rabotnicka, Katowice.
Tsurkoven Vestnik, Munich.
Ucitelska Noviny, Prague.
Ukrainian Review, London.
Ukrainski Visty, Edmonton.
Ungarische Passion, Konigstein
U.S. News & World Report, Washington, D.C.
Uzbekistan Communisti, Tashkent.

Valstiecu Laikrakstis, Vilnius.
Vatican Radio, Vatican City.
Vestnik, Munich.
Vilna Ukraina, Lvov.
Vital Speeches of the Day, Southold, New York.
Voice of America, European Station.
Volksbote, Munich.
Voprosy filosofii. Moscow.
Voyovnychy ateist, Kiev.
Wall Street Journal, Chicago.
Yunost, Moscow.
Zarya Vostoka, Tiflis.
Zeri i Popullit, Tiflis.
Zhurnal Moscovskoi Patriarkhii, Moscow.

MAJOR ETH—